PUBLIC LIBRARY CATALOG

1974 SUPPLEMENT
TO THE
SIXTH EDITION, 1973

EDITED BY
ESTELLE A. FIDELL
AND
GARY L. BOGART

THE H. W. WILSON COMPANY
NEW YORK
1975

Copyright © 1975
By The H. W. Wilson Company

Printed in the United States of America

International Standard Book Number 0-8242-0518-9

Library of Congress Catalog Card Number 74-656

PREFACE

This 1974 Supplement should be used with the Sixth Edition, 1973 of PUBLIC LIBRARY CATALOG. The number of books entered and number of analytical entries are as follows:

> Books entered 831
> Number of analytical entries 1316

Some new editions of works that are listed in the basic volume are entered in this 1974 Supplement, if the new edition represents a substantial revision, or if significant new material has been added.

Readers are urged to read "Directions for Use" before consulting the Catalog. An historical account of its beginnings and growth, as well as a fuller introduction to the Catalog as a whole, is included in the Preface to the Sixth Edition.

The Catalog provides a classified list of titles selected by a representative group of practicing librarians, who have been chosen with the advice and assistance of the Public Library Association and the Association of College and Research Libraries, divisions of the American Library Association. The librarians are staff members of public or academic libraries. A list of library systems participating in the compilation of this Catalog appears below.

While originally intended for use in the small and medium-sized library, the Catalog has also been found valuable in college and large public libraries. The Catalog is intended as an aid toward, and not a substitute for, good book selection. Selection should always respond to the special needs and interests of a particular library. Larger libraries, with greater staff and facilities will, of course, need to expand this list.

The publisher is glad to acknowledge its debt to the staff members of the following library systems for participating in the selection of titles for this Supplement:

Public Library of Cincinnati
   and Hamilton County
   Cincinnati, Ohio

Free Public Library
   East Orange, N.J.

Jacksonville Public Library
   Jacksonville, Fla.

Memphis Public Library
   Memphis, Tenn.

Free Public Library
   Montclair, N.J.

Public Library
   Mount Vernon, N.Y.

(continued page iv)

Norfolk Public Library System
  Norfolk, Va.

Reed College Library
  Portland, Ore.

Salt Lake Public Library
  Salt Lake City, Utah

San Antonio Public Library
  San Antonio, Tex.

Ventura County Free Library
  Ventura, Calif.

Mullen Memorial Library
  The Catholic University of America
  Washington, D.C.

Public Library
  Winnipeg, Manitoba, Canada

Martin Memorial Library
  York, Pa.

TABLE OF CONTENTS

Preface	iii
Directions for use	vi
Part 1. Classified Catalog	1
Part 2. Author, Title, Subject, and Analytical Index	111
Part 3. Directory of Publishers and Distributors	163

DIRECTIONS FOR USE

PART 1. CLASSIFIED CATALOG

Use as a guide in book selection. For this purpose the books listed are arranged by Dewey Decimal Classification numbers. Information about publisher, price, and annotations are given in this section.

Use also as a cataloging tool, since the subject headings for each book are indicated in this section.

An outline of the Dewey Decimal Classification appears on page x of the Sixth Edition, 1973.

PART 2. ALPHABETICAL INDEX

Use as an index to Part 1. Here in one alphabet are author, title, and subject entries for all books, as well as analytical entries under author, title, or subject for parts of books.

PART 3. DIRECTORY OF PUBLISHERS AND DISTRIBUTORS

Use to locate full names and addresses of publishers and distributors of books listed.

PUBLIC LIBRARY CATALOG

1974 Supplement

CLASSIFIED CATALOG

000 GENERALITIES

001.6 Data processing. Computer programming

Diebold, John
(ed.) The world of the computer. Random House 1973 457p $12.50 **001.6**
 1 Electronic data processing 2 Computers 3 Technology and civilization
 ISBN 0-394-47150-4 LC 73-3994
 Analyzed in Essay and general literature index
 This is "one of the most comprehensive, understandable, and coherently organized books on computers to have been published. Diebold's introduction is excellent—not superficial, yet accessible even to those who are most intimidated by computers. The clarity of the selections, which chronologically trace the computer's development and application in various fields, makes even the most technical of the pieces enjoyable to read. The philosophical and moral questions raised by the computer as well as the relevant technological changes are handled thoughtfully and fairly." Library J

Sippl, Charles J.
 Computer dictionary and handbook, by Charles J. Sippl and Charles P. Sippl. [2d ed] Sams 1972 778p illus $16.95 **001.6**
 1 Electronic data processing—Dictionaries 2 Computers—Dictionaries
 ISBN 0-672-20850-4 LC 70-175572
 Earlier edition entered in main catalog
 First published 1966. The 1974 edition "has been thoroughly updated to reflect the changes in this dynamic area. Definitions have been changed, new words have been added, and obsolete terms have been dropped." Cur Ref Bks

Sondak, Norman
 The layman's dictionary of computer terminology, by Norman and Eileen Sondak. Hawthorn Bks 1973. 203p $10.95
 001.6
 1 Electronic data processing—Dictionaries 2 Computers—Dictionaries LC 75-39269
 "The computer has become all-pervasive, and written and spoken language is becoming more and more replete with computer terms. This work provides simple, straightforward definitions of over 2,000 such terms. There are definitions for the acronyms that sprinkle computer talk, for the terms from ordinary language (e.g., garbage, hash) that have special computer-related meanings, and for a great many of the technical terms unique to the field. Pronunciations are provided for a few difficult or oddly pronounced terms. Definitions range in length from a sentence to a paragraph, and clear typography makes for easy use. Libraries whose patrons have difficulty understanding the definitions in the larger or more technically oriented dictionaries that exist will want to consider this handy volume." Cur Ref Bks

001.9 Controversial and spurious knowledge

Däniken, Erich von
 The gold of the gods; tr. by Michael Heron. Putnam 1973 210p illus $6.95 **001.9**
 1 Curiosities and wonders 2 Civilization, Ancient 3 Archeology
 SBN 399-11208-1 LC 73-78588
 Original German edition 1972
 The author "claims to have seen a vast 'Zoo,' a subterranean storehouse of gold animal statues, and an astonishing 'Metal Library,' containing thousands of embossed gold-leaf 'documents,' in caves 800 feet beneath Peru and Ecuador. These caves prove, he contends, visits by our astral ancestors." Newsweek
 "He produces photos (his book contains 100 photos and drawings, some in color), comparing prehistoric wall painting, an Inca gold plaque, etc., with similar 'proof' from other remarkable and apparently man-made tunnel systems around the world to support his thesis. Poorly organized, naively exclamatory—but the 'and yet' factor still exerts a mesmerizing pull." Pub W

 In search of ancient gods; my pictorial evidence for the impossible; tr. by Michael Heron. Putnam [1974 c1973] 249p illus maps **001.9**
 1 Curiosities and wonders 2 Civilization, Ancient 3 Man, Prehistoric
 ISBN 0-399-11346-0 LC 73-93725
 Original German language edition 1973
 The author presents illustrated evidence to support his theory that the earth was visited long ago by exraterrestrial astronauts who brought information enabling man to develop from a primitive to a civilized being
 Bibliography: p245-47

Napier, John
 Bigfoot; the Yeti and Sasquatch in myth and reality. Dutton 1973 [c1972] 240p illus $8.95 **001.9**
 1 Sasquatch 2 Yeti
 ISBN 0-525-06658-6 LC 71-179857
 First published 1972 in England
 The author "begins with a chronological account of Yeti sightings in the Himalayas—the first in 1832, the latest on the Annapurna expedition of 1970. He goes on to discuss the principal sightings of the Sasquatch, the monster of the Northwest Coast, one who, in 1924 according to a lumberman, kidnapped him and brought him to its own Sasquatch family for observation. He also tells of the Minnesota Iceman, a man-ape frozen in a block of ice, who, in 1968, convinced an eminent scientist of his authenticity." Publisher's note
 "Napier, a humorous and charming writer as well as a scientist, examines the evidence for the existence of the whole Abominable Snowman tribe with professional knowledge and proper skepticism. . . . Anyone with the slightest interest in the Bigfoot business will find the book stimulating." Atlantic
 Bibliography included in Notes: p223-30

UFO's—a scientific debate; ed. by Carl Sagan and Thornton Page. Cornell Univ. Press 1972 xxxi, 310p illus $12.50 **001.9**
 1 Flying saucers
 ISBN 0-8014-0740-0 LC 72-4572
 "Fifteen documented papers, elucidated with figures and tables, presented at a symposium sponsored by the American Association for the Advancement of Science in 1969 . . . show the unanswered questions that persist after the roundup of information in the 'Final Report of the scientific study of unidentified objects' by E. U. Condon [entered in main catalog under Colorado. University]. . . . Coverage includes a collection of UFO cases substantiated by location, time, and type of sighting and later discussed from various points of view, and essays on the background of UFO, observations, social and psychological aspects, and retrospective and perspective views. The editors summarize the symposium discussion in the addendum." Booklist
 "This work ranks with the Condon Report in importance. Happily, most will find it easy to read, with only a small amount of heavy going." Choice
 Includes bibliographical notes

015.73 National bibliographies—U. S.

Wynkoop, Sally
 (comp.) Subject guide to government reference books. Libs. Unlimited 1972 276p $11.50 **015.73**
 1 U.S.—Government publications—Bibliography 2 Reference books—Bibliography
 ISBN 0-87287-025-1   LC 72-83382

"Some works published during 1968-1971 are included in this bibliography, but fuller coverage for these years will be found in the biennial series, 'Government Reference Books' [entered in main catalog under title]." Introduction

This volume is "extremely useful. . . . Its four parts cover general reference sources (catalogs, bibliographies by country, biographical sources, library science, etc.); social sciences, (further subdivided by subjects and then by forms); science and technology, and a final short section on humanities, since the government is not distinguished for reference publications in literature, the fine arts, and music. For each of the 1050 well-annotated entries, the compiler gives entry, paging, price, LC card number, SuDocs classification, and if reprinted . . . price and publisher are noted. The index includes specific subjects, titles, and personal and corporate authors. We join the compiler in the hope that this much-needed subject guide 'will assist librarians and patrons of all types of libraries to utilize more fully the rich resources of government publications.'" Ref Services Rev

016 Subject bibliographies

Museum media; a biennial directory and index of publications and audiovisuals available from United States and Canadian institutions. Paul Wasserman, managing editor; Esther Herman, associate editor. Editorial staff: Gary Blemaster [and others]. Gale Res. 1973 455p $62   **016**
 1 U.S.—Galleries and museums—Bibliography 2 Canada—Galleries and museums—Bibliography 3 U.S.—Galleries and museums—Directories 4 Canada—Galleries and museums—Directories
 ISBN 0-8103-0385-X   LC 73-16335

"The first edition of what is planned as a biennial directory of the publications of museums in the U.S. and Canada. It includes books, pamphlets, catalogs of exhibits, films and filmstrips published by 732 museums, art galleries, zoos, botanical gardens, and national parks. The first section is an alphabetical listing of institutions and their publications, followed by a . . . title and keyword index and lists of museums by subject and geographical area. The directory indicates whether reproductions of art works are available but does not list specific offerings." Choice

The index lists not only titles of materials but also the artists, works, media, periods, subjects, movements and countries mentioned in the titles. The index is well done and will lead the user to much hitherto unavailable materials. . . . The only drawback is the price—quite expensive, but worth the price if your patrons are media-minded." Cath Lib Assn

Wynar, Christine L.
 Guide to reference books for school media centers. Libs. Unlimited 1973 473p $17.50   **016**
 1 Reference books—Bibliography 2 School libraries
 ISBN 0-87287-069-3   LC 73-87523

This volume contains 2,575 annotated entries of reference books and selection tools for use in elementary, junior, and senior high schools. The subjects treated are those generally included in school curricula, plus extra curricular topics such as pets, hobbies, clubs, etc. Entries are arranged alphabetically by author under 54 main subject headings. Paperback editions and prices are shown. Index includes author, title and subject entries

"The main advantage here will be breadth and up-to-dateness. . . . One could quibble that some titles are too specialized for school libraries or that some very useful titles are omitted. However, this will be a useful list for collection building and for reminding librarians or patrons of sources to use on particular problems." Cur Ref Bks

016.05 Bibliographies of serials

Katz, Bill
 (ed.) Magazines for libraries; for the general reader, and school, junior college, college, and public libraries. 2d ed. supplement. [Ed. by] Bill Katz and Berry Gargal, science editor. Bowker 1974 328p $16.50 **016.05**
 1 Periodicals—Bibliography
 ISBN 0-8352-0761-7

"This Supplement to the second edition of 'Magazines for Libraries' [entered in main catalog] describes approximately 1,800 periodicals and journals selected for the general reader and student. . . . When used with the second edition volume, which contains 4,500 magazine annotations, content analysis and ordering details are provided for about 6,300 publications. . . . A special time-saving feature of this Supplement is the combined index to both the Supplement and the second edition, which provides one source for locating publications in the two volumes. . . . The Supplement includes selected new journals and magazines published since the second edition cut-off date, spring 1972, and up to the spring of 1974, and journals and magazines, published prior to 1972, that for one reason or another were not included in the second edition. Titles that appeared in the second edition are not updated in terms of price, address, editor's name, etc. Some publications are covered again if there were major changes in ownership, publication schedule, or editorial policy. . . . In addition to enlarging the basic selection, an effort was made to 'back and fill' various subjects." Preface

New serial titles; a union list of serials commencing publication after December 31, 1949. Lib. of Congress per year $170   **016.05**
 1 Periodicals—Bibliography
 ISSN 0028-6680   LC 53-60021

Eight monthly issues with quarterly and annual cumulations. First published 1950 with title: Serial titles newly received

Succesor to the Union list of serials in the libraries of the United States and Canada. 3d edition entered in main catalog

"Prepared under the sponsorship of the Joint Committee of the Union List of Serials." Title page

1950-1970 cumulation available in four volumes from Bowker $190 (ISBN 0-8352-0556-8)

Bibliographical data provided includes the name of an issuing body, the place of publication and the beginning and ending dates of the serial. Frequency, address of the publisher, and annual subscription price to U.S. subscribers is also given in the monthly and quarterly issues. One or two subject classification numbers are also provided for each title

016.3 Bibliographies of the social sciences

White, Carl M.
 Sources of information in the social sciences; a guide to the literature [by] Carl M. White and associates. 2d ed. A.L.A. 1973 702p $25   **016.3**
 1 Social sciences—Bibliography
 ISBN 0-8389-0134-4   LC 73-9825

First published 1964 by Bedminster Press

"Logically arranged, with a general overview of the whole field, it lumps such reference materials used in all social sciences under form, e.g. bibliographies, directories, encyclopedias, journals, statistics, handbooks, and yearbooks. Each succeeding chapter follows

White, Carl M.—*Continued*
the same pattern; basic works, or a summary of the field and guides to the literature. The latter are fully annotated. The eight fields so admirably covered are history, geography . . . economics and business administration . . . sociology, anthropology, psychology, education, and political science." Ref Services Rev

016.31 Bibliographies of statistics

Statistics sources. . . . 4th ed. Paul Wasserman, managing editor; Joanne Paskar, associate editor. Gale Res. 1974 892p $45
            016.31
1 Statistics—Bibliography
ISBN 0-8103-0396-5   LC 74-2163
Earlier edition entered in main catalog
"A subject guide to data on industrial, business, social, educational, financial, and other topics for the United States and internationally." Subtitle
First published 1962. The 1974 edition has been revised and "the selected and annotated bibliography of key statistical sources has been updated and enlarged to provide details for a basic collection of current and key statistical sources as of the end of 1973." Preface

016.3713 Bibliographies of teaching methods

National Information Center for Educational Media
[NICEM Indexes to nonbook media] The Center   016.3713
1 Audio-visual materials—Catalogs
Contains indexes to: 16mm educational films (3v) $99.50; 35mm filmstrips (2v) $78.50; Educational overhead transparencies (2v) $68.50; Educational audio tapes $42.50; Educational video tapes $26.50; Educational records $42.50; 8mm motion cartridges $42.50; Educational slides $38.50; Producers and distributors $19.50; Psychology—multimedia $26.50; Vocational and technical education—multimedia $26.50; Health and safety education—multimedia $26.50; Black history and studies—multimedia $19.50; Ecology—multimedia $19.50
Also available is an updated subscription service, called Update of nonbook media $388.50 for ten yearly volumes beginning in 1973

016.78 Bibliographies of music

Chicorel Bibliography to books on music and musicians; ed. by Marietta Chicorel. Chicorel Lib. Pub. Corp. 1974 487p $49.50
            016.78
1 Music—Bibliography 2 Musicians
ISBN 0-87729-023-1   LC 74-161012
"Chicorel Index series"
An "unannotated, unselective bibliography of materials on all aspects of music for all age levels . . . [with] a convenient listing of in-print items from a wide range of publishers. Smaller and less wealthy libraries will have to rely on 'Subject Guide to Books in Print,' where most of the cited items can be found—albeit under less convenient headings and in a format that is much harder to read. Chicorel lists some 10,000 works, arranged under broad headings, with finer subdivisions. Both books of music and books about music are listed. Some sections seem very complete, bringing to the attention of the user a wide range of titles for many levels of sophistication. Others, e.g., ballet, are quite weak." Cur Ref Bks

Duckles, Vincent
(comp.) Music reference and research materials: an annotated bibliography. 3d ed. Free Press 1974 526p $10.95 016.78
1 Music—Bibliography
ISBN 0-02-907700-1   LC 73-10697
Earlier edition entered in main catalog
First published 1964. The 1974 edition "lists more than 600 new entries, pointing out new editions, new numbers in important series, and reprints of older but valuable reference sources. By and large, the organization of the work remains the same, except for a new section on 'Music History in Pictures' and new categories treating individual composers." Cur Ref Bks

016.7902 Bibliographies of performing arts

Chicorel Bibliography to the performing arts; ed. by Marietta Chicorel. Chicorel Lib. Pub. Corp. 1972 498p $49.50 016.7902
1 Performing arts—Bibliography
ISBN 0-87729-222-1   LC 73-155102
"Chicorel Index series"
A compilation "listing 9,000 entries under 35 main subject headings and 300 subheadings relating to most performing arts areas, this ambitious and often useful work is marred by omissions and several mysterious inclusions. . . . Most entries are books in English, either current books in print or reprints. . . . An author index would have increased this work's viability. Despite its limitations, however, this work will still be useful as a one-volume compilation, especially to undergraduate reference libraries. The editor promises supplementary listings." Choice

016.8 Bibliographies of literature

McGarry, Daniel D.
World historical fiction guide; an annotated, chronological, geographical and topical list of selected historical novels. 2d ed. by Daniel D. McGarry and Sarah Harriman White. Scarecrow 1973 629p $15 016.8
1 Historical fiction—Bibliography
ISBN 0-8108-0616-9   LC 73-4367
First published 1963 with title: Historical fiction guide
The authors "provide an . . . annotated listing of fiction works in English that deal with historical topics and periods from antiquity to 1900. There are chronological, geographical, and topical breakdowns, with author and title indexes. This edition lists some 6,500 titles." Cur Ref Bks
The work "provides brief sentence fragment annotations for each entry. For the purpose of this bibliography the authors define historical fiction to include references to customs, conditions, identifiable persons, or events in the past. The work is selective and intends to include only better works of fiction meeting such criteria as literary excellence, readability, and historical value. Although designed especially for use by adults and students in senior high schools, colleges, and universities, the bibliography can also be used by students at the junior high school level. Books suitable for such grades are identified as 'Y.A.'" Booklist

016.8092 Bibliographies of drama criticism

Palmer, Helen H.
(comp.) European drama criticism. Supplement I-II; comp. by Helen H. Palmer and Anne Jane Dyson. Shoe String 1970-1974 2v v 1 $6.50, v2 $8.50 016.8092
1 Drama—History and criticism—Bibliography
2 Theater—Bibliography
ISBN 0-208-01044-0; 0-208-01422-5
           LC 67-24188
Supplementary volumes to basic volume entered in main catalog
The first supplement updates the basic bibliography to January 1970 and adds interpretations from three additional journals. The second supplement includes critical articles through 1972 and adds a few new playwrights as well as critical material from earlier dates not included in the earlier editions

016.813 Bibliographies of American fiction

Eichelberger, Clayton L.
 (comp.) A guide to critical reviews of United States fiction, 1870-1910, v2. Scarecrow 1974 351p $10   016.813
  1 American fiction—History and criticism—Bibliography 2 Book reviews—Bibliography 3 Periodicals—Indexes
  ISBN 0-8108-0701-7   LC 77-149998
  Earlier volume entered in main catalog
  This second volume lists approximately nine thousand additional contemporary critical notices of fiction produced by United States writers and published during the 1870-1910 period, thus expanding the original listing to over twenty thousand items

016.82 Bibliographies of English literature

The New Cambridge Bibliography of English literature, v 1: 600-1660. Ed. by George Watson. Cambridge 1974 xxxi, 2491p [i.e. 2476 columns, 15p] $49.50   016.82
  1 English literature—Bibliography
  ISBN 0-521-20004-0   LC 73-82455
  Volumes 2, 3, and 4 entered in main catalog. This volume completes the revised bibliography, which now supersedes The Cambridge Bibliography of English literature, also entered in main catalog

021.7 Promotion of libraries

Coplan, Kate
 Effective library exhibits; how to prepare and promote good displays; introduction by Gerald W. Johnson. 2d ed. Oceana 1974 176p illus $10   021.7
  1 Public relations—Libraries 2 Enoch Pratt Free Library, Baltimore
  ISBN 0-379-00265-5   LC 74-4428
  Earlier edition entered in main catalog
  First published 1958. In the 1974 edition "it seemed appropriate to revise certain sections, in keeping with developments of recent years. Accordingly, we have replaced a majority of the illustrations contained in the work, inserting contemporary topics among the suggested displays. Also, we have amended the chapter on Library Book Fairs; updated the bibliography; expanded the list of free and inexpensive display materials; added to the sources of supplies and equipment, and appended a new index." Acknowledgments

025.2 Acquisitions

Broadus, Robert N.
 Selecting materials for libraries. Wilson, H.W. 1973 342p $12   025.2
  1 Book selection
  ISBN 0-8242-0510-3   LC 73-3406
  "Addressed to students of librarianship yet valuable to practicing librarians, the book defines selection principles for medium-sized public libraries with some attention given to college, university, school, and special collections. The first two chapters identify guiding concepts of book selection, note general publishing aids, and describe the work of representative publishers; succeeding sections cover selection of particular types of print and nonprint materials and explain policies for purchase of government documents and out-of-print items. . . . Brief bibliographies are given to indicate further sources of information." Booklist
  "In discussing aids to selection within each chapter, Broadus makes a good choice among available material—although one could quarrel with the quality of some of his annotations. . . . Broadus readily admits that some topics have been omitted entirely (materials for children and 'library organization for selection'), while other topics have been treated far less fully than they deserve (such as the literature of science and technology, some areas of nonbook materials, the underground or alternative press, and the freedom to read issue." Library J

Carter, Mary Duncan
 Building library collections. 4th ed. by Mary Duncan Carter, Wallace John Bonk [and] Rose Mary Magrill. Scarecrow 1974 415p $9   025.2
  1 Book selection 2 Acquisitions (Libraries)
  ISBN 0-8108-0730-0   LC 74-7359
  Earlier edition entered in main catalog
  First published 1959. The 1974 edition has been considerably revised, expanded and updated with a redesigned format. Newly added are "the texts of twelve A.L.A. Council statements relating to the U.S. Constitution, and the text of the June, 1973 Supreme Court decision on obscenity." Publisher's note
  Includes bibliographies

Ford, Stephen
 The acquisition of library materials. A.L.A. 1973 237p $9.95   025.2
  1 Acquisitions (Libraries)
  ISBN 0-8389-0145-X   LC 73-9896
  Designed for use as a textbook in library schools and as a conceptual manual for practicing acquisitions librarians, the author examines all aspects of acquisitions in 16 chapters. Among these are purchasing domestic books, foreign books, and serial publications; procurement of materials through gift and exchange; purchasing of out-of-print books, reprints, and microforms. In addition to these specific acquisition efforts, Mr. Ford discusses principles of searching, sound order routines, centralized processing, and automation of order routines
  "Many added references are appended, as well as a subject index and glossary, which includes acronyms as well as terms. Remember, this is on acquisition, not book selection." Ref Services Rev
  Includes bibliographies

025.3 Cataloging

Piercy, Esther J.
 Commonsense cataloging; a manual for the organization of books and other materials in school and small public libraries. 2d ed. rev. by Marian Sanner. Wilson, H.W. 1974 233p illus $9   025.3
  1 Cataloging
  ISBN 0-8242-0009-8   LC 73-7573
  Earlier edition entered in main catalog
  First published 1965. For the 1974 edition "the reviser has retained the arrangement of the first edition, proceeding 'from the general to the specific, from principles to practices.' The chapters on Subject Cataloging and Audiovisual and Other Nonbook Materials have been expanded. The rules presented in this revision are based on those contained in 'Anglo-American Cataloging Rules' and in 'Non-book materials: the Organization of Integrated Collections;' many of the rules have been rephrased for simplicity but retain the principles enunciated in the two codes." Preface to the Second Edition
  The appendixes include routines, a glossary and a bibliography

025.5 Services to patrons. Reference

Katz, William A.
 Introduction to reference work. 2d ed. McGraw 1974 2v (McGraw-Hill Ser. in library education) v 1 $9.50, v2 $8.50   025.5
  1 Libraries—Reference service 2 Reference books—Bibliography
  LC 73-8658

Katz, William A.—*Continued*
First published 1969
Contents: v 1 Basic information sources (ISBN 0-07-033353-X); v2 Reference services and reference processes (ISBN 0-07-033354-8)
"The 2v set serves as a basic text for the study of reference work. [In] v 1 . . . basic reference sources are grouped by type, and many are treated at some length; v2 is concerned with the principles and practices of reference service." Winchell. Guide to Reference Books. 8th edition, 3d Supplement, 1969-1970 [Review of first edition]
"Students and teachers of librarianship, librarians who have missed out on a formal reference course, and interested laymen will benefit particularly from the broad, creative interpretation of the nature of reference work and of the scope and use of reference sources. . . . A worthwhile accompaniment to Winchell's Guide to reference books." Booklist [Review of first edition]

026 Libraries devoted to special subjects

Ash, Lee
(comp.) Subject collections; a guide to special book collections and subject emphases as reported by university, college, public, and special libraries and museums in the United States and Canada. Comp. by Lee Ash, with the assistance of William Miller and Alfred Waltermire, Jr. 4th ed. rev. & enl. Bowker 1974 908p $38.50   **026**
1 Libraries, Special
ISBN 0-8352-0453-0   LC 74-19331
Earlier edition entered in main catalog
First published 1958. The 1974 edition has been revised and updated

026.025 Special libraries—Directories

Directory of special libraries and information centers. 3d ed. Edited by Margaret Labash Young, Harold Chester Young, and Anthony T. Kruzas. Gale Res. 1974 v 1 $55, v2 $35, v3 by subscription only $57.50   **026.025**
1 Libraries, Special—Directories
ISBN v 1 0-8103-0279-9; v2 0-8103-0280-2; v3 0-8103-0281-0   LC 74-3240
Earlier edition entered in main catalog under the editorship of Anthony T. Kruzas
First published 1963. The 1974 edition has been revised and contains nearly 4,000 new entries

027.4 Public libraries

The **Metropolitan** library; ed. by Ralph W. Conant and Kathleen Molz. MIT Press 1972 333p $10   **027.4**
1 Public libraries   2 Metropolitan areas
ISBN 0-262-03041-1   LC 72-4338
Sequel to: The public library and the city, entered in main catalog, class 021, under Conant
This volume contains contributions by librarians and persons active in other fields, including urban studies, communication, sociology, publishing, political science, and journalism. Among the topics considered are the library in "society and in governmental setting, recognizing the user, the financial concerns, publishing, technology, telecommunications, [and] education of librarians." Library J
This "is a fine collection of pertinent pieces on a subject of continuing importance." Library Q
Metropolitan area library problems: an annotated bibliography: p299-327

027.5 Government libraries

Goodrum, Charles A.
The Library of Congress. Praeger 1974 292p illus (Praeger Lib. of U.S. Government departments and agencies) $10   **027.5**
1 U.S. Library of Congress   LC 72-189909
"A concise introduction for the general reader to what the author calls (with qualification) the world's largest library: its history, development, organization, programs, divisions, collections, and services, and its relationship to Congress, the nation, and the world of learning. Appendixes give information on careers at the Library of Congress and a list of the men who have served as Librarian of Congress. Bibliography." Booklist

027.62 Libraries for children and young adults

Edwards, Margaret A.
The fair garden and the swarm of beasts; the library and the young adult. Rev. and expanded. Hawthorn Bks. 1974 194p $5.95   **027.62**
1 Libraries, Young adults'   2 Books and reading   LC 74-4166
Earlier edition entered in main catalog
First published 1969. The 1974 edition has been expanded and brought up to date
A bibliography for the librarian working with teen-agers: p179-82

028.7 Use of books and other records as sources of information

Gates, Jean Key
Guide to the use of books and libraries. 3d ed. McGraw 1974 308p $6.95   **028.7**
1 Reference books   2 Libraries—Handbooks, manuals, etc.
ISBN 0-07-022984-8   LC 73-9502
Earlier edition entered in main catalog
First published 1962. The 1974 edition has been revised and brought up to date. Emphasis is on titles published since 1968

031 American encyclopedias

Encyclopaedia Britannica. 15th ed. Encyclopaedia Britannica 1974 30v illus maps   **031**
1 Encyclopedias and dictionaries
ISBN 0-85229-290-2   LC 73-81025
Prices vary according to binding
Earlier edition entered in main catalog
The ten-volume Micropedia "is both the index to the 'Macropaedia' and an independent ready reference source offering some 102,214 articles ranging from a few lines up to 750 words in length. The nineteen-volume 'Macropaedia' comprises 4,207 'in depth' articles, none of which is less than 1,000 words in length. These are signed articles by a worldwide roster of authorities, and include selective, briefly annotated bibliographies." College & Research Libs

The **World** book encyclopedia. Field Enterprises 22v illus maps   **031**
1 Encyclopedias and dictionaries
ISBN 0-7166-0073-0   LC 74-189336
Prices vary according to editions and bindings
First published 1917-1918. Beginning with 1972 edition, the set contains 22 volumes
This encyclopedia "was created to serve the needs of the entire family, but with emphasis on usefulness to students in the upper elementary grades through high school, and even through beginning college. It serves libraries, homes, and offices as an everyday reference tool, and is as popular with adults as with

The **World** book encyclopedia—*Continued*
young people.... It deals in depth with all areas of knowledge in an unbiased and impartial manner, while emphasizing those subjects most often required by students in the broad areas of the sciences (this coverage is especially fine), the arts, literature, technology, and biography. The latter category alone comprises more than 5,000 detailed entries." Walsh. General Encyclopedias in Print, 1971-72

Kept up to date by: The World book Yearbook

For a fuller review of the latest edition see: The Booklist and Subscription Books Bulletin, December 15, 1973

050 Periodical indexes

Humanities index. Wilson, H.W. service basis   **050**

1 Periodicals—Indexes

Quarterly with bound annual cumulations

Started publication in June 1974 as a result of the division with increased coverage of the Social sciences & humanities index, entered in main catalog, into Humanities index, and Social sciences index, the latter now listed in class 300.5

"The main body of the Index consists of author and subject entries to periodical articles. In addition there is an author listing of citations to book reviews, following the main body of the Index. Subject fields indexed include archaeology and classical studies, area studies, folklore, history, language and literature, literary and political criticism, performing arts, philosophy, religion and theology, and related subjects." Prefatory note

051 American periodicals

The **Best** of Life. Time-Life Bks. [distributed by Little] 1973 302p illus $19.95   **051**

1 Photography   LC 73-79056

"Editor: David E. Scherman"

"A spectacular selection of the magazine's photo-coverage by lensmen who achieved fame in its pages and by lesser-known photographers who had their inspired moments. Here are Eisenstaedt, Bourke-White, Capa, Elisofon, Parks, Mydans, Duncan, Gene Smith and the whole 'Life' gang. Their often historic photos leap at the eye: the 1937 explosion of the 'Hindenburg'; Rosenthal's classic Iwo Jima flagraising; the assassinations of JFK, King and Robert Kennedy; men-on-the-moon and so much more. The book's 20 sections, inevitably crowded but generally well laid out with many excellent full-color reproductions, make a visual panorama of drama and change reflecting wars from Spain to Vietnam, sports, science, kids, glamor-people, nature." Pub W

069.025 Museums—Directories

Museums of the world; a directory of 17000 museums in 148 countries, including a subject index [comp. by Eleanor Braun]. Bowker 1973 762p illus $47.50   **069.025**

1 Museums—Directories

ISBN 3-7940-3419-8   LC 73-155445

Title page and prefatory material in English and German

"Art museums, natural science and technical museums, ancient history and archaeological museums, local historical museums and historic sites are included. For each, when the information was available, the name of the museum, complete address, year of foundation, name of the director, type of museum, and information on the scope of its collection are given. The volume is arranged by continent, then by country, then subdivided again by city. Unfortunately, this arrangement makes it somewhat difficult to use the U.S. section because museums of cities of different states come together, e.g., Bloomington, California and Bloomington, Illinois and Bloomington, Indiana are grouped in the same section. Fortunately, the indexes make it possible to circumvent this awkward arrangement and locate any museum quickly. Three separate indexes:

one by subject covers everything from acoustics to tombstones; the second is a name index; and the last, a geographical index. The only up-to-date work in English covering museums in almost all the countries of the world and presenting its information conveniently, this work is highly recommended." Choice

100 PHILOSOPHY

110 Metaphysics (Speculative philosophy)

Heidegger, Martin

The end of philosophy; tr. by Joan Stambaugh. Harper 1973 110p $4.95   **110**

1 Metaphysics 2 Ontology

ISBN 0-06-063856-7   LC 73-6338

These four essays "give the best available picture of Heidegger's doctrine of the history of Being, and are thus helpful towards understanding his thought, particularly in its latest phases. The translation is very good.... 'Metaphysics as History of Being,' is quite thorough and intelligible; and the last, 'Overcoming Metaphysics,' is especially good on the point of the place of modern technology in the history." Library J

128 Man—his life and death

Kübler-Ross, Elisabeth

Questions and answers on death and dying. Macmillan Pub. Co. 1974 177p $4.95   **128**

1 Death

ISBN 0-02-567120-0   LC 73-19046

The answers concern the acceptance of the end of life, suicide, terminal illness, and euthanasia. The author also discusses ways of telling the patient he is critically ill and deals with the special difficulties surrounding death. The questions were asked by professional people and families arising out of their experiences with the terminally ill

This "book was written with no theological pretensions yet there is ample food for the believer here since she deals with the ultimate Christian question of how we face death, how we deal with it—or for that matter, what we think it is." America

Neale, Robert E.

The art of dying. Harper 1973 158p $5.95   **128**

1 Death

ISBN 0-06-066090-2   LC 72-11361

The author offers advice on "experiencing the fears of death and the fears of life, the dimensions of suicide and grief [and] the images and concepts of death." Library J

"A clear, contemplative and penetrating exploration of human attitudes toward death. Robert Neale has designed his book as a series of 'exercises' intended to raise and possibly transform the reader's own conscious or unconscious feelings and attitudes. There is, however, no formidable, dull or preachy didacticism here. Such exercises as Neale outlines are mere suggestions for the troubled." Pub W

Selected bibliography: p151-58

131 Popular psychology. Happiness

Teilhard de Chardin, Pierre

On happiness; tr. by René Hague. Harper [1974 c1973] 93p $3.95   **131**

1 Happiness

ISBN 0-06-061794-2   LC 73-9333

Original French edition 1966. This translation first published 1973 in England

This volume contains a lecture given by the author in Peking in 1943 and the comments he made at three weddings in 1928, 1935 and 1948. All are concerned with life's joy and life's meaning

Teilhard de Chardin, Pierre—*Continued*

This is a "tiny gem of a book. . . . [The author's] definition of three types of humankind and his call for humanity to strive for a higher state of consciousness surely offer nothing new to readers familiar with his work. But in this short book his mood is contagious, his style elegant. His stirring message of aspiration and hope is a welcome one at a time of widespread cynicism and despair." Christian Century

133.3 Divinatory arts

Gibson, Walter B.
The complete illustrated book of divination and prophecy, by Walter B. Gibson and Litzka R. Gibson; drawings by Murray Keshner. Doubleday 1973 336p illus $7.95
    133.3

1 Divination
ISBN 0-385-03599-3   LC 71-103748

"From aeromancy (prophecy by atmospheric conditions and heavenly bodies) to zoomancy (portents involving imaginary animals), a guide to the various methods of foretelling the future. The methods of divination covered include oracles, numerology, the 'I ching,' tarot and card reading, tasseomancy, and palmistry with history, explanations, instructions, and advice on how to prognosticate the fickle hand of fate with cards, coins, buttons, daisies, numbers, tea leaves, and coffee grounds." Booklist

This is "a good comprehensive collection of techniques used to foretell the future. . . . The chapters read well and explore each method more comprehensively than the usual surveys. Excellent glossary. The major failing (one common to most books on the occult) is its lack of scholarly credentials: no references; no bibliography. But it will provide an excellent starting point for those interested in foretelling the future." Choice

Nostradamus
The prophecies of Nostradamus; tr. ed. and introduced by Erika Cheetham. Putnam [1974 c1973] 439p $8.95   **133.3**

1 Prophecies
SBN 399-10995-1   LC 73-78957

"Capricorn books"
Another edition of a work entered in main catalog with title: The complete prophecies of Nostradamus

133.4 Demonology

Woods, William
A history of the devil. Putnam [1974 c1973] 251p illus $6.95   **133.4**

1 Demonology 2 Paganism
ISBN 0-399-11327-4   LC 73-93751

First published 1973 in England
The author "sees the devil as a remnant of an older, more primitive folk religion. This early devil was a god of nature, neither evil incarnate nor good personified. It was only with the increasing political power of the Church that the familiar horned god took on more and more of his allegedly malevolent traits, and his followers had to go underground, eventually to surface as witches and sorcerers. Woods's book spends a great deal of space castigating the Church and tracing its destruction of heretical groups as well as its imitation and assimilation of earlier festivals and holidays from the older religions." Library J

"His position has its limitations, but it does offer a refreshing distraction from the current Exorcist hullabaloo." Atlantic
Bibliography: p235-37

137 Personality analysis. Graphology

Hartford, Huntington
You are what you write. Macmillan Pub. Co. 1973 380p illus $8.95   **137**

1 Graphology   LC 72-91262

The author "traces a short history of writing and the beginnings of graphology and explains those elements of handwriting—rhythm, speed, pressure, connective form, slant, spacing, capitals, and small letters—which can be interpreted. [He] also investigates how accurate these interpretations can be and how health, mental disease, and the criminal mind can affect handwriting. . . . Numerous writing samples, reference sources, and bibliography." Booklist

"Will appeal to those interested not only in the background, but in the handwriting of famous personalities, like Marie Curie, Thomas Jefferson, and Abraham Lincoln." Ref Services Rev

150.19 Psychology systems, schools, viewpoints

Carpenter, Finley
The Skinner primer: behind freedom and dignity. Free Press 1974 224p $7.95   **150.19**

1 Behavior 2 Free will and determinism 3 Skinner, Burrhus Frederic
ISBN 0-02-905310-2   LC 73-16603

"A practical survey of operant behaviorism, the doctrine affirmed by Harvard psychologist B. F. Skinner. [The author] explains Skinnerian principles, judges their strengths and weaknesses, and examines similarities and contrasts between his and behaviorist views of freedom. In the critique of hypothetical societal situations governed by Skinner's theories, Carpenter asserts that one's psychological health can be maintained only by clinging to notions of personal freedom and determinism. Reading lists appended to several chapters. Very brief index." Booklist

Hall, Calvin S.
A primer of Jungian psychology [by] Calvin S. Hall and Vernon J. Nordby. Taplinger 1973 142p $5.95   **150.19**

1 Jung, Carl Gustav 2 Psychoanalysis
ISBN 0-8008-6554-5   LC 73-7255

"Brief, lucid introduction for students and the general reader to the voluminous writings of Carl Jung. Following a short biographical sketch the authors present an intelligible digest of Jung's theories on the personality, its structure, dynamics, development, types, and its relation to symbols and dreams. The presentation is expository and no attempt is made to deal with either criticism, evaluation, comparison, or consideration of Jung's ideas on abnormal personality. . . . Bibliography and reading guide to Jung's works and a list of recommended commentaries on Jung." Booklist

Skinner, B. F.
About behaviorism. Knopf 1974 256p $6.95   **150.19**

1 Behaviorism (Psychology)
ISBN 0-394-49201-3   LC 73-20768

The author "leads the reader through his investigation of the causes of behavior, through his own concepts of innate behavior, operant behavior, and verbal behavior, of thinking and knowing, and finally into . . . questions of emotion and the sense of Self. . . . He [seeks to] make clear his own beliefs about the workings of the human animal . . . with . . . the hope of identifying and implementing a science to improve human life." Publisher's note

Skinner "gives a good, slightly popularized introduction to behaviorist principles and attempts, especially in the 'Summing Up,' to refute his most persistent critics. However, he is more likely to confirm their views that his interpretation of human feelings, cognition, values, and accomplishments is reductionistic, his methodology open to question, and his ideas for the application of behavior control techniques a threat to freedom and dignity. Still his spirited defense of his philosophy should be made available so that laymen as well as professionals in psychology may draw their own conclusions." Library J
Bibliography: p253-56

152.4 Emotions and feelings

Fromm, Erich
The anatomy of human destructiveness. Holt 1973 521p $10.95 **152.4**
1 Aggressiveness (Psychology) 2 Violence
ISBN 0-03-007596-3   LC 73-3698

"In Parts 1 and 2, the author confronts the errors and inadequacies he finds in previous efforts to explain the origins and causes of aggression. . . . In Part 3, Fromm distinguishes 'biologically adaptive aggression which serves life,' whether in the world of animals or man, from malignant aggression or destructiveness. This destructiveness is specifically human and results from the interaction of various social conditions with man's existential needs.' Fromm then examines this interaction . . . [and argues] his theory with case studies of Stalin, Himmler, and Hitler." Library J

This work "will be welcomed by many as a wholesome reaction to the widely accepted views of some neo-instinctivists and neo-behaviorists. . . . The hasty reader may sometimes find the going a bit slow. But Fromm is always worth reading, even when he indulges in what may look like a detour. His book ends on a note of cautious optimism." Commonweal

Bibliography: p479-98

153.1 Memory and learning

Lorayne, Harry
The memory book, by Harry Lorayne and Jerry Lucas. Stein & Day 1974 237p $7.95   **153.1**
1 Memory
ISBN 0-8128-1664-1   LC 73-90705

The authors seek to show "that any new item can be remembered if one associates it in a ridiculous way with a memory 'peg.' Paying close attention when encountering whatever one wishes to remember is fostered by this trick." Library J

"Reading the book suggests that the system may work as advertised." Time

Piaget, Jean
Memory and intelligence [by] Jean Piaget and Bärbel Inhelder in collaboration with Hermine Sinclair-De Zwart; tr. from the French by Arnold J. Pomerans. Basic Bks. 1973 414p illus $12.50   **153.1**
1 Memory
SBN 465-0445-X   LC 72-89197

Original French edition published 1968

In this volume "the authors extend their study of children's developing ability to understand logical, numerical, and causal structures. Children aged three to six were asked to describe or reproduce from memory objects and relationships seen weeks or months previously. Of particular interest is the finding that as children's mental operational abilities develop over a period of months their reconstructions from 'memory' may in fact be superior to those produced immediately after first exposure to stimuli." Choice

Includes bibliographical references

155.4 Child psychology

Gesell, Arnold
Infant and child in the culture of today; the guidance of development in home and nursery school [by] Arnold Gesell, Frances L. Ilg, Louise Bates Ames, in collaboration with Janet Learned Rodell. Rev. ed. Harper 1974 420p illus $9.95   **155.4**
1 Child study 2 Infants
ISBN 0-06-011506-8   LC 73-4083

Earlier edition entered in main catalog

First published 1943. The 1974 edition has been brought up to date and includes material on a new behavior level: three and a half years, accelerated learning, the relationship between organism and environment, the challenge of individuality, and the changing culture. There is a new section on the guidance nursery school. Other material updated includes such currently revived practices as natural childbirth, peer learning, and breast-feeding." Publisher's note

Books for children: p391-98. Selected reading: p399-405

Joint Commission on Mental Health of Children
Mental health: from infancy through adolescence; reports of Task Forces I, II, and III and the Committees on Education and Religion. Harper 1973 470p $15   **155.4**
1 Child study 2 Mental health 3 Adolescence
SBN 06-012228-5   LC 78-123939

This book "reviews mental health aspects of human development in three stages: infancy to age five, kindergarten through eighth grade, and adolescence. Enhancement of mental development at each stage, effect of interrelated factors in achievement and productivity, and specialization of prevention and treatment at each level are emphasized. Two additional reports discuss the common relevance and goals of education and mental health, along with legislative considerations to promote these goals, and the place of religion in mental growth, particularly in forming and transmitting values. . . . Contains appendixes, tables, references, bibliographies, and indexes." Booklist

"This well-written volume . . . results from the commission's continuing effort to enlighten the public on contemporary needs of children and youth. . . . [The book] contains carefully conceived recommendations for improvement, touching on topics from birth control and teacher-training programs to a comprehensive system for coping with the manifold mental health needs of children and youth." Library J

158 Applied psychology

Newman, Mildred
How to be your own best friend; a conversation with two psychoanalysts [by] Mildred Newman & Bernard Berkowitz with Jean Owen. Random House [1973 c1971] 56p $4.95   **158**
1 Psychology, Applied
ISBN 0-394-48769-9   LC 73-4029

First published 1971 by Lark Publishing Company

"Jean Owens, a freelance writer grounded in philosophy and psychology, holds an extended conversation with a man-and-wife team of New York psychoanalysts. . . . Miss Owens draws out of Mildred Newman and Bernard Berkowitz a deceptively simple wisdom which goes beyond Coué and the 'positive thinking' school of self-help by presenting a rounder, more self-tolerant view of the human personality. Too many troubled people enjoy putting themselves down, they say; the way to enter adulthood is to 'let go of that fantasy of childhood safety,' accept maturity as a never-completed adventure, learn to loosen up." Pub W

"An accurate but sometimes over-simplified account of how to achieve emotional well-being." Library J

O'Neill, Nena
Shifting gears; finding security in a changing world [by] Nena O'Neill & George O'Neill. Evans, M.&Co. 1974 255p $7.95   **158**
1 Psychology, Applied
ISBN 0-87131-145-3   LC 73-91884

Th authors offer advice to help "a person develop a life strategy to meet change and personal crises. Their hypothesis is that, given the tools, an individual under stress can grow and mature and thus be able to change direction toward a more fulfilling life. They prescribe various techniques, such as 'centering' on one's values and needs, 'focusing' on the specific problem and appropriate solution, and 'committing' oneself to a chosen course of action." Library J

"The O'Neills propose a life strategy based on our real needs for continuing growth, and an understanding of how those needs change in the course of the life cycle. . . . The model

O'Neill, Nena—*Continued*

or process is realistic and enables one to become creative and mature in his own right. It is not like the other fads being pushed on the gullible public; it requires an honest effort on the part of the individual to understand the process of shifting gears to help live in our changing society." Best Sellers

Bibliography: p250-55

174 Euthanasia

Mannes, Marya

Last rights. Morrow 1974 [c1973] 150p illus $5.95   **174**

1 Euthanasia 2 Suicide 3 Death
ISBN 0-688-00211-0   LC 73-9881

"The book describes how the terminally ill are treated medically, psychologically and sociologically; it seeks, through the experiences of many different people, to analyze what death itself is really like; examines various ethical and religious attitudes toward life and death; and offers some alternatives to a prolonged, painful, costly and undignified death. Finally, Mannes sets forth her own provision for a 'decent' death." Pub W

"Written by a humanist for humanists, 'Last Rights' will have a sympathetic following. Christian readers who can identify with the sufferings of Christ will have many questions and misgivings. Right to Life proponents should read this book, if only to know the arguments they will encounter. The book contains a good deal of emotion masquerading as logic; it also contains some logic." Best Sellers

Bibliography: p143-44

181 Oriental philosophy

Forem, Jack

Transcendental meditation; Maharishi Mahesh Yogi and the science of creative intelligence. Dutton 1973 274p illus $7.95   **181**

1 Transcendental meditation
ISBN 0-525-22225-1   LC 72-96900

This is an introduction to the theoretical science of creative intelligence (SCI) and its practical technique, transcendental meditation (TM). The author believes that SCI and TM followers can experience and apply the source of one's inner creative intelligence. Results include the attainment of sounder physical and mental health, the increased competence to think, act and work efficiently, and the ability to experience more meaningful interpersonal relations. This book does not offer TM instruction, but rather describes SCI principles and goals, reviews scientific research on TM, and points out practical applications to individual and social problems. He draws parallels between the teachings of Maharishi, the movement's leader, and contemporary physics, education and psychology. A history of the movement is included

Includes bibliographic references

Manheim, Werner

Martin Buber. Twayne 1974 106p (Twayne's World authors ser) $6.95   **181**

1 Buber, Martin
ISBN 0-8057-2182-7   LC 72-13373

The author "has produced the best overview of Buber available yet in English, neglecting no major area. . . . [He has given] the almost impossible: an overview in depth. . . . [Manheim] has the breadth of scholarship and understanding needed to examine the literary, religious, philosophic, and contemporary character of Buber's work. He has produced a work **faithful to the variety of Buber himself,** managing real attractiveness of style with depth of grasp." Choice

Selected bibliography: p102-04

191 American philosophy

Dewey, John

The philosophy of John Dewey; ed. with an introduction and commentary by John J. McDermott. Putnam 1973 2v (xli, 723p) ea $7.95   **191**

1 Philosophy
SBN 399-10956-0; 399-10957-9   LC 73-175269

"Capricorn books"

Analyzed in Essay and general literature index

Contents: v 1: The structure of experience; v2: The lived experience

"For smaller collections which do not have extensive representation of Dewey's works a digest of the American philosopher's writings is supplied in two volumes of extracts from Dewey's most important works. The wide scope of his thoughts and insights on metaphysics, the scientific method of inquiry, the problem of knowledge, and value theory is presented in volume one while the second volume is concerned with ethics, aesthetics, pedagogy, politics, and the philosophy of culture. Identical biographical introductions, prefaces, chronologies, and bibliographies of Dewey's works are contained in both volumes." Booklist

194 French philosophy

Grene, Marjorie

Sartre. New Viewpoints 1973 301p $8.95   **194**

1 Sartre, Jean Paul
ISBN 0-531-06358-5   LC 73-1311

This is a study of the French author as both philosopher and writer. The author focuses on Sartre's place in the history of philosophy. She deals with his relationship with Descartes and his special debt to the school of phenomenology, particularly as represented by Husserl and Merleau-Ponty. Professor Grene also brings out the influence of Kierkegaard and Heidegger on Sartre's thought. Finally, she deals with his ambivalent relationship with Karl Marx, as reflected in "The Critique of Dialectical Reason"

"Grene, an accomplished scholar of existentialism, proposes that Sartre may be the last great Cartesian. Her study is not matched by any other in its comprehensiveness linked with critical appraisal. . . . While intelligible to any reader familiar with philosophy it is not a 'popular study.' " Choice

Bibliography: p289-91. Bibliographical references included in Notes: p293-300

200 RELIGION

203 Religion—Encyclopedias and dictionaries

The Oxford Dictionary of the Christian Church; ed. by F. L. Cross. 2d ed. Edited by F. L. Cross and E. A. Livingstone. Oxford 1974 xxxi, 1518p $35   **203**

1 Theology—Encyclopedias   2 Christianity—Encyclopedias
ISBN 0-19-211545-6

Earlier edition entered in main catalog

First published 1957. "This complete revision and updating has kept the high standards of the original publication. It has now brought within the scope of the 'Dictionary' the work of the Second Vatican Council and the attendant changes in the Roman Catholic Church, as well as the continuing developments in ecumenical work, theological modernization, and the emergence of new leadership since that time. The book has been expanded about one-tenth in size, and its helpful bibliography has been brought up to date." Choice

220 Bible

Eerdmans' Handbook to the Bible; ed. by David Alexander [and] Pat Alexander; consulting editors: David Field [and others]. Eerdmans 1973 680p illus maps $12.95   220

1 Bible—Handbooks, manuals, etc.
ISBN 0-8028-3436-1   LC 73-7638

This volume "is divided into four main sections: a section of general information about the Bible and biblical archaeology, two sections which treat the Old and New Testaments book by book, and a final section of brief entries on terms, people, and places. The handbook is written from the Protestant Christian viewpoint." Cur Ref Bks

This book "is written by 32 authorities representing British, Canadian, or Commonwealth institutions. The contributors are identified as to position, and the materials for which they are responsible are signed. Each has written on subjects for which he is qualified by background and experience. . . . The Foreword states: 'The editors of this book have selected and presented a variety of factual information in a simple, helpful, and visually interesting way. . . . The emphasis is always on the kind of information that is directly relevant for the Bible reader who is trying to increase his understanding of what the text before him has to say.' In general, the editors achieve their purpose. The book is designed by arrangement and organization to be consulted for specific information. . . . The entire text is liberally illustrated with maps, charts, tables, reproductions, and photographs. Users are to be reminded that the version of the Bible used as basis for the text is not specified. Eerdmans' Handbook to the Bible will be useful to those who need an easy-to-get-at introduction to Bible literature." Booklist

220.5 Bible. Modern versions

Bible
The Anchor Bible. Doubleday 1974 3v ea $8   220.5

Earlier volumes entered in main catalog
Contents: v34 Ephesians 1-3 (ISBN 0-385-04412-7); v34A Ephesians 4-6 (ISBN 0-385-0803-9); v42 I and II Esdras (ISBN 0-385-00426-5)

220.9 Bible—Geography

Baly, Denis
The geography of the Bible. New and rev. ed. Harper 1974 288p illus maps $10.95   220.9

1 Bible—Geography
ISBN 0-06-060371-2   LC 73-6340

Earlier edition entered in main catalog
First published 1957. In the 1974 edition "two new chapters have been added; the others have been rewritten; all maps have been redrawn and their total number is doubled; new photos have been added." Library J
Bibliography: p257-62

232 Jesus Christ and his family

Vermes, Geza
Jesus the Jew; a historian's reading of the Gospels. Macmillan Pub. Co. [1974 c1973] 286p $6.95   232

1 Jesus Christ   LC 73-18516

First published 1973 in England
"The work has two sections. The first is an exposition of the 'setting,' which concludes that Jesus was born in Nazareth of Joseph and Mary, probably never married and was an itinerant exorcist, healer, preacher and holy man (Hasid) not seriously in conflict with Jewish doctrine. The second and major section is a detailed examination of five titles given to Jesus." America

"Already regarded as a turn-in-the-road book, this historical study eschews most theological elements and jolts Christian readers into relocating Jesus in his original Jewish environment. Positive thinking about an often forgotten context; readable by non-specialists." Christian Century

233 Man. Sin

Menninger, Karl
Whatever became of sin? Hawthorn Bks. 1973 242p $7.95   233

1 Sin   LC 72-7776

"Convinced that the 'idea' of 'sin' has become lost in our time, behind such political terms as 'crime' and such medical terms as 'disease,' Menninger convincingly demonstrates that the 'reality' of sin is very much with us. Furthermore, moral health, social health, and mental health are intimately related, so that neglect of the moral brings sickness to the whole of life. Drawing upon his rich reservoir of experience as a psychiatrist, his penetrating insights as a social critic, the best theological studies on the issue, Menninger has written a compassionate and helpful book for the ordinary man." Choice

248 Personal Christian religion

Merton, Thomas
The Asian journal of Thomas Merton; ed. from his original notebooks by Naomi Burton, Patrick Hart & James Laughlin; consulting ed: Amiya Chakravarty. New Directions 1973 xxviii, 445p illus $12.50   248

1 Spiritual life 2 Meditations
ISBN 0-8112-0464-2   LC 71-103370

"Father Merton, the writer and Trappist monk who explored Hinduism, Buddhism, Zen and Sufi mysticism, and who died in Bangkok in December, 1968, kept a notebook which covered his first trip to Asia—'the home where I have never been in this body'—and the three months before his untimely death. Now, carefully edited and elaborated by a team of friends, scholars and fellow monks, this book shines with the familiar radiance of Merton's spirituality. A travelogue in one sense, it is also a compendium of quotations from Asian religious leaders which struck Merton as having universal validity. His three audiences with the Dalai Lama are particularly valuable for readers pursuing metaphysical wisdom and discipline." Pub W

Includes bibliography and a glossary

252 Sermons

Marshall, Peter
Mr Jones, meet the Master; sermons and prayers of Peter Marshall. Hall, G.K.&Co. 1973 [c1950] 330p $9.95   252

1 Sermons 2 Prayers
ISBN 0-8161-6132-1   LC 73-9911

A large print edition of a title first published 1950 by Revell and entered in main catalog

265 Rites, ceremonies, sacraments. Marriage

Brill, Mordecai L.
Write your own wedding; a personal guide for couples of all faiths [by] Mordecai L. Brill, Marlene Halpin [and] William H. Genné. Assn. Press 1973 127p illus pa $2.95   265

1 Marriage customs and rites
ISBN 0-8096-1855-9   LC 73-5927

"The authors—a Jewish rabbi, a Roman Catholic educator and a Protestant clergyman—

Brill, Mordecai L.—*Continued*
offer examples of liturgies and suggestions for original prayers and vows for couples who want to design their own marriage ceremonies." Christian Century
"The authors' tone throughout is thoughtful." Library J
Music for your wedding: p100-07. Other useful books: p127

277.3 Christian church in the U.S.

Marty, Martin E.
The fire we can light; the role of religion in a suddenly different world. Doubleday 1973 240p $5.95   277.3
  1 U.S.—Religion 2 Protestantism
  ISBN 0-385-07602-9   LC 73-83601
"A Christian century projection for the 1970s" The author surveys "the state of religion in America during the first term of President Nixon. He sees religion in this era taking a conservative turn, thus providing the ballast to help stabilize a turbulent society. However, he is critical of the churches' readiness to condone and prosper from the conservatism of the age, while neglecting to take a stand on urgent social problems. The work abounds with observations and interpretations of current religious phenomena, such as the renewed emphasis on the spiritual, the decline of some older Protestant denominations, the rise of newer ones, and the broadening of the Roman Catholic Church. Well-written, and timely." Library J
Reference notes: p234-40

291 Comparative religion and religious mythology

Noss, John B.
Man's religions. 5th ed. Macmillan Pub. Co. 1974 589p illus maps $9.95   291
  1 Religions
  ISBN 0-02-388440-1   LC 72-13972
Earlier edition entered in main catalog
First published 1949. In the 1974 edition among the passages "that are new or that have been reconsidered are such topics as these: the close interrelation of ritual and soma in early Hinduism; divination in early Chinese religion, especially as treated in the 'I Ching;' the large role of folk religion in Shinto; the taboo-breaking attempts of Hindu and Buddhist tantrists to experience reality directly while transcending the physical aspects of the experience; alchemy, hygiene, and group religious rites in Taoist magic and religion; medieval cathedrals and the masses performed in them; Vatican II on non-Christian religions; and the effects of Islam on architecture, learning, and literature." Preface to the 5th edition
Includes bibliographies

291.03 Comparative religion and religious mythology—Encyclopedias and dictionaries

Parrinder, Geoffrey
A dictionary of non-Christian religions. Westminster Press [1973 c1971] 320p illus $10.95   291.03
  1 Religions—Encyclopedias
  ISBN 0-664-20981-5   LC 73-4781
First published 1971 in England
This dictionary covers "the religions of the world, with the exception of Christianity and the Bible. . . . [Attention is given] to Hinduism, Buddhism and Islam. . . . Space is also devoted to other Far Eastern religions, to the classical worlds of ancient Persia, Mesopotamia, Egypt, Greece and Rome, and to Celtic, Teutonic and Scandinavian religions. Judaism is referred to in detail in the post-Biblical period, and . . . [included also] are discussions of some of the beliefs and customs of ancient American cultures: Mayas, Aztecs and Incas, and also those of Australasia and Africa." Introduction
"The attempts to say much about key terms, persons and events in the world's religions, all within the scope of 320 pages, may seem to be foolhardy. But those who would like very brief references to these will find Parrinder helpful. Illustrated, inelegantly." Christian Century
Further reading list: p318-20

299 Other religions

Castaneda, Carlos
The teachings of Don Juan; a Yaqui way of knowledge. Simon & Schuster 1973 [c1968] 288p $7.95   299
  1 Juan, Don, 1891- 2 Yaqui Indians—Religion and mythology 3 Hallucinogenic drugs
  ISBN 0-671-21555-8   LC 73-166188
Companion volume to the author's Journey to Ixtlan: the lessons of Don Juan and A separate reality, both entered in main catalog
A reissue of the title first published 1968 by the University of California Press
"This book is the record of a young anthropologist's experiences as the apprentice of a [Yaqui] Indian sorcerer. Over a period of four years, Mr. Castaneda paid intermittent visits to Don Juan, first in Arizona, then in Sonora, Mexico. The aim of his initiation [which he describes in the first part of the book] was to gain power over the demonic world through the ritualized ingestion of peyote and other hallucinogenic plants. . . . The second half of the book is called 'A Structural Analysis,' in which the author attempts to analyze his experiences in the language of the social sciences." N Y Times Bk R

300 THE SOCIAL SCIENCES

300.5 Social sciences—Periodicals —Indexes

Social sciences index. Wilson, H.W. service basis   300.5
  1 Social sciences—Periodicals—Indexes
Quarterly with bound annual cumulations
Started publication in June 1974 as a result of the division with increased coverage of the Social sciences & humanities index, entered in main catalog class 050, into Humanities index now listed in class 050, and Social sciences index
"The main body of the Index consists of author and subject entries to periodicals in the fields of anthropology, area studies, economics, environmental science, geography, law and criminology, medical sciences, political science, psychology, public administration, sociology and related subjects. In addition there is an author listing of citations to book reviews, following the main body of the Index." Prefatory note

301.2 Culture and cultural processes

Severin, Timothy
The Horizon Book of vanishing primitive man; foreword by Colin M. Turnbull. Editor: Alvin M. Josephy, Jr. Picture editor: Douglas Tunstell. Am. Heritage 1973 379p illus maps $22   301.2
  1 Society, Primitive
  ISBN 0-07-056348-9   LC 73-7781
This book describes the evolution of prehistoric man and explores the primitive societies of the Australian Aborigines, Polynesians, Melanesians, Pygmies, Bushmen, Cuna of Panama, Indians of the Amazon, Eskimos, Ainu of Japan and Lapps
"Among recent attempts to describe exotic but waning 'primitive' peoples, this volume is one of the better efforts. Severin dis-

Severin, Timothy—*Continued*
cusses ten different peoples by examining historical, anthropological and other outsiders' descriptions. . . . While basically sound in description and presentation, the book has the usual problem of oversimplification. . . . [It] is well produced and has many illustrations, both color and black-and-white. The general reader will find the volume useful, and Turnbull's introduction is an appropriate stage-setter." Science Bks

Recommended reading: p378. Bibliographical references included in Permissions: p379

301.29 Culture and cultural processes—Historical and geographical treatment

Patai, Raphael
  The Arab mind. Scribner 1973 376p $12.50   301.29
  1 Arabs
  ISBN 0-684-13306-7   LC 72-11120

  In this study of the Arab mind, the author "discusses 'Arab' and 'Muslim,' Bedouins and urbanites, dreams of unity and realities of conflict. He analyzes literary, religious and social traditions, laying stress on child-rearing patterns and such revealing Arab characteristics as the tendency to disregard time and take words for deeds. Finally he comes to nationalism, Israel, the impact of the 20th century on an essentially medieval society and this society's complex, basically hostile attitude toward the West." Pub W

  "A penetrating, lucid treatment of a difficult and sensitive subject. . . . Undoubtedly, a study on the mentality and behavior of a large, complex, and not-so-homogeneous population as the Arabs involves considerable generalizations, and some readers will take exception to many made in this book. . . . Nevertheless, this is a valuable and welcome contribution to the understanding of the people of the Middle East and commands the attention of both student and layman." Choice

  Bibliographical references included in Notes: p328-63

301.32 Populations

Kahn, E. J.
  The American people; the findings of the 1970 census [by] E. J. Kahn, Jr. Weybright & Talley 1974 340p $8.95   301.32
  1 U.S.—Population 2 U.S.—Census
  ISBN 0-679-40003-6   LC 73-84073

  "Here is a book dealing with the 1970 census data which does not include a single chart, map, or graph! Not only that but Kahn '(New Yorker)' even makes it interesting and entertaining. While poring over census reports it is often difficult to pick out significant details, important trends, directions, and fluctuations. This is an excellent reference work, which in plain, understandable language points up the relevent similarities and differences among our 210 million people in such areas as race, mobility, status, money, sex, and migration. The poor and the minorities, especially the blacks and the Chicanos, get extensive coverage. There is an excellent section on racial and ethnic intermarriage, with some surprising conclusions drawn on the basis of the data." Choice

301.34 The community

Banfield, Edward C.
  The unheavenly city revisited. Little 1974 358p $8.95   301.34
  1 Cities and towns—U.S. 2 Sociology, Urban
  ISBN 0-316-08014-4   LC 73-22876

  Earlier edition, entered in main catalog, has title: The unheavenly city

  First published 1970. The 1974 edition has been thoroughly revised and expanded to reflect changes in the problems of the cities and the growth and distribution of population. Includes a list of writings about: The unheavenly city

  Bibliographical references included in chapter notes

301.41 The sexes and their relations

Friedan, Betty
  The feminine mystique. 10th anniversary ed. Norton 1974 430p $8.95   301.41
  1 Women in the U.S. 2 Woman—Social conditions
  ISBN 0-393-08685-2   LC 74-160840

  Earlier edition entered in main catalog
  First published 1963. The 1974 edition has "a new five-page introduction and a new 17-page epilogue, both of which first appeared in the 'New York Times Magazine.'" Library J
  Includes bibliographical references

Howard, Jane
  A different woman. Dutton 1973 413p $7.95   301.41
  1 Women in the U.S. 2 U.S.—Social conditions
  ISBN 0-525-09310-9   LC 73-79557

  "The author went around the country for a period of two years and interviewed women of various backgrounds in an effort to find out where is the American woman and what does she want in life. Interspersed with these interviews are the author's recollections of her own life, her mother, and her sister. The portrait of the contemporary woman which is revealed is a complex one, involving controversy and disillusionment." Cath Lib World

  Jane Howard "has written a wholesome book about a lot of un-well-known American women whose lives are being affected by the wave of feminism sweeping the country. . . . With a not-too-radical stance the book explores what women think they are looking for. . . . And if people think a lot of women aren't hungry for this sort of reading they are all wrong. . . . The women Ms Howard cites are serious, very serious. But her telling is lightened by deft and funny touches." Christian Science Monitor

Montagu, Ashley
  The natural superiority of women. New rev. ed. Collier Bks. 1974 268p pa $1.95   301.41
  1 Woman
  ISBN 0-02-096080-8   LC 73-8087

  Earlier edition entered in main catalog
  First published 1953 by Macmillan. The 1974 edition is brought up to date with added material on the sexual superiority of the female. (Publisher)
  Includes bibliographical references

Rossi, Alice S.
  (ed.) The feminist papers: from Adams to de Beauvoir; ed. and with introductory essays. Columbia Univ. Press 1973 716p map $12.95   301.41
  1 Woman—Social conditions 2 Woman—Civil rights 3 Women's Liberation Movement
  ISBN 0-231-03795-3   LC 73-8828

  This "anthology of representative passages from intellectuals, crusaders, and activists who have consciously thought, written, and acted in an attempt to elevate the status of women opens with letters by Abigail Adams and concludes with writings by Virginia Woolf, Margaret Mead, and Simone de Beauvoir. The editor analyzes the historical, biographical, religious, and sociological aspects of feminist writers." Booklist

  "Here are, as Alice Rossi claims in her well-written preface, 'the essential works of feminism,' published over a period of 200 years. Her introductions to each section are informative and written with nonpolemical grace." New Repub

  Bibliography: p707-16

301.42 Marriage and family

Caine, Lynn
Widow. Morrow 1974 222p $6.95 301.42
1 Widows
ISBN 0-688-02850-0 LC 73-23124

The author's account of her husband's "death from cancer is the springboard for a narrative that carries the painful but ultimately reassuring message of her book: widowhood is a trauma that very few women are prepared to cope with. Mrs. Caine describes every step of her long struggle back to self-confidence expressing the plain truth about a widow's grief, her money anxieties, the subtle social ostracism inflicted by a world of 'couples,' the sexual pitfalls common to widows." Pub W

"Her style is tough and lucid. Self-humor, tact, and regard for the essential keep the book as well paced and fascinating as a mystery.... But the crux of the problem for the widow is never lost: how to become a discrete self, when you are no longer Mrs. John Smith. This book should be required reading for everyone over 18." Choice

Klein, Carole
The single parent experience. Walker & Co. 1973 241p $7.95 301.42
1 Parent and child 2 Adoption
ISBN 0-8027-0371-2 LC 72-80536

The author's "examination of this relatively new variation on the family is based on interviews with a fairly large number of single parents, female, male, adoptive, natural, interracial, and some homosexuals. Motivations vary, and some of these single parents seem to have healthier attitudes than others.... Miss Klein is generally sympathetic to the single parent situation, but she is careful to record negative reactions by psychiatrists and warnings about some of the things that can go wrong.... A useful compendium of adoption agencies is included." Pub W

"An informal, impressionistic, and vivid account.... Written in an engaging and highly anecdotal style, the book... [is] highly recommended for general audiences but too limited and superficial for scholarly libraries." Choice
Bibliography: p239-41

Krantzler, Mel
Creative divorce; a new opportunity for personal growth. Evans, M.&Co. 1974 268p $6.95 301.42
1 Divorce
ISBN 0-87131-131-1 LC 73-82863

The author "touches all the bases: how to come to terms with past marriage; how to release and cope with anger; how to keep from avoiding the opposite sex; how to stop repeating destructive patterns in human relationships." Pub W

"Krantzler's chapter on children in divorce [is] full of humane and common-sense comfort to parents.... [His] approach is not far from the new, popular psychoanalytical field of transactional analysis, in which emphasis is on the notion that within each grownup the child he used to be lives on, and that within each child there is a little adult, worthy of respectful consideration." New Repub

Landis, Judson T.
Building a successful marriage [by] Judson T. Landis [and] Mary G. Landis. 6th ed. Prentice-Hall 1973 526p illus $9.95 301.42
1 Marriage 2 Family life education
ISBN 0-13-086991-0 LC 72-11889

Earlier edition entered in main catalog
First published 1948. The 1973 edition has been updated and includes new material on premarital sex, mixed marriage, women's liberation, abortion, and changing attitudes on sexual behavior
Includes bibliographies

301.43 Specific age levels

Curtin, Sharon R.
Nobody ever died of old age 301.43
1 Aged—U.S. 2 Aged—Dwellings

Some editions are:
Hall, G.K.&Co. $7.95 Large print edition (ISBN 0-8161-6107-0)
Little $6.95 An Atlantic Monthly Press book (ISBN 0-316-16546-8)

First published 1972
"A first-person narrative of [author's] experiences with problem situations involving the aged, partially in her capacity as a nurse.... Although subjective, it pinpoints what this reviewer has also long posed as a major problem of the aged poor. The loss of dignity is imposed on the aged through the myriad agencies that a person must demeaningly approach and sacrifice his privacy to in order to supplement inadequate Social Security payments. The government persistently adds a pittance to the Social Security check and then takes it back via another agency, or even adds an agency, rather than putting it all into one check and restoring dignity to the aged." Choice

These stories "are told with anger and always with compassion but never with sentimentality. Curtin believes that motivation for any real change must come from old people themselves.... But her overriding concern is with the attitudes our society has formed toward aging, and her lucid, intelligent, often moving book is meant to serve, at least in part, as a reminder that those we now consider a 'problem' will one day be ourselves." Sat R Sci

Holt, John
Escape from childhood. Dutton 1974 286p $7.95 301.43
1 Children—Civil rights 2 Parent and child 3 Children—Management 4 Youth
ISBN 0-525-099557 LC 73-18060

Holt maintains that children are "humiliated and degraded by our society.... [He wants] to give them freedom of choice in education... the vote, financial independence, the right to choose their guardians and... 'the right to do, in general, what any adult may legally do.'... [He seeks] to show that the family as we know it is a modern phenomenon, and that childhood itself is an historical invention.... Prolonged childhood is partly an attempt to protect the child from exploitation by society, partly an attempt to keep him out of an overcrowded job market.... [The author also argues] that, in many respects, our power to protect becomes the power to abuse." N Y Times Bk R

"His claims of children's responsibility and competency in decision-making give the work a flavor of wild idealism. He underestimates the consequences of such changes on the family and the social structure.... Holt's book is light reading and has many examples from the author's experience with children. It is intended for a general audience and would be of special interest to parents who might find the ideas thought-provoking although somewhat sensational." Choice

Smith, Bert Kruger
Aging in America. Beacon Press 1973 239p $8.95 301.43
1 Aged—U.S. 2 Old age
ISBN 0-8070-2768-5 LC 72-6232

"The author bases this book on her intimate knowledge of the emotional, financial and physical needs of the older people in this country. She proves her thesis, that there are as many different kinds of aged and aging folk as there are younger people. One retiree is still vigorous and working part time as a consultant for the firm which formerly employed him full time. In desperate contrast are the plights of others with no occupation, no friends and no money. Even those with their own homes and social security find their welfare threatened because of inflation. An encouraging appendix lists by states those organizations which concerned people can call on to help them help the aged and/or themselves." Pub W

"Smith is knowledgeable and articulate, and the book reads easily and commands the full attention of the reader. Well referenced, the book should be a valuable volume to all students interested in the study of aging. Further it should have interest for persons who deal with problems associated with aging in this society." Choice

Includes bibliographcal references

Thompson, Thomas
 Richie; the ultimate tragedy between one decent man and the son he loved. Saturday Review Press 1973 308p illus $7.95   **301.43**
 1 Diener family 2 Conflict of generations 3 Drugs and youth
 ISBN 0-8415-0249-8   LC 72-88667
 "This book recounts the ironic mix of events, personal backgrounds, and relationships which led to the 1972 murder of an East Meadow, Long Island teenage drug-user by his straight, middle-class father." Library J
 "Meticulously, without heavy hindsight, Thompson traces the factors in the calamity that befell the Dieners. He has a telling chapter on the general ignorance about the dangers of readily available 'downers' when pot, LSD and heroin were widely publicized. . . . Not everyone will agree with the sympathetic portrayal of George Diener. . . . The final confrontation on the cellar stairs silences any easy attribution of blame: this is a terrible story, told thoughtfully and movingly." Newsweek

301.45 Nondominant aggregates of racial, ethnic and national origins

Aptheker, Herbert
 (ed.) A documentary history of the Negro people in the United States. Citadel 1973-1974 2v ea $17.50   **301.45**
 1 Negroes—History—Sources 2 Negroes—Civil rights   LC 51-14828
 Volume I entered in main catalog as a two volume set
 Contents: v2 1910-1932 [From the emergence of the N.A.A.C.P. to the beginning of the New Deal] Preface by Charles H. Wesley (ISBN 0-8065-0362-9); v3 1933-1945 [From the beginning of the New Deal to the end of the Second World War] Preface by William L. Patterson (ISBN 0-8065-0438-2)

Baldwin, James
 A dialogue [by] James Baldwin [and] Nikki Giovanni; foreword by Ida Lewis; afterword by Orde Coombs. Lippincott 1973 112p $4.95   **301.45**
 1 Negroes—Psychology 2 U.S.—Race relations
 ISBN 0-397-00916-X   LC 73-4388
 This is a dialogue between "novelist and poet, black man and black woman, each facing up to the painful dilemmas of blackness in a white society. Their taped discussion was aired on public TV in December, 1971, and has been revised minimally. . . . Central to the dialogue . . . is Nikki Giovanni's 'demand' that black men no longer run out on their responsibilities to black women and their children." Pub W
 "When a poet turns to prose, when a fine prose writer reveals himself after all a poet, the resulting conversation is a privilege to read. Here are: an effective description of the writer and his task; an acute differentiation between love and lust; a mystical treatment of The Word; an expression of the saving grace of responsibility to children." Best Sellers

Birmingham, Stephen
 Real lace: America's Irish rich. Harper 1973 322p illus $10   **301.45**
 1 Irish in the U.S. 2 U.S.—Social life and customs
 ISBN 0-06-010336-1   LC 73-4061
 The author covers the political, financial and social rise of some of the descendants of Irish immigrants who came to this country during the famine years of the mid-nineteenth century. "Opening with the collapse of the brokerage firm of McDonnell and Co., he traces the rise and relationships of the McDonnells, Murrays and Cuddihys, jumps to the Dohenys and Teapot Dome, follows this with sections on the 'wheeler-dealers' (including the Kennedys), and on 'high society' (including the Buckleys), and concludes with a section in which the problems, corporate and personal, of the McDonnell-Murrays are further explored." Library J

"The most interesting information in the book concerns the wide variety of businesses and professions successfully undertaken by the Irish. The most obvious omission is any serious examination of the reasons for the social prejudice which, as Catholics, they encountered." Atlantic

Franklin, John Hope
 From slavery to freedom; a history of Negro Americans. 4th ed. Knopf 1974 xxv, 548, xlii p illus $13.95   **301.45**
 1 Negroes—History 2 Slavery in the U.S.
 ISBN 0-394-48786-9   LC 73-15590
 Earlier edition entered in main catalog
 First published 1947. The 1974 edition has been revised to include recent developments in the Black struggle for equality
 Bibliographical notes: p513-48

Golden, Harry
 Travels through Jewish America, by Harry Golden with Richard Goldhurst. Doubleday 1973 276p $7.95   **301.45**
 1 Jews in the U.S.
 ISBN 0-385-07811-0   LC 73-79635
 Golden and his son have produced a "collection distinguished by warmth, enthusiasm, and wit, if not by originality. Essays and social commentary on Jews and Jewish culture in contemporary America . . . offer a good look at 10 U.S. cities and the sense of Jewish community as it has evolved in the twentieth century." Booklist

Hughes, Langston
 A pictorial history of Blackamericans [by] Langston Hughes, Milton Meltzer, and C. Eric Lincoln. 4th rev. ed. of A pictorial history of the Negro in America. Crown [1974 c1973] 377p illus maps $7.95
   301.45
 1 Negroes—History 2 U.S.—Race relations 3 Slavery in the U.S.   LC 73-82942
 Earlier edition entered in main catalog
 First edition by Langston Hughes and Milton Meltzer published 1956. This edition has been updated and revised. Some of the "chapters that have been added deal with the ancient African civilizations, Afro-Americans, and Africa today, blacks in arts and letters, black motion pictures, the aftermath of Vietnam, sports and the Cinderella syndrome, and the communications gap." Publisher's note

Woodward, C. Vann
 The strange career of Jim Crow. 3d rev. ed. Oxford 1974 233p $8.95   **301.45**
 1 Negroes—Segregation
 ISBN 0-19-501804-4   LC 73-90370
 Earlier edition entered in main catalog
 First published 1955. In the 1974 edition the author "updates his classic study of Southern segregation by the addition of a concluding chapter covering events from 1965 Watts riots to . . . controversies under the Nixon administration, while concurrently shifting focus from problems in the South to those of Northern cities. Recent titles appear in appended reading list." Booklist

309.173 Social conditions of the U.S.

Moynihan, Daniel P.
 Coping; essays on the practice of government. Random House [1974 c1973] 430p $10   **309.173**
 1 U.S.—Social conditions 2 U.S.—Social policy
 ISBN 0-394-48324-3   LC 73-3983
 Analyzed in Essay and general literature index
 The subjects of these essays, which appeared in various journals between 1961 and 1973, "range from welfare to traffic safety, from political reform to the President's relationship with the press, from racial relations

Moynihan, Daniel P.—*Continued*
to education and urban affairs. Yet the essays all have a single theme: that to cope with specific public issues you must first define the nature of the problems involved." Publisher's note

'Coping' is really a series of lessons drawn from . . . [Moynihan's] experiences in Washington. . . . Generally . . . the articles maintain that high quality of analysis and thought that we have come to expect from Moynihan. The best selections are those focusing on areas where the author has done basic research; his articles on transportation, race relations, and welfare will remain required reading for some time to come." Library J

309.175 Social conditions of the Appalachian region

Kahn, Kathy
Hillbilly women; photographs by Al Clayton; migrant photographs by Frank Blechman, Jr. Doubleday 1973 230p illus map $7.95   309.175
1 Women in the U.S. 2 Appalachian region—Social conditions 3 Miners
ISBN 0-385-01411-2   LC 72-96246

The women of the Appalachian back country are presented "as members of families fighting for their rights, their lands, and their heritage of strong independence; the picture also has its brutal side, in the stories of harassment by mining interests and factory bosses." Library J

"Ms. Kahn etches a compelling portrait of the problems of southern Appalachia, but equally important, she suggests channels through which the inhabitants and outsiders can help." Sat R/World

320.03 Political science—Encyclopedias and dictionaries

Blevins, Leon W.
The young voter's manual; a topical dictionary of American government and politics. Littlefield 1973 366p pa $3.95   320.03
1 Political science—Encyclopedias 2 U.S.—Politics and government—Encyclopedias
ISBN 0-8226-0260-1   LC 73-10377

"A Littlefield, Adams Quality paperback"

"This is intended for new voters who want a quick reference to terms used in government and politics. It is arranged in broad subject areas, including branches of government, foreign policy, political dynamics, major Supreme Court cases, etc. Terms referred to elsewhere are italicized and have supernumbers indicating the chapter." Library J

"This volume's subtitle would seem more appropriate than the title, because it contains information that even the oldest of voters would find new and enlightening. . . . The internal cross-referencing between the separate sections is excellent and thorough. This book compares most favorably with 'The American political dictionary' by J. C. Plano and M. Greenberg [entered in main catalog]. It is not as long, does not go as deeply into specific governmental functions, e.g., labor, agriculture, etc. nor does it emphasize the significance of each definition, but there are more definitions in this book. . . . A must for reference shelves." Choice

321.8 Democratic forms of state

Padover, Saul K.
(ed.) Sources of democracy; voices of freedom, hope and justice; selected with commentary by Saul K. Padover. McGraw 1973 xxxiv, 402p $25   321.8
1 Democracy 2 Political science 3 Civil rights
ISBN 0-07-048073-7   LC 72-10247

This is a "source book of ideas and documents of democracy over the centuries. The selections range from the writings of Pericles and Aristotle to statements by U.S. Presidents and Supreme Court decisions and include documents from Roman Edicts to modern constitutions. Arranged chronologically within thematic sections the pieces encompass definitions, of democracy and republicanism, civil liberty, political and racial equality, freedom of communication and religion, voting rights, and the American self-image." Booklist

"The whole is introduced by an excellent, thoughtful essay by Padover, 'Reflections on democracy,' and each of the nine parts is prefaced by his commentary. Often such books as this lack continuity; this book is an exception. . . . The excerpts are put together with skill so that each succeeding one builds on its predecessors. It should be extremely useful for teaching in high schools and colleges, and lay persons should also find it fascinating. Handsomely put together; includes an excellent short bibliography; indexed." Choice

322.4 Political action groups

Meier, August
CORE; a study in the civil rights movement, 1942-1968 [by] August Meier and Elliott Rudwick. Oxford 1973 563p maps $15   322.4
1 Congress of Racial Equality 2 Negroes—Civil rights
ISBN 0-19-501627-0   LC 72-92294

"The emergence of CORE as a major force for black protest is traced from its origins as part of the Christian Pacifist movement, initially interracial in makeup and nonviolent in philosophy. The authors analyze the crisis of declining revenue and volatile personnel clashes that ironically undermined CORE just as major victories were achieved." Booklist

"Two distinguished historians of the American black experience have made a valuable contribution to Afro-American historiography with this work. Utilizing a prodigious amount of research from both archival and oral evidence [they] have written a model study. . . . They provide an inclusive chronological account of the activities of CORE's myriad chapters through-out the country." Library J
Notes on sources: p432-42

Sale, Kirkpatrick
SDS. Random House 1973 752p $15   322.4
1 Students for a Democratic Society 2 Right and left (Political science)
ISBN 0-394-47889-4   LC 72-12647

A "history of the Students for a Democratic Society, from its 1960 beginnings as a relatively insignificant left-liberal adjunct to the League for Industrial Democracy, to its flaming collapse in the factional disputes, the Weatherman fantasies, and the bomb factory in Greenwich Village in the 1970's." Library J

"This volume is, without doubt, the definitive study of the most important student organization of the 1960s. While Sale exhibits a sympathy for his subject, his treatment is generally fair-minded. Extensive interviews with key SDS leaders and use of primary documents are effectively combined to make the book particularly valuable." Choice
Bibliographical references in Notes: p695-726

323.44 Freedom of action

American Library Association. Office for Intellectual Freedom
Intellectual freedom manual; comp. by the Office for Intellectual Freedom of the American Library Association. A.L.A. 1974 xxx, various pagings $12.75   323.44
1 Intellectual freedom 2 Libraries—Censorship
ISBN 0-8389-3151-0   LC 73-22338

Hardbound, spiral binding

"This manual is designed to answer the many practical questions that confront librarians in applying the principles of intellectual freedom

American Library Association. Office of Intellectual Freedom—*Continued*

to library service. It is our hope that every librarian will keep this volume on his desk as a convenient reference work." Preface
Contents: Library Bill of Rights; Freedom to read; Intellectual freedom; Intellectual freedom and the law; Assistance from ALA
Includes bibliography

Thurman, S. David
The right of access to information from the Government. Oceana 1973 113p (Legal almanac ser) $4   323.44
1 Freedom of information 2 U.S.—Government publications
ISBN 0-379-11085-7   LC 73-7990
"The author covers the information needed to secure the documents and records from every department and organ of the federal government, together with relevant addresses, publications of interest and legal cases affecting the public's right to know as a result of the "Freedom of Information Act" of 1957
General bibliography: p85-86

327 International relations

Reischauer, Edwin O.
Toward the 21st century: education for a changing world. Knopf 1973 195p $5.95   327
1 International relations
ISBN 0-394-48881-4   LC 73-7264
The author discusses "the need to reshape education in order to survive in a rapidly changing world. Reischauer's thesis is that looming world problems will replace war among nations as the prime threat to man's future. These include population growth, food resources, ecology and natural conservation. In his view the successful confrontation of each of these can be achieved only by a synthesis of expert knowledge about every part of the world." Pub W
The problems discussed "have all been treated elsewhere in greater detail. Therefore, the real value lies in the author's deep historical sensitivity as well as his extensive background knowledge of the history and culture of Japan, a subject on which he is perhaps America's foremost expert; and Reischauer uses this expertise to good effect in presenting his major concepts." Library J

327.73 U.S. foreign policy

Kissinger, Henry A.
American foreign policy. Expanded ed. Norton 1974 304p $6.95   327.73
1 U.S.—Foreign relations
ISBN 0-393-09264-X   LC 74-4378
Earlier edition entered in main catalog
First published 1969. The 1974 edition includes Kissinger's recent public statements on United States foreign policy, our relations with our allies and adversaries, arms control, the Middle East and issues facing the United Nations

The Middle East; U.S. policy, Israel, oil and the Arabs. Congressional Quarterly 1974 100p maps pa $4   327.73
1 U.S.—Foreign relations—Near East 2 Near East—Foreign relations—U.S. 3 Jewish-Arab relations 4 Petroleum industry and trade
ISBN 0-87187-057-6   LC 74-5252
"A résumé of factors influential on Middle East countries at war and peace with parallel attention to recent changes in U.S. policies toward the region. Essentially a statement of attitudes and resultant actions, the concise review contains inset summaries on such topics as Israel's altered social attitudes after the 1973 war, the rise of Arab terrorism, and the origin of the arms race. Statistical data concern U.S. economic aid to the region from 1946 to 1973 and Arab oil revenues. Thumbnail histories of Arab countries, a lengthy-chronology of Middle East events from 1945 and 1973, and a brief bibliography [are] appended." Booklist

328.73 Legislative branch of U.S. government

Barone, Michael
The almanac of American politics; the Senators, the Representatives—their records, states and districts [by] Michael Barone, Grant Ujifusa [and] Douglas Matthews. Gambit illus $15   328.73
1 U.S.—Congress—Directories 2 U.S.—Politics and government—Yearbooks
1972 edition entered in main catalog
First published 1972. Revised and updated biennially

Congressional districts in the 1970s. 2d ed. Congressional Quarterly 1974 236p illus pa $10   328.73
1 U.S. Congress. House
ISBN 0-87187-063-0   LC 72-94078
First published 1973
This "book brings together statistical and descriptive profiles of all 435 congressional districts based on the 1970 census and subsequent reapportionment and redistricting decisions. Also given are data on the official 1972 election returns with comparisons made to the 1968 and 1970 results. Maps of all states are provided showing district lines with added maps of cities containing several districts. In addition to the strictly electoral data information on major military, space, and atomic energy facilities in each district is set forth together with lists of major industries, universities, newspapers, and television stations located in each area. A history of reapportionment and redistricting is appended." Booklist
"A very useful reference book. . . . It is recommended to fill a gap in most reference collections." Library J [to the 1973 edition]

329 Practical politics. Political parties

Atkins, Chester G.
Getting elected; a guide to winning state and local office, by Chester G. Atkins with Barry Hock & Bob Martin. Houghton 1973 202p $6.95   329
1 Politics, Practical 2 Elections—U.S.
ISBN 0-395-16614-4   LC 72-12401
The chapters proceed in the following sequence: "The decision to run, Precampaign activities, The organization, The budget, Fundraising, Tactics, Opinion polling, Issues, Literature and advertising, and The press, following which are several case studies of hypothetical candidates and a chapter on being a candidate." Choice
"This simply written handbook for winning state and local elections is intended for candidates with limited practical experience in the mechanics of running for office." Library J

Chisholm, Shirley
The good fight. Harper 1973 206p illus $6.95   329
1 Presidents—U.S.—Election 2 U.S.—Politics and government—1961- 3 Negroes—Political activity
ISBN 0-06-010764-2   LC 72-10680
"A Cass Canfield book"
The author, a Congresswoman from New York City, describes how, as a Black woman, she ran as a candidate for the Presidency. The book is also the story of her continuing struggle for the reform of American politics
"It is in the last few chapters, where Chisholm focuses pragmatically upon the failure of the McGovern campaign and the future role of minorities in politics, that the book offers some valuable insights. Recommended more for the author's prominence on the contemporary liberal political scene and for the last few sections than for the main body of its analysis. Selections from Chisholm's 1972 position papers and campaign speeches are contained in two appendixes." Library J

Johnson, Donald Bruce
(comp.) National party platforms, 1840-1972; comp. by Donald Bruce Johnson and Kirk H. Porter. Univ. of Ill. Press 1973 889p $20   329

1 Political parties
ISBN 0-252-00414-0   LC 73-81566

Earlier edition entered in main catalog under Porter, with title: National party platforms, 1840-1968
First published 1956. The 1973 edition brings the material up to date through the election of 1972

McGovern, George
An American journey; the Presidential campaign speeches of George McGovern. Random House 1974 246p illus $8.95   329

1 Presidents—U.S.—Election 2 U.S.—Politics and government—1961-
ISBN 0-394-48944-2   LC 73-20595

"In addition to the author's announcement of his candidacy, his acceptance of the nomination, and his concession speech, the book includes the speeches in which McGovern expressed his views on the economy, integrity in government and the rights of all citizens, and his constant pleas for peace

Minow, Newton N.
Presidential television [by] Newton N. Minow, John Bartlow Martin [and] Lee M. Mitchell. Basic Bks. 1973 232p $8.95   329

1 Television in politics 2 Presidents—U.S.
ISBN 0-465-06274-1   LC 73-81134

"A Twentieth Century Fund report"
The authors are "superbly qualified in the legal problems of the media [and] they have produced a coherent, readable account of the increasing fascination of Presidents, Congress and politicians generally with television. They have also reduced to understandable language the incredible complications of the 'fairness doctrine' and the failure of the Federal Communications Commission to produce standards that insure 'balance' in the presentation of political issues." N Y Times Bk R
Among the remedies suggested are "regular prime-time coverage of congressional debates, the deregulation of presidential and opposition television, and improved coverage of the Supreme Court. . . . Like most of the written products of foundation-funding and the committee mind, the book is built with wooden prose. . . . No matter. It is a very important book." New Repub
Bibliography: p219-21

Political parties in American history. General editor: Morton Borden. Putnam [1974 c1973-1974] 3v (xliv, 1324p) illus ea $8.95   329

1 Political parties   LC 73-76139

Contents: v 1 1789-1828, edited by Winfred E. A. Bernhard (ISBN 0-399-10991-9); v2 1828-1890, edited by Felice A. Bonadio (ISBN 0-399-10992-7); v3 1890-Present, edited by Paul L. Murphy ((ISBN 0-599-10993-5)
"As a total project this three-volume anthology constitutes a major scholarly work. The editors of each volume have selected articles and chapters from the works of leading scholars. The study's main thesis is that an understanding of the development of the American nation cannot be achieved unless the role and impact of political parties are taken into consideration. In each volume the work is divided into several sections for which the editors have written short introductions. Each selection is preceded by a well-written, succinct headnotes. The selections are footnoted. There is a good basic bibliography at the end of each volume." Choice

White, Theodore H.
The making of the President, 1972. Atheneum Pubs. 1973 391p $10   329

1 Presidents—U.S.—Election 2 U.S.—Politics and government—1961-
ISBN 0-689-10553-3   LC 72-94252

The fifth in the author's series, first begun with the 1960 Presidential campaign; the earlier volumes are entered in main catalog

This chronological account of the 1972 Presidential campaign in the United States discusses the candidates, their parties, the issues, the political conventions, and the factors involved in the results
The author "skillfully blends autobiography, political journalism and history into a precise, carefully conceived, and well organized document. If there is one basic flaw in this present book it is that White tries to be overly fair with both Mr. McGovern and Mr. Nixon. White does not hide facts and indeed gives the readers enough detail to make up their own minds about the candidates. He does however, tend to make excuses for the candidates." Best Sellers
Maps on lining-papers

330 Economics

Myrdal, Gunnar
Against the stream; critical essays on economics. Pantheon Bks. 1973 336p $10   330

1 Economics 2 Social sciences
ISBN 0-394-48682-X   LC 73-4753

Analyzed in Essay and general literature index
"A collection of essays based in large part on Myrdal's earlier writings and long-time criticisms of many of the traditional approaches and theories still relied upon in present-day economics. A broad and recurring theme throughout the book is that of the need for value premises (as opposed to pure objectivity) in economic analysis. Other major topics of discussion involve the problem of 'stagflation' that currently characterizes many Western economies, the need for transdisciplinary scholarship in the social sciences, the continuing problem of world poverty, the need for radical domestic reforms with respect to inequality, land reform, population growth, etc., and observations of the progress and experience of America since the writing of 'An American dilemma.' [entered in main catalog, class 301.451]." Choice
"The essays in this new book are particularly strong in their plea to economists to consider all of a society's institutions, and the value assumptions that lie behind policy making. . . . Separate chapters on America and India provide a strong indictment of America's moral position abroad today, and the program for social justice cum growth in India." Christian Science Monitor
Includes bibliographical notes

330.973 U.S.—Economic conditions

Harris, Fred R.
The new populism. Saturday Review Press 1973 209p $6.95   330.973

1 U.S.—Economic conditions—1961- 2 U.S.—Social conditions
ISBN 0-8415-0244-7   LC 72-88653

"The former Senator from Oklahoma directs his attack against the large industrial monopolies, e.g., the automobile, steel, transportation, and oil industries. He charges that these industries control prices by eliminating competition and they eat up billions of tax dollars via federal subsidies; at the same time, they pay only a fraction of the taxes they owe by the exercise of various tax loopholes. Harris sees the solution to these problems . . . in the true exercise of the free enterprise system, which stimulates competition and preserves the small competitor." Library J
"Notwithstanding the title, there is nothing startlingly new or different in this book, although it reads well, presents quite a bit of supporting data and information, and is fairly stated." Choice
Includes bibliographies

331.2 Conditions of employment

Nader, Ralph
You and your pension [by] Ralph Nader and Kate Blackwell. Grossman Pubs. 1973 215p $5.95   331.2

1 Old age pensions
ISBN 0-670-79390-6   LC 72-81084

Nader, Ralph—*Continued*

An examination of current practices and conditions in the American system of retirement pensions and an outline for basic reform measures necessary to fulfill private pension promises

"Sufficiently broad to provide overall coverage for most readers, this book is certainly a valuable addition to the 'public service' function of a general library collection. It should be useful to social workers and other professional helpers, especially those who attempt to help community and institutional groups organize on their own behalf." Choice

Bibliography included in Notes: p198-207

Pearson, John Ward

The 8-day week. Harper 1973 161p illus $6.95   331.2

1 Hours of labor 2 U.S.—Social conditions 3 Leisure
ISBN 0-06-013316-3   LC 72-9104

The author "proposes a system of four days of work and four days off; business would be open every day for ten hours. Half the people would be at work while the other half would be off. He feels such a system would bring great economic, social, and psychological rewards; employment would increase, and capital equipment would be more efficiently used. Even air pollution would be reduced. Pearson realized his system would have a number of complications for working families, small businesses, schools, and churches, but he attempts to prove that most obstacles can be overcome with planning." Choice

"Pearson outlines a most intriguing plan. . . . He discusses, somewhat superficially, the various aspects of the scheme and tackles, with mixed success, many practical objections. However, Pearson's plan is exciting; and, because of its obvious potential impact on our life styles, it is likely to provoke much interest." Library J

For further reading: p151

Terkel, Studs

Working; people talk about what they do all day and how they feel about what they do. Pantheon Bks. 1974 xliv, 589p $10   331.2

1 Labor and laboring classes—U.S. 2 Work 3 U.S.—Social conditions
ISBN 0-394-47884-3   LC 73-18037

"Terkel ranged over the U.S. talking with people and tape-recording the conversations. In all, 134 men and women's thoughts and feelings regarding their work appear here. The types of work represented are, e.g., barber, auditor, hooker, car hiker, film critic, bus driver, professor of communication, model, press agent, farm worker, etc. . . . What emerges is people's search for, and finding more often than one might expect, affirmation in their work that what they are doing daily is worth doing, needs doing, and therefore the person who does it has dignity." Choice

"The result is not a dry, academic treatise but a sensitive portrayal of the experience of working, with all its pain, tension, frustrations, and occasional satisfactions. . . . [Terkel] is ever-present as the master interviewer. Undoubtedly, he must be a sympathetic listener to get his subjects to talk so uninhibitedly about their jobs. And undoubtedly, he is a man very much in love with the power of spoken English to select such moving accounts for his oral anthology. Through this effort, Studs Terkel has created a monument, if not to the dignity of work at least to the strength of the worker." Best Sellers

331.4 Women workers

Bird, Caroline

Everything a woman needs to know to get paid what she's worth; ed. by Helene Mandelbaum. McKay 1973 304p $8.95   331.4

1 Woman—Employment   LC 73-79946

"Organized in a question-answer style the inclusive guide . . . outlines techniques useful to women in achieving personal satisfaction and equal monetary reward in employment. Covering professional, blue-collar, self-employed, and even household cleaning positions, the book suggests helpful job hunting and interview methods for prospective employees, spells out ways to insure promotions, explains legal ramifications of equal-pay cases with data on where to secure assistance, and describes women's role in union machinery." Booklist

"A competent survey of problems faced by ambitious working women. . . . Of particular help are specific questions dealing with illegal practices and questions which tell where and how to complain. Also valuable is the resource section of books and agencies to consult for further help." Library J

332.03 Financial economics—Encyclopedias and dictionaries

Munn, Glenn G.

Glenn G. Munn's Encyclopedia of banking and finance. 7th ed. Rev. and enl. by F. L. Garcia. Bankers Pub. 1973 953p illus $49.75   332.03

1 Finance—Encyclopedias 2 Banks and banking—Encyclopedias 3 Banks and banking—U.S.
ISBN 0-87267-019-8   LC 73-83395

Earlier edition entered in main catalog

First published 1924. In the 1973 edition "new terms, organizations, and symbols have been added, many of them with added references appended." Ref Services Rev

332.6 Investment finance

Rukeyser, Louis

How to make money in Wall Street. Doubleday 1974 271p $7.95   332.6

1 Investments 2 Speculation 3 Stocks
ISBN 0-385-07505-7   LC 73-14055

The author describes the world of stocks, bonds, commodities, and mutual funds. He answers such questions as whether you really belong in Wall Street in the first place, how to select and deal with a broker, how to decide what kind of securities to buy, how to pick stocks, how to invest for growth and how to invest for income, how to use options and other trading techniques, how to choose mutual funds, and when to sell stock

"The author's erudite wit, given only flash exposure on the TV show [Wall Street Week] is here provided a format allowing for more leisurely development. . . . In one paragraph on the very first page are casually tossed out such phrases as un-chic materialism, corollary assumption, and moral tutelage. Such verbal hurdles aside, the book is thorough in its coverage of what the investor should know, and sound in its conservative advice on what and when to buy and sell. . . . The choice of this book over others as a guide to making money on Wall Street turns on preferences in style." Christian Science Monitor

333.8 Utilization of subsurface (mineral) resources

Energy crisis in America. Congressional Quarterly 1973 93p illus map pa $4   333.8

1 Power resources 2 Natural resources—U.S.
ISBN 0-87187-038-X   LC 72-92522

"This book contains chapters dealing with gasoline prices, the Alaska pipeline, strip mining, nuclear power, the environment and pollution, and new sources of energy. A chronology of relevant U.S. Supreme Court decisions and congressional legislation is given in the last two chapters." Library J

Bibliography of materials on energy problems: p93

335 Socialism and related systems. Utopias

Kinkade, Kathleen
 A Walden Two experiment; the first five years of Twin Oaks Community; foreword by B. F. Skinner. Morrow 1973 271p $7.95
 335
 1 Utopias 2 Twin Oaks Community
 ISBN 0-688-00020-7 LC 72-8090
 "Kathleen Kinkade was one of the original members and planners of the Virginia commune, Twin Oaks, founded to test the ideas of community propounded by B. F. Skinner in his 'Walden Two.' Five years later Ms. Kinkade remains at Twin Oaks, the only one of the original members to stay on. This [is a] lucid account of the commune's trials and tribulations, both emotional and economic, its membership problems and its continuing belief in structured freedom and the possibility of utilizing technology toward a fuller life." Pub W
 "This is an amazingly well balanced account of one attempt at a new life style, and the reader comes away with the feeling that communal, rural living is a viable alternative for those who choose to learn a great deal about human interaction and simple agriculture as well. This is not a book about another group of freaks; rather, it is a simple progress report." Library J

335.4 Marxian systems (Marxism)

Marx, Karl
 On the First International; arranged and ed. with an introduction and new tr. by Saul K. Padover. McGraw 1973 lix, 623p illus (The Karl Marx lib. v3) $20 335.4
 1 Communism 2 The International
 ISBN 0-07-048076-1
 "The International Working Men's Association—known as the First International—was the first successful attempt at a worldwide radical organization. A pioneering effort, its attempts to unify European and American workers for their common interests came to disaster after the Franco-Prussian War of 1870. For at that time no single organization could contain both the turbulent anarchist Michael Bakunin and the philosophical Karl Marx—the one representing revolutionary violence with no government, and the other, careful preparation and organized political action. Nevertheless, the International's valiant attempt to unify and give overall direction to radical and revolutionary working people in England, Germany, France, Belgium, Switzerland, Poland, Italy, Spain, and the United States made it, in Marx's words, 'the fighting organization of the proletariat.'" Publisher's note
 Bibliography: p585-87

336.2 Taxes and taxation

Stern, Philip M.
 The rape of the taxpayer. Random House 1973 483p $10 336.2
 1 Income tax
 ISBN 0-394-46998-4 LC 72-11368
 "The author stresses the point that our tax system is riddled with large loopholes, which allow some people with large incomes to pay very little or no taxes, and giant corporations to avoid paying taxes, even though they show earned profits and pay dividends to their stockholders. This book . . . limits its coverage to personal and corporate income taxes, and inheritance and gift taxes. . . . The author recommends that we close all loopholes at once, instead of doing the patchwork that Congress has been doing so far, and treat all incomes alike, regardless of whether they come from wages, interest on municipal bonds, capital gains, or any other source." Best Sellers
 He "presents our tax system as a national mess, maintained and constantly expanded by politicians who have to rely for their campaign financing on the very people who have the most to lose from any fair tax plan. It is all the more convincing because Stern, the heir to a Sears, Roebuck fortune who admits to using the shelters he wants to see abolished, would presumably be one of the victims of his own plan." Time
 Includes bibliographical references

338.2 Mineral industries

Cooper, Bryan
 Alaska: the last frontier. Morrow [1973 c1972] 248p illus $7.95 338.2
 1 Petroleum industry and trade 2 Alaska—Economic conditions 3 Alaska—Description and travel
 ISBN 0-688-00016-9 LC 78-182955
 "This book is only partly about the Alaskan oil rush, following the discovery on the North Slope of one of the world's largest oilfields. It is also about Alaska itself—its history, land and people. The author discusses the conservation conflict that has arisen because of the need to protect the wildlife and environment of America's last frontier." Book Rev Digest
 "Working primarily through the medium of empirical investigation (except for brief introductory material on Alaskan history), Cooper has written in somewhat 'chatsy' documentary form a history of the discovery and attempted exploitation of the North Slope oil fields on the Arctic coast of Alaska. Well described and most interesting is the fact that this discovery of the largest oil field in the U.S. comes at a time when conservation of the environment conflicts with the growing need for oil and oil products in the U.S. Thus, this is a timely work of interest to conservationists, industrialists, and the general reader. Maps, charts, photographs, index, and excellent bibliography." Choice

338.4 Secondary industries

The Updated Last Whole earth catalog; access to tools. All listings accurate as of May 1974. [Portola Institute; distributed by Random House] 1974 447p illus $25, pa $5 338.4
 1 Manufactures—Catalogs 2 Mail-order business—Catalogs
 ISBN 0-394-49503-9; 0-394-70943-8 LC 74-9085
 Earlier edition entered in main catalog with title: The Last Whole earth catalog
 Edited by Steward Brand
 First published 1968 with title: Whole earth catalog. The 1974 edition has been completely revised and brought up to date to include current prices, sources, and items no longer available

338.973 U.S.—Economic policy

Galbraith, John Kenneth
 Economics and the public purpose. Houghton 1973 334p $10 338.973
 1 Industry and state—U.S. 2 U.S.—Economic conditions—20th century 3 Corporations
 ISBN 0-395-17206-3 LC 73-8750
 "After summarizing the theories of conventional 'neoclassical' economists—and showing how full of holes they are . . . [Galbraith] gives his version of a realistic statement of the economic state of the world today and the unsolved problems of unequal distribution of power and wealth, recurring monetary crises, government intervention or nonintervention, pollution, and multi-national corporations. He devotes the final third of his book to specific recommendations for reforming the system." Pub W
 "As the eternal gadfly of American capitalism, he has played a considerable role in popularizing once radical economic theory. . . . [This] book is a slow and often taxing read. But at a time when the old economic rules 'are not working quite the way they used to' . . . it is probably a necessary read as well." Time

340 Law

The **Family** legal advisor; a clear, reliable and up-to-date guide to your rights and remedies under the law; ed. by Alice K. Helm, assisted by: Allen H. Brill [and] Kenneth Birnbaum; foreword by Theodore R. Kupferman. Greystone [distributed by Crown] 1974 480p illus $9.95 **340**

1 Law—U.S.
LC 73-93374

First published 1950, under the authorship of Albert W. Gray

This volume contains basic information about legal problems which confront the layman. Among the topics discussed are marriage, divorce, inheritance, citizenship, the mentally ill, libel, and insurance laws

"While it cannot replace a good lawyer, this work will supplement other popular guides and will help persons avoid legal problems or deal with them in an informed manner." Cur Ref Bks

Dictionary of common legal terms: p455-67

Sloan, Irving J.
Youth and the law; rights, privileges & obligations. 2d ed. Oceana 1974 121p (Legal almanac ser) $4 **340**

1 Law—U.S.
ISBN 0-379-11097-0
LC 74-6493

Earlier edition entered in main catalog

First published 1970. The 1974 edition has been revised as to incorporate the new laws and regulations on narcotics, alcohol and voting. This edition also has two new chapters on selective service, the standby draft; and on the environment

Glossary of legal terms: p77-87

344 Social law

Fraenkel, Osmond K.
The rights we have. 2d ed. . . . Crowell 1974 246p $6.95 **344**

1 Civil rights
ISBN 0-690-00585-7
LC 74-5428

Earlier edition entered in main cataog, class 323.4

First published 1971. The 1974 edition has been "revised to include the most important decisions of the U.S. Supreme Court through 1973." Title page

344.3 Social law. Welfare

Law, Sylvia
The rights of the poor; with a chapter on the rights of migrants by Burt Neuborne. Sunrise Bks. [1974 c1973] 176p (An American Civil Liberties Union Handbook) $6.95 **344.3**

1 Public welfare—Laws and regulations
ISBN 0-87690-139-9
LC 74-75008

"A Richard Baron book"

This is a guide to welfare rights in the United States. The author describes eligibility criteria for each type of assistance, how to apply, and where to appeal if the application is denied This book provides insight into the ways in which welfare agencies operate at the local, state and federal levels

Bibliographical references included in footnotes. Includes a chart of welfare rights in each state

344.7 Social law. Education and schools

Levine, Alan
The rights of students; the basic ACLU guide to a student's rights [by] Alan Levine, with Eve Cary and Diane Divoky. Sunrise Bks. [1974 c1973] 160p (An American Civil Liberties Union Handbook) $6.95 **344.7**

1 Students—Civil rights
ISBN 0-87690-137-2
LC 73-84703

"A Richard Baron book"

A concise guide treating the civil rights of public school students in such areas as: personal appearance, rights under the First Amendment, due process in disciplinary proceedings, records, grades, marriage and pregnancy

"Several publications are available on the rights of college students: Levine's book seems to be one of the few available on student rights in public high schools. . . . Answers include references to more than 500 legal citations, though the lack of an index makes it difficult to locate specific items. Intended for the students themselves, but administrators may also benefit from reading it." Library J

Selected bibliography and informational sources: p139-46

Rubin, David
The rights of teachers; the basic ACLU guide to a teacher's constitutional rights. Richard W. Baron [distributed by Dutton] 1973 175p (An American Civil Liberties Union Handbook) $6.95 **344.7**

1 Teachers—Civil rights
ISBN 0-87777-037-9
LC 72-87846

First published 1972 in a paperback edition by Discus Books

"Addressed to teachers at the elementary and secondary levels, guidance here offered is also relevant to related rights of educators at colleges and universities. . . . Rubin in a question-and-answer format describes developments in constitutional law concerning the professional and personal rights of teachers, discusses variations in teacher's rights depending on particular state laws, local rules, and contractual provisions, and points out when to seek legal assistance and/or enlist the aid of teacher organizations. . . . Rubin encourages educators to maintain their rights by exercising them. Documentary notes at end of chapters. Selected bibliography appended." Booklist

"A practical guide for teachers, [this book] . . . is also very useful for school administrators, school boards, schools of education, parents and students, and the general public. Heavily documented." Choice

345 Criminal law

Rosengart, Oliver
The rights of suspects [by] Oliver Rosengart, with Gail Weinheimer. Sunrise Bks. [1974 c1973] 122p (An American Civil Liberties Union Handbook) $5.95 **345**

1 Criminal law 2 Civil rights
ISBN 0-87690-138-0
LC 74-76009

"A Richard Baron book"

Contents: Rights in individual confrontations with the police; Rights upon arrest; Rights in court; Remedies

"This book does not attempt to discuss all of the rights that suspects and defendants have throughout the entire criminal process. Rather it concentrates on the rights of persons before they have been charged with a crime, when they are arrested and up until the time they finally go to trial." Introduction

Rudovsky, David
The rights of prisoners; the basic ACLU guide to a prisoner's rights. Richard W. Baron [distributed by Dutton] 1973 128p (An American Civil Liberties Union Handbook) $4.95 **345**

1 Prisons—U.S.—Laws and regulations 2 Civil rights 3 Criminal law
ISBN 0-87777-040-9
LC 72-96828

"This handbook provides guidance in the areas of due process, freedom from cruel and unusual punishment, free communication and access to the courts and the problems of prison censorship. The author discusses religious and racial discrimination, political rights, privacy and personal appearance, medical care, rehabilitation and protection from sexual assault. Questions are answered about jail conditions, pre-trial confinement and parole." Publisher's note

Rudovsky, David—*Continued*
"A valuable and useful guide to the legal rights of those convicted of crime and those awaiting trial and jailed (for want of bail in most instances). A question and answer format is used. Stylistic qualities are excellent. Footnotes appear at the ends of chapters. Citations of cases are in legal form. . . . An appendix lists legal organizations active in prisoners' rights litigation. There is also a brief (13-item) selected bibliography." Choice

345.7 Trials

Tidyman, Ernest
Dummy. Little 1974 277p $6.95   345.7
1 Deaf   2 Trials
ISBN 0-316-84510-8   LC 73-19966
This is the account of a "criminal case in which [Donald Lang], a young black deaf-mute, incapable of intellectual communication with anyone by any means, was charged with the murder of a prostitute. How to prosecute, how to defend, what to do about the man at all, were unprecedented legal problems." Atlantic
"A thorny, problematical book whose questions are not entirely answered by which painfully lays bare the plight of society's victims and unconscionable lapses in the American legal system." Booklist

346 Private law

Bander, Edward J.
Change of name and law of names. Oceana 1973 116p (Legal almanac ser) $4
    346
1 Names, Personal—U.S.—Laws and regulations
ISBN 0-379-11088-1   LC 73-11060
First published 1954 under the authorship of Lawrence G. Greene with title: How to change your name, and the law of names
This volume covers the legal aspects of name changing such as changes in the records, conducting business under an assumed name, the married women and her name. The author includes a summary of state laws relating to the subject and provides examples of forms, petitions and certificates involved
Bibliography: p111-14

Ennis, Bruce
The rights of mental patients; the basic ACLU guide to a mental patient's rights [by] Bruce Ennie [and] Loren Siegel. Richard W. Baron [distributed by Dutton] 1973 336p (An American Civil Liberties Union Handbook) $5.95   346
1 Mental illness—Laws and regulations
ISBN 0-87777-039-5   LC 72-96829
This book includes a general description of the laws that affect mental patients. It discusses problems which arise in every state, the ways in which some of the more important court decisions have resolved those problems and suggestions for other methods of resolution. Such topics as emergency hospitalization, release procedures, rights in the hospital, and discrimination against former patients, are covered. The book also contains specialized information about the law on a state-by-state basis
"Written primarily for lawyers and law students, but very useful for the medical profession, social scientists, families of the mentally ill, and for many of the mentally ill themselves." Choice

Ross, Susan C.
The rights of women; the basic ACLU guide to a woman's rights. Sunrise Bks. [1974 c1973] 384p (An American Civil Liberties Union Handbook) $7.95   346
1 Woman—Civil rights
ISBN 0-87690-136-4   LC 73-84702
"A Richard Baron book"
This guide to women's rights under existing American laws discusses the Constitutional concept of "equal protection," the proposed Equal Rights Amendment to the Constitution, rights against discrimination in employment and education, the treatment of women in the mass media, laws affecting women as criminals and as victims of rape, birth control (including abortion and sterilization), divorce, changing names, etc. Appendices include charts of state laws concerning name changes and discrimination in employment, public accommodations, housing and education; listings of organizations and publications offering legal aid and advice; and, listings of women's organizations and their publications

Wilkerson, Albert E.
(ed.) The rights of children; emergent concepts in law and society; with an introduction by Justine Wise Polier. Temple Univ. Press 1973 313p $10   346
1 Children—Civil rights   2 Child welfare—Laws and regulations
ISBN 0-87722-052-2   LC 73-79230
Analyzed in Essay and general literature index
"An important book which bases itself four-square on the 1959 U.N. Declaration of the Rights of the Child. . . . Divided into three parts—'The Child as a Person,' 'Guarantees for the Child,' 'Decisions About the Child'—it is a well-organized gathering of the sometimes clashing views of a wide range of this country's most respected judges, legislators, social workers and lawyers. Their focus is on existing conditions affecting children's rights and lives, and on social and legal concepts emerging from issues making news today: adoption, custody, abortion, child abuse, legitimacy, inheritance and juvenile 'criminality.' [The editor] sums up the issues fairly, humanely and affirmatively. Indispensable for concerned adults and the libraries serving them." Pub W

346.1 Domestic relations

DeCrow, Karen
Sexist justice. Random House 1974 329p $7.95   346.1
1 Woman—Civil rights   2 Women in the U.S.   3 Sex discrimination   4 Domestic relations—Laws and regulations
ISBN 0-394-48403-7   LC 73-15835
The author "identifies existing laws that can protect men and women from legal sexism, and discusses how sexism affects money and employment, fair representation, the job market, credit, motherhood and abortion, education and the passage of the Equal Rights Amendment. There are individual chapters on criminal, family and estate law." Pub W
"Ms. DeCrow is a lawyer and well equipped to pin down, case by case and statute by statute, the misogyny which permeates both the structure and the application of our laws. She does it clearly, with a minimum of ill temper, and a decent consideration of the historical roots of the situation. This is a valuable reading both for feminine activists and for those who still wonder what the girls are complaining about." Atlantic
Bibliography in Notes: p304-29

Wheeler, Michael
No-fault divorce. Beacon Press 1974 194p $7.50   346.1
1 Divorce—Laws and regulations
ISBN 0-8070-4482-2   LC 73-17421
A "study of current divorce legislation, the trend toward no-fault divorce, and the different forms reform has taken in various states, especially California. In custody issues, Wheeler urges emphasis on the child's welfare, not on the use of punitive or arbitrary standards. Conciliation programs and alimony are also discussed. There are numerous cases cited and opinions included from judges, lawyers, and laymen." Library J
"A one-sided discussion of the case for 'no-fault' divorce, this book deals well with the inequities in present-day divorce laws and practices but glides past many problems in any forthcoming no-fault systems." Christian Century
Bibliography: p187

350 Public administration

The **CQ** Guide to current American government. Congressional Quarterly pa ea $3
350

1 U.S.—Politics and government—Periodicals 2 Legislation—Periodicals
ISBN 0-87187-023-1   LC 72-87225

Semiannual. Began publication with edition called 1961/62, issued in fall 1961

Information is obtained and culled from both Congressional Quarterly Weekly Reports and Congressional Quarterly Almanac. They are then presented in summary or digest form. "The 'Guide' is now issued in January and in late August. It 'contains the most useful and instructional of recent CQ research material, rearranged and rewritten for classroom and study use' and is designed to illustrate 'the continuing interplay of forces which constitute our political system' and to encourage 'discussion and individual research in the day-to-day operations of government.'" Wynar. Guide to Reference Books for School Media Centers

351.9 Malfunctioning of government

Berger, Raoul

Impeachment: the constitutional problems. Harvard Univ. Press 1973 345p (Studies in legal history) $14.95   351.9

1 Recall 2 U.S. Constitution
ISBN 0-674-44475-2   LC 73-75055

This work is "concerned with the possible use of impeachment proceedings as a way to enforce legislative accountability upon the Chief Executive. . . . [Included is a] survey of the English sources and usages contemporary with the framing of the Constitution. [Berger argues] . . . that while impeachment is a remedy of last resort, it is and ought to be considered an available remedy for the political misconduct of Presidents and other high officials." Choice

"For today this volume is important not for its notions about judicial removal, but for the historical exegesis of the origins and meanings of the constitutional provision. And, as he says, 'One thing is clear: in the impeachment debate the Convention was almost exclusively concerned with the President.' Indeed, the fact that the book focused on judicial problems lends it a special credibility, for it was obviously not written to prove or disprove the claims of the President's critics or defenders." N Y Times Bk R

Bibliography: p313-22

Bernstein, Carl

All the President's men [by] Carl Bernstein [and] Bob Woodward. Simon & Schuster 1974 349p illus $8.95   351.9

1 Watergate Affair, 1972- 2 The Washington Post
ISBN 0-671-21781-X   LC 73-22334

The two Washington Post reporters whose investigative journalism first revealed the Watergate scandal tell the way it happened from the first suspicions, through the trail of false leads, lies, secrecy, and high-level pressure, to the final moments when they were able to put the pieces of the puzzle together and write the series that won the Post a Pulitzer Prize

"The book with its pervasive feeling of justified paranoia has the qualities of a superior who-done-it; there are descriptions of secret night meetings with an informant described only as 'Deep Throat' in a deserted underground garage, meetings in a garden with Benjamin Bradlee, the executive editor of 'The Post,' to avoid their conversations being bugged, and constant competition with other topnotch reporters from 'Time, The New York Times,' and others. Equally interesting are the insights into the operation of a major newspaper which takes its mission very conscientiously. The methods used by the newspapermen are also eye-opening to a layman—the enormous (and thick-skinned) persistence in following any lead, the assembling of an outline from seemingly unrelated detail, and the painstaking subsequent filling in. There are no surprises about Watergate itself to the diligent newspaper reader, but the book is highly recommended as a permanent part of the Watergate story and as a first-rate, firsthand description of big-time journalism." Choice

Cohen, Richard M.

A heartbeat away; the investigation and resignation of Vice President Spiro T. Agnew [by] Richard M. Cohen [and] Jules Witcover. Viking 1974 373p illus $10   351.9

1 Agnew, Spiro Theodore 2 Corruption (in politics)
SBN 670-36473-8   LC 74-28

"A Washington Post book"

"The first part of the book deals with the discovery of evidence that indicated that Agnew was involved in income-tax evasion and in taking bribes. The book then follows the highly complicated investigation process to the plea bargaining stage and ends when the Vice President pleaded 'nolo contendere' before a Maryland state judge." Choice

"The drama and ironies of the Agnew saga are the stuff of a fast-paced novel, and the authors' comprehensive research and smoothly understated writing make it just that. It is a suspenseful account even though the Agnew denouement from its beginning was but an isolated shock wave in the unending earthquake of Watergate." Christian Science Monitor

The **Presidential** transcripts; in conjunction with the staff of The Washington Post. Delacorte Press 1974 xl, 693p $10   351.9

1 Watergate Affair, 1972- —Sources 2 Nixon, Richard Milhous, President U.S.
ISBN 0-440-06056-7   LC 74-175957

Transcripts of Watergate-related conversations between President Nixon and his chief advisors with commentary by the staff of The Washington Post, including Bob Woodward, Carl Bernstein, Haynes Johnson and Lawrence Meyer

Watergate: chronology of a crisis. Congressional Quarterly 1973-1974 2v illus pa v 1 $7.50, v2 $6   351.9

1 Watergate Affair, 1972-
ISBN 0-87187-049-5; 0-87187-059-2 LC 73-12792

Volume I "detailed the initial unfolding of the Watergate scandal and focused on the activities of the Senate Select Committee on Presidential Campaign Activities. A major portion of the book was devoted to the hearings conducted by that committee before a nationwide television audience during the summer of 1973. . . . Volume I concluded with the completion in early August of the first round of Senate committee hearings and President Nixon's Aug. 15, 1973, speech responding to damaging testimony presented during the hearings." Preface

Volume II covers the period from August 22, 1973 through May 1974, when the House Judiciary Committee formally opened its impeachment hearings

353.007 Specific executive departments in federal government. C.I.A.

Marchetti, Victor

The CIA and the cult of intelligence [by] Victor Marchetti and John D. Marks; introduction by Melvin L. Wulf. Knopf 1974 xxvi, 398, xxi p $8.95   353.007

1 U.S. Central Intelligence Agency
ISBN 0-394-48239-5   LC 74-4995

This book examines the organization and operations of the Central Intelligence Agency and seeks to show how its original purpose—the gathering and processing of intelligence information—has been subverted by its obsession with clandestine operations. Passages censored by the CIA are indicated

"Balked in its intelligence function, the CIA began during the 1950s to deploy its Clandestine

Marchetti, Victor—*Continued*
Services branch in paramilitary adventures in the Third World, where easier results could be achieved and the agency's existence justified. Marchetti and Marks provide fresh details on such interventions. . . . Even in this mutilated form, [the authors] presentation is crisp, finely detailed and devastating." Newsweek

353.03 Executive branch of federal government

Berger, Raoul
Executive privilege; a Constitutional myth. Harvard Univ. Press 1974 430p (Studies in legal history) $14.95   353.03
  1 Executive power—U.S. 2 U.S.—Constitutional history
  ISBN 0-674-27425-3   LC 73-93837

The author analyzes the "myth" of executive privilege as put forth by recent Presidents. "Superbly organized, his analyses range historically from the British Parliament's 'inquiries into the Crown in the 18th century and the debate as to the President's powers (and their limits) among the Constitution's framers, to Watergate and its continuing fallout in 1974. Berger touches every base from Jefferson's role in the trial of Burr to Nixon's arguments for withholding his tapes from Jaworski and the House Impeachment Inquiry. The twin shibboleths of government secrecy and an 'executive privilege' unique to Presidents are devastated down to the last constitutional crumb. Documentary appendices; general and 'case' indices." Pub W
"Dense reading, but important and by no means too technical for a non-lawyer's comprehension." Atlantic
Bibliography: p391-99

Hughes, Emmet John
The living Presidency; the resources and dilemmas of the American Presidential office. Coward, McCann & Geoghegan 1973 377p $10.50   353.03
  1 Executive power—U.S. 2 Presidents—U.S.—History
  SBN 698-10500-1   LC 72-87580

The author seeks to show how men and moments have shaped Presidential power. He ranges "back and forth in history, makes observations on most of our Presidents and explores the idea of the Presidency: the range of its powers and limitations, changes in the office effected by time, problems of managing the Presidency and dangers inherent in the office." Newsweek
This "analysis of the institution of the Presidency of the U.S. is a good one—scholarly but not stuffy, thoughtful without propounding glib answers. . . . Hughes was a speechwriter for Eisenhower in 1953, has been a close President watcher ever since, and delivers his ideas persuasively. . . . An interesting appendix, 'The Presidency as I Have Seen It,' contains short essays by a dozen men who have been close to the institution in various ways—from Sherman Adams and Abe Fortas to Averell Harriman and Nelson Rockefeller." Pub W
Notes and sources: p295-307

Schlesinger, Arthur M.
The imperial Presidency [by] Arthur M. Schlesinger, Jr. Houghton 1973 505p $10
353.03
  1 Executive power—U.S. 2 Presidents—U.S.—History
  ISBN 0-395-17713-8   LC 73-15805

This work on Presidential power is a "survey of nearly 200 years of conflict . . . arising from the Constitution's establishment of an inherently unstable division of powers. . . . [The author addresses] the general question of a 'runaway Presidency'—an executive branch virtually unchecked in foreign policy and in the employment of armed force overseas, moving in recent years toward plebiscitary power—the mystique of the 'mandate'—and accountable only once every four years in the voting booth. . . . The central dilemma of the American Constitution, in Schlesinger's view, has always been the war power . . . and the domestic disgraces of the Nixon Administration seem to Schlesinger to offer an occasion to restore Constitutional balance." Newsweek
"Schlesinger has produced his best work since the Roosevelt trilogy. Although there is still too much lavish praise for liberal Democratic Presidents, he has become one of the first of the leading historians to admit publicly that many Americans (including intellectuals) have turned their backs on the creation of the 'imperial Presidency' because they agreed with an administration's policies. . . . Those who look for an easy, foolproof escape from the Watergate syndrome will come away shorthanded. In Schlesinger's mind, only the Congress, the courts, the American public, the press, the universities, etc. acting in concerned concert can alter the evolutionary pattern. A solid library acquisition." Choice
Bibliographical references included in Notes: p423-66

361.7 Private welfare work

Katz, Harvey
Give! Who gets your charity dollar? Anchor Press 1974 252p $6.95   361.7
  1 Charities 2 Fund raising
  ISBN 0-385-02220-4   LC 73-9163

The author "recites some horror stories of notorious swindles of the past, then shows the everyday workings of five charities facing different kinds of problems, includng the Red Cross, Disabled American Veterans, and the Damon Runyon Fund. . . . He also feels there should be compulsory disclosure of annual income and detailing of expenses. In spite of many irregularities, he does not preach nongiving, but instead counsels: 'Give carefully! Give wisely!' An appendix lists some large charities, with income-expense information where he could get it." Pub W
"Concerned contributors might find this investigative work to their liking." Library J

Kutz, Myer
Rockefeller power. Simon & Schuster 1974 288p $7.95   361.7
  1 Rockefeller family
  ISBN 0-671-21718-6   LC 73-21050

Kutz's premise "is that the Rockefeller family has used its money and prestige not only for philanthropy but also—and more importantly—for self-aggrandizement and power. The narrative begins by recounting the first John D. Rockefeller's money making/giving philosophies and it ends with a description of Nelson Rockefeller's handling of the 1971 Attica prison uprising." Library J
"The money amassed by John D. Rockefeller not only enabled him to rise from poverty, but gave him power never before seen in this country. How the money was amassed, and the use of the power that came with it, begins Mr. Kutz's book. . . . [His] coverage of the Rockefeller empire is a powerful account." Best Sellers
Selected bibliography: p269-74

362.2 Mental illness

Szasz, Thomas S.
(ed.) The age of madness; the history of involuntary mental hospitalization presented in selected texts; ed. with preface, introduction, and epilogue. Anchor Bks. 1973 372p pa $2.95   362.2
  1 Mentally ill—Institutional care
  ISBN 0-385-04638-3   LC 72-89952

"A Doubleday Anchor original"
"Writings by Daniel Defoe, Anton Chekov, Karl Kraus, Jack London, James Thurber, Sylvia Plath, and several others offer views of involuntary mental confinement from 1650 to the present. There are 33 selections (short stories, reports, articles, etc.), and each is introduced by a short explanatory note." Library J

362.6 Problems of aged people

Mendelson, Mary Adelaide
 Tender loving greed; how the incredibly lucrative nursing home "industry" is exploiting America's old people and defrauding us all. Knopf 1974 245p $6.95 362.6
 1 Aged—Institutional care
 ISBN 0-394-47597-6   LC 73-17312
 "This slashing exposé decries the corruption that permeates the nursing-home industry, leaving patients abused and neglected and the operators of the homes waxing fat on the riches of exploitation. Miss Mendelson shows that Medicare and Medicaid have put federal funds into the hands of the sick and aged but have not protected them against systematic abuses. And so they have been beset by an army of predators—among them the home operators, doctors, pharmacies, and hospital suppliers. In a seris of rogues' gallery sketches Miss Mendelson introduces us to some of the con men who operate these homes. . . . She [also] tells you about the real fat cats: the invisible owners, chain operators, and stock manipulators." Sat R/World
 The "book is muckraking in the best tradition." N Y Times Bk R

362.7 Problems of young people and their alleviation. Adoption

Breitbart, Vicki
 (comp.) The day care book; the why, what, and how of community day care; with articles by: Lucille Abbott [and others]. Designed and illus. by Marcia Salo Rizzi. Knopf 1974 211p illus $7.95 362.7
 1 Day nurseries 2 Children—Care and hygiene
 ISBN 0-394-48070-8   LC 73-7294
 A book that springs from the growing movement for universal day care facilities, intended to show how knowledge, effort, and action can lead to better lives. Arguing that the best possible day care system would be funded by the government, managed by the families involved, and made available to everyone regardless of financial circumstance, the author also makes clear how individual families can work to create rational, caring programs for their own and their neighbors' children. A guide to available materials, books, funds; an illustrated "how-to" section of homemade toys and furniture; a suggested "curriculum" and staffing policy

Fontana, Vincent J.
 Somewhere a child is crying; maltreatment—causes and prevention. Macmillan Pub. Co. 1973 xx, 268p $6.95 362.7
 1 Cruelty to children   LC 73-10566
 The author "presents startling descriptions and statistics of a major national problem which demands action. His concept of the 'child maltreatment syndrome' encompasses all forms of child neglect and abuse, the 'battered child' being the most extreme. He cites evidence of increasing incidence, and argues that it must be perceived and treated within the social environmental structure. Fontana's concern for both child and parent, his plea for recognition of the rights of children, and his suggestions for improving both legislation and procedures for detecting, investigating, and preventing maltreatment make this book vital reading for concerned layman and professional alike." Library J
 "This book should be universally required reading, particularly by the young who are looking for a cause, though reading it is like taking a walk in hell. . . . His book is an impassioned plea to an aroused, concerned citizenry to assist the innocent victims and their 'guardians.'" Pub W

Griffin, Al
 How to start and operate a day care home. Regnery 1973 233p $7.95 362.7
 1 Day nurseries
 ISBN 0-8092-9120-7   LC 72-11177

 "This comprehensive guide should be included in every public library, not only to provide sound advice on improving child care home facilities, but also, hopefully, to lure qualified mothers who might not have considered the possibility of caring for children in their homes. The chapters on licensing, equipment, schedules, meals, and naps include helpful lists and outlines. Griffin's discussions of child development and potential problems are short and not always authoritative, but he insists that operators take their jobs very seriously, by undertaking further reading and course work. The book includes a lengthy annotated bibliography and a list of licensing agencies." Library J

Helfer, Ray E.
 (ed.) The battered child; ed. by Ray E. Helfer and C. Henry Kempe. 2d ed. Univ. of Chicago Press 1974 262p illus $15 362.7
 1 Cruelty to children
 ISBN 0-226-32629-2   LC 73-87303
 Earlier edition entered in main catalog
 First published 1968. In the 1974 edition "the editors have deleted material no longer applicable, updated other contributions, and added more recent information. A chapter on the New York experience has been added. The section on the reporting laws, pathology, and X-ray has been . . . revised." Preface to the second edition
 Includes bibliographies

Klibanoff, Susan
 Let's talk about adoption [by] Susan and Elton Klibanoff. Little 1973 263p $7.95 362.7
 1 Adoption
 ISBN 0-316-49845-9   LC 73-10401
 A "book that provides answers to some common questions about adoption and at the same time introduces the whole subject reassuringly. Mrs. Klibanoff offers a mother's-eye view of the problems she and her husband (a man involved in the reform of Massachusetts adoption laws) solved in adopting a baby girl. The rest of the book is a well-organized look at the diverse reasons for adopting a child, the way adoption 'happens,' the kinds of adoption (transracial, older children, children with special needs, single-parent adoption, etc.), some of the history of adoption, legal controversies (religious restrictions and other issues). The appended state-by-state list of Adoptive Parents' Groups is most valuable." Pub W
 Includes bibliographical references

Raymond, Louise
 Adoption and after; rev. by Colette Taube Dywasuk. Harper 1974 257p $6.95 362.7
 1 Adoption
 ISBN 0-06-013531-X   LC 73-14285
 Earlier edition entered in main catalog
 First published 1955. The 1974 edition has been revised to bring the material up to date
 Bibliography: p251-52

363.2 Police services

Whittemore, L. H.
 The super cops; the true story of the cops called Batman and Robin. Stein & Day 1973 359p $7.95 363.2
 1 Greenberg, David 2 Hantz, Robert 3 New York (City)—Police 4 Crime and criminals—U.S.
 ISBN 0-8128-1538-6   LC 72-96377
 This is an account of the work of two "police officers who teamed up on a private anticrime crusade in the police academy and in Brooklyn's Bedford-Stuyvesant area from 1968 to 1972. They earned the nicknames Batman and Robin because of their unorthodox methods (one was to watch victims from rooftops, and then swoop down on them via ropes and grappling hooks). These methods appear unusually effective; but their phenomenal success proved embarrassing to the rest of New York's finest. Therefore, the police establishment used various means to thwart their efforts." Library J
 This action filled narrative "would make fine reading as a supplement to a detailed text in police work, for general reading in the fields of criminology and law enforcement, or for pleasure." Best Sellers

363.3 Maintenance of public safety

Sherrill, Robert
The Saturday night special, and other guns with which Americans won the West, protected bootleg franchises, slew wildlife, robbed countless banks, shot husbands purposely and by mistake, and killed presidents —together with the debate over continuing same; illus. by Julio Fernandez. Charterhouse Bks. 1973 338p illus $8.95   363.3
    1 Firearms—Laws and regulations 2 Firearms industry and trade 3 National Rifle Association of America
    ISBN 0-88327-016-1   LC 73-84076

This is an "inquiry into the type of society that let the gun problem spiral out of control . . . [as well as a study] of the gun trade and its techniques for survival." N Y Times Bk R
"Not only a reference-work loaded with cool statistics, this book is, for those with the guts to face facts, an indispensable warning of the crime that threatens the survival of the nation." Best Sellers
Bibliography: p325-28

364.1 Criminal offenses

Wambaugh, Joseph
The onion field. Delacorte Press 1973 427p $8.95   364.1
    1 Murder 2 Hettinger, Karl 3 Campbell, Ian James 4 Powell, Gregory Ulas 5 Smith, Jimmy Lee   LC 73-7540

The author "tells what happened in the wake of the 1963 kidnapping, by two hoodlums, of two Los Angeles cops who had tried to arrest them. In a moonlit onion field near Bakerfield one of the officers was killed in cold blood; his partner escaped. The killers were caught hours after the crime—but the case was closed only after more than six years of legal gymnastics. There was a complex trial, an appeal, a retrial and more appeals. In the end the main killer adjusted to life in San Quentin, but the good-guy cop who escaped was a broken man. Wambaugh's spare, vivid documentary style draws the marrow out of police, court and psychiatric records while shaping a strong case for the reform of American criminal justice." Pub W

365 Penal institutions

Charrière, Henri
Banco; the further adventures of Papillon; tr. from the French by Patrick O'Brian. Morrow 1973 270p $7.95   365
    ISBN 0-688-00218-8   LC 73-13897
    Sequel to: Papillon, entered in main catalog
    Original French edition, 1972

"Imprisoned for life in Devil's Island on a false murder charge, Henri Charrière ('Papillon') escaped after 14 years and gained freedom in Venezuela. This book describes the rest of his life there: first as a miner who was tempted to steal a gold horde, then as a crooked dice player and would-be bank robber, and finally—after meeting Rita, his wife, who insisted that he go straight—as hotelier, restaurateur and fishing-fleet operator." Pub W
Charrière's "moving narrative is a convincing document of self-understanding and an exciting story as well." Library J

Mitford, Jessica
Kind and usual punishment; the prison business. Knopf 1973 340p illus $7.95   365
    1 Prisons—U.S.
    ISBN 0-394-47602-6   LC 73-7263

This exposé of the American penal system "examines the indeterminate sentence, the parole and work furlough systems . . . the convict's vulnerability to medical experimentation, the 'creative editing' of crime statistics by the police, the implications of the new prison technology and the new double-think that clothes ugly realities in bland jargon." Pub W
"Deliberately 'uncouched in the mind-glazing language of sociology,' [the author's] book is carefully documented. The author . . . met with criminologists, prison administrators, ex-convicts, legislators, lawyers, and spent a night in a women's prison. She does not, however, issue forthright alternatives to imprisonment nor call for outright abolition. . . . [Her treatise] stands in sharp contrast to most corrections literature, done by 'experts' or scholars often too close to the problem." Christian Science Monitor
Bibliography included in Notes: p311-40

Solzhenitsyn, Aleksandr I.
The Gulag archipelago, 1918-1956; an experiment in literary investigation. [Pt] I-II tr. from the Russian by Thomas P. Whitney. Harper 1974 660p illus $12.50   365
    1 Political prisoners 2 Russia—Politics and government—1917-
    ISBN 0-06-013914-5   LC 73-22756
    Original Russian edition published 1973

The "archipelago" of the title refers to the system of forced labor camps run and augmented by the Soviet secret police and its institutions. "Gulag" is the acronym of the central office that administered the penal colonies. This volume follows scores of victims on their journey from arrest to first cell and interrogation through transit prisons across the country to the ports and ships of the archipelago
This book "is written by a man whose courage, whose integrity, and whose experience will give it overwhelming authority throughout the world. It is a truly exceptional work: For in it literature transcends history, without distorting it." Sat R/World
Glossary: p621-41

369 Miscellaneous kinds of associations

Anderson, Peggy
The Daughters; an unconventional look at America's fan club—the DAR. St Martins 1974 360p $10   369
    1 Daughters of the American Revolution
    LC 73-87396

"The author finds the Daughters of the American Revolution more than a bunch of elderly tea drinkers, but less than perfect. Few members of the public know that the D.A.R. supports schools, gives scholarships to American Indians, has furnished Independence Hall, etc. Instead, people remember the 1939 Marian Anderson incident and the ridiculousness of the D.A.R.'s annual resolutions. Anderson (no relation to Marian Anderson) examines in a sometimes rambling way the D.A.R. functions and concerns: the difficulties in searching out one's genealogy, operations on a chapter level, and the duties and concerns of the leadership. She suggests that the D.A.R. modernize itself, make the resolutions more realistic, and try to attract black members." Library J
"Miss Anderson puts the D.A.R. into perspective, and she does so with considerable grace and style." N Y Times Bk R
Bibliography: p343-45

370.15 Educational psychology

Jensen, Arthur R.
Educability and group differences. Harper 1973 407p illus $10   370.15
    1 Educational psychology 2 Intellect
    ISBN 0-06-012194-7   LC 72-9126

In this "analysis of the genetic factor in intelligence and educability, [the author] argues that those qualities which seem most closely related to educability cannot be accounted for by a traditional environmentalist hypothesis. It is more probable, he claims, that they have a substantial genetic basis. Educability as defined in this book is the ability to learn the traditional scholastic subjects, especially the three R's, under ordinary conditions of classroom instruction." Publisher's note

Jensen, Arthur R.—*Continued*

"The author is skilled at conveying complex statistical ideas. Nevertheless, considerable background in statistics and research design is needed to evaluate his arguments. This may prove convenient for some extreme environmentalists, who will have decided he's wrong before they open the book. The work is well organized. At times, Jensen comes close to writing more like an advocate than a searcher for truth, but on the whole he makes a rather objective presentation." Best Sellers

References: p376-96

370.19 Education and society

Toffler, Alvin
(ed.) Learning for tomorrow; the role of the future in education. Random House 1974 xxvi, 421p $10   **370.19**
1 Education—U.S. 2 Civilization, Modern—1950-
ISBN 0-394-48313-8   LC 73-12914

"These 16 papers focus on role images, curricula, and directions and resources for the future in education. Topics discussed include the roles of women and blacks; programs in the sciences, social sciences, and humanities; and the use of such tools as games and science fiction. The writers generally support Toffler's thesis that 'all education springs from some image of the future,' and assert students' need to learn to 'future-plan.' . . . They view the school as a change agent, and advocate strong teacher commitment. A 'status report' lists sample syllabuses and a 'directory of future studies.' Much here is suggestive of Dewey, reconstructionism, and the experience-centered pedagogy of the 1930's." Library J

For each of the "contributors, the school of the future would manage things quite differently. Discussing what those differences could be makes for exciting, if uneven, reading. Toffler's introductory essay—which treats the future not as something impersonal and 'out there' but as susceptible to individual manipulation—is particularly intriguing." Christian Science Monitor

370.3 Education—Encyclopedias and dictionaries

The Encyclopedia of education. Lee C. Deighton, editor-in-chief. Macmillan Pub. Co. 1971 10v $199   **370.3**
1 Education—Encyclopedias   LC 70-133143

"In more than 1,000 articles . . . [the set] offers a view of the institutions and people, of the processes and products, found in educational practice. The articles deal with history, theory, research, and philosophy, as well as with the structure and fabric of education." Preface

This "is an entirely new work conceived . . . to fill a long-felt need for a modern overview of education. . . . [This work] cannot be considered a handbook or manual of operation for educators, but rather an authoritative source of background information in many areas of concern. . . . Most articles examined were adequate, and many were excellent. The style of writing is generally clear and understandable by the layman, the exception being technical articles directed toward scholars and graduate students. . . . The encyclopedia can be considered a well-organized and useful reference set for educators, students, and nonprofessional users. Purchase is recommended to all libraries serving adult readers." Booklist

371 The school

Esty, John C.
Choosing a private school [by] John C. Esty, Jr. Dodd 1974 267p $6.95   **371**
1 Private schools
ISBN 0-396-06861-8   LC 73-11550

The author answers "such questions as why choose a private school, who should go, how much do they cost, what do boarding schools offer, etc. In attempting to cover the field from local parochial schools to elite boarding schools . . . [the author] draws a general picture which does not always adequately cover the various alternatives; but the sections on selecting a school are very useful, and the work will, on the whole, be informative to parents considering this form of education. Appendixes cover directories of schools, guidance and placement agencies, and accrediting associations." Library J

Selected reading and references: p257-60

371.3 Methods of instruction and study

Montessori, Maria
Childhood education; tr. by A. M. Joosten. Regnery 1974 137p $5.95   **371.3**
1 Montessori method of education
ISBN 0-8092-9102-9   LC 73-20433
Original Italian edition published 1949. English translation first published 1955

"This work does not pretend to be a detailed explanation of how the Montessori schools were designed and operated. It is, rather, an explanation of Montessori's basic philosophy of child development and of how she came to hold her views. She believed that the basis of education reform must be built on the scientific study of man and his place in the cosmic order, and that we must seek an understanding of how the child learns in his psychological nature (she felt the optimum age for a child to learn to write and to read, in that order, is four years, when his interest is still spontaneous). Her ideas are still relevant today." Library J

From childhood to adolescence; including Erdkinder and The function of the university. Schocken 1973 146p $6.95   **371.3**
1 Montessori method of education   2 Child study
ISBN 0-8052-3516-7   LC 72-91607
Translated from the French by the Montessori Educational Research Center

Montessori first discusses the characteristics and needs of children from seven to twelve. This is followed by chapters concerning experimentation and study in such areas as organic and inorganic chemistry. Included in the Appendix are articles which were first published in Amsterdam in 1939 under the titles "The Erdkinder: A Scheme for a Reform of Secondary Education," "The Reform of Education During and After Adolescence," and "The Function of the University." This book was conceived as a series of lectures "Despite the deficiencies of the editorial compilation . . . the profound thinking of Montessori . . . is always exciting and provides thought-provoking reading. . . . This book is recommended for inclusion in undergraduate education libraries." Choice

371.9 Special education

Levy, Harold B.
Square pegs, round holes; the learning-disabled child in the classroom and at home. Little 1973 250p $7.50   **371.9**
1 Mentally handicapped children—Education 2 Problem children—Education
ISBN 0-316-52232-5   LC 73-3422

The author explains "that academic learning is dependent upon integrity of the central nervous system, and that children with minimal brain dysfunction will exhibit behavioral deviations. His book represents an appeal from medicine to pedagogy to recognize and accept a group of children heretofore misunderstood and consequently mismanaged. He points out the prevalence of specific learning disabilities, but he discourages those who would be case-finding agents for the purpose of referring problem children out of the educational mainstream." Foreword

"Dr. Levy's insight into the learning-disabled child and his use of a clear vocabulary in writing for parents and teachers make this book an outstanding contribution to the lit-

Levy, Harold B.—*Continued*
erature on learning disabilities. . . . This book is highly recommended for teachers, particularly elementary and junior high school teachers, to arouse awareness of these children and to kindle the desire for further study directed toward more productive teaching. An excellent list of suggested additional readings adds to the value of the book as a reference source." Science Bks

MacCracken, Mary
A circle of children. Lippincott 1973 239p $6.95   371.9

1 Problem children—Education
ISBN 0-397-00994-1   LC 73-10054

"The appealing personal account of a young society matron who visited a school for emotionally disturbed children and was so fascinated that she came back, first as a volunteer, then as a teacher. MacCracken's main theme throughout is that a worker with love and understanding can do more for these children than can one with several education degrees. Her inspiring account should encourage more enthusiasm—especially among ambitious college-age readers—for teaching such youngsters." Library J

372.1 Elementary education

Silberman, Charles E.
(ed.) The open classroom reader. Random House 1973 xxiii, 789p illus $12.50
372.1

1 Education—Experimental methods
ISBN 0-394-48221-2   LC 72-11430

Companion volume to: Crisis in the classroom, entered in main catalog, class 370
The first "section describes English and American primary classrooms. The second section includes the aims of education and learning theory. . . . The third section combines practical suggestions about classroom arrangements, materials, and planning with discussions of the teacher as adviser, facilitator, learner, and senior partner. . . . [The final section describes language arts, mathematics, science, and the arts." Choice
"A well-coordinated and interlocking presentation of the open-classroom concept. . . . Undoubtedly, this book will become required reading for all prospective educators." America

372.7 Mathematics

Kline, Morris
Why Johnny can't add: the failure of the new math. St Martins 1973 173p illus $6.95
372.7

1 Mathematics—Study and teaching
                  LC 72-80894

The author seeks to show that the new math is a failure because it is directed toward the minute fraction of students who will someday become professional mathematicians while the rest are left with scarcely enough mathematical capability to perform simple arithmetic operations. He recognizes that the old methods of teaching math were imperfect, but he argues that a theory of teaching mathematics that excludes numbers in favor of empty sets, is not satisfying the needs and desires of the overwhelming majority of America's students
The "list of criticisms Kline presents is impressive. Equally noteworthy is his recounting of the reasons for the unhappy history." Christian Science Monitor
Bibliography: p171-73

378 Higher education

Du Bois, W. E. B.
The education of Black people; ten critiques, 1906-1960; ed. by Herbert Aptheker. Univ. of Mass. Press 1973 171p $10   378

1 Negroes—Education 2 Education, Higher
ISBN 0-87023-130-8   LC 72-90495

"In 1940, DuBois assembled and wrote brief introductions for seven of these ten essays on Negro education; but that collection was never published. For the current edition, Aptheker, literary custodian of the DuBois papers, has selected three later DuBois essays and provided introductory comments for them. . . . [These] essays (nine were speeches delivered at Negro colleges) chronicle DuBois' . . . fight for quality higher education for American blacks. . . . Aptheker's overall introduction and his bibliography of DuBois' published writings on education complement this important collection. . . . [These essays] not only provide valuable insight into the history of the Negro college's role in American life; but they also serve as a monument to DuBois' influence and foresight in black education." Library J

378.1 Institutions of higher education

Barron's How to prepare for the College Level Examination Program CLEP. William C. Doster, editor [and others]. Barrons Educ. Ser. 1973 633p illus pa $5.95
378.1

1 Educational tests and measurements 2 Colleges and universities—Entrance requirements
ISBN 0-8120-0420-5   LC 71-1628

Based on what an average college sophomore has studied, the CLEP examines educational growth achieved in or independent of a college curiculum. This book aims to help the user score high on the CLEP. It contains approximately 4700 test items arranged into five subject sections: English composition, humanities, mathematics, natural sciences, and social sciences. A complete sample CLEP battery is included
Includes bibliographies

Davies, Peter
The truth about Kent State; a challenge to the American conscience [by] Peter Davies and the Board of Church and Society of the United Methodist Church. Farrar, Straus 1973 241p illus maps $10   378.1

1 Ohio. State University, Kent
ISBN 0-374-27938-1   LC 72-94722

A "damning book concerning the Kent State tragedy of May 4, 1970. Using official reports, documents, and some new information, Davies chronicles the events at Kent State and makes a strong case against the National Guard for their firing at students. The carefully assembled set of photographs of the events provide dramatic, if extremely depressing, supporting evidence for Davies' contentions. Davies not only points out the 'errors' which were made by authorities at Kent State, but alleges that there was a conspiracy by the National Guard to 'cover up' what really happened. Just as important, the author indicates, were the many efforts by the government to 'cover up' the real situation. Davies carefully analyzes the actions (and inactions) of the Justice Department and various other state and federal agencies." Choice
This book was published before the trial and dismissal of charges against the Ohio guardsmen
Bibliography: p229-30

378.3 Student finances

Proia, Nicholas C.
Barron's Handbook of American college financial aid. Rev. by Nicholas C. Proia [and] Vincent M. Di Gaspari. Barrons Educ. Ser. 1974 508p pa $6.95   378.3

1 Scholarships, fellowships, etc. 2 Student loan funds
ISBN 0-8120-0406-X   LC 79-121890

Earlier edition entered in main catalog
First published 1971. The 1974 edition has been revised to include "data for more than 1400 four-year private and public colleges that offer financial assistance." Introduction
Glossary of educational terms: p10-19

385.09 Railroad transportation—History

The Railroaders, by the editors of Time-Life Books, with text by Keith Wheeler. Time-Life Bks. [distributed by Little] 1973 240p illus maps (The Old West) $9.95   385.09

1 Railroads—History 2 The West—History
LC 73-84316

This book, illustrated with photographs, maps, drawings and newspaper clippings of the period, shows the advent of the railroad into the Old West, and its effect on the wilderness and settlers of the late nineteenth century
Bibliography: p236-37

391 Costume and personal appearance

Schoeffler, O. E.
Esquire's Encyclopedia of 20th century men's fashions [by] O. E. Schoeffler and William Gale. McGraw 1973 709p illus $35   391

1 Men's clothing 2 Costume—History
ISBN 07-055480-3   LC 72-9811

"Profusely illustrated with sketches and photographs from Bettmann Archives and such firms as Hickey-Freeman, this guide to what the well-dressed man has worn from 1900 to the present is organized by type of clothing, then chronologically. Suits, coats, shoes, belts, all sorts of sport clothes, from skiing to horseback riding, toilet articles, hats and ties, all are covered in this well-researched encyclopedia. In addition to descriptions, there are accounts of such facts as when the first pair of levis was manufactured, biographies of designers and their philosophy of design, and a glossary of fashion-related terms." Ref Services Rev

391.03 Costume—Encyclopedias and dictionaries

Picken, Mary Brooks
The fashion dictionary; fabric, sewing, and apparel as expressed in the language of fashion. Rev. and enl. Funk 1973 434p illus $12.95   391.03

1 Clothing and dress—Dictionaries 2 Textile industry and fabrics—Dictionaries
ISBN 0-308-10052-2   LC 72-83771

First published 1939 with title: The language of fashion

Over 200 black and white photographs and "800 drawings illustrate this collection of descriptions of 10,000 fashion terms, alphabetically arranged from aal (a red dye) to Zulu cloth, a fabric used as foundation for crewel work. Most definitions are very brief, but some larger subjects, such as leather and wool, are treated more fully. Illustrations are separately indexed." Ref Services Rev

392 Customs of life cycle. Weddings

Seligson, Marcia
The eternal bliss machine; America's way of wedding. Morrow 1973 304p $7.95   392

1 Marriage customs and rites
ISBN 0-688-00158-0   LC 72-126

This is an exposé of American wedding customs and the businesses which profit from those customs with "examples from the first contacts with caterer and orchestra, florist and bridal salon, to the honeymoon experiences in the Poconos. Included are the catered affair, the odd couple, ethnic, Hollywood, Texas and White House weddings." Pub W

This is a "bright and peppy review of American marital extravagances. Its story of consumerism and grossness is appropriately appalling." Christian Century
Bibliography: p289-91

398 Folklore

Coffin, Tristram Potter
(ed.) Folklore from the working folk of America; selected and ed. by Tristram Potter Coffin and Hennig Cohen, from the leading journals and archives of folklore. Anchor Press 1973 xxxviii, 464p illus music $8.95   398

1 Folklore—U.S.
ISBN 0-385-03874-7   LC 79-97699

"Originating with the occupations pursued down through U.S. history the selections, including words and music for 27 songs, form an anthology that salutes and memorializes the workers of the nation. The introduction describes the divisions into which the material presented is arranged: part one contains clearly literary pieces, part two encompasses nonliterary cultural expressions passed on traditionally, and the third and final grouping is devoted to folklore inspired by notable characters, and legendary heroes comprising songs, verse, stories, and related items concerning working peoples." Booklist

"The end notes provide descriptive source information as well as references to other material. This excellent collection provides access to many items from sources that are normally available to only a few scholars." Library J

Titles and first significant lines of songs and verse: p460-62

400 LANGUAGE

401 Language and languages—Philosophy and theory

Farb, Peter
Word play; what happens when people talk. Knopf 1974 [c1973] 350p $8.95   401

1 Language and languages—Psychology
2 Communication
ISBN 0-394-48675-7

"The latest knowledge of tongues—an interdiscipline involving psychology, sociology and even a touch of metaphysics—is summed up here for the layman. . . . A portion of what Farb says has been said by the old semanticists and, in fact, by such commentators on the vagary of words as Lewis Carroll. Farb's achievement is to organize today's theories into a primer, systematically discounting or rejecting outworn conceptions and myths which he feels may be lodged in the minds of his readers. . . . In his enthusiasm for 'body language'—the things said by facial expressions, gestures, posture—Farb goes far beyond most scholars of the new linguistics. . . . When the theorizing becomes heavy, Farb knows how to entertain himself and his reader with a rich miscellany of random facts and provocative (if not always documented) opinions that spill beyond his outline." Time
Bibliography: p335-50

413 Polyglot dictionaries and lexicography

Paxton, John
(ed.) Dictionary of abbreviations. Rowman & Littlefield 1974 384p $11.50   413

1 Abbreviations—Dictionaries 2 Dictionaries, Polyglot
ISBN 0-87471-188-6   LC 73-5881

Half title: Everyman's Dictionary of abbreviations

"A useful compilation of some 25,000 entries with over 37,000 definitions, many of them ex-

Paxton, John—*Continued*
plained. Included are contractions, shortened forms, initials and their variants, acronyms, and signs and symbols from international sources. Special emphasis is given economic and commercial matters, particularly including employers' associations and trade union organizations. Though coverage is global, the work is beamed toward British and Commonwealth users." Library J

"There is a good deal of overlap with standard sources; however, there are some terms and definitions not to be found elsewhere, especially terms from England and Europe. Sometimes the various sources include different definitions of the same abbreviation, thereby increasing the chances of finding the one intended by author being read." Cur Ref Bks

420 English language

Laird, Charlton
You and your language. Prentice-Hall 1973 182p illus $6.95   420
1 English language
ISBN 0-13-976977-3   LC 73-15654
"A Spectrum book"

An examination of our language and how we use it, as well as the way it shapes our thinking. The author also provides a chapter on how to stretch your brain power with words, a chapter which tells why slang ain't so bad, and another on the bureaucratese of government and the other special languages developed by business and the professions

"Laird touches many subjects but never quite settles down to examine any in great detail. Fortunately, Laird is a popularizer with an enjoyable style; he admonishes us to 'have fun,' as indeed he does. His enthusiasm is contagious and will, hopefully, encourage the reader to dip deeper into other sources." Library J

421.03 Written and spoken codes of standard English—Dictionaries

De Sola, Ralph
Abbreviations dictionary: abbreviations; acronyms; anonyms; contractions; initials and nicknames; short forms and slang shortcuts; signs and symbols. New international 4th ed. Am. Elsevier Pub. Co. 1974 428p $24.50   421.03
1 Abbreviations—Dictionaries 2 Acronyms—Dictionaries 3 Signs and symbols
ISBN 0-444-00139-5   LC 73-7687
First published 1958 by Duell, Sloan and Pearce

Contains "Automatic data-processing abbreviations for zip-coded mail; Chemical element symbols, atomic numbers, and discovery data; Civil and military time systems compared; Diacritical and punctuation marks; Greek alphabet; International civil aircraft markings; International radio alphabet and code; Numbered abbreviations; Numeration; Proofreader's marks; Railroads of the world; Roman numerals; Russian alphabet (transliterated); Ship's ly used; Steamship lines; U.S. Naval ship symbols; Weather symbols; Beaufort scale; Zodical signs." N Y New Tech Bks

422 Etymology of standard English

Pei, Mario
Double-speak in America. Hawthorn Bks. 1973 216p $6.95   422
1 English language—Etymology 2 English language—Terms and phrases 3 Words, New
    LC 78-39894

"Pei examines the semantics of advertising, academe, women's lib, politics, the Pentagon, the black culture, and sex, to mention only a few. The book's strength lies in the abundant examples, for the only semblance of a thesis is Pei's underlying desire to acquaint the reader with the dangers of language that calls attention to itself rather than to its actual meaning. What Pei shows us about 'double-speak' is a timely reminder that Orwell's 'Newspeak' is only 11 years away. Two excellent indices: (1) index of persons, places, titles, and things and (2) index of words and expressions." Choice

"The book could serve as a supplement to dictionaries that are struggling, valiantly to keep up with the changes; and, of course, it can be read on its own—it's more amusing, and more opinionated, than a dictionary." Library J

422.03 Etymology of standard English—Dictionaries

Carroll, David
The dictionary of foreign terms in the English language. Hawthorn Bks. 1973 212p $9.95   422.03
1 English language—Foreign words and phrases—Dictionaries   LC 70-39281

The author presents "one-sentence definitions or translations of some 7,000 foreign terms and phrases that appear frequently in written and spoken English. There is a predominance of Latin phrases (e.g., mottos, aphorisms), as well as many French terms and phrases. Other languages ranging from Arabic to Turkish and Yiddish are also represented. Words and phrases are listed alphabetically, and for each entry the language of origin and the meaning are presented. Infrequently, an etymology is provided.... This source will be a very convenient one for quick assistance to patrons whose understanding of what they have heard or read is inhibited by a sprinkling of foreign words and phrases." Cur Ref Bks

"Strictly foreign terms are given in italics, but foreign terms now common in the English language are in Roman type. The language or origin and a cosmic meaning are given, but no attempt has been made to indicate pronunciation." Library J

423 Dictionaries of standard English

The Barnhart Dictionary of new English since 1963 [ed. by] Clarence L. Barnhart, Sol Steinmetz [and] Robert K. Barnhart. Barnhart/Harper 1973 512p $12.95   423
1 Words, New—Dictionaries 2 English language—Dictionaries
ISBN 0-06-010223-3   LC 73-712

This dictionary contains about 5,000 new words and terms resulting from recent scientific and technical achievements and cultural and social changes. Each entry includes a definition and at least one quotation to convey its meaning and flavor. Pronunciations, etymologies and usage notes are provided in many cases

"For native speakers, editors, English scholars, writers, and all word enthusiasts, this is a useful supplement to standard dictionaries." Minnesota

427 Nonstandard English

Moss, Norman
What's the difference? A British/American dictionary. Harper 1973 138p $6.95   427
1 English language—Terms and phrases 2 Americanisms 3 English language—Dictionaries
ISBN 0-06-013096-2   LC 73-9140

The author presents a list of "words that are different in the two languages in their common usage. The criterion is whether a word is familiar to most people in one country or the

Moss, Norman—*Continued*

other, not whether it is listed in a dictionary. ... Where it is appropriate ... [he includes] an indication of the verbal or social context in which a word is likely to be used, as well as a definition." Introduction

"Mr Moss has done amazingly well, and for one rather simple reason: he is perfectly serious. He likes his little joke, best of all with a blue tinge. ... But for all his fun, he is never arch; nor are the jokes the point of the book. This is a workmanlike little dictionary, genuinely useful, and with a great deal of work behind it." Economist

495.1 Chinese language

Lin, Yutang

Lin Yutang's Chinese-English dictionary of modern usage. The Chinese Univ. of Hong Kong [distributed by McGraw 1973 c1972] lxvi, 1720p $39.50   **495.1**

1 Chinese language—Dictionaries
ISBN 0-07-099695-4   LC 72-3899

First published 1972 in Hong Kong

This volume "attempts to present idiomatic English equivalents for all the words in the Chinese national language (the guoyuu) that the modern reader is likely to encounter. It represents several departures in Chinese-English dictionary making. First, it emphasizes 'words,' whether monosyllabic or polysyllabic, rather than the monosyllabic 'characters.' It treats the words linguistically, indicating parts of speech and meanings derived from context. Contrary to past practice, the language as it is spoken is given prime importance. The handsome volume is well provided with introductory and explanatory material, as well as good keys to use. Although scholars of Chinese language may not be in unanimous agreement with this approach to dictionary making, this is sure to be a landmark work." Cur Ref Bks

500 PURE SCIENCES

500.9 Natural history

Abbey, Edward

Cactus country, by Edward Abbey and the editors of Time-Life Books. Time-Life Bks. [distributed by Little] 1973 184p illus (The American wilderness) $7.95   **500.9**

1 Natural history—Sonoran Desert
LC 72-91599

This book describes 69,000 square miles of southern Arizona and northern Mexico, an arid wilderness which represents about half of the Sonoran Desert. Cacti, animal life and geological features are discussed and several personal experiences are recounted
Bibliography: p180

Borland, Hal

Seasons; photographs by Les Line. Lippincott 1973 108p illus $14.95   **500.9**

1 Nature
ISBN 0-397-00996-8   LC 73-5988

"Each season is given its own photo portfolio and introductory essay; and the combination of Borland's nostalgic, lyrical prose and Line's stunning color photographs is pure delight, whether for reading, looking, or dreaming." Library J

Brown, Dale

Wild Alaska, by Dale Brown and the editors of Time-Life Books. Time-Life Bks. [distributed by Little] 1972 184p illus (The American wilderness) $7.95   **500.9**

1 Natural history—Alaska
LC 74-190658

In text and photographs, the author describes the geology and the plant and animal life of our northernmost state
Bibliography: p180

Carr, Archie

The Everglades, by Archie Carr and the editors of Time-Life Books. Time-Life Bks. [distributed by Little] 1973 184p illus map (The American wilderness) $7.95   **500.9**

1 Everglades 2 Natural history—Florida
LC 72-96548

Text and numerous illustrations portray the flora, fauna and ecology of the Florida Everglades
Bibliography: p180

Clement, Roland C.

Hammond Nature atlas of America. ... Hammond 1973 255p illus maps $17.95   **500.9**

1 Natural history—North America
ISBN 0-8437-3511-2   LC 73-7524

This title supersedes: Hammond's Nature atlas of America, by E. L. Jordan, entered in main catalog

"A Ridge Press book"

"Reptiles & amphibians, insects, birds, wildflowers, trees, rocks & minerals, fishes, mammals." Title page

"This book is essentially a color photo sampler covering geologic, botanical, and zoological features of America; clearly written descriptions (about 150 words each) accompany each pictured example. The claim to the title 'atlas' lies in the range maps, which show regional distributions for a sampling of animals, plants, minerals, weather conditions, and physiographic features." Library J

"The illustrations are colorful, accurate, and graphic. Particularly noteworthy are the special maps. ... Written in clear, succinct language readily understood by the student or layman [this work] is an excellent introduction to the ecology of the United States." Booklist
Glossary: p249. Suggested reading: p251

For a fuller review see: Reference and Subscription Books Reviews, February 1, 1974

Dillard, Annie

Pilgrim at Tinker Creek. Harpers Mag. Press 1974 271p $7.95   **500.9**

1 Nature 2 Natural history—Virginia
ISBN 0-06-121980-0   LC 73-18655

Starting with January, Dillard "records the seasons as they come and go at Tinker Creek in Virginia. ... She points out the sights: the creek, 17 ft. wide; a favorite Osage orange tree ... woods leading up to the Blue Ridge Mountains; Brushy, McAfee's Knob Dead Man. [She also records] the death of a small frog sucked dry by a giant water bug, and ... an afternoon she spent sitting beside a copperhead." Time

This work is "in an honored tradition of literature; not quite environmentalism and not the philosophy of science, it is rather the refraction of natural philosophy through the prismatic conscience of art. Highly recommended for the general reader—any general reader, anywhere—who wishes to deepen his awareness of his yard of world and to reflect upon it more profoundly." Choice

Johnson, William Weber

Baja California, by William Weber Johnson and the editors of Time-Life Books. With photographs by Jay Maisel. Time-Life Bks. [distributed by Little] 1972 184p illus (The American wilderness) $7.95   **500.9**

1 Natural history—Baja California 2 Baja California—Description and travel
LC 72-85157

This book describes the wilderness and plant and animal life of Baja California, the 800 mile long peninsular Mexican state which lies south of California between the Pacific Ocean and the Gulf of California
Bibliography: p180

Knauth, Percy

The north woods, by Percy Knauth and the editors of Time-Life Books. Time-Life Bks. [distributed by Little] 1972 184p illus map (The American wilderness) $7.95 **500.9**

1 Natural history—Canada 2 Natural history—Minnesota 3 Forests and forestry
LC 72-88525

Knauth, Percy—Continued

Text and numerous illustrations portray the seasonal changes of the flora and fauna of the north woods which extend from northern Minnesota to embrace parts of four Canadian provinces as well as the Northwest Territories
Bibliography: p180

Leonard, Jonathan Norton

Atlantic beaches, by Jonathan Norton Leonard and the editors of Time-Life Books. Time-Life Bks. [distributed by Little] 1972 184p illus map (The American wilderness) $7.95   500.9

1 Natural history—Atlantic States
LC 72-79775

Covering the Atlantic coastline from Cape Cod to North Carolina, this book describes the different types of beaches, how they form and decline, and the variety of plant and animal life
Bibliography: p180

National Geographic Society

Wilderness U.S.A. The Society 1973 344p illus maps $10.65   500.9

1 Wilderness areas 2 Natural history—U.S. 3 Camping
ISBN 0-87044-116-7   LC 73-10213

A book about America's surviving wildernesses, why men go to them, and what they are doing to save them from the relentless push of people and progress. Outdoorsmen, naturalists, scientists, townsmen, and backcountry woodsmen—all take turns filling this book with their experiences and observations. In 344 large-format pages, with 360 color views, they survey the Nation's wildernesses from Florida's tip to Alaska's North Slope

"This splendid volume invites the reader to sample the unspoiled beauty of wilderness mountains, forests, deserts, prairies, swamps, and waterways. . . . Appended are a backpacking primer and sources for additional information. The binding is sturdy, end papers are handsome, and the price is reasonable." Library J

Russell, Franklin

The Okefenokee Swamp, by Franklin Russell and the editors of Time-Life Books; with photographs by Patricia Caulfield. Time-Life Bks. [distributed by Little] 1973 184p illus map (The American wilderness) $7.95   500.9

1 Natural history—Georgia 2 Okefenokee Swamp 3 Marshes   LC 73-78582

Illustrated with photographs, this book describes the history and ecology of the Okefenokee swamplands on the Georgia-Florida border
Bibliography: p180

Walker, Bryce S.

The Great Divide, by Bryce S. Walker and the editors of Time-Life Books. Time-Life Bks. [distributed by Little] 1973 184p illus maps (The American wilderness) $7.95   500.9

1 Natural history—Rocky Mountains
LC 73-81327

This book relates the natural history of the Rocky Mountain region known as the Great Continental Divide, the 1700 mile ridge which separates the east and west flowing streams. Physical features including glaciers, geysers, mountain ranges, parks, and plant and animal life are described
Bibliography: p180

Wallace, Robert

Hawaii, by Robert Wallace and the editors of Time-Life Books. Time-Life Bks. [distributed by Little] 1973 184p illus maps (The American wilderness) $7.95   500.9

1 Natural history—Hawaii   LC 73-75608

This natural history of Hawaii surveys the islands' varied animal life, vegetation, volcanoes, and other geological features. Scientists' observations and personal accounts are included
Bibliography: p180

501 Science—Philosophy

Bronowski, J.

The ascent of man. Little [1974 c1973] 448p illus $15   501

1 Science—Philosophy 2 Science—History 3 Man
ISBN 0-316-10930-4   LC 73-20446

First published 1973 in England, based on the BBC television series

The author surveys "the scientific and intellectual history of Man—a history that reveals Man as unique among the animal species. Bronowski explores the great monuments of human ideas and inventions from the origin of Man to our own day, from primitive tool to relativity. This is an informal account of Man's search to understand Nature, and it is the human qualities of thought and imagination that have led Man to analyze the physical world." Choice

This "is an inspiring account of man in his prouder moments being true to himself. It provides the reader with a viewpoint by which he can make some sense out of the present knowledge explosion. It organizes the bits of half-thoughts with which we are bombarded daily and provides us with a challenge of our own if we are to be involved in the ascent of man." Best Sellers
Bibliography: p440-42

508 Science—Collections

Asimov, Isaac

Today and tomorrow and . . . Doubleday 1973 321p $6.95   508

1 Science
ISBN 0-385-03247-1   LC 72-89819

This collection of 32 essays covers "such diverse topics as biological clocks, women in space, global villages, and the possibility of mass-transference." Chicago

The tragedy of the moon. Doubleday 1973 220p $6.95   508

1 Science
ISBN 0-385-07221-X   LC 73-79641

This collection includes seventeen essays reprinted from the Magazine of Fantasy and Science Fiction on subjects ranging from the work of Pasteur in developing his germ theory to speculations on what would have happened to early astronomy and religions if earth had been moonless

The author's "handling of scientific facts is authoritative, and a lot is compressed into an admirably brief space. However, Asimov loves to interject anecdotes about himself, and the resultant arch, chatty style is sometimes distracting." Choice

519.4 Applied numerical analysis

Adler, Irving

Thinking machines. Rev. and enl. A layman's introduction to logic, Boolean algebra, and computers; with diagrams by Ruth and Peggy Adler. Day 1974 222p illus $6.95   519.4

1 Computers 2 Mathematics
ISBN 0-381-98220-3   LC 73-19704

Earlier edition entered in main catalog
First published 1961. The 1974 edition explains new developments made possible by integrated circuits and the invention of higher-level programming languages
Bibliography: p218-19

523 Descriptive astronomy

Alter, Dinsmore

Pictorial astronomy. 4th rev. ed. [by] Dinsmore Alter, Clarence H. Cleminshaw [and] John G. Phillips. Crowell 1974 328p illus maps $10   523

1 Astronomy
ISBN 0-690-00095-2   LC 73-15577

Alter, Dinsmore—*Continued*
Earlier edition entered in main catalog
First published 1948 by Griffith Observatory. The 1974 edition has been updated and expanded to cover developments in the field resulting from our increased understanding of pulsars, neutron stars, black holes, quasars, the interstellar medium and the galactic structure as well as the formation of the moon and planets
Glossary: p313-20

Asimov, Isaac
Asimov on astronomy. Doubleday 1974 238p illus $8.95   523
1 Astronomy
ISBN 0-385-04111-X   LC 73-80946
These essays were originally published in The Magazine of Fantasy and Science Fiction. They were selected from five earlier collections of science essays and updated with footnotes where necessary
"Asimov wanders all over the solar system and beyond in these 17 essays, asking excruciatingly complex questions and giving witty, tentative answers in terms intelligible to anyone with high school physics and math. Why doesn't earth have as many craters as the moon and Mars? How do you calculate the brightness of stars? Are there any planets in our solar system out beyond Pluto? What planets are most likely to support life? How do tides work?" Pub W

[Moore, Patrick]
The concise Atlas of the universe. Rand McNally 1974 190p illus $19.95   523
1 Astronomy
ISBN 0-528-83031-7   LC 74-421
Earlier edition, which is still available, January 1975, is entered in main catalog with title: The atlas of the universe
First published 1970. The 1974 edition has been thoroughly revised and updated to include later developments as the Russian moon lander, Comet Kohoutek, and Pioneer 10 photos of Jupiter, while coverage of the moon has been condensed and the afterword commentary dropped
Glossary of terms used in astronomy: p180-85

523.8   Stars

Moore, Patrick
Color star atlas. Crown 1973 112p illus $7.95   523.8
1 Stars—Atlases
ISBN 0-517-51403-6   LC 73-88403
"A guide to the heavens written for the layman by an English astronomer. . . . The volume is primarily intended as a descriptive guide for the amateur observer using either the naked eye or a small telescope. The first half of the book contains descriptions of stars, clusters, nebulae, and galaxies, and is . . . illustrated in color. The last half is a detailed introduction to the identification of stars and constellations in the sky." Choice
"The maps themselves, along with well written notes, manage to convey a great deal of information on stars, star groups, and constellations. Most reference collections should already contain one or more standard star atlases, which should be adequate, but amateur star watchers will appreciate being able to take this handy guide home." Cur Ref Bks

549   Mineralogy

Desautels, Paul E.
Rocks & minerals; from the collection of the Smithsonian Institution; with photographs by the author. Grosset 1974 159p illus (Collector's ser) $12.95   549
1 Mineralogy 2 Rocks—Collectors and collecting
ISBN 0-448-11540-9   LC 73-91134
"A Ridge Press book"
"The inherent physical beauty of mineralogical specimens is emphasized in these highly subjective color photographs which treat rocks and crystals as art objects in their own right rather than objective presentations of scientific facts. A brief text and additional black-and-white photographs provide more precise information on types of rocks and minerals, aspects of collecting, and terminology." Booklist

551.03   Physical and dynamic geology—Encyclopedias and dictionaries

Challinor, John
A dictionary of geology. 4th ed. Oxford 1974 [c1973] 350p $13   551.03
1 Geology—Dictionaries
ISBN 0-19-519719-4
Earlier edition entered in main catalog
First published 1961 in Wales. First American edition 1962. The present "greatly enlarged edition is extensively revised and completely rest." Preface to the fourth edition

551.4   Geomorphology

National Geographic Society
World beneath the sea; prepared by the Special Publications Division. [2d ed] The Society 1973 204p illus $4.75   551.4
1 Oceanography—Research 2 Underwater exploration
ISBN 0-87044-046-2   LC 71-173305
Earlier edition by James Dugan, entered in main catalog
First published 1967. The 1974 edition has been revised and updated by contributing authors Bill Barada, George F. Bass and others
Additional references: p202

560   Paleontology. Paleozoology

Life before man, by the editors of Time-Life Books. Time-Life Bks. [distributed by Little 1973 c1972] 160p illus (The Emergence of man) $7.95   560
1 Fossils 2 Evolution   LC 72-86602
This book describes prehistoric animal life and the environmental and evolutionary changes which occurred prior to early man's emergence, about five and a half million years ago. It includes information about dinosaurs and some paleozoologists, and compares the anatomy and behavior of several modern animals
Bibliography: p153

572   Human races

Montagu, Ashley
Man's most dangerous myth; the fallacy of race. 5th ed. rev. and enl. Oxford 1974 542p $15   572
1 Race 2 Race problems
ISBN 0-19-501775-7   LC 73-92869
Earlier edition entered in main catalog
First published 1942. The 1974 edition "has been revised to include three new chapters. Additional material includes commentary published between 1969-1972 on Jensen and his critics, the American Indian, and sociogenic brain damage. General updating has made use of current findings in anthropology, biology, and sociology." Booklist
Bibliography: p449-528

573   Physical anthropology

Constable, George
The Neanderthals, by George Constable and the editors of Time-Life Books. Time-Life Bks. [distributed by Little] 1973 160p illus (The Emergence of man) $7.95   573
1 Neanderthal race   LC 72-96553

Constable, George—*Continued*

The author surveys the physical characteristics and way of life of the Neanderthals. Picture essays describe modern methods of investigating this primitive race

"The European evidence is stressed, and little is said of Afro-Asian fossils. Neanderthal man's immediate ancestors from the later Mid-Pleistocene are wisely included. The main contribution of this book is the persuasive argument supporting the relatively advanced state of Neanderthal culture and intelligence, although the illustrations do not depict him as well-equipped culturally as does the text." Science Bks

Bibliography: p153

The First men, by the editors of Time-Life Books. Time-Life Bks. [distributed by Little] 1973 160p illus maps (The Emergence of man) $7.95 **573**

1 Man—Origin and antiquity 2 Man, Prehistoric LC 72-93968

This book examines the physical characteristics, mental capacity, tools, hunting, language and social patterns of the species homo erectus, or erect man, which evolved 1.3 million years ago. There are also accounts of anthropological field work and of the primitive Tasaday people

Bibliography: p151

573.2 Organic evolution and genetics of man

Edey, Maitland A.

The missing link, by Maitland A. Edey and the editors of Time-Life Books. Time-Life Bks. [distributed by Little] 1972 160p illus map (The Emergence of man) $7.95 **573.2**

1 Man—Origin and antiquity 2 Evolution LC 72-89569

This book describes the invention of language, domestication of animals, and mastery of metalworking by early man. It "reviews the evidence for the earliest phase of man's evolution: the crucial period when he separated from the common ancestor he shares with the African apes. . . . The peculiar quality of this ancestral species from man's most distant past —this missing link—is pieced together . . . from the evidence of excavation, and from observations of the behavior of our living primate relatives." Introduction

Bibliography: p153

574.01 Biology—Philosophy

Thomas, Lewis

The lives of a cell; notes of a biology watcher. Viking 1974 153p $6.95 **574.01**

1 Biology—Philosophy
ISBN 0-670-43442-6 LC 73-18888

A collection of twenty-nine short essays, in which the author observes recent biological discoveries on tiny microorganisms and relates "them to the totality of human society. He has perceptive and surprising things to say about our reluctance to discuss death, the gap between basic and applied science, misplaced priorities in medical research, the efficiency of termite societies as opposed to human, as well as apt comments on computers, bureaucrats, space research and linguistics. Occasionally the layman might have to consult the dictionary on words like 'eukaryotes' and 'mycetocytes,' but on the whole the provocative message of each essay comes across clearly." Pub W

"The author does not confine his scientist's eye to a microscope. He takes a much wider view of the world, looking at insect behavior and the possibility of intelligent life in outer space or bird songs and the evolution of language. He also offers a modest proposal for saving ourselves from nuclear self-destruction." Time

Bibliography: p149-53

574.02 Biology—Handbooks, manuals, etc.

Altman, Philip L.

(ed.) Biology data book; comp. and ed. by Philip L. Altman and Dorothy S. Dittmer. 2d ed. Federation of American Societies for Experimental Biology 1972-1974 3v (Biological handbooks) ea $30, set $75 **574.02**

1 Biology—Handbooks, manuals, etc.
LC 72-87738

First published 1964 in one volume

"A basic reference for biology, organized into quantitative and descriptive tables, charts, and diagrams. Many citations to standard authorities." A L A Reference Books for Small and Medium-sized Public Libraries [1973 edition]

574.5 Ecology

Kirk, Ruth

Desert: the American Southwest; illus. with photographs by Ruth and Louis Kirk. Houghton 1973 361p illus (The Naturalist's America) $10 **574.5**

1 Desert ecology 2 Natural history—Southwest, New
ISBN 0-395-17209-8 LC 73-9902

Following a brief survey of the "five major deserts in the United States, this work . . . concentrates on the hottest, driest, and biologically most varied—the Sonoran Desert of Arizona and adjacent Mexico. Drawing on both long personal experience and published research, Kirk presents a . . . picture of its topography, flora, and fauna and of their shaping by the dominant realities of aridity and heart." Library J

"Particular chapters stand out because of the wealth of material presented. . . . The book contains a selective list of scientific names, maps on the inside covers, a good index, an abundance of excellent photographs and a rather complete bibliography." Science Bks

574.92 Hydrographic biology

Cousteau, Jacques

Oasis in space. World Pub. 1972 144p illus maps (The Ocean world of Jacques Cousteau) $7.95 **574.92**

1 Marine biology
ISBN 0-529-04936-8 LC 72-87710

The author describes "provisions of the ocean as they change with the seasons, as they support their brilliant varieties of life, as they are swept by storms and currents. . . . [He tells] about the essential drives of the creatures of the sea—their needs to feed, to mate, to defend themselves, to find hospitable environments, to depend upon one another, to play a role in the balance of nature, and ultimately to die." Publisher's note

This book "is distinguished by Cousteau's clear, direct writing and by hundreds of illustrations. Throughout the book, Cousteau expresses urgent concern about the destruction of ocean life. The main features of each section (on deep sea life, reef builders, marine birds, etc.) are described very briefly; and almost every page of text is accompanied by from one to seven full-color illustrations. Most of these are photographs (there are some drawings) and they are, for the most part, clear, helpful, and interesting." Library J

Window in the sea. World Pub. [distributed by Abrams] 1973 144p (The Ocean world of Jacques Cousteau) $7.95 **574.92**

1 Marine biology 2 Marine animals 3 Underwater exploration
ISBN 0-529-05049-8 LC 74-157855

Text and numerous illustrations explore the deep sea world without sun, with individual chapters on: Why is the sea blue; Man's direct vision; Man's indirect vision; **The gift of the sun**

581 Botany

Tompkins, Peter
The secret life of plants [by] Peter Tompkins and Christopher Bird. Harper 1973 402p $8.95   581

1 Plants
ISBN 0-06-014326-6   LC 72-9160

"The authors report on some recent discoveries relating to plants and electronics, discoveries unacknowledged by orthodox scientists. . . . [They discuss human-plant telepathy, plant sensitivity to both sound and color wave-lengths, and the possibility of conscious perception and motivation within the plant kingdom.] There is a discussion of related research in the U.S.S.R.; sketches of some pioneers of plant mysteries; material on organic gardening, alchemy and dowsing. The final chapter is an account of communication with the plant world." Pub W

The authors "blend selected works of numerous scientists, pseudo-scientists and mystics into a hard-sell attempt to prove that plants have a nervous system, can transmute chemical elements, exude a mysterious aura, and respond to music and such human emotions as love and hate. . . . It is unfortunate that the authors have written so subjectively that the reader cannot clearly distinguish fact from fantasy." Science Bks

581.6 Economic botany

Gibbons, Euell
Stalking the faraway places; illus. by Freda Gibbons. McKay [1974 c1973] 279p illus $6.95   581.6

1 Plants, Edible 2 Natural history—North America 3 Wilderness survival
ISBN 0-679-50394-3   LC 73-79955

The author teaches how to recognize and enjoy wild foods in relating his forays in the United States, Canada and Mexico. "He stalks the wild foods of the West, both desert and mountain; he returns to Bald Island for a tidal feast, stalks in New York State and San Francisco (easy!), visits Baja California. Additional chapters deal with trees and wildflowers, organic farming and ecology; this section concludes with four pieces of biological doggerel." Pub W

"This is "a folksy, lively chronicle. . . . [The] fine, delicate sketches of edible wild plants are especially helpful as the book rarely gives descriptions or directions more explicit than 'We peeled off the dark outside rind, sliced the roots thinly, and started experimenting.'" Christian Science Monitor

582 Trees

Collingwood, G. H.
Knowing your trees, by G. H. Collingwood and Warren D. Brush. Rev. and ed. by Devereaux Butcher. Am. Forestry Assn. illus maps $7.90   582

1 Trees   LC 73-83868

First published 1937. Revised with each printing

"The appearance of the tree is described, its economic importance is indicated, and its range is shown on a small map of the United States. Good photographs show a mature tree and the leaf and bark. Deciduous broadleafed trees, are pictured in summer and winter. Index of scientific and common names." Am Forests
Includes bibliography

Johnson, Hugh
The international book of trees; a guide and tribute to the trees of our forests and gardens. [Simon & Schuster 1973] 288p illus maps $29.95   582

1 Trees
ISBN 0-671-21607-4   LC 73-3974

Backed by "superb writing and observation, a very unusual and fully illustrated book on world trees has at last been created. The work is divided into four sections: (1) how a tree grows, including descriptions of tree parts, man and the forest, use of trees in gardening and landscaping, and pruning and other arts; (2) the conifers; (3) the broad-leaves; (4) a reference section and index, which includes tree pests and tree diseases, a guide to choosing trees, the meaning of botanical names, and numerous other facts. Unusually beautiful color photography of trees in their native habitat, an historical narrative, and detailed photo studies of twigs, leaves, flowers, and fruit are tastefully combined with a treatment of man's use of the trees in landscape structure. It is difficult to do justice to this volume's photography, text, and organization in a short review. There are many books on trees, but Johnson's transcends all of these, if for nothing else, then for vast scope." Choice

591 Zoology

Vanishing species, by the editors of Time-Life Books; with an introductory essay by Romain Gary. Time-Life Bks. [distributed by Little] 1974 264p illus $14.95   591

1 Rare animals   LC 73-87751

Editor: Kathleen Brandes

Text and color photographs describe over 100 endangered mammals, amphibians, reptiles and birds

"While this book makes no claim to completeness, only to a representative listing, it is more complete than many books on the subject. What makes it exceptional, though, are some 200 incredibly beautiful pictures. These would be difficult to find in other sources, and the impact of seeing these animals adds a dimension to the tragedy that words and statistics cannot." Cur Ref Bks

591.03 Zoology—Dictionaries and encyclopedias

Grzimek, Bernhard
(ed.) Animal life encyclopedia. Van Nostrand-Reinhold 1973-1974 4v illus ea $29.95   591.03

1 Zoology—Encyclopedias   LC 79-183178

Earlier volumes of this set are entered in main catalog
Contents: v 1 Lower animals (ISBN 0-442-22944-5); v3 Mollusks (ISBN 0-442-22943-7); v4 Fishes 1 (ISBN 0-442-22937-2) v5 Fishes 2 and Amphibians (ISBN 0-442-22938-0)

Leftwich, A. W.
A dictionary of zoology. [3d ed] Constable [distributed by Crane, Russak] 1973 478p $13.50   591.03

1 Zoology—Dictionaries
ISBN 0-8448-0845-8   LC 73-161027

Earlier edition entered in main catalog
First published 1963 by Van Nostrand. In the 1973 edition the new definitions from the 1967 edition "and some 1,600 others are incorporated into the alphabetical sequence. Also added . . . is a section of English common names of animals, with references to the definitions of scientifically named families, etc." Cur Ref Bks
Bibliography: p475-78

591.5 Animal ecology

Durrell, Gerald
A bevy of beasts; illus. by Edward Mortlemans. Simon & Schuster 1973 253p illus $7.95   591.5

1 Animals—Habits and behavior 2 Zoological Society of London. Gardens. Whipsnade Park
ISBN 0-671-21457-8   LC 72-87945

The author describes his experiences "as student keeper at Whipsnade, the huge country zoo of the Zoological Society of London. . . .

Durrell, Gerald—*Continued*

He shares his introduction to the delightful 'bevy of beasts' housed there and to the equally heartwarming assortment of men who cared for them. Durrell eventually founded his own zoological park in Jersey in the Channel islands; and, in his epilogue, he describes the efforts of his Jersey Wildlife Preservation Trust to save some species from extinction." Library J

"Anyone familiar with Gerald Durrell's books which he seems to toss off with the ease of old socks, will know what to expect—amusing adventures with animals that have distinctive personalities. . . . Durrell's style is easy and charming, and as usual there are serious observations about animals scattered throughout the book." N Y Times Bk R

591.9 Zoology—Geographical treatment

Allen, Thomas B.
 Vanishing wildlife of North America; foreword by Gilbert M. Grosvenor. Prepared by the Special Publication Division. Natl. Geographic Soc. 1974 207p illus $4.75   591.9
   1 Rare animals   2 Wildlife—Conservation   3 Animals—North America
   ISBN 0-87044-129-9   LC 73-833

"After gathering information on 109 species or subspecies on the federal list of endangered wildlife while traveling extensively in the U.S., Allen gives [an] . . . account of the work of scientists who are trying to save these creatures from extinction. He uses many examples of habitat disruption which has brought biologists into conflict with industry, developers, and agriculturalists and comments on the lack of concern over the fate of lesser creatures like salamanders, fish, and frogs. Damage done by exotic plants, fish, birds and pesticides is also discussed." Booklist

"A comprehensive, profusely illustrated account of the myriad problems involved in the struggle to save at least some of the many endangered species in North America. . . . Highly recommended both for the interested layperson and for the serious student." Library J
 Additional reading: p207

591.92 Marine zoology

Cousteau, Jacques
 The act of life. World Pub. [distributed by Abrams] 1972 144p illus (The Ocean world of Jacques Cousteau) $7.95   591.92
   1 Marine animals 2 Reproduction
   ISBN 0-529-04937-6   LC 74-682

Text and numerous colored illustrations explore the reproduction process of various sea creatures with chapters devoted to: Controlling factors and the balance of nature; Survival of the fittest; Internal parental protection; Parental care for the young; Perversions

 The art of motion. World Pub. [distributed by Abrams] 1973 144p illus (The Ocean world of Jacques Cousteau) $7.95   591.92
   1 Marine animals 2 Animal locomotion
   ISBN 0-529-05073-0   LC 74-154492

This study of animal movement focuses on the systems of propulsion found in the ocean among various marine creatures and how and why fish movements vary

594 Mollusks and mollusk-like animals

Cousteau, Jacques-Yves
 Octopus and squid; the soft intelligence [by] Jacques-Yves Cousteau and Philippe Diolé; tr. from the French by J. F. Bernard. Doubleday 1973 304p illus maps (The Undersea discoveries of Jacques-Yves Cousteau) $9.95   594
   1 Octopus 2 Squids
   ISBN 0-385-06896-4   LC 72-76141

Text and photographs depict the world of octopus and squid, discussing their physiology, propulsion, intelligence, sensory apparatus, mating habits and arts of camouflage

"Lavishly illustrated with many of the finest color photographs of cephalopods ever published. . . . Coverage is broader than the title indicates and the narrative [also] contains many fascinating accounts of the authors' undersea experiences with cuttlefishes, nautiluses, and other cephalopods. . . . [The] book is well written, reasonably scientific, and designed for the popular market. It will appeal to most naturalists." Choice
 Illustrated glossary: p287-300. Bibliography: p301-02

597 Fishes. Ichthyology

Sweeney, James B.
 A pictorial history of sea monsters and other dangerous marine life. Crown 1972 314p illus maps $9.95   597
   1 Sea monsters 2 Fishes
   ISBN 0-517-50112-0   LC 76-185087

"A historical survey of aquatic monster sightings of all types constitutes the first third of this . . . book, the rest being concerned with sharks, manta rays, giant squids, stinging coral, groupers that have swallowed divers whole, and other unfriendly residents of the world's oceans. Several chapters, on red tides and other natural or man-induced marine disasters, discuss the perilous nature of ecological balance in the sea." Library J

"There is nothing illogical in the idea that the deep caverns of the sea are inhabited by monsters that rarely surface. Mr. Sweeney makes his point by the juxtaposition of reports of sea serpents with a catalogue of what could reasonably be called existing sea monsters. . . . [This is one] of the most interesting conservation-cum-ecology-cum-science-fiction books to appear for some time, but do not read Mr. Sweeney late at night if you suffer from nightmares." Economist
 Bibliography: p304-06

598.1 Reptiles. Turtles

Ernst, Carl H.
 Turtles of the United States [by] Carl H. Ernst & Roger W. Barbour. Univ. Press of Ky. 1972 347p illus $22.50   598.1
   1 Turtles
   ISBN 0-8131-1272-9   LC 72-81315

"A survey of current knowledge concerning the life histories of the forty-nine species of turtles native to the United States and Canada. A series of . . . color photographs shows each turtle in its natural setting, and black and white photographs depict the skulls and details of physical structure. . . . Maps indicate the range of each species in the United States." Publisher's note

"Lay readers may find the physical description of each species somewhat technical; the descriptions of habitat, behavior, reproduction, and growth are clear and interesting. . . . There is also an informative chapter about the 'Care of Turtles in Captivity' that turtle owners of all ages should find helpful." Sat R Sci
 Glossary of scientific names: p292-94. Bibliography: p295-342

Minton, Sherman A.
 Giant reptiles [by] Sherman A. Minton, Jr. and Madge Rutherford Minton. Scribner 1973 345p illus $9.95   598.1
   1 Reptiles
   ISBN 0-684-13267-2   LC 72-9770

The authors "have gathered information from their own experiences with wild and captive reptiles, from visits to herpetologists in the U.S. and in other countries, and from a search of the scientific and popular literature extending from about 450 B.C. (Herodotus) to 1971. Topics include the dinosaurs, crocodilians, turtles, lizards, and snakes. Woven through the main biological theme is the thread of man's encounters with reptiles, his myths about them, and his use of reptiles for food and medicine. . . . Glossary, index, and selected bibliography." Choice

599 Mammals

Collins, Larry R.
Ling-Ling and Hsing-Hsing; year of the panda [by] Larry R. Collins and James K. Page, Jr. Anchor Press 1973 164p illus $6.95
599

1 Pandas
ISBN 0-385-04803-3   LC 73-10535

"This engaging book chronicles the first year at Washington's National Zoo of the two pandas presented to this country by the People's Republic of China. The general public usually thinks of pandas as cute and cuddly playthings, but they're actually full of surprises—and they're not always good-natured (one trainer narrowly escaped serious injury when chased by Ling-Ling). Included here are observations of the two animals, background information on pandas, and material on some animals thought to be related to the panda." Library J

Lawick, Hugo van
Solo: the story of an African wild dog; with an introduction by Jane van Lawick-Goodall, and drawings by David Bygott. Houghton 1974 [c1973] 159p illus $6.95 599

1 Dogs
ISBN 0-395-18321-9   LC 73-19747

First published 1973 in England

"The first half of this narrative concerns van Lawick's observations of a pack of African wild dogs—the matings of two wild bitches, their consequent struggle for superiority, and the survival of their young. The second half is devoted to his attempt to save the life of lone surviving pup—Solo." Library J

McNulty, Faith
The great whales; illus. by Richard Cuffari. Doubleday 1974 100p illus $4.95   599

1 Whales
ISBN 0-385-00297-1   LC 72-96270

This "text should convince any reader that the whale is a marvelous creature that deserves much better treatment from humans. . . . 'Men have pursued whales for centuries, and killed them with unbounded cruelty and in staggering numbers, without learning much more than the simplest facts. . . .' The author goes on to detail reports of slaughter which have decimated the great whale herds and, more welcome news of conservationists who are dedicated to saving them. The book closes with a heartening story of Gigi, a female baby which was captured and raised successfully at Sea World, then freed to rejoin other whales. An irresistable reading experience." Pub W

Mowat, Farley
A whale for the killing. Little 1972 239p $6.95
599

1 Whales
ISBN 0-316-58691-9   LC 72-5157

"An Atlantic Monthly Press book"

This is the story of the killing of a Fin whale "that became entrapped in a tiny bay near a Newfoundland village in 1967. Local 'sports'—not the local fishermen who made their living from the sea—made the whale a captive target for buzzing with their motor-boats, for practice harpooning, for shooting with whatever guns were handy. The whale died horribly. Mowat uses the tragedy as touchstone for his plea on behalf of what is left of the whale species and as a microcosm of senseless human cruelty." Pub W

"Mowat makes the reader root for the whale and feel angry at its terrible death. . . . His book is a plea for environmental sanity, an effective chapter, let us hope, in the larger saga that is already a tragedy and may well become one of irreparable loss." Sat R

Map on lining-papers

Schaller, George B.
Serengeti: a kingdom of predators. Knopf 1972 114p illus map $12.95   599

1 Animals—Africa, East 2 Serengeti National Park
ISBN 0-394-47242-X   LC 75-171119

This is a study of "the behavior of free-living lions—the formation of prides, male-female and cub-adult relations, population dynamics, hunting patterns, . . . mating habits, facial expressions, and so on. The lion is seen as an integral part of the African ecosystem, and the book delves . . . into its relation with and to other wild animal species, the prey and rival predators—leopards, zebras, cheetahs, gazelles, hyenas, wilde-beests, buffaloes—of the Serengeti wilderness." Sat R

"The photographs are clear, colorful, stop-action things, and for the greater part are in splendid color; they are chiefly concerned with carnivores on the prowl, attacking, or devouring prey. Realistic." Best Sellers

Selected readings: p115

600 TECHNOLOGY (APPLIED SCIENCES)

603 Technology—Encyclopedias and dictionaries

Pugh, Eric
Second dictionary of acronyms & abbreviations; more abbreviations in management, technology and information science. Archon Bks. 1974 410p $16.50   603

1 Technology—Dictionaries 2 Management—Dictionaries 3 Information sciences—Dictionaries 4 Abbreviations—Dictionaries 5 Acronmys—Dictionaries
ISBN 0-208-01354-7   LC 74-4271

Supplementary volume to the authors: A dictionary of acronyms and abbreviations entered in main catalog

This volume contains approximately 10,000 entries together with updated entries covering recent changes in the titles of some organizations, etc. contained in the second edition

610.9 Medicine—History

Marks, Geoffrey
The story of medicine in America [by] Geoffrey Marks and William K. Beatty; illus. with photographs. Scribner [1974 c1973] 416p illus $10   610.9

1 Medicine—History
ISBN 0-684-13537-X   LC 73-1369

This book "traces practitioners and their practices from the Virginia and New England colonies, describes the development of early medical schools, the direction toward specialization, the problems of epidemics and public health, the recognition of the need for medical research, and brings us right up to today's investigations into nuclear and aerospace medicine. [Includes] numerous illustrations of the people and places involved, [and] ample reference notes." Best Sellers

It "is well organized, the writing is clear and it should find many interested readers. Those interested in medicine and historical development will find this presentation far more than a simple survey or dry recounting of the facts." Science Bks

Selected bibliography: p388-401

612 Human physiology

Grollman, Sigmund
The human body; its structure and physiology. 3d ed. Macmillan Pub. Co. 1974 612p illus $10.95   612

1 Physiology 2 Anatomy
ISBN 0-02-348100-5   LC 72-91266

Earlier edition entered in main catalog

First published 1964. In the 1974 edition "changes have been made in the chapters on the cell, the nervous system, and the endocrine system. Typical of the new material is a section on the articulatory system. There are enlarged sections on cellular energetics, the

Grollman, Sigmund—*Continued*
thalamus, hypothalamus, reticular activating system, amygdala and synaptic transmission, and the actions of hormones and enzymes. In addition, many new tables, electron micrographs, and illustrations have been included to provide more detailed information and comprehension of both anatomical and physiological concepts as well as to reinforce those concepts." Preface
Includes chapter bibliographies

Hackett, Earle
Blood. Saturday Review Press 1973 288p illus $9.95   **612**

1 Blood 2 Blood—Diseases
ISBN 0-8415-0215-3   LC 72-88895

The author, a medical doctor gives an "account of the history of ideas about the functions of the blood, from antiquity . . . to the present day. . . . [Hackett seeks] to explore and explode the myths of folklore. Words and phrases still in use—blood-thirsty, bloody, cold-blooded, sangfroid . . . [are examined] and an explanation of the schoolboy deep-breathing fainting trick [given]. He [also] has an . . . account of his own investigation into the clotting effect of a cobweb on a wound." Economist
Further reading: p278

612.6 Reproduction, development, maturation

Child Study Association of America
What to tell your child about sex. Rev. ed. Prepared by the staff of Child Study Association of America. Wel-Met inc. Foreword by Mary S. Calderone. Child Study Press 1974 97p illus $4.95   **612.6**

1 Sex instruction
ISBN 0-87183-241-0

Earlier edition entered in main catalog
First published 1954 with title: Facts of life for children. The 1974 edition contains new illustrative drawings and the young adult section has been completely revised and updated
Selected reading for parents, children, and young people: p85-93

Pomeroy, Wardell B.
Your child and sex; a guide for parents. Delacorte Press 1974 206p $6.95   **612.6**

1 Sex instruction
ISBN 0-440-08866-6   LC 73-15508

Questions explored in this book include: How can parents cope with the sexual climate of today? How can they help their children cope with it? What should they know for their own sake—and their child's? What is the value of sex education in school? What should be taught at home? What is the effect of pornography on sexual behavior? Of nudity? How should a parent deal with homosexuality
Bibliography: p197-99

613.8 Addiction and health. Alcoholism

United States. Department of Health, Education and Welfare
Alcohol and health; report from the Secretary of Health, Education and Welfare. Scribner 1973 xxv, 372p illus pa $3.95   **613.8**

1 Alcoholism
ISBN 0-684-13271-0   LC 72-11115

"The Scribner Lyceum editions"
First published 1971 with title: First special report to the U.S. Congress on alcohol & health
"Prepared under the auspices of the U.S. Department of Health, Education, and Welfare: Office of the Assistant Secretary for Health and Scientific Affairs; Health Services and Mental Health Administration; National Institute of Mental Health; National Institute on Alcohol Abuse and Alcoholism. Editorial staff: Mark Keller, Consulting editor; Shirley Sirota Rosenberg, editor [and others]." Facing title-page
"This special report to the Congress of the United States brings together a substantial portion of the current scientific knowledge on the health consequences of using, and especially of abusing, alcoholic beverages. The information is presented within the perspective of the history and epidemiology of alcohol use, as well as its effects on both the central nervous system and other body organs, tissues, and systems. The causal theories, treatment, methods, and legal status of alcohol-related problems are reviewed. In addition, directions for future action are charted in research, training, treatment, and prevention for the field of alcohol abuse and alcoholism." Publisher's note
Reference notes: p327-60

613.9 Birth control and sex hygiene

Arnstein, Helene S.
What every woman needs to know about abortion. Scribner 1973 144p $5.95   **613.9**

1 Abortion
ISBN 0-684-13547-7   LC 73-5168

"The author gives a very brief history of social and legal views of abortion before and after the 1970 Supreme Court decision. She then continues to explore the decision-making process a woman experiences when she discovers she is unexpectedly pregnant. Arnstein describes the various methods of abortion and gives suggestions for aftercare; she also discusses methods of contraception and alternatives to abortion. Emphasis is placed on seeking counseling through reputable, nationally known organizations; and addresses and telephone numbers are provided for each organization mentioned." Library J

Fleishman, Norman
Vasectomy, sex and parenthood [by] Norman Fleishman and Peter L. Dixon; foreword by Alan F. Guttmacher. Doubleday 1973 128p $5.95   **613.9**

1 Sterilization (Birth control)
ISBN 0-385-00123-1   LC 72-76152

This is a discussion of the physical, moral, legal and psychological implications of the procedures involved in male birth control. Questions explored include: What is it? What are the pros and cons? How much will it cost? Where can you get one? Will your sex life be affected? Can it be safely reversed?
"Much of the book deals with the cost of unwanted children; and while the authors generally make a solid case, a good deal of their argument is overly emotional and unnecessarily aggressive." Library J

Rosenfeld, Louis J.
The truth about vasectomy [by] Louis J. Rosenfeld and Marvin Grosswirth. Prentice-Hall [1973 c1972] 156p illus $4.95   **613.9**

1 Sterilization (Birth control)
ISBN 0-13-931170-X   LC 72-8341

A conversational account of the male form of birth control. "After providing 35 questions and answers that are likely to turn up in any discussion of vasectomy, they review the history of contraception, the male reproductive system, and the vasectomy operation. . . . The next chapters deal with the doctor-patient relationship, the feelings of the men and women involved, and possible side effects. Here the authors' personal tone is quite helpful in leading the reader to think about the various aspects of his life involved in this operation. The book concludes with five case histories of candidates, with the reader asked to decide which are good risks. There is the usual appendix listing facilities where vasectomies are performed." Library J

614 Public health. Forensic medicine

Cooper, Paulette
The medical detectives; introduction by Milton Helpern. McKay 1973 238p $6.95 **614**

1 Medical jurisprudence 2 Medicine
ISBN 0-679-50382-X   LC 73-79947

This is the story "of the men who practice forensic medicine—coroners, medical examiners, pathologists. The focus is not who-done-it, but what-done-it. . . . [The author discusses] the Sheppard case, the Sharon Tate murders, JFK's assassination and other crimes, as well as paternity suits and death under suspicious circumstances." Pub W

Suggested readings: p236-38

614.8 Safety (Accidents and their prevention)

Red Cross. United States. American National Red Cross
Advanced first aid and emergency care; prepared by the American National Red Cross for the instruction of advanced first aid classes; with 353 illus. Doubleday 1973 318p illus $3.95 **614.8**

1 First aid
ISBN 0-385-05902-7   LC 73-76727

This book is designed for those administering emergency care to the sick and injured. First aid instructions are provided for wounds, injuries to specific parts of the body, shock, respiratory emergencies and artificial respiration, water accidents, poisoning, drug abuse, burns, exposure to extreme radiation, cold, heat, and bone and joint injuries, sudden illnesses, childbirth, emergency rescue and transfer, and extrication

Standard first aid and personal safety; prepared by the American National Red Cross for the instruction of first aid classes; with 206 illustrations. Doubleday 1973 268p illus $3.50 **614.8**

1 First aid
ISBN 0-385-05908-6   LC 73-76726

This book describes emergency first aid treatment and offers information about personal safety and accident prevention. Wounds, specific injuries, shock, artificial respiration, swallowed objects, poisoning, drug abuse, burns, dressings and bandages, and short-distance transfers are among the topics considered

615 Pharmacology and therapeutics

Montgomery, Ruth
Born to heal; the astonishing story of Mr A and the ancient art of healing with life energies; introduction by Dena L. Smith **615**

1 Mental healing 2 A, Mr
Some editions are:
Coward, McCann & Geoghegan $6.95 (ISBN 0-698-10493-5)
Hall, G.K.&Co. $8.95 Large print edition (ISBN 0-8161-6109-7)

" 'Mr. A' claims to have had the gift of healing by the 'laying on of hands' as a child. He believes that through this gift (he's not a doctor, has little formal education) he has cured malignant tumors, arthritis, heart ailments, glaucoma, paralysis and innumerable other physical complaints. He explains his gift as a mysterious ability to focus generated energy onto injured nerves, and claims a nearly 100% success." Pub W

"Unfortunately, although there are many case histories included, the book is not documented; like many testimonials of its kind, it must be taken on faith. Not an essential purchase, although public libraries may have to buy it in order to meet a probably fairly high demand from Montgomery's readers." Library J

Tan, Leong T.
Acupuncture therapy; current Chinese practice [by] Leong T. Tan, Margaret Y.-C. Tan [and] Ilza Veith. Foreword by Walter R. Tkach. Temple Univ. Press 1973 159p illus $15 **615**

1 Acupuncture
ISBN 0-87722-025-5   LC 72-96004

This work "includes a brief history, philosophy, and description of acupuncture in general, as well as a description of the acupuncture points and treatment for selected conditions. . . . One full chapter (out of four) is devoted to aspects of acupuncture anesthesia, a newcomer to acupuncture therapy. The test also includes a discussion of the practical application of acupuncture, legal implications, and several theories regarding its action." Choice

"The indexes are good. It is regrettable that the authors do not reflect here on their own experience or evaluate the efficacy of acupuncture treatment on various ailments. However, this book will serve well as a primer for physicians interested in learning acupuncture." Library J

Bibliography: p147-48

616.1 Diseases of cardiovascular system

Alsop, Stewart
Stay of execution; a sort of memoir. Lippincott 1973 312p illus $8.95 **616.1**

1 Leukemia—Personal narratives
ISBN 0-397-00897-X   LC 73-13691

The author, a "journalist, recounts his thoughts, and recollections from July 1971 when he was first diagnosed as having acute myeloblastic leukemia, with an expected survival of one year, through the early months of 1973 by which time the diagnosis had been changed to 'smoldering' or aleukemic leukemia, survival time unknown." Library J

"This memoir is in no way depressing or morbid, although naturally the author has despondent moments. Nor is it especially dramatic or moving, since the approach is so objective and clinical. Even in this ultimate crisis, Alsop remains a detached reporter." Pub W

Brams, William A.
Managing your coronary; illus. by Hertha Furth. 4th ed. Lippincott 1974 187p $6.95 **616.1**

1 Heart—Diseases
ISBN 0-397-01010-9   LC 73-13869

Earlier edition entered in main catalog
First published 1953. The 1974 edition has been revised to reflect advances in diagnostic and surgical treatment

Stichman, JoAnn
How to survive your husband's heart attack; what you both need to know to put your lives back together [by] JoAnn Stichman [and] Jane Schoenberg. McKay 1974 306p $7.95 **616.1**

1 Heart—Diseases
ISBN 0-679-50445-1   LC 74-76722

This book "covers the entire spectrum of heart attack experience from the onset—the emergency paramedic attendance, the coronary care unit, the recovery period, home rehabilitation, preventive measures to avoid another attack, and finally the restoration of full participation in marital life and the return to an accustomed occupation. This is not a book of prohibitions, but rather one of helpful suggestions from two women, each of whom has coped successfully with her husband's heart attack." Foreword

616.8 Diseases of nervous system

Schreiber, Flora Rheta
Sybil. Regnery 1973 350p $8.95 **616.8**

1 Personality disorders
ISBN 0-8092-0001-5   LC 72-11188

Schreiber, Flora R.—*Continued*

"A free-flowing account of a young woman's life drama as it unfolds over an eleven-year span in psychotherapy, including hypnotherapy. As made clear by a visit of her father with her psychiatrist, Sybil, in her formative years, was exposed to incongruent and inhuman conditions. Against these she defended herself by metamorphosizing into 16 different persons, some in sequence, others concurrently. In the supportive care of her therapist, she was guided on tortuous paths that brought her inner conflicts into consciousness. Once there, she eventually was able to relinquish her hold on the past and come to grips with her real self." Choice

"The multiple personality thriller is on its way to becoming a standard genre. Sybil provides [fascinating] material. . . . If we can accept the basic truth of this highly novelistic, sometimes novelettish, account, it has extraordinary interest both as a psychological document of a woman who is said to have had sixteen personalities and as a moving human narrative." N Y Rev of Books

616.9   Other diseases. Cancer

Crile, George
What women should know about the breast cancer controversy. Macmillan (N Y) 1973 179p $4.95   **616.9**

1 Cancer
   LC 73-7142

"Designed to inform women of varied methods of treatment available and enable the patient to exercise freedom of choice, the book includes definitions of medical terms and a thorough review of Criles position recommending greater discretion by surgeons in the fiel l. Ethical considerations are made and reasons given why in Crile's opinion U.S. surgeons have been slow to abandon the practice of radical mastectomy. The advantages and disadvantages of different operations for breast cancer are set forth with citations of case histories." Booklist

"His philosophy of treatment is simply that a patient should be told the pros and cons of various treatments and should, in most cases, be allowed to make the decision herself. He documents his position and concludes the book with a list of positively stated 'Important Do's and Don'ts.' This thought-provoking book, which combines humanity and science, should be in public and medical libraries." Library J

Includes bibliographical references

618.2   Obstetrics

Bradley, Robert A.
Husband-coached childbirth. Rev. ed. Harper 1974 214p illus $6.95   **618.2**

1 Childbirth
ISBN 0-06-010444-9   LC 73-14247
First published 1965

This book on natural childbirth indicates for the husband how to help his wife from earliest pregnancy through birth and after, including the nursing period

"The mothers and fathers who will read it will feel like pioneers, too, if, as I hope, they decide to adopt and follow Dr. Bradley's recommendations, for they will be pioneering in the most important of all frontiers; the making of good human beings in a good family. The family is the basis of society. As the family is, so is the society, and it is human beings who make a family—not the quantity of them, but the quality of them. As a contribution toward improving the quality of the family, Dr. Bradley's book is of major importance." Foreword

Zimmerman, David R.
Rh; the intimate history of a disease and its conquest. Macmillan Pub. Co. 1973 371p illus $8.95   **618.2**

1 Infants—Diseases 2 Blood groups
   LC 72-90280

"Erythroblastosis fetalis or Rh hemolytic disease killed and crippled thousands of babies each year before the development of a successful vaccine in the 1960s and its clinical use beginning in 1968. [The author] a medical journalist, has pieced together the complex history of this scientific achievement from interviews, manuscripts, and published sources, and has written this account of it for a general audience. Since the book, as he says, is about creativity in medical research, he pays considerable attention to the origin and development of the ideas, the difficulties of research and analysis, and the relations between the investigators." Choice

The author "has written a detailed, clear, and exciting account. . . . He interviewed many of the people who have worked to identify and treat the disease and consulted a substantial amount of primary material." Library J

Glossary: p353-60

618.9   Pediatrics and geriatrics

Clarke, Louise
Can't read, can't write, can't takl too good either; how to recognize and overcome dyslexia in your child. Walker & Co. 1973 280p illus $7.95   **618.9**

1 Dyslexia
ISBN 0-8027-0392-5   LC 72-80537

"Through a case study of the author's son who has persevered and succeeded in living with the problems of dyslexia the book spells out the symptoms of the handicap, describes complications in word perception, visual and physical coordination, and in speech patterns that are evident in persons who are so afflicted." Booklist

Stewart, Mark A.
Raising a hyperactive child [by] Mark A. Stewart and Sally Wendkos Olds. Harper 1973 299p $8.95   **618.9**

1 Exceptional children
ISBN 0-06-014121-2   LC 72-79696

"The range of subjects covered includes causes and characteristics of hyperactivity and various treatment modes such as counseling and psychotherapy for parents and children, parent discussion groups, remedial educational programs, and drugs. Detailed sections on how to help the child at home and in school offer many creative as well as practical ideas on how to cope with the hyperactive child. Finally, problems which typify the hyperactive child at the various stages of development are enumerated." Library J

References: p287-92

Wender, Paul H.
The hyperactive child; a handbook for parents. Crown 1973 120p $3.95   **618.9**

1 Exceptional children
ISBN 0-517-503522   LC 72-96670

"A pediatric psychiatrist discusses the nature, causes, and treatment of hyperactive children for parents, professionals working with children, and concerned laymen. Wender explains various symptoms and shows how the school and family must work together to make certain that hyperactive children are not misunderstood. He suggests helpful things to be done at home, points out the kind of schools that are best, calls attention to sports that are good and activities that help, and explains the use of drugs." Booklist

621   Applied physics, Electrical

Graf, Rudolf F.
How it works, illustrated: everyday devices and mechanisms, by Rudolf F. Graf and George J. Whalen and the editors of Popular Science; illus. by Farmlett, Barsanti, & Wood, Inc. Harper 1974 184p illus $10.95   **621**

1 Electric engineering 2 Mechanical movements 3 Household equipment and supplies
ISBN 0-06-011589-0   LC 73-80716

"A Popular Science book"

"With simple drawings and concise explanations the workings of such mysterious devices as the automatic orange juicer, electronic

Graf, Rudolf F.—*Continued*

watches, aerosol dispensers and over 80 other mechanical wonders are clearly laid out. The **emphasis is on why and how** things work and on the technology and operating principles involved; intricate details and repair information have been deliberately omitted. A browser's treasure trove." Booklist

621.43 Internal-combustion engines

Chilton's Repair and tune-up guide: small engines. Chilton Bk. Co. 1974 198p illus $8.95
621.43

1 Gas and oil engines—Repairing
ISBN 0-8019-515-6   LC 74-779

"Maintenance procedures for a variety of small industrial engines and one lawn mower engine are detailed and general discussions of single-cylinder engines precede individual chapters arranged by manufacturer. Specific information and instructions are aided with numerous diagrams, statistical charts, and black-and-white photographs. Conversion tables appended." Booklist

621.5 Pneumatic, vacuum, low-temperature technology

Elonka, Stephen Michael
Standard refrigeration and air conditioning questions and answers [by] Stephen Michael Elonka [and] Quaid Walton Minich. 2d ed. McGraw 1973 321p illus $12.50
621.5

1 Refrigeration and refrigerating machinery 2 Air conditioning
ISBN 0-07-019291-X   LC 72-13017

First published 1961

This book provides information on the operation and maintenance of refrigeration and air conditioning equipment and systems in question and answer format

Partial contents: Fundamentals; Refrigerants; Compressors; Condensers; Evaporators; Electric controls; Piping and fittings; Lubrication; Defrosting; Practical calculations; Refrigeration applications; Air conditioning; Cooling water and brine; Safety; Cryogenics; License requirements for refrigeration and air conditioning engineers in the United States and Canada

Includes chapter bibliographies

622 Mining engineering and related operations

Pearl, Richard M.
Handbook for prospectors. 5th ed. . . . McGraw 1973 472p illus $14.50   622

1 Prospecting
ISBN 0-07-049025-2   LC 72-11749

"A revision of Handbook for prospectors and operators of small mines by M. W. von Bernewitz [first published 1926]." Title page

Partial contents: The art and science of prospecting; Aids to prospectors; Prospecting equipment; Camping, clothing, cooking; Health and safety; Basic prospecting; Sampling, testing, assaying; Staking a mining claim; Elementary mineralogy; Precious metals; Lightweight metals; Other major metals; Gemstones; Abrasives; Metallurgical materials; Manufacturing materials; Opening a mine; Mineral processing

"Enough elementary material on geology and mineralogy is included to make the book self-sufficient for the layman. Each chapter is quite condensed, but numerous references to books, reports, and addresses of organizations will help line up more detailed information, especially in the U.S. and Canada. . . . Clearly written with a good sense of humor this is a must for . . . beginning prospectors." Choice

Glossary of terms: p431-48. Includes bibliographies

623.82 Nautical craft

Chilton's Repair and tune-up guide: inboard/outdrives. Prepared by the Automotive Editorial Department. . . . Chilton Bk. Co. 1973 251p illus $6.95
623.82

1 Marine engines—Repairing 2 Motorboats
ISBN 0-8019-5781-8   LC 73-1268

Title on cover: Chilton's Inboard/outdrives: repair tune-up guide

"Managing editor: John D. Kelly; assistant managing editor: Peter J. Meyer; senior editor: Kerry A. Freeman; technical editors: Robert J. Brown [and] Philip A. Canal; copy editor: Eric J. Roberts." Title page

"A guide to the tune-up, repair troubleshooting, and maintenance of the most popular models of inboard boat engines and outdrives manufactured by Kiekhaefer Mercury, Outboard Marine Corporation's Evinrude and Johnson, and Chrysler/Volvo Penta. Introductory chapters detail general boating instructions, safety precautions, and emergency procedures, while other sections give specific information on individual models. Numerous charts, drawings, and black-and-white photographs illustrate for the owner-mechanic procedures ranging from spark plug specification to complete tune-up and rebuilding." Booklist

Chilton's Repair and tune-up guide: outboard motors 30 horsepower & over. Prepared by the Automotive Editorial Department. . . . Chilton Bk. Co. 1973 284p illus $6.95
623.82

1 Marine engines—Repairing 2 Motorboats
ISBN 0-8019-5722-2   LC 72-11533

Title on cover: Chilton's 30 horsepower and over, outboard motors: repair & tune-up guide

"Managing editor: John D. Kelly; assistant managing editor: Peter J. Meyer; editor: Kerry A. Freeman; technical editors: Robert J. Brown [and] Philip A. Canal." Title page

This is a guide for the tune-up, repair, troubleshooting, and repair of the most popular American-made outboard motors, covering models from 1966 through 1972

623.88 Seamanship. Knots

Montgomery, Edward
Useful knots for everyone. Scribner 1973 128p illus $5.95   623.88

1 Knots and splices
ISBN 0-684-13382-2   LC 73-2551

Illustrated with step-by-step diagrams, this book offers instructions for tying and untying household knots (as distinct from scout and nautical knots). After explaining eight basic knots, the author describes binding and loop knots, hitches, bends, and some special purpose knots The final two chapters describe parcel, garden plant and kitchen knots, and how to prevent cord or rope ends from unraveling

629.133 Aircraft

Angelucci, Enzo
Airplanes from the dawn of flight to the present day; color illus. and design by Marco Rota. McGraw 1973 287p illus $14.95
629.133

1 Airplanes—History
ISBN 0-07-001807-3   LC 72-12755

Original Italian edition published 1971

"Essentially a picture book, it contains at least one illustration of every aircraft and numerous color plates, half-tones, and small three-view drawings of an imposing selection of planes. Each major era and each major type of plane is prefaced by a cogent overview, and the majority of the planes pictured have historical thumbnail sketches." Library J

Bibliography: p271-74

629.2 Motor land vehicles. Automobiles

Billiet, Walter
Automotive engines: maintenance and repair. 4th ed. Am. Tech. Soc. 1973 516p illus $9.95
629.2

1 Automobiles—Engines
ISBN 0-8269-0062-3 LC 72-88611

Earlier edition by Ernest Venk and Walter Billiet entered in main catalog
First edition by Ernest Venk published 1951. The 1974 edition has been revised and updated to reflect new technical developments in the field and illustrations have been added to cover these developments. "In addition, a new section has been added covering the operating principles of the Wankel engine . . . [and a] new chapter has been added covering emission systems including tune-up, service, and troubleshooting information." Preface to the fourth edition

Chilton's Auto air conditioning manual. . . . Prepared by the Automotive Editorial Department. . . . Chilton Bk. Co. 1974 824p illus $16
629.2

1 Automobiles—Air conditioning
ISBN 9-8019-5773-X LC 72-12459

Title on cover: Chilton's Auto heating & air conditioning manual
"General manager: William D. Byrne; editor-in-chief: Jack Kelly; managing editor: John H. Weise; assistant managing editor: Peter J. Myer; senior editor: Leo A. Mealey; service editors: John M. Baxter [and others]." Title page
"General and model-by-model descriptions of automobile air conditioning and heating units and their maintenance and repair. Covers American autos [and selected trucks] and Volkswagen from 1966 through 1974 models. Abundant illustrations include diagrams, photographs, tables and trouble-shooting charts. The highly detailed table of contents beginning each section makes up for the lack of a general index. Information in the manual is based on industry sources. For the public library, automobile reference collections and interested laymen." N Y New Tech Bks

Dark, Harris Edward
The Wankel rotary engine; introduction and guide. Ind. Univ. Press 1974 145p illus $6.95
629.2

1 Wankel engine
ISBN 0-253-19021-5 LC 73-16676

"A history and layman-level technical description of rotary-type internal combustion engines with heavy emphasis on those designed by Felix Wankel." N Y New Tech Bks
"Harris quotes sources which almost invariably sing the Wankel's praises. . . . He omits any mention of the testing by Consumers Union, over the past several years, of Wankel-equipped Mazda automobiles. The union found—and Harris seems to have ignored—a number of serious problems associated with the rotary." Library J
Bibliography: p139-40

629.22 Types of vehicles. Motorcycles

Griffin, Al
Motorcycles; a buyer's & rider's guide. Rev. ed. Regnery 1974 317p illus $10
629.22

1 Motorcycles
ISBN 0-8092-8996-2 LC 73-20682

Earlier edition entered in main catalog
First published 1972. The 1974 edition has been enlarged and updated to include material on all available models through 1974

629.28 Tests, operation, maintenance, repairs

Carlson, Margaret Bresnahan
How to get your car repaired without getting gypped [by] Margaret Bresnahan Carlson with Ronald G. Shafer. Harper 1973 278p illus $6.95
629.28

1 Automobiles—Repairing
SBN 06-010612-3 LC 72-11811

In this book car owners are warned about common fraud practices in automotive repair facilities. Also included is information on how to tell what repairs are necessary, where to go for repairs, self-protection against fraud and action to be taken against fraudulent repair concerns. Appendices list estimated cost of running a car, major recall campaigns, places to write with complaints, small claims courts, and a glossary of parts

Chilton's Auto troubleshooting guide. Prepared by the Automotive Editorial Department. Chilton Bk. Co. 1973 120p illus pa $3.95
629.28

1 Automobiles—Repairing
ISBN 0-8019-5745-1 LC 73-4259

This guide covers the major automotive systems, showing how each system works and giving tests for the determination of specific repair needs. An appendix includes conversion tables, decimal equivalents, and anti-freeze information

Chilton's Motorcycle troubleshooting guide; prepared by the Automotive Editorial Department. . . . Chilton Bk. Co. 1973 165p illus $7.95
629.28

1 Motorcycles—Repairing
ISBN 0-8019-6081-9 LC 73-5753

"Managing editor: John D. Kelly; assistant managing editor: Peter J. Meyer; senior editor, motorcycles: Michael S. Yampolsky; editors: James H. Johnson [and] Joseph F. Pelliccioti." Title page
Contents: Introduction to troubleshooting; Two-stroke engine troubleshooting; Four-stroke troubleshooting; Fuel system troubleshooting; Electrical system troubleshooting; Clutch and transmission troubleshooting; Chassis troubleshooting
"Written in a rather chatty but highly effective style for the motorcycle enthusiast who is having (or contemplating) trouble. Diagrams and photographs are excellent." N Y New Tech Bks

Chilton's Repair and maintenance guide: truck campers; prepared by the Automotive Editorial Department. Recreational Vehicles. . . . Chilton Bk. Co. 1973 99p illus $5.95
629.28

1 Travel trailers and campers—Repairing
ISBN 0-8019-5744-3 LC 73-4840

Title on cover: Chilton's Truck campers: repair & maintenance
"Managing editor: John D. Kelly; assistant managing editor: Peter J. Meyer; senior editor, recreational vehicle department: Kerry A. Freeman; editor: Philip A. Canal; technical editor: Robert J. Brown; copy editor: Eric J. Roberts." Title page
"A complete handbook for care and reconditioning of slide-in, chassis-mount, and pick-up-style campers offers full data on both automotive and interior maintenance. Accompanied by black-and-white photographs and diagrams of parts and techniques the book defines and classifies campers, explains vehicle components, and reviews fuel and heating procedures. The handbook covers water and sewage as well as electrical and refrigeration processes that may need repair. Conversion and antifreeze tables are appended." Booklist

Coles, Clarence W.
Glenn's Complete bicycle manual: selection, maintenance, repair, by Clarence W. Coles and Harold T. Glenn. Crown 1973 339p illus $7.95
629.28

1 Bicycles and bicycling—Repairing
ISBN 0-517-50092-2 LC 70-185100

Coles, Clarence W.—*Continued*

"A superior guide to the selection, maintenance, and repair of American, European, and Japanese bicycles. Step-by-step instructions are given for complete disassembly, assembly, adjustment, and maintenance, with photographs and detailed drawings showing what is to be done and how to do it. It is better on the more complicated procedures than on the simple ones. Information on choosing a bike includes a discussion of various types and price ranges, and a formula for determining the correct size to buy. A short sketch of the development of cycling and hints on cycling safety broaden the interest of this very practical bicycle manual." Cur Ref Bks

629.45 Manned flight

Collins, Michael

Carrying the fire; an astronaut's journeys; with a foreword by Charles A. Lindbergh. Farrar, Straus 1974 478p illus $10   629.45

1 Apollo project 2 Space flight to the moon
ISBN 0-374-11917-1   LC 74-7211

"Despite the voluminous press coverage of recent years, and a fair number of books, especially after Apollo 11, people still don't have the vaguest idea of what it was like 'up there,' or what pre- and post-flight activities were necessary and how they affected the lives of those involved. I wrote this book to do that, tracing my participation in the astronaut selection process, subsequent training, the frustration of being so close yet so far away, making it on Gemini 10, being assigned to the first circumlunar flight and getting bounced off by spinal surgery, and finally orbiting the moon while Armstrong and Aldrin walked on it." Preface

This "is a magnificent piece of exposition alive with humor, candid in its anxiety, very sensitive in its appreciation of the men involved. . . . Twenty-three astronauts were involved in the final phase [of the moon program], and Collins gives a frank man-to-man estimate of each. He is equally frank about the medics, whose worries he did not accept. . . . This is a splendid and affirmative book which tells the nation of the amazingly precise training these men went through and of what they endured." Atlantic

Cooper, Henry S. F.

Thirteen: the flight that failed [by] Henry S. F. Cooper, Jr. Dial Press 1973 [c1972] 199p $5.95   629.45

1 Apollo project   LC 72-13676

This "deals with the flight of Apollo 13, which suffered a disastrous explosion in the depths of space that threatened the lives of the astronauts. . . . The story is unfolded from several points of view. The spacecraft is dissected to explain exactly what went wrong. The contrast is brought out between the attitudes of the crew, understandably worried, and the ground controllers, unruffled at first because of their faith in the reliability of their machines. In the end, the greatest threat to the safety of Lovell, Haise, and Swigert was their growing exhaustion: because of the need to save battery power it became very cold in the spacecraft, and none of them slept much for several days. It was a very close call." Library J

"For me its interest is less in the suspense than in a concentration that economy and restraint—and the nature of Apollo 13—turn upon the technology, the operational process and parts, the real thing or at least its hard embodiment. . . . Certainly the book will intrigue those who think technology boring." N Y Times Bk R

630.1 Agricultural life

Tabler, Gladys

Country chronicle   630.1

1 Country life—Connecticut 2 Cookery

Some editions are:
Hall, G.K.&Co. $8.95 Large type edition
Lippincott $6.95 (ISBN 0-397-01023-0)

First published 1974 by Lippincott

"In this calendar of seasons at Stillmeadow in the New England countryside, Taber . . . recites the charms of yesterday and of the enduring rural life. The book is almost worth reading for the recipes alone ('Alma's orange delight,' baked stuffed mushroom caps, etc.). Her simple homey philosophy is at times a bit woolly, but on the whole, this book is charming and reasonably fresh." Library J

630.2 Agriculture—Miscellany

Logsdon, Gene

Homesteading; how to find new independence on the land. Rodale 1973 256p $7.95   530.2

1 Agriculture—Handbooks, manuals, etc. 2 Agriculture—U.S. 3 Farm management
ISBN 0-87857-068-3   LC 73-5159

"Independence on the land is sought by thousands of young people and it is to this group that the experienced homesteader has addressed himself. Depending on where you live, you can catch the snapping turtle, raise hogs, who are not as lovable as the author thinks, raise sheep, though he doesn't consider it practical on a small place, or better still, raise the fertile rabbit. Of course the practical organic vegetable garden includes such sturdy fare as kale, turnips, and kohlrabi, as well as the more succulent rhubarb." Ref Services Rev

Bibliography: p249-51

635 Garden crops

Crockett, James Underwood

Vegetables and fruits, by James Underwood Crockett and the editors of Time-Life Books. Watercolor illus. by Richard Crist. Time-Life Bks. [distributed by Little] 1972 160p illus (The Time-Life Encyclopedia of gardening) $6.95   635

1 Vegetable gardening 2 Fruit culture 3 Herbs
LC 78-93862

"This book discusses the latest techniques in food gardening and includes an encyclopedia with characteristics, planting dates and growing times of all popular varieties." Publisher's note

Bibliography: p155

Dietz, Marjorie J.

(ed.) 10,000 garden questions answered by 20 experts. 3d ed. Originally ed. by F. F. Rockwell. New drawings for the 3d ed. by Reisie Lonette. Doubleday 1974 1421p illus $10.95   635

1 Gardening
ISBN 0-385-00479-6   LC 73-17596

"An American Garden Guild book"

Earlier edition entered in main catalog under F. F. Rockwell

First published 1944. The 1974 edition has been thoroughly revised and enlarged. The botanical names of plants have been up-dated to conform as nearly as possible to the International Code for the Nomenclature of Cultivated Plants, and numerous new illustrations have been included

Sources for further information: p1354-80

Faust, Joan Lee

(ed.) The New York Times Garden book; with a preface by Hal Borland. 2d ed. rev. Knopf 1973 xxv, 370p illus $10   635

1 Gardening
ISBN 0-394-48335-9   LC 72-11016

First published 1962 with New York Times as author

A compendium of "gardening information taken from the gardening pages of the 'New York Times,' horticultural experts detail every phase of gardening activity from lawn care and landscape design to the propagation and culture of trees, shrubs, flowers, fruits, vegetables, and house plants. . . . An appendix lists various sources of plant and gardening supplies. Bibliography." Booklist

635.9 Flowers and ornamental plants (Floriculture)

Elbert, George A.
The indoor light gardening book. Crown 1973 250p illus $10.95 635.9
1 Gardening—Lighting
ISBN 0-517-50095-7 LC 72-84298

"After discussing fluorescent light facts, fixtures, and accessories and plant light requirements, [the author] furnishes details on creating fluorescent-illuminated shelf and case units, stacked arrangements, wall gardens, and more, and effective soilless and soil mixes. He considers appropriate fertilizers and other chemicals, ventilation, humidity, watering, propagation and pesticides, herb gardens, and plants for children. Plants of choice to grow under lights and their needs occupy several chapters. . . . Appendix of plant and equipment sources and data and reading list." Booklist

Evans, Charles M.
The terrarium book [by] Charles M. Evans with Roberta Lee Pliner; illus. by Betty Fraser. Random House 1973 102p illus $7.95 635.9
1 Terrariums 2 Plants
ISBN 0-394-48564-2 LC 72-11388

"A beginner's guide to an increasingly popular method of growing green things in sealed glass containers. The authors give brief but expert advice on the choice of containers, various types of plants and their required environments, soils, planting, and maintenance of terrariums. Numerous line drawings illustrate plants, procedures, and finished planters. Most plant names are given in the scientific Latin from (genus and species) but common names are provided in an appendix of plant names and occasionally in the text." Booklist

Faust, Joan Lee
The New York Times Book of house plants; illus. by Allianora Rosse. Quadrangle Bks. 1973 274p illus $9.95 635.9
1 House plants
ISBN 0-8129-0309-9 LC 72-91701

"Basic instructions are followed by a calendar of plant care and a section on 100 popular plants to grow. Arranged alphabetically by plant, this section provides capsule growing instructions and attractive identifying watercolor illustrations for each plant. Gardening under lights, office plants, topiary, and other special features are discussed subsequently. Helpful photographs and line drawings and appendix, lists of plant societies, suppliers, and books to consult round out an unusually easy-to-follow guide." Booklist

"Mothers will like the chapters on plants for children to raise, and ardent growers will find the list of societies convenient." Ref Services Rev

Northern, Henry T.
Greenhouse gardening [by] Henry T. Northern [and] Rebecca T. Northen. 2d ed. Ronald 1973 388p illus $10.50 635.9
1 Plants, Ornamental 2 Greenhouses
LC 75-190208

First published 1956 with title: The complete book of greenhouse gardening

This manual includes information about the selection, building and management of greenhouses, soils, methods of plant propagation and growth control, pests and diseases, and temperature suitability of various plants. Additional chapters describe types of ornamental plants, including begonias, ferns, orchids, succulents, members of bulb families, and greenhouse-grown vegetables

Terrariums & miniature gardens, by the editors of Sunset Books and Sunset magazine. Lane Bk. Co. 1973 80p illus pa $1.95 635.9
1 Terrariums 2 Gardens, Miniature
ISBN 0-376-03781-4 LC 72-92519

"A Sunset book"

"Step-by-step instructions in artificial lighting and in creating imaginative bottle gardens, vivariums, underwater gardens, and gardens with moats." Chicago

636.08 Production, maintenance training of animals. Pets

Carson, Gerald
Men, beasts, and gods; a history of cruelty and kindness to animals. Scribner [1974 c1972] 268p illus pa $3.95 636.08
1 Animals—Treatment
ISBN 0-684-13716-X LC 72-1216

First published 1972

"The author broadly traces the history of man-animal interactions from prehistory to the present, including the religious and mythological uses of animals. At the beginning of civilization, man still felt spiritually close to the animal world, as indicated by his admiration and even deification of some beasts. A gradual shifting of attitutdes, especially in the Judeo-Christian area of influence, resulted in animals being considered inferior, exploitable objects. Animal cruelty (domestic, sport, scientific and commercial exploitation) for the 'benefit' of man is documented admirably. The attitudes which permit cruelty and exploitation are well presented and analyzed. Various social pressure groups as well as legislative developments for the protection of animals receive their share of attention." Scienc Bks

"Although this book is a polemic, an indictment of past and present treatment of animals, it still provides a respectable amount of information. . . . [The book's] thesis is that man's attitude toward the other animals with whom he shares the world is an expression of his attitude toward himself. A readable, interesting, and useful survey." Choice

McKeown, Donal B.
Your pet's health from A to Z, by Donal B. McKeown and Earl O. Strimple. Luce, R.B. 1973 255p $7.50 636.08
1 Pets 2 Pets—Diseases and pests
ISBN 0-88331-063-5 LC 73-9057

The authors have compiled a "cross-referenced dictionary of topics most frequently on the mind of pet owners. Most entries deal with various organs, diseases, deficiencies, nutrition, poisoning, and disorders of pets. Each topic is usually one paragraph; others, needing further clarification, cover several pages. Several home remedies are listed; however, diagnosis is pointed out as the function of the vet. This book should be in the hands of all pet owners, in school libraries, and on the shelf of life science teachers who keep laboratory animals." Science Teacher

Villiard, Paul
Raising small animals for fun and profit. Winchester Press 1973 160p illus $6.95 636.08
1 Animals
ISBN 0-87691-084-3 LC 72-79368

The author "has raised most of the animals described; and in short sketches covering species that range from microscopic freshwater forms available in the nearest pond to the sophisticated mink (for profit) and flying squirrels. . . . He presents the pros and cons of small-animal rearing and directions for handling and feeding the creatures and discusses marketing problems. Although the treatment for each animal is limited to a few pages, instructions are clearly written and adequate for the beginner." Library J

An appendix lists American and Canadian governmental agencies, on national and regional levels, which provide wildlife information. Some United States government publications are specified

636.103 Horses—Encyclopedias

Hope, C. E. G.
(ed.) The encyclopedia of the horse; ed. by C. E. G. Hope and G. N. Jackson; advisory editor: William Steinkraus; picture editor: Diana R. Tuke. Viking 1973 336p illus maps $22.50 636.103
1 Horses—Encyclopedias 2 Horsemanship—Encyclopedias
ISBN 0-670-29402-0 LC 72-90351

Hope, C. E. G.—*Continued*
"A Studio book"

This book "presents information on every recognized breed of horse and pony in the world. A list of 'Horses of the World' at the beginning of the volume, alphabetically arranged by country, then by breed, precedes a list of 'Horse and Pony Societies,' first internationally by country, followed by a more detailed list of the breed and activity organizations in the United Kingdom and the United States. The articles range in length from simple phrases, e.g., 'mare, an adult female horse,' to several pages, e.g., 'Long distance riding' and 'Show jumping.' The scope is not limited to articles on breeds, methods of riding, tack, horse activities, noted horsemen and stables, and maintenance and diseases, but also includes information on the horse in literature, in art and in the motion pictures, and on the stage, among others." Ref Services Rev

"This one volume encyclopedia is comprehensive, well written and illustrated, with 32 color plates and over 300 black and white illustrations of consistently fine quality. It is not only an excellent reference work for the professional, but a helpful textbook for the novice." Christian Science Monitor

636.109 Horses—History

Braider, Donald
The life, history, and magic of the horse. Grosset 1973 247p illus $14.95   636.109
1 Horses—History
ISBN 0-448-02169-2   LC 72-77107
"A Madison Square Press book"

This "volume traces the ancestry of the horse, reviews the origin and attributes of specific breeds, and tells how medieval man used and thought about the animal. Chapters are also devoted to the horse in art and in literature with excerpts appended from writings by Shakespeare, Jonathan Swift, and later writers. Black-and-white and colorplates represent ancient and modern artists' conceptions of the horse and show, among many items, nineteenth-century U.S. vehicles pulled by horses, races and games using horses, and horses in the circus and movies." Booklist

636.8 Cats

Fox, Michael W.
Understanding your cat. Coward, McCann & Geoghegan 1974 221p illus $7.95   636.8
1 Cats
ISBN 0-698-10603-2   LC 73-93763

This book is more a "guide to cat behavior and psyche than to health and disease problems which are briefly touched. Fox focuses on such aspects of the cat as its brain and senses, social life and communication, behavior disorders, and relationship with man. He concludes with a selection of questions and answers." Booklist
Bibliography: p205

Gallico, Paul
Honorable cat; photographs by Osamu Nishikawa; additional photographs by Virginia Gallico. Crown 1972 159p illus $10   636.8
1 Cats 2 Cats—Poetry
ISBN 0-517-50049-3   LC 72-84297

The author examines the cat in all his infinite variety and moods and from every aspect—psychological, social, intellectual, and historical. He debunks many of the myths that have developed about cats: that black cats mean bad luck, that they scratch, that they prowl and kill, that they are the familiars of witches, that they cause terrible disasters. He shows the cat in all his environments, how he responds to them, and how he reacts to humans

"The first fourth of the book is an unabashed appreciation of the cat's superiority to other creatures, including man. The remainder consists of marvelous color photographs of cats and kittens in winning action or striking pose coupled with . . . [Haiku] verses by Gallico. . . . [This book will] be relished by the confirmed cat lover." Booklist

636.803 Cats—Encyclopedias and dictionaries

Henderson, G. N.
(ed.) The international encyclopedia of cats; ed. by G. N. Henderson and D. J. Coffey. Consultant: Leslie S. Smith; photographs by Anne Cumbers; drawings by Annabel Milne. McGraw 1973 256p illus $17.95   636.803
1 Cats—Encyclopedias
ISBN 0-07-028163-7   LC 72-10958

Arranged alphabetically, this volume includes information for cat owners—breeding, buying, grooming, and health. Newly developed species are described as well as the big cats and the well known breeds. Line drawings and black-and-white and color photographs accompany the text

This book "provides much factual information. The text, especially the sections on diseases, veterinary procedures, and anatomy is illustrated with many diagrams and photographs. Although much of the text is oriented to the British cat fancier, the information on cat physiology, care, and treatment is detailed and applies to all cats. . . . Enough different information is provided to make it a suitable addition to a library which already has Grace Pond's 'The Complete Cat Encyclopedia' [entered in main catalog]." Library J

637 Dairy and related technologies

Alth, Max
Making your own cheese and yogurt. Funk 1973 226p illus $5.95   637
1 Cheese 2 Yogurt
ISBN 0-308-10081-6   LC 73-11111

An "introduction to basic principles governing preparation of cheese and yogurt addressed to the novice. . . . Historical references to cheese and yogurt are given and nutritional values fully explained both in the text and in appended tables; instructional drawings amplify the discussion of techniques. Required equipment is explained as are formulae that determine the kind of cheese and yogurt desired. Recipes for both included and final processes such as storage, pressing, sealing, and packaging are discussed." Booklist
Bibliography: p225-26

639 Nondomesticated animals. Sealing

Mowat, Farley
Wake of the great sealers; prints and drawings by David Blackwood. Little 1973 157p illus $19.95   639
1 Sealing
ISBN 0-316-58649-8   LC 73-14315
"An Atlantic Monthly Press book"

"Utilizing actual accounts of late 19th-Century Newfoundland sealers in a first-person narrative style, Mowat powerfully conveys a feeling for these individuals, their lives, and times. The combination of simple text and beautifully executed, darkly powerful prints and drawings recreates a life of stark hardship. . . . It is a moving illustration of the triumph of human spirit over nearly unsurmountable adversity. Seemingly expensive for only 157 pages, but the quality of the plentiful artwork justifies the price." Library J

640 Home economics

Habeeb, Virginia T.
The Ladies' Home Journal Art of homemaking; everything you need to know to run your home with ease and style; with drawings by Loretta Trezzo. Simon & Schuster 1973 588p illus $9.95   640
1 Home economics
ISBN 0-671-21487-X   LC 72-90393

Habeeb, Virginia T.—Continued

This book provides basic how-to information on various household tasks including decorating, cleaning, repairing, freezing, and household budgeting

"This up-to-date volume contains special sections not found in other recent books and more detail in essential areas; for example, there are sections on living with pets, moving, and safety as well as details on the ingredients and chemical reactions of cleaning agents. A clear format, lively prose style, and helpful lists and charts also make this a good choice if a basic homemaking book is needed." Library J

Bibliography: p537-45

United States. Department of Agriculture

Handbook for the home; the yearbook of agriculture, 1973. Supt. of Docs. [1973] 388p illus $5.70   **640**

1 Home economics 2 Consumer education

"Suggests ways that families can live fuller, more secure, and more satisfying lives, and helps them avoid costly pitfalls of all kinds. It gathers a great wealth of consumer material into some 400 compact pages. This is a book for families. It centers around the home—whether home is a suburban house, a country place, or a city apartment." Foreword

Bibliography at ends of chapters

640.73 Consumer education

Ross, Donald K.

A public citizen's action manual. Grossman Pubs. 1973 237p $5.95   **640.73**

1 Consumer protection
SBN 670-58201-8   LC 72-9904

The author "provides guidelines for exercising citizen power. Drawing primarily on the work of Nader-associated groups, the author suggests specific action projects (of varying complexity) on health care, consumer abuses, equal opportunity, property tax inequities, and government responsiveness. He fully outlines how to test, expose, and remedy various abuses, and provides sources of relevant material. Ross also explains how to organize citizen groups and discusses the role of the Public Interest Research Group (PIRG) movement. . . . This is an important and practical manual." Library J

Thomas, Sarah M.

A guide to sources of consumer information, by Sarah M. Thomas and Bernadine Weddington; with a foreword by Virginia H. Knauer. Information Resources Press 1973 177p illus $10.50   **640.73**

1 Consumer education—Handbooks, manuals, etc. 2 Consumer education—Bibliography
ISBN 0-87815-010-2   LC 73-77342

"A useful little guide to materials and organizations concerned with consumer problems. . . . Twenty-four textbooks are listed with annotations, as are 116 books, pamphlets, and reports on a variety of specific products and problems and 65 consumer oriented periodicals. Federal government agencies and offices are listed with notes on their function. Consumer protection agencies for the various states are indicated, and 89 national nongovernment organizations are briefly described. This latter listing includes the consumer education programs of some commercial concerns (e.g., Safeway Stores, J. C. Penney Co.)." Cur Ref Bks

641.3 Foods and foodstuffs

Evans, Travers Moncure

The meat book; a consumer's guide to selecting, buying, cutting, storing, freezing, & carving the various cuts, by Travers Moncure Evans and David Greene; with illus. by Dana Greene. Scribner 1973 310p illus $8.95   **641.3**

1 Meat
ISBN 0-684-13565-5   LC 73-1337

"A former meatcutter and wholesale meat distributor . . . has shared with a writer and good food lover his knowledge of how to buy and eat better meat economically. A timely book for non-vegetarians. Beef, pork, and the lesser used liver, tongue, sweetbreads, heart, kidney, brains, tripe, and oxtail are discussed, with a separate chapter for the happy few who are able to buy a side of beef. Well indexed." Ref Services Rev

Glossaries and a bibliography are included

Goldbeck, Nikki

The supermarket handbook; access to whole foods [by] Nikki and David Goldbeck; drawings by Ellen Weiss. Harper 1973 413p illus $7.95   **641.3**

1 Food 2 Consumer education 3 Cookery
ISBN 0-06-011581-5   LC 73-4084

"A shopping tour of the supermarket from the dairy case to the meat counter gives . . . information on buying and evaluating food which is free from unnecessary additives, preferably unadulterated but not necessarily organic. Recommended products and brands along with recipes are noted and consumer-oriented data on labeling, dating codes, ecology, food substitution, and a glossary are also provided." Booklist

"The volume takes a common-sense approach, urging the consumer to read labels carefully and to use good judgment. . . . Sensible and quite readable." Library J

641.5 Cookery

The American Heart Association cookbook; recipes selected, compiled, and tested under the direction of Ruthe Eshleman and Mary Winston; illus. by Tonia Hampson. McKay 1973 xxxiv, 412p illus $7.95   **641.5**

1 Cookery   LC 72-97548

"Emphasis is placed on fat control in a comprehensive cookbook which spells out ways to avoid harmful fats while enjoying a well-balanced pleasing diet. The recipes are carefully tested and standardized and stress use of polyunsaturated oils, but the book does not include low sodium dishes; all recipes are for foods with some nutritive value. Among special features are shopping and cooking tips, vegetarian, rice, and pasta recipes, menus for holidays and special occasions, ways to adapt one's own recipes to fat control rules, definitions of pertinent scientific terms, hints for eating out, and a fat-cholesterol chart." Booklist

Bibliography: p391

Berglund, Berndt

Wilderness cooking; a unique illustrated cookbook and guide for outdoor enthusiasts, by Berndt Berglund and Clare E. Bolsby; illus. by E. B. Sanders. Scribner 1973 192p illus $7.95   **641.5**

1 Outdoor cookery 2 Cookery—Game and game birds
ISBN 0-684-13335-0   LC 72-12158

"Addressed to outdoorsmen and valuable as a guide to Indian and frontier cooking practices viable today the inclusive book explains wilderness techniques such as hunting by bow and arrow or with firearms, tells ways to dress, butcher, and cure game in the field, notes wilderness measurements, and describes wild seasonings. The recipes collected for meat, birds, fish, and desserts stem from pioneer or Indian sources and for the most part contain wilderness ingredients and natural vegetables. Instruction is given for preparation of breads, beverages, corn, sugar, and syrups and wild game meats such as skunk, buffalo, pheasant, and squirrel. Many recipes suggest time required for full realization of satisfaction to be derived from the wilderness foods suggested." Booklist

Blevin, Margo

The low blood sugar cookbook [by] Margo Blevin and Geri Ginder; foreword by Herbert B. Goldman. Doubleday 1973 520p $8.95   **641.5**

1 Cookery for hypoglycemics
ISBN 0-385-05174-3   LC 72-79378

Blevin, Margo—*Continued*

This cookbook for people who suffer from hypoglycemia, a disease characterized by low blood sugar includes recipes, a selection of charts and lists of allowed and not allowed foods and a 'unit system' for planning menus

"Good suggestions are made for guest, ethnic, and holiday menus; for the special needs of children and teens; and for emergencies. Unfortunately, the bibliography is skimpy, and even though fatty meals can predispose one to vascular damage, little attention is given to the maintenance of a saturated-unsaturated fat balance in the diet." Library J

Davis, Francyne

The low blood sugar cookbook; foreword by Carlton Fredericks; introduction by Marilyn Hamilton Light. Grosset 1973 xxiii, 199p $6.95 **641.5**

1 Cookery for hypoglycemics
ISBN 0-448-01576-5   LC 72-90832

"Written for the hypoglycemic patient, (one whose pancreas produces too much insulin and who must have a high-protein, low-carbohydrate diet), this cookbook includes lists of allowable foods and foods to avoid, sample menus, and more than 200 recipes. . . . It is especially valuable that this cookbook includes recipes for acceptable breads and desserts." Library J

The **Good** Housekeeping cookbook; ed. by Zoe Coulson; drawings by Murray Tinkelman; photographs by James Viles. Good Housekeeping 1973 811p illus $8.95 **641.5**

1 Cookery
ISBN 0-87851-014-1   LC 73-81131

The earliest version of this cook book appeared in 1903, compiled by Isabel Gordon Curtis, published by Phelps Publishing Company. First published with this title 1933. The 1963 edition has title: The New Good Housekeeping cookbook

Includes over 3000 recipes in 34 chapters. There are special chapters on entertaining; preparation of game and fowl; use of wine; cooking for two; cooking for a crowd; outdoor cookery; diet recipes; canning, preserving, and freezing; and storage of food. Index is cross referenced

Myers, Norma

Gifts from the kitchen, by Norma Myers and Joan Scobey; illus. by Jean La Vigna. Doubleday 1973 298p illus $6.95 **641.5**

1 Cookery 2 Gifts
ISBN 0-385-02477-0   LC 72-96250

This "book features recipes suited to all types of people and occasions. These recipes go beyond the usual offerings of jams and pickles, and include several sophisticated dishes. Soups and casseroles may be hard to visualize as gifts, but they are perfect for certain occasions. And there are new ideas for containers—an important part of each gift. Many of the recipes have special storage or handling notes that should accompany the gift when it is given. . . . The recipes are easy enough for the novice." Library J

Nidetch, Jean

Weight Watchers Program cookbook. Hearthside Press 1973 320p illus $6.95 **641.5**

1 Cookery 2 Weight control
ISBN 0-8208-0216-6   LC 72-79087

First published 1966

This cookbook "is built around a nutritionally sound regimen and 'legal' foods. Some rules continue unchanged: no alcohol, no skipping meals, no calorie counting. Happily though, the lists of 'legal' foods have been broadened and subdivided, with the result that weight watchers may now have easier to prepare meals with greater variety and economy and with less bulk. . . . [The book] reflects the program changes: bread and cereal; daily choice (bread substitutes); liver, a weekly must; use-as-desired bonus foods; and leveling and maintenance plans." Library J

641.8 Composite dishes

Beard, James

Beard on bread; drawings by Karl Stuecklen. Knopf 1973 230p illus $7.95
641.8

1 Bread
ISBN 0-394-47345-0   LC 73-7266

The famous chef "is more interested in good taste and gives us a collection of personal recipes, not a comprehensive bread cookbook. There is a brief section on ingredients and tools and a helpful section on choosing the right bread. The first of the recipes is given in detail for the benefit of beginners; then there follows a selection of some 100 recipes. . . . The most helpful feature is Beard's discussion of each bread, for he describes the distinctive characteristics of the bread before proceeding with the recipe. This volume is for the extensive cookbook collection." Library J

Good Housekeeping Complete book of cake decorating. Good Housekeeping Bks. 1973 192p illus $7.95 **641.8**

1 Cake decorating 2 Cake
ISBN 0-87851-012-5   LC 73-83959

A reissue of The Good Housekeeping Book of cake decorating, first published 1961 by Barrows

Includes recipes for a variety of cakes, from sponge cake to fruit cake, and for several frostings from quick and easy icings to rich butter-creams. Instructions are given for creating many decorations and designs

The book "describes specialized equipment well, includes an excellent chart of decorating tubes showing exactly what each can be used for and gives good directions for packing cakes and cookies to travel and for freezing them." Library J

643 The home and its equipment

The **Family** Handyman Home improvement book, by the editors of The Family Handyman magazine. Scribner 1973 498p illus $14.95 **643**

1 Houses—Repairing 2 Building—Repair and reconstruction
ISBN 0-684-12910-8   LC 72-1211

"A useful manual of design ideas, specifications, and step-by-step instructions in pictures, diagrams, and text for the home craftsman on improving or expanding his home himself. . . . Chapters deal with altering kitchens, gaining more space for children, achieving a satisfactory basement family fun room, creating added storage space, constructing a patio or other outdoor installations for family activities, and many other projects. Information on establishing and equipping a workshop and ready-reference charts and tables of materials standards occupy the two final chapters." Booklist

Hertzberg, Robert

The home owner handbook of electrical repairs; illus. by Henry Clark. Bounty Bks. 1974 125p illus $2.98 **643**

1 Household appliances, Electric—Repairing
ISBN 0-517-514400   LC 74-77426

This book first offers general background information deemed helpful for understanding and repairing electrical systems, such as fuses, circuits, tools, wiring and switches. Then the author goes on to describe the functions, operations, repairs and/or installations of more than 20 household electrical items, including lights, door chimes, freezers and televisions

Klamkin, Charles

How to buy major appliances. Regnery 1973 186p illus $6.95 **643**

1 Household appliances, Electric 2 Consumer education
ISBN 0-8092-9106-1   LC 72-11182

"Facts useful for the consumer considering purchase of a refrigerator, freezer, washer, dryer, dishwasher, range, air conditioner, de-

Klamkin, Charles—*Continued*
humidifier, television, stereo, or compact appliances. The advantages and drawbacks of current features and styling, deceptive advertising or sales pressure, the question of second year repair insurance contracts, and recourses if appliance is faulty and service is poor are discussed. For each appliance, the author makes recommendation of best made regardless of cost, and best value for cost."
Booklist

Mechanix Illustrated Fix-it home repairs handbook. Arco 1973 c1972 112p illus $3.95   **643**

1 Houses—Repairing
ISBN 0-688-02937-4   LC 72-95382

First published 1970 as a special issue of Mechanix Illustrated
This book describes basic tools and offers instructions for dozens of home repairs and improvements. Small electric appliances, lighting, plumbing, roofing, upholstering, locks, painting, and storage space are among the topics considered

646.2 Sewing and related operations

Better Homes and Gardens Sewing for your home. Meredith Corp. 1974 208p illus $7.95   **646.2**

1 Sewing 2 Interior decoration
ISBN 0-696-00570-0   LC 73-78907

Included in this book are sewing ideas and projects for home decoration. Fabric selection, planning, and construction of such items as drapes, bed linens, quilts, cushions, slipcovers, and table linen are discussed
Glossary: p202-03

649 Child rearing and home nursing

Pomeranz, Virginia E.
The first five years; a relaxed approach to child care, by Virginia E. Pomeranz, with Dodi Schultz. Doubleday 1973 248p $6.95   **649**

1 Infants—Care and hygiene 2 Children—Care and hygiene
ISBN 0-385-02015-5   LC 72-96254

Written by an experienced pediatrician "who has had some 20 years of experience dealing with children and their parents, felt that 'despite the proliferation of printed advice, parents are still at best confused, at worst trembling with self doubt.' Her aim is to convey the idea that there is no one right way to bring up a child; and she does this rather effectively. The work is written in a casual, interesting style; and numerous real-life examples enhance the presentation. The volume lacks detailed information concerning child development and rearing; rather, it focuses on the philosophical basis of parenting." Library J
"A checklist of commonly asked questions, a brief annotated list of readings, and sources of information for specific medical problems are appended." Booklist

Spock, Benjamin
Raising children in a difficult time; a philosophy of parental leadership and high ideals. Norton 1974 268p $7.95   **649**

1 Children—Management 2 Parent and child
ISBN 0-393-01106-2   LC 73-21848

Areas explored include "the liberation of women (which includes changing roles for parents), drug use, divorce, relationships with grandparents, the needs of children, the benefits of psychotherapy for those who need it, sex education, and . . . how to teach beliefs and ideas in a cynical age." Pub W
"The discussion appears to be honest, and Spock does not place himself above the average human. He does not even try to tell parents how to rear their children. Instead, he speaks as an experienced physician and parent and tells what he thinks his approach would be to current problems." Choice

651.02 Office services— Handbooks, manuals, etc.

Whalen, Doris H.
The secretary's handbook. Rev. ed. Harcourt 1973 236p illus pa $4.40   **651.02**

1 Secretaries 2 Office management—Handbooks, manuals, etc. 3 English language—Business English
ISBN 0-15-579297-0   LC 72-90643

First published 1968
"An up-to-date manual on grammar and usage and on the conventions of office procedure, organized for ready reference, with 60 sets of exercises for self-testing and review

657 Accounting

Century 21 accounting: Advanced course [by] Lewis D. Boynton [and others] South-Western Pub. illus $8.48   **657**

1 Bookkeeping 2 Accounting
ISBN 0-538-02980-3   LC 73-90594

Replaces the edition entered in main catalog with title: 20th century bookkeeping and accounting: Advanced course
First published 1912

658 General management

Drucker, Peter F.
Management: tasks, responsibilities, practices. Harper 1974 839p $15   **658**

1 Management
ISBN 0-06-011092-9   LC 72-79655

The author believes that "a responsible management is the only alternative to tyranny. . . . Dividing his work into three parts, Drucker first looks at the tasks of management; then he examines the manager himself; and finally he deals with top management, its tasks, structures, and strategy. His stress is on business management, but his ideas can be applied to the operation of any type of organization." Library J
This "work, a landmark in management studies attempting to set forth an organized body of knowledge, is well written [and] has a valuable bibliography. . . . It should be considered for acquisition by all libraries, large or small, with or without a collection of business books." Choice

How to run a small business. 4th ed. rev. and enl. by J. K. Lasser Tax Institute. Editor: Bernard Greisman. Directors: Bernard Greisman, Lee Gray, T. R. Lasser. McGraw 1974 306p $9.95   **658**

1 Small business
ISBN 0-07-036565-2

Earlier edition entered in main catalog under Lasser, J. K.
First published 1950 under the editorship of J. K. Lasser. The 1974 edition has been revised to reflect changed business conditions. Included are three new chapters dealing with franchising, mail order selling, and the management of a service firm

658.7 Management of materials

Aljian, George W.
(ed.) Purchasing handbook. . . 3d ed. McGraw 1973 1 v (various pagings) $29.50   **658.7**

1 Buying
ISBN 0-07-001068-4   LC 73-4544

First published 1958
"Standard reference book on policies, practices, and procedures, utilized in departments responsible for purchasing management or materials management." Title page
"Really an invaluable desk book for the purchasing agent, it is also a good survey of

Aljian, George W.—*Continued*
the field for the public library reference collection. Providing its information in 32 topically arranged sections, it covers forms, procedures, and techniques well." Cur Ref Bks
Includes bibliographies

658.8 Management of distribution. Garage sales

Ullman, James Michael
How to hold a garage sale. Scribner 1973 99p illus $5.95 **658.8**
ISBN 0-684-13283-4   LC 72-11300
"A Benjamin Company book"
The author "clearly knows his subject, writing concisely and clearly—especially keeping the absolute garage-sale beginner in mind—of every necessary step and phase of running one of those things. He accents the reasons people of all kinds go to such sales, tells just what happens at a typical garage (house, cellar, barn, backyard) sale, explains 'market research,' organizing, advertising, pricing, promoting, etc." Pub W
Includes a list of periodicals with buy-and-sell advertising

663 Beverage technology

Adams, Leon D.
The wines of America. Houghton 1973 465p illus $10.95   **663**
1 Wine and wine making
ISBN 0-395-15456-1   LC 73-75347
"A San Francisco Book Company/Houghton Mifflin book"
"Here is a comprehensive compendium of American wines, covering the history of winemaking, legends of the colorful winemakers, the growing of grapes, and the production of wines in nearly every state. More space is given to California wines than to those of any other region. Kosher winemakers and the wines of Canada and Mexico are also included." Pub W

668 Technology of organic products. Cosmetics

Krochmal, Connie
A guide to natural cosmetics. Quadrangle/The N.Y. Times Bk. Co. 1973 227p illus $8.95   **668**
1 Cosmetics
ISBN 0-8129-0362-5   LC 73-77028
This book "contains many recipes for preparing cosmetics for personal use. Measures are given in units commonly used in food preparation. Each list of ingredients is followed by brief mixing instructions." N Y New Tech Bks
"The large number of formulas covering cleansing substances, lotions and perfumes will make this a useful resource in collections whose cosmetics material is likely to be rather 'square' in orientation. . . . The amounts and directions for the recipes are generally clear, although the novice might wish for more guidance on proper application or use. Also, sometimes one wishes there were descriptions of how the resultant products should look or feel." Cur Ref Bks
Additional readings: p221-22

681 Precision instruments. Clocks and watches

Fried, Henry B.
The watch repairer's manual. 3d ed. Chilton Bk. Co. 1973 326p illus $9.95   **681**
1 Clocks and watches—Repairing
ISBN 0-8019-5916-0   LC 73-10193

Earlier edition entered in main catalog
First published 1949 by Van Nostrand. The 1973 edition has been updated introducing new descriptions and methods that have developed. Included is a new chapter on inserting and fitting watch crystals

683 Hardware

Nonte, George C.
Firearms encyclopedia, by George C. Nonte, Jr. Harper 1973 341p illus $11.95
683
1 Firearms—Encyclopedias   LC 73-80712
"An Outdoor Life book"
"Equipment, terms, and usage are defined and illustrated in an exceptionally well-designed reference source. Background material, care of equipment, and detailed articles on special aspects are included within the alphabetic arrangement. Eight appendixes supply charts of technical data, a directory of goods and services, a listing of associations, foreign gun terms, and abbreviations." Booklist
Bibliography: p273-80

684 Furnishings and home workshops

Scharff, Robert
Complete book of wood finishing. 2d ed. McGraw 1974 370p illus $9.95   **684**
1 Wood finishing
ISBN 0-07-055166-9   LC 73-22239
First published 1956
"Beginning with the fundamentals, the author guides the reader through a wide variety of wood finishing processes. At every stage, methods and materials are presented in . . . detail. Many alternatives are included to suit individual finances, skills, and equipment. Handy tips on reviving old paintbrushes, preventing varnish bubbles, applying quick-dry lacquers, repairing blistered veneer, and dozens of other practical pointers are provided. . . . Illustrated with photographs, drawings, charts, and schedules, this practical work contains a glossary of wood finishing terms and materials, and a comprehensive index for easy reference." Publisher's note

684.1 Furniture

Brumbaugh, James E.
Wood furniture, finishing, refinishing, repairing. Audel 1974 343p illus $6.95 **684.1**
1 Furniture—Repairing 2 Wood finishing
ISBN 0-672-23216-2   LC 73-91640
This book provides information on how to repair furniture and refinish wood surfaces. Included are sections on various wood grains, stains, and woodworking tools as well as on structural repairs, inlays, and decorative touches

Stevenson, Robert P.
How to build and buy cabinets for the modern kitchen. Rev. ed. Working drawings by Richard J. Meyer. Arco 1974 262p illus $10   **684.1**
1 Cabinet work 2 Kitchens
ISBN 0-668-03454-8   LC 72-85680
Earlier edition entered in main catalog with title: How to build cabinets for the modern kitchen
First published 1954 by Simmons-Boardman. The 1974 edition has been revised, out-of date plans have been dropped and replaced by new ones. New chapters on buying and ready-made cabinets have been added as well as ideas on updating old cabinets

690 Buildings

Neal, Charles D.
Do-it-yourself housebuilding step-by-step. Macmillan Pub. Co. 1973 246p illus $12 **690**
1 Building—Handbooks, manuals, etc.
LC 72-91256

Neal, Charles D.—Continued

This book gives "sound advice from the standpoint of a university professor who has planned and built two homes and written many books. This advice is aimed at the layman handy with tools. Planning, tools, financing, site selection, blueprints, exteriors and interiors, all are well treated, with an index, a glossary and many keys to better building added. Clear photographs throughout." Ref Services Rev

700 THE ARTS

701 The arts—Philosophy and theory

Barzun, Jacques
The use and abuse of art. Princeton Univ. Press 1974 150p $6.95   701

1 The arts—Addresses and essays 2 Art and society 3 Art, Modern—History and criticism
ISBN 0-691-09903-0   LC 73-16780

"Bollingen series"
"The A.W. Mellon lectures in the fine arts, 1973. The National Gallery of Art, Washington D.C."
Contents: Why art must be challenged; The rise of art as religion; Art the destroyer; Art the redeemer; Art and its tempter, science; Art in the vacuum of belief

These six essays "present with exceptional clarity their author's less-than-sanguine view of the state of modern art—chiefly the visual arts, but literature and music as well. Barzun examines the traditional functions of art from the Renaissance to Cubism and its proliferating successors. . . . This is debatable but provocative and civilized art criticism of a high order." Pub W

702.3 Art as a profession

Holden, Donald
Art career guide. 3d ed. rev. and enl. A guidance handbook for art students, teachers, vocational counselors, and job hunters. Watson-Guptill 1973 303p $7.95   702.3

1 Art as a profession 2 Art—Study and teaching
ISBN 0-8230-0251-9   LC 72-10192

First published 1961
This book discusses how to plan a high school program, and choose an art school. It describes the work, training, and opportunities in the fields of fine art (painting, sculpture, and printmaking), illustration, graphic design, fabric design, interior design, architecture, industrial design, photography, art teaching, are museum jobs, and crafts. It offers advice for recent graduates and professionals on writing a resumé, organizing a job hunt, planning a portfolio and handling job interviews. It includes directories of degree granting schools, professional organizations and guidance agencies, and lists sources of additional information

707 Art—Study and teaching

Read, Herbert
Education through art. [3d rev. ed.] Pantheon Bks. [1974] xxii, 328p illus 64 plates $10   707

1 Art—Study and teaching 2 Art—Psychology 3 Education—Philosophy
ISBN 0-394-49178-5   LC 74-163504

First published 1943 in England. First American edition published in 1948. This is a reissue of the third revised edition published in 1958

Drawing on findings and theories in the fields of psychology, education and esthetics, the author argues the thesis that art should be made the basis for education. A section of black and white reproductions of over 100 drawings and paintings by children with annotations indicating the mental type of the artist follows the main text

Contents: The purpose of education; The definition of art: On perception and imagination; Temperament and expression; The art of children; Unconscious modes of integration; The natural form of education; The aesthetic basis of discipline and morality; The teacher; Environment; The necessary revolution; Bibliography

709 Art—History

Kramer, Hilton
The age of avant-garde; an art chronicle of 1956-1972. Farrar, Straus 1973 565p illus $15   709

1 Art, Modern—19th century 2 Art, Modern—20th century 3 Art—History
ISBN 0-374-10238-4   LC 72-89885

"This book consists of 141 essays written between 1956 and 1972 (most from the last five or six years), mostly on painters and sculptors—from Turner and Courbet to the present (there are six essays on photographers, three on critics.) . . . In general, Kramer concentrates on artists whose work displays some kind of dialectic tension, some evidence of relation to or vital redefinition, of tradition, and comments rarely on more problematic modern developments or on 'modernist' art, much of which he finds 'devoid of moral intelligence and concerned too exclusively with aesthetic issues. As a consequence, the coverage of these essays, while broad, is erratic. . . . Despite its limitations as general art history, this is strongly recommended for all students of 19th- and 20th-century art." Choice

709.04 Art—History, 1900-

Phaidon Dictionary of twentieth-century art. Phaidon [distributed by Praeger] 1973 420p 48 plates $15   709.04

1 Art, Modern—20th century—Encyclopedias 2 Artists—Encyclopedias
ISBN 0-7148-1557-8   LC 72-86572

"Consists of some 1,750 entries of from one sentence to one page in length. About 150 of these define groups, concepts, and movements, and the rest are on painters, sculptors, and graphic artists important to the century. Artists from all over the world, both those universally recognized and those not so well known, are included. The articles are unsigned, but a list of forty authoritative contributors is given. Some bibliographic references are given, but cross-references are sparse." Cur Ref Bks

"Not included are architects, technical terms, and processes. An appendix of black-and-white reproductions of representative art works is provided. Intended for the non-specialists, the authoritative and well written text makes this a worthy addition to reference collections." Library J

709.2 Biographies of artists

Collective biographies

Havlice, Patricia Pate
Index to artistic biography. Scarecrow 1973 2v (1362p) $35   709.2

1 Artists—Indexes
ISBN 0-8108-0540-5   LC 72-6412

"Approximately 65,000 different artists from all periods, places, and backgrounds are listed in this effort to broadly index 64 basic works (in ten languages) devoted to full-length or 'who's who' type information about artists. Most source material was published in the 1960s, with a scattering earlier and a bit later. Arranged alphabetically by name, the index includes for each entry: dates, nationality, type of artist, and entry sources. . . . In addition to serving as an index, the work will be valuable for ready-reference searching to determine spelling of names, birth and death dates, and identification. (Where there are variant spellings, pseudonyms and alternate

Havlice, Patricia P.—*Continued*

names, this is so indicated.) A spot check indicates that the material, which apparently stops at about mid-1972, is accurate enough. Since there is nothing else quite like this, and given the majority of titles indexed by Havlice, the compilation will be of appreciable assistance to any large art library, as well as for numerous ready-reference sections." Choice

Bibliography: p v-viii

Individual biographies

Whistler, James Abbott McNeill

Weintraub, Stanley. Whistler; a biography. Weybright & Talley 1974 498p illus $12.50   **709.2**

ISBN 0-679-40099-0   LC 73-76570

"Whistler, always thought of as a flamboyant personality, emerges here as an extraordinary artist and a difficult person. Combative, eccentric, a perfectionist, he made enemies, masked his inner self with a bizarre façade, and always had the courage of his artistic convictions. American born, he took London as his home, though Paris, in its way, was kind to him. Ridiculed for years by the artistic establishment, he nonetheless persisted in his unique painterly vision." Pub W

The author "has met the challenge of . . . [his] rich subject with a sparkling narrative that gives us a very intimate account of the artist's life and a very illuminating portrait of the worlds in which he moved. . . . It is the artist's life to be sure, rather than his art that the biographer recounts for us with such absorbing detail." N Y Times Bk R

Sources: p469-81

709.66   History of West African art

Leuzinger, Elsy

The art of Black Africa. N.Y. Graphic 1972 378p illus $16.50   **709.66**

1 Art, African   2 Art, Primitive
ISBN 0-8212-0468-8   LC 70-186806

Original German edition published 1970

"This survey examines African art on a regional, tribal basis, with maps which locate the various types of work." Atlantic

"Although the map, index, and heavily Germanic bibliography are adequate, the sculptures shown in the plates range from indecipherable 'noble fragments' through well-loved classics and previously little-known masterpieces to recent patent fakes." Choice

Bibliography: p363-69

709.7   Indians—Art

Dockstader, Frederick J.

Indian art of the Americas; photography by Carmelo Guadagno. Mus. of the Am. Indian [1974 c1973] 304p illus maps $10   **709.7**

1 Indians—Art   LC 73-89979

Containing photographs of 500 art objects, including 24 in color, this is a catalog of a traveling exhibition whose scope "is the Indian of the North, Central and South American continents, from the time of the earliest surviving material culture to the expressions of contemporary Indian artists working in various media. . . . The selection is esthetic. . . . The source of these objects is entirely from one institution: the Museum of the American Indian, Heye Foundation, in New York City. . . . In an effort to more clearly aid in an understanding of Indian art, we have elected to present a general essay on the subject and then give a more specific consideration of items in the extended captions which accompany the specimens on exhibit. . . . For further reference, an extensive bibliography is provided." Foreword

709.73   History of art in the U.S.

The Britannica Encyclopedia of American art. Encyclopedia Britannica; distributed by Simon & Schuster [1973] 669p illus $29.95   **709.73**

1 Art, American—Encyclopedias   2 Artists, American
ISBN 0-671-21616-3   LC 73-6527

"A Chanticleer Press edition"

"A welcome addition to the increasing number of books dealing with the history of American art. The book covers the gamut of creative endeavor found in this country during the past 350 years; painting, architecture, sculpture, photography, printmaking, the decorative arts, and handcrafts are all dealt with in this compendium of American art. The 32 contributors to the encyclopedia are well-qualified historians, critics, and curators; though one may question various omissions or perhaps the selection of illustrations, the concise and informative entries are beyond reproach. The book is profusely illustrated with over 800 reproductions, 350 of which are in color. . . . [The appendices] include a guide to museums and public collections (which fails to cite some very fine, albeit small, collections of American art), a glossary of terms, and a useful bibliography." Choice

Davidson, Marshall B.

The American Heritage History of the artists' America, by Marshall B. Davidson and the editors of American Heritage. Am. Heritage [distributed by McGraw] 1973 402p illus $19.95   **709.73**

1 Art, American—History
ISBN 0-07-015437-6   LC 73-295

"The book is a kaleidoscopic view of the way American artists have seen the country's history and great personalities, the land's natural beauties and the folkways of the people. Davidson and his colleagues have written an enlightening and often anecdotal text to supplement their handsomely reproduced illustrations—some 300 in all (120 in full color), including paintings, drawings, furniture, architecture, sculpture and photos. Artists famous or little known are represented: the Peales, Copley, West, Remington, Russell and Schreyvogel, early and modern sculptors, the Ashcan School, 'naive' artists and moderns up to Pollock, Rothko et al." Pub W

"It's strictly a popular treatment and would be a good buy for smaller public libraries." Library J

724.9   20th century architecture

Scully, Vincent

Modern architecture; the architecture of democracy, by Vincent Scully, Jr. Rev. ed. Braziller 1974 158p illus (The Great ages of world architecture) $8.95   **724.9**

1 Architecture, Modern—20th century
ISBN 0-8076-0159-4   LC 74-157053

Earlier edition entered in main catalog

First published 1961. The 1974 edition "offers an opportunity to focus on the major new developments in architecture in the last twelve years, and in the light of those events, to revise and enlarge the view of modern architectural history as a whole which the original text presented. Unlike the earlier edition, the revision devotes considerable attention to city planning." Publisher's note

Bibliographical note: p135-36

728   Residential buildings. Barns

Arthur, Eric

The barn; a vanishing landmark in North America [by] Eric Arthur and Dudley Witney. N.Y. Graphic 1972 256p illus $25   **728**

1 Barns
ISBN 0-8212-0488-2   LC 72-80416

"An architect and a photographer-draftsman have produced a handsome, informative book on

Arthur, Eric—*Continued*
a building that no longer dominates the rural scene in eastern Canada and the northeastern United States. Text and pictures . . . present barns outside and in, showing clearly how the major types were constructed, explaining influences on design, and detailing the aspects that make them works of art. Colleges with art and architecture courses will want the book, as will public libraries serving artists and Americana buffs." Library J
Bibliography: p249-50

728.6 Suburban and rural type dwellings

Cobb, Betsy
Vacation houses; what you should know before you buy or build [by] Betsy & Hubbard Cobb. Dial Press 1973 261p illus $7.95
728.6
1 Houses LC 72-10831
This guide to summer houses covers financing and building costs, insurance, buying land, negotiating with real estate agents, hiring architects, blueprints, remodeling, styles and designs, and includes examples of a variety of houses (with floor plans)
All aspects of ownership "are described clearly in a comprehensive guide. Illustrated with small but clear black-and-white photographs of a wide variety of houses and vacation housing developments." Booklist

738.1 Ceramic arts—Techniques, apparatus, equipment, materials

Rhodes, Daniel
Clay and glazes for the potter. [Rev. ed] Chilton Bk. Co. 1973 330p illus $12.50 738.1
1 Pottery 2 Clay 3 Glazes
ISBN 0-8019-5633-1 LC 72-12887
First published 1957 by Greenberg
This book offers practical and technical information about ceramic materials and their use in pottery. The author first considers the composition, physical nature, drying and firing processes, various kinds, mixtures, and preparation of clay. He then focuses on the nature and early types of glazes, their reaction with oxides, glaze materials, technical calculations and formulas, compositions, textures, compounds and mixes, flaws, underglazes and overglazes, reduction firing, and special effects. The illustrations feature old and contemporary pieces from different cultures
Glossary: p306-09. Books on pottery and ceramics: p325

739.2703 Jewelry—Encyclopedias and dictionaries

Mason, Anita
An illustrated dictionary of jewellery; illus. by Diane Packer. Harper 1974 389p illus $8.95 739.2703
1 Jewelry—Encyclopedias
ISBN 0-06-012818-6 LC 73-11590
First published 1973 in England
"All aspects of jewelry, including tools and techniques, precious metals and gemstones, the history of jewelry, and biographies of notable jewelers of the past, are covered by the more than 3,000 terms defined and discussed in this volume. While there are a number of good books on each of these topics, this reviewer knows of no other that covers all fields and emphasizes concise information for easy reference. Entries range from a sentence to several pages (e.g., on bethrothal rings, necklaces, the jewelry of certain periods or locales). Line drawings illustrate many definitions. The student, craftsman, and interested layman should find this book helpful." Cur Ref Bks
Bibliography: p387-[90]

745 Decorative and minor arts. Folk art

Lipman, Jean
The flowering of American folk art, 1776-1876 [by] Jean Lipman and Alice Winchester. Viking in cooperation with the Whitney Museum of American Art 1974 288p illus $25 745
1 Folk art, American
ISBN 0-670-32120-6 LC 73-6081
"A Studio book"
"The diversity and inventive blending of the naive with a strong design sense characterize the first century of American folk art. Paintings, sculpture, exterior and interior ornamentation and constructions, and household furnishings are represented. From stitchery to paints, ironware to wood, the subject matter is prodigal as are the over 400 examples, more than 100 in color. All categories are introduced with an explanatory essay and each illustration is fully captioned. A valuable anthology, carefully researched and assembled." Booklist
Appendix includes a biographical index of artists and a bibliography

745.1 Antiques

Flayderman, Norman
Collecting tomorrow's antiques today [by] Norman Flayderman [and] Edna Lagerwall. Doubleday 1972 222p illus $7.95
745.1
1 Art objects—Collectors and collecting
ISBN 0-385-06175-7 LC 71-186021
"What items to look for among such suggested categories of twentieth-century collectibles as modern glass in limited editions or commemorative spoons, where to look and what firms or other sources account for the creations in question, and tidbits on price, potential value, and historical background compose the information gathered by the authors, experienced collectors, to whet novices' interest." Booklist
Bibliography: p176-81

745.59 Making specific objects

Newsome, Arden J.
Egg decorating, plain & fancy. Crown 1973 96p illus $5.95 745.59
1 Egg decoration
ISBN 0-517-50595-9 LC 73-82940
"Newsome takes decorated eggs out of the Easter basket and widens the inventive horizons. More than nature's eggs are dealt with—the author has numerous plans for gilding ceramic, plastic, glass, wood, wax, styrofoam, and papier maché eggs as well. Materials and methods are amply described for both real and artificial eggs. . . . The choice of decorative possibilities ranges from folk art motifs and contemporary, jeweled or painted surfaces to the elaborate hinged egg with scenic interior. An appended list of sources includes publications and a directory of suppliers, teachers, authors, and shops." Booklist

746.4 Needle- and handwork

Bacon, Lenice Ingram
American patchwork quilts; photography by Creative Photographers, Boston. Morrow 1973 190p illus $16.50 746.4
1 Coverlets
ISBN 0-688-00170-X LC 73-8041
"The history of quilt making from ancient times to the present is related in . . . narrative that draws on Bacon's own experience as a maker of quilts. The book explores quilts as practical bed coverings and as expressions of

Bacon, Lenice I.—*Continued*

ingenuity and beauty with examples handsomely presented in numerous black-and-white illustrations and colorplates. Data on making, collecting, and care of quilts is given in conclusion. Footnotes and a brief bibliography are appended." Booklist

"The book will appeal to the reader who does not wish to wade through an intense account of the evolution of patchwork, but the material here can be found in other sources." Library J

Bress, Helene

The macramé book. Scribner 1972 274p illus $12.50   746.4

1 Macramé
ISBN 0-684-12756-3   LC 79-37222

"This is the most comprehensive, useful, and attractive book on macramé to date. . . . Covering historical, instructional, and aesthetic angles, Bress has provided the complete guide for the 'macramaniac.' Clear photographs . . . portray practical and fanciful items made by the author and by macramé masters of the past and present. Large, easily interpreted diagrams accompany how-to instructions that are sufficient for beginners or for enthusiastic fans seeking new ideas. Valuable features include the chart of knots and the table of yarns (with properties, number of threads to the inch, and availability). The book also provides a list of suppliers, a bibliography, and an index. Sure to be the standard for years to come, this volume is an essential acquisition for library craft collections at all levels." Library J

Meilach, Dona Z.

Contemporary batik and tie-dye; methods, inspiration, dyes. Crown 1973 280p illus (Crown's Arts and crafts ser) $8.95   746.4

1 Batik   2 Dyes and dyeing
ISBN 0-517-50088-4   LC 72-84320

"Information about these popular dyeing techniques, from historical uses to modern applications. Basic materials and methods, as well as alternatives, are fully described, with useful diagrams." Chicago

"Special chapters treat paper batik, batik eggs, the display of finished works, and the creation of clothing and accessories. A glossary, sources of additional information, and a list of suppliers are provided." Booklist

Wilson, Erica

Erica Wilson's Embroidery book. Scribner 1973 374p illus $14.95   746.4

1 Embroidery
ISBN 0-684-10655-8   LC 78-123841

This book includes "full directions, with diagrams, for seven completely different types of embroidery: crewel, needlepoint, silk and gold thread, black work, white work, stump work, and applique." Chicago

The author "tells how to select materials, suggests methods of transferring the design, and gives excellent diagrams and clear instructions (accompanied by a sampler) for a large variety of stitches suitable to that particular type of embroidery. Even the prosaic cross stitch becomes elegant here, along with hundreds of others. Libraries will need . . . this book, which is as handsome as it is practical." Library J
Bibliography: p369

748   Glass

Goodell, Donald

The American bottle collector's price guide to historical flasks, pontils, bitters, mineral waters, inks & sodas; with photographs by Dugway Photography. Tuttle 1973 144p illus $6   748

1 Bottles—Collectors and collecting
ISBN 0-8084-1098-2   LC 72-89738

The range of values on collector's bottles are given along with a descriptive listing and hints on where to find the various types of bottles

"This guide will certainly be of value to the experienced collector as well as the novice. It gives good practical information on a subject in antiques where current knowledge is in great demand. The author has wisely chosen to indicate ranges of acceptable value rather than to cite specific prices for items listed. Libraries will find the book helpful." Library J
Bibliography: p141. Glossary: p143-44

751.4   Painting with specific mediums. Collage

Meilach, Dona Z.

Collage and assemblage; trends and techniques, by Dona Z. Meilach and Elvie Ten Hoor. Crown 1973 246p illus $8.95   751.4

1 Collage
ISBN 0-517-50577-0   LC 73-82320

Collage and assemblage are related composite media which use various materials. Collages are essentially two-dimensional and low relief pieces, while assemblages are high relief or three-dimensional sculptural forms. After an historical survey of earlier trends and movements, the authors concentrate on work executed since 1970. Considering collages first, they offer photographs along with step-by-step instructions which demonstrate various processes. These include work with papers, textured surfaces, and fabrics, transfo-collé, photo techniques and collagraphy. The descriptions and photographs in the final two chapters depict assemblages, including box assemblages

759.05   Painting—1800-1900

Clark, Kenneth

The romantic rebellion; romantic versus classic art. Harper [1974 c1973] 366p illus $15   759.05

1 Painting, Modern—19th century   2 Art, Modern—19th century   3 Artists
ISBN 0-06-010802-9   LC 72-9751

Analyzed in Essay and general literature index

First published 1973 in England

"The works of 13 artists are surveyed, and the period covered runs from the second half of the 18th century to the middle of the 19th century. Except for Goya, Piranesi, Fuseli, Constable, and Turner, all of the artists are French: David to Degas. The subtitle is somewhat misleading since the thesis of the book leads one to understand that the most 'romantic' of painters might well exhibit elements of 'classicism' in his painting. It is better to consider the author's intention as an exploration of the various elements of classicism, realism, and romanticism as they manifest themselves in the actual works of the art. The essays are eminently readable—as valuable for the specialist as for the general reader. Sir Kenneth is an extremely perceptive connoisseur of art, and he communicates his enthusiasm to the reader very effectively. While in no way a historical survey of romanticism in 19th-century painting . . . this new book is a definite contribution to studies in this area. The reproductions, both in black and white and in color, are excellent." Choice

759.13   Painting—U.S.

Tanner, Clara Lee

Southwest Indian painting; a changing art. 2d ed. Univ. of Ariz. Press 1973 477p illus map $35   759.13

1 Indians of North America—Art   2 Painting, American
ISBN 0-8165-0309-5   LC 74-160812

First published 1957

Indian tribes in Arizona and New Mexico were introduced to easel painting in the 1920's. This book describes the traditional stylistic aspects of this art form, traces its development from decorative art to easel art, and discusses the styles and work of many modern Southwest Indian painters
Bibliography: p453-58

Wyeth, N. C.
N. C. Wyeth: the collected paintings, illustrations, and murals, by Douglas Allen and Douglas Allen, Jr. With a foreword by Paul Horgan and an introduction by Richard Layton. Crown 1972 335p illus $29.95   **759.13**
ISBN 0-517-50054-X   LC 71-168323

"Tracing the career of N. C. Wyeth (father of Andrew) from early work with Howard Pyle through first successes with Western subjects for 'Scribner's' and on to 1945, this book forms an excellent survey of his achievements. ... Author Douglas Allen ... divides Wyeth's work into categories. He examines paintings of Indians and the West, religious paintings, rural scenes, advertisements, and the classics of literature. His love of the trappings of an historical era, particularly the Middle Ages and Colonial America, made his place in American art. The book is a valuable picture survey and bibliography of published works." Choice

759.4   French painting

Matisse, Henri
Henri Matisse; text by John Jacobus. Abrams 1973 184p illus (The Lib. of great painters) $22.50   **759.4**
ISBN 0-8109-0277-X   LC 72-6633

"This major monograph delves into all of Matisse's diverse talents. The emphasis is naturally on Matisse's paintings, but there are also discussions on the artist's mastery of sculpture, drawings, graphics, and book illustration. The biographical, critical essay explores the evolution of the artist's identity, mainly in terms of the artist's special interest in the human figure. Concern centers on his use of color and sense of the monumental. There are 48 excellent color plates accompanied by perceptive commentary. Numerous black-and-white illustrations, a biographical outline, and a bibliographical article are added features." Library J

"Taken as a survey of Matisse's entire oeuvre, the selection is unduly biased toward the earliest production." Choice

759.7   Russian painting

Haftmann, Werner
Marc Chagall; tr. by Heinrich Baumann and Alexis Brown. Abrams 1973 162p illus (The Lib. of great painters) $22.50   **759.7**
1 Chagall, Marc
ISBN 0-8109-0074-2   LC 73-7657

This volume "discusses in a well-translated introductory text the development of Chagall's themes, subjects, and style against the background of his biography and milieu; this section is illustrated with black-and-white illustrations. The main body of the book consists of a selection of good plates in black and white of the graphic work of the artist and of 48 superb color plates of major works. The latter are juxtaposed to full-page analytical and highly illuminating commentaries." Choice
Bibliography: p162

769   Prints

Hogarth, William
Engravings by Hogarth; 101 prints. Ed. by Sean Shesgreen. Dover [1974 c1973] xxxiii, 205p illus $13.50   **769**
ISBN 0-486-23023-6   LC 2-96411

First published 1973 in paperback
This volume reproduces 101 engravings and 10 study sketches and paintings by the eighteenth century English artist. Many of Hogarth's series or "progresses" are represented in their entirety, including A harlot's progress, A rake's progress, Before and after, and Marriage à la mode. Shesgreen offers an introductory essay which analyzes Hogarth's work and satiric, often hostile observations of contemporary England, a chronology, and editorial comments facing each of the illustrations
Bibliography: p xxxi-xxxiii

770   Photography and photographs

Feininger, Andreas
Darkroom techniques. Prentice-Hall 1974 2v ea $7.95   **770**
1 Photography   LC 73-82108

Contents: v 1 The darkroom, film development, basic photo-chemistry (ISBN 0-13-197517-X); v2 Equipment materials, contact printing, enlarging (ISBN 0-13-197533-1)

The author "supplies a detailed manual on what develops after the shutter is closed. Intended as an 'intelligent reader's guide to black-and-white darkroom techniques,' the handbook gives simple yet complete instruction for beginners and advanced photographers. ... Illustrations convey Feininger's points with added clarity, while common errors are pinpointed and methods of identifying and correcting mistakes are discussed. A short bibliography is supplied in volume one." Booklist

770.1   Photography—Philosophy and theory

Feininger, Andreas
Principles of composition in photography. Am. Photographic Bk. Pub. Co. [1972 c1973] 136p illus $6.95   **770.1**
1 Photography
ISBN 0-8174-0552-6   LC 72-77136

The author tells how to approach the tricky area of composition. In a visual exposition he leads the reader through the many elements that distinguish the technically good but artistically mediocre picture from the picture that expresses personal style

778.5   Motion pictures and television photography

Bobker, Lee R.
Making movies: from script to screen [by] Lee R. Bobker, with Louise Marinis. Harcourt 1973 304p illus $10   **778.5**
1 Moving picture photography
ISBN 0-15-155950-3   LC 72-93333

This book discusses the artistic and technical steps in the filmmaking process including the script and storyboard, production preparations, directing, cinematography, recording, editing, post-production sound, and distribution

The author "claims mainly to offer information about technical matters, but he does this within a narrow and simplistic theoretical context which limits the beginning filmmaker at the outset. Amateurs and movie fans might find 'Making movies' informative and entertaining." Choice
Includes chapter bibliographies

779   Collections of photographs

Bourke-White, Margaret
The photographs of Margaret Bourke-White; ed. by Sean Callahan; introduction by Theodore M. Brown; foreword by Carl Mydans. N.Y. Graphic 1972 208p illus maps $15   **779**
1 Photography, Journalistic 2 Photography, Artistic
ISBN 0-8212-0462-9   LC 72-80415

"From the thousands of photographs Margaret Bourke-White took during her long career, editor Sean Callahan (who worked with [the

Bourke-White, Margaret—*Continued*
photographer] during the last two years of her life) has selected more than one hundred and twenty-five representing her major interests from machines and industrial forms through to her photographic essays on people. . . . The photographs assembled range from those commissioned by the city of Cleveland and those commissioned from Fortune essays, through trips abroad to Russia, Poland and Czechoslovakia, to the years of the great drought in southwest U.S.A., the depression years, tours of South Africa and India." Best Sellers

This volume "reveals the major life works of a fine modern photographer. . . . Powerful stuff, not only of considerable technical accomplishment but exemplifying pictorial journalism of a high order and of considerable social and historic value. It also displays artistry in straight, strong compositions which pay tribute to the aesthetic superiority of black-and-white over colour." Times (London) Lit Sup

Selected bibliography: p203-08

780.1 Music—Philosophy and theory

Bookspan, Martin

101 masterpieces of music and their composers. Rev. and updated. Doubleday 1973 465p pa $2.95   780.1

1 Music—Analysis, appreciation 2 Music—History and criticism 3 Composers 4 Music—Discography
ISBN 0-385-05721-0   LC 72-84961

"Dolphin books"

First published 1968. Based on a series of articles published in Hi Fi/Stereo Review

This book provides analysis and historical background for 101 musical compositions by 36 composers from the standard concert repertoire. Included are classical European composers from Vivaldi and Bach to Bartok and Stravinsky and the American composers George Gershwin and Aaron Copland. There are biographical sketches of each composer and discussions of the best available record and tape recordings of each piece. Also included is a glossary of musical terms

Haggin, B. H.

The new listener's companion and record guide. 4th ed. Horizon Press 1974 399p music $10   780.1

1 Music—Analysis, appreciation 2 Composers 3 Music—Discography
ISBN 0-8180-1211-0   LC 73-21470

Earlier edition entered in main catalog

First published 1956 with title: The listener's musical companion. The 1974 "edition contains a supplement with additional new recordings since 1970." Publisher's note

Includes index of musical procedures, forms and terms, general index and index of performers

780.3 Music—Encyclopedias and dictionaries

Blom, Eric

(comp.) Everyman's Dictionary of music. Rev. by Sir Jack Westrup with the collaboration of John Caldwell, Edward Olleson and R. T. Beck. St Martins 1972 793p music $15   780.3

1 Music—Encyclopedias   LC 70-173562

First published 1946 in England

A "dictionary for quick reference, not for the specialist. Deals with Western music of the Christian Era. Includes terms, works, places, and biographical sketches." Winchell. Guide to Reference Books. 8th edition (Review of 4th edition)

"Music examples, some taken from composers' original scores, are reproduced, and all in all, this dictionary would seem to be invaluable to the music student or library." Pub W

Vinton, John

(ed.) Dictionary of contemporary music. Dutton 1974 834p illus music $25   780.3

1 Music—Encyclopedias 2 Musicians
ISBN 0-525-09125-4   LC 73-78096

"A handbook rather than a dictionary, this work furnishes information on questions that people are likely to have concerning concert music in the Western tradition. There are a great many articles on composers from all countries (primarily those born after 1880 or alive after 1930). Survey articles on technical and special subjects emphasize what is new and distinctive about this century's topics. There are useful articles on contemporary music in each of the major countries of the world. Many articles are signed, and most include bibliographical references. Articles on composers (perhaps three-fourths of the entries) contain basic biographical and career information, critical comments, listings of principal compositions, and bibliographical references. Jazz, popular music, Asian music, and folk music are covered only in general survey articles. Broadcasting, functional music, and music criticism are largely omitted. This work has been produced with high editorial standards, and it will admirably supplement standard music reference works in all types of libraries." Cur Ref Bks

780.9 Music—History

Jacobs, Arthur

A short history of Western music; a listener's guide. Drake Pubs. 1973 363p $8.95   780.9

1 Music, European—History and criticism 2 Composers
ISBN 0-87749-429-0   LC 72-11453

First published 1972 in England

"Nontechnical introduction for the music lover and beginning student to the history of European music from the thirteenth century down to the present day. . . . [The author] emphasizes music's chronological development from the secular songs of the troubadours to contemporary electronic compositions with discussions of the chief composers of each period and their major works, performance practices, innovations, changes in taste, and interaction with political, religious, and literary movements. Modern popular, jazz, and rock music are presented only as influences on serious classical music." Booklist

"Although this work covers much the same material as other musical histories, it should still be considered for purchase. . . . Only when the book reaches the mid-20th Century does the presentation become too cluttered. . . . For medium-sized and large libraries." Library J

The New Oxford History of music. Oxford 1973-1974 2v illus v7 $27.50, v10 $32.50   780.9

1 Music—History and criticism

Earlier volumes entered in main catalogs

Contents: v7 The age of the enlightenment, 1745-1790, ed. by Egon Wellesz (ISBN 0-19-316307-1); v10 The modern age, 1890-1960, ed. by Martin Cooper (ISBN 0-19-316310-1)

Includes bibliographies

Salzman, Eric

Twentieth-century music: an introduction. 2d ed. Prentice-Hall 1974 242p illus music (Prentice-Hall History of music ser) $8.95   780.9

1 Music—History and criticism
ISBN 0-13-935015-2   LC 73-17211

This is a survey of twentieth century music beginning with the late 19th century sources and the revolutionary works of Debussy, Stravinsky, Schoenberg, Berg and Webern, and continuing up to recent minimalist, concept, pop and multi-media developments. Includes chapter bibliographies

Partial contents: The breakdown of traditional tonality; The new tonalities: Atonality and twelve-tone music; The avant-garde and beyond; Appendix: Musical examples

780.92 Biographies of musicians

Collective biographies

Claghorn, Charles Eugene
   Biographical dictionary of American music. Parker Pub. Co. 1973 491p $12.95
                                     780.92

1 Musicians, American—Dictionaries
ISBN 0-13-076331-4   LC 73-5534

   Included are brief biographical sketches of over 5200 American composers, singers, teachers, and writers in all musical categories, from the Colonial period to the present. Listings are alphabetically arranged with cross references from composers and their works to lyricists and librettists

Green, Stanley
   The world of musical comedy; the story of the American musical stage as told through the careers of its foremost composers and lyricists; foreword by Deems Taylor. 3d ed. rev. and enl. Barnes, A.S. 1974 556p illus $17.50
                                     780.92

1 Composers, American 2 Librettists 3 Musical revues, comedies, etc.
ISBN 0-498-01409-6   LC 73-5777

   Earlier edition entered in main catalog
   First published 1960 by Ziff-Davis. The 1974 edition has been revised and brought up to date to include new material up to 1973

Pleasants, Henry
   The great American popular singers. Simon & Schuster 1974 384p illus $9.95
                                     780.92

1 Singers 2 Music, Popular (Songs, etc.)
SBN 671-21681-3   LC 73-16878

   The author "examines and evaluates the musical art of 22 . . . famous singers whose careers have spanned half a century. The criterion is that they have been originators of a style (Mildred Bailey, Bing Crosby, Elvis Presley, Jimmie Rodgers) or have carried a style to a high degree of artistic and technical fulfillment (Ella Fitzgerald, Mahalia Jackson, Peggy Lee, Frank Sinatra, Hank Williams). Jazz, blues, country-and-western, soul—the aficionados will find their favorites here. . . . Over 100 photos." Pub W
   "The author is a trained vocalist and long-established music critic who here offers a mature technical and artistic analysis. . . . Pleasants makes clear his admiration of these singers on their own grounds. . . . Few critics have combined such respectful appraisal with technical understanding of the craft. Recommended for any and all levels of libraries from high school to music school." Choice
   Glossary: p371-74

Wechsberg, Joseph
   The waltz emperors; the life and times and music of the Strauss family. Putnam 1973 272p illus $15
                                     780.92

1 Strauss family
ISBN 0-399-11167-0   LC 73-78610

   The author "interweaves the biographies of the Strausses—father Johann and his sons, Johann, Josef, and Eduard—with the pop-culture history of Vienna over the eighty-odd years they dominated the city's musical scene." New Yorker
   "The tone at times seems a bit defensive, and the generally readable, personal style is marred by an occasional banal comment. Nevertheless, this is an informative popular work—comfortable reading for the armchair musician." Library J

Individual biographies

Dylan, Bob
   Gray, Michael. Song & dance man; the art of Bob Dylan. Dutton 1972 336p illus $7.95
                                     780.92

1 Music, Popular (Songs, etc.)
ISBN 0-525-20685-X   LC 72-82693

   This book is intended as a study of Dylan's artistry. It contains an examination of his musical roots and an analysis of the influence on Dylan of such writers as Blake, Browning and T. S. Eliot. The chapters of the book correspond to the progression in Dylan's art as seen through the primary influences in each of his albums from the protest songs of his early work, the influences of drugs, mysticism and the dimensions of language Dylan is experimenting with
   "Gray has produced an insightful and comprehensive analysis. . . . By his dissection of the literary and musical influences on Dylan, by his careful analysis of Dylan's lyrics, and by his profound understanding of Dylan's significance to rock music, the author, a British teacher of literature, has convincingly placed the American composer-singer on an artistic plateau far above the average rock entertainer. . . . It will interest casual fans and serious students of contemporary popular music. Index and a useful annotated discography." Choice

Ellington, Edward Kennedy
   Music is my mistress. Doubleday 1973 522p illus $14.95
                                     780.92

1 Musicians, American
ISBN 0-385-02235-2   LC 73-83189

   "At 74, Duke Ellington reminisces about his pleasant childhood in old-fashioned Washington, D.C., his experiences with billiard sharks, gamblers and visiting pianists in Frank Holliday's poolroom, his introduction to New York's jazz world, his big bands, his fellow artists, and his State Department-sponsored travels to every part of the world. . . . [The book includes a] list of the Duke's honors and awards and a selected discography." Pub W
   The "memoirs are quintessential Ellington: articulate, witty, cosmopolitan, eclectic, and reverent. They recall only the good things, characteristically overlooking the mountains of racial and musical prejudice a middle-class black piano player has had to surmount in almost 50 years in popular music. . . . Some will be disappointed to find little here that is really about jazz; but the Duke is talking mostly of his joy in living. He also tries to describe his very personal feelings toward God." Library J
   Bibliography: p[523]

Gershwin, George
   Jablonski, Edward. The Gershwin years, by Edward Jablonski and Lawrence D. Stewart; with an introduction by Carl van Vechten. [2d ed] Doubleday 1973 416p illus $12.95
                                     780.92

1 Gershwin, Ira
ISBN 0-385-02847-4   LC 73-78334

   First published 1958
   This dual biography of the composer/lyricist brother team includes pictures and anecdotes about such associates and friends as Irving Berlin, Jerome Kern, Gertrude Lawrence, and Maurice Ravel. Snapshots of scenes from Gershwin musicals and movies are included along with family pictures. A bibliography, list of Gershwin compositions and a discography are appended
   This is a "pictorial biography—with a full, though rather too fond and defensive narrative text (why bother now, for instance, to further belittle the late Oscar Levant's claims to friendship with Gershwin?). The most valuable addition is a detailed, authoritative discography. . . . Gershwin's loyal friends have hindered as well as helped his biographers; and the devoted Ira Gershwin has laudably and understandably, played a part in perpetuating this simplified image of his younger brother." N Y Times Bk R

Miller, Glenn
   Simon, George T. Glenn Miller and his orchestra. Crowell 1974 473p illus $10
                                     780.92

1 Bands (Music)
ISBN 0-690-00470-2   LC 74-1017

   The author "observed at first hand Miller's development as musician, arranger, band organizer and leader, successful businessman. Here are full details of his personal and musical relationships, the world of big bands during the 30s and 40s; portraits of Miller as seen by friends and associates; nostalgic accounts of

Miller, Glenn—*Continued*

performances at the Glen Island Casino, Meadowbrook, the Palladium; Major Miller and his great AAF band." Pub W

"The definitive biography of Miller by the man most qualified to write it. . . . He explains the origins of the Miller style and also of the Miller personality, which most people only glimpsed. . . . It is replete with excellent photographs, carefully edited interviews, and historical documentation—all integrated with George Simon's characteristically polished writing." Choice

Recordings by Glenn Miller and his orchestras: p451-56

Rubinstein, Arthur

My young years. Knopf 1973 478p illus $10   780.92

ISBN 0-394-46890-2   LC 70-171147

This autobiography by the 86-year-old pianist recalls the time between his birth in Lodz, Poland, in 1887 and "May, 1917, when, just out of his twenties and already a figure on the world music scene, he sailed from Cadiz in Spain for his South American debut in Buenos Aires. Part 1, 'Childhood in Poland,' is an account of the little boy's predilection for music. . . . Three other parts, 'Growing Up in Berlin,' 'On My Own,' and 'England & the First World War' complete this . . . self-portrait." Christian Science Monitor

"One may wonder a little at the author's seemingly total recall of events 50 to 80 years ago but no one can possibly resist his fascinating reconstruction of the musical life of an era long since past. Rubinstein knew all the great musicians of Europe from the turn of the century on—Joachim Ysaye, Paderewski, Chaliapin, Saint-Saens, Szymanowski, Stravinsky, etc., as well as the great impresario Diaghilev and the leading members of high society in all the European capitals." Choice

Smith, Bessie

Albertson, Chris. Bessie. Stein & Day 1972 253p illus $7.95   780.92

1 Blues (Songs, etc.)
ISBN 0-8128-1406-1   LC 79-163353

This "biography of Bessie Smith, the greatest female blue singer who ever lived, is based mainly on interviews with Ruby Walker, her niece, and on statements from others who were close to Bessie. Albertson, a jazz promoter, critic, and writer, has uncovered certain information which directly contradicts previous assumptions about Smith. . . . This very readable story, which concentrates on Smith's problems and personal tragedies, will be required reading for all blues fans. There are many pictures which appear for the first time, as well as a discography of long-playing albums." Library J

Bibliography: p243-44

780.973 Music of the U.S.

Hitchcock, H. Wiley

Music in the United States: a historical introduction. 2d ed. Prentice-Hall 1974 286p music (Prentice-Hall History of music ser) $8.95   780.973

1 Music, American—History and criticism
ISBN 0-13-608398-6   LC 73-19751

First published 1969

This survey of American music contains information on colonial sacred, early American secular, nineteenth century vernacular and cultivated, and various types of twentieth century music, including jazz, electronic, pop and rock. The work of composers and performers is also considered

Includes chapter bibliographies

Pavlakis, Christopher

The American music handbook. Free Press 1974 xx, 836p $25   780.973

1 Music, American—Handbooks, manuals, etc. 2 Music, American—Directories
LC 73-2127

The author has compiled a "directory to many aspects of concert, serious, or classical music. Over 5,000 entries cover service institutions and organizations of all kinds, performing organizations, individual musicians and composers, music festivals and competitions, institutions that teach or provide access to music, communications media, and suppliers and manufacturers of instruments and other music materials. A name index provides detailed access to the 13 major sections. Pavlakis does not claim exhaustivity (e.g., only 166 of an estimated 1,204 symphony orchestras in this country are described). However, he usually outlines well justified criteria for his listings." Cur Ref Bks

781.5 Musical forms. Ragtime

Schafer, William J.

The art of ragtime; form and meaning of an original Black American art [by] William J. Schafer and Johannes Riedel; with assistance from Michael Polad and Richard Thompson. La. State Univ. Press 1973 249p illus music $10   781.5

1 Jazz music 2 Negro music
ISBN 0-8071-0220-2   LC 72-89115

This is a musicological study of ragtime piano music as well as a social history of the racial attitudes which temporarily minimized its influence. The compositions of Joplin, Scott, and Lamb are analyzed. Music for banjo and piano is included in appendix

"The strength of this fine book lies in its careful language about music and musical effects, notoriously difficult subjects. . . . Read the appropriate parts of [it] with a certain amount of care and you will know, in terms of music, everything there is to know about ragtime. [This is] a superb book." N Y Times Bk R

Bibliography of ragtime: p226-39

781.7 Music of ethnic and national orientation

Nettl, Bruno

Folk and traditional music of the western continents; with chapters on Latin America by Gérard Béhague. 2d ed. Prentice-Hall 1973 258p illus music (Prentice-Hall History of music ser) $8.95   781.7

1 Folk songs—History and criticism 2 Music, Primitive—History and criticism
ISBN 0-13-322941-6   LC 72-10010

First published 1965

After a description of the general characteristics of traditional music and its cultural context, this book considers European, sub-Sahara African, American Indian, Latin American, Afro-American and modern North American folk music

Includes chapter bibliographies and discographies

Roach, Hildred

Black American music: past and present. Crescendo Pub. 1973 199p illus maps music $9.50   781.7

1 Negro music—History and criticism 2 Negro musicians
ISBN 0-87597-079-6   LC 72-87762

This book begins with the slave era and the heritage of Africa, developing into various types of folk music from which emerge the first Black professionals, the composer-performers of the early minstrel shows, and eventually the originators of jazz. Also discussed are the art music composers who drew from non-Black sources. The author uses musical examples along with the text to describe music both as music and as it relates to the Black experience

Readings and recordings: p183-91. List of musical terms: p191-93

782.8 Theater music. Musical comedies

Burton, Jack
 The blue book of Broadway musicals; with additions by Larry Freeman. Century House [1974] 335p illus $18   782.8
 1 Music, Popular (Songs, etc.)—History and criticism   2 Musical revues, comedies, etc.
 Earlier edition entered in main catalog
 First published 1952. The 1974 edition has been revised and updated to include information on shows through 1974
 Includes discographies

Laufe, Abe
 Broadway's greatest musicals. Illus. ed. Funk 1973 502p illus $10   782.8
 1 Musical revues, comedies, etc.
                                       LC 72-7574
 Earlier edition entered in main catalog
 First published 1970. The 1973 edition "adds a few black-and-white illustrations to what is basically a reprint of the earlier edition for the first 360 pages, with a new section of some 15 pages on the late 1960s, and a new chapter of 20 pages on the early 1970s. The brief bibliography has not been revised, even to show new editions of standard works, although the appendix on longest running musicals has been updated through April 1972. . . . [Some libraries having earlier edition] might find that the additional information does not justify purchase." Cur Ref Bks

The New York Times Great songs of Broadway. Introductions by Alan Jay Lerner and Jule Styne. Quadrangle Bks. 1973 320p illus $17.50   782.8
 1 Musical revues, comedies, etc.   2 Songs
 ISBN 0-8129-0288-2   LC 72-85051
 Two songwriters "have arrayed chronologically, from 1904 to 1971, 73 songs from 63 Broadway shows, with composer and title indexes, and hopeful introductions by both of these gentlemen, who are optimistic that the Broadway musical of the old days will again become popular. Arranged for voice, piano and guitar, it is grand for nostalgic evenings with the guitar or at the piano, singing Cole Porter and Rodgers and Hart and Lerner and Styne, for the compilers haven't been too modest to rightfully include some of their own. Some small facsimiles of the front pages of playbills and songs are appended." Ref Services Rev
 "Recommended, especially for libraries that do not collect sheet music." Library J

784 Vocal music. Songs

The Best of Broadway. . . . Chappell Music Co. [distributed by Crown. 1974 c1973] 335p illus music pa $6.95   784
 "Complete words and music; 80 great songs of the American musical theatre arranged for piano, vocal and guitar; foreword by Richard Rodgers." Title page
 "The word 'best' in a title invariably invokes arguments. This book, in its inclusions and exclusions, is no exception, but it certainly contains many generally acknowledged best songs of the Broadway theater. . . . Some of what is included did not appear in the original production: e.g., lyrics to the title song of 'Fiddler on the Roof' and different lyrics to 'Sunrise, sunset.' Often the arrangements and continuity are not those of the stage productions. There is a useful foreword by Richard Rodgers giving a short history of the form." Choice

Fremont, Robert A.
 (ed.) Favorite songs of the nineties; complete original sheet music for 89 songs; with an introduction by Max Morath. Dover 1973 401p illus music pa $6.95   784
 1 Music, Popular (Songs, etc.)
 ISBN 0-486-21536-9   LC 72-92765
 "The Dover Series of playing editions"
 This book consists of reproductions of the sheet music for 89 popular songs written from the mid-1880's through the first decade of the twentieth century, including such perennial favorites as "After the ball," "The band played on," "Daisey Bell," "Give my regards to Broadway," and "My wild Irish Rose"

100 best songs of the 20's and 30's; introduction by Richard Rodgers. Harmony Bks. 1973 398p $15   784
 1 Music, Popular (Songs, etc.)
 ISBN 0-517-50368-9   LC 73-75348
 A "collection of popular songs of the 1920s and 1930s, drawn primarily from Broadway shows and motion picture scores. It contains original arrangements for voice, piano, and (occasionally) guitar. Because of copyright complications, the compilers have omitted some significant songs from the two decades. . . . The spiral binding and full-sized reproductions of the sheet music and lyrics make the collection practical as a song book for vocalists and instrumentalists. . . . And as a social document bringing together the popular music of two important decades of American history, the collection is cursory, yet provocative. . . . Four useful indices: title, chorus line, first line, and composer and lyricist." Choice

784.01 Vocal music—Indexes

Lewine, Richard
 Songs of the American theater; a comprehensive listing of more than 12,000 songs, including selected titles from film and television productions [by] Richard Lewine and Alfred Simon; introduction by Stephen Sondheim. Dodd 1973 820p $15   784.01
 1 Music, Popular (Songs, etc)—Indexes   2 Songs, American   3 Musical reviews, comedies, etc.
 ISBN 0-396-06657-7   LC 72-3931
 A successor to the author's Encyclopedia of theatre music, published in 1961
 This work lists all theater songs, from 1925 to 1971 and includes a selective list of the most important from 1900 to 1925. Theater songs, including selected songs from film and television, are first listed alphabetically by title together with the composer lyricist, show of origin, and date. Productions are then listed alphabetically by title giving the date, number of performances, the composer and lyricist, the songs in order of their appearance, and where applicable, cast albums, vocal scores, folio publications, and awards. The following section deals with shows chronologically
 "Without any descriptive matter, this is mainly an identification source for reference." Booklist
 Includes an index of composers and lyricists

785 Instrumental ensembles and their music

Ewen, David
 Orchestral music, its story told through the lives and works of its foremost composers. Watts, F. 1973 312p illus (Mainstreams of music v2) $9.95   785
 1 Orchestral music—History and criticism   2 Orchestra   3 Composers
 ISBN 0-531-02619-1   LC 72-10839
 Companion volume to the author's: Opera, entered in main catalog, class 782.1
 "An excellent introduction to orchestral music from its beginning in the 16th Century through the 20th Century. Mainstreams of development in European, Russian, Scandinavian, English, and American music are traced through the lives and works of trend-setting major composers (e.g., Haydn, Brahms, Berlioz, Grieg, Sibelius, Britten, Cage). Interweaving of biographical and musicological details . . . contribute to the copious background information. Also provided is a concise run-down on the modern symphony orchestra and sample seating arrangement chart. Clearly written generously illustrated with old prints and photographs, and including a glossary and index, this is an exceptionally attractive and informative reference book." Library J

790.2 The performing arts

The National directory for the performing arts and civic centers [1974]; author of the idea: Beatrice Handel, editors: Janet Spencer [and] Nolanda Turner. Handel & Co. 1973 604p $24   **790.2**

1 Performing arts—Directories 2 Centers for the performing arts—Directories
ISBN 0-913766-00-3

This is the first issue of a projected "annual directory to the dance, theater, and vocal and instrumental music arts in all 50 states. . . . [It] is arranged alphabetically state by state and by city under the states. All types of performing arts activities are identified. Facilities for performing are cited by name, address including zip code, and telephone number. Other . . . information given includes date of founding, name of manager and directors, type of organization (civic, profit, non-profit), season, sources of income, and seating capacity." Booklist

"Not only is this a publisher's first, but it also heralds the birth of a much needed reference annual on the nation's performing arts centers. . . . All major libraries . . . should find this work of immense value because of the increasing and demanding roles society's playing in the development and funding of the arts." Library J

791.43 Motion pictures

Adamson, Joe

Groucho, Harpo, Chico and sometimes Zeppo; a history of the Marx Brothers and a satire on the rest of the world. Simon & Schuster 1973 464p illus $10   **791.43**

1 Marx Brothers 2 Moving pictures
ISBN 0-671-2145-6   LC 72-87944

The author describes the film comedians' "early days in vaudeville and on Broadway (including . . . sketches of each brother), and shows how the varied elements of their later successes were created by trial and error before live audiences. Each film is . . . analyzed, and a detailed breakdown of the comedy sequences is interwoven with . . . selections of the wackier dialogue. . . . Adamson also chronicles and analyzes their sad decline as the later films degenerated into mechanical formula routines." Library J

"A thoroughly researched, thoroughly entertaining survey. . . . Adamson has included dozens of stills and provided an index, notes, and bibliography, all useful. . . . The author surveys, appreciates, and captures much of the Marx brothers' spirit—a refreshing change in an area too often dominated by the pathologically serious. . . . A useful addition to the history of American film comedy, for the general reader more than the film historian." Choice

Blum, Daniel

A new pictorial history of the talkies. Rev. and enl. by John Kobal. Putnam 1973 379p illus $10   **791.43**

1 Moving pictures—History
ISBN 0-399-11213-8   LC 73-77887

Earlier edition entered in main catalog
First published 1958 with title: A pictorial history of the talkies. The 1974 edition "has been updated and enlarged with text and illustrations through 1973." Library J

Finch, Christopher

The art of Walt Disney; from Mickey Mouse to the Magic Kingdoms; with a special essay by Peter Blake. Abrams 1973 458p illus $45   **791.43**

1 Disney, Walt 2 Disney (Walt) Productions
ISBN 0-8109-0122-6   LC 73-4639

"A lavish, expensive, and surprisingly informative study of the cinematic world of Walt Disney and the studio he created. Finch studies the many facets of the Disney empire from its modest beginnings to the apotheosis of Disneyland and provides significant details and assessments of the animated cartoons, live-action films, and especially the full-length animated features which were Disney's chief contribution to cinematic history. Finch also sketches Disney's role in the growth and development of the Disney Studio. . . . Excellent reproductions of sketches, studies, and complete animated frames along with particulars of animation techniques and problems give a good idea of the Disney Studio's artistic achievement. Less attention is paid to the offshoots of Disney films—comic strips, television programs—but several chapters are devoted to the social and cultural ramifications of Disneyland and Walt Disney World, including a study of Disney World as Experimental Prototype Community of Tomorrow." Booklist

Bibliography: p453-54

Higham, Charles

The art of the American film, 1900-1971. Doubleday 1973 322p illus $12.50   **791.43**

1 Moving pictures—History
ISBN 0-385-06935-9   LC 70-186026

This is a survey of American films and the personalities who produced and directed them

"This book may seem at first glance to be just one more history of the American motion picture. There are some distinctive features in it, however. For one, the approach is through directors and hence the history is only loosely chronological, despite the division into decades of film making; and besides, the comments are fresh and original." Best Sellers

Kael, Pauline

Deeper into movies. Little 1973 458p $12.95   **791.43**

1 Moving pictures
ISBN 0-316-48176-9   LC 72-11565

"An Atlantic Monthly Press book"
Analyzed in Essay and general literature index

This is a collection of over 150 movie reviews written between 1969 and 1972. "Kael writes so well, cares so deeply about motion pictures as a form of creative art, brings such knowledge to her criticism, that some readers may feel they derive more sheer enjoyment from her writing than from many of the films she writes about. She is a sophisticated critic, but does not posture: she is usually as indignant about sloppy sentimental cinema as she is about shock for shock's sake. She rejoices in the honest ethnic attempt in 'Fiddler on the Roof,' shows impatience with the purplish excess of 'Women in Love' and 'The Music Lovers.' As for foreign films, they're not all masterpieces —and she says why." Pub W

Kubrick, Stanley

A clockwork orange; based on the novel by Anthony Burgess. Abelard-Schuman 1972 unp illus $7.95   **791.43**

ISBN 0-200-00003-9   LC 72-10604

A shot-by-shot analysis of the film describing the exploits of Alex, a 15-year-old psychopath who roams the streets of London indulging in acts of violence and sadism. In this story set of the future, Alex undergoes a corrective brainwashing

'Spoken dialogue accompanies "the pictures at the appropriate point, so that what we have is an almost completely effective aide-mémoire for the film, which is, after all, one of the principal reasons for publishing a screenplay in the first place. It is an example which might well be followed for other screenplays in the future, because it is worth the extraordinary effort and checking that it takes. Recommended for all film collections and general collections on the arts." Choice

Robinson, David

The history of world cinema. Stein & Day 1973 440p illus $10   **791.43**

1 Moving pictures—History
ISBN 0-8128-1476-2   LC 76-187546

The scope of this volume "ranges from experiments with cinematography in 1895 through the achievements of Griffith in the U.S. and Eisenstein in Russia to present kinetic films and underground cinema. The author is concerned with four groups who in combination

Robinson, David—*Continued*
condition the enjoyment of films—artists, businessmen, technicians, and audiences. Three appendixes include a note on animated films, selected filmographies, and a multilingual bibliography." Booklist

Sarris, Andrew
The primal screen; essays on film and related subjects. Simon & Schuster 1973 337p $9.95   **791.43**

1 Moving pictures
ISBN 0-671-21341-5   LC 72-90401
Analyzed in Essay and general literature index
A collection of the author's articles of the 1960's and 1970's which have appeared previously in such publications as Film Culture, The New York Times, Mid-Century and The Village Voice
"Sarris, one of the two or three most significant critics of film in America, has done more than any other critic to reverse the trend of critical condescension towards American films. . . . These essays discuss the forties, some of his favorite stars, Rogers and Astaire, political films, Keaton, Sternberg, Lloyd, Judy Garland, and move off into some consideration of arts and letters. All of it is, of course, strongly 'auteuristic,' opinionated, dogmatic, frustrating, and stimulating. It is impossible to agree with any considerable quantity of Sarris, but to fail to read him or to fail to make him available to the student of film is to remain in a kind of critical ignorance." Choice

Solomon, Stanley J.
(ed.) The classic cinema; essays in criticism. Harcourt 1973 354p illus pa $3.95
791.43

1 Moving pictures
ISBN 0-15-507629-9   LC 72-94995
Analyzed in Essay and general literature index
"Fourteen films from the U.S., France, Germany, Italy, Russia, and Sweden are presented with a common format of film credits, editorial introduction, and several essays by outstanding critics such as Charles Higham, David Bordwell, and Pauline Kael, who comment on Welles' 'Citizen Kane,' and Stanley Kaufmann, Richard Roud, and John Bragin, who write on Antonioni's 'The red desert.' As in any anthology, one may question the choice from an artist's work. Why 'Vertigo' rather than 'Psycho' from Hitchcock? 'Satyricon' rather than 'La dolce vita' from Fellini. But Solomon's well-documented choices exercise his editorial privilege. Unless one has seen or knows of the films discussed, the text may seem esoteric; but for what it aims for and accomplishes this compilation of critical analyses deserves a hard cover for library acquisition." Choice
Filmographies and selected bibliographies: p339-50

Stephenson, Ralph
The animated film. Barnes, A.S. 1973 206p illus (The International Film guide ser) pa $2.95   **791.43**

1 Moving picture cartoons
ISBN 0-498-01202-6   LC 72-1785
First published in England 1967 with title: Animation in the cinema
"This history is based generally on an earlier work, 'Animation in the Cinema' and much of the material is the same." Author's note
Partial contents: Disney and his contemporaries; Animation in Canada and Britain; French animation from Cohl to Kamler; Puppets and cartoons in Czechoslovakia; Humour and artistry in Italy; Present trends, abstract and computer animation; Bibliography; Filmographies

Taylor, John Russell
The Hollywood musical [by] John Russell Taylor [and] Arthur Jackson. McGraw 1971 278p illus $12.95   **791.43**

1 Moving pictures—History 2 Musical revues, comedies, etc.—History 3 Moving pictures—Biography
ISBN 0-07-062953-6   LC 70-139565
"This book is much more than a romantic return to the past. This is a serious treatment of the musical comedy on the screen. It is not definitive, it handles too much material for any depth, but the observations on various screen musicals are sound and sometimes provocative. The first part of the book is analysis by trends, directors, stars, rather than by chronology. Then there is a fine filmography; it makes no attempt at completeness but contains a tremendous amount of material—year of making, director, cast, songs and who sang which one; the only thing missing is a summary. After that is an alphabetical list of artists and reference to their performances. The illustrations are abundant and good and they include some excellent stills from movies. Lacking at the end is an index to the perceptive ninety-page commentary that starts the volume." Best Sellers

791.4303 Motion pictures—Encyclopedias and dictionaries

Halliwell, Leslie
The filmgoer's companion. 4th ed. . . .
Hill & Wang 1974 873p $25   **791.4303**

1 Moving pictures—Encyclopedias
ISBN 0-8090-4484-6   LC 75-116875
Earlier edition entered in main catalog
First published 1965 in England. The 1974 edition has been "entirely revised, reset and much enlarged. Over 500 unusual illustrations." Title page

792 Theater (Stage presentations)

Moore, Sonia
The Stanislavski system; the professional training of an actor. Digested from the teachings of Konstantin S. Stanislavski. New rev. ed. Viking 1974 xxi, 106p $5.95
792

1 Stanislavskiĭ, Konstantin Sergeevich 2 Acting
ISBN 0-670-66694-7   LC 73-13290
Earlier edition entered in main catalog
First published 1960 with title: The Stanislavski method. The 1974 edition has been brought up to date in the light of recent publications on Stanislavski in the Soviet Union. It includes a new section on emotional memory

792.01 Theater—Indexes

The New York Times Directory of the theater; introduction by Clive Barnes. Arno Press published in cooperation with Quadrangle/The N.Y. Times Bk. Co. 1973 1009p illus $25   **792.01**

1 Theater—Indexes 2 Theater—New York (City)—Reviews 3 New York Times—Indexes
ISBN 0-8129-0364-1   LC 73-3054
"Primarily an index to the theater reviews published in the New York Times from 1920 to 1970. Most of the volume is a personal-name index listing all persons mentioned in the reviews (actors, producers, dramatists, adaptors, directors, designers, musical directors), with the names of the productions and the date of the 'Times' which carried the review. There is also a title index in the volume, as well as brief biographies of all the critics who served the paper during the half century, listings of recipients of the major theater awards of the period, and reprints of articles about the awards. The book is essential for maximum benefit usage of the reviews, but—with the depth of its indexing and the guide it provides to the American theater of the 20th Century—it is also helpful to collections which may not have the reviews." Library J

792.09 Theater—History

Atkinson, Brooks
Broadway. Rev. ed. Macmillan Pub. Co. 1974 564p illus $12.95   **792.09**

1 Theater—New York (City)—History
ISBN 0-02-504180-0   LC 74-12077

Atkinson, Brooks—*Continued*

Earlier edition entered in main catalog
First published 1970. The 1974 edition has been revised and expanded with "new chapters on the latest Tony awards, theater financing, Joe Papp and the Shakespeare Festival, and Blacks on Broadway; biographical sketches of Jason Robards, Colleen Dewhurst, Julie Harris, Zoe Caldwell, Christopher Plummer, Zero Mostel, Maureen Stapleton, George C. Scott, Geraldine Page, Jessica Tandy, and Hume Cronyn; thirty new photographs." Publisher's note

Wilson, Garff B.

Three hundred years of American drama and theatre; from Ye bear [sic] and ye cubb to Hair. Prentice-Hall 1973 536p illus $4.95
 792.09

1 Theater—U.S.—History 2 American drama—History and criticism
ISBN 0-13-920314-1 LC 72-3808

This study of the development of dramatic art in America from 1665 to 1972 explores the history of both drama and theatre and discusses the relation between the two and how they were influenced by the historical events of the country
Selected bibliography: p508-15

793.8 Magic

Christopher, Milbourne

The illustrated history of magic. Crowell 1973 452p illus $14.95 793.8

1 Magic—History 2 Magicians
ISBN 0-690-43165-1 LC 73-10390

The author's account of magicians from ancient times to the twentieth century "includes stories of the most famous illusions, feats of legerdemain and mind-reading along with biographies of Blitz, Carter, Nicola, Thurston, Houdini, Carl and Adelaide Herrmann and many others." Pub W

"A physically beautiful book, written in an interesting, informative style, it will be useful at any level and is far more than a coffee-table edition. The book is good reading, good viewing, and, perhaps most amazing of all, the author reveals very little of the secrets behind the tricks, while revealing quite a few little-known, spellbinding details about the idiosyncrasies of various magicians." Choice
Bibliography: p435-39

Kay, Marvin

The Stein and Day Handbook of magic; illus. by Al Kilgore. Stein & Day 1973 310p illus $10 793.8

1 Magic 2 Tricks
ISBN 0-8128-1628-5 LC 73-81793

"In order to 'show the unpolished performer how to become a magical entertainer,' the author depicts not only the rudiments of about 50 magic tricks, but emphasizes their display and effect. There are useful chapters on show planning and audience communication, including tips on do's and don'ts. Performing before children's groups, hospital groups, senior citizens, etc., is considered." Library J

"It is such an excellent treatise, lucidly written and illustrated, that if read and followed it can't help extending the intelligent practice and appreciation of conjuring." N Y Times Bk R

794.1 Chess

Horowitz, I. A.

Learn chess quickly [by] A. I. [sic] Horowitz; with photographs and diagrams. New, rev. and enl. ed. of A picture guide to beginner's chess. Doubleday 1973 218p illus $6.95 794.1

1 Chess
ISBN 0-385-06890-5 LC 73-14139

"A Chancellor Hall book"
First published 1956 by Harvey House
"The information is elementary and clearly presented with photographs and diagrams illustrating basic moves and ploys and the approach is intended to encourage the new player." Booklist
Glossary: p214-17. Bibliography: p218

The world chess championship [by] Al Horowitz; a history. Macmillan Pub. Co. 1973 291p illus $6.95 794.1

1 Chess LC 72-80175

"A survey of famous contestants and their important games from the first of the international chess tournaments in 1851 to the Fischer-Spassky match in 1972." Booklist
This "book can be recommended to younger and general readers; little technical knowledge of chess is necessary to enjoy the interesting story of events and personalities." Choice

Roberts, Richard

Fischer/Spassky: The New York Times Report on the chess match of the century, by Richard Roberts, with Harold C. Schonberg [and others]. Quadrangle Bks. 1972 218p illus $7.95 794.1

1 Chess 2 Fischer, Bobby 3 Spasskiĭ, Boris Vasil'evich
ISBN 0-8129-0302-1 LC 72-90465

"Background remarks on Iceland, site of the 1972 Fischer-Spassky chess match, general notes on pieces and plays, a rundown of each day's events and game, profile comments concerning both players, and appendixes of international tournament rules and regulations and special rules for the Fischer/Spassky match comprise [this] panoramic report." Booklist

795 Games of chance

Goren, Chas. H.

Goren's Modern backgammon complete. Doubleday 1974 208p illus $7.95 795

1 Backgammon
ISBN 0-385-01014-1 LC 73-14120

"A Chancellor Hall book"
This guide explains how the game is played, what the basic strategies are and what are the best moves for every possible opening throw
Glossary: p205-08

Scarne, John

Scarne's Encyclopedia of games. Harper 1973 628p illus $13.95 795

1 Cards 2 Games
ISBN 06-013813-0 LC 72-79691

"After an outline of the general rules applying to all card games, chapters are devoted to draw poker, stud poker, rummy games, gin rummy, canasta, bridge: contract and auction, other games in the whist family, pinochle with its many variations, other members of the Bezique family, cribbage and how it is played, casino, the Big Euchre family, the Heart Group, the All-Fours Group, Banking card games, the stops games, skarney children and family card games (including I Doubt It, Old Maid, Authors, War, Donkey, etc.), miscellaneous card games (including partnership tressette, briscola, German solo, etc.), solitaire and patience games, tile games (including dominoes, mah-jongg), dice and their many games, chess, checkers and teeko, games requiring special equipment (including backgammon, parcheesi, halma, mancala, solitaire, etc.), lottery and guessing games and parlour games for all." Ref Services Rev

This is "a very comprehensive and useful source of information on games. . . . All but the smallest library will want both reference and circulating copies on hand for parlor-sporting readers." Cur Ref Bks

Scarne's New Complete guide to gambling. Fully rev. expanded, updated ed. Simon & Schuster 1974 xxii, 871p illus $14.95 795

1 Gambling
ISBN 0-671-21734-8 LC 74-11701

Earlier edition entered in main catalog
First published 1961 with title: Scarne's

Scarne, John—*Continued*
Complete guide to gambling. The 1974 edition has been partly rewritten to include "the Law and Off-Track Betting; the changes in baseball, football, and basketball betting resulting from the various leagues' expansions and play-off systems; Greyhound Dog Racing; Jai-Alai; State Lotteries and Rules and Strategy; Contract Bridge; and Backgammon." Publisher's note
Glossary: p829-53

795.4 Card games

Gibson, Walter B.
Hoyle's Modern encyclopedia of card games; rules of all the basic games and popular variations. Doubleday 1974 398p illus pa $3.95   **795.4**
1 Cards
ISBN 0-385-07680-0   LC 73-163085
"A Dolphin handbook"
Arranged alphabetically according to the names of each specific game, this guide gives descriptions and explanations of rules and techniques for each game and its variations. Included are special sections for the varieties of pinochle, poker, and solitaire. A glossary-index featuring definitions of terms and page references is also included

Scarne, John
Scarne on cards. Updated enl. ed. 75 illus. by George Karger, including a photographic section on cheating at cards. Crown 1974 535p illus $9.95   **795.4**
1 Cards
ISBN 0-517-51541-5   LC 73-91527
Earlier edition entered in main catalog
First published 1949. For the 1974 edition "all the official rules are brought up to date to reflect the changes that have occurred over the years. Scarne includes new variations as well as new games and mathematical values of the games and the probabilities and percentages reflected by his latest researches. . . . All the original hundreds of favorite games are here, and for Bridge buffs there is a new section on Contract and Auction Bridge, including detecting cheating; new games such as Skarney, . . . Monte; and Chinese Fan Tan; and new, expanded chapters on Poker, Gin, Canasta, Baccarat, banking card games, and others." Publisher's note

796.03 Sports—Encyclopedias and Dictionaries

Guinness Sports record book . . . [comp.] by Norris McWhirter & Ross McWhirter. Sterling illus $3.95   **796.03**
1 Sports—Encyclopedias   LC 73-180468
"Taken from the Guinness Book of world records [entered in main catalog class 032]." Title page
First published 1972 and periodically revised to keep material up to date
This compilation presents records set in over sixty sports from archery to yachting and includes even such sports and games as auto racing, bridge, chess, scrabble and tiddleywinks

796.32 Basketball

Hollander, Zander
(ed.) The modern encyclopedia of basketball. Rev. ed. Four Winds 1973 xxi, 547p illus $14.95   **796.32**
1 Basketball—Encyclopedias 2 Basketball—Statistics   LC 70-81705
"An Associated Feature book"
First published 1969
This book "covers the sport from its invention in 1891, but emphasizes the modern era. Coverage is broad, including not only professional and college teams, but also State high school championship winners since 1938. Along with the usual statistics and team records, there are feature stories on the stars, teams, coaches, referees, and the Globetrotters." Cur Ref Bks
Further reading: p523-27

Holzman, Red
Holzman's Basketball: winning strategy and tactics [by] Red Holzman and Leonard Lewin. Macmillan Pub. Co. 1973 242p illus $6.95   **796.32**
1 Basketball   LC 72-90551
"This book is a complete guide to basketball. All fundamental phases of the game are carefully outlined from a professional standpoint. Adding to the book's interest are Holzman's personal observations of professional players making these fundamentals work for them. This in-depth book includes numerous diagrams and illustrations which clarify the various strategies and tactics of offense and defense." Library J
"The chapter on the player's viewpoint, explaining guard play, forward play, and center play, is a masterpiece. The book is very well written and Holzman's explanation of patterns, using the pro-basketball players names, results in better understanding of every aspect of play. This book can be read and understood thoroughly by basketball players from junior high through the college." Choice

796.352 Golf

Evans, Webster
(comp.) Encyclopedia of golf. [New ed] St Martins 1974 320p illus $10.95   **796.352**
1 Golf—Encyclopedias   LC 73-88040
First published 1971 in England. First American edition 1972
"Through the use of A to Z entries, Evans presents information on the game's history, origin and meaning of terms, development of clubs and balls, golf in various countries, rules, and biographies of leading personalities. . . . There are line drawings (sketches of notable golf courses might be a very useful feature in some libraries) and photographs." Cur Ref Bks

Golf Magazine's Encyclopedia of golf; ed. by Robert Scharff and the editors of Golf Magazine; assisted by Peter D. Eaton. Updated [ed.] Harper 1973 424p illus $13.95   **796.352**
1 Golf
ISBN 0-06-011569-6   LC 73-173401
First published 1970
The majority "of the material in this book appeared in one form or another in 'Golf' magazine during the more than ten years of its publication, some material was contributed from other sources." Acknowledgements
"The contents consist of a brief history of the game, results of tournaments and championships, a who's who, articles on golf equipment, the principles of golf, rules and etiquette, descriptions of championship courses and a glossary." Booklist [1970 edition]

Nicklaus, Jack
Golf my way, by Jack Nicklaus with Ken Bowden; illus. by Jim McQueen. Simon & Schuster 1974 264p illus $9.95   **796.352**
1 Golf
ISBN 0-671-21702-X   LC 73-14090
"This is the only book written by golf's number one player that covers in depth his entire technique of the game as he plays it, from top to bottom. The intellectual and scholarly dedication that Nicklaus brings to his game is explained fully, and the reader will find that there are many phases of his game that are unorthodox. . . . The book has 70 full-page and double-spread illustrations, 24 of which are in full color. These illustrations are excellent and well documented. . . . This book is highly recommended for all college and physical education libraries, and would be excellent reading for anyone interested in the game of golf." Choice

796.357 Baseball

The Baseball encyclopedia. Rev. and updated. The complete and official record of major league baseball. Macmillan Pub. Co. 1974 1532p $17.95   796.357

1 Baseball—Statistics   LC 73-21291

First published 1969 and entered in main catalog

The 1974 edition has been reset, revised and brought up to date to include the 1973 World Series statistics

Official baseball register. Publisher: C. C. Johnson Spink. Sporting News pa $5   796.357

1 Baseball—Statistics

Annual. First published 1940 with title: Baseball register

This book gives information, mostly in tabular form, about active players, managers, coaches and recently retired players in major league baseball. Included are place and date of birth; nicknames; whether right or left-handed; height and weight; hobbies; colleges attended; records and awards; yearly statistics for batting, fielding and pitching in the major and minor leagues and major league career totals; and team records of managers. Includes statistics for play in World Series and All-Star games

796.5 Outdoor life

Abel, Michael

Backpacking made easy. [Naturegraph] 1972 125p illus $5.95   796.5

1 Backpacking
ISBN 0-87961-009-3

This guide to backpacking "points out the pitfalls to avoid and gives many . . . suggestions for making plans where to go, what to take, how to increase endurance on your trips, grow in the skills of the outdoorsman, and how to select and wisely use the equipment and food needed." Publisher's note

References: p124-25

Bridge, Raymond

America's backpacking book. Scribner [1974 c1973] 417p illus maps $12.50   796.5

1 Backpacking
ISBN 0-684-13370-9   LC 73-1342

"Practical advice for the beginner with hints and suggestions for the experienced backpacker are conveyed in an inclusive, lively guide. Emphasizing that the less weight carried the more mobility will be gained in wilderness travels, detailed suggestions are given for choice of clothing, sleeping bags, pack styles, and related equipment suitable to conditions usually encountered by the camper. Survival techniques for outdoor living such as physical conditioning, desert and mountain walking, and backpacking with children. A few ideas on areas with backpacking opportunities and ways to preserve nature are given with lists of suppliers." Booklist

"The book is well illustrated [and] has good diagrams and charts, and has an adequate bibliography." Choice

Fletcher, Colin

The new complete walker; the joys and techniques of hiking and backpacking. 2d ed. rev. enl. and updated; illus. by Vanna Franks. Knopf 1974 470p illus $8.95   796.5

1 Hiking 2 Backpacking
ISBN 0-394-48099-6   LC 73-20763

Earlier edition entered in main catalog

First published 1969 with title: The complete walker. The 1974 edition has been revised to reflect the changes and improvements in equipment, freeze-dried and organic foods and our expanded knowledge of ecology and the environment

796.6 Cycling

Sloane, Eugene A.

The new complete book of bicycling. Simon & Schuster 1974 531p illus $12.50   796.6

1 Bicycles and bicycling
ISBN 0-671-27119-9   LC 73-9362

Earlier edition entered in main catalog

First published 1970 by Trident Press with title: The complete book of bicycling. The 1974 edition is "totally revised, expanded and updated, with 180 additional photographs." Publisher's note

A cycling dictionary of terms: p489-91. Bibliography: p507-09

796.9 Ice sports. Hockey

Beddoes, Richard

Hockey! The story of the world's fastest sport. New expanded ed. By Richard Beddoes, Stan Fischler [and] Ira Gitler. Macmillan Pub. Co. 1973 387p illus $9.95   796.9

1 Hockey   LC 72-176062

First published 1969

This work covers NHL beginnings and expansion; individual team biographies; famous —and infamous—games; great players past and present; the birth and growth of the upstart WHA; and a description of the confrontation between Team Canada and Russia

797.1 Boating

Angier, Bradford

Introduction to canoeing [by] Bradford Angier and Zach Taylor. Stackpole Bks. 1973 191p illus $5.95   797.1

1 Canoes and canoeing
ISBN 0-8117-0912-4   LC 73-519

"Far more than just an introduction for the novice to the challenging sport of canoeing, this is a comprehensive guide to the pastime. It very completely covers the various types of canoeing in sufficient detail to enable the tyro to master the various techniques, with sufficient practice. The book is well illustrated with many relevant sketches throughout, and the detailed treatment even extends to naming suppliers (with their addresses), canoes, and accessories, including a discussion of the relative merits of various brands." Choice

797.2 Swimming and diving

Council for National Cooperation in Aquatics

The new science of skin and scuba diving. 4th rev. ed. Illus. by James E. Young. Assn. Press 1974 288p illus $6.95   797.2

1 Skin diving
ISBN 0-8096-1876-1   LC 73-18139

Earlier edition entered in main catalog

First published 1957 by the Conference for National Cooperation in Aquatics with title: The science of skin and scuba diving. The 1974 edition has been revised with respect to new techniques in instruction and advances in technology

Glossary of skin and scuba diving terms: p279-84

798 Equestrian sports

Chew, Peter

The Kentucky Derby, the first 100 years. Houghton 1974 303p illus $15   798

1 Kentucky Derby
ISBN 0-395-18482-7   LC 74-625

The author "captures a brimming measure of the 100-year history, mystique, personalities,

Chew, Peter—*Continued*

lore and excitement of this annual emotional binge in his vividly written and excellently researched book. He chronicles the Derby from the great colt Aristide's triumph in the first race in 1875 to Secretariat's victory in 1973; his behind-the-scenes vignettes and profiles make it clear that for all its hokum and its aura of patrician snobbery, those magnificent horses make the Derby an exciting phenomenon." Pub W

799.1 Fishing

Gerlach, Rex
Creative fly tying and fly fishing; foreword by A. l. "Pal" Alexander. Winchester Press 1974 231p illus $10   **799.1**
1 Flies, Artificial 2 Fly-casting
ISBN 0-87691-122-X   LC 73-78831

"Mostly flies and fly tying, with a few chapters on fly fishing. The information on fishing is largely for the beginner and, while accurate, can be found elsewhere. The real strength of the book is in the chapters on flies and fly tying. Illustrations and good close-up photography show tying methods for standard as well as specialized patterns. Flies for such species as grayling, pike, and muskellunge are somewhat unusual and much appreciated." Library J
Bibliography: p223-24

Ovington, Ray
Basic fly fishing & fly tying. Stackpole Bks. 1973 192p illus $5.95   **799.1**
1 Fishing 2 Flies, Artificial
ISBN 0-8117-0200-6   LC 73-12849

"Of the many introductory books published with the novice fly fisher in mind none has been quite so successful as this. Simply written, it introduces the basics of fly fishing and fly tying and makes no attempt to carry the reader to more advanced levels. Complicated details are avoided, and factual instruction remains." Library J

Sand, George X.
The complete beginner's guide to fishing. Doubleday 1974 204p illus $4.95   **799.1**
1 Fishing
ISBN 0-385-09367-5   LC 73-11721

"Beginning with a discussion of hooks, the author describes fishing "equipment and its use, the location and characteristics of various species of American game fish as well as fishing from shore and in and on fresh and salt water, thoroughly covering fly, bait, and spin casting in addition to still fishing and trolling. Although not included in the index, safety measures may be found throughout the book. The appendix includes advice on making wading shoes, on kit fishing, fishing through ice, care of equipment, trailering a boat, and other useful information." Booklist

800 LITERATURE

801 Literature—Philosophy and theory

Handy, William J.
(ed.) Twentieth century criticism: the major statements; ed. by William J. Handy [and] Max Westbrook. Free Press 1974 499p $10.95   **801**
1 Criticism 2 Literature—History and criticism
ISBN 0-02-913710-1   LC 73-3898

"This collection of essays in literary criticism is divided as follows: formalist criticism, genre criticism, archetypal criticism, historical criticism and interdisciplinary criticism. Contributors included are: I. A. Richards, T. S. Eliot, Northrup Frye, Leslie Fiedler, Tdmund Wilson, Lionel Trilling and Susan Sontag

803 Literature—Encyclopedias and dictionaries

Fowler, Roger
(ed.) A dictionary of modern critical terms. Routledge 1973 208p $8.25   **803**
1 Literature—Dictionaries
ISBN 0-7100-7543-X   LC 73-89194

The editor and his team have "contributed some 160 entries which discuss and analyse critical concepts, and provide the inquiring reader with suggestions for further exploration." Economist

"An adequate reason for publishing this handbook is given in the preface. It was not designed to replace 'terminological handbooks, but to add to and qualify such aids.' It has the advantage of avoiding, as far as possible, the most technical of language in entries of a highly informative nature. The list of contributors is distinguished, and adequate assistance is given for seeking further information in the short bibliographies appended to key entries. Its particular asset is in the reflection of current scholarship and the attention to current literary trends." Choice

808 Rhetoric

Flesch, Rudolf
The art of readable writing; 25th anniversary edition; rev. and enl. with the Flesch readability formula. Harper 1974 271p illus $7.95   **808**
1 Rhetoric 2 English language—Composition and exercises
ISBN 0-06-011293-X   LC 73-14260

Earlier edition entered in main catalog
First published 1949. For the 1974 "edition the author has added postscripts to those chapters that needed updating." Library J
Includes bibliographical notes

Meredith, Scott
Writing to sell. 2d rev. ed. Harper 1974 232p $7.95   **808**
1 Authorship—Handbooks, manuals, etc. 2 Fiction—Technique
ISBN 0-06-012929-8   LC 74-1837

Earlier edition entered in main catalog
First published 1950. The 1974 edition brings the material up to date

808.3 Rhetoric of fiction

Burack, A. S.
(ed.) Techniques of novel writing. Writer 1973 305p $8.95   **808.3**
1 Fiction—Technique
ISBN 0-87116-000-5   LC 72-95433

"A collection of articles by 40 published novelists, well- and lesser-known, who discuss general and specific (gothic, mystery, adventure, etc.) aspects of novel writing. Perhaps its chief value to the fledgling novelist is the revelation that there are many ways of writing a novel: outline it completely or begin with only a character and no plot; work regular hours or catch-as-catch-can. . . . The book offers no fool-proof step by step formulas for novel writing, but it does offer nuggets of mostly useful advice which should encourage the beginner. It is also fun to read." Choice

Koontz, Dean R.
Writing popular fiction. Writers Digest 1972 232p $7.95   **808.3**
1 Fiction—Technique
ISBN 0-911654-21-6   LC 72-92664

This book is a step-by-step explanation of how to write various forms of popular, i.e., category fiction: science fiction, fantasy, suspence, mysteries, gothic romances, westerns, and erotica. Brief examples are quoted from published fiction. Also considered are such general questions as manuscript preparation, book titling, viewpoint of narrator, and nu-

Koontz, Dean R.—*Continued*
merous other practicalities. The book takes strictly a nuts-and-bolts approach to writing and is not concerned with literary quality, which cannot be taught anyway. One following these techniques could at least turn out a formula novel." Choice

808.8 Literature—Indexes

Chicorel Index to the spoken arts on discs, tapes, and cassettes; ed. by Marietta Chicorel. Chicorel Lib. Pub. Corp. 1973-1974 3v ea $60 **808.8**
1 Literature—Discography
ISBN 0-87729-003-9 (v7); 0-87729-004-2 (v7A); 0-87729-358-1 (v7B)

"Chicorel Index series; v7, v7A, v7B"
Each volume serves as a companion to the others but may be used independently
"Locates, analyzes and indexes plays, short stories, novels, speeches, commentaries, documents, conversations, poems and readings on . . . recorded media; includes U.S. and foreign productions. Indexes discs, tapes and video play performances." Ref Services Rev

808.82 Drama—Collections

The **Best** plays of 1973-1974; ed. by Otis L. Guernsey, Jr. Illus. with photographs and with drawings by Hirschfeld. Dodd 1974 516p illus $15 **808.82**
1 Drama—Collections 2 Drama 3 Theater—Yearbooks
ISBN 0-396-07017-5 LC 20-21432

"The Burns Mantle yearbook"
Earlier volumes entered in main catalog
Contains the following plays, abridged: The contractor, by D. Storey; Bad habits, by T. McNally; Find your way home, by J. Hopkins; Short eyes, by M. Piñero; Creeps, by D. E. Freeman; Noel Coward in two keys, by N. Coward; Jumpers, by T. Stoppard; The good doctor, by N. Simon; When you comin' back, Red Ryder, by M. Medoff; The sea horse, by E. J. Moore

The **Best** short plays, 1974; ed. and with an introduction by Stanley Richards. Chilton Bk. Co. 1974 348p (Best short plays ser) $8.95 **808.82**
1 Drama—Collections 2 One-act plays
ISBN 0-8019-5887-3 LC 38-8006

Earlier volumes entered in main catalog
Contents: An American sunset, by J. Prideaux; Welcome to Andromeda, by R. Whyte; The owl killer, by P. H. Dean; Let's murder Vivaldi, by D. Mercer; The ladies should be in bed, by P. Zindel; On vacation, by G. Hofmann; Present tense, by F. D. Gilroy; Vanilla crescents, by L. Ingrisch; Blank pages, by F. Marcus; Sitting, by J. Tobias; The last victim, by N. Holland; The wooing of Lady Sunday, by T. Pezzulo

Chicorel Theater index to plays in periodicals. Chicorel Lib. Pub. Corp. 1973 500p (Chicorel Index ser) $49.50 **808.82**
1 Drama—Indexes
ISBN 0-87729-005-1 LC 73-174118

A "guide to plays in 159 periodicals, ranging from the 19th century to the present. Sources are primarily English-language publications, including several from England and Ireland, although a few French and German-language periodicals are indexed. . . . The total number of entries is over 10,000 arranged in one alphabetical listing incorporating four types of categories: main entry, play title, author, and editor/adaptor/translator. Each play is identified as to place, time, and classification, although the latter is arbitrary and sometimes imprecise. . . . The total is impressive and the completeness and efficiency of the index make it the best up-to-date play index [to periodicals] available." Choice

Richards, Stanley
(ed.) Best short plays of the world theatre, 1968-1973; ed. with an introduction and prefaces to the plays by Stanley Richards. Crown 1973 303p $7.50 **808.82**
1 Drama—Collections 2 One-act plays
ISBN 0-517-50589-4 LC 73-82936

Earlier volume entered in main catalog
Richards "anthologizes 20 one-act plays reflecting the tempo and ambience of the period covered. Two are translations and another is based on a Chekhov short story. In his introduction Richards expresses personal views and opinions on theatrical entertainment and states his aim here is to 'involve, absorb, and entertain' the reader. Dramatists represented include Williams, Simon, Coward, Anouilh, Bellow, Inge, and Adrienne Kennedy." Booklist

808.85 Speeches—Collections

Prochnow, Herbert V.
(comp.) The speaker's and toastmaster's handbook; 1,000 quips, stories, and illustrations for all occasions. Denison 1973 220p $6.95 **808.85**
1 Public speaking—Handbooks, manuals, etc. 2 Anecdotes 3 Speeches, addresses, etc.
ISBN 0-513-01172-2 LC 72-92120

Witticisms, humorous stories, biographical illustrations and ideas for speeches or sermons are included in this book, which also gives examples for special days, introductions of speakers, and opening and closing remarks

809 History, description, critical appraisal of more than one literature

Auden, W. H.
Forewords and afterwords; selected by Edward Mendelson. Random House 1973 529p $12.50 **809**
1 Literature—History and criticism
ISBN 0-394-48359-6 LC 72-10230

Analyzed in Essay and general literature index
This collection contains 46 previously published prefaces, book reviews, and biographical and critical esays
"Whether he is writing about a composer—Wagner, Verdi—an artist—Van Gogh—a religious thinker—Kierkegaard, Luther—or an author—Lewis Carroll, Goethe, Tennyson, Mr. Auden zeroes in on the biographical detail, the revelatory flash of truth that illumines both the man and his life work. . . . Used wisely it will prove a golden thread, leading as all good books do, toward other good books. It condenses a lifetime of reading, reflecting and judging." Christian Science Monitor

Contemporary literary criticism; excerpts from criticism of the works of today's novelists, poets, playwrights, and other creative writers. Gale Res. ea $30 **809**
1 Literature—History and criticism
LC 76-38938

At head of title of v 1: CLC
First published 1973
Editor: 1973- Carolyn Riley
Each volume in the continuing series covers about 200 authors. Succeeding volumes in the series will contain criticism on authors not previously covered, plus new criticism on authors already treated in earlier volumes
Included are "excerpts from previously printed criticism on important contemporary literary figures . . . from various countries, who are living or have died since 1960, all excerpts are in English, and have been chosen from books and periodical articles published within the past twenty-five years. The authors included may have written science fiction, detective novels, or fantasy, as well as the more conventional types of fiction, drama, or poetry; some evaluations of nonfiction are also

Contemporary literary criticism—*Continued*
included if this genre is significant for a particular author. . . . A brief note on each author's significance usually includes a reference to his appearance in the Gale series 'Contemporary Authors [entered in main catalog].'" College & Research Libs

Seymour-Smith, Martin
 Funk & Wagnalls Guide to modern world literature. Funk 1973 xxi, 1206p $13.95 **809**
 1 Literature—History and criticism 2 Literature, Comparative—History and criticism
 ISBN 0-308-10079-4   LC 73-5931
 English title: Guide to modern world literature
 This account "attempts to cover all writers of interest whatever nationality who survived 31 December 1899, and . . . includes a few who died before that date. . . . The book is arranged in sections, each dealing with a national literature—African and Caribbean, Albanian, American, Arabic, and so on. Within each section the reader is offered a history of the literature concerned, roughly from the last twenty years of the 19th century to the present day, generally dealing with the novel, drama and poetry in separate sub-sections, and on occasion introducing further chronological divisions." Encounter

809.1 Poetry—History and criticism

Paz, Octavio
 Children of the mire; modern poetry from Romanticism to the avant-garde; tr. by Rachel Phillips. Harvard Univ. Press 1974 186p $7.95 **809.1**
 1 Poetry
 ISBN 0-674-11625-9   LC 73-88498
 "The Charles Eliot Norton lectures, 1971-1972"
 Paz contends that "the modern age and modern poetry are unique in the sense that past traditions are completely rejected, as the artist and society constantly pursue change. As soon as new discoveries are made, they are discarded and the search begins again. This characteristic is related to modern man's obsession with progress and his idolatry of the future, but it is drawing to a close because of disillusionment caused by negative results, such as pollution and frightening armaments." Library J
 "There are remarkable pages here on the German romantics and on Mallarmé, some useful guidelines to modernismo and its consequences in Latin America and Spain. There is a persuasive sketch of Symbolism in France as a late, reflexive form of what had been Romanticism in Germany, and there is a fine insight into analogy (as distinct from symbolism, or metaphor, or imagery, or imagism, or any other partial practice or faith) as the 'true religion of modern poetry.'" N Y Rev of Books
 Includes bibliographical references

809.3 Fiction—History and criticism

Bretnor, Reginald
 (ed.) Science fiction, today and tomorrow; a discursive symposium by Ben Bova [and others]. Harper 1974 342p $8.95 **809.3**
 1 Science fiction—History and criticism
 ISBN 0-06-010467-8   LC 73-4142
 Analyzed in Essay and general literature index
 "A collection of 15 essays on topics like the function of science fiction, its relationship to the visual media and to mainstream fiction, moral and religious preoccupations in the genre, critical and aesthetic questions in science fiction, and others. Contributors are practitioners, critics, and teachers in the field. . . . The anthology includes biographical sketches of, and a listing of primary sources by, contributors as well as a select bibliography of secondary sources dealing with science fiction." Choice
 "These intelligent essays go far beyond the sometimes self-serving utterances of genre writers. Just about anyone interested in popular fiction can find meat in this book." Pub W

810.3 American and Canadian literature—Encyclopedias and dictionaries

[Story, Norah]
 Supplement to The Oxford Companion to Canadian history and literature. General editor: William Toye: contributors: Alvine Bélisle [and others]. Oxford [1974 c1973] 318p $9.50 **810.3**
 1 Canadian literature—Encyclopedias 2 Canadian literature—Bio-bibliography
 ISBN 0-19-540205-7   LC 67-31959
 Title page date 1973
 Basic volume entered in main catalog
 This supplement containing nearly 200 biographical entries discusses novelists, poets, playwrights, historians, and other writers who have published significantly from the beginning of 1967 to the end of 1972
 "The book remains the most comprehensive and accessible source on recent Canadian writing." Library J

810.8 American literature—Collections

Wolfe, Tom
 (ed.) The new journalism; with an anthology ed. by Tom Wolfe and E. W. Johnson. Harper 1973 394p $10.95 **810.8**
 1 American literature—Collections 2 Journalism
 ISBN 0-06-014707-5   LC 71-123972
 A collection of 3 introductory essays by Wolfe are followed by 23 selections and excerpts from articles, books and magazines which exemplify "the new journalism," a fiction-like journalistic style. Rex Reed, Truman Capote, Terry Southern, Joe McGinniss, and Joan Didion are among the writers represented
 This is "a well-selected collection. . . . [In his introductory chapters, Wolfe] claims that the new journalism of the '60s and '70s has taken the place of the novel as the most revered literary form in America. He describes this new form as characterized by verbatim dialogue, scenes as the structural element, the third-person point of view, and the selection of details symbolic of the life style or status life of the characters. . . . The book draws attention to an important form of writing and uses a variety of examples which the general reader will find of interest in their own right." Choice

810.9 American literature—History and criticism

Cowley, Malcolm
 A second flowering; works and days of the lost generation. Viking 1973 276p illus $7.95 **810.9**
 1 American literature—History and criticism 2 Authors, American
 ISBN 0-670-62826-3   LC 72-78992
 Analyzed in Essay and general literature index
 "The writers and intellectuals who made Paris-in-the-20s their home away from home and earned, perhaps romantically, the generic appellation 'Lost Generation' come under affectionate scrutiny: . . . Fitzgerald, Hemingway, Dos Passos, Cummings, Wilder, Faulkner, Wolfe and Hart Crane. Cowley underscores the great impact of the first World War on these and some lesser-known but still significant writers born in those few years bracketing the century's turn; his analysis of their responses to the war and the subsequent mark their work made on American writing form both a tribute and a haunting retrospective study." Pub W
 These "essays are a skillful blend of criticism and biography—most suitable for a generation whose lives are as much discussed as its writings. . . . His essays on the individual

Cowley, Malcolm—*Continued*
writers, all of whom have been overobserved and overanalyzed, remain fresh and perceptive. . . . Cowley's book, I think, may be—and may remain—the best brief introduction to the generation." Newsweek

Literary history of the United States. Editors: Robert E. Spiller [and others]. 4th ed. rev. Macmillan Pub. Co. 1974 2v ea $25   **810.9**

1 American literature—History and criticism
2 American literature—Bibliography
ISBN   LC 73-14014

Earlier edition entered in main catalog
First published 1948 in three volumes. The 1974 edition has been enlarged and updated to reflect current directions and experimental techniques of the literature of the 60's and 70's. The second Bibliography supplement, published separately in 1972 has been incorporated into the Bibliography volume
Contents: v 1 History; v2 Bibliography

Malin, Irving
(ed.) Contemporary American-Jewish literature; critical essays. Ind. Univ. Press 1973 302p $8.95   **810.9**

1 American literature—History and criticism
2 Jewish literature—History and criticism
ISBN 0-253-31420-8   LC 72-75393

Analyzed in Essay and general literature index
"Through pages of qualification, debate, affirmation, and denial, the quest for the meaning, quality, and impact of Jewishness here attains luminous definition. First-rate critical minds (Solotaroff, David Daiches, Allen Guttman, et al.) join force to sort out findings and ambiguities, mainly about novelists and writers of short fiction. Although criteria differ and conclusions dissent, the cumulative effort delineates the meaning and impact of such ostensibly diverse talents of Jewish 'breakthrough' as Mailer, Bellow, Roth, Malamud, Shapiro, Friedman, Singer, and others. The comprehensive bibliography by Jackson R. Bryer further enhances this excellent symposium." Library J

811   American poetry

Berrigan, Daniel
Prison poems; foreword by Philip Berrigan. Unicorn Press 1973 124p $5.95   **811**
ISBN 0-87775-049-1   LC 73-76683

These poems were "written while Berrigan was imprisoned at Danbury Federal Penitentiary. . . . To his customary range of allusions Berrigan has added penitentiary life as well as references to his activities in opposition to the war." Choice
"Berrigan's faith and humor never seem to flag, even under the worst circumstances. . . . Berrigan insists on this stream-of-consciousness method and defiant sense of irony throughout the book, both I think to a poetic disadvantage." Best Sellers
"Many of the best poems in [this volume] . . . are political and we have not had better political poetry in America since the Depression. . . . The language of prisons, like the language of armies, is obscenity. That is because prisons, like armies, are obscenities. That is the message (if you must have message in your poetry) of Prison Poems." Christian Century

Selected and new poems. Doubleday 1973 293p $6.95   **811**
ISBN 0-385-03099-1   LC 72-118847

A seven part sequence of works by the radical Jesuit poet who was imprisoned for his draft resistance activities "selected from his previous volumes beginning with 'Time Without Number' and moving through his Vietnam awakening in 'False Gods, Real Men' and his . . . 'Trial Poems.' The singular coherence of Berrigan's passionate humanity, his mystically rooted sense of justice, love and redemption, carries into the 30 new poems—apparently written during and after his term in Danbury." Pub W
"This volume shows that Berrigan has developed as a poet over the passage of years. . . . In his later poetry he is much more open to experimentation in the use of alliteration, internal rhyme, and typography suggesting contemporaries like Charles Olson most particularly and another Black Mountain poet, Robert Creeley, in the wit and humor in the verse. Much more than they and many present-day poets Berrigan is highly topical. His verse is strewn with allusions to contemporary happenings and public figures, making great demands on the reader's knowledge of current events and concerns." Choice

Ferlinghetti, Lawrence
Open eye, open heart. [New Directions] 1973 148p $6.95   **811**
ISBN 0-8112-0488-X   LC 73-78784

"A New Directions book"
The poems in this collection concern "politics, love, loneliness, ecology, poetry, women, etc." Library J
"The verse, in a wide range of styles, reflects the usual West Coast mixture of Wobbly anarchism and Sunkist orientalism, but the famous Ferlinghetti swinging line still works, especially in those poems which fuse his unabashedly lyrical idiom with his mild-mannered and playful satirical bent. For a 'public poet,' there are a surprising number of poems in this volume about poetry, other poets, and 'after' other poems: but then Ferlinghetti has always been the most frankly literary of his group." Choice

Ginsberg, Allen
The fall of America; poems of these States, 1965-1971. City Lights Bks. 1972 188p pa $2.50   **811**
LC 72-84228

"The Pocket poets series"
"Ginsberg maintains strikingly variant tones and, to some extent, techniques in these 62 poems that sing, chant, and preach against the extent of mechanization of America and her vast machinery of destruction. Pollution of environment and of mind and soul are at the center of his concern. . . . Anyone who knows the poet only through 'Howl' would do well to read this excellent collection." Library J

Giovanni, Nikki
My house; poems. Morrow 1972 69p illus $5.95   **811**
ISBN 0-688-00025-5   LC 72-116

"36 poems, most written in late 1971 and in 1972. Generally in a gentler, more loving mood than in her first volume of poems she is nevertheless still capable of great bitterness, rage, and strong passion. As before a sense of black pride permeates her work, and with an effective economy of words she sets a scene and conveys an emotion." Booklist

Goodman, Paul
Collected poems; ed. by Taylor Stoehr; with a memoir by George Dennison. Random House [1974 c1973] xxx, 465p $12.50   **811**
ISBN 0-394-48358-8   LC 73-3979

This volume, which Goodman had nearly completed at the time of his death, includes all the poems from his earlier volumes and many previously unpublished poems. Contains index of titles and first lines
"The poems are not only moving but interesting—a rare enough accomplishment. And one way by which he made his cultural reference insistently, though indirectly, was the literary quality of his writing. . . . This collected edition is important for the poet's reputation and useful for us all. It contains many poems, at least a fourth of the total, never published before; some are splendid. The whole has great integrity and power, though like any poet's collected work it includes a number of inessential poems." N Y Times Bk R
Includes index of titles and first lines

Lowell, Robert
The dolphin. Farrar, Straus 1973 78p $6.95   **811**
ISBN 0-374-14140-1   LC 72-96315

Awarded the Pulitzer Prize, 1974
The poet describes "his experiences in England where he spent time in a hospital, recovered, and contemplated his relationship with

Lowell, Robert—Continued

his third wife. The dolphin of the title is a symbol of near-human life with which the poet attempts communication, reflective also of the mermaids of other poems as part human, part animal beings whom Lowell celebrates. The poems bespeak his anxieties over marriage, children, and his role as a parent and also treat his reaction to living abroad." Booklist

In this volume, "feeling is like an enveloping sack; Lowell is largely confined to his passions. If his mind transcends them, it is in wondering grief, occasionally in surprised joy, coming upon them almost always after the fact. Or such is his poetic, a poetic of taking stock." N Y Times Bk R

For Lizzie and Harriet. Farrar, Straus 1973 48p $6.95 **811**

ISBN 0-374-15729-4   LC 72-96316

The poems included appeared in other versions in the author's Notebook, entered in main catalog

"In all this work of the last six years, [Lowell] can be seen exercising and renewing his power over the basic line of English poetry most congenial to him, the Marlovian-Shakespearean pentameter. During a difficult period of his life, safety-belted into his fourteen-line stanza, he has been playing with it, deepening his grasp, seeing what it can accommodate in the way of mundane fact, prose loosening, supple understatement." Newsweek

History. Farrar, Straus 1973 207p $7.95 **811**

ISBN 0-374-17044-4   LC 72-96314

Comprises about 80 new poems, in addition to those appearing in his "Notebook", entered in main catalog. All these latter have been rewritten. The themes reflect the poet's outlook on world events, present as well as past

The poems are "arranged in chronological order from Genesis to My Lai. . . . What Lowell is contriving by means of the sonnet-sequence is a vehicle for his own particular blend of random jotting, reflections, observations. It is a vehicle both journalistic and mythic, comparable as the poet sees it to 'an eelnet made by man for the eel fighting.' Furthermore, as his practice in raiding 'Notebook' for the creation of new books reveals, it is a modular eelnet, in the best 20th-century architectural tradition, capable of extensions, regroupings, insertions and deletions." Christian Science Monitor

Nash, Ogden

Ave Ogden! Nash in Latin; tr. by James C. Gleeson and Brian N. Meyer; with drawings by Ken Maryanski. Little 1973 94p illus $5.95 **811**

ISBN 0-316-31590-7   LC 73-13586

In English and Latin

"Whatever the reasons, I do think the Nash buff will be entertained; certainly the Latinist will admire the cleverness of these 52 renditions and will be able to use them with good effect upon students. The shorter poems generally work best. The 14 drawings by Maryanski add to the spirit of the undertaking." Library J

"What is excellent about the Nash translations is not only that the English original is on the facing page (an indispensable prop to dignity) but that the poems are very short. . . . Nashian distortion is not handled really well . . . but translations that do not require puns or word twists are sometimes perfect." Time

Nemerov, Howard

Gnomes & occasions; poems. Univ. of Chicago Press 1973 79p $5.95 **811**

ISBN 0-226-57254-4   LC 72-90073

A collection of some fifty poems written by the poet since 1967. The "gnomes" of the title refers to the gnomic or epigrammatic character of a number of the offerings

Nemerov "responds suggestively to the evanescent gaiety of late butterflies, to the mysterious aspects of the heavens, to such seemingly minimal matters as stamps or the completing of a picture puzzle. . . . It is the union of wit and feeling that marks these poems, resulting in hilarity or, more often, in poignant irony." New Repub

Oates, Joyce Carol

Angel fire; poems. La. State Univ. Press 1973 62p $4.95 **811**

ISBN 0-8071-0222-9   LC 72-91189

"Dividing her poems in three groups and titling them 'Lovers' Bodies,' 'Domestic Miracles' and 'Revelations,' [the poet] lends universal meaning and order to what are, after all, deeply personal experiences. Her tone and imagery now begin to assume an almost feverish concreteness and imagery, owing less than ever to her reading or her metaphysical inclinations. Her throes-of-love passion enable her to paint indelible scenes." Pub W

"Miss Oates seems to have real poetic material at her fingertips in the rudiments of her powerful vision. But lacking is a strong formal principle to give the poetic energy direction, any direction. The poems transcend the 'real' universe by creating a coherent one of their own." Best Sellers

O'Hara, Frank

The selected poems of Frank O'Hara; ed. by Donald Allen. Knopf 1974 [c1973] 233p $8.95 **811**

ISBN 0-394-46026-X   LC 73-7302

The poems chosen for this collection, arranged chronologically, give voice to "a New York City artist of continuing critical importance. Polishing a variety of poetic styles to reflect his distinctive personality O'Hara pays tribute to artists, poets, and to friends of the urban milieu in which he moved. . . . A brief prefatory essay describes O'Hara's approach to poetry; appended are a chronology of his life and works from 1926 to 1966 and indexes of titles and first lines." Booklist

Rukeyser, Muriel

Breaking open. Random House 1973 135p $6 **811**

ISBN 0-394-48696-X   LC 73-5045

In this volume Rukeyser presents "poetry about her family, her friends, her country, her religion, herself, . . . [and a] section of 'Northern Poems,' translations of Eskimo songs." New Repub

"'What kind of woman goes walking and searching?' Rukeyser asks in 'Searching/Not Searching.' . . . Her poems answer the question: a sensual and sensitive urban woman attuned to her own inner shiftings and needs, strongly committed to nonviolent resistance in the major social/political struggles. . . . She is capable of the tightly crafted, sharply focused poem . . . but it is the looser, sometimes prosy poems celebrating her quests that one remembers as characteristic. Fifteen haunting, strangely blues-like Eskimo songs, translated with the late Paul Radin, complement many of her own poems in their directness." Library J

Sarton, May

Collected poems (1930-1973). Norton 1974 416p $10 **811**

ISBN 0-393-04386-X   LC 74-1259

"From the point of view of content, the book contains the major themes that Sarton has become known for, all culminating in a self-awareness and self-knowledge on the part of the writer. From the point of view of technique, the reader who follows the chronological order of the poems will be aware of the progression of manipulation and artistry on the part of the poet. The table of contents lists the poems as they appeared in various book collections, the index at the back of the book lists the poems by first lines. The reader who likes to skip around looking for old favorites will find them easily; the reader who just browses through the book will have many hours of pleasurable reading." Choice

Sexton, Anne

The death notebooks. Houghton 1974 97p $2.95 **811**

ISBN 0-395-18281-6   LC 73-17311

"Sexton is noted for an often harsh, almost imperious baring of her ecstasies and her sufferings. Here she is preoccupied with the fearful intimacies of death. The arterial beat of her language and the padded footsteps of

Sexton, Anne—*Continued*

peripheral madness haunt and color her surprising visions. Some poems have been published previously." Booklist

"There are few cheerful words in this volume. Sexton's style and poetics have reached exceptional polish . . . but the bleakness of her world continues to be too intense for all but the most avid of her readers." Choice

Van Doren, Mark

Good morning; last poems by Mark Van Doren; foreword by Richard Howard. Hill & Wang 1973 95p $6.95   **811**

ISBN 0-8090-5064-1   LC 73-80219

"Thoughtful, warm, and perceptive poems written during the final three years of Van Doren's life. . . . More important than the poet's humanistic bent and sensitivity to nature which are again revealed is the quiet acceptance of man's mortality expressed in most of the poems. A substantial foreword by Richard Howard introduces newcomers to Van Doren's well-liked conventional style and also serves as refresher for readers familiar with his lyrical gems." Booklist

Van Duyn, Mona

Merciful disguises; published and unpublished poems. Atheneum Pubs. 1973 245p $10   **811**

ISBN 0-689-10578-9   LC 73-78407

"In this collection of 85 poems (selected from four previously published volumes) and an additional 18 unpublished poems, . . . [the author examines] the implications of loving people, places, and things." Library J

The author "is a poet of great wisdom, skill, and versatility; she is able to sustain locally intense language over long narrative and meditative poems, in a variety of modes and voices." Va Q R

811.025 American poets—Directories

A Directory of American poets; including names and addresses of 1300 poets and contemporary writers whose work has been published in the United States. Poets & Writers 1973 119p map pa $4   **811.025**

1 Poets, American—Directories   LC 72-96830

"Intended for groups and individuals interested in locating and sponsoring contemporary American poets and some other writers, this directory lists 1300 writers state by state, giving addresses, teaching preferences, languages spoken, latest published volumes, and occasionally some indication of fee. . . . A separate listing of minority writers is helpful to those seeking black, Spanish speaking, Chicano, American Indian, or Asian-American writers. Also included are organizations interested in sponsoring poets, arranged by state, and a section devoted to anthologies of contemporary poets, films and videotapes, materials for writing teachers, information on little magazines, grants and awards. Prepared with the aid of a grant from the Literature Program of The National Endowment for the Arts, and modestly priced, it should be useful in all types of libraries." Ref Services Rev

811.08 American poetry—Collections

Adoff, Arnold

(ed.) The poetry of Black America; anthology of the 20th century; introduction by Gwendolyn Brooks. Harper 1973 xxxi, 552p $12.50   **811.08**

1 Negro poetry—Collections
ISBN 0-06-020089-8   LC 72-76518

"Reflects the personal choice of a black poet, scholar, and anthologist. Adoff presents over 600 poems, using 'quality' as his criterion. His scope allows demonstration of the range of major poets and the promise of some very young ones. There are the standard to-be-expected (and much needed) poems which appear in most anthologies, but there are many surprises also. . . . The inclusion of 145 biographical notes is a valuable addition." Choice

"More than anything else Adoff's anthology underscores powerfully the vigorous totality of the cultural breakthrough of black American poets in our day." Pub W

Bontemps, Arna

(ed.) American Negro poetry. Rev. ed. Edited and with an introduction by Arna Bontemps. Hill & Wang 1974 231p $6.95   **811.08**

1 Negro poetry—Collections
ISBN 0-8090-2521-3   LC 72-95044

"American century series"

Earlier edition entered in main catalog

First published 1963. In the 1974 edition "work of 12 contemporary poets (including Nikki Giovanni, Don L. Lee, Richard A. Long, and Audre Lorde) has been added." Library J

Included are biographical notes for each poet represented and an index of titles

Evans, David Allan

(ed.) New voices in American poetry: an anthology. Winthrop Pubs. 1973 265p pa $4.95   **811.08**

1 American poetry—Collections
ISBN 0-87626-613-8   LC 72-12943

"Although the quality is uneven this is an attractive and inviting anthology of poems by 45 new young poets, most relatively unknown but all published in a variety of periodicals and some in book form. A photograph, brief profile, and three or four poems are included for each poet, while the poets themselves have contributed essays on how they came to write one or more of the poems." Booklist

Rottmann, Larry

(ed.) Winning hearts & minds; war poems by Vietnam veterans; ed. by Larry Rottman, Jan Barry [and] Basil T. Paquet. McGraw 1972 116p illus $3.95   **811.08**

1 American poetry—Collections 2 War poetry
ISBN 0-07-054076-4   LC 72-185861

In this "anthology of war poems . . . the subjects usually involve mechanized slaughter, the agony of children or the difficulty of showing the Vietnamese what one feels. Futility figures largely in them. . . . [The poems also reveal] an appreciation of the people and the land . . . an awareness of . . . brutality . . . [and a] recognition of how the poet himself has been made brutal." Newsweek

"Don't beg off from this shattering little volume of Vietnam poems by veterans of that war on the grounds that it isn't Lenten reading. God help us, yes, it is very much Lenten reading. The title is an ironic use of the official slogan that has been used by the United States to describe its pacification program." America

811.09 American poetry—History and criticism

Aird, Eileen M.

Sylvia Plath. Barnes & Noble 1973 114p $5.25   **811.09**

1 Plath, Sylvia
ISBN 06-490038-X   LC 73-174111

This biographical and critical study of Plath's poetry and other writings provides an "overview of her poetry and prose from 1958 to 1963. [The author] demonstrates the ways in which Plath explores the tragic dimensions of domesticity and the feminine role and discusses the development of the major images of her work, the recurring battle to subdue inner conflict and alienation through the power of her imaginative vision, and her relation to her literary contemporaries." Library J

"Bogged down though it is in the heavy-handed style of the academic thesis, this is a

Aird, Eileen M.—Continued

useful guide to the poetry and the novel published by Plath. Aird relates The bell jar and the verse to events in Plath's short troubled life, and traces the influence on her work of Robert Lowell and Theodore Roethke, the outstanding 'confessional' poets of our time." Choice

Select bibliography: p113-14

Barry, Elaine

Robert Frost. Ungar [1974 c1973] 145p (Modern literature monographs) $6   811.09

1 Frost, Robert
ISBN 0-8044-2016-5   LC 72-79942

"This well-written and unpretentious little addition to the series will serve as a thoughtful introduction to Frost's poetry. It contains a useful chronology and a brief biographical introduction, as well as chapters on Frost's use of the lyric, dramatic narrative, and sonnet forms, and a concluding chapter on major themes. The author argues effectively throughout that Frost was a poet of depth as well as technical skill, and he illustrates that Frost's reserve and balance should not be mistaken for a lack of intellectual dimension." Library J

Bibliography: p135-38

Frost, Robert

Robert Frost on writing. [Comp. by] Elaine Barry. Rutgers Univ. Press 1973 188p $9   811.09

1 American poetry—History and criticism
ISBN 0-8135-0692-1   LC 73-10103

"Frost as a figure in American letters continues to gain strength. This gathering of his statements on writing, annotated and prefaced by Elaine Barry, reveals some of the reasons why. . . . The competent Barry preface sets forth the scope of Frost's criticism and discusses him as theorist and practical critic. But the real meat for Frost lovers will be found in the texts themselves: letters, prefaces, reviews, lectures, parodies, interviews (some new material included). Sheer pleasure to read, rewarding to ponder, and of course, a worthy addition to the growing Frost shelf." Pub W

Bibliography: p183-88

Gibson, Donald B.

(ed.) Modern Black poets; a collection of critical essays. Prentice-Hall 1973 181p $5.95
811.09

1 Negro poetry—History and criticism
ISBN 0-13-588392-X   LC 72-12811

"Twentieth century views. A Spectrum book"
"Anthology of criticism tracing the growing unity of black poetry as a distinct body of American literature. Following a historical introduction covering black poetry from the eighteenth century to today, 12 critical essays sketch the tradition of black poets in the U.S. from the Harlem Renaissance of the 1920s to the black rage of the 1970s. Separate critiques are devoted to the work of Langston Hughes, Countee Cullen, Melvin B. Tolson, Robert Hayden, and Imamu Amiri Baraka (LeRoi Jones)." Booklist

"An excellent collection of basic articles by well-known black critics. . . . Half of the essays were apparently written for this book (a rare procedure in the series), because Gibson has tried to give a balanced presentation. . . . Gibson's own introduction is excellent, especially for . . . readers unfamiliar with the black experience, but the book is only a beginning for such study. There is inadequate treatment of the interrelationship of black music and poetry, and no essays by the younger poets themselves. A good bibliography of 250 items deal specifically with eight important poets." Choice

Malkoff, Karl

Crowell's Handbook of contemporary American poetry. Crowell 1973 338p $10
811.09

1 American poetry—History and criticism
ISBN 0-690-22625-X   LC 73-14787

"Putting his emphasis on explanation rather than evaluation [the author] starts off with brief essays on the esthetic theories and methods of precontemporary poetry, and on certain seminal poems and movements (imagism, for example, beat poetry, the new black poetry); then in his second, larger section he provides brief biographical-cum-critical discussions of contemporary schools, movements and poets arranged in alphabetical order, beginning with A. R. Ammons and ending with James Wright." Pub W

Morris, Adalaide Kirby

Wallace Stevens: imagination and faith. Princeton Univ. Press 1974 205p (Princeton Essays in literature) $9.50   811.09

1 Stevens, Wallace
ISBN 0-691-06265-X   LC 73-2495

The author argues that the search for a substitute for religion occupies Stevens' poetic energy from his earliest to his latest work. It emerges in his patterns of speech, in his symbols, and in his poetic forms; it encompasses a critique of Christianity, often wryly humorous and sometimes bitterly satiric; and it results in a theory of poetry that becomes a mystical theology

Selected bibliography: p189-96

Perloff, Marjorie G.

The poetic art of Robert Lowell. Cornell Univ. Press 1973 209p $9.50   811.09

1 Lowell, Robert
ISBN 0-8014-0771-0   LC 72-12412

This study focuses on two questions: "what kind of poetry does Lowell write, and what is its value? To these ends the author devotes each of the book's chapters to an examination of a different literary aspect of Lowell's poetic practice. In turn, she analyzes his imagery, genre, convention, syntax, and tone; and she concludes by comparing his poetry with that of his contemporaries." Library J

"This book is an excellent survey of the poet's work; it is clearly written, with a minimum of technical jargon; and it should be in any library concerned with modern poetry." Choice

Bibliography in Notes: p185-203

Sibley, Agnes

May Sarton. Twayne 1972 160p (Twayne's United States authors ser) $6.95   811.09

1 Sarton, May   LC 70-187610

The author "brings to her detailed study of May Sarton's writing a sensitive awareness of May Sarton's qualities as a writer and as a person. She points out astutely the blending of attachment to a richly varied European tradition with an innate independence of spirit. Sibley is an excellent critic: intelligent, perceptive, sympathetic. She has packed a small book with careful analyses and illuminating insights into the work of a highly complicated mind. Her book is the first full-length study of May Sarton's work to appear." Choice

Bibliography: p155-57

Wagner, Jean

Black poets of the United States; from Paul Laurence Dunbar to Langston Hughes; tr. by Kenneth Douglas. Univ. of Ill. Press 1973 xxiii, 561p $15   811.09

1 Negro poetry—History and criticism
ISBN 0-252-00292-X   LC 72-075141

Original French edition, 1963

"The chronological focus of the book is a half-century of Afro-American poetry published from 1890 to 1940. In effect, two generations of black poets are treated in considerable depth: Paul Laurence Dunbar and his contemporaries, and the major poets of the Harlem Renaissance. . . . Wagner's central thesis is the interdependence of racial and religious feeling in American Negro poetry." Foreword

"An excellent critical study. . . . [It examines] the social conditions which are revealed in the poetry. The major poets are presented in detail—their lives as well as their works. The place of minor poets in literary history is also discussed. Appended is a selective . . . bibliography covering each of the authors studied as well as general works useful to a study of black American culture and literature." Cur Ref Bks

812 American drama

Baldwin, James
One day, when I was lost; a scenario based on Alex Haley's "The autobiography of Malcolm X." Dial Press 1973 [c1972] 280p illus $7.50   812

1 Malcolm X—Drama
ISBN 0-8037-6649-1   LC 72-10572

First published 1972 in England
This film script outlines the facts of Malcolm's life. The first part, using flashbacks, describes his early life. Part two, beginning with his conversion to Islam traces his career and closes with his assassination in 1965
"The first half of the book, which deals with Malcolm's past as a hustler in Harlem, is sharp, funny and precise and the second half, after his conversion, is slow-moving and suffused with a sentimentality." Times (London) Lit Sup

Heller, Joseph
Catch-22; a dramatization. Delacorte Press 1973 xxv, 228p illus $6.95   812

1 World War, 1939-1945—Drama
ISBN 0-440-01098-5   LC 72-10200

Characters: Large mixed cast. 2 acts. First produced July 13, 1971 at the John Drew Theater, East Hampton, New York
"Heller has edited and rearranged his novel into a rather terse . . . play. The source of conflict and development derives from Yossarian, the central character, and his battle for human dignity within the military establishment during . . . [World War II]. He faces the idiotic military bureaucracy; he struggles with the '1984' quality of twisted language; and, ultimately, he sees with bitter humor the insanity of risking death for a colonel's whim to up the number of flying missions in order for the colonel to become a general. . . . The play reads well; and . . . it would offer good theater, if, perhaps, a bit didactic." Library J

Jones, Tom
The fantasticks [and] Celebration; 2 musicals by Tom Jones and Harvey Schmidt. Drama Bk. Specialists/Pubs. 1973 232p illus $10   812

ISBN 0-910482-44-6   LC 73-5972

In The fantasticks, the love between a young couple is nurtured by a wall and the ingenue's father. Celebration borrows its theme from the ancient rituals which honored the cycle of rebirth. At a New Year's Eve party in a modern city, a young inexperienced man battles against an old decadent one for the favors of an ambitious young actress

Simon, Neil
The prisoner of Second Avenue; a new comedy. Directed on Broadway by Mike Nichols. Random House 1972 87p front $4.95
                                                               812

1 Apartment houses—Drama
ISBN 0-394-48259-X   LC 72-2743

Characters: 2 men, 4 women, 2 acts 5 scenes. First produced at the Eugene O'Neill Theater, November 11, 1971
Domestic comedy. Middle aged couple have to cope with declining facilities of New York (City) apartment houses, as well as tensions which metropolitan and national affairs engender, such as unemployment

The sunshine boys; a new comedy. Random House 1973 109p $4.95   812

ISBN 0-394-48808-3   LC 73-5049

Characters: 5 men, 2 women. First produced at the Broadhurst Theater, December 20, 1972
A comedy revolving about an attempt to reunite a vaudeville team, who, though they disliked each other, played together for 43 years. The crisis is reached when the team reluctantly agree to rehearse their old act for a history of comedy to be shown on television

Vonnegut, Kurt
Between time and Timbuktu; or, Prometheus-5; a space fantasy based on materials by Kurt Vonnegut, Jr.; designed by Joel Schick; with photographs by Jill Krementz and from the NET Playhouse production. Delacorte Press 1972 276p illus $8.95   812

1 Television plays   LC 72-2458

"A Seymour Lawrence book"
This "is the script of an NET Playhouse television program based mainly on [the novels] Cat's Cradle . . . and The Sirens of Titan, with material [added] in from two or three Vonnegut stories and his first novel, Player Piano. . . . Vonnegut apparently had a hand in stitching the script together." N Y Rev of Books
The basic story line: Young Stony Stevenson wins a jingle contest and, as his prize, is blasted off into the time-space warp. The country's first poet-astronaut thus experiences both past and future human history simultaneously. His observations on it consist mainly of dramatized selections from the author's works

Walker, Joseph A.
The River Niger; a play. Hill & Wang 1973 177p $7.95   812

1 Negroes—Drama
ISBN 0-8090-8239-X   LC 73-80218

"A Mermaid dramabook"
Characters: 7 men, 4 women. 3 acts. 1 set. First produced at St Mark's Playhouse, New York City, December 5, 1972
Johnny Williams, Harlem house painter, poet, devoted husband, father, and friend, is the central figure of the play. Johnny's quest for a battlefield on which to fight for the rights of all Black men is counter-pointed by his son Jeff's demand for individuality and self-expression within society's bounds. The play opens with Jeff's homecoming from military service and develops around the subsequent confrontation of tensions between generations, sexes, comrades, and philosophies
This play "was given the Obie award for the best Off-Broadway play, 1972-73. Although the drama seems to be worthy of the award, it is not without rather serious faults. . . . The plot is somewhat contrived and melodramatic. Then, too, Walker seems to be striving for shock effect through his overabundant use of unnecessarily coarse and bawdy language. Perhaps the play's greatest strength rests in character portrayal. All of the main characters are concretely and convincingly delineated, and thus most readers and spectators should have little difficulty in empathizing with them." Choice

Wheeler, Hugh
A little night music; a new musical comedy. Book by Hugh Wheeler; music and lyrics by Stephen Sondheim; suggested by a film by Ingmar Bergman; originally produced and directed on Broadway by Harold Prince; illus. with a drawing by Al Hirschfeld and photographs. Dodd 1973 174p illus $6.95   812

ISBN 0-396-06915-0   LC 73-19082

Characters: 7 men, 10 women. 2 acts. 17 scenes, prologue and entr'acte. First produced at the Shubert Theatre, New York City, February 25, 1973
Based on the Ingmar Bergman film: Smiles of a summer night, this musical comedy, set in turn of the century Sweden, deals with the love lives of youth and the middle aged and the retrospective affairs of the old

812.07 American drama—Awards

Bonin, Jane F.
Prize-winning American drama; a bibliographical and descriptive guide. Scarecrow 1973 222p $6.50   812.07

1 American drama—History and criticism 2 American drama—Bibliography 3 Literary prizes
ISBN 0-8108-0607-X   LC 73-3111

"This book, arranged chronologically by theatre season, lists prize-winning plays from 1917

Bonin, Jane F.—*Continued*
to 1971. The awards included are the Pulitzer Prize, the Critics' Circle Award, the Tony, the Obie, and the Players' Workshop Award. There is a brief synopsis of each play, its theatre history, critical response to the play, and biographical information about the author. Citations to representative reviews are included also. In general, the information given is far too brief to be of much use. All the information given here is available in much more detail in other standard reference sources, although there is the convenience of having the information summarized in one place." Cur Ref Bks

812.08 American drama—Collections

Hatch, James V.
(ed.) Black theater, U.S.A.; forty-five plays by Black Americans, 1847-1974. Ted Shine, consultant. Free Press 1974 886p $19.95   **812.08**
 1 Negro drama—Collections
 ISBN 0-02-914160-5   LC 75-169234

The selections range in attitude from plays in which Black characters and concerns are absent to contemporary expositions of rage and revolution. Among the playwrights represented are: Jean Toomer, Langston Hughes, Willis Richardson, Richard Wright, Stanley Richards, James Baldwin, Lorraine Hansberry, Alice Childress, Adrienne Kennedy, Imamu Amiri Baraka (LeRoi Jones), and Ed Bullins
"While the cumulative effect does not necessarily provide an index to the black theater as an institutional priority, the wide range of plays authored by blacks is quite revelatory. Most gratifying for any researcher is the reissue of plays that have long been out of print and inaccessible. It is also of interest to discover . . . obscure works. . . . The editors have been insightful in providing two sections of early and contemporary plays written by black women." Choice
Bibliographies: p875-80

812.09 American drama—History and criticism

Hayman, Ronald
Edward Albee. Ungar [1973 c1971] 151p illus (World dramatists) $6.50   **812.09**
 1 Albee, Edward
 ISBN 0-8044-2385-7   LC 71-153121
First published 1971 in England
In this study of Albee's work to date, Ronald Hayman sees a "natural" playwright whose remarkable talent is threatened by the "rival pulls of Beckett and Broadway." Albee's plays in the experimental and naturalistic traditions are examined in detail, as are those works—Tiny Alice, A Delicate Balance, and All Over—in which he attempts a fusion of two seemingly antithetical approaches to the drama
"This is a rather good book, but only for the first half. Literate and commonsensical. Hayman examines the plays as theater and literature; but almost exactly half way through he begins to evade basic thematic and plot concerns. . . . The strong concluding paragraph of the book seems hastily tacked on, hardly resulting from his previous commentary. But the plays are summarized (though misleadingly in the final two chapters), and there is a list of productions and five photos. The first four chapters are a good starting place for the Albee student." Choice
Bibliography: p143-44

813.09 American fiction—History and criticism

Bakish, David
Richard Wright. Ungar 1973 114p (Modern literature monographs) $5   **813.09**
 1 Wright, Richard
 ISBN 0-8044-2015-7   LC 71-190353

"Balanced if brief in coverage the book appraises Wright as a spokesman for black liberation whose writings served as precursors for present-day militant theorists. The study weighs the impact of Wright's political concepts and personal experiences as dominant factors in the formulation of his writing style and thorough synopses of both familiar and less-known works shows Wright's critical importance as a black author." Booklist
Bibliography: p107-09

Baum, L. Frank
The annotated Wizard of Oz; The wonderful Wizard of Oz; pictures by W. W. Denslow; with an introduction, notes, and bibliography by Michael Patrick Hearn. Potter, C.N. 1973 384p illus $15   **813.09**
 1 Baum, L. Frank. The wonderful Wizard of Oz
 ISBN 0-517-50086-8   LC 72-80842

This "introduction gives a brief biography of the author, spiced with contemporary and recent appraisals of his work, and an appendix is devoted to the illustrator of this first Oz book, W. W. Denslow, whose illustrations are reproduced in color, along with sketches, some of Denslow's other work, and photographs of various stage and screen productions of Oz stories. Hearn's notes run along with the original text. . . . For all readers who have loved the Oz books, this book is a must, and it offers a complete and attractive introduction to anyone new to the series." Choice

Costa, Richard Hauer
Malcolm Lowry. Twayne 1972 208p (Twayne's World authors ser) $6.95   **813.09**
 1 Lowry, Malcolm   LC 75-185451

For his "discussion of the composition of Lowry's 'Under the volcano' (1947) Costa examined the five extant drafts and 1,100 pages of working notes, interviewed Lowry's widow and such intimates as Conrad Aiken, Earle Birney, and David Markson, and followed Lowry's trail through Mexico to plot the close parallels between Lowry's life and art. . . . Discussing the rest of Lowry's fragmented work, Costa rejects the inflated claims of the cultists, and finds it to be of interest mainly in relation to 'Volcano,' the book Lowry never stopped writing even after publication. Of additional interest are the full account of Lowry's death, the intelligent discussion of Lowry's Canadianness, and a tantalizingly annotated bibliography." Choice

Fennimore, Keith J.
Booth Tarkington. Twayne 1974 167p (Twayne's United States authors ser) $6.50   **813.09**
 1 Tarkington, Booth
 ISBN 0-8057-0715-8   LC 73-16403

"Fennimore finds Tarkington, usually dismissed as merely a genial and slickly competent storyteller, perceptive as a social critic, well ahead of all but a few of his pre-World War I contemporaries. He notes in Tarkington's early novels (e.g. the Pulitzer prize-winning 'Magnificent Ambersons') threats of urban blight, air pollution caused by industrial development, even passion for the 'horseless carriage' that was to become a universal agency of change. . . . Fennimore concedes him a worthy position in our national letters." Choice
"A balanced volume which gives close attention to character analysis. . . . Since Tarkington, a once popular writer, seems due for renewed attention for a variety of reasons among which are revived interest in his era and his portraits of women), this volume will serve as a competent introduction." Library J
Selected bibliography: p157-61

Hardy, John Edward
Katherine Anne Porter. Ungar 1973 160p $6   **813.09**
 1 Porter, Katherine Anne
 ISBN 0-8044-2351-2   LC 72-79929

The author considers the meaning of Katherine Anne Porter's art through a review of what has been written about her life, followed by [an] . . . analysis of the stories them-

Hardy, John E.—*Continued*
selves. He approaches her work through a discussion of prominent themes which dominate the stories in different guises
"Hardy's interpretation of Porter's use of color, image, and symbolism avoids the murky prose of much literary criticism. . . . [New readers of Porter] will appreciate this simply organized, not overly academic study." Library J
Bibliography: p147-51

Hersey, John
(ed.) Ralph Ellison; a collection of critical essays. Prentice-Hall 1974 180p $5.95 **813.09**
1 Ellison, Ralph 2 Ellison, Ralph. Invisible man
ISBN 0-13-274357-4 LC 73-16224
"Twentieth century views. A Spectrum book"
This collection brings together selections by celebrated critics and authors such as Robert Penn Warren, Saul Bellow, Irving Howe, and Tony Tanner. They focus primarily on Invisible man, Ellison's symbolic, epic narrative of a Black man's maturation in white America. Also included is an interview with Ellison conducted by the editor
Selected bibliography: p179-80

Kazin, Alfred
Bright book of life: American novelists and storytellers from Hemingway to Mailer. Little 1973 334p $8.95 **813.09**
1 American fiction—History and criticism
ISBN 0-316-48418-0 LC 72-13748
"An Atlantic Monthly Press book"
Analyzed in Essay and general literature index
The author "carries his continuing interpretation of American fiction to 1971. He looks back again at Hemingway and Faulkner . . . and then picks up with the postwar generation: the war novelists, the Jewish novelists, the new generation of Southern writers, the women writers prophesying doom, [and] a few of the American absurdists." Newsweek
"Kazin has his obscure passages when he telescopes his ideas, but he is, for the most part, clear and graceful. His book is useful to the foreign reader for he has read everything worth reading from Hemingway onwards, but it is more than a work reference. . . . He goes for the essence of his novelists, major and minor, rather than for the social or metaphysical conundrums surrounding them. He is a catholic and discursive commentator who makes excellent asides. He knows where his argument is going as the novel leaves the confidence of the Hemingway period for the brilliant assertions that have marked the disintegration of forms we are now getting used to." N Y Times Bk R

Klinkowitz, Jerome
(ed.) The Vonnegut statement; ed. by Jerome Klinkowitz & John Somer. Delacorte Press 1973 286p $7.95 **813.09**
1 Vonnegut, Kurt
ISBN 0-440-09482-8 LC 72-5161
"The book includes a long and revealing Robert Scholes interview with Vonnegut, an affectionate tribute by fellow Hoosier novelist Dan Wakefield, a small group of serious and penetrating essays, a very comprehensive bibliography, and a lot of chatter about the Vonnegut kids and the emerging cult of Vonnegut. But it is not an impartial book. . . . [It] reveals something of the charisma of Vonnegut and includes some very solid essays about his novels; therefore, promotional stunt or not, it is essential for any library of contemporary literature." Choice

Lundquist, James
Sinclair Lewis. Ungar [1972 c1973] 150p (Modern literature monographs) $6 **813.09**
1 Lewis, Sinclair
ISBN 0-8044-2562-0 LC 72-76774
"Capsule evaluation of Lewis' novels and essays that respects its subject while laying bare stylistic atrocities. Lundquist assesses Lewis' survival value, examining ironic undertones, preoccupation with fundamental moral values, and satiric treatment of Minnesotans. The author's understanding depiction of Lewis enriches the lucid analysis." Booklist
Bibliography: p137-42

Powers, Lyall H.
(ed.) Henry James's major novels: essays in criticism; ed. with an introduction. Mich. State Univ. Press 1973 461p $12.50 **813.09**
1 James, Henry
ISBN 0-87013-142-7 LC 73-140679
Analyzed in Essay and general literature index
"With one exception, all of the essays have been published within the past twenty years. . . . Some of [them] are strictly explicative—F. C. Crews' on The Ambassadors, [L. H. Powers'] on The Portrait of a Lady, and H. K. Girling's on The Golden Bowl. . . . In other essays the explication serves to relate the novel in question to major motifs of European literature of the nineteenth and twentieth centuries—e.g. Edward Engelberg's on Roderick Hudson, Lionel Trilling's and Frederick I. Hoffman's on The Princess Casamassima." Preface
The collection "is discriminating and highly selective." New Eng Q
Selected bibliography: p459-61

Rank, Hugh
Edwin O'Connor. Twayne 1974 197p (Twayne's United States authors ser) $7.50 **813.09**
1 O'Conner, Edwin
ISBN 0-8057-0555-4 LC 73-17301
"Well-written, packed with information, this critical-biographical study soundly sets forth the case for O'Connor's importance as an American novelist. It argues for his artistic merit and the thematic importance of his contributions to the Irish-American and American-Catholic fictional traditions." Library J
Bibliography: p193-94

Ratner, Marc L.
William Styron. Twayne 1972 170p (Twayne's United States authors ser) $6.50 **813.09**
1 Styron, William LC 70-169632
"Outlines Styron's development, considers his use of satire, forwards what are believed to be his views on sex, violence, and contemporary American social life, and attempts to demonstrate that regarding Styron simply as a regional author is to read his works in error. One is, at book's end, willing to concede this point but not, perhaps, willing to accept the premise that Styron's poetic gifts 'approximate' those of William Faulkner. A sound and straightforward account that ought to be of interest to all libraries with even modest collections of works by and about Styron. Contains chronology, notes, bibliography, and index." Choice

Schulz, Max F.
Black humor fiction of the sixties; a pluralistic definition of man and his world. Ohio Univ. Press 1973 156p $8.50 **813.09**
1 American fiction—History and criticism.
ISBN 0-8214-0125-4 LC 72-85538
Analyzed in Essay and general literature index
"The method and subject of black humor, which Schultz states remains a predominantly American phenomenon of the 1960s, are here analyzed and exemplified. Schulz regards the genre multistranded and restricts discussion to one or two authors for each point—the writings of Barth in relation to the metaphysics of multiplicity, Vonnegut for unconfirmed thesis, Pynchon in relation to the politics of parody, and Friedman for conformist heroes. Bibliography of text references and summaries of novels discussed are appended. Chapter notes include bibliographical references." Booklist
"Excerpt for isolated magazine articles, little that is definitive has been written to date about black humor—so Schulz' book fills a gap. It is fully footnoted and indexed; and a final section supplies summaries of 26 black-humor works discussed in the text." Choice

Stephens, Martha
The question of Flannery O'Connor. La. State Univ. Press 1973 205p (Southern literary studies) $8.50 **813.09**
1 O'Connor, Flannery
ISBN 0-8071-0000-5 LC 73-77656

Stephens, Martha—*Continued*

Stephens discusses O'Connor's two novels, Wise blood and The violent bear it away, and the major short stories, 'A good man is hard to find,' 'Temple of the Holy Ghost,' 'A circle in the fire,' and 'Parker's back'. "Included in the discussions are ... illustrative quotations from the novels and stories.... [The author discusses also] O'Connor's religious beliefs and her search for artistic truth ... her background, her illness, writers with whom she shares a common bond ... [and] her limitations; the focus of the book, however, remains ... on O'Connor the artist and the 'tonal dimension' which characterizes her work," Choice

Bibliography: p197-202

Walters, Dorothy
Flannery O'Connor. Twayne 1973 172p (Twayne's United States authors ser) $7.50
813.09

1 O'Connor, Flannery
ISBN 0-8057-0556-2   LC 72-934

"This book aims to explore as fully as possible Flannery O'Connor's fictional universe, focusing on the many dualities and contrarieties which are inherent in her work.... It explores the major themes and subjects: man's painful progress toward salvation, the sacramental nature of human experience, the many convergences—of races, generations, and beliefs—which continually disrupt life in the earthly city." Publisher's note

Bibliography: p163-69

814   American essays

Pound, Ezra
Selected prose, 1909-1965. Ed. with an introduction by William Cookson. New Directions 1973 475p $15
814

ISBN 0-8112-0465-0   LC 72-93978

"A New Directions book"
Among the topics included in this collection of 66 essays are religion, Confusion, Mencius, American historical figures, civilization, economics, poetry, and Pound's contemporaries. The essay, Patria mia, is included

This collection of Pound's writing demonstrates "how wide ranging his concerns could be, and how good-humoredly and without excessive authoritarianism he could, when he chose, discuss them. It is a big book intelligently divided by subject, with the heaviest and longest section properly devoted to 'Civilisation, Money and History.' A major contribution to the Pound file." New Repub

817   American satire and humor

Armour, Richard
Going like sixty; a lighthearted look at the later years
817

1 Old age—Anecdotes, facetiae, satire, etc.

Some editions are:
Hall. G.K.&Co. $6.95 Large print edition (ISBN 0-8161-6222-0)
McGraw $5.95 (ISBN 0-07-002291-7)

First published 1974
Armour's devotees "will welcome his latest work, devoted to the exploration of some common verities—and fallacies—that surround the process of growing old." Library J

It all started with freshman English; a survival kit for students and teachers of English and a relaxed review for those who are happily past it all. McGraw 1973 161p $5.95
817

1 English literature—Anecdotes, facetiae, satire, etc. 2 American literature—Anecdotes, facetiae, satire, etc.
ISBN 0-07-002301-8   LC 73-461

This is a "collection of light verse and prose selections from Armour's previously published books and from 'Saturday Review' columns, with new supplemental and explanatory materials added. His unconventional approach to punctuation, grammar, Shakespeare, and English and American literature includes parodies and a liberal sprinkling of puns along with wise and witty remarks on the art of teaching." Booklist

"There is some good, lighthearted banter in this little book and it has passages which will induce wry smiles, particularly among teachers in colleges. The parodies are lengthy and somewhat amusing, but the three principal subjects—'Hamlet,' 'David Copperfield,' and 'The Scarlet Letter'—easily lend, and have lent, themselves to parody. The verses are so typical of inferior student papers that they are apt to make a reader squirm with embarrassment." Best Sellers

Bombeck, Erma
I lost everything in the post-natal depression; illus. by Loretta Krupinski. Doubleday 1973 161p illus $4.95
817

ISBN 0-385-02904-7   LC 72-97269

In this "expanded collection of items from her syndicated column 'At Wit's End' ... [the author gives] humorous comments on the current middle class suburban life-style." Library J

"The least exciting events in day-to-day living are satirized and made into hilarious experiences.... Many modern and up-to-date notions are presented in the author's account. Edith Bunker, Flip Wilson, Carol Burnett, and other T.V. notables are used to contemporize her comic incidents. Such mention makes this a 'now' book because in time these events will become cliches, but for the reader who wants to be amused, who wants to laugh at himself and his family in twentieth-century U.S.A., this book is a winner." Best Sellers

Buchwald, Art
I never danced at the White House. Putnam 1973 249p $6.95
817

1 U.S.—Civilization—Anecdotes, facetiae, satire, etc.
ISBN 0-399-11212-X   LC 73-78585

This "is a compilation of the columnist's essays written in 1971, 1972, and the first half of 1973.... Included here are pieces on the 1972 Presidential campaign, U.S. policy in Indochina, Nixon's trip to China, and the Administration's economic policies. Further afield, Buchwald has included essays on women's lib, the media, youth, the trials and tribulations of family life, and travel problems." Library J

"Buchwald treats crucial issues of domestic and foreign policy with a wry wit that reveals his clear eye for the potential humor in the most serious situation which he turns to the best critical advantage." Booklist

Levenson, Sam
In one era and out the other. Simon & Schuster 1973 190p $6.95
817

ISBN 0-671-21578-7   LC 73-5250

Comedian and former schoolteacher Sam Levenson, who was brought up in a background of poverty and Jewish orthodoxy, presents humorous reminiscences and comments on changing times and values

"Sam Levenson's humor may not always produce gales of laughter, but most of us will be hard put not to find chuckles and, at the very least, rueful smiles in his new book." Pub W

818   American miscellany

Capote, Truman
The dogs bark; public people and private places. Random House 1973 419p $8.95
818

ISBN 0-394-48751-6   LC 73-3988

This collection of essays, profiles, travel pieces and observations includes The muses are heard, and Local color, originally published 1956 and 1950 respectively

This book "bulges with sharp, subtle observations of people, fascinating reminiscences and travel jottings, wonderful sketches, anecdotes and yarns, and, among other things, the most frightening horror story you've ever heard. Not a deep plate of soup, perhaps, but a marvelously tasty one. Capote is an incomparable stylist and entertainer." N Y Times Bk R

Fuller, R. Buckminster
Buckminster Fuller to children of earth; comp. and photographed by Cam Smith. Doubleday 1972 unp illus pa $3.95   **818**
ISBN 0-385-02979-9   LC 72-86571

"Buckminster Fuller, designer of the geodesic dome, is a modern philosopher with a vision of the universe as an educative experience. This small book is a collaboration with Cam Smith, a wildlife photographer. Her photographs, combined with Fuller's aphorisms, strongly enforce his vision of the earth. Fuller sees the beauty of nature, the creative forces of man, and the natural inquisitiveness of children. Although this is slight, it will appeal to YA's [and others] concerned with the environment." Library J

Kesey, Ken
Kesey's Garage sale. Viking 1973 238p illus $8.95   **818**
ISBN 0-670-41268-6   LC 77-186734

"A lunacy offering, illustrated by a delirious crawl of cartoons by 'artist extraordinaire' Paul Foster, and based on the freaked-out lives of Kesey and his friends. It's a 'joint' effort in the form of a 'garage sale' of memorabilia, memories and prophecies out of the post-Beat past; one might in fact call it an event in Americana played out on the fringe of the fringe. The book's Hot Items are: Kesey's vignette-crowded recall of life in a 'local VA nuthouse'; his screenplay 'Over the Border,' a raw recap of the adventures of his band of X-iles in Mexico; a choice selection from 'The Last Supplement to the Whole Earth Catalog'; a nostalgic chest of 'truth-tools' drawn from the Kesey-Cassady-Ginsberg past; Paul Krassner's serious-wacky interview with Kesey. Yeats's center that cannot hold holds beautifully for Arthur Miller, whose introduction linking his generation's protest with Kesey's is one of his most mature writings." Pub W

Kinnamon, Keneth
(ed.) James Baldwin; a collection of critical essays. Prentice-Hall 1974 169p $6.95   **818**

1 Baldwin, James
ISBN 0-13-055566-5   LC 74-6175

"Twentieth century views. A Spectrum book"
"Fourteen critics evaluate Baldwin's literary achievements and influences, giving widely varying interpretations of the author's moral and social themes. Essays include speculation on the degree to which Baldwin's personal deprivations confine his work to a racial statement or are a depiction of contemporary ordeals. Studies by Irving Howe, Calvin Hernton, Eldridge Cleaver, and Benjamin DeMott are included among the well-chosen selections. Chronology, notes on contributors, and a select bibliography are appended." Booklist

Levertov, Denise
The poet in the world. [New Directions] 1973 275p $9.50   **818**
ISBN 0-8112-0492-8   LC 73-78785

"A New Directions book"
"Drawing on formal essays, notebook jottings, work sheets, rally speeches, and symposium talks, Levertov offers a . . . sample of her prose writings; statements on poetics; political comments based on a trip to Hanoi; accounts of teaching experiences (both the successes and fiascos) at Drew, CCNY, Vassar, and Berkeley; 'fictive or semi-fictive' pieces . . . and reviews of several modern poets." Library J
This is an "uneven, occasionally exasperating and always sincere collage of essays. . . . Of its five sections—'Work and Inspiration,' 'Life at War,' 'The Untaught Teacher,' 'Perhaps Fiction,' and 'Other Writers'—by far the most interesting is the first. Miss Levertov can, and does, write lucidly of the blunders, prizes and tenacities of the poet sweating out her poem; and . . . she has some sharply accurate things to say of the flabbiness of much current poetry. . . . Her analysis of the uses of myth in poetry, of the numinous metaphor, is an intelligent discussion of the poverty of urban cynicism. . . . When she writes of teaching . . . her veracity and her empathy with students of any age and background are most appealing." New Repub
Includes bibliographical references

McKay, Claude
The passion of Claude McKay; selected poetry and prose, 1912-1948; ed. with an introduction and notes by Wayne F. Cooper. Schocken 1973 363p illus (Sourcebooks in Negro history) $10.95   **818**
ISBN 0-8052-3498-5   LC 72-95662

This collection of Claude McKay's writings includes "his first articles in 1918; his comments on the year spent in Russia (1922-23); his best poems written between 1912 and 1925; and the essays and personal letters during his expatriate years, 1925-32. Unpublished letters and other writing appear here for the first time." Choice
Bibliography: p340-58

Mencken, H. L.
The young Mencken; the best of his work; collected by Carl Bode. Dial Press 1973 xxxii, 576p illus $15
ISBN 0-8037-9816-4   LC 72-13534

This is a "collection of Mencken's early writing in chronological order, from 1896 to 1917, with a reverent introduction and sectional notes by Carl Bode. . . . Verse, short stories, social criticism, and essays on music and literature, reprinted from the 'Baltimore Sun' and the magazine 'Smart Set,' display Mencken's relish at his public posture of gadfly and scourge of pomposity." Booklist
Here are "early position papers and tomfooleries by a master of English prose." Library J

Thoreau, Henry David
The illustrated Walden; with photographs from the Gleason collection. Text ed. by J. Lyndon Shanley. Princeton Univ. Press 1973 xxxv, 352p illus $15   **818**
ISBN 0-691-06266-8   LC 73-8266

Another edition of a work entered in main catalog with title: Walden

Vonnegut, Kurt
Wampeters, foma & granfalloons (opinions) [by] Kurt Vonnegut, Jr. Delacorte Press 1974 xxvii, 285p $8.95   **818**
ISBN 0-440-08717-1   LC 73-22462

"Vonnegut's attitudes on contemporary existence surface in this compilation of previously published articles gathered from various periodicals. Topics range from a transplantee reduced to life at the mercy of plastic tubes and computerized organs to a mellow journey down the East Coast Inland Waterway. In reviews, essays, speeches, a play, and a 'Playboy' interview, the author manifests serious meditations as well as slamming satire in frank but pleasurable style." Booklist

820.3   English literature— Encyclopedias and dictionaries

Freeman, William
Dictionary of fictional characters. Rev. by Fred Urquhart; with indexes of authors and titles by E. N. Pennell. Writer [1974 c1973] 579p $8.95   **820.3**

1 English literature—Dictionaries 2 American literature—Dictionaries 3 Characters and characteristics in literature—Dictionaries
ISBN 0-87116-085-4   LC 73-18065

Earlier edition entered in main catalog
First published 1963. This edition first published 1973 in England. "Urquhart has eliminated about 400 characters listed in the first edition (1963) and has added 1614 new references, which provide data on more than 2000 characters from 360 novels and plays." Library J

820.8 English literature—Collections

The Oxford Anthology of English literature. General editors: Frank Kermode and John Hollander. Oxford 1973 2v illus maps ea $9.95   820.8

1 English literature—Collections
LC 72-92355

Each of the six parts collected here were published separately and are available in paperback at $3.95 each
Contents: v 1 The Middle Ages through the eighteenth century: Medieval English literature [ed. by] J. B. Trapp, The literature of Renaissance England [ed. by] John Hollander and Frank Kermode; The Restoration and the eighteenth century [ed. by] Martin Price (ISBN 0-19-501657-2); v2 1800 to the present: Romantic poetry and prose [ed. by] Harold Bloom and Lionel Trilling; Victorian prose and poetry [ed. by] Lionel Trilling and Harold Bloom; Modern British literature [ed. by] Frank Kermode and John Hollander (ISBN 0-19-501658-0)
"This is an excellent handsome anthology of English literature. Its editors are widely known for their scholarship, and the introductions are good if not always excellent. It is, however, very like other anthologies. The weakest section in the Oxford is the Victorian. . . . The medieval and Renaissance sections are excellent, better than any available anthology. Eighteenth-century selections are very good; good notation. A very small or very large library might purchase these two volumes. One distinctive feature of the set is the use of illustrations." Choice
Includes a glossary, suggestions for further reading, an author and title index and an index of first lines

821 English poetry

Browning, Elizabeth Barrett
The poetical works of Elizabeth Barrett Browning; with a new introduction by Ruth M. Adams. Houghton 1974 xxii, 548p front $10   821
ISBN 0-395-18485-1   LC 73-20373
"Cambridge edition"
Another edition of a title first published 1900 with title: The complete poetical works of Elizabeth Barrett Browning, and entered in main catalog
Includes indexes of first lines and titles

Coward Noël
The lyrics of Noël Coward. Overlook Press [1973 c1965] 418p $12.95   821
ISBN 0-87951-011-0   LC 73-77884
This is a reprint of a book first published 1965 in England
Arranged by the decades in which they were written, this book includes the lyrics to songs by Noël Coward spanning from the 1920's to the 1960's

Durrell, Lawrence
Vega, and other poems. Overlook Press 1973 54p $5.95   821
ISBN 0-87951-009-9   LC 73-75122
Love and philosophy are the concerns of this collection of verse by the English writer
"These poems are more focused and more clearly grounded in the recognition of mortality than those in Durrell's last book, The Ikons [and other poems, entered in main catalog]. A few of the love lyrics and a number of the more philosophical poems are as sure as those earlier poems which captured the essence of things or sketched in short biographies the dualism of heart and head. As always in Durrell's poetry, the allegiance is to experience, not to reason." Library J

Graves, Robert
Poems, 1970-1972. Doubleday 1973 [c1972] 83p $5.95   821
ISBN 0-385-06269-9   LC 72-84917
A collection of 83 poems. "The first two sections contain love poems; the last consists of satire and contemporary comment." Library J
"His prosody becomes most forceful when he uses no end rhymes but lets the rhythms flow. Graves confesses his debt to Welsh metrics. It has been a good influence. Diction and imagery move in lovely concordance, apparently with ease but thoroughly crafted by a great consciousness." Choice

821.08 English poetry—Collections

Chicorel Index to poetry in collections in print, on discs and tapes: poetry on discs, tapes, and cassettes; ed. by Marietta Chicorel. Consulting editors: Mariella Bednar [and others]. Chicorel Lib. Pub. Corp. 1972 443p $49.50   821.08

1 English poetry—Indexes 2 American poetry—Indexes
ISBN 0-87729-004-9   LC 73-160763
"Chicorel Index series"
"The reader will find approximately 700 collections of recorded poetry analyzed on more than 1,800 discs and tapes, in a record 25,000 entries." Ref Services Rev

The Oxford Book of children's verse; chosen and ed. with notes, by Iona and Peter Opie. Oxford 1973 xxxi, 407p illus $10   821.08

1 Children's poetry—Collections
ISBN 0-19-812140-7   LC 73-76871
Arranged chronologically, these 332 selections from British and American children's poetry include works by such poets as Chaucer, Charles and Mary Lamb, Kipling, Farjeon, Milne, Eliot and Nash. Poets still living are not included
This "volume serves as a solid base for a logical presentation of the historical devolpment of children's verse. . . . Although few child readers will find the collection especially exciting because of the clear connections of the verses with the historical periods that produced them, scholars at last have an intelligent, comprehensive anthology of verse for children or about children that clearly demonstrates changing attitudes and values. An excellent chronological collection that should be in every library." Choice
Includes sources and biographical notes and indexes of authors, first lines and familiar titles

The Oxford Book of twentieth-century English verse; chosen by Philip Larkin. Oxford 1973 1, 641p $12.50   821.08

1 English poetry—Collections
ISBN 0-19-812137-7   LC 73-159943
This anthology of more than 600 poems by more than 200 twentieth-century British writers includes works by John Mansfield, T. E. Eliot, W. B. Yeats, W. H. Auden, Dylan Thomas and Alan Sillitoe
"A strong vein of neo-Georgianism runs throughout the book, resulting in a clear partiality for work that is explicitly, even documentarily, English in locale, for poems that are narrative or anecdotal, for neat, well-populated fables and for moralistic ruminations. . . . [Larkin] has played safe with major figures, and by exhibiting commitments both wide enough and shallow enough to seem blandly noncommital . . . he has contrived neither to offend nor cheer the living." New Statesman
Includes indexes of first lines and authors

Sylvester, Richard S.
(ed.) The Anchor Anthology of sixteenth-century verse; ed. with an introduction and notes. Anchor Bks. 1974 xxxiv, 624p pa $6.95   821.08

1 English poetry—Collections
ISBN 0-385-00286-6   LC 73-8496
"This excellent anthology presents generous selections of 16th-Century English poetry in the original spelling, including major works of 11 poets, such as Wyatt, [Skelton], Surrey, Gascoigne, Raleigh, Spenser, Sidney, Marlowe, and Campion, and giving careful attention to 14 sonneteers, among them Watson, Lodge, Fletcher, Constable, Daniel, Drayton, and Greville. Professor Sylvester's preface succeeds

Sylvester, Richard S.—*Continued*

in informing the reader and in engaging his attention to the poetry. His selection brilliantly represents both the scope and emphasis of the period and this confirms the reader's interest; his notes provide information essential to further study." Library J

Indexed by author, title and first line. Contains biographical and bibliographical notes for each author and a general bibliography

Untermeyer, Louis

(ed.) 50 modern American & British poets, 1920-1970; ed. with a biographical and critical commentary. McKay 1973 xxv, 358p $7.95

821.08

1 English poetry—Collections 2 American poetry—Collections
ISBN 0-679-30230-1   LC 72-89118

Poets represented in this anthology include: Frost, Stevens, Williams, Pound, Moore, Eliot, Cummings, Langston Hughes, Auden, Dylan Thomas and Allen Ginsberg

This "is the kind of book that makes an ideal gift, a gift not for the adept or the connoisseur; but for that species of common reader 'who doesn't like modern poetry.' Untermeyer's '50' are skillfully chosen to persuade that reader, to lure, to initiate, to win over. It begins with the familiar . . . and it ends with the unfamiliar, with Erica Jong's 'The Eggplant Epithalamion.' . . . The concluding quarter of this book is made up of commentaries on each poet. Here, veteran anthologist Louis Untermeyer offers helpful interpretations of individual poems, occasional quotations from critics, and titles for further reading. He is never obtrusive, often illuminating." Christian Science Monitor

Includes title, author and first line indexes

821.09 English poetry—History and criticism

Crowell, Norton B.

A reader's guide to Robert Browning. Univ. of N.Mex. Press [1973 c1972] 268p $12

821.09

1 Browning, Robert
ISBN 0-8263-0265-3   LC 72-86825

The author singles out twenty-three of the poet's major short poems for discussion, incorporating into his own analyses a summary of the major critical opinions about each and adding to every chapter an annotated list of suggested readings

"In this guide an established Browning scholar provides a useful tool. . . . Crowell's criticism, if not strikingly innovative, is straightforward and perceptive; his work will serve many readers well." Library J

Bibliography of works published on Browning, 1945-1969: p243-65

Oates, Joyce Carol

The hostile sun; the poetry of D. H. Lawrence. Black Sparrow Press 1973 60p pa $3

821.09

1 Lawrence, David Herbert
ISBN 0-87685-168-5   LC 73-8763

The author "pays intelligent tribute to a great predecessor to whom she feels indebted. Her assessment of Lawrence's poetry is hardly startling, but her interpretations are insightful and have the strength of conviction. Admirers of Oates will be particularly interested in this handsome little item, and serious readers of Lawrence will want to know about it too." Library J

822.09 English drama—History and criticism

Nicoll, Allardyce

English drama, 1900-1930; the beginnings of the modern period. Cambridge 1973 1083p $55

822.09

1 English drama—History and criticism 2 Theater—Great Britain—History 3 English drama—Bibliography
ISBN 0-521-08416-4   LC 70-171679

In this "survey of the theatre from 1900 to 1930, Professor Nicoll discusses not only the works of the more prominent playwrights (from Pinero and Jones, through Shaw, Barrie, Galsworthy, Maugham, Davies, Calderon, Granville-Barker, Milne, and on to Coward), but also those of the now lesser-known but once successful and influential authors, including writers of melodramas, musical comedies, pantomimes, music hall one-act plays, revues, propagandist plays, pageants and other usually neglected forms of theatre. [Included is a] . . . general hand-list of plays, long and short, acted and printed during these years, with information on production dates and publication." Publisher's note

"It is useful to those scholars and students needing detailed information concerning the work of minor as well as major playwrights." Choice

822.3 William Shakespeare

Quennell, Peter

Who's who in Shakespeare [by] Peter Quennell and Hamish Johnson. Morrow 1973 287p illus $14.95

822.3

1 Shakespeare, William—Characters 2 Shakespeare, William—Dictionaries
ISBN 0-688-00192-0   LC 73-10404

In this guide to Shakespearean characters "entries are arranged alphabetically and are liberally illustrated with playbills and photographs. Each entry describes the character and establishes the character's importance in the plays. For most important Shakespeare characters, quotations are included from famous early critics such as Jonson, Coleridge, and Hazlitt." Booklist

This work "will serve its intended function of ready reference. They are all here: Cinna the Conspirator and Cinna the Poet; Falstaff's Bardolph and Lord Bardolph; the bit-player Berkeley in Richard II and his mute namesake in Richard III; and over a thousand others. . . . The entries are seasoned with quotations from the plays and extracts from 'famous early critics'. . . . We are also briefly informed about the actual careers of historical personages, and about dates and sources. . . . [The pictures] especially the posters are handsome enough." Times (London) Lit Sup

Author's acknowledgements: p9-10

Rowse, A. L.

Shakespeare the man. Harper 1973 284p illus $10

822.3

1 Shakespeare, William—Biography 2 Shakespeare, William—Criticism, interpretation, etc.
ISBN 0-06-013691-X   LC 72-10683

"A Cass Canfield book"

The author "describes the rich background of Shakepeare's life and works. He dismisses the notion that little is known about Shakespeare but shows him very 'much a reading man,' traveling frequently between London and Stratford. Rowse's Shakespeare is untroubled by the mental strain and philosophical dilemmas that vex his dramatic characters. This is no psychological study but a straightforward historical narrative." Christian Science Monitor

"A book [which] ought to delight general readers and scholars alike. . . . [Rowse] brings historical perspective to the usual account of Shakespeare as Stratford boy and London actor, the poet who left fractual records of his business ventures, but only dubious allusions to himself in his plays and poems. But bold authority becomes daring speculation as the historian sweeps through the sonnets with a new theory." Library J

Shakespeare, William

The Riverside Shakespeare; textual editor: G. Blakemore Evans; general introduction: Harry Levin. [Editors:] Herschel Baker [and others] with an essay on stage history by Charles H. Shattuck. Houghton 1974 1902p illus $14.95

822.3

ISBN 0-395-04402-2   LC 73-10712

Another edition of a work entered in main catalog with title: The complete works of William Shakespeare

Spevack, Marvin
 The Harvard Concordance to Shakespeare. Harvard Univ. Press 1973 1600p $45   **822.3**

1 Shakespeare, William—Concordances
ISBN 0-674-37475-4   LC 73-76385

"Belknap Press"
 "In 1968-70 the six volume 'A Complete and Systematic Concordance to the Works of Shakespeare,' by Marvin Spevack, was published [in Germany]. While this work has been considered an essential work for libraries supporting study of Shakespeare, many libraries could not afford the price tag of some $300, and others wished it had a more convenient format. Now, Harvard University Press has come out with a one-volume edition of the most useful parts of the [computer-generated] 'Concordance' (Volumes IV-VI). Based on the modern-spelling Riverside text of Shakespeare, edited by G. Blakemore Evans, it provides entries for every one of the more than 29,000 different words used by the bard. Since contexts are provided, it will serve as a complete quotations dictionary to the plays and poems. (if a patron gets even one key word right in a half-remembered line, one can find it here.) Also, information on the frequency of each word, indication of whether a specific instance of use is in verse or prose, and abundant cross references between variant forms of words enhance the value of the work. Most general libraries will want this fine volume." Cur Ref Bks

Wagenknecht, Edward
 The personality of Shakespeare. Univ. of Okla. Press 1972 190p $5   **822.3**

1 Shakespeare, William—Biography 2 Shakespeare, William—Criticism, interpretation, etc.
ISBN 0-8061-1028-7   LC 72-868

"What can the poems and plays tell us about the temperament of our most impersonal of authors? That is the question Wagenknecht asks.... All who love Shakespeare will enjoy this rare glimpse of the middle ground between embellished reviews of the dull facts of his life and disembodied criticisms of his plays. As they would expect, the rural mind of the boy from Stratford lives again in the vibrant allusions to flowers, sports, and cats. As they would conclude, an ideal of decency pervades both heroic and ordinary characters." Library J

823.03 English fiction—Encyclopedias and dictionaries

Greaves, John
 Who's who in Dickens. Taplinger [1973 c1972] 231p $6.95   **823.03**

1 Dickens, Charles—Characters 2 Dickens, Charles—Dictionaries
ISBN 0-8008-8266-0   LC 73-5335

First published 1972 in England
 This volume lists "in alphabetical order by name, the many characters found throughout the novels [and] stories ... of Dickens.... Each entry includes a brief description and lists ... the title in which the character appears.... Cross references, [and] a list of names (arranged by title, with chapter) ... is included." Library J
 This work "does not contain entries on the characters in the plays or Christmas Stories, or accounts of the essay collections.... But on the novels and Christmas Books, Mr Greaves—whom few other Dickens-buffs could meet in a Dickens-quiz without quailing, for he is the omniscient secretary of the Dickens Fellowship—is unfailingly accurate, succinct and genial." Times (London) Lit Sup

823.09 English fiction—History and criticism

Hardwick, Michael
 (comp.) The Charles Dickens encyclopedia; comp. by Michael and Mollie Hardwick. Scribner 1973 531p $15   **823.09**

1 Dickens, Charles—Encyclopedias
ISBN 0-684-13562-0   LC 73-7212

This volume contains information on the writing and publications of Dickens' work and plot summaries. The long section of quotations is followed by an index which forms a rudimentary concordance to Dickens. Other interesting features are biographies of the members of Dickens' circle, a chronology of the novelist's works, and a time chart covering events in the writer's life, in his writing career, and in the rest of the world, all laid out in parallel columns for quick reference. Finally, a gazetteer in two parts, inside and outside London, explains the significance of the names of geographical locations, both to Dickens' life and to his works." Choice
 "Admirably fulfills its claim as 'the most comprehensive and accurate encyclopedia' of its kind." Ref Services Rev

 A guide to Anthony Trollope. Scribner 1974 219p $6.95   **823.09**

1 Trollope, Anthony
ISBN 0-684-13823-9   LC 73-21144

English title: The Osprey Guide to Anthony Trollope
 This guide to the nineteenth century English writer's 47 novels is divided into two sections. The first offers plot summaries and descriptions of circumstances involving the novels' writing and publishing. The second section is a dictionary of nearly 500 characters who appear in Trollope's Barchester and Palliser novel series
 This book is "interesting as [a] popular guide or refresher." Library J

 A guide to Jane Austen. Scribner 1973 237p $6.95   **823.09**

1 Austen, Jane
ISBN 0-684-13824-7   LC 73-21143

This book provides a précis of Jane Austen's ten novels, "with the circumstances of their writing and publishing history; an alphabetical list of all the characters with a note of their function in the story ... and a brief 'life' of the author." Publisher's note
 "Hardwick supplies an appreciative introduction ... but there are no footnotes or bibliography." Library J

Mansell, Darrell
 The novels of Jane Austen; an interpretation. Barnes & Noble 1973 226p $13   **823.09**

1 Austen, Jane
ISBN 0-06-494548-0   LC 73-166540

This book "concentrates on the process of psychological reformation each of the heroines is forced to undergo. Each begins in a state of illusion, imposing her own private vision of the world. In the course of the novel she slowly gives up her illusion as she reluctantly accepts a few isolated, recalcitrant 'facts that she cannot change to suit her own private purposes, and that for Jane Austen represent a 'real' world into which the heroine is being initiated. Mr Mansell's book develops the thesis that this psychological reformation of the heroine is the very centre of Jane Austen's art." Publisher's note
 "The most forceful and clear explanation of Austen's six novels to appear in some time.... [The author plays] no psychoanalytic games. The ladies are mentally reformed, to be sure; but Mansell explains their reformation in traditionally allegorical terms, the journey from ignorance to knowledge.... Mansell's intellectual scheme, if sometimes brittle, is always forthright and is a no-nonsense alternative to much that has been done on Austen." Library J

Schlueter, Paul
 The novels of Doris Lessing; with a preface by Harry T. Moore. Southern Ill. Univ. Press 1973 144p (Crosscurrents/modern critiques) $6.95   **823.09**

1 Lessing, Doris
ISBN 0-8093-0612-3   LC 72-10281

On spine: Doris Lessing
 The work "is divided into five chapters. After a brief introduction Lessing's first book, The Grass Is Singing, is analyzed; in the next two chapters, the ... five-volume Children of Violence and The Golden Notebook—regarded as Lessing's central statement—are taken up. A final section deals with the ... Retreat to Innocence and the recent ... Briefing for a Descent into Hell." Christian Century

Schlueter, Paul—*Continued*

"In the long chapter on 'The Golden Notebook' Schlueter combines Lessing's comments on her novel with his own analysis to provide a very clear guide to the structure of that exceedingly complex work. The bibliography is fine, too; and this Lessing monograph, narrow and occasionally superficial though it is, is a good buy." Library J

Small, Christopher

Mary Shelley's Frankenstein; tracing the myth. Univ. of Pittsburgh Press [1973 c1972] 352p $9.95   823.09

1 Shelley, Mary Wollstonecraft (Godwin). Frankenstein 2 Shelley, Percy Bysshe
ISBN 0-8229-3276-8   LC 73-80072

First published 1972 in England with title: Ariel like a harpy

"Attempting to exemplify the 'natural history of metaphor,' Small traces the 'myth' of Frankenstein from its origin in the youthful imagination of Mary Shelley to its current manifestations in film and science fiction." Library J

"Well and probingly researched, the book pre-supposes a familiarity with Shelley's circle and work as it traces the genesis of the Frankenstein tale—its literary and social sources—the Promethean myth, Godwinism, and its relationship to Shelley himself." Pub W

Bibliography: p244-45

Walling, William A.

Mary Shelley. Twayne 1972 173p (Twayne's English authors ser) $6.50   823.09

1 Shelley, Mary Wollstonecraft (Godwin)
LC 75-161820

"Without relaxing critical standards, Walling's able scholarship demonstrates convincingly that the dimensions of Mary's fictional talents do not stop with 'Frankenstein.' Her commitment to finding a form that would bridge ideology and fiction led her into new areas of experimental novel-making. Walling gives priority to this aspect of Mary's genius, rending his discussions of her 'lost' novels, 'Valperga,' 'The last man,' 'Lodore,' and, 'Falkner' the strongest feature of his study. Although Walling produces no new biographical facts, this book is not another re-profiling: rather it is a reassurance that Mary has deservedly become a woman set free from the historical rumor that she merits attention only because she was Shelley's wife." Choice

Bibliography: p161-67

828 English miscellany

Greene, Graham

The portable Graham Greene; ed. by Philip Stratford. Viking 1973 xxiii, 610p $7.95   828
ISBN 0-670-56566-0   LC 72-78990

"The Viking Portable library"

This collection contains ten selections from autobiographical writings; twelve short stories; two complete novels, The heart of the matter and The third man; nine critical literary essays; and statements about political and social issues

"This imaginatively and carefully edited volume should help to give momentum to the growing interest in all of Greene's work.... Although one might quibble with certain of the editor's choices, this book is finally one that every library should have since it not only includes some of the best of Greene's work but also provides invaluable scholarly aids such as a full chronology, bibliographies, and the splendid introduction." Choice

Helms, Randel

Tolkien's world. Houghton 1974 167p $5.95   828

1 Tolkien, John Ronald Reuel
ISBN 0-395-18490-8   LC 74-1240

The author's "book is an admiring and searching study of Tolkien's total 'oeuvre.' Fellow devotees of 'The Hobbit' and 'Lord of the Rings' will find their appreciation deepened by this book. Most interesting is a chapter in which Helms contrasts the beliefs of William Blake and Tolkien. Blake's posture is that Eros is the ally of the good soldier in the fight against Thanatos (evil and death), while Tolkien insists that Eros is the ally,' ... even the servant, of Thanatos.' In other sections, we find confirmation of Tolkien's stature as the author who gave this generation a unique and necessary fantasy." Pub W

"Helms innovatively deals in depth with the totality of the Tolkien canon, using the scholarly, critical, and minor fiction writings to illuminate the Ring trilogy." Library J

Includes bibliographical references

Kenner, Hugh

A reader's guide to Samuel Beckett. Farrar, Straus 1973 208p $7.95   828

1 Beckett, Samuel
ISBN 0-374-24095-7   LC 73-183234

This survey is designed to give the reader a review of each of Beckett's works. "The stress falls on the uniqueness of each work, and the impression I hope to leave is one of surprising variety." Introduction

The author focuses "on Beckett's verbal craftsmanship and 'unceasingly inventive technique.' ... Usually Kenner's wit is incisive, but sometimes it lapses into preciousness.... Students of contemporary literature will be grateful for the service rendered by [this study]." Library J

Bibliography: p201-02

833.09 German fiction—History and criticism

Gray, Ronald

Franz Kafka. Cambridge 1973 220p $11.50
833.09

1 Kafka, Franz
ISBN 0-521-20007-5   LC 72-83576

In this critical introduction to the writings of Kafka, Gray surveys the most important of the novels and short stories as well as the religious or confessional writings. He presents an account of Kafka's personal and artistic development and its meaning and value for us. There are chapters on the best known and largest works, The Castle, The Trial and America, but Dr Gray argues that the early short stories, especially the Metamorphosis, are the most finished and controlled

"Carefully written and researched, aware of secondary literature, novel in some aspects but not opinionated, this book will truly facilitate the study of this enigmatic writer for non-German readers. Anyone who desires a guide in his searchings for Kafka's meaning will do well to read this book from cover to cover." Choice

Select bibliography: p215

834 German essays

Hesse, Hermann

My belief; essays on life and art. Ed. and with an introduction by Theodore Ziolkowski; tr. by Denver Lindley; with two essays tr. by Ralph Manheim. Farrar, Straus 1974 xxii, 393p $8.95   834
ISBN 0-374-21666-5   LC 72-84782

Analyzed in Essay and general literature index

This collection of 74 essays written between 1904 and 1961 includes "bits of autobiography, literary criticism, political and cultural commentary, intellectual history and pieces on Oriental literature." Pub W

In these essays "all of Hesse's abundant meditative energy, his proliferation of poles and counterpoles and syntheses, his masterly studies of Dostoevsky and Jean Paul and Hölderlin, his frank and penetrating discussion of moral and political and cultural issues show him struggling to overcome the dichotomies of past and present, science and poetry, and espousing the belief 'that there are not various peoples and minds but only One Humanity, only One Spirit.' At times both the predicament and the resolve are stated quite baldly.... But more representative of Hesse's style are those qualities of

Hesse, Hermann—*Continued*
modesty, delicacy, and tact, the aura of what he calls 'magical thinking' which illuminate even the most casual excursion and disarm us by the earnestness and purity of his voice."
N Y Rev of Bks

841 French poetry

Chanson de Roland
The song of Roland; tr. with an introduction and notes by Howard S. Robertson. Dent [distributed by Rowman & Littlefield 1973 c1972] 140p $5.75   841
ISBN 0-460-00777-7
Another edition of a title entered in main catalog
Includes bibliography, notes, and glossary

Villon, François
The legacy, the testament, and other poems of François Villon; tr. by Peter Dale. St Martins 1973 159p illus $15   841
LC 72-85557
This translation of works by the fifteenth century French poet "incorporate Villon's ballade style and changes of tone, exclamations, and seeming irrelevancies. A discussion of Dale's problems of translation and a biographical sketch of Villon procede the poems." Booklist
"Strictly metrical, the translation is a tour de force that captures the various aspects of the poetry, its coarseness and beauty, humor and profundity. Since the work is not intended as a scholarly edition or a school text, notes are short and of minimal assistance." Library J

841.09 French poetry—History and criticism

Lombard, Charles M.
Lamartine. Twayne 1973 132p (Twayne's World authors ser) $5.95   841.09
1 Lamartine, Alphonse Marie Louis de
LC 72-3449
The author "seeks to provide an analysis of Lamartine's works and career which will help to clarify the role of this Romantic poet in French literature. In order to accomplish this goal, Lombard devotes the main part of his study to a summary and concise critical analysis of each of Lamartine's works.... The final chapter consists of a valuable, well-balanced summary of Lamartine's reputation and influence both during and after his lifetime." Library J

842.09 French drama—History and criticism

Abraham, Claude
Pierre Corneille. Twayne 1972 169p (Twayne's World authors ser) $6.95   842.09
1 Corneille, Pierre   LC 76-186715
The author has given us "a scholarly and interesting book, quite possibly unequaled in English at the present time. After an introductory biographical chapter, all of the plays are carefully studied. Abraham tries, among other things, to correct the tendency of many critics to abstract criteria of 'Cornelian' standards.... He sees, rather, in the whole body of Corneille's dramatic production, along with a fidelity to certain basic principles, a steady evolution which reaches its climax in the final masterpiece, 'Surena.' The evolution is seen, in part, in the youthful heroes of the earlier plays, exuberant and instinctive in their reactions, gradually giving way to more reasoning, urbane, and human figures, and in the heroines, who, although always mindful of their obligations to themselves and their reputation, abandon their 'assumption of a masculine mystique' for a growing awareness of their true feminine nature. The selected, annotated bibliography will be very helpful, especially to readers of French." Choice

Lewis, Allan
Ionesco. Twayne 1972 119p (Twayne's World authors ser) $5.50   842.09
1 Ionesco, Eugène   LC 75-187630
The author has written summaries of Ionesco's major plays for the non-scholarly reader
Bibliography: p99-101

Webb, Eugene
The plays of Samuel Beckett. Univ. of Wash. Press 1972 160p $7.95   842.09
1 Beckett, Samuel
ISBN 0-295-95202-4   LC 72-2901
"A thematic study of Beckett's dramatic output—plays, mimes, and film—done with clarity and sensitivity.... Webb shows that thorough familiarity with the intellectual roots of the modern mind is one of the principal sources of Beckett's powers. He interprets each Beckett play individually, reveals the continuities among the plays, and groups them as they tend to emphasize either analysis of or exploration into the meaning of life. Chapter notes, chronology of first performances, and bibliography of first editions and selective list of criticism appended." Booklist

843.09 French fiction—History and criticism

Wallace, A. H.
Guy de Maupassant. Twayne 1973 156p (Twayne's World authors ser) $5.95   843.09
1 Maupassant, Guy de   LC 72-11000
A study of what Maupassant accomplished and how his achievement is both the result and revelation of his life
Bibliography: p151-54

861 Spanish poetry

Neruda, Pablo
New poems (1968-1970); edited, tr. and with an introduction by Ben Belitt. Grove 1972 xxxii, 153p $5.95   861
ISBN 0-394-48286-7   LC 72-3709
English and Spanish on opposite pages
"The several translations which have appeared in U.S. literary journals are among a majority of poems in a new collection that reflect an apolitical refinement and mellower resignation not usually associated with Chilean poet Neruda but retain quixotic characteristics which intrigue admirers. More than 50 poems, vitalistic yet disengaged, confirm Neruda's virtuosity and intense foci and are preceded by an erudite essay on the poet by Belitt." Booklist
Includes bibliographical references

864 Spanish essays

Paz, Octavio
Alternating current; tr. from the Spanish by Helen R. Lane. Viking 1973 215p $7.95   864
ISBN 0-670-11526-6   LC 72-76796
Partially analyzed in Essay and general literature index
"A Richard Seaver book"
"Paz presents a collection of criticism ranging over most of contemporary intellectual life. Partly reflections on his art by a working poet, partly superb critical synthesizing of other men's thought, the book ranges from literature —mainly Spanish-American and French— through painting, to religion, drugs, politics, and philosophy. The pieces are mostly short ... [and consider such topics as] the place of Surrealism in modern art, analogies between

Paz, Octavio—Continued

Eastern and Western thought, post-Nietzschean atheism, changing conceptions of time—and the idea of revolution among them." Library J

An important selection "by a distinguished Mexican author. . . . The difficult challenge of translating the complex content of the essays and of doing justice to the artistic and vibrant style of the author has been successfully met by the translator, thus making available to a broad public the work of a thinker rated . . . among the leading minds in the Hispanic world. This selection is a stimulating book reaching far beyond those interested in Latin American matters only." Choice

868 Spanish miscellany

Di Giovanni, Norman Thomas
(ed.) Borges on writing; ed. by Norman Thomas di Giovanni, Daniel Halpern, and Frank McShane. Dutton 1973 173p $6.95 **868**

ISBN 0-525-06997-6   LC 72-94692

This volume contains transcriptions of three discussions which took place in 1971. They deal with Borges' prose writing, with a focus on his short story: The end of the duel; his poetry; and problems of translating his work from the Spanish into literary English

"The value of this book lies primarily in the revelation of the personality of Borges and the elucidation of his own method of writing, as well as presenting his work to a North American readership. . . . [Readers] will be charmed by the sense of immediacy in the presentation." Choice

874.09 Latin lyric poetry—History and criticism

Quinn, Kenneth
Catullus; an interpretation. Barnes & Noble 1973 305p $12.75 **874.09**

1 Catullus
ISBN 0-06-495757-8   LC 73-157934

"My object has been to offer a reasonably full selection of poems in the context of an interpretation of the Catullan collection as a whole. . . . Chapter 1 discusses the collection, as it has come down to us, in general terms; Chapter 2 deals with the Lesbia poems, taking them pretty much in the order in which they stand in the collection; Chapter 3 tackles the . . . question of the relationship of the poems to what is known, or supposed, about the facts of the affair between Catullus and the women he called Lesbia; Chapter 4 discusses the relationship of the Lesbia poems to what I have called the poems of social comment." Preface

"Quinn surveys and extends the conclusions of modern scholarship regarding a Latin poet important in the Western poetic tradition. . . . His observations on both personal and social poems and his conclusions regarding the artistry of the collection as a whole and its place in Latin literary history are sensitive and provocative." Library J

Bibliography in notes: p283-98

882 Classical Greek dramatic poetry and drama

Sophocles
Antigone; tr. by Richard Emil Braun. Oxford 1973 101p (The Greek tragedy in new translations) $5.95 **882**

LC 73-83943

Another edition of a title entered in main catalog

883 Classical Greek epic poetry and fiction

Homer
The Iliad; tr. by Robert Fitzgerald; with drawings by Hans Erni. Anchor Press 1974 594p front $15 **883**

1 Trojan War
ISBN 0-385-05940-X   LC 74-3528

Another edition of the title entered in main catalog

884 Classical Greek lyrical poetry

Pindar
Pindar's odes; tr. with preface, introduction, and notes, by Roy Arthur Swanson. Foreword by Kimon Friar. Bobbs 1974 lvii, 358p illus $8.95 **884**

ISBN 0-672-51543-1   LC 72-90908

"The Library of liberal arts"

Another edition of the work entered in main catalog with title: The odes of Pindar

888 Classical Greek miscellany

Aristotle
Introduction to Aristotle. 2d ed. rev. and enl. with a new general introduction and new introductions to the particular works, by Richard McKeon. Univ. of Chicago Press [1974 c1973] lii, 759p $3.45 **888**

ISBN 0-226-56032-5   LC 73-87305

Earlier edition entered in main catalog

First published 1947 by Modern Library

Contents: Analytics posteriora (Posterior analytics); Physica (Physics) the second of the eight books; De anima (On the soul); De partibus animalium (On the parts of animals) book I, chapter 1; Metaphysica (Metaphysics) the first and twelfth of the fourteen books; Ethica Nicomachea (Nicomachean ethics); Politica (Politics) the first and third of the eight books; Poetica (Poetics); Rhetorica (Rhetoric) book I, chapters 1-4, book II, chapters 18-22

Russell, D. A.
Plutarch. Scribner 1973 183p illus (Classical life and letters) $8.95 **888**

1 Plutarch
ISBN 0-684-13351-2   LC 72-12156

This "fresh literary evaluation of Plutarch aims to help all students—whether students of Greek or not—to read Plutarch. In addition to discussing Plutarch's language, style, and form, Russell presents him as a scholar with his book, a philosopher and his religion, a moralist and his fellow men. The philosopher-historian comes to life in many well-chosen, well-translated excerpts from his works. After an effective introductory guide to the 'Lives,' 'Alcibiades' is analyzed with generous samples. A short chapter, 'From Plutarch to Shakespeare,' is mainly an outline of the judgments passed on Plutarch and on translations of his writings." Choice

Includes bibliographies

891.7 Russian literature

Dyck, J. W.
Boris Pasternak. Twayne 1972 206p (Twayne's World authors ser) $6.95 **891.7**

1 Pasternak, Boris Leonidovich   LC 79-187631

"The stated purpose of this volume is to present the non-expert reader with a critical analysis that takes into account biographical and historical material necessary for an understanding, appreciation, and assessment of Boris Pasternak's entire literary output. In this the author has succeeded extremely well. His study

Dyck, J. W.—*Continued*
is well organized and written in a concise and clear style. It includes a chronology of Pasternak's life and work, valuable notes and references, and seven chapters, which pass in review most adequately, particularly for the average student and layman interested in Russian literature, all that Pasternak has written as a poet, novelist, or translator. A most useful little study." Choice

Jackson, Robert Louis
(ed.) Twentieth century interpretations of Crime and punishment; a collection of critical essays. Prentice-Hall 1974 122p $5.95
891.7
1 Dostoevsky, Fyodor. Crime and punishment
ISBN 0-13-193086-9   LC 73-15716
"A Spectrum book"
"These critical essays by Russian, European and American critics examine, analyze and assess the novel, its main characters, social setting, the questions of guilt and evil and the integral role played by the epilogue
This "slender volume achieves cohesiveness not only in an evenness of quality and originality of its contributions but also in the organization of all its material. His book follows, in a sense, the chronology and development of the novel itself, dealing with its beginnings, progression, and basic focus. A scholarly yet highly readable book." Choice
Selected bibliography: p122

Lindstrom, Thais S.
Nikolay Gogol. Twayne 1974 216p (Twayne's World authors ser) $6.95   891.7
1 Gogol', Nikolaĭ Vasil'evich
ISBN 0-8057-2377-3   LC 73-17457
"This book begins and ends with a literary biographical chapter and touches upon all of Gogol's works. Besides giving a thorough summary of each work, the author analyzes the compositional and the stylistic features in their development. Gogol's style, especially the nature of his humor and grotesque, is directly related to the theme of the work, which is Gogol's modernity, i.e., estrangement from society. While the discussion of the grotesque is extensive (though not new), its relationship to the theme, as well as the author's use of the concept of estrangement, is loose." Library J
Bibliography: p209-11

Mandelstam, Osip Emilevich
Complete poetry of Osip Emilevich Mandelstam; tr. by Burton Raffel and Alla Burago; with an introduction and notes by Sidney Monas. State Univ. of N.Y. Press 1973 353p illus (Russian literature in translation) $15   891.7
ISBN 0-87395-210-3   LC 76-38004
Written by the twentieth century Russian poet, this collection is an "important step toward making Mandelstam accessible to the English-speaking public. . . . Monas' running commentary . . . [is] helpful, but there [is] not enough of [it]. . . . Virtually all of Mandelstam's poetry is in rhymed, accented verse. He is a melodic poet: rhythm and sound patterns play a very active role in his poetry. It is this level that is most difficult to analyze and most difficult to translate. . . . Raffel has not only decided against trying to duplicate Mandelstam's rhythms and sound patterns: he also avoids 'melodious' lines where they naturally suggest themselves." New Repub
Includes a title index

Solzhenitsyn, Aleksandr
Candle in the wind; tr. by Keith Armes in association with Arthur Hudgins; with an introduction by Keith Armes. Univ. of Minn. Press 1973 141p $6.95   891.7
ISBN 0-8166-0681-1   LC 73-77712
Original Russian edition copyright 1960
In this play "the protagonist, Alex Coriel, a 40-year-old mathematician closely resembling Solzhenitsyn himself, returns a changed man after nine years in a prison camp on false charges (the locale is a fictional 'Caledonia,' not Russia). Despite misgivings—he now mistrusts the scientific engineering of human lives—he participates in a 'neurostabilization' experiment on his girl-cousin Alda, repenting bitterly when he sees the results. He argues eloquently with friends and colleagues about the morality of state-dominated biocybernetics but is left despondent when Alda 'voluntarily' goes along with the scientists. The theme is powerfully presented." Pub W

900 GEOGRAPHY AND HISTORY

901.9 Civilization

Brinton, Crane
Modern civilization; a history of the last five centuries [by] Crane Brinton, John B. Christopher [and] Robert Lee Wolff. 3d ed. Prentice-Hall 1973 xcv, 1216p illus maps $12.50   901.9
1 Civilization, Modern—History
ISBN 0-13-590059-X   LC 76-39237
First published 1957
"In preparing this new edition of 'Modern Civilization,' we have taken as the main body of our text the chapters from our book 'A History of Civilization' [entered in main catalog] that deal with the period 1300 to the present. . . . To these chapters from our parent work we have prefaced two introductory chapters, the first one 'The Ancient and Medieval Background of Modern Civilization,' the second 'Europe at the Close of the Middle Ages.' Illustrations, maps, and reading lists are new." Preface
This book deals primarily with the development of Western civilization, although political developments in other parts of the world during the 20th century and, more briefly, during earlier Western colonialism are covered. In addition to political history, developments in the arts, philosophy, religion and science are discussed

901.93 Civilization—1500-1900

Jones, Howard Mumford
Revolution & romanticism. Belknap Press 1974 487p front $15   901.93
1 Eighteenth century 2 Romanticism 3 Revolutions
ISBN 0-674-76710-0   LC 73-84398
The relationship between "the democratic revolution of the late eighteenth century, especially the American and French revolutions [and] . . . the new 'movement' of thought and expression that made itself felt at about the same time . . . is Jones's theme. In the textbook conception of the relationship romanticism is a reaction to revolution. . . . Jones rejects [this interpretation] . . . and argues that romanticism was casually related to revolution, at least in Europe. . . . [Of these two] forces, he thinks that romanticism, with its basic postulating of every human being an end in himself, has had the more enduring influence." Va Q R
"The nonspecialist reader, for whom this stimulating, rather lengthy study of the origins of modern Western man is intended, must read with close attention if he is not to lose his way among its branching themes. . . . If the book is less than shattering or profound, it's dotted with fine insights and the opposite of stodgy." Pub W
Includes bibliographical references

901.94 Civilization—1900-

Fuller, R. Buckminster
Utopia or oblivion: the prospects for humanity. Overlook Press [1972 c1969] 365p illus $11.95   901.94
1 Civilization, Modern—1950-
ISBN 0-87951-003-X   LC 72-81085
First published 1969 in paperback by Bantam, still available for $1.25
"The book comprises a series of talks given by the author, whose central thesis is that

Fuller, R. B.—*Continued*

mankind is obsessed with the fear of scarcity in the world and fails to see the potential inherent in comprehensive world-wide information resources, which can be applied for the benefit of man through design technology and can lead to the ability to do more with less. Instead of entropy and oblivion, the realignment of science and society offers mankind the abundance of Utopia." Library J
Bibliography: p365

Trilling, Lionel

Mind in the modern world. Viking [1973 c1972] 41p pa $2.50   **901.94**

1 Civilization, Modern—1950- 2 Civilization—Philosophy 3 Mind and body
ISBN 0-670-00377-8   LC 72-86631

"Jefferson lecture in the humanities, 1972"
"Although 'Mind in the Modern World' eschews any single critical posture, it evokes Trilling's past mind-culture commentaries as it centers on the diminished status of rationality. Simply stated, it urges renewed confidence in intellectual life and an active use of the mind so that culture can be affected rather than just reflected." Library J

904 Collected accounts of specific events. Disasters

Hoehling, A. A.

Disaster: major American catastrophes. Hawthorn Bks. 1973 208p illus $6.95   **904**

1 Disasters   LC 75-29277

"The major American catastrophies described encompass approximately 100 years, from the draft riots of 1863 to Hurricane Agnes in 1972; and they include both natural disasters and those resulting from human causes. Some, such as the burning of the 'Hindenburg' and the Hartford circus fire, have been covered before; but others, like the Galveston tidal wave of 1900 and the mine disaster at Monongah, are less well known. Interspersed with the vivid descriptions of the disasters themselves are poignant accounts of miraculous escapes and many true tales of heroism. The events are recounted in chronological order." Library J
Includes bibliographical references

909.82 World history—1900-1999

Laqueur, Walter

A dictionary of politics. Rev. ed. Edited by Walter Laqueur, with the assistance of Evelyn Anderson [and others]. Free Press [1974 c1973] 565p $14.95   **909.82**

1 World politics—Dictionaries 2 History, Modern—20th century—Dictionaries   LC 74-9232

Earlier edition entered in main catalog
First published 1971. In the revised edition all entries have been updated to 1971 and in some cases to early 1973. The intention is to give concise historical background on contemporary politics and information on changes in terminology

910.1 Geography—Indexes

National Geographic Magazine

Handy key to your "National Geographics"; subject and picture locater. Underhill, C.S. pa $3   **910.1**

1 National Geographic Magazine—Indexes 2 Pictures—Indexes
ISBN 0-9600268-3-5   LC 56-1375

Biennial. First published 1954. Since 1962, all issues have been cumulative from 1915
Compiler: 1954- C. S. Underhill
The index is arranged "to locate in a single alphabetical listing all the incomparable educational and pictorial wealth to be found in the 'National Geographic Magazine' in any year for which requests are likely to be made, providing at the same time a quick means of selecting the most useful articles in order of preference up to the last December. . . . The arrangement of citations under headings and subheadings is seldom alphabetical. Under certain headings the order is geographical, from north to south, from the Western Hemisphere to the Eastern; under others, such as historical, it is chronological; under others, like Aviation or Birds, it is by types, which may be combined with the other methods. In short, related subjects will usually be found in close proximity, even if the relationship is not stated. As with any reference tool, it takes a little familiarity to use it best. The basic treatment of the 'Geographic' is by region. References here are usually to entire articles. In other headings such as Industry or Sports, citations are usually to parts of articles only and may require some searching in the issues named. However, there is always a picture to help locate the reference. For all articles, colored illustrations, duotones, paintings, etchings, picture-maps, and foldouts are clearly indicated." Foreword [to the 1974 edition]

910.2 Geography—Miscellany. Travel guides

Bracken, Peg

But I wouldn't have missed it for the world! The pleasures and perils of an unseasoned traveler. Harcourt 1973 270p $6.95   **910.2**

1 Travel
ISBN 0-15-114984-4   LC 73-8678

Among the familiar topics covered by the author "are airplane experiences and memorable meals, a few words about calories, clothes and lodgings, personal pleasures and disasters, the always entertaining language barrier, and occasional reports of personal encounters. This one-woman view of travel east, west, south—Europe, Mexico, North Africa, Japan, Hawaii, etc.—will undoubtedly amuse the distaff side and strike some familiar travellers' chords. Ms. Bracken includes some canny tips to females faced with wardrobe and itinerary problems, but don't read this one for insights into unknown lands and people. Rather, enjoy her good talk, recipes, quotes and wit." Pub W

Clark, Sydney

All the best in. . . . [series] Dodd **910.2**
ISBN 0-396-06952-5

This series, entered in main catalog, now includes a guide book for Mexico

910.4 Accounts of travel. Shipwrecks

Burton, Hal

The Morro Castle. Viking 1973 182p lilus $7.95   **910.4**

1 Morro Castle (Steamship)
ISBN 0-670-48960-3   LC 72-91826

A reconstruction "of events leading to the 1934 fire and destruction of the Ward Line cruise ship Morro Castle. The ship, on her return run from Havana, was cruising through a northeaster off the New Jersey coast when fire was discovered just before 3:00 a.m. It soon raged out of control; and, in the ensuing confusion, many passengers were killed." Library J
"Documentary writing in good classic disaster style by a newspaperman who covered the 'Morro Castle' tragedy when it happened, and now returns to the old files, adding present-day interviews with the survivors." Pub W
Includes bibliographical references

912 Atlases

Rand McNally Illustrated world atlas. Rand McNally 1973 222p illus maps $2.95 **912**

1 Atlases
ISBN 0-528-83009-0   LC 73-3912

"This inexpensive little pocket atlas has detailed physical and thematic maps of the world,

Rand McNally Illustrated world atlas—*Cont.*
classified under such topics as the planet earth in space and time, nations of the world (flags and information tables), the earth in maps, with both subject and geographic indexes. Principal urban centers are shown in enlarged scale. Good color." Ref Services Rev

913 Geography of and travel in ancient world. Prehistory archeology

Hawkins, Gerald S.
Beyond Stonehenge. Harper 1973 319p illus $10   913

1 Archeology 2 Astronomy—History
ISBN 0-06-011786-9   LC 72-79671

Companion volume to Stonehenge decoded, entered in main catalog, class 913.362

The author describes study expeditions to sites containing astro-archaeological remains. He explores the possible astronomical use by the ancients of sites such as "Stonehenge; Machu Picchu, the shores of Lake Titicaca and other sites in Peru; geometric mounds in the U.S.; Mayan remains in Mexico; the statues of Easter Island; the pharaoh temples of Egypt; and megalithic remains in Scotland." Pub W

"An appended magazine article, bibliography, photographs, and line drawings round out a somewhat technical attempt at popularization best suited for the layman with a scientific bent." Booklist

Woolley, Sir Leonard
Digging up the past. [3d ed] Rowman & Littlefield 1973 141p illus $5   913

1 Excavations (Archeology)
ISBN 0-510-03504-3   LC 73-166198

First published 1930 in England. First American edition published 1931 by Scribner

This work, based on a series of talks broadcast by the BBC, attempts to explain to the layman the principles and methods of archeology. It describes how the field archeologist organizes an expedition, selects a site and conducts an excavation. There are chapters on working on a town site, grave-digging and the use and interpretation of archaeological material. The author refers to examples from his own work and that of other prominent archeologists

913.32 Egypt to 640 A.D.

Edwards, I. E. S.
The treasures of Tutankhamun; foreword by Lord Trevelyan. Viking [1973 c1972] 47p 110 plates $14   913.32

1 Egypt—Antiquities 2 Tutenkhamûn, King of Egypt
ISBN 0-670-72723-7   LC 73-1025

"A Studio book"
Text first published 1972 in England
This is "the catalog from the British Museum's 1972 exhibition of the contents of Tutankhamun's tomb." Library J

"For those who remain fascinated with the rich legend of Tutankhamun, this book will provide hours of absorbing reading. . . . [It] contains 160 photographs, a history of the young pharoah's rule and the discovery of his tomb, as well as a descriptive analysis of the 50 objects lent to Britain by the Egyptian Government." Christian Science Monitor
Includes bibliography

913.37 Italian peninsula and adjacent territories to 476 A.D.

Menen, Aubrey
Cities in the sand. Dial Press 1973 [c1972] 272p illus $15   913.37

1 Rome—Civilization 2 Rome—History—Empire, 30 B.C.-476 A.D. 3 Cities and towns, Ruined, extinct, etc.
ISBN 0-8037-1329-0   LC 72-96

First published 1972 in England
The author views "impressive archaeological ruins in their historical setting. Chapters present a motley variety of subjects: including vignettes of relevant late Roman emperors; the focal point is the splendor of the remains at Leptis Magna, Timgad, Palmyra, and Petra." Library J

"Menen has written an attractive book. . . . In the course of reading his descriptions and comments, and gazing at some worthy photographs of this eminently photogenic material, an uncomfortable feeling arises: unless one has visited the places already, or plans to do so in the very near future, this may be all that one will ever see of them. . . . The narrative is lively and spicy for so were the unreliable ancient originals on which it is based." Times (London) Lit Sup
A short reading list: p260

914 Geography of and travel in Europe

Automobile Association
AA Guide to continental motoring. The Association; distributed by Harper illus maps pa $4.95   914

1 Europe—Description and travel 2 Hotels, motels, etc.—Europe

Annual. First published in England. Title varies

This volume begins with general information and motoring advice for the traveller in Europe. The bulk of the book is arranged by countries into over 20 sections. These describe major approach routes and other information of particular interest to automobile drivers, points of interest, and annotated listings which rate about 7,000 hotels
Folded map in end-paper pocket

Baxter, Robert
Baxter's Eurailpass travel guide; with illus. by Alice Muller. Rail-Europe illus maps pa $3.95   914

1 Europe—Description and travel 2 Railroads —Europe   LC 74-169913

Biennial. First published 1971 by Eurail with title: Eurail 71-72

A Eurailpass is a ticket which is issued for a specific period and valid for unlimited first class train travel on the national railways of thirteen European countries. Separate chapters for each of the participating countries offer descriptions of the countries, rail stations (with sketches), public city transportation between stations, main inter-city rail services, suggested excursions, and international connections to other Eurailpass countries, as well as miscellaneous information useful for better rail travel. Additional chapters describe the Trans Europe Express (TEE) trains, some Eurailpass bonuses (e.g. steamer trips and discounts), and suggested itineraries. There are also vocabulary lists of French, Portuguese and Spanish words for train passengers

Dunn, William J.
Enjoy Europe by car. Scribner 1973 284p illus $9.95   914

1 Europe—Description and travel 2 Automobiles—Road guides
ISBN 0-684-13254-0   LC 72-7940

This book is divided into three parts. The first part offers general information of particular interest for the motoring tourist. Brief essays consider car selection, tours, roads and their markings, fuels and service stations, maps and guides, types of hotels and restaurants, auto clubs, currency exchanging, customs, ferries, and hitchhikers. The second section describes places of interest in over 16 European countries, with lists of their travel offices in North America. The final part of the volume is a set of appendices which offers information and tabulations about specific makes of automobiles, fuel prices, mountain passes, and mileage between cities. Useful phrases in six languages are also listed

Fodor's Europe on a budget. McKay illus maps pa $4.95   914

1 Europe—Description and travel   LC 72-76243

Annual. First published 1972
Editors: 1972- Eugene Fodor and Robert C. Fisher

This guide book is designed to help the cost-conscious tourist plan a European vacation. It

Fodor's Europe on a budget—*Continued*
includes information about different kinds of transportation and suggests specific package tours, hotels, restaurants, sights, shops and "offbeat resorts" in over 25 eastern and western European countries

Hadley, Leila
Fielding's Guide to traveling with children in Europe. Rev. ed. Field Publications 1974 504p $9.95   914
1 Europe—Description and travel
ISBN 0-688-61159-1   LC 74-171891
Earlier edition entered in main catalog
First published 1972. The 1974 edition "has been completely revised and updated, with an entirely new section on Greece added, bringing the total number of countries covered to nineteen." Publisher's note

Kane, Robert S.
Grand tour A to Z: the capitals of Europe. Doubleday 1973 515p map $9.95   914
1 Europe—Description and travel
ISBN 0-385-00441-9   LC 72-79401
"There are 23 cities covered, from Amsterdam to Vienna, giving historical background, sightseeing, museums, places to stay in and eat and drink in, entertainment, shopping directions, etc., with notes on travel, climate, currency, tipping, and other matters, including sources for other information. All concisely put, but too big a volume to carry under one's arm." Pub W

Rand, Abby
How to get to Europe and have a wonderful time. Rev. and updated. Scribner 1974 275p $7.95   914
1 Europe—Description and travel
ISBN 0-684-13874-3   LC 73-19259
Earlier edition entered in main catalog
First published 1971. The 1974 edition has been revised and updated including information on new group flights
Includes bibliographical references

Rand McNally Road atlas of Europe. Rand McNally maps pa $2.95   914
1 Automobiles—Road guides 2 Europe—Description and travel
First published 1970
"About 150 colored maps of countries and cities are included in this inexpensive source of added information on distances, motorail service, and advice on what to do in case of an accident. Also included are official sources for travel and visa information." Ref Services Rev

Rowland, Howard S.
The New York Times Guide to student adventures and studies abroad, 1974, by Howard S. Rowland and Beatrice L. Rowland. Quadrangle/The N.Y. Times Bk. Co. 1974 550p illus pa $4.95   914
1 Europe—Description and travel
ISBN 0-8129-0331-5   LC 72-90454
"After a chapter of practical advice on a summer abroad, including an informative section on criteria for choosing a summer program, the [authors] offer information on programs relating to special interests, such as Israeli excavations, Brazilian art studies, and farming in Greece. Finally, there is a section on individual countries. All through, there are organizations to contact, tips on adventuring and learning, and details to aid in planning. . . . [This volume] will be an important factual source of information about studying and traveling abroad." Cur Ref Bks

914.2 Geography and travel in the British Isles

Automobile Association
AA Britain's heritage; castles, houses, gardens, museums, wild life parks. The Association; distributed by Harper illus maps pa $2.95   914.2
1 Great Britain—Description and travel

Annual. First published 1966 in England with title: Castles, houses and gardens, and other places of interest. Subtitle varies
This guide book lists over 2,000 sights arranged alphabetically into three sections: England and Wales, Scotland, and Northern Ireland. Descriptions of places of interest include location, history, and hours and prices of admission. There are indexes of counties and special interests, biographies of architects, a brief history of British architecture, and an atlas

Commager, Henry Steele
(ed.) Britain through American eyes; edited, with an introduction and commentaries. McGraw 1974 767p $17.50   914.2
1 National characteristics, British 2 Great Britain—Social conditions 3 Americans in Great Britain
ISBN 0-07-012366-7   LC 73-8686
This is a compilation of "104 excerpts from published letters, journals, and essays by prominent Americans who visited Britain from 1777 to 1948. The selections are arranged chronologically and we can see how attitudes changed from Revolutionary hatred to veneration in the Victorian era culminating in the realignment of American interests away from Britain. A lengthy introduction and brief biographical sketches for each writer are included. Generally the selections are interesting and informative though writers such as Bryant, Prescott, Stowe, and Holmes are neglected. . . . This sourcebook should interest students of Anglo-American affairs." Library J

Gathorne-Hardy, Jonathan
The unnatural history of the nanny. Dial Press 1973 [c1972] 350p illus $8.95   914.2
1 Children—Care and hygiene 2 Household employees 3 Great Britain—Social life and customs   LC 73-255
First published 1972 in England with title: The rise and fall of the British nanny
"The author describes his book as a study of a unique . . . way of bringing up children, which evolved among the upper and middle classes during the 19th century, flourished for approximately 80 years and then, with the second world war, disappeared." New Statesman
"This is not a book for the nursery teatable. It is not a nice book at all. There are 'sexual detours' . . . a section on the nanny as murderess . . . potted psychology . . . and endless passages on child cruelty. . . . And yet, maddeningly, there is a lot of good, original social history and research in this book. . . . His study of nineteenth-century advertisements for domestic staff and the Victorian household hierarchy is genuinely new and interesting. There is folklore in his collection of nanny sayings." Economist
Bibliography: p337-39

Priestley, J. B.
The English. Viking 1973 256p illus $17.95
914.2
1 National characteristics, British 2 Great Britain—Biography
ISBN 0-670-29630-9   LC 73-1638
"A Studio book"
Priestley seeks "to define his concept of Englishness as a way of mind which owes much to softness of boundaries, absence of hard philosophical edges, a system which will always defy the rational in favor of the reasonable, a mental climate of hazy confidence. . . . [His] thesis is that the English are a haunted people. . . . [They have an] obsession with ghosts. . . . Priestley makes this traffic between the conscious and the unconscious one of his defining themes." Christian Science Monitor
"Writing with his usual facility Priestley highlights British men and women of high and common class who personify Englishness and takes a perceptive look at the arts, humor, and hobbies. He includes a personal 'National Portrait Gallery' or profiles of seven figures—Raleigh, Pepys, Samuel Johnson, Charles Lamb, Michael Faraday, R. F. Burton, and C. B. Fry —whom he considers all English 'in bone and marrow.'" Booklist

914.21 London

Kane, Robert S.
London A to Z. Doubleday 1974 199p $6.95
914.21

1 London—Description
ISBN 0-385-08637-7   LC 73-9035

"A useful but 'unabashedly subjective' guide for the London-bound traveler. The novice is directed to 12 prime attractions (The Tower, Westminster Abbey etc.); but experienced visitors will profit from the lengthy catalog of both famous and obscure museums, churches, parks, stately homes, shops, restaurants, hotels, etc. Text and descriptions are brief and personal. . . . Although a more detailed pocket guide will be required, this is an excellent reference for identifying the worthwhile sights of London." Library J

914.4 France

Hibbert, Christopher
Versailles, by Christopher Hibbert and the editors of the Newsweek Book Division. Newsweek 1972 172p illus (Wonders of man) $10
914.4

1 Versailles
ISBN 0-88225-016-7   LC 76-163363

This book describes the growth and historical importance of the royal French château at Versailles, and profiles many of its residents and visitors. The text traces the complex from 1661, when Louis XIV decided to transform his father's modest country house into a palace on a grandiose scheme, to its takeover by a French Revolutionary mob in 1789 and finally to its present status as a restored national museum. One chapter contains passages excerpted from the writings of French and foreign observers, including the Marquise de Sévigné and Samuel Langhorne Clemens. There are also a chronology of French history from 1594 to 1970, with special attention given to Versailles related entries, a genealogical chart of French royalty, and a brief descriptive guide to 9 other French châteaux. Over 150 modern photographs and reproductions of historical paintings and engravings illustrate this volume
Selected bibliography: p168

Kane, Robert S.
Paris A to Z. Doubleday 1974 199p $6.95
914.4

1 Paris—Description
ISBN 0-385-08650-4   LC 73-9036

"This volume is intended for on-site use, but the sightseeing sections—which are organized by type (museums, parks, churches, etc.) rather than by area of the city—may serve better in the planning stages than for actually trying to locate points of interest in a given district. The book gives a fairly balanced, up-to-date once-over-lightly, of the basic information of interest to most tourists, from coping with the Métro to attending the Opéra. Hotel, shopping, and restaurant suggestions are aimed mainly at travelers of moderately affluent means." Library J

914.94 Geography of the Alps

National Geographic Society
The Alps; prepared by the Special Publications Divisions. The Society 1973 207p illus maps $4.25
914.94

1 Alps
ISBN 0-87044-109-4   LC 72-75384

"An attractive, personal account of the widely diverse experiences to be found in the Alps of the countries sharing this mountain range (Switzerland, France, Liechtenstein, Germany, Italy, Austria, Yugoslavia). . . . The tone throughout is enthusiastic; and the first-person narrations should have avid travelers phoning the airlines as they read. Scenes range from the cultivated formality of Lake Como to the traditional transhumance (migration of herds to summer pasturage). Maps and historical information are supplied; and the photographs are very appealing." Library J
Additional reading: p207

915.1 Geography of China

Galbraith, John Kenneth
A China passage; illus. with photographs by Marc Riboud, and endpaper map by Samuel H. Bryant. Houghton 1973 143p illus $5.95
915.1

1 China (People's Republic of China, 1949-)—Description and travel 2 China (People's Republic of China, 1949-)—Economic policy
ISBN 0-395-16615-2   LC 72-11340

"Based on the standard visitor's tour [Galbraith analyzes] . . . that portion of China's economy that [he] was permitted to see." Christian Science Monitor
"Professor Galbraith's journal of his . . . visit to China is short, amusing and unpretentious. He clearly enjoyed the trip and admired most of what he saw while remaining well aware that much was not being shown, a condition that has caused him to present his conclusions about the Chinese economy with uncharacteristic diffidence." Atlantic

Salisbury, Charlotte Y.
China diary. Walker & Co. 1973 210p $6.95
915.1

1 China (People's Republic of China, 1949-)—Description and travel
ISBN 0-8027-0406-9   LC 72-95761

"A diary of a trip to the People's Republic of China in the summer of 1972. The author accompanied her husband Harrison E. Salisbury on a six-week visit to Peking, Shanghai, Siam, Wuhan, Changsha and other areas
"She is much interested in the people and the human dimensions of life in Mao's China. . . . She has a shrewd eye . . . and a pleasant feminine mystique. And she has a practical approach. To her diary she has appended a useful section of Travel Tips to aid people going to China (clothing for both women and men, winter and summer; a listing of things that can be purchased in China; another of 'Be sure to take' items)." N Y Times Bk R

Salisbury, Harrison E.
To Peking—and beyond; a report on the new Asia. Quadrangle/The N.Y. Times Bk. Co. 1973 308p illus $7.95
915.1

1 China (People's Republic of China's 1949-) 2 Asia—Politics
ISBN 0-8129-0333-1   LC 72-90467

In the early part of May, 1972, Salisbury, associate editor of the New York Times spent two weeks visiting the Democratic People's Republic of Korea, and then joined his wife Charlotte in Peking for a six-weeks trip through China. He reports on Sino-Soviet relations, the 'New Chinese Man,' the Chinese population problem, and describes interviews with Chou En-lai, Madame Soong Ching-ling, Prince Sihanouk, Premier Kim Il Soong of North Korea as well as with other people in many walks of life
"Though handicapped by his inability to speak Chinese, Salisbury's long experience as a journalist reporting from Communist states both in Europe and in Asia greatly enriches this book. Indeed, its special virtue is in the comparisons that Salisbury is able to make between China and other Communist nations—particularly the Soviet Union. Both in these comparisons and in its general outlook, this book is clearly favorable to China. . . . This well-written and informative book should have a wide readership." Choice

Toynbee, Arnold
(ed.) Half the world; the history and culture of China and Japan; texts by E. Glahn [and others]. Holt 1973 368p illus $30
915.1

1 China—Civilization 2 Japan—Civilization
ISBN 0-03-010716-4   LC 73-4198

Thirteen essays by Owen Lattimore, J. J. Y. Liu, Donald Keene, Charles Sheldon, Carmen Backer, S. Nakayama, P. A. Cohen, Jean Chesneaux, and others. Chronology. Bibliography
"The 13 essays together constitute an up-to-date high popularization which, without losing readability, just barely falls short of the detailed treatment of China and Japan one would expect in a first-rate textbook. Only Jean

Toynbee, Arnold—*Continued*
Chesneaux's doctrinaire Marxist treatment of 19th- and 20th-century China strikes a somewhat sour, though still lucid, note. The illustrations are large, clear, relevant, and keyed to the narrative by marginal notations in the text." Choice

916 Geography of Africa

Kane, Robert S.
  Africa A to Z. Rev. ed. Doubleday 1972 430p $8.95 **916**
  1 Africa—Description and travel
  ISBN 0-385-02679-X   LC 75-175386
  First published 1961
  A travel guide for the active as well as the armchair traveler. Index

916.6 Geography of West Africa

Moorhouse, Geoffrey
  The fearful void. Lippincott 1974 288p illus maps $10 **916.6**
  1 Sahara—Description and travel
  ISBN 0-397-01019-2   LC 73-19977
  This is an account of the author's attempt to cross the Sahara Desert by camel which he started alone in October 1972 in Mauritania and ended in March at Tamanrasset, Algeria
  Moorhouse's "book is both the account of the journey from Nouakchott . . . to the Algerian Sahara, where exhausted and ill [he] gave up, and the musings of a sensitive and very human man as he experiences appalling physical deprivation and discomfort, severe illness, disgust and contempt for the way of life and character of the desert people and the imminent prospect of the annihilation he set out to face. On both levels it is fascinating." Economist

917.3 Geography of the U.S.

Boorstin, Daniel J.
  Democracy and its discontents; reflections on everyday America. Random House 1974 136p $5.95 **917.3**
  1 U.S.—Civilization
  ISBN 0-394-49185-8   LC 73-20571
  "Two dominant themes in essays by a noted historian whose critical views and optimism are closely allied suggest that technological success in the United States with its floods of information via television, advertising myths, and pollster opinion-measuring and hucksterism, creates more long-term problems than pleasures and that, on the other hand, U.S. institutions remain fundamentally viable thanks to American powers of renewal. Essentially a minor supplement to Boorstin's major studies, this readable if somewhat repetitive collection consists of revised lectures of a series delivered in 1972 at the University of Michigan and some additional pieces." Booklist
  "Boorstin's ironic sense of the self-limiting paradoxes in modern American life informs every insight in this provocative book." Pub W

Great historic places, by the editors of American Heritage. Editor in charge: Beverley Da Costa; introduction by Richard M. Ketchum. Am. Heritage 1973 319p illus $6.95 **917.3**
  1 U.S.—Historic houses, etc. 2 National parks and reserves—U.S.
  ISBN 0-07-001171-0   LC 73-8836
  "An American Heritage guide"
  "National and military parks, battlefields, and state memorials are among the 1,000 historic sites covered in a gazetteer alphabetically arranged by state and town and illustrated with black-and-white photographs of the postcard variety. Seasons and hours open are given in the brief descriptions coded to indicate places of interest during the U.S. Bicentennial and buildings listed in the 'National register of historic places.' Convenient." Booklist

Hayes, Bob
  The Black American travel guide. Rev. ed. [Straight Arrow Bks. 1973] 349p pa $4.95 **917.3**
  1 U.S.—Description and travel
  ISBN 0-87932-057-5   LC 73-88278
  Earlier edition entered in main catalog
  First published 1971. The 1973 edition up-dates the material in the previous volume and contains information on three new cities—Atlanta, Dallas and Detroit

National Geographic Society
  American mountain people; prepared by the Special Publications Division. The Society 1973 198p illus maps $4.75 **917.3**
  1 U.S.—Social life and customs 2 Mountains
  ISBN 0-87044-126-4   LC 73-829
  "Five writers visited people living in Southern Appalachia, the Ozarks, the Rockies, and the mountains of the far West and write of the countryside, the inhabitants' homes and occupations. . . . Each author found that the mountains have a hold on the residents and that in spite of hardships and poverty many people have no desire to leave their locality. About twice as many pages are devoted to Southern Appalachia as to the other regions." Booklist
  "The text is anecdotal and informative; the photographs are simply superb." Library J
  Additional reading: p199

  Life in rural America; prepared by the Special Publications Division. The Society 1974 207p illus $4.25 **917.3**
  1 Country life—U.S. 2 Farm life—U.S. 3 U.S.—Social life and customs
  ISBN 0-87044-146-9   LC 74-1562
  This book "emphasizes the virtues of rural life. The arrangement is topical rather than geographic, and covers small towns, work, leisure, and fellowship. The emphasis is on a nostalgic yearning for a simpler, more fundamental life style; and the sometimes harsh realities of rural life, particularly the grinding poverty of subsistance farming and the suppressive provinciality found in many small towns, are missing here. The photographs, which emphasize people at work and play, are excellent; the text is journalistic and anecdoatal. On the whole, a pleasant armchair excursion." Library J
  Additional reading: p206

Natural wonders of America, by the editors of American Heritage. Editor in charge: Beverley da Costa; introduction by Alvin M. Josephy, Jr. Am. Heritage 1972 319p illus map $6.95 **917.3**
  1 Natural monuments—U.S. 2 National parks and reserves—U.S. 3 U.S.—Description and travel
  ISBN 0-07-001155-9   LC 72-80700
  "An American Heritage guide"
  This book "lists and describes a representative sampling of the natural wonders of each State. The over 1,000 sites are arranged alphabetically within each State, and include National Park Service properties (parks, lakeshores, seashores, recreation areas, riverways, trails, scenic monuments, memorials), all 155 national forests, selected State, county, and municipal parks and forests with extraordinary scenic features, and outstanding sites that are privately owned but open to the public. Locations are given, and information on hours and fees follow each entry where applicable. The only map in the book is one keyed to a list of National Park Service properties. . . . This is a very worthwhile, compact, inexpensive reference work, which will help fill the need for travel information for all libraries." Cur Ref Bks

Nye, Russel Blaine
  Society and culture in America, 1830-1860. Harper 1974 432p illus (The New American nation ser) $10 **917.3**
  1 U.S.—Civilization 2 U.S.—History—1815-1861 3 U.S.—Intellectual life
  ISBN 0-06-013229-9   LC 73-14277
  "Nye's previous volume 'The cultural life of the new nation, 1776-1830' [entered in main catalog] was devoted to features that typified

Nye, Russel B.—*Continued*

the formative years in America; the current book examines the ways in which these features became transformed. A heightened sense of self-discovery in the arts and literature is seen to develop along with efforts at achieving a philosophic perfection whose expression ranged from social reforms to utopian movements. The pending crisis of the Civil War provides the darker matrix for the events that Nye finds most significant." Booklist

"Rich in detail and synthesis [this work] is a superb example of Nye's ability to present a plethora of fact and commentary in an artful format. Many historical figures are rescued from obscurity and little-known, but significant phenomena demand the reader's attention and interest. . . . Although the work is of interest to the general reader, it is an invaluable tool for the serious student of American social history and an absolute prerequisite for teachers." Choice
Bibliography: p401-16

917.7 Geography of Middle West

Burman, Ben Lucien
  Look down that winding river; an informal profile of the Mississippi; with a foreword by John K. Hutchens; illus. by Alice Caddy. Taplinger 1973 192p illus $7.95   917.7
  1 Mississippi River
  ISBN 0-8008-4960-4   LC 72-6610

Included here are "anecdotes from the old days of steamboating; Mr Burman was once a cub pilot himself and . . . recalls the characters who steered the big ships down the treacherous, boundless river. He eavesdrops on the roust-abouts, rides a show boat and then, in his last chapter, boards one of the modern, radar-equipped towboats that now ply the Mississippi. For all the mechanization, he concludes, the river is the same." N Y Times Bk R
  This book "is, as Mr. Burman calls it, an 'informal portrait.' It's a delightful portrait, conversational in tone and deeply satisfying." Best Sellers

917.8 Geography of Western States

The Magnificent Rockies; crest of a continent; by the editors of American West. Am. West 1973 285p illus (The Great West ser) $18.50   917.8
  1 Rocky Mountains
  ISBN 0-919118-27-2   LC 72-82181

"The lucid text is a careful blending of natural history, such as geologic formation) and intriguing stories of human history (such as of the fur traders). The book is beautifully illustrated with photos (many in color), maps, and charts; and though the subject matter is regional, it will have great appeal to most lay readers." Library J

917.95 Geography of the Pacific Northwest

The Great Northwest; the story of a land and its people, by the editors of American West. Am. West 1973 285p illus maps (The Great West ser) $18.50   917.95
  1 Northwest, Pacific
  ISBN 0-910118-32-9   LC 72-90946

"The natural history, geography, geology, and early exploration of the U.S. Pacific Northwest are outlined in a popularized illustration of how nature shapes human history. Characteristic natural beauties of the region and the broad range of contrasting geographical features found in the area are portrayed in numerous photographs, paintings, and drawings in color and in black and white. The original Indian inhabitants, explorers in search of adventure and land from the sixteenth century on, development schemes in the nineteenth century, and ecological concerns in the wake of twentieth-century progress are also dealt with." Booklist
  Sources and suggested reading: p281

917.98 Geography of Alaska

Alaska; [ed. by Dorothy Krell; design: Joe Seney; cartography and illustrations: Dick Cole] Lane Mag. & Bk. Co. 1974 207p illus maps $12.95   917.98
  1 Alaska
  ISBN 0-376-05151-5   LC 73-89586

"A Sunset pictorial"
  In brief text and numerous photographs, the editors take the reader on a region by region tour of our northernmost state. Included are descriptive looks at the natural wonders, as well as shared visits with the people as they go about the daily activities of their Arctic life
  Selected readings: p206-07

918 Geography of South America. Andes

Read, Piers Paul
  Alive; the story of the Andes survivors. Lippincott 1974 352p illus maps $10   918
  1 Survival (after airplane accidents, shipwrecks etc.) 2 Andes 3 Cannibalism
  ISBN 0-397-01001-X   LC 73-22269

On October 13, 1972, a plane carrying forty Uruguayans and a crew of five crashed in the Argentinian Andes. The sixteen survivors were not rescued until December 21. This book describes how they stayed alive, resorted to cannibalism; and were finally rescued when two who left camp reached help
  "Amid instances of ignoble pilfering and despair, which Read wisely refuses to suppress, 'Alive' records a remarkable communal feat of heroism. It will become a classic in the literature of survival." Newsweek

920 BIOGRAPHY

Books of biography are arranged as follows: 1 Biographical collections (920) 2 Biographies of individuals alphabetically by names of biographees (92)

920 Collective biography

For the convenience of having collective biography together in one alphabet, 920 is used here for all classes except artists and musicians. The latter are classified in 709.2 and 780.92 respectively

Cowles, Virginia
  The Rothschilds; a family of fortune. Knopf 1973 304p illus $17.50   920
  1 Rothschild family
  ISBN 0-394-48773-7   LC 73-3663

The author "traces the family fortunes from the Frankfurt ghetto, where Mayer Amschel founded both business and dynasty, on to the next generation of five sons, who became leading bankers throughout Europe. The reader moves with the Rothschild descendants through history to the 20th Century, meeting Zionists, bankers, scientists, winegrowers, and patrons of the arts. This biography is fascinating and well written. Some of the anecdotes have appeared before, but much of the material is new. And the illustrations are an important plus." Library J
  Includes bibliographical references

Daniels, Jonathan
  The Randolphs of Virginia. Doubleday 1972 362p illus $10   920
  1 Randolph family
  ISBN 0-385-00299-8   LC 72-76146

"From the union of William and Mary Isham Randolph in 17th-century Virginia have come descendants who have played parts—often very prominent parts—in virtually every important event in colonial and U.S. history. Their offspring include Thomas Jefferson, John Marshall, Robert E. Lee, J. E. B. Stuart, Lady Astor, the 'Gibson girl,' several governors of

Daniels, Jonathan—*Continued*
Virginia, several presidents of William and Mary College, several national cabinet members (including Franklin Roosevelt's Attorney General Biddle), and others too numerous to mention. Jonathan Daniels author of 18 other books on American life, traces the Randolph line from William (1651?-1711) down to Randolphs of the mid-20th century, concentrating on the more colorful family members of the 18th and 19th centuries whether they be famous and accomplished or stained by dark deeds." Choice
Bibliography: p335-45

Freidel, Frank
Our country's Presidents. Prepared by National Geographic Special Publications Division. Natl. Geographic Soc. illus $4.25
 920
1 Presidents—U.S. 2 U.S.—History
1972 edition entered in main catalog
First published 1966. Periodically revised
Includes bibliography

Gielgud, Sir John
Distinguished company. Doubleday 1973 179p illus $5.95 920
1 Actors and actresses, British
ISBN 0-385-04563-8 LC 72-96237
First published 1972 in England
"Born into a distinguished theatrical family, Gielgud further enhanced the Terry tradition by becoming a celebrated actor, director, and patron of the arts. 'Distinguished company,' his collection of striking portraits, includes recollections not only of the famous actors and actresses he has known both on and off stage but also of his own illustrious relations—the 'immortal' Ellen Terry and the brilliant Edward Gordon Craig. In this candid and affectionate book, Sir John reveals the wit, artistry, and foibles of his subjects while evoking the full flavor of the culture that produced them. Although all the portraits included in the volume are fascinating, those of Mrs. Patrick Campbell, Charles Laughton, and Vivian Leigh are outstanding." Choice

Hatch, Alden
The Lodges of Massachusetts. Hawthorn Bks. 1973 360p illus $10.95 920
1 Lodge family 2 Cabot family LC 72-4922
"A sympathetic and well-written account of an illustrious political family by a prolific freelance writer. The book focuses upon Henry Cabot Lodge, the distinguished Massachusetts senator of the early 20th century, and his two grandsons: Henry Cabot Lodge Jr., senator and diplomat, and John Davis Lodge, movie star governor of Connecticut, and ambassador to Spain. Other family members given coverage include patriarch George Cabot, an influential late 18th-century figure who certainly deserves more than the six pages devoted to him, and George Cabot 'Bay' Lodge, the nonconformist son of Henry Cabot Lodge. This work will not command the attention of serious scholars, but it will make enjoyable reading for the general public." Choice
Includes bibliographical references

Kane, Joseph Nathan
Facts about the Presidents; a compilation of biographical and historical data. 3d ed. Wilson, H.W. 1974 407p illus $15 920
1 Presidents—U.S.
ISBN 0-8242-0538-3 LC 74-5297
Earlier edition entered in main catalog
First published 1959. The 1974 edition "has been brought up to date as of December 1973." Preface

Markmann, Charles Lam
The Buckleys; a family examined. Morrow 1973 364p $8.95 920
1 Buckley family 2 Buckley, James Lane 3 Buckley, William Frank
ISBN 0-688-00152-1 LC 72-13137
In his introductory chapters the author "provides an overview of the founder of the dynasty, William Frank Buckley Sr. (1881-1958), and his ten offspring; but Markmann's major attention is focused throughout upon the careers of the two most famous sons, columnist William Jr. and James, the present U.S. Senator from New York. The author's underlying thesis is that the Buckleys, despite distinct parallels with he Kennedy family, constitute a far more serious threat on the American political scene due to the selfless, almost fanatical, character of their beliefs." Library J
Principal bibliographical references: p351-52

Rogers, J. A.
World's great men of color; ed. with an introduction, commentary, and new bibliographical notes by John Henrik Clarke. Macmillan Pub. Co. 1972 2v illus ea $9.95 920
1 Negroes—Biography LC 73-186437
Reissue of a work first published 1946-47 by J. A. Rogers
Volume I includes biographical sketches of fifty-two great Black figures of the pre-Christian era and of Asia and Africa. Volume II introduces sixty-four individuals of Black heritage who made contributions to European and New World history
"Rogers wrote what amounts to a biographical dictionary in order to refute arguments of Negro inferiority. He hoped to do this by calling attention to great persons in the past who had at least one-eighth Negro ancestry. . . . Rogers relies on flimsy evidence at times, claiming ancestry on the basis of physical appearance or on reputed attribution of parents. His book is representative of more than 100 years of effort to show black achievement by historical biography and, while it seems dated, it is a useful reference." Choice
Includes bibliographies

920.025   Biography—Directories

American men and women of science. . . . Ed. by the Jaques Cattell Press. 12th ed. The social and behavioral sciences. Bowker 1973 2v ea $42.50 920.025
1 Scientists—Directories LC 72-622716
"Formerly American men of science; a biographical directory founded in 1906." Title page
Earlier edition entered in main catalog with title: American men of science. The social and behavioral sciences
Contents: v 1 A-K (ISBN 0-8352-0600-9); v2 L-Z (ISBN 0-8352-0601-7)
Alphabetically arranged Discipline indexes are available at $25 each for this directory, and its companion directory, The physical and biological sciences, entered in main catalog

920.03   Biography—Dictionaries

Celebrity register. Simon & Schuster 1973 $35 920.03
1 U.S.—Biography—Dictionaries
First published 1959 by Celebrity Register with title: International Celebrity register. The 1963 edition published by Harper
Frequency is irregular. Editor: 1959 and 1963 Cleveland Amory; 1973 Earl Blackwell
"A compilation of brief unconventional biographical sketches of newsworthy U.S. residents or visitors, many in the entertainment world or sports." Booklist
"The sketches, all accompanied by photographs, are not terribly skimpy, they actually give a fair amount of knowledge about the people presented, and they say just the right things for the information seeker. Moreover, they are well written. The volume is at present [1973] right up to date, and it deals with the living, not with the dead, except for those most recently deceased. . . . Generally a great book for anyone who is trying to put his finger on some concrete information about some well known person." Best Sellers
A Directory of addresses is appended

Contemporary authors; a bio-bibliographcial guide to current authors and their works. First rev. v9-12. Clare D. Kinsman, Mary Ann Tennenhouse, editors. Gale Res. 1974 994p $28 920.03
1 U.S.—Bio-bibliography 2 Authors, American
ISBN 0-8103-0002-8 LC 67-9634
Earlier volumes of this set are entered in main catalog

Dictionary of scientific biography. Charles Coulston Gillispie, editor in chief. Scribner 1974 2v ea $40 920.03
1 Scientists—Dictionaries LC 69-18090
"Published under the auspices of the American Council of Learned Societies." Facing title page
Earlier volumes entered in main catalog
Contents: v9 A. T. Macrobius—K. F. Nauman (ISBN 0-684-10120-3); v10 S. G. Navashin—W. Piso (ISBN 0-684-10121-1)

Herdeck, Donald E.
African authors; a companion to Black African writing; v 1: 1300-1973; contributors: Abiola Irele, Lilyan Kesteloot, Gideon Mangoaela. Black Orpheus Press 1973 605p illus maps $27.50 920.03
1 Authors, African—Dictionaries 2 African literature—Bio-bibliography
ISBN 0-87953-008-1 LC 73-172338
The first of a projected series to be updated and expanded by biennial supplements "Short sketches, alphabetically arranged, of 594 poets, novelists, critics, dramatists, and journalists of sub-Saharan African, Malagasy, and Mauritius constitute the major portion of the work. Biographies, designed to give a survey of a writer's life and work and a 'reasonably complete summary of his achievements both in and outside of literature,' include dates, education, professional training, position, honors, genres and languages, and complete citations to publications. A hundred pages of appendixes include essays and bibliographies on various aspects of African literature, lists of authors by genre, languages, sex, dates, and directories of publishers, journals, and bookshops." College & Research Libs
For a more complete review see: The Booklist, January 15, 1974

The McGraw-Hill Encyclopedia of world biography; an international reference work. McGraw 1973 12v illus maps $275 920.03
1 Biography—Dictionaries
ISBN 0-07-079633-5 LC 70-37402
Here are "5,000 articles ranging from 800 to 3,000 words; 200 maps; 5,500 half-tone pictures, not simply portraits; and finally, 32 full-color plates. Articles are both profusely illustrated and captioned. In addition each article has the vital statistics synopsized as a lead. . . . The 'further readings' suggestions refer inquiries to pertinent contemporaries and to study guides; however, the titles listed in the bibliographies are most often out of print or there is a heavy emphasis on history, especially American, with refreshing though brief forays into Australian, Canadian, and Latin-American history. . . . All nationalities are covered: Chinese, Arab, etc., even Finnish; and all minorities: Amerindians, blacks, and women, though admittedly the coverage is light until more recent times. The crux of a reference book is its index, which must offer easy access to the materials. This index, once one deciphers the typography, takes on all comers. The reader can trace a biography through names and misspellings of places, wars, battles, buildings, book titles, tribes, inventions, theories, world's fairs, vocations, etc. . . . This set fills the gap between simple identification and full-blown biography." Choice
For a fuller review see: The Booklist, October 5, 1973

Notable names in American history; a tabulated register. 3d ed. of White's Conspectus of American biography. White 1973 725p $44.95 920.03
1 U.S.—Biography
ISBN 0-88371-002-1 LC 73-6885
Earlier edition entered in main catalog with title: White's Conspectus of American biography
First published 1909 with title: The conspectus of American biography. The 1973 edition "has been completely revised and updated, and a 110-page index of more than 50,000 separate entries has been added." Library J
For a fuller review see: The Booklist, June 1, 1974

Shockley, Ann Allen
Living Black American authors: a biographical directory [by] Ann Allen Shockley and Sue P. Chandler. Bowker 1973 220p $12.95 920.03
1 Negro authors—Bio-bibliography 2 American literature—Bio-bibliography
ISBN 0-8352-0662-9 LC 73-17005
"Approximately 450 living black authors are listed in this biographical directory. Arrangement is alphabetical by name, with each entry providing information on occupation, place and date of birth, education, family, professional experience, memberships, awards, publications and mailing address. This work includes a list of black publishers, and a title index." Ref Services Rev
"The combination of a broad definition of 'author' and a scope limited to the living has produced a very useful current directory. . . . There is a list of active black publishers, many of whom can also be found in other listings." Cur Ref Bks

92 Individual biography

Lives of artists and musicians will be found in this catalog in class 709.2 and 780.92, respectively
Lives of individuals are arranged alphabetically under the name of the person written about

Aaron, Henry
Aaron. Rev. ed. by Henry Aaron with Furman Bisher. Crowell 1974 236p illus $6.95 92
1 Baseball—Biography
ISBN 0-690-00509-1 LC 74-566
First published 1968 by the World Publishing Company with title: "Aaron, r.f."
This autobiograpy of the baseball player traces his career from 1954, when he was a rookie with the Indianapolis Clowns, to the end of his 1973 season with the Atlanta Braves when he hit his 713th home run
"There is little that sets this sports biography apart from so many others like it, but baseball fans will enjoy reading about this nice guy who made it in the Big Leagues." Library J

Adams, Henry
The education of Henry Adams. Ed. with an introduction and notes by Ernest Samuels; Jayne N. Samuels, assistant editor. Houghton [1973 c1918] xxx, 705p $10 92
ISBN 0-395-16810-4 LC 73-6411
'Riverside editions'
Another edition of a title entered in main catalog
Bibliography: p537-38

Adams, John, President U.S.
John Adams; a biography in his own words. Ed. by James Bishop Peabody; with an introduction by L. H. Butterfield, Joan Paterson Kerr, picture editor. Newsweek; distributed by Harper 1973 416p illus map (The Founding Fathers) $15 92
ISBN 0-06-013308-2 LC 72-92141
This book is based on Adams' Diary and autobiography, entered in main catalog, and Adams family correspondence
In this volume "comes alive a passionate, human Adams, his remarkable and adored wife Abigail and their international world. . . . Pictures and text make it easily the most accessible entry into the mind, character and career of John Adams." N Y Times Bk R
Selected bibliography: p408

Aldrin, Edwin E.
Return to earth [by] Edwin E. "Buzz" Aldrin, Jr., with Wayne Warga. Random House 1973 338p illus $7.95 92
1 Apollo project
ISBN 0-394-48832-6 LC 73-4364
One of the first astronauts to set foot on the moon, "Buzz Aldrin, a superachiever from

Aldrin, Edwin E.—*Continued*

way back, was catapulted to a fame for which he was ill prepared. . . . Getting his feet on the ground involved a near breakup of his marriage, a bout with mental illness and a complete break with the cocoon of military life. As Aldrin recounts his childhood, years at West Point and his career in the Air Force, he realizes that it all added up to programming for success. He describes in detail the preparation for Apollo 11 and its historic voyage, the receptions afterward and the world goodwill tour; he presents [a] picture of a man exhausted and troubled, heading for a nervous breakdown." Pub W

"There are times in reading through this book that one may become bored by its attention to detail. . . . Yet, upon reflection these very specifics add up to a profound realization that we are truly in touch with a fine human being." Best Sellers

Angelou, Maya

Gather together in my name. Random House 1974 214p $5.95

ISBN 0-394-48692-7   LC 73-20570

Continues the autobiography begun with: I know why the caged bird sings, entered in main catalog

"As an unmarried teenage mother trying to find love and a place in life for herself and her son she has a series of men and jobs including, for a brief time, work in a house of prostitution to help a man she loves who turns out to be a pimp keeping more than one woman. The book ends on an upbeat note as at nineteen she rejects escape through narcotics and looks to a better future." Booklist

"Ms. Angelou describes the confusion and disillusionment that struck the Black community when all the economic progress achieved during World War II evaporated into peacetime air. The astonishing adventures are her own, but her bewildered bouncings from unpleasant pillar to illegal post stand for the troubles of a whole generation." Atlantic

Balzac, Honoré de

Pritchett, V. S. Balzac. Knopf 1973 272p illus $15

ISBN 0-394-48357-X   LC 72-8681

The author outlines the "life of the great French novelist. Beginning with Balzac's inauspicious birth at Tours in 1799, following him through his family's troubles, his amours, his business ventures, his politics and his social affectations, Pritchett builds the background from which came Balzac's epic contributions to literature." Pub W

"If one is searching for a good concise life of Balzac to put into the hands of a student or reader who is coming to this prolific author for the first time, then Pritchett's work will admirably serve the purpose. The magnificent illustrations, many of them in full color, recreate Balzac's world for the modern reader as much as does the fast-moving text. Pritchett has profited from all the latest Balzacean scholarship." Choice

Select bibliography: p264-65

Beaconsfield, Mary Anne (Evans) Disraeli, Viscountess

Hardwick, Mollie. Mrs Dizzy; the life of Mary Anne Disraeli, Viscountess Beaconsfield. St Martins [1973 c1972] 218p illus $7.95

LC 72-89422

This is the life story of Mary Anne Lewis who "was forty-five years old when in 1838, after a brief widowhood, she married Disraeli, who was twelve years younger. . . . [She] delighted in her husband's political fame and subordinated herself completely to the taxing demands it made on her own social activities. . . . Her peerage as the sole resignation honour of 1869 gave her much pleasure. . . . Death followed three years later." Times (London) Lit Sup

"Mary Anne's story, as told here, will make pleasant reading for those who enjoy the lighter aspects of social history, though it's hard not to wish that a little less were told of 'her' and a little more of her fascinating husband." Pub W

Bibliography: p205-06

Bell, Alexander Graham

Bruce, Robert V. Bell: Alexander Graham Bell and the conquest of solitude. Little 1973 564p illus $12.50

ISBN 0-316-11251-8   LC 72-11572

"Conditioned by the backgrounds of his father and grandfather, both actors and teachers of English and elocution, Alexander Graham Bell worked with his father in teaching Visible Speech—a system that used a phonetic alphabet that could help deaf persons or stammerers reproduce sounds of speech. Bell taught at schools for the deaf in Boston and Hartford, where his wife had been one of his pupils. During his teaching career he carried on experiments, reproducing sounds through the use of electromagnets and diaphragms, and working on his harmonic multiple telegraph system. Robert Bruce tells the story of Bell and his work." Pub W

"This is a sound, scholarly, thoroughly documented biography that will appeal both to specialists and the general reader. . . . The many illustrations are well chosen and add greatly to the interest of the work. It should stand as the definitive biography for many years." Library J

Bibliography: p501-03

Carrighar, Sally

Home to the wilderness. Houghton 1973 330p illus $7.95

ISBN 0-395-15461-8   LC 72-6807

In the author's "recollections of her unhappy childhood she tells how, even at six years of age, she adjusted to her mother's hatred and cruelty by taking refuge in her own thoughts and in her study of music. Although her mother's ridicule and distrust kept her from being friends with her peers or with animals, she rejoices in some unusually amicable relationships with several adults outside the family. She covers briefly her two deeply happy years at Wellesley and in more detail the build-up of despondency as she searched for a satisfying career. She considers herself most fortunate in finding an able psychoanalyst who helped straighten out her life and a singing mouse who started her on her successful wildlife study and writing." Booklist

"The book chronicles monstrous disturbing cruelty that ends in triumph. That triumph, that settling of one's mind and feeling of one's own pulse is an incredible story. . . . This author writes from the deepest level and withholds nothing." Best Sellers

Catherine II, Empress of Russia

Coughlan, Robert. Elizabeth and Catherine; empresses of all the Russias; ed. by Jay Gold. Putnam 1974 347p illus $10

1 Elizabeth, Empress of Russia 2 Russia—History

ISBN 0-399-11250-2   LC 73-87181

"These two extraordinary women, who ruled respectively from 1741-61 and 1762-96, are justly considered, together with their exemplar Peter the Great, the founders of modern Russia. Coughlan writes of all three in this . . . study but concentrates on Catherine (the Great) whose achievements crowned those of the other two. All were outsize, supremely Russian personalities, insatiably greedy for life and power, compassing extremes of asceticism and sensuality, of—at least in Peter's case—cruelty and compassion." Pub W

"Coughlan's 'foreword' points out that this book 'does not pretend to be a historiographical work.' It is, rather, a very lively, brightly written tale of court intrigues, 'affairs,' games, scandals, and so on, which also pays intermittent attention to such things as the Seven Years War, partitions of Poland, and the Pugachev rebellion. Sensible, if unoriginal, judgments are offered regarding many such serious matters, but the focus is clearly elsewhere. . . . The general reader may find it fascinating, as indeed it is, but he needs to be well informed." Choice

Bibliography: p335-36

Cavett, Dick

Cavett [by] Dick Cavett and Christopher Porterfield. Harcourt 1974 373p illus $8.95

1 Television broadcasting

ISBN 0-15-116130-5   LC 74-8492

Cavett, Dick—*Continued*

This is a series of autobiographical interviews between the television talk-show host and his college room mate

"There is an appealing account of Cavett's boyhood in Nebraska as the son of schoolteachers and grandson of a Baptist minister. . . . Cavett talks fascinating shop. He pays touching homage to his idols Groucho Marx and Stan Laurel. . . . The usual thing said about [Cavett] in front of TV sets is not that he's talented—which he is—but that he would be nice to know. The book confirms it." Newsweek

Charles Edward, the Young Pretender

Daiches, David. The last Stuart; the life and times of Bonnie Prince Charles; with 31 illus. Putnam 1973 335p illus maps $10 92

1 Jacobite Rebellion, 1745-1746
ISBN 0-399-11109-3   LC 72-94434

This biography of the grandson of the deposed King James II of England is presented partly through passages from contemporary 18th century documents. "A vain but dashing and not unlikable man, Charles spent his youth on the Continent, nurtured on dreams of Stuart restoration. Seeing his chance in 1745, he crossed to Scotland, rallied the Highland clans and reached Derby on his way to London. There he quarreled with his best general and began a course of retreat that swiftly led to Culloden, the grave of both his army and his cause. A brief period of romantic flight in the Highlands was followed by 40 years of exile marked by continual wandering, an unhappy marriage and wilting dreams." Pub W

"This learned and readable biography tells an absorbing, if sad, story and also manages to illuminate any number of things, from the sources of Scottish nationalism to the politics of an era moving, so to speak, from baroque certainties to the shiftier subtleties of rococo." New Yorker

Bibliography: p326-29

Chesterton, Gilbert Keith

Barker, Dudley. G. K. Chesterton; a biography. Stein & Day 1973 304p illus $8.95   92

ISBN 0-8128-1544-0   LC 72-95988

"Neglected in recent years, Chesterton (1874-1936) may be due for a comeback. He was a formidable figure— in physical bulk, in energy, in intellect, one might almost say in amiability; in debate the match of Bertrand Russell and Bernard Shaw. Barker . . . adds this elegant, well-rounded portrait of the well-rounded G.K.C., giving interesting insights into his youth and marriage and allowing a share of the spotlight to his distinguished friends Hilaire Belloc and Maurice Baring. Chesterton spent the most productive years of his life as a 'Jolly Journalist' of Fleet Street, dashing off a prodigious quantity of journalistic and literary work, often on buses, in wine-shops, or even afoot." Pub W

"Barker has written a life that is lucid and convincing, and that treats Chesterton as more important than a Jolly Journalist, and more interesting than a Roman Catholic saint; and because most of the previous books on Chesterton have been adulatory and parochial, this is a valuable and necessary achievement." Times (London) Lit Sup

Bibliography: p289-95

Cody, William Frederick

Burke, John. Buffalo Bill: the noblest whiteskin. Putnam 1973 320p illus $7.95   92

ISBN 0-399-11060-7   LC 72-87607

The author's "aim: to show how the Buffalo Bill legend was put to use—by himself and his exploiters. While he might seem to be cutting Cody down to human size in portraying him warts-and-all, Burke actually makes the man quite appealing, even 'lovable,' and in the end—he died in 1917, a mere employee for the Wild West show that was once his own—a really sad old man. After his death the Medal of Honor given him for 'heroism' in an Indian fight on the Platte in 1872 was rescinded. Burke traces Cody's life from boyhood through his youthful cattle-herding, scouting and hunting days and his first fame when the dime-novel king Ned Buntline made him the prototype Indianfighter of the West. Cody's later career as world-traveled showman belongs to the gaudy annals of American press-agentry." Pub W

Bibliography: p305-06

Cohan, George Michael

McCabe, John. George M. Cohan: the man who owned Broadway. Doubleday 1973 296p illus $7.95   92

ISBN 0-385-01578-X   LC 72-89328

"The talent and exuberance suffused on the Broadway scene by patriotic showman Cohan for more than 30 years animate a felicitous portrayal of the creative spirit and personal sentiments of the theatrical marvel as well as unqualified successes as entertainer, director, writer, and producer are zestfully related and illustrated with photographs of career highlights and of his family. A list of Cohan's New York productions and appearances, names and dates of plays authored by Cohan, and acknowledgments are appended." Booklist

"A rather breezily written biography, with a clear and amusing style. While the author . . . makes no attempt at any deep analysis of Cohan's playwriting and performing skills, he does deal knowledgeably with his artistic success. Anecdotes abound and the reader feels that he has 'met' Cohan." Choice

Columbus, Christopher

Bradford, Ernle. Christopher Columbus. Viking 1973 288p illus maps $16.95   92

1 America—Discovery and exploration
ISBN 0-670-22156-2   LC 73-6080

"A Studio book"

The author "vividly re-creates the life of Columbus whom he portrays as indomitable, forebearing, exceptionally devout, sincere, and lucky. The core of the handsomely illustrated biography is, of course, Columbus' voyages of discovery but also described in some detail are his years of striving and waiting for royal backing, his triumphant return from the first voyage, his weaknesses as a colony administrator and his humiliating downfall. Bilingual bibliography." Booklist

Cosell, Howard

Cosell, by Howard Cosell with the editorial assistance of Mickey Herskowitz. Playboy Press 1973 390p illus $8.95   92

1 Television broadcasting 2 Sports
        LC 73-84918

The controversial sportscaster "acknowledges that the nasty things some people have said about him—'obnoxious' sums them up—are true. But fair-minded fans . . . will likely agree he's a helluva man in many admirable ways after reading his sports autobiography. This is a hard-to-put-down book, one that expresses Cosell's underlying serious concern for the contract of fairness and decency in every aspect of amateur or professional sports. Its toughness stems from its author's characteristically frank exposure of sham, hypocrisy, cruelty and unfairness wherever he finds them. For many his moving reminiscences of Jackie Robinson and Vince Lombardi will prove the high spots of his book, which never shortchanges the reader and is as frequently fervent in praise of some sports greats as it is critical of others. Cosell always pinpoints the 'man' and his mark on his times." Pub W

Coward, Noël Pierce

A last encore; words by Noël Coward; pictures from his life and times; ed. by John Hadfield. Little 1973 144p illus $12.95   92

1 Music, Popular (Songs, etc.)   LC 73-10352

"Completed since Sir Noel Coward's death early this year, this is a warmly nostalgic romp through one area of Coward's talent—sophisticated and sometimes endearing lyrics, songs and sketches for which he has been famous since the 1920s, and through which he reflected and upheld the spirits of the English people through sobering times. Americans who, as it were, linked arms with the English from one war to another, will relish John Hadfield's selection and 'arrangement' of a boater-full of Coward's songs." Pub W

"Like all blithe spirits who go away, Noel Coward is not easily recaptured in a replay of aspects of his busy, successful life." Chirstian Science Monitor

Coward, Noël P.—*Continued*

Castle, Charles. Noël. Doubleday 1973 [c1972] 272p illus $12.95
ISBN 0-385-00422-2 LC 72-89296

First published 1972 in England

"A gorgeous, nostalgic, complimentary book, without a bit of critical insight, this splendid collection of visuals and anecdotal memorials by such as Beaton, Thorndike, Gingold, Gielgud, and Niven is meant to entertain in breezy British manner. Coward, by catching that manner, personified both an age and a style. His art is here attributed to 'wit,' 'love,' and 'hard work.' A rudimentary biography in roman type splices together italicized paragraphs from his autobiographies with italicized interviews of those acquaintances and co-workers sufficiently familiar, famous, or talkative and, in contrasting typewriter type, Coward songs and scene snippets. This audio-text accompanies a rich black-and-white video of playbills, drawings, and photographs of people and productions from 1904 to 1972. . . . The remarkable illustrations as well as the text are usefully indexed." Choice

Cromwell, Oliver

Fraser, Antonia. Cromwell, the Lord Protector. Knopf 1973 xx, 774p illus maps $12.50

1 Great Britain—History—Civil War and Commonwealth, 1642-1660
ISBN 0-394-47034-6 LC 73-7270

Published in England with title: Cromwell: our chief of men

This book presents a portrait of the 17th-century genius, who in roles of legislator, soldier, and ruler dominated Britain during and after the Great Civil War

The author has "presented her findings in a smooth-flowing narrative which is a pleasure to read. . . . Her treatment of the political events which led to the constitutional crisis of the early 1640s is skimpy . . . and in general she is cursory in analysing the intellectual currents which galvanised the parliamentary party. To some extent the book lacks historical background and depth. But as a portrait of a man it is a genuine work of art: complete, subtle, understanding and convincing. This biography . . . will go a long way to redress the distortions from which Cromwell has suffered." New Statesman

Reference books: p728-44

Dayan, Moshe

Teveth, Shabtai. Moshe Dayan: the soldier, the man, the legend; tr. from the Hebrew by Leah and David Zinder; illus. with photographs. Houghton 1973 [c1972] 372p illus maps $8.95

1 Israel—Politics and government
ISBN 0-395-15475-8 LC 72-5221

Original Hebrew edition copyrighted 1972

This biography examines "the sources of Dayan's attitudes on Jews, Zionism, and Israel. . . . Native-born, his understanding and appreciation of the Arab Palestinians today is shown to be the result of his childhood experiences with the Arab community. His military career is drawn . . . through the pre-State period . . . the planning of the Suez operation in 1956, and his direction of the 1967 war." Library J

This "is a serious piece of work, well-researched and crisply written, with clear accounts of his campaigns and only occasional lapses into sentiment. The story of Dayan's early life is fascinating." Economist

De Mille, Agnes

Speak to me, dance with me. Little 1973 404p illus $8.95

1 Ballet
ISBN 0-316-18038-6 LC 72-10732

"An Atlantic Monthly Press book"

Much of this volume consists of letters the author/dancer/choreographer wrote to her mother from May 1933 to November 1934. "In point of time this book comes between 'Dance to the Piper' and 'And Promenade Home' [both entered in main catalog] and covers the three years between 1932 and 1935." Best Sellers

"Though not a well-written book a scholar will find it worthwhile as a primary source for 20th-century American and British dance because it recounts the experiences of Agnes de Mille and her artistic colleagues on both sides of the Atlantic." Choice

De Mille, Cecil Blount

Higham, Charles. Cecil B. DeMille. Scribner 1973 335p illus $10

1 Moving pictures
ISBN 0-684-13379-2 LC 73-1119

"The life and work of the ultimate Hollywood director whose career spanned several eras of cinematic development from early silent pictures to the most vulgar and popular spectacles of the 1950s. In a refreshing switch from the usual tinsel atmosphere of gossip and transgression which infest film celebrity biography (although the reader is not spared repeated examples of DeMille's foot fetish), Higham concentrates on DeMille's career as a moviemaker. Higham's research tries to upgrade DeMille's underrated reputation by exploring the now neglected films which best represent the director's art and recognizing the important innovations DeMille incorporated into many of his films. In addition to this serious material Higham provides a plethora of anecdotes. . . . Includes a chronological listing of DeMille's pictures and their stars." Booklist

Douglas, Stephen Arnold

Johannsen, Robert W. Stephen A. Douglas. Oxford 1973 993p illus $19.95

1 U.S.—Politics and government—1815-1861
ISBN 0-19-501620-3 LC 72-92293

This biography "sets Douglas against the texture of his times and assesses the man and his role in American political life in the years preceding the Civil War." Pub W

"If the details of political maneuvering seem excessive now and then, the reader must bear in mind that, to a large degree, such details formed the very stuff of Douglas's career. The book demonstrates the virtues of largescale straight-forward narrative biography at its best. This is no 'life and times'—Douglas himself is always in the foreground, though he is clearly related to the events in which he had a part. Its completeness and objectivity will make it the standard authority for many years to come." N Y Times Bk R

Bibliography included in Notes: p875-965

Douglas, William O.

Go East, young man: the early years; the autobiography of William O. Douglas. Random House 1974 493p illus $10

LC 73-5025

In this first volume of a projected two volume autobiography, Douglas recollects his life from his poor beginnings in Yakima, Washington to his appointment as Supreme Court Justice in 1939. Accounts of overcoming the effects of polio, love for the outdoors, working his way through law school, friendship with Franklin D. Roosevelt, and appointment as Securities and Exchange Commission Chairman are included

Douglas writes "with warmth and humor. . . . Yet, he is sharp and incisive in dissecting the character and ability of leading Americans of his time. Unfailingly, the author's love of nature and nation, of man and his democratic institutions shines like a beacon light. This is a soaring message of faith in America which will inspire its readers, and cause them to say 'more.'" Library J

Dylan, Bob. See class 780.92

Edward IV, King of England

Clive, Mary. This sun of York; a biography of Edward IV. Knopf 1974 [c1973] xlvi, 312p illus maps $10

1 Great Britain—History—Wars of the Roses, 1455-1485
ISBN 0-394-48591-2 LC 73-7296

First published 1973 in England

As a King, Edward IV was "strong, vain, amorous, business-like, highly successful in war though no lover of it [and] one of the last great scions of a dying medieval order. He managed to hold England together after

Edward IV, King of England—*Continued*

the saintly dimwit Henry VI had made it a sparring ground for voracious barons. . . . [Some of the other historical figures involved in this biography and history of the War of the Roses period include] Queen Margaret, Louis XI of France, Buckingham, Clarence [and] Gloucester (later Richard III)." Pub W

The author "has dug down into the past to show . . . historic personalities as they were, and a tougher, greedier, wickeder gang than the royalty and nobility of fifteenth-century England is hard to conceive. Yet the book is by no means unpleasant, or even hard going, for the author is an easy, chatty writer, who takes pains to explain the period. The other, middle-class point of view she presents helps us to understand, if not to like the grandees—the men who were willing to defraud, betray, and even kill their blood relations for cash, acreage, or power." New Yorker

Selected bibliography: p307-12

Eisenhower, John S. D.

Strictly personal. Doubleday 1974 412p illus $10.95   92

ISBN 0-385-07071-3   LC 73-20510

"As the son of an American president, John Eisenhower has known both rewards and problems accompanying the relationship. . . . He recalls his childhood as an Army brat, his years at West Point, the brief periods on active duty in Europe and Korea. His White House duties involved trip-planning; he travelled with the Prseidential party, taking copious notes at meetings, some of which he reconstructs here. He describes the family's readjustment to private life, his father's death and his stint as Ambassador to Belgium." Pub W

"Accurately titled, this is a very personal account of . . . struggling to shape a life and career in the shadow of a great-man father. While the memoir provides insight into the difficulties of the son-father relationship and private glimpses of the eminent men the author was able to observe, it adds little to what is already known of the war in Europe and the Eisenhower Administrations." Choice

Eliot, Thomas Stearns

Matthews, T. S. Great Tom; notes towards the definition of T. S. Eliot. Harper 1974 219p illus $8.95   92

ISBN 0-06-012838-0   LC 73-14068

In this account of Eliot's life and literary career, Matthews deals with "Eliot's family background and early years in Saint Louis and at Harvard . . . [which he assesses] in relation to the larger context of Eliot's emotional and creative development, his . . . unhappy first marriage to Vivienne Haigh-Wood, and his subsequent decision to become an Anglo-Catholic. . . . [Matthews also discusses] how the . . . moral puritanism of [Eliot's] Unitarian upbringing was . . . influential in the formation of the poet and the public personality." Sat R/World

"What T. S. Matthews' unofficial interim biography does, with considerable grace and affection, is bring Eliot back onstage. His portrait is of a tormented, intensely private man who hid his true face as he hid the meanings of his poems. . . . Faults and all, the book may help stir fresh interest in what is central: those crystalline obscurities, Eliot's poems." Time

Bibliography: p207-09

Ellington, Edward Kennedy. See class 780.92

Ervin, Samuel James

Clancy, Paul R. Just a country lawyer; a biography of Senator Sam Ervin. Ind. Univ. Press 1974 310p illus $8.50   92

1 U.S.—Politics and government—20th century

ISBN 0-253-14540-6   LC 73-16528

Biography of the Senator from North Carolina who presided over the committee investigating the Watergate case

"It is a biography that is gently adulatory, occasionally uncomplimentary, and neither stirring nor controversial. . . . [Ervin's dedication and character] come forth—and Clancy is fair and kind in his portrayal. . . . Chapters 13 and 14 dealing with Watergate are worth reading." Best Sellers

Sources: p301-04

Faulkner, William

Blotner, Joseph. Faulkner; a biography. Random House 1974 2v (1846, 269p) illus $25   92

ISBN 0-395-47452-X   LC 72-11370

"This is meant to be a biography of William Faulkner's works as well as of their creator; since each element of them was in some sense a product of his total life experience, I have tried to present the life as fully as possible. Because he drew more extensively on family and regional lore than any other major American writer, I have treated these backgrounds in detail. . . . In treating the works I have tried to use a developmental approach: insofar as possible to show authorial intent as each work grew, together with the themes and techniques linking it to other elements in both the canon and the life." Foreword

"Blotner will no doubt be criticized for a kind of academic overkill, as well as for his open, occasionally fawning, admiration for his subject. . . . His main thesis—that Faulkner's work springs directly from particular people and places—poses an insurmountable technical problem for it requires incessant plot summation. . . . Blotner has written an old-fashioned biography, free of interpretation and analytic cant, which allows us to draw our own conclusions about a truly exemplary life. And that's plenty far enough." Harper

Includes bibliographic references

Fields, W. C.

W. C. Fields by himself; his intended autobiography. Commentary by Ronald J. Fields. Prentice-Hall 1973 510p illus $10   92

ISBN 0-13-944462-9   LC 73-3086

"Maybe the late W. C. Fields, film comic and nostalgia hero of almost legendary stature, truly intended to write his autobiography, but this isn't it. Lacking the real thing, Field's own grandson has come up with a book that's next best—a book that's a mammoth yet perfectly fascinating grab bag of Fieldsiana: letters, skits, sketches, unpublished scripts and assorted memorabilia all tied together with brief but helpful biographical-explanatory notes. It's an indispensable addition to whatever libraries Fields fans may cherish." Pub W

"As a particularly large bonus, the book carries some of the most hilarious radio scripts in the history of the medium; all one need do is picture Fields delivering the lines." Best Sellers

Ford, Gerald R. President U.S.

Vestal, Bud. Jerry Ford, up close; an investigative biography. Coward, McCann & Geoghegan 1974 214p illus $7.95   92

ISBN 0-698-10606-7   LC 74-78008

This biography traces Ford's life from his youth in Grand Rapids through his political career in the House of Representatives and appointment to the Vice Presidency by vote of Congress

Frost, Robert

Morrison, Kathleen. Robert Frost; a pictorial chronicle. Holt 1974 133p $10.95   92

ISBN 0-03-012601-0   LC 74-3383

"A very sympathetic memoir of Frost's last years written by his manager during that time. The book consists of a series of anecdotes about his farming, lecturing, public life, and death." Library J

"Not intended to be scholarly in tone, the essays, including interviews with James Dickey and John Ciardi, are engaging and consistently readable. Identification of contributors and a sketchy index are appended." Booklist

Gable, Clark

Harris, Warren G. Gable and Lombard. Simon & Schuster 1974 189p illus $7.95   92

1 Lombard, Carole

ISBN 0-671-21744-5   LC 74-117

This biography of Hollywood film stars Clark Gable and Carole Lombard highlights their

Gable, Clark—*Continued*

romance and marriage in the '30s and the tragedy of Lombard's death in a plane crash in 1942

"The story is replete with nuances of show business, reflecting conversational anecdotes and behavior patterns of the Hollywood scene, as must be. It name-drops from beginning to end." Best Sellers

George IV, King of Great Britain

Hibbert, Christopher. George IV: Prince of Wales, 1762-1811. Harper [1974 c1972] 338p illus $10   92

ISBN 0-06-011884-9   LC 72-9122

"A Cass Canfield book"
First published 1972 in England

In this book, the first of a projected two volume biography of England's King George IV, the author "does not succumb to the occupational disease of biographers, that of whitewashing his subject. . . . [He] handles the Prince of Wales sympathetically but firmly. . . . On the whole the author is more interested in the Prince's personal life than in his politics, an appropriate approach to the man who, in effect if not by intention, presided over the final withdrawal of the crown from the nation's government. George's role, as Prince of Wales in the society of his day is well brought out." Economist
Sources: p311-19

Gershwin, George. See class 780.92

Gibbon, Edward

Parkinson, R. N. Edward Gibbon. Twayne 1973 158p (Twayne's English authors ser) $6.50   92

ISBN 0-8057-1218-6   LC 72-13382

"An informative little book demonstrating the interplay of values inherent in Gibbon's judgments on the fall of Rome, 18th-century faith in reason, and the man Gibbon, his personal life and values. This results in an enriched understanding of the 'mirror image of the ordered . . . world' Gibbon lived in and projected as a criterion onto the past. . . . Briefly annotated, with select bibliography, this should prove an excellent introduction." Choice

Gish, Lillian

Dorothy and Lillian Gish; ed. by James E. Frasher. Scribner 1973 311p illus $19.95   92

1 Gish, Dorothy
ISBN 0-684-13571-X   LC 73-1111

"Oldsters will get a nostalgic thrill from this handsome book containing some 800 rare photos from Lillian Gish's private collection. Younger readers. so many of them film buffs, will be enthralled by its decade-by-decade revelations of the development of American movies from nickelodeon days to the 1970s— and its charming portraits of the fragile and gossamer Gish sisters in their many films and stage plays." Pub W

"Miss Gish takes the reader through her professional photograph album much as though she were entertaining at her own coffee table —a little kindly gossip, a little affectionate reminiscence, and considerable delicate humor." Atlantic

Goudge, Elizabeth

The joy of the snow. Coward, McCann & Geoghegan 1974 319p illus $8.95   92

ISBN 0-698-10605-9   LC 73-93757

"A charming potpourri of reminiscences of places and people Goudge has loved, comments on being a writer, discussions of her religious beliefs (including some intriguing anecdotes and theories about ghosts and ESP), and descriptions of her Edwardian childhood. While not strictly an autobiography, the narrative does give a clear picture of the influence of her parents and grandparents, of her homes throughout the years, and her schooling on her writing." Library J

Graham, Martha

The notebooks of Martha Graham; with an introduction by Nancy Wilson Ross. Harcourt 1973 464p $25   92

1 Dancing
ISBN 0-15-167265-2   LC 73-6517

"A rare opportunity to view the creative process at work. Graham does not hesitate to admit her borrowings of other's thoughts, theories, and insights, and these notebooks reveal many of her sources. They also indicate how she allied them with her own vision and craft to transform them into her own unique dances. More valuable than biography and more interesting than mere descriptions of the final works, these notes take us into the heart and soul of her art. The work is also a beautiful job of bookmaking: the look and feel of notebooks has been re-created in type. Beautiful full-page photographs by Barbara Morgan, Martha Swope, and others further enhance the book. Details of first performances of dances discussed in the notebooks are included." Library J

Hellman, Lillian

Pentimento. Little 1973 297p $7.95   92

ISBN 0-316-35520-8   LC 73-7747

A continuation of: An unfinished woman—a memoir, entered in main catalog

This volume offers sketches of events and people from the author's past. She reminisces about her childhood in the South, some of her eccentric relatives including Cousin Bethe and Uncle Willy, Julia, her childhood friend who was trapped by the Nazis, Dashiell Hammett, who was her lover, and her experiences in the theater

Hellman tries to see her subjects "in perspective. Hence her title: an artist's term for a painting that was reworked but whose original details emerge as the paint thins out. The profiles don't go deep. . . . One character stands forth sharply from her pages however—L. H. herself. In short, apart from its readability, Pentimento is valuable as a picture of a woman and writer in the making." New Repub

Herriot, James

All creatures great and small   92

1 Veterinary medicine

Some editions are:
Hall, G.K.&Co. $10.95 Large type edition (ISBN 0-8161-6095-3)
St Martins $7.95

"A warm and graphic account of the author's life as a young veterinarian in Yorkshire, England, during the 1930s. . . . [This was] a time when vets had an extraordinarily close relationship with farmers and their animals, and rugged as the life was, young James got used to being routed out of bed to assist at difficult animal births or to agonize with farmers when prized beasts were threatened with a trip to the knacker. Some of Herriot's stories are gripping, some quite touching, many hilarious. During his country apprenticeship the author had a romance with a farmer's daughter, and the book ends with young James a full partner with Dr Farnon and a newly married man happily honeymooning with his bride—testing herds for TB! Herriot has a real flair for writing and his book is a treat." Pub W

All things bright and beautiful. St Martins 1974 378p $8.95   92

1 Veterinary medicine   LC 73-87407

Sequel to: All creatures great and small, entered above

"A continuation of delightfully written episodes in the practice of a veterinarian in rural Yorkshire, England. Herriot's literary skill is uncanny in its mixture of humor, sympathy, joy. and sorrow—he has a rare gift of insight into the lives of animals and people. In this book, James is married to the lovely Helen and still a partner of the remarkable Farnon brothers. Each chapter is written so that it could stand alone as a complete incident, but many of the same animal and human characters weave in and out of the stories, bringing the varied life and beautiful setting of the Yorkshire dales into clear focus. A sequel rarely attains the same degree of excellence as the first book, but this one is a winner." Library J

Hess, Rudolf

Manvell, Roger. Hess: a biography [by] Roger Manvell and Heinrich Fraenkel. Drake Pub. 1973 256p illus $7.95   92
ISBN 0-87749-428-2   LC 72-10526

"The eccentricity and bravado of one of Hitler's closest deputies, author of the Nuremberg laws, emerges in a study centered on Hess' abortive flight to England in 1941. Manvell suggests that Hess' peace mission, designed to thwart ties between England and the Soviet Union, earned him the unabated enmity of the Russians, who remain adamant in their refusal to permit his release from life imprisonment. Hess' published and unpublished letters, interviews with his wife and son, and the reports and comments of associates shed a somewhat bizarre light on the sole occupant of Spandau Prison, who marks time with his classical recordings and cups of instant coffee." Booklist

Bibliography: p219-20

Hitler, Adolf

Fest, Joachim C. Hitler; tr. from the German by Richard and Clara Winston. Harcourt 1974 844p illus $15   92
1 Germany—Politics and government—1933-1945
ISBN 0-15-141650-8   LC 73-18154
"A Helen and Kurt Wolff book"

The author traces "Hitler's development, ideas, and reactions to events [within the] diplomatic, political, and social history of the period. . . . [Fest does not claim] that Nazism was the inevitable outcome of the weaknesses of Weimar, or, on the other hand, that the Third Reich was a terrible break in German continuity brought about by the madness of one individual and without an organic relationship to the past and the future." N Y Rev of Bks

"One general criticism: while Fest shows very well how Hitler operated at the personal level, he does not provide much detail about how Hitler worked institutions to secure his ends. There was more, for example, to gaining control of the bureaucracy than outmaneuvering the people at the top. Still, highly recommended for most libraries." Library J

Bibliography: p817-29

Payne, Robert. The life and death of Adolf Hitler. Praeger 1973 623p illus $12.95   92
LC 72-92891

This account of the life and career of Hitler tells "how the solitary schoolboy of Linz . . . the . . . peddler of postcards in Vienna . . . the dispatch-runner of World War I . . . became the ruler of an empire greater than Alexander's or Napoleon's, and ultimately caused the death of 40 million men, women and children." Christian Science Monitor

"Undergraduates will enjoy Payne's purple prose more than Bullock's often colorless narrative, but they will learn more about the Nazi era from Bullock's [Hitler, entered in main catalog]. Interesting features of Payne's book include a chapter on Hitler's little-known trip to England and pages from Eva Braun's diary. This biography is recommended for all libraries because it is a new, readable interpretation of Hitler, but it will not displace Bullock's biography." Choice

Bibliography: p607-12

Huxley, Julian

Memories II. Harper [1974 c1973] 269p illus $8.95   92
ISBN 0-04-925009-2   LC 70-138737

Earlier volume entered in main catalog

"Huxley ends this second volume of memoirs in his 84th year, still optimistic that man will reconcile his problems 'in some overall progress towards safeguarding our planet's future.' To the last, Huxley remains committed to reason and scientific humanism. He makes this clear in these recollections of his tenure as the first Director-General of UNESCO, his activities in behalf of arms control and peace, and his continuing professional interest in ecology and environmental studies. The book, Huxley notes, is 'almost a personal Baedeker' with its accounts of his extensive travels and his observations on man and nature." Library J

Jefferson, Thomas, President U.S.

Brodie, Fawn M. Thomas Jefferson, an intimate history. Norton 1974 591p illus $12.50   92
ISBN 0-393-07480-3   LC 73-11348

The author "seeks to draw a portrait of the man, and to correlate his public and private lives. . . . In so doing [she] reveals a Jefferson we have barely glimpsed before. In probing the man's personal ambiguities—attitudes toward the church, slavery, women, revolution—she constructs [an] . . . inner portrait, one that surfaces in his relationships with women and with figures such as Madison, Adams, Burr, and Hamilton." Pub W

"Whereas the formalists have given us the public career and Jefferson the intellectual, Brodie gives us the private life: repressed impulses as well as some he did not repress but did not wish to reveal. Brodie is a distinguished and candid biographer. Her research is very thorough; and she has refined her interpretations through discussions with experienced and reliable psycho-biographers. Her judgment of Jefferson's response to slavery may be less reliable than her insights into Jefferson's uneasy relationships with women. But, all in all, a compelling book." Choice

Bibliography: p555-65

Malone, Dumas. Jefferson and his time v5: Jefferson the President, second term, 1805-1809. Little 1974 704p $14.50   92
ISBN 0-316-54465-5   LC 48-5972

Earlier volumes entered in main catalog

This volume covers Jefferson's "last years as President when he unified party, government and country but was beset by factionalism at home and abroad. These were the years of Lewis and Clark, the Burr conspiracy, the embargo, the waning of presidential leadership." Pub W

"Malone's somewhat pedantic writing and mild pro-Jefferson bias (an occupational hazard with biographers) are more than offset by the detailed, exhaustive research which has obviously gone into this work. Malone painstakingly examines issues from both Republican and Federalist viewpoints, and, while generally agreeing with the former, in some cases concedes the reasonableness of the latter. While meant to be evaluated with the whole biography, the volume stands nicely alone. A useful chronology is included." Library J

John XXIII, Pope

Eliott, Lawrence. I will be called John; a biography of Pope John XXIII. Readers Digest Press [distributed by] Dutton 1973 338p illus $10   92
ISBN 0-88349-002-1   LC 72-95036

This biography of the pontiff traces his peasant childhood, seminary life, and subsequent career: as a young priest, papal emissary in the Middle East, papal nuncio in Paris, Patriarch of Venice, and Pope. It describes his efforts to bring about peace with all men, and his convocation of the Second Vatican Council

"Mr. Elliott, himself a non-Catholic, has produced a meticulously researched and eminently readable book. . . . Throughout this book one admires John's ability, tact, wit, wisdom, gentleness, and love as they are amply revealed. . . . Mr. Elliott's work differs from previous biographies, perhaps, in its greater use of interviews with John's relatives and of letters and telegrams between them." Best Sellers

Bibliography: p323-25

Johnson, James Weldon

Levy, Eugene. James Weldon Johnson, Black leader, Black voice. Univ. of Chicago Press 1973 380p illus (Negro American biographies and autobiographies) $14.50   92
ISBN 0-226-47603-0   LC 72-95124

This is a biography of a man who, during the first 40 years of the 20th century, was a "novelist, journalist, song writer, diplomat, and . . . champion of black rights." Choice

A "soundly researched and well-written biography. . . . Although the lack of sources sometimes causes Johnson to be lost among

Johnson, James W.—*Continued*

more general accounts, this biography contains considerable new material about a man who sought to navigate the difficult course between black and white." Library J
Bibliography: p531-68

Johnson, Lyndon Baines, President U.S.

Harwood, Richard. Lyndon [by] Richard Harwood and Haynes Johnson. Praeger 1973 187p illus $6.95   92

1 U.S.—Politics and government—1961-
LC 73-5226

"A Washington Post book"
The authors "have produced a sympathetic yet realistic book of 'impressions' of LBJ. . . . Harwood and Johnson hone in on this larger-than-life Texan in a sequence of vivid close-ups that show him in all his sweating ribaldry and 'cornpone' exuberance. They bring him to life on every page from his Texas boyhood and his earliest Washington days when he caught the eye of his idol, Franklin Roosevelt, to his traumatic retirement on the Pedernales. The authors have woven together a marvelous 'bait' of Johnson stories which, by showing Johnson's complex humanity and the intensity of his ambition to become a great President, serve to emphasize the tragedy of his fall." Pub W
"Pictures are an exciting part of the book. But few readers will have the background knowledge that these two newspaper men possess, and the absence of explanations or captions for many of the photographs is regrettable." Christian Science Monitor

Johnson, Samuel, 1709-1784

Quennell, Peter. Samuel Johnson: his friends and enemies. Am. Heritage [1973 c1972] 272p illus $12.95   92

ISBN 0-07-051040-7   LC 72-3470

"Focusing primarily on the circle which gathered at one time or another at the Streatham estate of the Thrales, Quennell spotlights most of the well-known and a good many of the lesser-known friends, acquaintances, and enemies of Johnson. Through these brief characterizations the reader comes to know not only those on both the inner and outer circles of Johnson's world, but also Johnson himself in considerably more depth. As a result, he becomes a less formidable and more human Johnson. Not necessarily a specialized work, Quennell's study is indeed a beautiful one, with rarely seen illustrations on nearly every page. It belongs on the shelves of everyone even remotely interested in the 18th century, and is a delight for even the Johnson scholar." Choice
Bibliography: p265-66

Joplin, Janis

Friedman, Myra. Buried alive; the biography of Janis Joplin. Morrow 1973 333p illus $7.95   92

ISBN 0-688-00160-2   LC 78-189274

"The author who worked for Janis Joplin's manager and befriended Joplin during the last three years of her life approaches the singer's life and career realistically and with sympathy in a biography based in part on interviews with family, friends, and others and in part on first-hand knowledge. Friedman stresses Joplin's essential loneliness and need for approval as evidenced by her frantic chase after thrills through sex, drink, speed, and heroin but never actually pinpoints why she was driven to self-destruction." Booklist
"Friedman is a gifted writer although her prose at times seems to run a temperature of 110 degrees. To read this deeply moving book is to understand how much Janis's art expressed her tragic life. Its title derives from one of her favorite songs: 'All caught up in a landslide, bad luck pressing in from all sides/Got bucked off my easy ride, buried alive in the blues.'" Newsweek

Kennedy, Joseph Patrick

Koskoff, David E. Joseph P. Kennedy: a life and times. Prentice-Hall 1974 643p illus $10   92

ISBN 0-113-511154-4   LC 73-21578

The author of this biography of the father of President Kennedy maintains that "in both public and private life, [Joseph P.] Kennedy brought drive and determination to his enterprises, but these characteristics were always coupled with conceit, vanity, and pomposity. In his concluding chapter, Koskoff implies that the legacy of Joseph P. Kennedy was duly transmitted to his sons and is in evidence in their respective political careers." Library J
The author's "historical contribution is sound, when it isn't in danger of falling under the weight of his own footnotes. Koskoff's 144 pages of footnotes and bibliography become compelling for the political aficionado the way boxscores sometimes obscure the game for the baseball buff." N Y Times Bk R
Bibliography: p616-29

Kennedy, Rose Fitzgerald

Times to remember. Doubleday 1974 536p illus $12.50   92

1 Kennedy family
ISBN 0-385-01625-5   LC 73-79682

"A wife-and-mother's-eye-view of her husband, ambassador to England, of the late President Kennedy, and the other, by now well-known, deceased and surviving members of the Kennedy family and their circle of friends and wellwishers. . . . Mrs. Kennedy tells of her faith, her schooling, her ideas of rearing children, and hundreds of small events and details." Choice
Mrs Kennedy's book "is conversational, unpretentious and above all, authentic. It . . . sounds as if it were written by a turn-of-the-century graduate of Dorchester High who went to finishing school in Europe and who still swims and says the rosary every day. And as a political document, of course, it is the most revealing tract on the Kennedys in all the shelves of Kennedy literature. . . . What Mrs Kennedy contributes to the story is . . . what most Americans are bedazzled by: how a family like that functions. . . . The most touching universal and affecting passages in the book deal with [the author's] religious faith." N Y Times Bk R

King, Billie Jean

Billie Jean, by Billie Jean King with Kim Chapin. Harper 1974 208p illus $6.95   92

1 Tennis—Biography
ISBN 0-06-012392-3   LC 73-4099

This is Billie Jean King's story of her tennis life including "her development from tomboyish junior tennis freak through her first Wimbledon singles championship in 1966 to her present pioneering role in women's pro tennis and Women's Lib." Pub W
"The only issues the book stays away from completely are the stickier subjects of lesbianism in women's tennis and drugs in athletics. If there is a real weakness to 'Billie Jean,' it is that Mrs. King is an on-going personality, continuously changed by events and her book is outdated by its own deadline." Christian Science Monitor

Krents, Harold

To race the wind; an autobiography. Hall, G.K.&Co. 1974 [c1972] 506p $11.95   92

ISBN 0-8161-6172-0   LC 73-20333

A large print edition of a title first published 1972 and entered in main catalog

Lenin, Vladimir Il'ich

Warth, Robert D. Lenin. Twayne 1973 198p (Twayne's Rulers and statesmen of the world ser) $6.95   92

1 Communism—Russia 2 Russia—History
ISBN 0-8057-3055-9   LC 73-1760

"A literate and thoughtful short biography of the founder of Bolshevism. Specialists and advanced students of Soviet history will find nothing new in these pages and will, perhaps, quarrel with some of Warth's interpretations —he argues, for example, that Lenin 'cannot be charged with direct responsibility for Stalinism'—and find some omissions, but neophytes could do worse than begin their study of Lenin with this volume. . . . Short annotated bibliography; index." Choice

Lincoln, Mary (Todd)

Ross, Ishbel. The President's wife: Mary Todd Lincoln; a biography. Putnam 1973 378p illus $8.95   92

ISBN 0-399-11132-8   LC 72-97309

"The best researched in a long series of biographies of notable American women by a capable popularizer of history. Ross covers fully the life of the brilliant but erratic wife of President Lincoln. She emphasizes the unhappy postwar period of the First Lady's life and debunks her reputation as a termagant. The writing is smooth, and the reading is easy. The book is without footnotes but carries adequate bibliographical references (lacking exact citations, however) in a chapter-by-chapter arrangement, as well as a good bibliography. Ross has leaned heavily on Ruth Painter Randall's 'Mary Lincoln; biography of a marriage' (1953) [entered in main catalog]. Randall's book stands as the more scholarly record, but this interpretation is recommended for undergraduate colletcions and also for high-school and public libraries." Choice

Bibliography: p361-66

Lindbergh, Anne Morrow

Bring me a unicorn; diaries and letters of Anne Morrow Lindbergh, 1922-1928. Hall, G.K.&Co. 1973 [c1972] 465p $11.95   92

ISBN 0-8161-6160-7   LC 73-14871

A large print edition of a title first published 1972 by Harcourt and entered in main catalog

Hour of gold, hour of lead; diaries and letters of Anne Morrow Lindbergh, 1929-1932   92

ISBN 0-15-142176-5

Some editions are:
Hall, G.K.&Co. $11.95 (ISBN 0-8161-6184-4)
Harcourt $7.95 A Helen and Kurt Wolff book (ISBN 0-15-142176-5)

The second volume of the author's diaries begun with Bring me a unicorn, entered in main catalog and above

"This book is, for the greater part, composed of diary entries of the author, and letters sent by her to members of her family. The 'Hour of Gold' refers to the period in which she met, became engaged to, and married the hero of the hour, Charles A. Lindbergh, who was the first man to fly across the Atlantic ocean. . . . When the time approached for the birth of their first baby, the Lindberghs went to Englewood, N.J., where Charles A. Lindbergh, Jr., was born on June 22, 1930. The joy this child brought to his parents was short-lived. On March 1, 1932, the baby was kidnapped from his home. This was, indeed, the author's 'Hour of Lead.' " Best Sellers

"By the last entries, the reader can only wince as credit is again given to others for vision and power that surely are the writer's own. This private record of an extraordinary young American woman in a time of crisis reminds us of our wealth and our waste." Choice

Followed by: Locked rooms and open doors

Locked rooms and open doors; diaries and letters of Anne Morrow Lindbergh, 1933-1935   92

Some editions are:
Hall, G.K.&Co. $13.95 Large type edition (ISBN 0-8161-6231-X)
Harcourt $7.95 A Helen & Kurt Wolff book (ISBN 0-15-152958-2)

First published 1974

The third volume of the author's diaries begun with Brings me a unicorn, entered in main catalog, and Hour of gold, hour of lead

The "author records a long journey: five months of Atlantic air-route survey flight; the completion of her book 'North of the Orient'; a new career beginning; and finally the prospect a new home. In this new memoir Anne Morrow Lindbergh describes enthrallingly the closeness of family ties and her joy in her child while recording her most intimate doubts and anguish on the way to a hard-earned wisdom that enabled her to open doors to a new life of accomplishment." Pub W

Livingstone, David

Jeal, Tim. Livingstone. Putnam 1973 427p illus maps $10   92

1 Africa—Discovery and exploration
ISBN 0-399-11215-4   LC 73-82030

This is a "picture of Livingstone as a failure —as a missionary, as a husband, as a father, as an explorer. But Jeal's reevaluation of Livingstone as a man also results in a reevaluation of Livingstone's contributions to British colonial politics and here Jeal's treatment shows a remarkable success in Livingstone's role in the determination of Africa's future. The paradoxes and self-deceptions of Livingstone and the entire Victorian era are . . . [documented in this] chronicle of a once popular and still important figure." Booklist

"Jeal set out to tell the truth about Livingstone with a harshness that is often painful. . . . [He] has reconstructed Livingstone's life with remarkably few distortions, and has eliminated a great many made by earlier writers." N Y Times Bk R

Sources: p391-94

Macaulay, Thomas Babington Macauley, 1st Baron

Clive, John. Macaulay: the shaping of the historian. Knopf 1973 499, xxxvi p illus $15   92

ISBN 0394-4728-0   LC 72-8727

"In this masterful and definitive biography of the great whig historian, Clive covers the major events and periods in Macaulay's life: his education, his career as an 'Edinburgh Reviewer,' his meteoric parliamentary appearance, and his 'exile' in India." Library J

"Magisterial in learning, gentle in tone, it most elegantly mingles the analysis of Macaulay's writings and ideas, the narrative of the development of his mind and career, the assessment of scholarship on a myriad of relevant questions, and the examination of the case for and against Macaulay in his controversies. It is, above all, a supremely positive work." N Y Times Bk R

Includes bibliographical footnotes

Magruder, Jeb Stuart

An American life; one man's road to Watergate. Atheneum Pubs. 1974 338p illus $10   92

1 U.S.—Politics and government—1961- 2 Watergate Affair, 1972-
ISBN 0-689-10603-3   LC 74-78466

While awaiting sentence following his 1973 conviction for perjury in connection with the Watergate case, Magruder, the former presidential aide, describes his life and attempts to suggest some of the personal and political factors that led to the Watergate Affair

"Since Magruder was actively involved in the original planning which led to the Watergate bugging and burglary and the subsequent cover-up, and since he does not seem to have concealed much of his role at least, all academic and public libraries should buy this book both for its historical value and its narrative fascination." Choice

Malcolm X

Goldman, Peter. The death and life of Malcolm X. Harper 1973 xx, 438p illus $8.95   92

ISBN 0-06-011582-3   LC 70-138726

"This volume concentrates on the later years of Malcolm's life, especially after his split with Elijah Muhammad. Nearly a fourth of the book is 'a detective story' reviewing the circumstances surrounding Malcolm's murder and the conviction of his killers. In the wake of the myths that have surrounded the charismatic Malcolm's life and death, it is significant for both black and white understanding of the man that a white man has written this serious biography to evaluate Malcolm's contribution to the black struggle in America. The book is enhanced by 26 photographs, notes on sources, and an index." Choice

This book is a "thoughtful re-evaluation of one of the most important black leaders who emerged in the 20th century and is highly recommended to both academicians and general readers. It adds vividly to our understanding of the complexities of racial ideology." America

Includes bibliographical references

Mandelstam, Nadezhda

Hope abandoned; tr. from the Russian by Max Hayward. Atheneum Pubs. 1974 687p $13.95

1 Mandel'shtam, Osip Emil'evich 2 Russia—Politics and government—1917– 3 Russia—Intellectual life

ISBN 0-689-10549-5   LC 76-871412

Sequel to the author's: Hope against hope, published 1970

"When Osip Mandelstam, the great Russian poet, chose to die in prison rather than seek a 'detente' with the Soviet government, his wife dedicated herself to keeping his works alive. She includes interpretations of his writings, which illuminate them and help explain his beliefs, stories of their life together and of their friendships, details of his arrests, and final end and of her own persecution during the years of his imprisonment." Pub W

"Mrs. Mandelstam's new book is not, strictly speaking, a sequel to her first one. . . . The emphasis is now . . . on the author herself, her views and her opinions. The . . . writing manner is as flamboyantly virtuosic as in the first book. (Hayward . . . has unfortunately toned down the brilliance and verbal exuberance of Mrs. Mandelstam's Russian style . . . to eliminate her occasional flights of colorful vulgarity.) But there is a new element: 'In my old age, there awoke in me a woman convinced of her own infallibility,' Nadezhda Mandelstam confesses at one point. It is this infallible woman who now sits in judgment not only over Mandelstam's enemies and persecutors, but over the whole of Russian 20th-century culture." N Y Times Bk R

Miller, Glenn. See class 780.92

Monroe, Marilyn

Mailer, Norman. Marilyn: a biography; pictures by the world's foremost photographers. [Grosset 1973] 270p illus $19.95   92

ISBN 0-448-01029-1   LC 73-6899

A study of Marilyn Monroe which describes her life and career as an actress. It is illustrated with over 100 photographs, many in color

"About half of 'Marilyn' is great as only a great writer, using his brains and feelers could make it. . . . But it's a good-bad book. . . . The second half of the book is supremely cruel to [Arthur] Miller." N Y Times Bk R

Muggeridge, Malcolm

Chronicles of wasted time. Morrow 1973-1974 [c1972-1973] 2v v 1 $6.95, v2 $7.95   92

LC 7-8707

Contents: v 1 The green stick (ISBN 0-688-00191-2); v2 The infernal grove (ISBN 0-688-00300-1)

These first and second volumes of a projected three volume autobiography, were first published 1972 and 1973, respectively, in England

In The green stick "Muggeridge, writer and former 'Punch' editor, recounts his early life from maturation in a socialist home and later teaching days in India through work as a press correspondent in Egypt and Russia, largely for the 'Manchester Guardian.' . . . Items for his concern include the popularity of wars, university education, the downfall of English imperialism, success, and authority. . . . On the positive side, he proclaims his general happiness through 'love:' love of humanity and of life itself, and particularly love of his wife, Kitty." Library J

In The infernal grove "after describing his early experiences as a journalist in England and India, he focuses on World War II, in particular his slightly comic and his not-at-all comic work with British Intelligence in Lisbon, Mozambique, Paris and elsewhere, often in cooperation with Graham Greene and the notorious Kim Philby. He precisely records this 'floating world,' but he sees it as a convinced Christian: hence his wry appreciation that it 'is' floating and his acidulous view of big words like democracy, freedom, socialist brotherhood, and of those who use them." Pub W

"The variety of Muggeridge's experiences, his watchful presence at innumerable key junctures, his capacity to arrange his vast cast of characters, and his constant changes of scene within the strict framework of a consistent if painful philosophy promise to make this one of the outstanding memoirs of our time." Choice

Mussolini, Benito

Mussolini, Rachele. Mussolini: an intimate biography, by his widow, Rachele Mussolini, as told to Albert Zarca. Morrow 1974 291p illus $8.95   92

ISBN 0-688-00266-8   LC 74-1129

Original French edition, 1973. English translation first published 1973 in England with title: The Real Mussolini

"This is the biography of a man who has become an integral part of history. The book, though, is not about his political doctrines, or national or international achievements, but about the man, the husband and father, whom destiny catapulated onto the Italian national scene and the world stage, and who, for better or for worse, reshaped Italy's life for over twenty years. It presents the human side of Mussolini's life as seen by his widow." Best Sellers

"Most startling about these memoirs is the fact that Rachele, usually depicted as apolitical, kept far from the photographer's eye and always at home, emerges as an acute political observer. . . . Completely absent are any footnotes or bibliography for this is a totally personal account—unique in many ways. While some of the materials may prove to be more myth than truth, this is an important and refreshing biography." Choice

Nassar, Gamal Abdel, President United Arab Republic

Lacouture, Jean. Nasser; a biography; tr. from the French by Daniel Hofstadter. Knopf 1973 399p $10   92

1 Egypt—Politics and government
ISBN 0-394-46625-X   LC 71-154914

Original French edition, 1971

This biography "examines Nasser's family and public life, his career and achievements, strengths and failures, attitudes toward Arabism, socialism, communism, and religion, his place in history and possible effect on Egypt's future." Pub W

"Impressionistic, sketchy, with background and sidelights incomplete and much omitted, it is nonetheless deeply perceptive, lucid, and essentially fair to that prodigious man—triumph, failure, flaws and all." N Y Times Bk R

Bibliography: p397-99

Newton, Huey P.

Revolutionary suicide [by] Huey P. Newton, with the assistance of J. Herman Blake. Harcourt 1973 333p illus $8.95   92

1 Black Panther Party
ISBN 0-15-177092-1   LC 72-93749

In an "account that is more autobiography than political tract Newton, cofounder of the Black Panther Party, focuses on his own background growing up in Oakland, California and on his long ordeal in prison and in court after he was accused of killing an Oakland policeman in 1967. Although he is vague about the future direction of the Party he describes with clarity its beginnings and goals and highlights some of its efforts in the black liberation movement." Booklist

"Author Newton is a high-talented man who often considers himself to be above the law; by his own description he has been a criminal, a liberator, a kind of con artist, a guerrilla theatre type, and all-around leader. Revelatory of a mentality that bourgeois America can only fantasize about, this book becomes a prime document on black revolution—on that shelf with works by Eldridge Cleaver and a few others." Christian Century

Nin, Anaïs

The diary of Anaïs Nin, 1947-1955; ed. and with a preface by Gunther Stuhlmann. Harcourt 1974 275p $7.95   92

ISBN 0-15-125593-8   LC 66-12917

Earlier volumes entered in main catalog

Nin's journal [a fifth installment] is not only a record of her life but an investigation into its meaning, quite another matter, and the source of material and inspiration for her highly stylistic novels. The present segment begins with a description of an interlude in Acapulco and concludes with an account of

Nin, Anaïs—*Continued*
an experiment with LSD, a manner of provoking visions that she comes to reject. The personages appearing in this volume are James Herlihy, Christopher Isherwood, Caresse Crosby, Richard Wright, and Henry Miller." Choice
"This autobiography lacks the polish and organization (e.g. in relating isolated incidents and thoughts without transitions) of her novels and her scholarly studies, but her impassioned writing resounds true and clear." Library J

Olivier, Sir Laurence Kerr
Gourlay, Logan, ed. Olivier. Stein & Day [1974 c1973] 208p illus $8.95   92
ISBN 0-8128-1648-X   LC 73-88745
In this "collection of interviews, 20 personalities, including Michael Redgrave, Alec Guinness, Noel Coward and Douglas Fairbanks, dissect the intricate character of Sir Laurence Olivier and the special genius he brings to his trade. Although their comments have the overly generous ring of testimonial speeches for a good friend, they still present a compelling portrait of 'Larry' at many stages in his life. Fiercely egotistical and at the same time a possessor of great humility, sexy and yet self-conscious about his physical shortcomings, Olivier is clearly first and foremost an actor obsessed with his art. The interviewees analyze his roles from his halcyon days at the Old Vic to his conquest of Hollywood." Pub W
"The really illuminating material comes from the time of the Royal Court and the National Theatre. . . . Tony Richardson and John Osborne give extremely candid accounts of The Entertainer rehearsals." Times (London) Lit Sup
Theatre and film chronology: p196-208

O'Neill, Eugene Gladstone
Gelb, Arthur. O'Neill [by] Arthur & Barbara Gelb. Harper [1974 c1973] xx, 990p illus $17.50   92
ISBN 0-06-011487-8   LC 73-6760
Earlier edition entered in main catalog
First published 1972. "The addition of a 20-page epilogue treating the 17-year period by which Carlotta Monterey O'Neill survived her husband is the major revision of this definitive study." Choice

Sheaffer, Louis. O'Neill. Little 1968-1973 2v illus ea $15   92
Contents: v 1 O'Neill: son and playwright (ISBN 0-316-78335-8); v2 O'Neill: son and artist (ISBN 0-316-78336-6)
Volume one "covers O'Neill up to his emergence as a new force in American dramaturgy, with the 1920 production of 'Beyond the Horizon.'" N Y Times Bk R
Volume two, which was awarded the Pulitzer Prize for biography in 1974 traces the life of the "dramatist from his introduction to Broadway with 'Beyond the Horizon' through his many public triumphs (three Pulitzer awards, the Nobel Prize for Literature), his several marriages and long incapacitating illness, until his death in 1953 at the age of 65." N Y Times Bk R
Bibliography: v 1 p507-13; v2 p675-80

Paine, Thomas
Hawke, David Freeman. Paine. Harper 1974 500p illus $15   92
ISBN 0-06-011784-2   LC 73-14264
This is an account of the life and career of Thomas Paine from his obscure beginnings in England through the roles he played in the American and French Revolutions, his friendships with Benjamin Franklin, Thomas Jefferson, and James Monroe, his imprisonment in France during the Terror, his trial and banishment from England for The Rights of Man, and the tragedy of his declining years
This "study of Paine maintains a judicious balance between life and times, keeping a firm focus on Paine's career yet always placing it clearly within the age of democratic revolution. Hawke also takes a . . . detached view of Paine—his laziness, his drunkenness, his wanderlust as well as his consistent revolutionary idealism. Expecting a broader interest in the American Revolution during the bicentennial, this biography is aimed at both general and scholarly reading audiences." Choice
Bibliography: p463-74

Patton, George Smith
Blumenson, Martin, ed. The Patton papers, 1940-1945; illus. with photographs and maps by Samuel H. Bryant. Houghton 1974 889p illus maps $20   92
1 World War, 1939-1945—Campaigns and battles
ISBN 0-395-18498-3   LC 76-156490
Earlier volume entered in main catalog
This second "volume of General Patton's 'papers' (diary, military documents, letters) covers the years of his command in World War II—the man and the general in his prime, commanding the first U.S. tank brigade, out-Panzering the Panzers in his dash into Germany. Here is Patton in a revealing self-portrait, a man of passions, temperament and contradictions—easily misunderstood in his complex humanity. Complementing Patton, editor Blumenson judiciously includes other men's versions of some events; the result is a multi-dimensional and dynamic view of the war in Belgium, France, North Africa, Sicily and Germany." Pub W

Pearson, Drew
Diaries, 1949-1959; ed. by Tyler Abell. Holt 1974 592p $15   92
1 U.S.—Politics and government—20th century
ISBN 0-03-001426-3   LC 72-78142
"The first of three volumes of what, in the end, will include about one-third of a diary from 1949 to 1969, in which Drew Pearson recorded his friendships, rivalries, causes and passions, and many of the stories he was forced to suppress from his columns and broadcasts. Here Pearson reveals the indiscretions, illnesses, dubious acts or vindictiveness of Truman, Eisenhower, Nixon, Johnson, Ickes, Rayburn, Humphrey, Forrestal, Wayne Morse, and hundreds of other riders of the Washington Merry-Go-Round. Pearson not only aimed for big stories and big scoops; he battled corruption and made many enemies." Pub W
"I found the Drew Pearson diaries enjoyable and consistently readable. . . . He had the curiosity, the physical energy, the quickness of mind and the gritty determination to be on top of every story and to elbow himself to the front of every crowd that mark the journalist in his purest form. . . . If you enjoyed his hectic journalistic performance, whether or not you approved of it, you can enjoy it all over again in this fat book." N Y Times Bk R

Pepys, Samuel
The diary of Samuel Pepys; a new and complete transcription ed. by Robert Latham and William Matthews. Contributing editors: William A. Armstrong [and others]. v8: 1667. Univ. of Calif. Press 1974 626p illus map $15   92
1 Great Britain—History—Stuarts, 1603-1714—Sources 2 Great Britain—Social life and customs
ISBN 0-520-02095-2   LC 70-96950
Earlier volumes of this projected eleven volume edition are entered in main catalog in variant listings

Pickford, Mary
Windeler, Robert. Sweetheart; the story of Mary Pickford   92
Some editions are:
Hall, G.K.&Co. $10.95 Large print edition (ISBN 0-8161-6224-4)
Praeger $7.95 (ISBN 0-275-51410-5)
First published 1973 in England. First American edition published 1974 by Praeger
This biography begins with "the Broadway scene circa 1901-1902—the season the four Smiths (Mary, Lottie, Jack and their mother) arrived in the city. Mary became 'Mary Pickford,' demure in curls, and went on to enormous popularity as a screen actress and later success behind the scenes in the booming film industry." Pub W
Includes bibliography

Proust, Marcel
Sansom, William. Proust and his world. Scribner [1974 c1973] 128p illus $7.95   92
1 Proust, Marcel—Contemporary France
ISBN 0-684-13831-X   LC 74-980
First published 1973 in England
In this study Sansom "deals with every

Proust, Marcel—*Continued*

phase of [Proust's] life from childhood to his death at the age of fifty-one." Times (London) Lit Sup

"In the final analysis, it is a feeling the book provides that makes it an admirable introduction to Proust and his society. Admittedly, Sansom does not attempt to cite all the individuals and experiences that influenced Proust's characterizations; rather he shows how Proust mixed fact and fiction in an attempt to prove his theory of 'involuntary memory.' The book is a tribute to the novelist's definition that art serves to preserve eternally the past, for Sansom describes an era, a society, and a man with clarity and candor." Library J
Bibliographical note: p126

Raleigh, Sir Walter

Lacey, Robert. Sir Walter Ralegh. Atheneum Pubs. 1974 [c1973] 415p illus $10.95
92

ISBN 0-689-10570-3　　　LC 73-80750

First published 1973 in England

This is an account of the life and career of Sir Walter Raleigh, as a soldier, courtier, poet, historian, privateer and politician—both in his triumphs and failures

It "is a straightforward biography, held close to the narrative of Ralegh's life. Lacey . . . is less concerned to discover Ralegh through his written words than in his actions, and as Ralegh's life was replete with action and drama, the pace of the book is stupendous. I had to read it at a sitting. . . . What emerges is a wholly credible human being, not a character actor in the theater of the world." N Y Times Bk R

Randolph, Asa Philip

Anderson, Jervis. A. Philip Randolph; a biographical portrait. Harcourt 1973 398p illus $12.50
92

1 Negroes—Civil rights

ISBN 0-15-107830-0　　　LC 73-159449

A "full-length study of one of the most significant figures in black history, the history of American Socialism, and the American labor movement. The Randolph story covers important developments such as post-W.W.I. militancy among black workers; the emergence of militant black Socialists associated with 'The Messenger' (edited by Randolph and Chandler Owen); the long, bitter, and successful struggle to organize black Pullman porters; the movement to achieve employment for blacks during World War II which produced F.E.P.C.; the battle to force organized labor to eliminate racism; and finally the civil rights struggle since the 1950s. In each of these major developments, Randolph was a key figure." Choice
Bibliography: p353-84

Rogers, Will

Ketchum, Richard M. Will Rogers, his life and times; in co-operation with the Will Rogers Memorial Commission and staff of the Will Rogers Memorial, Claremore, Oklahoma. Am. Heritage 1973 415p illus (An American Heritage Biography) $15
92

ISBN 0-07-034411-6　　　LC 73-8713

"In today's time of troubles, Will Rogers' acerbic, astute, and humorous reflections on the daily chaos would be a welcome and needed respite. In his columns politicians were reduced to mere mortals. This study of Rogers as cowboy, vaudevillian, radio and movie star, and homespun philosopher-columnist is a panoramic view of popular American culture from the Gilded Age to his untimely death in 1935. The Rogers appeal seemed genuine; his constituency included young and old. Democrats and Republicans, intellectuals and middle-Americans. His only rivals for the hearts of his countrymen in the 1930s were President Roosevelt and Shirley Temple. Ketchum's readable treatment is obviously nostalgic, but it also faithfully portrays an unusual personality and his 'Zeitgeist.' The illustrations and quotations greatly enhance this volume. There is one caveat: some background material (such as that on Indians, vaudeville, and the movies) while interesting is not that pertinent." Choice

Roosevelt, Franklin Delano, President U.S.

Freidel, Frank. Franklin D. Roosevelt. Little 1952-1973 4v ea $15
92

1 U.S.—Politics and government—1919-1933

Contents: v 1 The apprenticeship (ISBN 0-316-29304-0); v2 The ordeal (ISBN 0-316-29305-9); v3 The triumph (ISBN 0-316-29306-7); v4 Launching the New Deal (ISBN 0-316-29303-2)

"One of this country's distinguished historians here continues his magisterial study of FDR and his times. Preceded by three other books on FDR, the latest deals with the acute depression crisis of 1932-33. . . . This is an indispensable book for any American who would understand this crucial part of our history and the part played by FDR in saving the country from chaos." Pub W

Roosevelt, Elliott. An untold story; the Roosevelts of Hyde Park, by Elliot Roosevelt and James Brough. Putnam 1973 318p illus $7.95
92

1 Roosevelt, Eleanor (Roosevelt)

ISBN 0-399-11127-1　　　LC 72-97308

"Elliott Roosevelt writes of 'the father we loved and the mother we respected,' portraying Franklin and Eleanor in . . . the context of their family relationships. . . . [He] gives a son's view of family celebrations, living arrangements and family finances [and] he tells of his mother's growing independence while his father pursued his political ambitions." Pub W

"The story is presented here . . . with enough affection, candor, and charm to make it one of the most interesting books yet written about that hopelessly incompatible but intriguing couple. . . . While the account of marital conflict is admittedly the most fascinating part of the book . . . Elliott also details Christmas at Hyde Park, summers at Campobello, F.D.R.'s courageous fight against polio [and] Louis Howe's fanatical devotion." Sat R Soc

Rubinstein, Arthur. See class 780.92

Sackville-West, Hon. Victoria Mary

Nicolson, Nigel. Portrait of a marriage. Atheneum Pubs. 1973 249p illus $10
92

1 Nicolson, Sir Harold George

ISBN 0-689-10574-6　　　LC 73-80754

A revelation by Nigel Nicolson offering a "presentation of and commentary on a manuscript written by his mother, the novelist Vita Sackville-West, in 1920, which he found carefully preserved in her study upon her death in 1962. In real life the wife of the diplomat-historian-author Harold Nicolson, V. Sackville-West reveals in this memoir her passionate love affair with Violet Keppel Trefusis. Nigel Nicolson, through the judicious use of his mother's letters and diaries, elaborates on the memoir and carries the tale on further to encompass her subsequent affair with Virginia Woolf. The importance of the work lies in its absolutely convincing portrayal of a marriage that, although between two persons who found most of their sexual release in homosexual contacts, was a loving partnership that far surpassed in feeling most conventional marriages. Nigel Nicolson deserves enormous credit himself for the great artistry with which he has set forth the whole story." Choice

Sarton, May

Journal of a solitude. Norton 1973 208p illus $6.95
92

ISBN 0-393-07474-9　　　LC 72-13464

This "is a journal kept over the course of a year in which [the poet and novelist] came to terms with a number of things: the poor reception of her latest book, the gradual ending of a love affair, a long depression and, simply, a reassessment of her life and work." Pub W

"The inner explosions are here; likewise the anguish of unutterable loneliness and spiritual conflict, honestly and painfully recorded along with glimpses of a New Hampshire garden in all weathers, perceptive comments on artistic, literary, and political figures as well as neighbors in the village, quotations from admired writers interspersed with shrewd judgments on what irritates the author to the point of rage. 'Journal of a solitude' will be a surprise (possibly distressing) only to those readers who romanticize a favorite author and so fail to note the signs of fire." Choice

Serpico, Frank

Maas, Peter. Serpico. Viking 1973 314p illus $7.95   92

1 New York (City)—Police
ISBN 0-670-63498-0   LC 72-79002

"Called a 'psycho' by some of his superiors in the New York Police Department, a 'rat—and worse'—by many of his fellow policemen, Patrolman Frank Serpico spent many of his 11 years on the force pushing for exposure of widespread corruption. Eventually his efforts resulted in the now-famous Knapp Commission hearings. [The author tells here the story of Serpico's police career]." Christian Science Monitor

"The emotionalized exposé shows how the patrolman's profound disillusionment with compromises, rationalizations, expediencies, and graft engaged in by fellow policemen tarnished even the promotion and honors which finally were awarded him for what he thought were the wrong reasons." Booklist

Smith, Bessie. See class 780.92

Stalin, Iosif

Ulam, Adam B. Stalin; the man and his era. Viking 1973 760p $12.95   92

1 Russia—History—1925-1953
ISBN 0-670-66683-1   LC 73-6226

Ulam's book covers the range of Russian history in this century, as he gives a detailed account of Stalin's political development, his relationship with Lenin, the reasons for the Great Purge and for the purges that occurred during the last decade of Stalin's life, his leadership during the Second World War, and his diplomatic triumphs. From his assessment of Stalin's role in history, of his achievements, and of the price the Russian people paid for them the author concludes that twenty years after his death, Soviet Russia is still in many ways Stalin's Russia

Ulam "is particularly effective in explaining the background and development of such extraordinary phenomena as the adoption of terror as a technique of government. He writes well, often briskly, [and] is never dull." Newsweek

Includes bibliographical references

Steffens, Lincoln

Kaplan, Justin. Lincoln Steffens; a biography. Simon & Schuster 1974 380p illus $10   92

ISBN 0-671-21592-2   LC 73-15486

"Kaplan's approach is a traditional, chronological one, carrying the reader from Steffens' California boyhood through his early years as a journalist-reformer, and then to his dalliance with Bohemia, his flirtation with fascism, and to the connubial bliss he ultimately found with Bolshevism. It is the portrayal of this intellectual and emotional odyssey from reformer to revolutionary that rightfully stands out and probably will be of most interest to scholars and layman. Certain lapses—the author's penchant for minimizing his subject's acceptance of Stalin's brutalities, for example—flaw but do not seriously detract from the book's overall excellence." Choice

Includes bibliographical references

Stein, Gertrude

Mellow, James R. Charmed circle: Gertrude Stein & company. Praeger 1974 528p illus $12.95   92

ISBN 0-275-50430-1   LC 73-7473

The author offers an account of "the spirit of the group of artists, writers and musicians who attended Gertrude Stein's salon in early 20th century Paris. She was 'an American expatriate, an experimental stylist in prose, a collector of paintings and a . . . propagandist for modern art. . . . To her Saturday evenings at her studio . . . came Max Jacob, Apollinaire, Marie Laurencin, Max Weber and Rousseau. . . . Later, Erik Satie and Blaise Cendrars appeared, and Cocteau and Duchamp, Lincoln Steffens, Ezra Pound, Man Ray came by, and so did Sherwood Anderson, Hemingway and Fitzgerald.'" Newsweek

"Mellow's affectionate and sensible chronicle, the biography of a milieu, is not disfigured by partisanship. Drawn primarily from memoirs and letters, [this study] consolidates rather than extends our understanding of an extraordinary time and its heroic actors." N Y Times Bk R

Bibliography: p507-14

Stevenson, Adlai Ewing, 1900-1965

The papers of Adlai E. Stevenson. Walter Johnson, editor; Carol Evans, assistant editor. Little 1973-1974 2v v3 $15, v4 $17.50   92

1 U.S.—Politics and government—20th century   LC 73-175478

Earlier volumes entered in main catalog
Contents: v3 Governor of Illinois, 1949-1953 (ISBN 0-316-46752-9); v4 "Let's talk sense to the American people," 1952-1955 (ISBN 0-316-46753-7)

Adlai Stevenson "was an exceptionally true man and it is abundantly clear through these letters and speeches that his character did not alter in the slightest even through the ordeal of running for the Presidency. He remained faithful to his family, to his friends, to his supporters and to the electorate." Best Sellers

Sulzberger, C. L.

An age of mediocrity; memoirs and diaries, 1963-1972. Macmillan Pub. Co. 1973 828p illus $12.95   92

LC 73-2746

The third volume of the author's memoirs begun with: A long row of candles, and The last of the giants, both entered in main catalog

"Students of history and American foreign policy will find the dated journal entries and personal vignettes about world figures at critical moments in the recent past as frank, revealing, and readable as the previous volumes. Sulzberger's insightful explanations of why he considers political makers and shapers of the past decade less than giants yet influential within the arena of international affairs contain many quotable statements." Booklist

Postscript with a Chinese accent; memoirs and diaries, 1972-1973. Macmillan Pub. Co. 1974 401p illus $10   92

1 China (People's Republic of China. 1949-)—Description and travel
ISBN 0-02-615320-3   LC 74-10507

The fourth volume of the author's memoirs, sequel to the volume entered above

This volume of the New York Times columnist's diaries covers his travels during 1972 and 1973. He recounts his meetings with world leaders and details his trip to China

The author "shares some good stories about Ike, Kissinger, André Malraux, and even Milovan Djilas. The China diaries, which make up about one quarter of the book, point up the problems of traveling and writing, and offer lessons in observing and recording that other travelers to China might emulate. For those who like their China visit accounts with a touch of class . . . Sulzberger's memoir will make good reading." Library J

Thompson, Dorothy

Sanders, Marion K. Dorothy Thompson: a legend in her time. Illus. with photographs and drawings. Houghton 1973 428p illus $10   92

ISBN 0-395-15467-7   LC 72-9013

"One of the most famous reporters of the 30s and 40s, a world-traveled sophisticate at home anywhere in the world, Dorothy Thompson remained at heart the Methodist preacher's daughter she was when growing up in upstate New York at the turn of the century. . . . In this full-blown biography Marion Sanders portrays her sympathetically and vividly; she draws heavily on Dorothy Thompson's private papers and the memories of family and friends, writing with candor but never losing sight of her subject's warm humanity and, at the end, the essential nobility of her character. She describes Dorothy pushing herself from obscurity to front-page fame as she reported from Ireland, Italy and Eastern Europe, and in mid-career, already

Thompson, Dorothy—*Continued*

something of a legend, waging a journalistic war against Nazism. An early suffragist, she found an ironic fulfillment in 'serving' the man who gave her the most unhappiness—Sinclair Lewis, the second of her three husbands. Women readers will especially enjoy this biography, although feminists may cavil." Pub W

Includes bibliographical references

Tillich, Paul

May, Rollo. Paulus; reminiscences of a friendship. Harper 1973 113p $5.95   92

ISBN 0-06-065535-6   LC 72-78075

The author "has written a striking personal portrait of Paul Tillich in which he combines his personal respect and love for his friend with psychological and theological insight. The brief book brings to life the 'presence' of Paulus, who lived Dionysian and thought Apollonian, and who therefore existed with ecstatic reason, in the agony of doubt, before a God beyond God, on the boundaries between opposing forces in hazardous and questioning times. Though one may raise questions about the extent of the effect of the death of Paulus' mother on his later life, one can certainly appreciate May's insight into the profound eros of Tillich, his love-hate-relations, his need for the presence of others as well as for solitude, and his approach to the 'dying day.'" Choice

Includes bibliographical references

Toklas, Alice B.

Staying on alone; letters of Alice B. Toklas; ed. by Edward Burns, with an introduction by Gilbert A. Harrison. Liveright 1973 xxii, 426p illus $11.95   92

1 Stein, Gertrude
ISBN 0-87140-569-5   LC 73-82424

This book "chronicles, through her letters, Alice Toklas's life after the death of Gertrude Stein in 1946. She corresponds with lawyers, critics and institutions; she writes friends . . . like Carl Van Vechten and Cecil Beaton. . . . Occasionally she unmasks her grief. . . . She sees people, keeps house and . . . works for the publication of Gertrude Stein's manuscripts. . . . She [also] writes about politics, fashion, Lillian Russell, Henry James and Hoover vacuum cleaners." Newsweek

These letters "show [Alice] as a brilliant, perceptive individual: witty, shrewd, often piercing, who could be extremely tactful or equally blunt as it suited her. . . . But most beguilingly the letters . . . tell what was going on in the world of art, writing, music and theater. . . . [They] are profusely and fascinatingly illustrated." Christian Science Monitor

Tolstoĭ, Lev Nikolaevich, Graf

Crankshaw, Edward. Tolstoy; the making of a novelist. Viking 1974 276p illus $16.95   92

ISBN 0-670-71861-0   LC 73-6078

"A Studio book"

An overview of the full span of Tolstoy's creative life, from: Childhood, Boyhood, and Youth to Anna Karenina. "Starting from biography and working toward critical statements, Crankshaw seeks to provide a key to understanding Tolstoi and his works. Tolstoi's temperament, his family problems, the events surrounding the writing of individual works are all touched upon." Choice

"Though not a full-length biography [this] is a full-bodied study, and a fine one, of the formative years of a genius encumbered with every handicap that insecurity, hypocrisy, envy, guilt, and fear of life can mount. . . . This is not only a most absorbing book but also a most beautiful one, illustrated with many photographs, paintings, and drawings, some in color." New Yorker

Bibliography: p272

Truman, Harry S. President U.S.

Miller, Merle. Plain speaking; an oral biography of Harry S. Truman. Berkley; distributed by Putnam 1974 448p $8.95   92

1 U.S.—Politics and government—1945-1953
ISBN 0-399-11261-8   LC 73-87198

Parts of this book deal with the memories of people who knew the president before 1935, the year he first went to Washington as Senator from Missouri. Other parts deal with his presidency and the period following it. The work is based on tapes Miller compiled from interviews with Truman and others in 1961 and 1962 in Independence, Missouri

"This is the most refreshing book that has ever been written about an American president. . . . [It] is absolutely crammed with Trumanisms on every conceivable subject, most of them revealing of the man. . . . [The book] is full of rough and vulgar language, on which Mr. Truman holds no monopoly. . . . The plain speaking gets very earthy at times. But, all such reservations apart, an extraordinarily direct, clear, usually straight-thinking human being is recorded in this book." Christian Science Monitor

Truman, Margaret. Harry S. Truman. Morrow 1973 [c1972] 602p illus $10.95   92

1 U.S.—Politics and government—1945-1953
ISBN 0-688-00005-3   LC 73-170238

"Margaret Truman writes affectionately but honestly of her father, combining tidbits of family and personal happenings with an inside, albeit mostly personal, view of Truman's political career and his Presidency." Booklist

"Apparently the greatest single advantage Miss Truman has enjoyed over other chroniclers of her father's career is free access to a calendar-diary he kept on his desk and on which he jotted down his instant-replay reactions to the people and events that marched past his desk. There are many delectable tidbits and a few meaty morsels among these entries, but they tell us a good deal more about Harry Truman's temperament and crotchets than about the problems he dealt with." New Repub

Vlad the Impaler, Dracula, Prince of Wallachia, 1431-1476

Florescu, Radu. Dracula; a biography of Vlad the Impaler, 1431-1476 [by] Radu Florescu and Raymond T. McNally. Hawthorn Bks. 1973 239p illus $7.95   92

LC 73-364

Companion volume to the authors': In search of Dracula, entered in main catalog, class 398

This is a study of the historical Dracula "Vlad III, a fifteenth century prince or princeling of Wallachia, a territory embracing the Carpathian Mountains. His father, Vlad II, bore the name of Dracul (probably because he belonged to the Order of the Dragon—that being the meaning of 'dracul'). Although the authors try to be scrupulously fair, Vlad III emerges from this study a supermonster responsible for the deaths, usually by impalement, of tens of thousands of people, and a sexual psychopath as well. That he stood bravely against the Ottoman Turks seems largely irrelevant. Working from very few primary sources, the authors do a good job of historical reconstruction, but the writing is leaden and the book will disappoint most horror buffs." Pub W

Bibliography: p215-28

Waugh, Evelyn

Pryce-Jones, David, ed. Evelyn Waugh and his world. Little 1973 248p illus $12.95   92

LC 73-5746

This collection of 16 essays by various British hands "presents a vast amount of new, informative, and sometimes startling data mostly about Waugh's life. . . . In every essay some fresh insights and knowledge of Waugh's career appear, e.g., his life at Lancing and at Oxford, his first wife examined, his religious conversion, his military service in World War II, etc. Numerous original letters and postcards are printed, and almost 100 photographs and illustrations adorn the book—the largest gathering of such material ever released." Choice

These "sometimes brilliant Waugh anecdotes and letters all provide vital evidence for anyone who wants to find out what this writer was about. The book is to the point, and at the same time it is fun; serious but unsolemn, it is in short a remarkable testimonial." Times (London) Lit Sup

Wellington, Arthur Wellesley, 1st Duke of

Longford, Elizabeth. Wellington. Harper [1970 c1969-1973 c1972] 2v illus maps ea $12.50   92

1 Great Britain—Politics and government—19th century 2 Great Britain—History, Military   LC 75-95793

Contents: v 1 The years of the sword (ISBN 0-06-012669-8); v2 Pillar of state (ISBN 0-06-012671-X)

In v 1 the author covers Wellington's early life and early political career with emphasis on his military achievements after 1808 when he fought and won the Peninsular war and the Waterloo campaign

v2 emphasizes Wellington's career as a Cabinet Minister, Premier and elder statesman

Wells, Herbert George

MacKenzie, Norman. H. G. Wells; a biography, by Norman and Jeanne MacKenzie. Simon & Schuster 1973 487p illus $10   92

ISBN 0-671-21520-5   LC 73-1184

A study of the man who "fought his way out of genteel poverty and in the first two decades of this century established himself as probably the West's leading popular interpreter of the ideas of science, in or out of fiction, as well as a beguiling storyteller, a champion of social justice and an uncanny futurist. Henry James, Bennett, Conrad, Shaw and Orwell figure in the story, as friends, ex-friends or adversaries, and so do numerous women, among them Rebecca West." Pub W

This biography "is quite possibly definitive; the MacKenzies write with that professional clarity and grace that is self-effacing. Their book proves to be a very personal account of the man who could write an 'Outline of history' and 'The history of Mr. Polly' 'The war of the worlds' and 'Mr. Britling sees it through.' At the same time, even though it contains straightforward accounts of Wells' personal peccadillos . . . and his trenchant debates . . . this book is also a microcosmic history of Western culture, clustering as it does around the commonsensical tendencies of Great Britain during the years 1870, roughly, to 1946, and the death of Wells." Choice

Bibliography: p469-74

West, J. B.

Upstairs at the White House; my life with the First Ladies, by J. B. West with Mary Lynn Kotz. Coward, McCann & Geoghegan 1973 381p illus $8.95   92

1 Presidents—U.S.—Family
ISBN 0-698-10546-X   LC 73-78738

Offering anecdotes about Presidential families from the Franklin Delano Roosevelts to the Nixons, a majordomo describes his twenty-eight years of service in the White House

"At various points dramatic, gossipy, humorous, and deeply touching but always discreet, West complements his reminiscences with photographs from his own collection. The author reveals knowledge and understanding of politics and feminine psychology through intriguing episodes of the daily lives and styles of six presidential families. He depicts the standards and idiosyncracies of each First Lady and points out the special imprint she made upon the president's house and chronicles her contributions to the heritage of the U.S. Signal events of each administration and perceptive views of each president enrich the contents." Booklist

Bibliography: p369-71

West, Jessamyn

Hide and seek; a continuing journey. Harcourt 1973 310p $7.50   92

ISBN 0-15-140215-9   LC 72-88797

The author "reminisces about her childhood and youth, depicting family life and travels. Along the way she reflects on a variety of subjects, such as education, language, death, love, religion, dreams. A nature lover, she finds much in common with Thoreau, quoting him frequently and even naming her trailer 'Walden on Wheels.'" Library J

This "is a rich book: an account and celebration of three months of solitude on the bank of the Colorado River; the memoir of a writer of intelligence and wit; an insightful and humorous reflection on continuity and change in the American culture over a period of years. The author's perception of nature, the culture, and herself is informed by literature and her intimate relationship with literature. Those readers who have enjoyed her essays, screenplays, and fiction will also take pleasure in this book." Choice

Whistler, James Abbott McNeill. See class 709.2

Wright, Frank Lloyd

Twombly, Robert C. Frank Lloyd Wright; an interpretative biography. Harper 1973 373p illus $10   92

1 Architecture, Modern—20th century
ISBN 0-06-14467-X   LC 72-9248

"This is an assessment of Wright's philosophy, architectural practice and theory and his private life. Twombly traces Wright through childhood, college, work with Louis Sullivan, problems and accomplishments. There are many photographs, some small, of Wright's creations, chapter notes and a lengthy bibliography of primary and secondary sources." Wis Lib Bul

"His source notes, most of which spill out like the particles of a split atom, are staggering. But his writing is rarely pedantic. . . . Faced with the enormous body of Wright's buildings and projects, Twombly is forced to be both synoptical and highly selective. . . . In those of Wright's designs which he does discuss at any length, Twombly's remarks are incisive and sound." Arch Forum

Wright, Richard

Fabre, Michel. The unfinished quest of Richard Wright; tr. from the French by Isabel Barzun. Morrow 1973 xx, 652p illus $15   92

ISBN 0-688-00163-7   LC 73-4227

This is a "picture of the life of the black American novelist who became a precursor of angry third world writers and a chronicler of the emerging black consciousness. Fabre traces Wright's evolution as an artist from his early days in Mississippi to his exile in France and relates the development of Wright's controversial international reputation, particularly the author's formative contacts with communism, existentialism, Pan-Africanism, and the third world. Fabre also provides brief but incisive critical reassessments of Wright's works." Booklist

"One of the values of Fabre's study is that it . . . challenges many traditional notions of Wright, as well as traditional ways of looking at Afro-American literature." N Y Times Bk R

Selected bibliography: p625-38

Yeats, W. B.

Memoirs: Autobiography—first draft [and] Journal; transcribed and ed. by Denis Donoghue. Macmillan (N.Y.) [1973 c1972] 318p illus $7.95   92

LC 72-11279

First published 1972 in England

"In 1921 W. B. Yeats sealed in an envelope the rough first draft of his 'Autobiography,' noting that the material was, 'private . . . containing much that is not for publication now, if ever.' This draft [written between 1915 and 1916 or 1917 and] now made available in its entirety for the first time, covers the years from 1887 down to 1898. . . . The present volume [also contains] the first printing of a 'Journal' which Yeats began in 1908 and added to intermittently until 1930. Here again we are confronted with complete frankness, with candid appraisals of Lady Gregory, George Moore, J. M. Synge, and other colleagues in the Irish dramatic revival; there are first drafts of many of the poems; and there are interesting insights into much of the 'system' worked out in detail in 'The Vision.'" Best Sellers

"'Memoirs' is indispensable to any student of poetry or modern literature and to any person professionally concerned with Yeat's work. Beyond that, however, its interest extends to the general world of letters and it provides in many ways a more ingratiating entry to Yeats's life and work than the hieratic final version." N Y Times Bk R

930-999 HISTORY

930 The ancient world to ca. 500 A.D.

Starr, Chester G.
A history of the ancient world. 2d ed. Oxford 1974 742p illus maps $15.95   **930**

1 History, Ancient
ISBN 0-19-501814-1   LC 74-79633

Earlier edition entered in main catalog
First published 1965. In the 1974 edition the author "has completely rewritten the opening chapters on early man and Near Eastern development; in later sections he takes into account recent contributions by archeological investigations and scholarly studies. Newly revised bibliographical essays direct the reader to . . . modern works as well as to archeological sources." Publisher's note
General bibliography: p717-28

940.4 World War I, 1914-1918 (Military conduct of the war)

Simpson, Colin
The Lusitania. Little 1973 303p illus $8.95   **940.4**

1 Lusitania (Steamship)
ISBN 0-316-79178-4   LC 73-91

"The 'unarmed' passenger ship Lusitania was sunk by a German U-boat off the south coast of Ireland on May 7, 1915, causing the loss of 1,198 lives, many of them American . . . According to Simpson's . . . enquiry, which is based on admiralty and U.S. National archives, documents relating to trial proceedings on both sides of the Atlantic, and other material, some of it secret until recently, the circumstances in which the ship would be attacked were created by prominent officials both British and American [including] Churchill who wanted to draw America into the war. . . . [The author, a journalist with the London Times, seeks to prove] that on its fatal voyage the Lusitania was armed, loaded with munitions and deliberately left to fend for herself in her hour of greatest peril." Pub W

"This analysis effectively shatters the old belief that the 'Lusitania' was simply the victim of German ruthlessness." Choice

The author's "bibliography is stupendous, his index huge, his footnote's are multitudinous, his expressions of opinion and characterization are unrestrained." Best Sellers

940.54 World War II, 1939-1945 (Military conduct of the war)

Boldt, Gerhard
Hitler: the last ten days. Coward, McCann & Geoghegan 1973 224p illus maps $6.95   **940.54**

1 Hitler, Adolf 2 World War, 1939-1945—Personal narratives 3 Germany—Politics and government—1933-1945
ISBN 0-698-10531-1   LC 72-97575

New English edition translated from the German by Sandra Bance
The author a young aide de camp to the Chief of the German General Staff, was in Hitler's Bunker at the fall of Berlin. "Escaping from the bunker at the last moment, he wrote down the details, and these he . . . published together with some account of his own . . . military career." N Y Times Bk R

At last this is "available in English. . . . [Boldt's] knowledgeable, far-ranging, and candid reminiscences are likely to interest both the professional soldier and the general reader." Economist

Conrat, Maisie
Executive order 9066: the internment of 110,000 Japanese Americans [by] Maisie & Richard Conrat. With an introduction by Edison Uno and an epilogue by Tom C. Clark; photographs by Dorothea Lange and others. MIT Press for the California Hist. Soc. 1972 120p illus pa $3.95   **940.54**

1 Japanese in the U.S.—Pictorial works 2 World War, 1939-1945—Evacuation of civilians—Pictorial works 3 Concentration camps
ISBN 0-262-53023-6   LC 72-9024

"A very moving collection of 62 photographs carefully selected from some 25,000 showing the results of Franklin Delano Roosevelt's order 9066 which interned 110,000 Japanese Americans in 1942. The introduction writtten by a man who was a child when he was interned with his family at Manzanar tells of the feelings of the Japanese. A short essay by two Caucasians explains the growth of anti-Orientalism in western U.S. Although the photographs speak in themselves of shock, tragedy, bewilderment, or resignation, headlines from newspaper and quotations from many sources accompany some of the photos. . . . Tom C. Clark summarizes the lesson to be learned from Executive order 9066." Booklist

Piekalkiewicz, Janusz
Secret agents, spies, and saboteurs; famous undercover missions of World War II; tr. from the German by Francisca Garvie and Nadia Fowler. Morrow [1974 c1973] 528p illus $12.50   **940.54**

1 World War, 1939-1945—Secret service 2 Spies
LC 74-182962

"Having gained access to the archives of several countries and accounts from eyewitnesses, Piekalkiewicz recorded for television the bare outlines of undercover missions during World War II. Twenty-seven of these activities are here amplified, each accompanied by photographs from both enemy and Allied files. Some of these adventures appeared earlier in full-length books which gave more detailed information." Booklist

"There is plenty of violence and of sorrow, hushed up for the greater part, but it all makes the dreadful world of war vivid, and also the tremendous world of heroism." Best Sellers

Whaley, Barton
Codeword BARBAROSSA. MIT Press 1973 376p illus $10   **940.54**

1 World War, 1939-1945—Secret service 2 World War, 1939-1945—Germany 3 World War, 1939-1945—Russia
ISBN 0-262-23062-3   LC 72-10882

The author has examined "the memoirs and intelligence literature of a dozen countries to . . . [compile] the signs that should have warned Stalin of Hitler's intention to attack him in June, 1941. His hypothesis is that not only did Hitler achieve total surprise so far as Stalin himself was concerned . . . but that . . . 'only a handful of the world's many intelligence chiefs, national policy makers or press pundits unambiguously foresaw the development.' . . . [The author] lists 84 'warnings' to Stalin of Hitler's intentions." N Y Times Bk R

"'Barbarossa' is a disturbing, fascinating, documented insight into the world of political espionage and military intelligence." Library J
Glossary of abbreviations, acronyms, codewords, and definitions: p361-64. Bibliography: p311-59

Young, Peter
(ed.) Atlas of the Second World War; cartography by Richard Natkiel. Putnam [1974 c1973] 288p illus maps $17.95   **940.54**

1 World War, 1939-1945—Campaigns and battles 2 World War, 1939-1945—Maps
ISBN 0-399-11182-4   LC 73-78626

First published 1973 in England
This atlas covers the military operations on land, sea and air from 1939 to 1945. It is divided into sections corresponding to the major theaters or campaigns of the war, each

Young, Peter—*Continued*

individual battle having a selection of pertinent maps accompanied by explanatory text, balance charts and illustrations
"This volume includes numerous photographs, a wealth of good, clear maps, and a text that is direct, uncomplicated, and provocative. Although some of the 215 maps are small and consequently do not provide minute detail, they are nevertheless clearer and more detailed than many other maps which accompany monographs on specific battles or campaigns; the larger, strategic maps are most satisfactory. Another praiseworthy feature is that maps of a particular campaign appear together with the appropriate text." Library J

942 British Isles

The Horizon History of the British Empire. Editor: Stephen W. Sears. Am. Heritage; distributed by McGraw 1973 511p illus maps $35   **942**

1 Great Britain—Colonies—History
ISBN 0-07-630354-1   LC 73-8684

"Based on material originally produced by Time-Life Books in association with the broadcast of the television series, The British Empire by BBC-TV." Verso of title page
"Written by some 30 authors, most of whom are acknowledged authorities [this book] provides a lively, readable account of the most splendid of all imperial edifices. As is appropriate in a general survey, both the first and second British Empires are covered. Clearly designed for a popular audience, the work tends to over-emphasize spectacular achievements and notable (or notorious) individuals at the expense of more mundane but important subjects such as administration and policy formulation. However, the lavish illustrations are superb . . . and the material usually reflects recent interpretations as well as considerable research." Choice

Smith, Goldwin
A history of England. 4th ed. Scribner 1974 924p illus maps $12.50   **942**

1 Great Britain—History
ISBN 0-684-13759-3   LC 73-19355
First published 1949
A survey of the English people from earliest times to the present
Bibliography: p863-900

Trevelyan, G. M.
History of England. New illus. ed. With an introduction by Asa Briggs; illus. selected by Penelope Brown and others. Longman 1973 xxxiii, 913p illus maps $15   **942**

1 Great Britain—History
ISBN 0-582-48471-5
1956 edition still available from McKay with title: Illustrated history of England, entered in main catalog
First published 1926. The 1973 edition has a new introduction, the illustrations have been completely reselected and the maps redrawn
Select bibliography of recent works: p881-91

943.08 Germany since 1866

Lorant, Stefan
Sieg Heil! (Hail to victory) An illustrated history of Germany from Bismarck to Hitler. Norton 1974 352p illus $14.95   **943.08**

1 Germany—History—1866-1918—Pictorial works 2 Germany—History—1918-1933—Pictorial works 3 Germany—History—1933-1945—Pictorial works
ISBN 0-393-05501-9   LC 73-20410

"The hundreds of photographs in black and white are . . . expressive of the age that led up to the rise and fall of Hitler. . . . To show that Hitler was a natural outcropping of history . . . Lorant has gone back to Bismarck and Bismarck's . . . statesmanship that limited German freedom and tolerated poverty but kept and increased Germany's sovereignty; then he goes through Wilhelm II's break with Bismarck and the events that led to the first World War. . . . [Included are] the era between the wars [and] the second World War." Best Sellers

"There is no other book in English (or German) which covers the 80 years of German history from the coronation of Wilhelm I as King of Prussia in 1861 through the end of Hitler's Third Reich in 1945 with anything even approaching its pictorial detail and wealth. . . . Despite the weaknesses of the text . . . it is a useful educational tool if corrected by a knowledgeable historian." Choice

947.085 Russia—Later 20th century, 1953-

Khrushchev, Nikita Sergeevich
Khrushchev remembers: the last testament. Tr. and ed. by Strobe Talbott; with a foreword by Edward Crankshaw and an introduction by Jerrold L. Schecter. Little 1974 xxxi, 602p illus $12.95   **947.085**

1 Russia—Politics and government—1953-   LC 74-4095

The second and concluding volume of Khrushchev's memoirs, the earlier volume of which is entered in main catalog class 947.084
In this volume Khrushchev sheds "insights on the Kremlin's political system. The flow of information blocked; admirals and generals who lacked vital weapons information; bureaucratic red tape. . . . [He tells] how he viewed power, himself, his people, bureaucrats, the military . . . foreign leaders, domestic and foreign policy, crisis 'management' at home and abroad." Best Sellers

"Should engross students of human nature as well as Soviet specialists and political scientists." Pub W

Solzhenitsyn, Aleksandr I.
Letter to the Soviet leaders; tr. from the Russian by Hilary Sternberg. Index on Censorship in association with Harper 1974 59p $3.50   **947.085**

1 Russia—Politics and government 2 Russia—Foreign relations 3 Civilization, Modern
ISBN 0-06-013913-7   LC 74-4191

This is a translation of a modified version of the letter Solzhenitsyn sent to the leaders in the Kremlin in September 1973. In it he "proclaims that the chief dangers facing the [Soviet Union] are those of a war with China and of the contamination of the environment—the exhaustion of natural resources owing to excessive industrialization and urbanization. He regards both dangers as having been engendered by blind adherence to ideas imported from the West: to the dogma of unlimited scientific-technical progress . . . and in particular to Marxist dogma, which he regards as the embodiment of the anti-religious lack of spirituality in the West." N Y Rev of Books

"Solzhenitsyn's eminence as a novelist warrants respectful consideration of his political writing. In this work, however, he falls far short of the achievement of his creative works. He urges the Soviet leaders to renounce their Communist ideology in order to avert war with China. Some of his arguments are cogent, and dramatically offered, but they betray naïveté and his own confusion on ideology." Library J

948.5 Sweden

Moberg, Vilhelm
A history of the Swedish people; tr. from the Swedish by Paul Britten Austin. Pantheon Bks. 1972-1974 2v illus ea $6.95   **948.5**

1 Sweden—History
ISBN 0-394-48192-5   LC 72-3411
Contents: v 1 From Odin to Engelbrekt; v2 From Renaissance to revolution
In volume 1, the author seeks to cover Sweden's history concentrating on Sweden's common people, and covers its prehistory through the Middle Ages
"The second volume takes up the saga of Sweden from the fifteen century to a significant revolution, the Dacke rebellion, in the sixteenth century." Booklist

952 Japan

Busch, Noel F.
The Horizon Concise history of Japan. Am. Heritage 1972 217p illus map $8.95
          952
1 Japan—History
ISBN 0-07-009299-0   LC 73-189384

The author presents the long, history of the Japanese people "beginning with the first imperial family in 660 B.C. to Perry's 'opening' of the country to the West in 1853 and events as recent as the Osaka World's Fair. The viewpoint is middle-of-the-road; Busch is not concerned with penetrating analyses of Japanese character or history, so his attitude—especially toward contemporary mercantile Japan with its unprecedented prosperity—is largely one of 'wait and see.' The book is neither more nor less than its title implies: a compact lucid introduction to Japan. More than 100 illustrations." Pub W

"A public library will be tempted, and probably should have the book. It would be unfortunate if it did not have something else as well, such as Edwin O. Reischauer's Japan; the story of a nation [entered below] as a counterpoint. Busch's history will appeal to a general audience which, unfortunately, will have little background from which to judge the material and may be misled." Choice

Najita, Tetsuo
Japan. Prentice-Hall 1974 152p maps (The Modern nations in historical perspective) $6.95   952
1 Japan—History
ISBN 0-13-509455-0   LC 74-3337
"A Spectrum book"

The author believes that the development of Japanese history has been far from unilinear. He contrasts alternating periods of bureaucracy and bureaucratic loyalism, a legacy of the Tokugawa period (1600-1868), with the ideological action fundamental to the Meiji period (1868-1912) which brought about the destruction of the feudal order. The final chapters of this volume describe the frontier development of political change. Emphasis is on the redefinition of constitutional politics and ideology, and on the growing discontent in the 1930's, especially among nationalists, liberals, socialists, and radical restorationists

Reischauer, Edwin O.
Japan: the story of a nation. Rev. ed. Knopf 1974 387, xx p maps $7.95   952
1 Japan—History
ISBN 0-394-49510-1   LC 74-7683

Earlier edition entered in main catalog
First published 1970 as a successor to the author's Japan, past and present, which first appeared in 1946. The 1974 edition has been revised and updated with a largely new final chapter and a few changes in the chapter before it as well as the addition of a chronology at the end
Bibliographical note: p383-87

959.704 Vietnam—Independence, 1949-

Herbert, Anthony B.
Soldier [by] Anthony B. Herbert with James T. Wooten. Holt 1973 498p illus maps $10.95   959.704
1 Vietnamese Conflict, 1961- —Personal narratives
ISBN 0-03-091456-6   LC 72-78121

In this account of his military career the author focuses on the corruption and negligence of the U.S. Army in Vietnam. He claims that his superior officers, the "commander and deputy commander of [his] Vietnam unit ... had refused to investigate or act upon eight incidents of murder, torture or mistreatment of prisoners he called to their attention." Newsweek

"As a case study it provides a unique perspective on frustrations of Viet-Nam policies and operations and reflects the dilemmas of recent societal impacts on traditional military dogma. Recommended for all general collections." Choice

960 Africa

Hallett, Robin
Africa since 1875; a modern history. Univ. of Mich. Press 1974 807, lix p maps (Univ. of Mich. History of the modern world) $15
      960
1 Africa—History
ISBN 0-472-07170-X   LC 72-91505

Companion volume to the author's: Africa to 1875, entered in main catalog

"The narrative begins in 1875 at a time when the majority of African peoples still preserved their old-established social and political structures. In the course of the next sixty years virtually the entire continent was brought under European hegemony—only to be followed by the rise of an African nationalism that has all but swept away, in a wave of independent nationhood, the dominions established by the European powers. Modern transformations wrought by the discovery of valuable minerals, the industrialization of the continent, and the spread of Western ideas have touched every aspect of African society, from Cairo to Cape Town.... [The author offers an] account and analysis of this dramatic period, and includes both an introductory overview of the century and a concluding consideration of the process of change in modern African history." Publisher's note
Suggested readings: p773-807

970.1 Indians of North America

La Farge, Oliver
A pictorial history of the American Indian; rev. by Alvin M. Josephy, Jr. Crown 1974 288p illus map $9.95   970.1
1 Indians of North America—History 2 Indians of North America—Pictorial works
      LC 74-78424

Earlier edition entered in main catalog
First published 1956. The 1974 edition has been brought up to date

Scientific American
Early man in America; readings from Scientific American; with an introduction by Richard S. MacNeish. Freeman 1973 93p illus $5.95   970.1
1 Indians—Origin 2 America—Antiquities
ISBN 0-7167-0864-7   LC 72-12251

A collection of articles for the novice which introduces archaeology as a stepping stone to studying issues surrounding the people of the new world

970.3 Specific Indian tribes. Aztecs

Davies, Nigel
The Aztecs; a history. Putnam [1974 c1973] 363p illus maps $10   970.3
1 Aztecs
ISBN 0-399-11331-2   LC 73-92595

First published 1973 in England

This is an account "of the outstanding events and personalities of the Mexica Aztec political-military history. Davies covers such topics as Mexica religion, social and economic organization, and the roles and views of other ethnic groups in the Valley of Mexico only as they are necessary to understand the outline of Mexica political history." Library J

This "is an excellent book, and not only on the centuries of migration by this hungry tribe before they reached dominance under the two Moctezumas. [Davies] carries on to the phases through which Spanish colonial history passed in the century following the Conquest and the bitter controversies between the colonists and the far more humane Spanish government at home. There is of course an enormous literature on this subject from Las Casas onwards; Mr Davies sifts it and (most important) puts each phase of the quarrels of colonisation fairly before the reader." New Statesman
Bibliography: p348-54

970.4 Indians in specific places

The Indians, by the editors of Time-Life Books; with text by Benjamin Capps. Time-Life Bks. [distributed by Little] 1973 240p illus maps (The Old West) $9.95   970.4

1 Indians of North America—The West
ISBN 0-8094-1454-6   LC 72-93991

Illustrated with photographs, paintings, drawings and maps, this book describes the history, customs, ceremonies and ways of life of western American Indians as well as their peaceful and belligerent relations with the white man. Among the topics discussed are the influence of the introduction of the horse on Indian life, buffalo hunting, the role of women in Indian society, Indian religious practices and the defeat of Custer at the Battle of the Little Bighorn, including excerpts from a pictographic account of the battle by an Indian participant
Bibliography: p236-37

970.5 Government relations with Indians

Deloria, Vine
Behind the trail of broken treaties; an Indian declaration of independence [by] Vine Deloria, Jr. Delacorte Press 1974 263p $8.95   970.5

1 Indians of North America—Government relations
ISBN 0-440-01404-1   LC 74-1153

The Indian author and lawyer argues "that the best solution to the 'Indian problem,' for Indians and the federal government alike, is to honor old treaties and to develop a new treaty relationship which gives tribes the status of quasi-international independence (with the U.S. acting as protector). The legal and moral arguments are set into historical developments; and the major objections to restoration of tribal sovereignty are countered with reason and with examples from around the world. Deloria does not proclaim this proposal as a panacea but simply as a necessary first step to permit Indian tribes, their lands, and their ways of life to survive so they can meet the difficulties of their political, economic, and cultural existence." Library J

"This is a book highly recommended to thoughtful whites interested in constructing a viable as well as moral solution to our government's self-created dilemma with respect to the Indian nations, and to Indians interested in broadening their knowledge of the treaty-making basis." Best Sellers

The Soldiers, by the editors of Time-Life Books with text by David Nevin. Time-Life Bks. [distributed by Little] 1973 239p illus maps (The Old West) $9.95   970.5

1 Indians of North America—Wars 2 U.S. Army—Military life 3 Frontier and pioneer life—The West   LC 73-79475

This book offers accounts of Indian wars and U.S. Army life west of the Mississippi from 1865 to 1876. During that time, over 15,000 soldiers engaged in battles, protected trails, surveyed railroad lines, and defended settlers, miners, cattlemen, and construction crews. There are details of battles, including the Fetterman and Sand Creek Massacres and the Battle of Little Big Horn. Prominent officers, such as Chivington and Custer, are also described. The book is illustrated with contemporary photographs and paintings
Bibliography: p234-35

973 United States

Billington, Ray Allen
Westward expansion; a history of the American frontier [by] Ray Allen Billington, with the collaboration of James Blaine Hedges. 4th ed. Macmillan Pub. Co. 1974 840p maps $12.95   973

1 U.S.—Territorial expansion 2 U.S.—History 3 Mississippi Valley—History 4 The West—History
ISBN 0-02-309840-6   LC 73-4044

Earlier edition entered in main catalog
First published 1949. In the 1974 edition "one new chapter has been added, a half-dozen more have been almost completely rewritten, and portions of nearly all the remainder altered to incorporate fresh material and interpretations. . . . Four chapters that appeared in the first three editions have been compressed into one. . . . The bibliography has also been completely revised, with many outmoded books and articles omitted, and with all significant new works published between 1967 and 1972 added." Preface to the fourth edition
Bibliography: p663-805

Cooke, Alistair
Alistair Cooke's America. Knopf 1973 400p illus $15   973

1 U.S.—History
ISBN 0-394-48726-5   LC 73-7268

An expanded narrative from the author's 13-part television series exploring the history of the building and growth of his "adopted country—through each of its phases from the Revolution to its present-day struggles to renew and extend the ideals of the Founding Fathers." Pub W

This "is a superb book . . . in its depth and its extraordinary coverage. . . . [It is] the consideration of a man of objectivity who loves this land. It is a book lavish in its illustrations, color and black-and-white, with paintings and drawings, with maps and an index." Best Sellers

Freidel, Frank
(ed.) Harvard Guide to American history. Rev. ed. Frank Freidel, editor, with the assistance of Richard K. Showman. Belknap Press 1974 2v (xxx, 1290p) set $45   973

1 U.S.—History—Bibliography 2 U.S.—History—Study and teaching
ISBN 0-674-37560-2   LC 72-81272

Earlier edition entered in main catalog under the editorship of Oscar Handlin
First published 1954 in one volume. The 1974 edition has been revised and greatly expanded to reflect the shifting interests and growth in the literature of American history during the past two decades. About one third of the entries are new and coverage includes demography, social structure, ethnicity and the new urban and cultural dimensions of history

Hofstadter, Richard
The American political tradition, and the men who made it; 25th anniversary edition; with a foreword by Christopher Lasch. Knopf 1973 xxxiii, 378p $7.95   973

1 U.S.—Politics and government 2 U.S.—Biography
ISBN 0-394-48880-6   LC 73-7291

Earlier edition entered in main catalog
First published 1948. The 1974 edition contains the original text with a new foreword and preface
Bibliographical essay: p349-78

200 years; a bicentennial illustrated history of the United States. U.S. News & World Report [1973] 2v illus $32.50   973

1 U.S.—History   LC 73-77836

"Although extensive in scope, no cumbersome elements detract from this spirited sweep through American history. Accent is on the ideas and successes of the individuals who in two centuries have shaped the U.S. into a nation both flourishing and unique. The lavishly illustrated volumes are uniform in format: each is divided into three chronological units appended with portraits and biographical data on chief executives and a reading portfolio of period speeches, writings, and clippings." Booklist
Includes bibliographical references

Wolff, Robert Paul
(ed.) 1984 revisited; prospects for American politics; original essays by Todd Gitlin [and others]. Knopf 1973 201p $6.95   973

1 U.S.—Politics and government 2 U.S.—Social conditions 3 Right and left (Political science)
ISBN 0-394-48188-7   LC 72-653

Wolff, Robert P.—*Continued*

"These six essays, written by academics formerly active in the New Left, are predictions of the future of America's politics leading to 1984. Prepared for this volume, the essays analyze recent history; and they are uniform in their prediction that repression lies ahead." Library J

"Edited by a philosopher who has written some of the best critiques of liberalism from the left, this volume purports to present radical causal theories of American politics, by mostly young scholars, oriented toward the period from the present to 1984. . . . There is no apparent common theoretical orientation, although Wolff suggests that Marxism is such a structure. Would be useful as an example of current radical left thinking in the U.S." Choice

Includes bibliographical references

973.3 U.S.—Revolution and confederation, 1775-1789

Chidsey, Donald Barr

The Loyalists; the story of those Americans who fought against independence. Crown 1973 213p illus $5.95   973.3

1 American Loyalists 2 U.S.—History—Revolution
ISBN 0-517-504200   LC 73-79619

"The author explains who The Loyalists were, why they held the opinions they did, and what happened to them. Even in so brief an account not too much space is given to direct treatment of the Loyalists; there are many asides, some brief, others quite long, discussing such topics as the Sons of Liberty, the Stamp Act, Boston riots, the activities of the Continental Congress, campaigns of Washington, Greene, etc. Mr. Chidsey emphasizes the lack of leadership and united action of the Loyalists and the failure of the British to offer encouragement or make use of their help." Best Sellers

"With a vigorous, staccato style, Chidsey draws exciting sketches of such leading Tories as Massachusetts Governor Thomas Hutchinson, Benjamin Church of South Carolina with his mistress problems, Benjamin Thompson who became a Bavarian count, James Rivington who doubled as an agent for George Washington, and the traitor Benedict Arnold. Drafted entirely from secondary works, the book is aimed at the general reader." Choice

Bibliography: p193-209

Stember, Sol

The bicentennial guide to the American Revolution. Saturday Review Press 1974 3v maps v 1 $12.95, v2-3 ea $8.95   973.3

1 U.S.—History—Revolution 2 U.S.—Description and travel   LC 73-23108

Contents: v 1 The war in the North (ISBN 0-8415-0310-9); v2 The middle colonies (ISBN 0-8415-0312-5); v3 The war in the South (ISBN 0-8415-0314-1)

"A travel guide to Revolutionary War sites in the North, South, and middle colonies. Stember supplies personalized descriptions, advice, and suggested routes in a state-by-state, area-by-area survey of forts, battlefields, and other historical locations. In Stember's narrative enough attention is paid to historical significance to give a good sense of perspective to the nation's early development and growth. Bibliographies are included in each volume." Booklist

973.303 U.S.—Revolution and confederation, 1775-1789— Encyclopedias and dictionaries

Boatner, Mark Mayo

Encyclopedia of the American Revolution, by Mark Mayo Boatner III. Bicentennial ed. [Rev. and expanded] McKay 1974 1290p maps $17.50   973.303

1 U.S.—History—Revolution—Encyclopedias
ISBN 0-679-50440-0   LC 73-91868

Earlier edition entered in main catalog

First published 1966. For the 1974 edition an attempt has been made to revise some articles and to correct errors. In addition a topical index has been added along with a brief addendum to the bibliography

973.7 U.S.—Administration of Abraham Lincoln, 1861-1865 (Civil War)

Catton, Bruce

Gettysburg: the final fury. Doubleday 1974 114p illus maps $8.95   973.7

1 Gettysburg, Battle of, 1863
ISBN 0-385-02060-0   LC 73-11896

An account of the causes, events and consequences of the Civil War battle which turned the tide in favor of the Union forces

"What is truly distinguished about Catton's retelling of the Gettysburg story is his nearly total focus on the significant human and military details and, most important, the lucid serenity of his descriptive writing. . . . This is pure narrative, unburdened by scholarly obtrusions, heightened by many photos, drawings, paintings and maps." Pub W

Nevins, Allan

Ordeal of the Union; selected chapters; comp. and introduced by E. B. Long. Scribner 1973 500p maps $12.50   973.7

1 U.S.—History—Civil War
ISBN 0-684-13414-4   LC 73-5189

A collection of fourteen chapters selected from the author's eight volume series about the Civil War: Ordeal of the Union, entered in main catalog in classes 973.6 and 973.7

Among the topics considered are: slavery and emancipation, American culture, political and military organization and leaders, and several battles

Bibliographic footnotes are included

Stampp, Kenneth M.

(ed.) The causes of the Civil War; newly rev. Prentice-Hall 1974 182p (Eyewitness accounts of American history) $6.95   973.7

1 U.S.—History—Civil War—Causes 2 U.S.—History—Civil War—Sources
ISBN 0-13-121202-8   LC 74-892

"A Spectrum book"

First published 1959

This book of 82 selections integrates the conclusions of various post-war historians with the thoughts of contemporary commentators like Jefferson Davis, Horace Greeley, and Lincoln. Political, cultural and economic aspects are emphasized

973.8 U.S.—Later 19th century, 1865-1901 (Period of reconstruction)

Benedict, Michael Les

The impeachment and trial of Andrew Johnson. Norton 1973 212p (The Norton Essays in American history) $6.95   973.8

1 Johnson, Andrew, President U.S. 2 U.S.—History—1865-1898
ISBN 0-393-05473-X   LC 72-10883

"The approach taken towards the impeachment of President Andrew Johnson in this . . . study suggests it was a justifiable if unsuccessful move reluctantly undertaken by a coalition of radical and conservative Republicans who felt the President acted outside his prerogatives. Johnson's character is shown as vitally important in determining the nature of his political decisions since he was a man of inflexible will governed by principles which once adopted he refused to modify. The course of political, social and legislative events that led to Johnson's impeachment and final acquittal in court are closely reviewed." Booklist

"This is an "excellently clear and compressed account of extraordinarily confused maneuverings. . . . [Benedict] paints a convincing and

Benedict, Michael L.—*Continued*
depressing picture of Johnson's incredible loner tactics, and argues that the failure of the impeachment proceedings was a conclusive demonstration of congressional impotence, both legally and politically, to act against a man who had gravely and stupidly exceeded the powers of his office." New Repub
A bibliographical review: p192-202

973.917 U.S.—Administration of Franklin D. Roosevelt, 1933-1945

Perrett, Geoffrey
Days of sadness, years of triumph; the American people, 1939-1945. Coward, McCann & Geoghegan 1973 512p $10   973.917

1 U.S.—History—1933-1945 2 World War, 1939-1945—U.S. 3 U.S.—Social conditions
ISBN 0-698-10488-9   LC 72-87594

"Perrett's focus is on civilian life in the U.S. from September 1939 to August 1945. His thesis is that 'the closest thing to a real social revolution the United States has known in this century came during those years'; and . . . he documents broad advances in such matters as education, standards of living, and social justice. 'The war years,' Perrett says, 'provided the last great collective social experience in the country's history'; and in a . . . concluding chapter, he suggests that the present generation must find its own source of similar political and social unity." Library J
The author "surveys every imaginable corner of American life, drawing on newspaper accounts, interviews, popular literature. He brings the scene to life vividly—citizens saving tin cans, women in defense plants, the impact of Pearl Harbor, FDR's leadership. Perrett's focus on the community response to the tragedy and challenges of war makes his history an impressive, enspiriting American 'cavalcade.' " Pub W
Bibliographical references included in Notes: p447-78. Selected bibliography: p481-96. Glossary: p497

Tugwell, Rexford G.
In search of Roosevelt. Harvard Univ. Press 1972 313p $12.95   973.917

1 U.S.—History—1933-1945 2 Roosevelt, Franklin Delano, President U.S.
ISBN 0-674-44625-9   LC 72-76559

"The essays in this collection were written over the past 20 years and most have been previously published. Tugwell, one of the original of FDR's brain trust, uses each essay to delve into Roosevelt's response to a particular set of circumstances or to a specific problem in an attempt to understand some aspect of the President's character." Library J
The author "avoids conclusive statements but points out Roosevelt's reliance for courage on his simple but profound religious faith and calls attention to the humanity of Roosevelt as reflected in his social reforms." Booklist
Includes bibliographical references

973.924 U.S.—Administration of Richard M. Nixon, 1969-1974

Mankiewicz, Frank
Perfectly clear; Nixon from Whittier to Watergate. Quadrangle Bks. 1973 239p $8.95   973.924

1 Nixon, Richard Milhous, President U.S. 2 U.S.—Politics and government—1961- 3 Watergate Affair, 1972-
ISBN 0-8129-0405-2   LC 73-82532

"Mankiewicz dissects 27 years of President Nixon's political career which he believes to be the inescapable precursor to the Watergate events. The fraud, deceit, and generally seamy underside of all the Nixon campaigns, the hardening of the views, and the secrecy of his maneuvers are documented. The ramifications of Watergate are recounted and the evidence for constitutional impeachment is marshalled." Booklist

"Mankiewicz could hardly be expected to give a totally impartial account of the Watergate scandal. . . . This is surely not a definitive account of Watergate, but it should be of value to libraries building a comprehensive collection on the subject." Library J

Osborne, John, 1907-
The fourth year of the Nixon watch; cartoons by Paul Conrad. Liveright 1973 218p illus $6.95   973.924

1 U.S.—Politics and government—1961- 2 Nixon, Richard Milhous, President U.S.
ISBN 0-87140-560-1   LC 72-97490

"This book consists of articles that appeared in the New Republic between January 1972 and January 1973." Verso of title page
The author "covers the entire year of Nixon's political tactics and self-conscious 'history making' in China, Russia and Miami Beach." Pub W
"Osborne's incisive writing pictures a President who achieved much success in foreign affairs, but who could not rise above domestic partisan politics. The author's insightful comments explain the climate created by secrecy and a desire to win reelection—a climate that appears to have led to Watergate. Editorial cartoons by Conrad of the 'Los Angeles Times' are good if not inspired." Library J

The fifth year of the Nixon watch; caricatures by David Levine. Liveright 1974 241p illus $7.95   973.924

1 U.S.—Politics and government—1961- 2 Watergate Affair, 1972- 3 Nixon, Richard Milhous, President U.S.
ISBN 0-87140-582-2   LC 73-93125

"This book consists of articles that appeared in The New Republic, between January 1973 and January 1974." Verso of title page
The author "analyzes the actions of an administration enmeshed in Watergate. He describes the President as a man trapped by his own errors as well as by external events—a President whose personal style added to his problems. The author does cover other areas, such as Kissinger's increased influence in foreign policy, but Watergate dominates here." Library J
"As one of the most respected and most fair-minded of veteran Washington journalists, Osborne has consistently leaned over backward to report Nixon and his administration objectively. In this . . . collection . . . however, he confesses to a long-held sense that Nixon's character is 'shoddy' and less than presidential. . . . Osborne's honesty has an agate hardness as his melancholy chronicle ranges from Nixon's 'peace' in Vietnam to Nixon-at-bay by the year's end. David Levine's savage Nixon caricatures . . . surface the emotions that Osborne's reportage rejects." Pub W

974.7 New York

Carmer, Carl
The Hudson; illus. by Stow Wengenroth. Holt [1974 c1939] 434p illus (Rivers of America) pa $4.95   974.7

1 Hudson River 2 Hudson Valley—History 3 New York (State)—Social life and customs
ISBN 0-03-089387-9   LC 73-10985

A reprint with new introduction of title first published 1939 by Farrar
"Famous boats, eminent men, beautiful scenery, and hot political strife have combined to make the Hudson one of the most storied rivers in this country, and Mr. Carmer has captured most engagingly its charm and its spirit." Cincinnati
Bibliography: p408-21

977 North central states

Havighurst, Walter
The heartland: Ohio, Indiana, Illinois. Rev. ed. Illus. by Grattan Condon. Harper 1974 430p illus maps (A Regions of America bk) $10   977

1 Illinois—History 2 Indiana—History 3 Ohio—History
ISBN 0-06-011781-8

Havighurst, Walter—*Continued*

Earlier edition entered in main catalog
First published 1962. The 1974 edition brings the region's history up to the present and includes a new chapter forecasting the area's growth, new innovations by state and local governments and the expanded awareness and participation of the communities
Bibliography: p407-17

978 Western states

The **Cowboys**, by the editors of Time-Life Books, with text by William H. Forbis. Time-Life Bks. [distributed by Little] 1973 240p illus maps (The Old West) $9.95   **978**

1 Cowboys   LC 72-87680

"The lore of the western frontier is graphically presented in this diverting look at the world of the American cowboy and the heyday of the cattle barons from the early 1860s through the late 1880s on the western plains of the U.S. where upwards of 40,000 cowboys rounded up and drove herds of longhorns to market. According to the author the mythical ideal of a cowboy as tanned, mature, and heroic is unrealistic; most cowboys were in their early twenties and a third were either blacks or Mexicans. Life on the range was not the romantic adventure of a Remington or Russell picture but dirty, difficult, and tiring work evocatively portrayed in the book's descriptions of roundups and cattle drives. Separate sections within the text give additional cowboy lore and information on branding, roping, apparel, provisions, saddles, and trappings. Among the 250 illustrations of paintings, maps, posters, and other documents are a number of excellent period photographs." Booklist

"Summation of the cattle industry, its booms and its problems are well presented. Much of the source material comes directly from accounts and interviews of those who were a part of this early industry." Choice
Bibliography: p236

979.7 Washington (State)

Holbrook, Stewart Hall

The Columbia; illus. by Ernest Richardson. Holt [1974 c1956] xxiv, 393p illus (Rivers of America) pa $4.95   **979.7**

1 Columbia River 2 Northwest, Pacific—History
ISBN 0-03-089388-7   LC 73-10986

A reprint with new introduction of title first published 1956 by Rinehart

The author describes the history and folklore of the Columbia River and the part of the Pacific Northwest through which it flows
Bibliography: p377-81

AUTHOR, TITLE, SUBJECT, AND ANALYTICAL INDEX

This index to the books in the classified part includes author, title, subject and analytical entries, arranged in one alphabet.

The number in boldfaced type at the end of each entry in this index refers to the Dewey Decimal Classification number where the main entry for the book will be found.

General subjects are indicated by classification number only. The individual books on that subject are not usually listed here unless they are classified in another class, i.e.

> Negroes **301.451**

Subdivisions of a subject are indicated by a dash indention under the subject, i.e.

> Negroes **301.451**
> —Bibliography **016.3014**

Another title by the same author is introduced by a dash (—) instead of repeating the name, i.e.

> Ewen, David. George Gershwin: his journey to greatness **780.92**
> —New Complete book of the American musical theater **782.8**

Analytical entries are introduced by the word *In*. They indicate (1) the page numbers in the book where the material is to be found unless the material is widely scattered throughout the book; (2) the class number of the book.

Title entries are given for each book unless the title of the book and its subject heading are identical or when the title is not distinctive.

A, Mr. See pages
  In Montgomery, R. Born to heal **615**
AA Britain's heritage. Automobile Association **914.2**
AA Guide to continental motoring. Automobile Association **914**
Aaron, Henry. Aaron **92**
Abandoned towns. See Cities and towns, Ruined, extinct, etc.
Abbey, Edward. Cactus country **500.9**
Abbreviations
—Dictionaries **421.03**; also pages
  In Paxton J. ed. Dictionary of abbreviations **413**
  In Pugh, E. Second dictionary of acronyms & abbreviations **603**
Abbreviations dictionary. De Sola, R. **421.03**
Abel, Michael. Backpacking made easy **796.5**
Abolition of slavery. See Abolitionists
Abolitionists. See pages
  In Franklin, J. H. From slavery to freedom p188-98 **301.45**
  In Hughes, L. A pictorial history of Black-Americans p78-153 **301.45**
  In Nye, R. B. Society and culture in America, 1830-1860 p61-70 **917.3**
Abortion **613.9**; also pages
  In De Crow, K. Sexist justice p223-49 **346.1**
—Laws and regulations. See pages
  In Wilkerson, A. E. ed. The rights of children p47-71 **346**
About behaviorism. Skinner, B. F. **150.19**
Abraham, Claude. Pierre Corneille **842.09**
Academic freedom. See pages
  In Rubin, D. The rights of teachers p24-74 **344.7**
Accidents. See Disasters; First aid
Accounting **657**
Acculturation. See East and West
Acheson, Dean Gooderham. See Pages
  In Miller, M. Plain speaking; an oral biography of Harry S. Truman p369-87 **92**
The acquisition of library materials. Ford, S. **025.2**
Acquisitions (Libraries) **025.2**
  See also Book selection
Acronyms
—Dictionaries **421.03**; also pages
  In Pugh, E. Second dictionary of acronyms & abbreviations **603**

The act of life. Cousteau, J. **591.92**
Acting **792**
Actors and actresses
—British. See pages
  In Gielgud, Sir J. Distinguished company **920**
Actresses. See Actors and actresses
Acupuncture **615**
Acupuncture therapy. Tan, Leong T. **615**
Adams, Henry. The education of Henry Adams **92**
Adams, John. John Adams **92**
Adams, Leon D. The wines of America **663**
Adamson, Joe. Groucho, Harpo, Chico and sometimes Zeppo **791.43**
Addresses. See Speeches, addresses, etc.
Adler, Irving. Thinking machines **519.4**
Administration. See Management
Adolf, Arnold, ed. The poetry of Black America **811.08**
Adolescence. See pages
  In Joint Commission on Mental Health of children. Mental health: from infancy through adolescence **155.4**
Adoption **362.7**; also pages
  In Klein, C. The single parent experience **301.42**
  In Landis, J. T. Building a successful marriage p450-62 **301.42**
Adoption and after. Raymond, L. **362.7**
Advanced first aid and emergency care. Red Cross. United States. American National Red Cross **614.8**
Advertising. See pages
  In Boorstin, D. J. Democracy and its discontents p26-42 **917.3**
Aeronautics. See Flying saucers
Aesthetics. See Esthetics
Africa
—Description and travel **916**
—Discovery and explorations. See pages
  In Jeal, T. Livingstone **92**
—History **960**; also pages
  In Franklin, J. H. From slavery to freedom p3-13 **301.45**
  In The Horizon History of the British Empire p176-259 **942**
—Social life and customs. See pages
  In Franklin, J. H. From slavery to freedom p14-29 **301.45**

PUBLIC LIBRARY CATALOG
1974 SUPPLEMENT

Africa, East
—Animals. See Animals—Africa, East
Africa A to Z. Kane, R. S. 916
Africa since 1875. Hallett, R. 960
African Americans. See Negroes
African art. See Art, African
African authors. See Authors, African
African authors. Herdeck, D. E. 920.03
African hunting dog. See Lycon pictus
African literature
—Bio-bibliography. See pages
   In Herdeck, D. E. African authors 920.03
—History and criticism. See pages
   In Herdeck, D. E. African authors p481-96 920.03
Afro-Americans. See Negroes
After-dinner speeches. See Speeches, addresses, etc.
Against the stream. Myrdal, G. 330
Age. See Old age
The age of avant-garde. Kramer, H. 709
The age of enlightenment, 1745-1790. Wellesz, E. ed.
   In The New Oxford History of music v7 780.9
The age of madness. Szasz, T. S. ed. 362.2
An age of mediocrity. Sulzberger, C. L. 92
Aged
—Dwellings. See pages
   In Curtin, S. R. Nobody ever died of old age 301.43
—Institutional care 362.6
—United States 301.43
Aggressiveness (Psychology) 152.4
Aging in America. Smith, B. K. 301.43
Agnew, Spiro Theodore. See pages
   In Cohen, R. M. A heartbeat away 351.9
   In Obsorne, J. The fifth year of the Nixon watch p151-69 973.924
Agreements. See Contracts
Agricultural chemistry. See Soils
Agricultural laborers. See Migrant labor
Agriculture
—Economic aspects. See Farm management
—Handbooks, manuals, etc. 630.2
—United States. See pages
   In Logsdon, G. Homesteading 630.2
Ahmed, Mohammed. See Mahdi
Ahuitzotl. See pages
   In Davies,N. The Aztecs p180-200 970.3
Ainos. See Ainu
Ainu. See pages
   In Severin, T. The Horizon Book of vanishing primitive man p225-46 301.2
Air. See pages
   In Asimov, I. Today and tomorrow and . . . p61-71 508
Air conditioning 621.5
  See also Automobiles—Air conditioning
Aird, Eileen M. Sylvia Plath 811.09
Airplanes
—History 629.133
Airplanes from the dawn of flight to the present day. Angelucci, E. 629.133
Akhenaton. See Amenhetep IV, King of Egypt
Akhnaton. See Amenhetep IV, King of Egypt
Alakai Swamp. See pages
   In Wallace, R. Hawaii p140-49 500.9
Alaska 917.98
—Description and travel. See pages
   In Cooper, B. Alaska: the last frontier 338.2
—Economic conditions. See pages
   In Cooper, B. Alaska: the last frontier 338.2
—Natural history. See Natural history—Alaska
Alaska: the last frontier. Cooper, B. 338.2
Albee, Edward. See pages
   In Hayman, R. Edward Albee 812.09
Albertson, Chris. Bessie [Smith] 780.92
Alcohol and health. United States. Department of Health, Education and Welfare 613.92
Alcoholism 613.8
Aldridge, Ira. The Black doctor
   In Hatch, J. V. ed. Black theater, U.S.A p3-24 812.08

For material about this author see Aldridge, Ira Frederick

Aldridge, Ira Frederick. See pages
   In Wilson, G. B. Three hundred years of American drama and theatre p89-103 792.09
Aldrin, Edwin E. Return to earth 92
Alekhin, Aleksandr Aleksandrovich. See pages
   In Horowitz, A. The world chess championship p94-116 794.1
Alekhine, Alexander. See Alekhin, Aleksandr Aleksandrovich
Alexander, David, ed. See Eerdmans' Handbook to the Bible 220
Aliens. See Citizenship
Alive. Read, P. P. 918
Alijan, George W. ed. Purchasing handbook 658.7
All creatures great and small. Herriot, J. 92
All the best in. . . . [Mexico]. Clark, S. 910.2
All the President's men. Bernstein, C. 351.9
All things bright and beautiful. Herriot, J. 92

Allen, Donald, ed. See O'Hara, F. The selected poems of Frank O'Hara 811
Allen, Douglas. See Wyeth, N. C. N. C. Wyeth: the collected paintings, illustrations, and murals 759.13
Allen, T. B. Vanishing wildlife of North America 591.9
Alligators. See pages
   In Allen, T. B. Vanishing wildlife of North America p38-49 591.9
Alloway, Lawrence. See pages
   In Sarris, A. The primal screen p66-80 791.43
The almanac of American politics. Barone, M. 328.73
Alps 914.94
Alsop, Stewart. Stay of execution 616.1
Alter, Dinsmore. Pictorial astronomy 523
Alternating current. Paz, O. 864
Alth, Max. Making your own cheese and yogurt 637
Altman, Philip L. ed. Biology data book 574.02
Alvaro Tezozomoc, Fernando. See pages
   In Davies, N. The Aztecs p49-60 970.3
The amen corner. Baldwin, J.
   In Hatch, J. V. ed. Black theater, U.S.A. p514-46 812.08
Amen Hotep. See Amenhetep IV, King of Egypt
Amenhetep IV, King of Egypt. See pages
   In Rogers, J. A. Great men of color p57-66 920
Amenhotep. See Amenhetep IV, King of Egypt
Amenophis. See Amenhetep IV, King of Egypt
America
—Antiquities. See pages
   In Scientific American. Early man in America 970.1
—Discovery and exploration. See pages
   In Bradford, E. Christopher Columbus 92
America. Alistair Cooke's. Cooke, A. 973
American architecture. See Architecture, American
American art. See art, American
American artists. See Artists, American
American arts. See The arts, American
The American bottle collector's price guide to historical flasks, pontils, bitters, mineral waters, inks & sodas. Goodell, D. 748
American characteristics. See National characteristics, American
American Civil Liberties Union. See Ennis, B. The rights of mental patients 346
—See Law, S. The rights of the poor 344.3
—See Levine, A. The rights of students 344.7
—See Rosengart, O. The rights of suspects 345
—See Ross, S. C. The rights of women 346
—See Rubin, D. The rights of teachers 344.7
—See Rudovsky, D. The rights of prisoners 345
American civilization. See United States—Civilization
American composers. See Composers, American
American drama 812
—Bibliography. See pages
   In Bonin, J. F. Prize-winning American drama 812.07
—History and criticism. See pages
   In Bolin, J. F. Prize-winning American drama 812.07
   In Wilson, G. B. Three hundred years of American drama and theatre 792.09
American essays 814
American fiction
—History and criticism 813.09; also pages
   In Nye, R. B. Society and culture in America, 1830-1860 p89-100 917.3
—History and criticism—Bibliography 016.813
American folk art. See Folk art, American
American folk songs. See Folk songs—United States
American foreign policy. Kissinger, H. A. 327.73
The American Heart Association cookbook 641.5
American Heritage. See Davidson, M. B. The American Heritage History of the artists' America 709.73
An American Heritage guide
  Great historic places 017.3
  Natural wonders of America 917.3
The American Heritage History of the artists' America. Davidson, M. B. 709.73
American history. See United States—History
American Indians. See Indians of North America
American-Jewish literature, Contemporary. Malin, I. ed. 810.9
An American journey. McGovern, G. 329
American Library Association
—Publications
  American Library Association. Office for Intellectual Freedom. Intellectual freedom manual 323.44
  Ford, S. The acquisition of library materials 025.2
American Library Association. Office for Intellectual freedom. Intellectual freedom manual 323.44

AUTHOR, TITLE, SUBJECT, AND ANALYTICAL INDEX
1974 SUPPLEMENT

An American life. Magruder, J. S. 92
American literature
  See also Latin American literature
  —Anecdotes, facetiae, satire, etc. See pages
    In Armour, R. It all started with freshman English 817
  —Bibliography. See pages
    In Literary history of the United States 810.9
  —Bio-bibliography. See pages
    In Shockley, A. A. Living American authors 920.03
  —Collections 810.8
  —Dictionaries. See pages
    In Freeman, W. Dictionary of fictional characters 820.3
  —History and criticism 810.9; also pages
    In Nye, R. B. Society and culture in America, 1830-1860 p71-126 917.3
    In Seymour-Smith, M. Funk & Wagnalls Guide to modern world literature p23-170 809
  —Southern States. See pages
    In Wagner, J. Black poets of the United States p48-72 811.09
American Loyalists 973.3
American men and women of science: The social and behavioral sciences 920.025
American men of science. See American men and women of science: The social and behavioral sciences 920.025
American mountain people. National Geographic Society 917.3
American music. See Music, American
The American music handbook. Pavlakis, C. 780.973
American musicians. See Musicians, American
American national characteristics. See National characteristics, American
American National Red Cross. See Red Cross. United States. American National Red Cross
American Negro poetry. Bontemps, A. ed. 811.08
American painting. See Painting, American
American patchwork quilts. Bacon, L. I. 746.4
The American people. Kahn, E. J. 301.32
American philosophy. See Philosophy, American
American poetry 811
  See also Negro poetry
  —Collections 811.08; also pages
    In Untermeyer, L. ed. 50 modern American & British poets, 1920-1970 821.08
  —History and criticism 811.09; also pages
    In Coffin, T. P. ed. Folklore from the working folk of America p112-43 398
    In Nye, R. B. Society and culture in America, 1830-1860 p115-26 917.3
  —Indexes. See pages
    In Chicorel Index to poetry in collections in print, on discs and tapes: poetry on discs, tapes, and cassettes 821.08
American poets. See Poets, American
The American political tradition, and the men who made it. Hofstadter, R. 973
American Red Cross. See Red Cross. United States. American National Red Cross
American Revolution. See United States—History—Revolution
American satire and humor 817
American science. See Science—United States
American sculpture. See Sculpture, American
An American sunset. Prideaux, J.
  In The Best short plays, 1974 p 1-22 808.82
American West. See The Great Northwest 917.95
  —See The Magnificent Rockies 917.8
Americanisms 427; also pages
  In Mencken, H. L. The young Mencken p318-32 818
Americans in Great Britain. See pages
  In Commager, H. S. ed. Britain through American eyes 914.2
America's backpacking book. Bridge, R. 796.5
Ames, Louise Bates, jt. auth. See Gesell, A. Infant and child in the culture of today 155.4
Amish. See pages
  In National Geographic Society. Life in rural America p173-92 917.3
Amonhotep. See Amenhetep IV, King of Egypt
Amon-Ra. See Karnak, Egypt. Temple of Ammon
Amory, Cleveland. See Celebrity register 920.03
Amphibians. See pages
  In Clement, R. C. Hammond Nature atlas of America p176-93 500.9
  In Vanishing species p144-53 591
Amsterdam
  —Description. See pages
    In Kane, R. S. Grand tour A to Z: the capitals of Europe p22-51 914
Amusements. See Play
Anatomy. See pages
  In Grollman, S. The human body 612
  —Comparative. See pages
    In Life before man p9-23, 99-121 560

The anatomy of human destructiveness. Fromm, E. 152.4
The Anchor Anthology of sixteenth-century verse. Sylvester, R. S. ed. 821.08
The Anchor Bible v34, v34A, v42. Bible 220.5
Ancient civilization. See Civilization, Ancient
Ancient history. See History, Ancient
Anderson, Garland. Appearances
  In Hatch, J. V. ed. Black theater, U.S.A. p100-34 812.08
Anderson, Jervis. A. Philip Randolph 92
Anderson, John Henry. See pages
  In Christopher, M. The illustrated history of magic p111-30 793.8
Anderson, Marian. See pages
  In Anderson, P. The Daughters p109-54 369
Anderson, Peggy. The Daughters 369
Andes 918
Anecdotes. See pages
  In Prochnow, H. V. comp. The speaker's and toastmaster's handbook 803.85
Angel fire. Oates, J. C. 811
Angelou, Maya. Gather together in my name 92
Angelucci, Enzo. Airplanes from the dawn of flight to the present day 629.133
Angier, Bradford. Introduction to canoeing 797.1
Angling. See Fishing
Anicet-Bourgeois, Auguste. The Black doctor; adaptation. See Aldridge, I. The Black doctor
Animal behavior. See Animals—Habits and behavior
Animal intelligence. See Animals—Habits and behavior
Animal life encyclopedia. Grzimek, B. ed. 591.03
Animal locomotion. See pages
  In Cousteau, J. The art of motion 591.92
Animals. See pages
  In Villiard, P. Raising small animals for fun and profit 636.08
  See also Desert animals; Marine animals; Pets; and names of animals, e.g. Cats
  —Africa, East 599
  —Aquatic. See Marine animals
Animals
  —Cruelty to. See Animals—Treatment
  —Everglades. See pages
    In Carr, A. The Everglades p60-107 500.9
  —Fossil. See Fossils
  —Habits and behavior 591.5; also pages
    In Fromm, E. The anatomy of human destructiveness p98-129 152.4
    In Life before man p122-49 560
  —Laws and regulations. See pages
    In The Family legal advisor p325-38 340
  —Marine. See Marine animals
  —Movement. See Animal locomotion
  —North America 591.9
  —Protection. See Animals—Treatment
  —Rare. See Rare animals
  —Rocky Mountains. See pages
    In Walker, B. S. The Great Divide p110-27, 136-44 500.9
  —Treatment 636.08
Animated cartoons. See Moving picture cartoons
The animated film. Stephenson, R. 791.43
The annotated Wizard of Oz. Baum, L. F. 813.09
Annulment of marriage. See Divorce
Anouilh, Jean. Episode in the life of an author
  In Richards, S. ed. Best short plays of the world theatre, 1968-1973 p113-25 808.82
Anthology of English literature, The Oxford 820.8
Anthology of sixteenth-century verse, The Anchor. Sylvester, R. S. ed. 821.08
Anthony, Susan Brownell. See pages
  In Rossi, A. S. ed. The feminist papers; from Adams to de Beauvoir p378-96 301.41
Anthropology
  —Bibliography. See pages
    In White, C. M. Sources of information in the social sciences p307-74 016.3
Antigone. Sophocles 882
Antiques. See Art objects
Antiquities. See Archeology; and names of countries, cities, etc. with the subdivision Antiquities, e.g. America—Antiquities
Antonioni, Michelangelo. See pages
  In Solomon, S. J. ed. The classic cinema p273-94 791.43
Apartment houses
  —Drama 812
Apollo project 629.45; also pages
  In Aldrin, E. E. Return to earth 92
Appalachian Mountains
  —Social life and customs. See pages
    In National Geographic Society. American mountain people p32-99 917.3
Appalachian region
  —Social conditions 309.175
Appearances. Anderson, G.
  In Hatch, J. V. ed. Black theater, U.S.A. p100-34 812.08

Appliances, Electric. See Household appliances, Electric
Applications for positions. See pages
In Holden, D. Art career guide p190-203 702.3
Applied psychology. See Psychology, Applied
Appreciation of music. See Music—Analysis, appreciation
The apprenticeship. Freidel, F.
In Freidel, F. Franklin D. Roosevelt v 1 92
Aptheker, Herbert, ed. A documentary history of the Negro people in the United States 301.45
Arab-Jewish relations. See Jewish-Arab relations
The Arab mind. Patai, R. 301.29
Arabic arts. See The arts, Islamic
Arabic language. See pages
In Patai, R. The Arab mind p41-72 301.29
Arabs. See pages
In Patai, R. The Arab mind 301.29
Arch, Joseph. See pages
In Commager, H. S. ed. Britain through American eyes p441-50 914.2
Archeology 913; also pages
In Däniken, E. von. The gold of the gods 001.9
See also Cities and towns, Ruined, extinct, etc.; Excavations (Archeology)
Architects. See Architecture as a profession
Architecture
—American—History. See pages
In Nye, R. B. Society and culture in America, 1830-1860 p188-98 917.3
—Domestic. See Houses
—Modern—20th century 724.9; also pages
In Twombly, R. C. Frank Lloyd Wright 92
Architecture as a profession. See pages
In Holden, D. Art career guide p118-28 702.3
Are you now or have you ever been; excerpt. See Bentley, E. Larry Park's day in court
Ariel like a harpy. See Small, C. Shelley's Frankenstein 823.09
Aristotle. Introduction to Aristotle 888
—Nicomachean ethics
In Aristotle. Introduction to Aristotle p337-581 888
—On the soul
In Aristotle. Introduction to Aristotle p153-245 888
—Poetics
In Aristotle. Introduction to Aristotle p668-713 888
—Posterior analytics
In Aristotle. Introduction to Aristotle p8-111 888
Aristotle (as subject) See pages
In Handy, W. J. ed. Twentieth century criticism: the major statements p134-45 801
Armies
—Medical and sanitary affairs. See Medicine, Military
Armour, Richard. Going like sixty 817
—It all started with freshman English 817
Armstrong, Louis. See pages
In Pleasants, H. The great American popular singers p97-110 780.92
Army life. See United States. Army—Military life
Arnstein, Helene S. What every woman needs to know about abortion 613.9
Art
See also Esthetics
—African 709.66
—American—Encyclopedias 709.73
—American—History 709.73; also pages
In Nye, R. B. Society and culture in America, 1830-1860 p158-98 917.3
—Analysis, interpretation, appreciation. See Art—Study and teaching
—Colectors and collecting. See pages
In Kutz, M. Rockefeller power p116-42 361.7
—Education. See Art—Study and teaching
—History 709
—Indian. See Indians—Art; Indians of North America—Art
—Modern—19th century. See pages
In Clark, K. The romantic rebellion 759.05
In Kramer, H. The age of avant-garde 709
—Modern—20th century. See pages
In Kramer, H. The age of avant-garde 709
—Modern—20th century—Encyclopedias 709.04
—Modern—History and criticism. See pages
In Barzun, J. The use and abuse of art 701
—Primitive. See pages
In Leuzinger, E. The art of Black Africa 709.66
In Severin, T. The Horizon Book of vanishing primitive man p309-17 301.2
See also Indians—Art
—Psychology. See pages
In Read, H. Education through art 707
—Study and teaching 707; also pages
In Holden, D. Art career guide 702.3

Art and religion. See pages
In Barzun, J. The use and abuse of art p24-46 701
Art and society 701
Art as a profession 702.3
Art career guide. Holden, D. 702.3
Art education. See Art—Study and teaching
Art objects
—Collectors and collecting 745.1
The art of Black Africa. Leuzinger, E.709.66
The art of dying. Neale, R. E. 128
Art of homemaking. The Ladies' Home Journal. Habeeb, V. T. 640
The art of motion. Cousteau, J. 591.92
The art of ragtime. Schafer, W. J. 781.5
The art of readable writing. Flesch, R. 808
The art of the American film, 1900-1971. Higham, C. 791.43
The art of Walt Disney. Finch, C. 791.43
Art schools. See Art—Study and teaching
Arthur, Eric. The barn 728
Artificial flies. See Flies, Artificial
Artificial insemination
—Laws and regulations. See pages
In Wilkerson, A. E. ed. The rights of children p72-85 346
Artificial intelligence. See pages
In Diebold, J. ed. The world of the computer p438-49 001.6
Artistic biography, Index to. Havlice, P. P. 709.2
Artists. See pages
In Clark, K. The romantic rebellion 759.05
See also Art as a profession; Children as artists
—American. See pages
In The Britannica Encyclopedia of American art 709.73
—Encyclopedias. See pages
In Phaidon Dictionary of twentieth-century art 709.04
—Indexes. See pages
In Havlice, P. P. Index to artistic biography 709.2
The artists' America, The American Heritage History of. Davidson, M. B. 709.73
The arts
—Addresses and essays. See pages
In Barzun, J. The use and abuse of art 701
—American. See pages
In Mencken, H. L. The young Mencken p334-48 813
—Arabic. See The arts, Islamic
—Islamic. See pages
In Patai, R. The Arab mind p167-79 301.29
—Muslim. See The arts, Islamic
—Study and teaching. See pages
In Silberman, C. E. ed. The open classroom reader p749-89 372.1
Arts, Fine. See The arts
The ascent of man. Bronowski, J. 501
Ash, Lee, comp. Subject collections 026
Asia
—Politics. See pages
In Salisbury, H. E. To Peking—and beyond 915.1
The Asian journal of Thomas Merton. Merton, T. 248
Asimov, Isaac. Asimov on astronomy 523
—Today and tomorrow and . . . 503
—The tragedy of the moon 508
Assateague Island. See pages
In Leonard, J. N. Atlantic beaches p104-12 500.9
Assemblage (Art) See pages
In Meilach, D. Z. Collage and assemblage p185-241 751.4
Astronautics. See Space flight to the moon
Astronautics as a profession. See Women in astronautics
Astronomical instruments. See Telescope
Astronomy 523; also pages
In Asimov, I. Today and tomorrow and . . . p19-48 503
See also Moon
—Atlases. See Stars—Atlases
—History. See pages
In Hawkins, G. S. Beyond Stonehenge 913
Asylums. See Mentally ill—Institutional care
Athens
—Description. See pages
In Kane, R. S. Grand tour A to Z: the capitals of Europe p52-71 914
Atkins, Chester G. Getting elected 329
Atkinson, Brooks. Broadway 792.09
Atlantic beaches. Leonard, J. N. 500.9
Atlantic States
—Birds. See Birds—Atlantic States
—Natural history. See Natural history—Atlantic States
Atlas of the Second World War. Young, P. ed. 940.54

AUTHOR, TITLE, SUBJECT, AND ANALYTICAL INDEX
1974 SUPPLEMENT

Atlas of the universe, The concise. [Moore, P.] 523
Atlases 912
 See also Bible—Geography
 —Astronomical. See Stars—Atlases
 —Bibliography
  In Katz, W. A. Introduction to reference work v 1 p287-316 025.5
Attention. See Boredom
Attica. See New York. State Prison, Attica
Attitude (Psychology) See Public opinion
Auden, W. H. Forewords and afterwords 809
Audio-visual materials. See pages
 In Broadus, R. N. Selecting materials for libraries p127-54 025.2
 In Katz, W. A. Introduction to reference work v2 p169-201 025.5
 —Catalogs 016.3713
Austen, Jane. See pages
 In Hardwick, M. A guide to Jane Austen 823.09
 In Mansell, D. The novels of Jane Austen 823.09
Australia
 —History. See pages
  In The Horizon History of the British Empire p112-27, 270-77 942
Australian aborigines. See pages
 In Severin, T. The Horizon Book of vanishing primitive man p41-63 301.2
Australian literature
 —History and criticism. See pages
  In Seymour-Smith, M. Funk & Wagnalls Guide to modern world literature p175-89 809
Austria. See pages
 In National Geographic Society. The Alps p172-203 914.94
Authors
 —African—Dictionaries 920.03
 —American. See pages
  In Contemporary authors. First revision v9-12 920.03
  In Cowley, M. A second flowering 810.9
Authorship
 See also Fiction—Technique
 —Handbooks, manuals, etc. 808
Auto air conditioning manual, Chilton's 629.2
Auto troubleshooting guide, Chilton's 629.28
Autobiography. Yeats, W. B.
 In Yeats, W. B. Memoirs: Autobiography—first draft [and] Journal p19-134 92
Automatic computers. See Computers
Automatic data processing. See Electronic data processing
Automation. See pages
 In Diebold, J. ed. The world of the computer p364-78 001.6
 See also Libraries—Automation; Management—Automation
Automobile Association. AA Britain's heritage 914.2
 —AA Guide to continental motoring 914
Automobile engines. See Automobiles—Engines
Automobile guides. See Automobiles—Road guides
Automobile insurance. See Insurance, Automobile
Automobiles
 —Air conditioning 629.2
 —Engines 629.2
 See also Wankel engine
 —Laws and regulations. See pages
  In Moynihan, D. P. Coping p79-99 309.173
 See also Traffic regulations
 —Motors. See Automobiles—Engines
 —Repairing 629.28
 —Road guides. See pages
  In Dunn, W. J. Enjoy Europe by car 914
  In Rand McNally Road atlas of Europe 914
Automotive engines: maintenance and repair. Billiet, W. 629.2
Avant-garde, The age of. Kramer, H. 709
Ave Ogden! Nash in Latin. Nash, O. 811
Aztecs 970.3

Babies. See Infants
Back packing. See Backpacking
Backgammon 795
Backpacking 796.5
Backpacking made easy. Abel, M. 796.5
Backster, Cleve. See pages
 In Tompkins, P. The secret life of plants p3-16 581
Backward areas. See Underdeveloped areas
Bacon, Lenice Ingram. American patchwork quilts 746.4
Bad man. Edmonds, R.
 In Hatch, J. V. ed. Black theater, U.S.A. p241-51 812.08

Bailey, Mildred. See pages
 In Pleasants, H. The great American popular singers p143-56 780.92
Baja California
 —Description and travel. See pages
  In Johnson, W. W. Baja California 500.9
Baking. See pages
 In The Good Housekeeping cookbook p413-62, 501-70 641.5
 See also Bread; Cake
Bakish, David. Richard Wright 813.09
Balance of power. See pages
 In Reischauer, E. O. Toward the 21st century: education for a changing world p34-52 327
Baldwin, James. The amen corner
 In Hatch, J. V. ed. Black theater, U.S.A. p514-46 812.08
 —A dialogue 301.45
 —One day, when I was lost 812
Baldwin, James (as subject) See pages
 In Kinnamon, K. ed. James Baldwin 818
Ballet. See pages
 In De Mille, A. Speak to me, dance with me 92
Balo. Toomer, J.
 In Hatch, J. V. ed. Black theater, U.S.A. p218-24 812.08
Baltimore
 —Description. See pages
  In Mencken, H. L. The young Mencken p268-81 818
Baly, Denis. The geography of the Bible 220.9
Balzac, Honoré de 92
Banco. Charrière, H. 365
Band music. See Bands (Music)
Bander, Edward J. Change of name and law of names 346
Bands (Music) See pages
 In Simon, G. T. Glenn Miller and his orchestra 780.92
Banfield, Edward C. The unheavenly city revisited 301.34
Banks and banking
 —Encyclopedias. See pages
  In Munn, G. G. Glenn G. Munn's Encyclopedia of banking and finance 332.03
 —United States. See pages
  In Munn, G. G. Glenn G. Munn's Encyclopedia of banking and finance 332.03
Baraka, Imamu Amiri. The slave
 In Hatch, J. V. ed. Black theater, U.S.A. p812-25 812.08

 For other works by this author see Jones, LeRoi

Barbecue cooking. See Outdoor cookery
Barbour, Roger W. jt. auth. See Ernst, C. H. Turtles of the United States 598.1
Barker, Dudley. G. K. Chesterton 92
The barn. Arthur, E. 728
Barnhart, Clarence L. ed. See The Barnhart Dictionary of new English since 1963 423
The Barnhart Dictionary of new English since 1963 423
Barns. See Farm buildings
Barone, Michael. The almanac of American politics 328.73
Barron's Handbook of American college financial aid. Proia, N. C. 378.3
Barron's How to prepare for the College Level Examination Program CLEP 378.1
Barry, Elaine. Robert Frost 811.09
 —comp. See Frost, R. Robert Frost on writing 811.09
Barry, Jan, jt. ed. See Rottman, L. ed. Winning hearts & minds 811.08
Barth, John. See pages
 In Schultz, M. F. Black humor fiction of the sixties p17-42 813.09
Barzun, Jacques. The use and abuse of art 701
Baseball
 —Biography. See pages
  In Aaron, H. Aaron 92
 —Statistics 796.357
The Baseball encyclopedia 796.357
Baseball register. See Official baseball register 796.357
Basic fly fishing & fly tying. Ovington, R. 799.1
Basketball 796.32
 —Encyclopedias 796.32
 —Statistics 796.32
Bastardy. See Illegitimacy
Batik 746.4
The battered child. Helfer, R. ed. 362.7
Battered child syndrome. See Cruelty to children
Baum, L. Frank. The annotated Wizard of Oz 813.09
 —The wonderful Wizard of Oz; criticism
  In Baum, L. F. The annotated Wizard of Oz 813.09
Bavaria. See pages
 In National Geographic Society. The Alps p100-19 914.94

Baxter, Robert. Baxter's Eurailpass travel guide 914
Baxter's Eurailpass travel guide. Baxter, R. 914
Beaches. See Seashore
Beaconsfield, Mary Anne (Evans) Disraeli, Viscountess 92
Beard, James. Beard on bread 641.8
Beard on bread. Beard, J. 641.8
Beatty, William K. jt. auth. Marks, G. The story of medicine in America 610.9
Beauty, Personal. See Cosmetics
Beckett, Samuel. See pages
 In Kenner, H. A reader's guide to Samuel Beckett 828
 In Webb, E. The plays of Samuel Beckett 842.09
Beddoes, Richard. Hockey 796.9
Bedouins. See pages
 In Patai, R. The Arab mind p73-117 301.29
Bedspreads. See Coverlets
Beerbohm, Sir Max. See pages
 In Auden, W. H. Forewords and afterwords p367-83 809
Beethoven, Ludwig van. See pages
 In Ewen, D. Orchestral music p52-66 785
 In Jacobs, A. A short history of Western music p197-208 780.9
The beggar's opera. Gay, J.
 In The Oxford Anthology of English literature v 1 p1963-2010 820.8
Béhague, Gérard. See Nettl, B. Folk and traditional music of the western continents 781.7
Behavior. See pages
 In Carpenter, F. The Skinner primer: behind freedom and dignity 150.19
Behaviorism (Psychology) 150.19; also pages
 In Fromm, E. The anatomy of human destructiveness p42-45, 69-76 152.4
 See also Behavior
Behind the trail of broken treaties. Deloria, V 970.5
Being. See Ontology
Belitt, Ben, ed. See Neruda, P. New poems (1968-1970) 861
Bell, Alexander Graham 92
Bell, Alexander Graham Bell and the conquest of solitude. Bruce, R. V. 92
Belle de jour (Motion picture) See pages
 In Solomon, S. J. ed. The classic cinema p295-316 791.43
Bellow, Saul. Mr Sammler's planet; criticism
 In Malin, I. ed. Contemporary American-Jewish literature p117-33 810.9
—Orange soufflé
 In Richards, S. ed. Best short plays of the world theatre, 1968-1973 p168-76 808.82
Bellow, Saul (as subject) See pages
 In Kazin, A. Bright book of life; American novelists and storytellers from Hemingway to Mailer p125-38 813.09
Benedict, Michael Les. The impeachment and trial of Andrew Johnson 973.8
Bentley, Eric. Larry Parks' day in court
 In Richards, S. ed. Best short plays of the world theatre, 1968-1973 p224-40 808.82
Beowulf. Beowulf
 In The Oxford Anthology of English literature v 1 p20-98 820.8
Bequests. See Gifts; Wills
Berger, Raoul. Executive privilege 353.03
—Impeachment: the constitutional problems 351.9
Berglund, Berndt. Wilderness cooking 641.5
Bergman, Ingmar. See pages
 In Solomon, S. J. ed. The classic cinema p223-45 791.43
Berkowitz, Bernard, jt. auth. See Newman, M. How to be your own best friend 158
Berlin, Irving. See pages
 In Green, S. The world of musical comedy p85-107 780.92
Berlin
—Description. See pages
 In Kane, R. S. Grand tour A to Z: the capitals of Europe p72-87 914
Bermondsey. Mortimer, J.
 In Richards, S. ed. Best short plays of the world theatre, 1968-1973 p213-23 808.82
Berne
—Description. See pages
 In Kane, R. S. Grand tour A to Z: the capitals of Europe p88-101 914
Bernewitz, M. W. von. See Von Bernewitz, M. W.
Bernhard, Winfred E. A. ed. See Political parties in American history 329
Bernstein, Carl. All the President's men 351.9
Bernstein, Leonard. See pages
 In Green, S. The world of musical comedy p289-95 780.92
Berrigan, Daniel. Prison poems 811
—Selected and new poems 811
Bessie [Smith]. Albertson, C. 780.92
The Best of Broadway 784

The Best of Life 051
The Best plays of 1973-1974 808.82
The Best short plays, 1974 808.82
Best short plays of the world theatre, 1968-1973. Richards, S. ed. 808.82
Better Homes and Gardens Sewing for your home 646.2
Between time and Timbuktu. Vonnegut, K. 812
Beverages. See pages
 In The Good Housekeeping cookbook p595-612 641.5
A bevy of beasts. Durrell, G. 591.5
Beyond Stonehenge. Hawkins, G. S. 913
Biafran War. See Nigeria—History—Civil War, 1967-1970
Bible. The Anchor Bible v34, v34A, v42 220.5
Bible (as subject)
—Geography 220.9
—Handbooks, manuals, etc. 220
—Maps. See Bible—Geography
Bibliography. See names of persons, places and subjects with the subdivision Bibliography, e.g. English drama—Bibliography
—Reference books. See Reference books—Bibliography
Bibliography of English literature, v 1 600-1660, The New Cambridge 016.82
The bicentennial guide to the American Revolution. Stember, S. 973.3
The bicycle thief (Motion picture) See pages
 In Solomon, S. J. ed. The classic cinema p199-221 791.43
Bicycles and bicycling 796.6
 See also Motorcycles
—Repairing 629.28
Big Cypress Swamp. See pages
 In Carr, A. The Everglades p42-59 500.9
Big white fog. Ward, T.
 In Hatch, J. V. ed. Black theater, U.S.A. p278-319 812.08
Bigfoot. Napier, J. 001.9
Billie Jean. King, B. J. 92
Billiet, Walter. Automotive engines: maintenance and repair 629.2
Billington, Ray Allen. Westward expansion 973
Bio-bibliography. See Authors; and subjects with subdivision Bio-bibliography, e.g. African literature—Bio-bibliography
Biographical dictionary of American music. Claghorn, C. E. 780.92
Biography
 See also names of classes of persons (e.g. Artists; Authors; Musicians, etc.); names of countries, etc. and special subjects with the subdivision Biography, (e.g. U.S.—Biography; Baseball—Biography; etc.) and names of persons for biographies of individuals
—Bibliography
 In Katz, W. A. Introduction to reference work v 1 p211-48 025.5
—Dictionaries 920.03
Biology. See pages
 In Asimov, I. Today and tomorrow and . . . p3-18 503
 See also Reproduction
—Handbooks, manuals, etc. 574.02
—Marine. See Marine biology
—Philosophy 574.01
Biology data book. Altman, P. L. ed. 574.02
Bionics. See Artificial intelligence
Bird, Caroline. Everything a woman needs to know to get paid what she's worth 331.4
Bird, Christopher, jt. auth. See Tompkins, P. The secret life of plants 581
Birds. See pages
 In Vanishing species p188-247 591
 In Villiard, P. Raising small animals for fun and profit p130-48 636.08
—Atlantic States. See pages
 In Leonard, J. N. Atlantic beaches p149-67 500.9
—Everglades. See pages
 In Carr, A. The Everglades p98-107 500.9
—Habits and behavior. See pages
 In Russell, F. The Okefenokee Swamp p94-105 500.9
—Protection. See pages
 In Allen, T. B. Vanishing wildlife of North America p58-73 591.9
—United States. See pages
 In Clement, R. C. Hammond Nature atlas of America p140-75 500.9
Birmingham, Stephen. Real lace: America's Irish rich 301.45
Birth. See Childbirth
Birth control. See pages
 In Arnstein, H. S. What every woman needs to know about abortion p91-117 613.9
 In Landis, J. T. Building a successful marriage p424-43 301.42
 See also Sterilization (Birth control)
—Laws and regulations. See pages
 In Ross, S. C. The rights of women p192-207 346

AUTHOR, TITLE, SUBJECT, AND ANALYTICAL INDEX
1974 SUPPLEMENT

Birth rate. See Birth control; Population
Bisher, Furman. See Aaron, H. Aaron 92
Black American music; past and present. Roach, H. 781.7
The Black American travel guide. Hayes, B. 917.3
Black Americans. See Negroes
The Black doctor. Aldridge, I.
  In Hatch, J. V. ed. Black theater, U.S.A. p3-24 812.08
Black humor fiction of the sixties. Schulz, M. F. 813.09
Black Panther Party. See pages
  In Newton, H. P. Revolutionary suicide 92
Black people. The education of. Du Bois, W. E. B. 378
Black poets of the United States. Wagner, J. 811.09
Black theater, U.S.A. Hatch, J. V. ed. 812.08
Blacks (United States). See Negroes
Blackstone, Harry. See pages
  In Christopher, M. The illustrated history of magic p368-87 793.8
Blackwell, Earl, ed. See Celebrity register 920.03
Blackwell, Elizabeth. See pages
  In Rossi, A. S. ed. The feminist papers: from Adams to de Beauvoir p323-46 301.41
Blackwell, Emily. See pages
  In Rossi, A. S. ed. The feminist papers: from Adams to de Beauvoir p323-46 301.41
Blackwell, Kate, jt. auth. See Nader, R. You and your pension 331.2
Blake, William. See pages
  In Clark, K. The romantic rebellion p147-74 759.05
Blank pages. Marcus, F.
  In The Best short plays, 1974 p231-45 808.82
Blavatsky, Helene Petrova (Hahn-Hahn) See pages
  In Vonnegut, K. Wampeters, foma & granfalloons (opinions) p121-37 818
Blevins, Margo. The low blood sugar cookbook 641.5
Blevins, Leon W. The young voter's manual 320.03
Blitz, Antonio. See pages
  In Christopher, M. The illustrated history of magic p97-110 793.8
Blk love song I. Ferdinand, V.
  In Hatch, J. V. ed. Black theater, U.S.A. p864-74 812.08
Blom, Eric. comp. Everyman's Dictionary of music 780.3
Blood 612
—Diseases. See pages
  In Hackett, E. Blood 612
Blood groups. See pages
  In Zimmerman, D. R. Rh 618.2
Bloom, Harold. ed. Romantic poetry and prose
  In The Oxford Anthology of English literature v2 p3-786 820.8
Blotner, Joseph. Faulkner 92
The blue book of Broadway musicals. Burton, J. 782.8
Blues (Songs, etc.) See pages
  In Albertson, C. Bessie [Smith] 780.92
Blum, Daniel. A new pictorial history of the talkies 791.43
Blumenson, Martin, ed. The Patton papers, 1940-1945 92
Boarding schools. See Private schools
Boatner, Mark Mayo. Encyclopedia of the American Revolution 973.303
Boats and boating. See Canoes and canoeing; Motorboats
Bobker, Lee R. Making movies: from script to screen 778.5
Boccaccio, Giovanni. The Decameron; criticism
  In Hesse, H. My belief p294-304 834
Bock, Jerry. See pages
  In Green, S. The world of musical comedy p359-69 780.92
Body, Human. See Physiology
Body and mind. See Mind and body
Bogs. See Marshes
Boldt, Gerhard. Hitler: the last ten days 940.54
Bolsby, Clare E. jt. auth. Berglund, B. Wilderness cooking 641.5
Bombeck, Erma. I lost everything in the postnatal depression 817
Bonadio, Felice A. ed. See Political parties in American history 329
Bonds. See Stocks
Bonin, Jane F. Prize-winning American drama 812.07
Bonk, Wallace John, jt. auth. See Carter, M. D. Building library collections 025.2
Bonner, Marita. The purple flower
  In Hatch, J. V. ed. Black theater, U.S.A. p201-07 812.08
Bonnie Prince Charlie. See Charles Edward, the Young Pretender

Bontemps, Arna, ed. American Negro poetry 811.08
Book industries and trade. See pages
  In The Metropolitan library p57-72 027.4
Book of children's verse, The Oxford. 821.08
Book of house plants, The New York Times. Faust, J. L. 635.9
Book of twentieth-century English verse, The Oxford 821.08
Book of vanishing primitive man, The Horizon. Severin, T. 301.2
Book reviews. See pages
  In Broadus, R. N. Selecting materials for libraries p69-84 025.2
—Bibliography. See pages
  In Eichelberger, C. L. comp. A guide to critical reviews of United States fiction, 1870-1910, v2 016.813
Book selection 025.2
Book trade. See Book industries and trade; Publishers and publishing
Bookkeeping 657
Books
—Appraisal. See Book reviews; Book selection; Books and reading; Criticism; Literature—History and criticism
—Reviews. See Book reviews
—Selection. See Book selection
Books and reading. See pages
  In Edwards, M. A. The fair garden and the swarm of beasts 027.62
  In Hesse, H. My belief p101-07, 153-62 834
  In The Metropolitan library p37-56, 289-98 027.4
Booksellers and bookselling. See Book industries and trade
Bookspan, Martin. 101 masterpieces of music and their composers 780.1
Boorstin, Daniel J. Democracy and its discontents 917.3
Boots. See Shoes and shoe industry
Boredom. See pages
  In Fromm, E. The anatomy of human destructiveness p242-51 152.4
Borges, Jorge Luis. The end of the duel; criticism
  In Di Giovanni, N. T. ed. Borges on writing p15-53 868
—See Di Giovanni, N. T. ed. Borges on writing 868
Borges on writing. Di Giovanni, N. T. ed. 868
Borland, Hal. Seasons 500.9
Born to heal. Montgomery, R. 615
Bose, Sir Jagadis Chunder. See pages
  In Tompkins, P. The secret life of plants p81-103 581
Botany
  See also Plants; Seeds; Trees
—Economics. See Plants, Edible
Bottles
—Collectors and collecting 748
Botvinnik, Michael. See Botvinnik, Mikhail Moiseyevich
Botvinnik, Mikhail Moiseyevich. See pages
  In Horowitz, I. A. The world chess championship p144-76 794.1
Bourgeois, Auguste Anicet- See Anicet-Bourgeois, Auguste
Bourke-White, Margaret. The photographs of Margaret Bourke-White 779
Bouton, Henri. See Blackstone, Harry
Bowden, Ken. See Nicklaus, J. Golf my way 796.352
Bowen, John. The waiting room
  In Richards, S. ed. Best short plays of the world theatre, 1968-1973 p264-76 808.82
Boynton, Lewis D. See Century 21 accounting: Advanced course 657
Boys. See Youth
Bracken, Peg. But I wouldn't have missed it for the world! 910.2
Bradford, Ernle. Christopher Columbus 92
Bradley, Robert A. Husband-coached childbirth 618.2
Brahms, Johannes. See pages
  In Ewen, D. Orchestral music p113-23 785
Braider, Donald. The life, history, and magic of the horse 636.109
Brain
—Diseases. See pages
  In Marks, G. The story of medicine in America p292-306 610.9
—Electronic. See Computers
Brams, William A. Managing your coronary 616.1
Branch, William. In splendid error
  In Hatch, J. V. ed. Black theater, U.S.A. p587-614 812.08
Brand, Stewart, ed. See The Updated Last Whole earth catalog 338.4
Brando, Marlon. See pages
  In Capote, T. The dogs bark p308-53 818
Braun, Eleanor, comp. See Museums of the world 069.025
Braun, Richard Emil, tr. See Sophocles. Antigone 882

Bread 641.8
See also Baking
Breaking open. Rukeyser, M. 811
The breast cancer controversy. What women should know about. Crile, G. 616.9
Breitbart, Vicki, comp. The day care book 362.7
Bress, Helene. The macramé book 746.4
Bretnor, Reginald. ed. Science fiction, today and tomorrow 809.3
Breton, André. See pages
  In Paz, O. Alternating current p47-61 864
Bridal customs. See Marriage customs and rites
Bridge, Raymond. America's backpacking book 796.5
Bright book of life: American novelists and storytellers from Hemingway to Mailer. Kazin, A. 813.09
Brill, Mordecai L. Write your own wedding 265
Bring me a unicorn. Lindbergh, A. M. 92
Brinton, Clarence Crane. See Brinton, Crane
Brinton, Crane. Modern civilization 901.9
Britain through American eyes. Commager, H. S. ed. 914.2
Britain's heritage, AA. Automobile Association 914.2
The Britannica Encyclopedia of American art 709.73
British actors and actresses. See Actors and actresses, British
British characteristics. See National characteristics, British
The British Empire, The Horizon History of 942
British national characteristics. See National characteristics, British
Broadcasting. See Television broadcasting
Broadus, Robert N. Selecting materials for libraries 025.2
Broadway. Atkinson, B. 792.09
Broadway, The best of 784
Broadway musicals, The blue book of. Burton, J. 782.8
Broadway's greatest musicals. Laufe, A. 782.8
Brodie, Fawn M. Thomas Jefferson, an intimate history 92
Bronowski, J. The ascent of man 501
Brooklyn
—Description. See pages
  In Capote, T. The dogs bark p40-49, 131-49 818
Brotherhood of Sleeping Car Porters. See pages
  In Anderson, J. A. Philip Randolph: a biographical portrait p151-225 92
Brough, James. See Roosevelt, E. An untold story [biography of Franklin Delano Roosevelt] 92
Brown, Dale. Wild Alaska 500.9
Brown, Sterling Allen. See pages
  In Wagner, J. Black poets of the United States p475-503 811.09
Brown, William Wells. The escape
  In Hatch, J. V. ed. Black theater. U.S.A. p34-58 812.08
The brown overcoat. Séjour, V.
  In Hatch, J. V. ed. Black theater. U.S.A. p25-33 812.08
Browne, Theodore. Natural man
  In Hatch, J. V. ed. Black theater. U.S.A. p360-81 812.08
Browning, Elizabeth Barrett. The poetical works of Elizabeth Barrett Browning 821
Browning, Robert. See pages
  In Crowell, N. A reader's guide to Robert Browning 821.09
Bruce, Robert V. Bell: Alexander Graham Bell and the conquest of solitude 92
Brumbaugh, James E. Wood furniture, finishing, refinishing, repairing 684.1
Brush, Warren D. jt. auth. See Collingwood, G. H. Knowing your trees 582
Brussels
—Description. See pages
  In Kane, R. S. Grand tour A to Z: the capitals of Europe p110-28 914
Brutality. See Cruelty
Buber, Martin. See pages
  In Manheim, W. Martin Buber 181
Buchwald, Art. I never danced at the White House 817
Buckley, James Lane. See pages
  In Markman, C. L. The Buckleys 920
Buckley, William Frank. See pages
  In Markman, C. L. The Buckleys 920
Buckley family. See pages
  In Markman, C. L. The Buckleys 920
The Buckleys. Markmann, C. L. 920
Buckminster Fuller to children of earth. Fuller, R. B. 818
Buddha and Buddhism. See pages
  In Noss, J. B. Man's religions p118-83 291
Buffalo Bill [Cody] the noblest whiteskin. Burke, J. 92

Bugs. See Insects
Building
—Handbooks, manuals, etc. 690
—Repair and reconstruction 643
Building a successful marriage. Landis, J. T. 301.42
Building library collections. Carter, M. D. 025.2
Building materials. See Wood
Bullins, Ed. Goin' a Buffalo
  In Hatch, J. V. ed. Black theater. U.S.A. p826-53 812.08
Buñuel, Luis. See pages
  In Solomon, S. J. ed. The Classic cinema p295-316 791.43
Burack, A. S. ed. Techniques of novel writing 808.3
Burgess, Anthony. A clockwork orange; adaptation. See Kubrick, S. A clockwork orange 791.43
Buried alive; the biography of Janis Joplin. Friedman, M. 92
Buried cities. See Cities and towns, Ruined, extinct, etc.
Buried treasure. See pages
  In National Geographic Society. World beneath the sea p117-40 551.4
Burke, John. Buffalo Bill [Cody] the noblest whiteskin 92
Burman, Ben Lucien. Look down that winding river 917.7
Burr, Aaron. See pages
  In Brodie, F. M. Thomas Jefferson, an intimate history p393-411 92
Burrill, Mary. They that sit in darkness
  In Hatch, J. V. ed. Black theater. U.S.A. p178-83 812.08
Burton, Hal. The Morro Castle 910.4
Burton, Jack. The blue book of Broadway musicals 782.8
Busch, N. F. The Horizon Concise history of Japan 952
Bushmen. See pages
  In Severin, T. The Horizon Book of vanishing primitive man p165-84 301.2
Business. See Accounting; Corporations; Economic conditions; Industrial management
Business English. See English language—Business English
Business letters. See English language—Business English
But I wouldn't have missed it for the world! Bracken, P. 910.2
Butcher, Devereaux, ed. See Collingwood, G. H. Knowing your trees 582
Buyers' guides. See Consumer education
Buying 658.7

CIA. See United States. Central Intelligence Agency
The CIA and the cult of intelligence. Marchetti, V. 353.007
CLC. See Contemporary literary criticism 809
CORE. See Congress of Racial Equality
CORE. Meier, A. 322.4
The CQ Guide to current American government 350
The cabinet of Dr Caligari (Motion picture)
  In Solomon, S. J. ed. The classic cinema p39-64 791.43
Cabinet work 684.1
  See also Veneers and veneering
Cabot family. See pages
  In Hatch, A. The Lodges of Massachusetts 920
Cactus. See pages
  In Abbey, E. Cactus country p52-61, 78-91 500.9
Cactus country. Abbey, E. 500.9
Caine, Lynn. Widow 301.42
Cake 641.8
Cake decorating 641.8
Caleb the degenerate. Cotter, J. S.
  In Hatch, J. V. ed. Black theater. U.S.A. p61-99 812.08
Calendars. See pages
  In Asimov, I. The tragedy of the moon p27-49 508
Cambodia. See pages
  In Salisbury, H. E. To Peking—and beyond p176-88 915.1
Cambridge Bibliography of English literature, v 1: 600-1660. The New 016.82
Camp cooking. See Outdoor cookery
Campaigns, Presidential. See Presidents—United States—Election
Campbell, Ian James. See pages
  In Wambaugh, J. The onion field 364.1
Campbell, James Edwin. See pages
  In Wagner, J. Black poets of the United States p129-38 811.09
Campbell, Mrs Patrick. See pages
  In Gielgud, Sir J. Distinguished company p45-54 920

AUTHOR, TITLE, SUBJECT, AND ANALYTICAL INDEX
1974 SUPPLEMENT

Campers and trailers. See Travel trailers and campers
Camping. See pages
  In Angier, B. Introduction to canoeing p163-79 797.1
  In National Geographic Society. Wilderness U.S.A. 500.9
  See also Backpacking; Outdoor cookery; Wilderness survival
Canada
—Galleries and museums—Bibliography. See pages
  In Museum media 016
—Galleries and museums—Directories. See pages
  In Museum media 016
—History. See pages
  In The Horizon History of the British Empire p57-63, 261-69 942
—Museums. See Canada—Galleries and museums
—Natural history. See Natural history—Canada
Canadian literature
—Bio-bibliography. See pages
  In [Story, N.] Supplement to the Oxford Companion to Canadian history and literature 810.3
—Encyclopedias 810.3
—History and criticism. See pages
  In Seymour-Smith, M. Funk & Wagnalls Guide to modern world literature p331-41 809
Cancer 616.9
Candle in the wind. Solzhenitsyn, A. 891.7
Candy. See Confectionery
Cannibalism. See pages
  In Read, P. P. Alive 918
Canning and preserving. See pages
  In The Good Housekeeping cookbook p691-703 641.5
Canoes and canoeing 797.1
Can't read, can't write, can't takl too good either. Clarke, L. 618.9
Capablanca, José Raoul. See pages
  In Horowitz, A. The world chess championship p71-93 794.1
Cape Cod. See pages
  In Leonard, J. N. Atlantic beaches p31-41 500.9
Capitalization (Finance) See Corporations—Finance
Capote, Truman. The dogs bark 818
—Local color
  In Capote, T. The dogs bark p21-104 818
—The muses are heard
  In Capote, T. The dogs bark p161-307 818
Capote, Truman (as subject) See pages
  In Kazin, A. Bright book of life: American novelists and storytellers from Hemingway to Mailer p207-19 813.09
Capps, Benjamin. See The Indians 970.4
Carbon. See pages
  In Asimov, I. The tragedy of the moon p79-103 508
Carcinoma. See Cancer
Card games. See Cards
Cardiac diseases. See Heart—Diseases
Cards 795.4; also pages
  In Scarne, J. Scarne's Encyclopedia of games 795
  In Scarne, J. Scarne's New Complete guide to gambling p625-794 795
Caribbean literature. See West Indian literature
Carlson, Margaret Bresnahan. How to get your car repaired without getting gypped 629.28
Carlyle, Thomas. See pages
  In Commager, H. S. ed. Britain through American eyes p253-63 914.2
Carmer, Carl. The Hudson 974.7
Carpenter, Finley. The Skinner primer: behind freedom and dignity 150.19
Carpentry. See Building
Carpets. See pages
  In Habeeb, V. T. The Ladies' Home Journal Art of homemaking p179-95 640
Carr, Archie. The Everglades 500.9
Carrighar, Sally. Home to the wilderness 92
Carroll, David. The dictionary of foreign terms in the English language 422.03
Carroll, Lewis. See Dodgson, Charles Lutwidge
Carrying the fire. Collins, M. 629.45
Carson, Gerald. Men, beasts, and gods 636.03
Carter, Mary Duncan. Building library collections 025.2
Cartoons and caricatures. See Moving picture cartoons
Carver, George Washington. See pages
  In Rogers, J. A. Great men of color v2 p462-73 920
Carving (Meat, etc.) See pages
  In Evans, T. M. The meat book p253-70 641.3
Cary, Eve. See Levine, A. The rights of students 344.7
Cascade Mountains. See pages
  In The Great Northwest p49-65 917.95
Cash, Johnny. See pages
  In Pleasants, H. The great American popular singers p291-305 780.92

Cassettes, Chicorel Index to the spoken arts on discs, tapes, and 808.8
Castaneda, Carlos. The teachings of Don Juan 299
Castle, Charles. Noël [biography of Noël Coward] 92
Castles, houses and gardens, and other places of interest. See Automobile Association. AA Britain's heritage 914.2
Cataloging 025.3
Cataloguing. See Cataloging
Catastrophes. See Disasters
Catch-22. Heller, J. 812
Catherine II, Empress of Russia 92
Cats 636.8
—Encyclopedias 636.803
—Poetry. See pages
  In Gallico, P. Honorable cat 636.8
Cattell (Jaques) Press, Temple, Ariz. See American men and women of science; The social and behavioral sciences 920.025
Catton, Bruce. Gettysburg: the final fury 973.7
Catullus. See pages
  In Quniin, K. Catullus 874.09
The causes of the Civil War. Stampp, K. M. ed. 973.7
Cavafy, Constantine P. See Kabaphēs, Kōnstantinōs Petrou
Cavett, Dick. Cavett 92
Cecil, Lord David. Max; criticism
  In Auden, W. H. Forewords and afterwords p367-83 809
Celebration. Jones, T.
  In Jones, T. The fantastics [and] Celebration p97-218 812
Celebrity register 920.03
Censorship. See Freedom of the press
Census
—United States. See United States—Census
Centers for the performing arts
—Directories. See pages
  In The National directory for the performing arts and civic centers [1974] 790.2
Central Intelligence Agency. See United States. Central Intelligence Agency
Century 21 accounting: Advanced course 657
Ceramic materials. See Clay
Ceramics. See Pottery
Chagall, Marc. See pages
  In Haftmann, W. Marc Chagall 759.7
Chaka, Zulu chief. See pages
  In Rogers, J. A. Great men of color v 1 p265-75 920
Challinor, John. A dictionary of geology 551.03
Chandler, Sue P. jt. auth. See Shockley, A. A. Living Black American authors 920.03
Change
—Social. See Social change
Change of name and law of names. Bander, E. J. 346
Chanson de Roland. The song of Roland 841
Chapin, Kim. See King, B. J. Billie Jean 92
Chaplin, Charles Spencer. See pages
  In Solomon, S. J. ed. The classic cinema p89-107 791.43
Character education. See pages
  In Read, H. Education through art p265-84 707
Characters and characteristics in literature
  See also Women in literature and art
—Dictionaries. See pages
  In Freeman, W. Dictionary of fictional characters 820.3
Chardin, Pierre Teilhard de. See Teilhard de Chardin, Pierre
Charitable institutions. See Charities; Mentally ill—Institutional care
Charities 361.7
—Public. See Public welfare
Charity organization. See Charities
Charles, Martie. Job security
  In Hatch, J. V. ed. Black theater, U.S.A. p765-71 812.08
Charles, Ray. See pages
  In Pleasants, H. The great American popular singers p247-61 780.92
Charles Edward, the Young Pretender 92
Charmed circle: Gertrude Stein & company. Mellow, J. R. 92
Charrière, Henri. Banco 365
Chavante Indians. See pages
  In Severin, T. The Horizon Book of vanishing primitive man p319-37 301.2
Cheese 637
Cheetahs. See pages
  In Schaller, G. B. Serengeti: a kingdom of predators p42-53 599
Cheetham, Erika, ed. See Nostradamus. The prophecies of Nostradamus 133.3
Chekhov, Anton. The safety match; dramatization. See Ginsbury, N. The safety match
Chemical elements. See pages
  In Asimov, I. Today and tomorrow and ... p49-60 503
Chess 794.1

Chesterton, Gilbert Keith 92
Chew, Peter. The Kentucky Derby, the first 100 years 798
Chicago
—Haymarket Square Riot, 1886. See pages
  In Havighurst, W. The heartland: Ohio, Indiana, Illinois p289-305 977
Chicorel, Marietta, ed. See Chicorel Bibliography to books on music and musicians 016.78
—ed. See Chicorel Bibliography to the performing arts 016.7902
—See Chicorel Index to poetry in collections in print, on discs and tapes: poetry on discs, tapes, and cassettes 821.08
—See Chicorel Index to the spoken arts on discs, tapes, and cassettes 808.8
—ed. See Chicorel Theater Index to plays in periodicals 808.82
Chicorel Bibliography to books on music and musicians 016.78
Chicorel Bibliography to the performing arts 016.7902
Chicorel Index to poetry in collections in print, on discs and tapes: poetry on discs, tapes, and cassettes 821.08
Chicorel Index to the spoken arts on discs, tapes, and cassettes 808.8
Chicorel Theater index to plays in periodicals 808.82
Chidsey, Donald Barr. The Loyalists 973.3
Child abuse. See Cruelty to children
Child and parent. See Parent and child
Child development. See Child study
Child psychology. See Child study
Child study 155.4; also pages
  In Montessori, M. From childhood to adolescence 371.3
  See also Exceptional children; Parent and child; Play
Child Study Association of America. What to tell your child about sex 612.6
Child welfare
  See also Children—Care and hygiene; Cruelty to children; Day nurseries
—Laws and regulations. See pages
  In Wilkerson, A. E. ed. The rights of children 346
Childbirth 618.2
Childhood education. Montessori, M. 371.3
Children
  See also Child study
—Adoption. See Adoption
—Care and hygiene 649; also pages
  In Breitbart, V. comp. The day care book 362.7
  In Gathorne-Hardy, J. The unnatural history of the nanny 914.2
  See also School children—Food
—Civil rights 346; also pages
  In Holt, J. Escape from childhood 301.43
—Cruelty to. See Cruelty to children
—Discipline. See Children—Management
—Education. See Education, Elementary
—Exceptional. See Exceptional children
—Illegitimate. See Illegitimacy
—Institutional care. See Day nurseries
—Laws and regulations. See pages
  In The Family legal advisor p81-98 340
—Management 649; also pages
  In Holt, J. Escape from childhood 301.43
  In Kinkade, K. A Walden Two experiment p130-46 335
  See also Cruelty to children
—Nutrition. See School children—Food
—Psychology. See Child study
Children as artists. See pages
  In Read, H. Education through art p108-70 707
Children in Europe, Fielding's Guide to traveling with. Hadley, L. 914
Children in the Near East. See pages
  In Patai, R. The Arab mind p25-40 301.29
Children of the mire. Paz, O. 809.1
Children's courts. See Juvenile courts
Children's poetry
—Collections 821.08
Childress, Alice. Mojo
  In Richards, S. ed. Best short plays of the world theatre, 1968-1973 p126-37 808.82
—Wine in the wilderness
  In Hatch, J. V. ed. Black theater, U.S.A. p737-55 812.08
Chilton's Auto air conditioning manual. 629.2
Chilton's Auto heating & air conditioning manual. See Chilton's Auto air conditioning manual 629.2
Chilton's Auto troubleshooting guide 629.28
Chilton's Motorcycle troubleshooting guide 629.28
Chilton's Repair and maintenance guide: truck campers 629.28

Chilton's Repair and tune-up guide: inboard/outdrives 623.82
Chilton's Repair and tune-up guide: outboard motors 30 horsepower & over 623.82
Chilton's Repair and tune-up guide: small engines 621.43
China
—Civilization 915.1
—Foreign relations—United States. See pages
  In Osborne, J. The fourth year of the Nixon watch p16-37 973.924
—Religion. See pages
  In Noss, J. B. Man's religions p240-307 291
China (People's Republic of China, 1949-) 915.1
—Description and travel 915.1; also pages
  In Sulzberger, C. L. Postscript with a Chinese accent 92
—Economic policy. See pages
  In Galbraith, J. K. A China passage 915.1
China diary. Salisbury, C. Y. 915.1
A China passage. Galbraith, J. K. 915.1
The Chinese. Schisgal, M.
  In Richards, S. ed. Best short plays of the world theatre, 1968-1973 p152-67 808.82
Chinese-English dictionary of modern usage, Lin Yutang's. Lin, Yutang 495.1
Chinese language
—Dictionaries 495.1
Chisholm, Shirley. The good fight 329
Choice of books. See Book selection
Choosing a private school. Esty, J. C. 371
Chou, En-lai. See pages
  In Salisbury, H. E. To Peking—and beyond p246-60 915.1
  In Sulzberger, C. L. Postscript with a Chinese accent p377-89 92
Christ. See Jesus Christ
Christian life. See Spiritual life
Christianity. See pages
  In Noss, J. B. Man's religions p417-506 291
—Encyclopedias. See pages
  In The Oxford Dictionary of the Christian Church 203
Christology. See Jesus Christ
Christopher, John B. jt. auth. See Brinton, C. Modern civilization 901.9
Christopher, Milbourne. The illustrated history of magic 793.8
Christopher Columbus. Bradford, E. 92
Chronicles of wasted time. Muggeridge, M. 92
Chronology. See Calendars
The church fight. Gaines-Shelton, R.
  In Hatch, J. V. ed. Black theater, U.S.A. p188-91 812.08
Church history
—Primitive and early church. See pages
  In Woods, W. A history of the devil p93-107 133.4
Churchill, Sir Winston Leonard Spencer. See pages
  In The Horizon History of the British Empire p455-64 942
Cinema. See Moving pictures
A circle of children. MacCracken, M. 371.9
Cities and towns 301.34; also pages
—United States
  In Moynihan, D. P. Coping p210-32 309.173
  In Wolff, R. P. ed. 1984 revisited p139-201 973
Cities and towns, Ruined, extinct, etc. See pages
  In Menen, A. Cities in the sand 913.37
Cities in the sand. Menen, A. 913.37
Citizen Kane (Motion picture) See pages
  In Sarris, A. The primal screen p111-36 791.43
  In Solomon, S. J. ed. The classic cinema p171-97 791.43
Citizenship. See pages
  In Ross, D. K. A public citizen's action manual p211-37 640.73
—Laws and regulations. See pages
  In The Family legal advisor p129-46 340
Civics. See Political science
Civil government. See Political science
Civil liberty. See Liberty
Civil rights. See pages
  In The Family legal advisor p147-58 340
  In Fraenkel, O. K. The rights we have 344
  In Padover, S. K. ed. Sources of democracy 321.8
  In Rosengart, O. The rights of suspects 345
  In Rudovsky, D. The rights of prisoners 345
  See also Children—Civil rights; Woman—Civil rights
—History. See pages
  In Perrett, G. Days of sadness, years of triumph p87-103, 216-30, 357-67 973.917
Civil service
—Great Britain. See pages
  In The Horizon History of the British Empire p310-25 942
Civil War
—England. See Great Britain—History—Civil War and Commonwealth, 1642-1660

AUTHOR, TITLE, SUBJECT, AND ANALYTICAL INDEX
1974 SUPPLEMENT

Civilization
 See also Archeology; Education; Society, Primitive; Science and civilization; Technology and civilization; also names of countries, states, etc. with the subdivision Civilization, e.g. United States—Civilization
—Ancient. See pages
 In Däniken, E. von. The gold of the gods 001.9
 In Däniken, E. von. In search of ancient gods, 001.9
—Modern. See pages
 In Solzhenitsyn, A. I. Letter to the Soviet leaders 947.085
—Modern—History 901.9
—Modern—1950- 901.94; also pages
 In Toffler, A. ed. Learning for tomorrow 370.19
—Philosophy. See pages
 In Trilling, L. Mind in the modern world 901.94
Civilization and science. See Science and civilization
Civilization and technology. See Technology and civilization
Claghorn, Charles Eugene. Biographical dictionary of American music 780.92
Clancy, Paul R. Just a country lawyer; a biography of Senator Sam Ervin 92
Clark, George Rogers. See pages
 In Havighurst, W. The heartland: Ohio. Indiana, Illinois p58-70 977
Clark, Kenneth. The romantic rebellion 759.05
Clark, Sydney. All the best in . . . [Mexico] 910.2
Clarke, John Henrik, ed. See Rogers, J. A. World's great men of color 920
Clarke, Louise. Can't read, can't write, can't talk too good either 618.9
The classic cinema. Solomon, S. J. ed. 791.43
Classical Greek dramatic poetry and drama 882
Classical Greek epic poetry and fiction 883
Classical Greek lyric poetry 884
Classical literature. See Greek literature
Clay 738.1
Clay and glazes for the potter. Rhodes, D. 738.1
Cleaning. See House cleaning
Cleaning compounds. See pages
 In Habeeb, V. T. The Ladies Home Journal Art of homemaking p61-72 640
Clement, Roland C. Hammond Nature atlas of America 500.9
Cleminshaw, Clarence H. jt. auth. See Alter, D. Pictorial astronomy 523
Cleopatra, Queen of Egypt. See pages
 In Rogers, J. A. Great men of color v 1 p121-30 920
Clive, John. Macaulay: the shaping of the historian 92
Clive, Mary. This sun of York; a biography of Edward IV 92
Clocks and watches
—Repairing 681
A clockwork orange. Kubrick, S. 791.43
Cloth. See Textile industry and fabrics
Clothing, Men's. See Men's clothing
Clothing and dress. See pages
 In Bridge, R. America's backpacking book p147-57 796.5
—Dictionaries 391.03
—Repairing. See pages
 In Habeeb, V. T. The Ladies' Home Journal Art of homemaking p389-403 640
Coal miners. See Miners
Cobb, Betsy. Vacation houses 728.6
Cobb, Hubbard, jt. auth. See Cobb, B. Vacation houses 728.6
Codeword BARBAROSSA. Whaley, B. 940.54
Cody, William Frederick 92
Coffey, D. J. jt. ed. See Henderson, G. N. ed. The international encyclopedia of cats 636.803
Coffin, Tristram Potter, ed. Folklore from the working folk of America 398
Cognition. See Knowledge, Theory of
Cohan, George Michael 92; also pages
 In Green, S. The world of musical comedy p25-35 780.92
Cohen, Hennig, jt. ed. See Coffin, T. P. ed. Folklore from the working folk of America 398
Cohen, Richard M. A heartbeat away 351.9
Coinage of words. See Words, New
Cole, Nat King. See pages
 In Pleasants, H. The great American popular singers p213-26 780.92
Coles, Clarence W. Glenn's Complete bicycle manual: selection, maintenance, repair 629.28
Collage 751.4
Collage and assemblage. Meilach, D. Z. 751.4
Collected poems (1930-1973) Sarton, M. 811
Collecting tomorrow's antiques today. Flayderman, N. 745.1
Collective settlements. See names of individual communes, e.g. Twin Oaks Community
College entrance requirements. See Colleges and universities—Entrance requirements

Colleges and universities
 See also Education, Higher
—Entrance requirements 378.1
Collingwood, G. H. Knowing your trees 582
Collins, Larry R. Ling-Ling and Hsing-Hsing 599
Collins, Michael. Carrying the fire 629.45
Color star atlas. Moore, P. 523.8
Colored people (United States) See Negroes
The Columbia. Holbrook, S. H. 979.7
Columbia River. See pages
 In The Great Northwest p133-41 917.95
 In Holbrook, S. H. The Columbia 979.7
Columbus, Christopher 92
Come as your are: Bermondsey. See Mortimer, J. Bermondsey
Comets. See pages
 In Alter, D. Pictorial astronomy p137-49 523
 In Asimov, I. Asimov on astronomy p127-40 523
Commager, Henry Steele, ed. Britain through American eyes 914.2
Commercial law. See Contracts—Laws and regulations
Committee on Finance. See United States. Congress. Senate. Committee on Finance
Committee on Ways and Means. See United States. Congress. House. Committee on Ways and Means
Commonsense cataloging. Piercy, E. J. 025.3
Commonwealth of England. See Great Britain—History—Civil War and Commonwealth, 1642-1660
Communication. See pages
 In Farb, P. Word play 401
 See also Language and languages
Communism 335.4
—Russia. See pages
 In Warth, R. D. Lenin 92
Communist China. See China (People's Republic of China, 1949-)
Community life. See pages
 In United States. Department of Agriculture. Handbook for the home p33-82 640
Companies. See Corporations
Comparative anatomy. See Anatomy, Comparative
The complete beginner's guide to fishing. Sand, G. X. 799.1
Complete bicycle manual: selection, maintenance, repair, Glenn's. Coles, C. W. 629.8
Complete book of bicycling, The New. Sloane, E. A. 796.6
The complete book of greenhouse gardening. See Northen, H. T. Greenhouse gardening 635.9
Complete book of wood finishing. Scharff, R. 684
Complete guide to gambling. Scarne's New. Scarne, J. 795
The complete illustrated book of divination and prophecy. Gibson, W. B. 133.3
Complete walker, The New. Fletcher, C. 796.5
Composers. See pages
 In Bookspan, M. 101 masterpieces of music and their composers 780.1
 In Ewen, D. Orchestral music 785
 In Haggin, B. H. The new listener's companion and record guide 780.1
 In Jacobs, A. A short history of Western music 780.9
—American. See pages
 In Green, S. The world of musical comedy 780.92
Computer dictionary and handbook. Sippl, C. J. 001.6
Computers 001.6; also pages
 In Adler, I. Thinking machines 519.4
—Dictionaries 001.6
Computing machines (Electronic) See Computers
Conant, Ralph W. ed. See The Metropolitan library 027.4
Concentration camps. See pages
 In Conrat, M. Executive order 9066: the internment of 110,000 Japanese Americans 940.54
Conception
—Prevention. See Birth control
The concise Atlas of the universe. [Moore, P.] 523
Concise history of Japan, The Horizon. Busch, N. F. 952
Concordance to Shakespeare, The Harvard. Spevack, M. 822.3
Confectionery. See pages
 In The Good Housekeeping cookbook p583-94 641.5
 See also Cake decorating
Confessional. Williams, T.
 In Richards, S. ed. Best short plays of the world theatre, 1968-1973 p 1-21 808.82
Conflict of generations 301.43
 See also Parent and child

PUBLIC LIBRARY CATALOG
1974 SUPPLEMENT

Confucius and Confucianism. See pages
  In Noss, J. B. Man's religions p270-307 **291**
Congress
—United States. See United States. Congress
Congress of Racial Equality **322.4**
Congressional districts in the 1970s **328.73**
Congressional Quarterly, Inc. See Congressional districts in the 1970s **328.73**
—See Energy crisis in America **333.3**
—See The Middle East **327.73**
—See Watergate: chronology of a crisis **351.9**
Congreve, William. The way of the world
  In The Oxford Anthology of English literature v 1 p1673-1733 **820.8**
Conjuring. See Magic
Connecticut
—Country life. See Country life—Connecticut
Conrat, Maisie. Executive order 9066: the internment of 110,000 Japanese Americans **940.54**
Conrat, Richard, jt. auth. See Conrat, M. Executive order 9066: the internment of 110,000 Japanese Americans **940.54**
Consciousness, Multiple. See personality disorders
Conservation of natural resources. See pages
  In Kutz, M. Rockefeller power p143-98 **361.7**
  In Reischauer, E. O. Toward the 21st century: education for a changing world p53-64 **327**
Conservation of wildlife. See Wildlife—Conservation
Conspectus of American biography, White's. See Notable names in American history **920.03**
Constable, George. The Neanderthals **573**
Constable, John. See pages
  In Clark, K. The romantic rebellion p265-83 **759.05**
Constitutional history. See Democracy; United States—Constitutional history
Constitutional law. See Civil rights
Construction. See Building
Consumer education. See pages
  In Goldbeck, N. The supermarket handbook **641.3**
  In Habeeb, V. T. The Ladies' Home Journal Art of homemaking p513-35 **640**
  In Klamkin, C. How to buy major appliances **643**
  In United States. Department of Agriculture. Handbook for the home **640**
—Bibliography. See pages
  In Thomas, S. M. A guide to sources of consumer information **640.73**
—Handbooks, manuals, etc. **640.73**
Consumer protection **640.73**
Consumers' guides. See Consumer education
Contemporary American-Jewish literature. Malin, I. ed. **810.9**
Contemporary authors. First revision v9-12 **920.03**
Contemporary batik and tie-dye. Meilach, D. Z. **746.4**
Contemporary literary criticism **809**
Contraception. See Birth control
Contractions. See Abbreviations
Contracts
—Laws and regulations. See pages
  In Sloan, I. J. Youth and the law p23-36 **340**
Convicts. See Crime and criminals
Cook, James. See pages
  In The Horizon History of the British Empire p96-111 **942**
Cook books. See Cookery
Cooke, Alistair. Alistair Cooke's America **973**
Cookery **641.5**; also pages
  In Goldbeck, N. The supermarket handbook **641.3**
  In Taber, G. Country chronicle **630.1**
  See also Bread; Outdoor cookery
—Game and game birds. See pages
  Berglund, B. Wilderness cooking **641.5**
Cookery for hypoglycemics **641.5**
Cookery for the sick. See Cookery for hypoglycemics
Cooking, Outdoor. See Outdoor cookery
Cooking utensils. See Household equipment and supplies
Cooling appliances. See Refrigeration and refrigerating machinery
Cooper, Bryan. Alaska: the last frontier **338.2**
Cooper, Henry S. F. Thirteen: the flight that failed **629.45**
Cooper, Martin, ed. The modern age, 1890-1960
  In The New Oxford History of music v10 **780.9**
Cooper, Paulette. The medical detectives **614**
Copenhagen
—Description. See pages
  In Kane, R. S. Grand tour A to Z: the capitals of Europe p129-56 **914**

Coping. Moynihan, D. P. **309.173**
Coplan, Kate. Effective library exhibits **021.7**
Corn. See pages
  In Havighurst, W. The heartland: Ohio, Indiana, Illinois p338-50 **977**
Corneille, Pierre. See pages
  In Abraham, C. Pierre Corneille **842.09**
Cornwallis-West, Beatrice Stella (Tanner) See Campbell, Mrs Patrick
Corny. See Owen, A. Male of the species: Corny
Coronary heart diseases. See Heart—Diseases
Corporations. See pages
  In Galbraith, J. K. Economics and the public purpose **338.973**
—Finance. See pages
  In Stern, P. M. The rape of the taxpayer p206-27 **336.2**
Corruption (in politics) See pages
  In Cohen, R. M. A heartbeat away **351.9**
Cortés, Hernando. See pages
  In Davies, N. The Aztecs p242-82 **970.3**
Cosell, Howard. Cosell **92**
Cosmetics **668**
Costa, Antone C. See pages
  In Vonnegut, K. Wampeters, foma & granfalloons (opinions) p65-76 **818**
Costa, Beverley da. See Da Costa, Beverley
Costa, Richard Hauer. Malcolm Lowry **813.09**
Costume
  See also Clothing and dress
—History. See pages
  In Schoeffler, O. E. Esquire's Encyclopedia of 20th century men's fashions **391**
Costume design
  In Schoeffler, O. E. Esquire's Encyclopedia of 20th century men's fashions p602-42 **391**
Cottages. See Houses
Cotter, Joseph S. Caleb the degenerate
  In Hatch, J. V. ed. Black theater, U.S.A. p61-99 **812.08**
Coughlan, Robert. Elizabeth and Catherine; empresses of all the Russias **92**
Coulson, Zoe, ed. See The Good Housekeeping cookbook **641.5**
Council for National Cooperation in Aquatics. The new science of skin and scuba diving **797.2**
Country chronicle. Taber, G. **630.1**
Country life
—Connecticut **630.1**
—United States. See pages
  In National Geographic Society. Life in rural America **917.3**
Coups d'état. See Revolutions
Courting. See Dating (Social customs)
Courtship. See Dating (Social customs)
Cousteau, Jacques. The act of life **591.92**
—The art of motion **591.92**
—Oasis in space **574.92**
—Octopus and squid **594**
—Window in the sea **574.92**
Coverlets **746.4**; also pages
  In Better Homes and Gardens Sewing for your home p74-93 **646.2**
Coward, Noël. A last encore **92**
—The lyrics of Noel Coward **821**
—A song at twilight
  In Richards, S. ed. Best short plays of the world theatre, 1968-1973 p51-80 **808.82**
  For material about this author see Coward, Sir Noël Pierce
Coward, Noël Pierce **92**
Cowboys **978**
Cowles, Virginia. The Rothschilds **920**
Cowley, Malcolm. A second flowering **810.9**
Cozzens, James Gould. See pages
  In Kazin, A. Bright book of life: American novelists and storytellers from Hemingway to Mailer p95-105 **813.09**
Crane, Hart. See pages
  In Cowley, M. A second flowering p191-215 **810.9**
Crankshaw, Edward. Tolstoy **92**
Creation (Literary, artistic, etc.) See pages
  In Bretnor, R. ed. Science fiction, today and tomorrow p135-47, 235-57 **809.3**
Creative divorce. Krantzler, M. **301.42**
Creative fly tying and fly fishing. Gerlach, R. **799.1**
Creativeness. See Creation (Literary, artistic, etc.)
Credit. See Loans
Crile, George. What women should know about the breast cancer controversy **616.9**
Crime and criminals. See pages
  In Mitford, J. Kind and usual punishment p47-78 **365**
  See also Criminal law; Murder; Rape
—United States. See pages
  In Whittemore, L. H. The super cops **363.2**
Crime and punishment, Twentieth century interpretations of. Jackson, R. L. ed. **891.7**

122

AUTHOR, TITLE, SUBJECT, AND ANALYTICAL INDEX
1974 SUPPLEMENT

Criminal law 345; also pages
  In DeCrow, K. Sexist justice p185-222 346.1
  In The Family legal advisor p419-46 340
  In Ross, S. C. The rights of women p164-89 346
  See also Punishment
Criminals. See Crime and criminals
Criticism 801
Crockett, James Underwood. Vegetables and fruits 635
Cromwell, the Lord Protector. Fraser, A. 92
Crosby, Bing. See pages
  In Pleasants, H. The great American popular singers p126-42 780.92
Crosby, Harry Lillis. See Crosby, Bing
Cross, F. L. ed. See The Oxford Dictionary of the Christian Church 203
Crowell, Norton B. A reader's guide to Robert Browning 821.09
Crowell's Handbook of contemporary American poetry. Malkoff, K. 811.09
Cruelty, See pages
  In Fromm, E. The anatomy of human destructiveness p51-63 152.4
Cruelty to animals. See Animals—Treatment
Cruelty to children 362.7; also pages
  In Wilkerson, A. E. ed. The rights of children p174-89 346
'Cruiter. Matheus, J.
  In Hatch, J. V. ed. Black theater, U.S.A. p225-32 812.08
Cukor, George Dewey. See pages
  In Higham, C. The art of the American film, 1900-1971 p178-87 791.43
Cullen, Countee. See pages
  In Gibson, D. B. ed. Modern Black poets p69-83 811.09
  In Wagner. J. Black poets of the United States p283-347 811.09
Cultural change. See Social change
Cummings, Edward Estlin. See pages
  In Cowley, M. A second flowering p90-113 810.9
Cuna Indians. See pages
  In Severin, T. The Horizon Book of vanishing primitive man p116-27 301.2
Curiosities and wonders 001.9
Currency question. See Inflation (finance)
Current American government, The CQ Guide to 350
Curtains. See Drapery
Curtin, Sharon R. Nobody ever died of old age 301.43
Custer, George Armstrong. See pages
  In The Soldiers p181-220 970.5
Cybernetics. See pages
  In Diebold, J. ed. The world of the computer p274-86 001.6
Cycles, Motor. See Motorcycles
Cycling. See Bicycles and bicycling; Motorcycles
Cyclopedias. See Encyclopedias and dictionaries
Czech literature
—History and criticism. See pages
  In Seymour-Smith, M. Funk & Wagnalls Guide to modern world literature p349-62 809

DAR. See Daughters of the American Revolution
DNA. See pages
  In Asimov, I. The tragedy of the moon p131-41 508
Da Costa, Beverley, ed. See Great historic places 917.3
—ed. See Natural wonders of America 917.3
Daiches, David. The last Stuart; the life and times of Bonnie Prince Charlie 92
Dairy products. See Cheese; Yogurt
Dancing
  In Graham, M. The notebooks of Martha Graham 92
Daniels, Jonathan. The Randolphs of Virginia 920
Däniken, Erich von. The gold of the gods 001.9
—In search of ancient gods 001.9
Dante. See pages
  In Christopher, M. The illustrated history of magic p368-87 793.8
Dark, Harris Edward. The Wankel rotary engine 629.2
Darkroom techniques. Feininger, A. 770
Darwinism. See Evolution
Data processing. See Electronic data processing
Dating (Social customs). See pages
  In Landis, J. T. Building a successful marriage p33-67 301.42
  See also Marriage
The Daughters. Anderson, P. 369
Daughters of the American Revolution 369

Davidson, Marshall B. The American Heritage History of the artists' America 709.73
Davies, Nigel. The Aztecs 970.3
Davies, Peter. The truth about Kent State 378.1
Davis, Francyne. The low blood sugar cookbook 641.5
The day care book. Breitbart, V. comp. 362.7
Day care centers. See Day nurseries
Day nurseries 362.7; also pages
  In Joint Commission on Mental Health of Children. Mental health: from infancy through adolescence p61-76 155.4
Day of absence. Ward, D. T.
  In Hatch, J. V. ed. Black theater, U.S.A. p695-710 812.08
  In Richards, S. ed. Best short plays of the world theatre, 1968-1973 p34-50 808.82
Dayan, Moshe 92
Days of sadness, years of triumph. Perrett, G. 973.917
Deaf. See pages
  In Tidyman, E. Dummy 345.7
Dean, Phillip Hayes. The owl killer
  In The Best short plays, 1974 p61-92 808.82
Death 128; also pages
  In Mannes, M. Last rights 174
The death notebooks. Sexton, A. 811
De Chardin, Pierre Teilhard. See Teilhard de Chardin, Pierre
Decoration, Interior. See Interior decoration
Decoration and ornament. See Egg decoration; Interior decoration; Table setting and decoration
Decorative arts. See Interior decoration
De Crow, Karen. Sexist justice 346.1
Deeper into movies. Kael, P. 791.43
Degas, Edgar. See Degas, Hilaire Germain Edgar
Degas, Hilaire Germain Edgar. See pages
  In Clark, K. The romantic rebellion p309-29 759.05
De Gourmont, Rémy. See Gourmont, Rémy de
De Goya y Lucientes, Francisco Jose. See Goya y Lucientes, Francisco Jose de
Deighton, Lee C. ed. See The Encyclopedia of education 370.3
Dejection. See Depression, Mental
Delacroix, Eugène. See pages
  In Clark, K. The romantic rebellion p199-220 759.05
De La Mare, Walter John. See pages
  In Auden, W. H. Forewords and afterwords p384-94 809
De Lamartine, Alphonse Marie Louis. See Lamartine, Alphonse Marie Louis de
Deloria, Vine. Behind the trail of broken treaties 970.5
De Maupassant, Guy. See Maupassant Guy de
De Mille, Agnes. Speak to me, dance with me 92
De Mille, Cecil Blount 92
Democracy 321.8; also pages
  In Dewey, J. The philosophy of John Dewey v2 p620-43 191
Democracy and its discontents. Boorstin, D. J. 917.3
Democratic Party. See pages
  In Moynihan, D. P. Coping p53-68 309.173
Demonology 133.4
Deoxyribonucleic acid. See DNA
Department of Health, Education and Welfare. See United States. Department of Health, Education and Welfare
Depression
—Mental. See pages
  In Fromm, E. The anatomy of human destructiveness p242-52 152.4
Depressive psychoses. See Depression, Mental
Desautels, Paul E. Rocks & minerals 549
Desert animals. See pages
  In Abbey, E. Cactus country p126-41 500.9
Desert ecology 574.5
Desert: the American Southwest. Kirk, R. 574.5
Deserts. See pages
  In Bridge, R. America's backpacking book p323-32 796.5
  See also Desert animals
De Sica, Vittorio. See pages
  In Solomon, S. J. ed. The classic cinema p199-221 791.43
De Sola, Ralph. Abbreviations dictionary 421.03
Desoxyribonucleic acid. See DNA
Design, Decorative. See pages
  In Wilson, E. Erica Wilson's Embroidery book p357-65 746.4
Detectives. See pages
  In Wolfe, T. ed. The New journalism p259-80 810.8
Determinism and indeterminism. See Free will and determinism
Developing countries. See Underdeveloped areas
Devil. See Demonology
Dewey, John. The philosophy of John Dewey 191

A dialogue. Baldwin, J. 301.45
Diaries, 1949-1959. Pearson, D. 92
The diary of Anaïs Nin, 1947-1955. Nin, A. 92
The diary of Samuel Pepys v8. Pepys, S. 92
Dickens, Charles. See pages
  In Hardwick, M. comp. The Charles Dickens encyclopedia 823.09
—Characters. See pages
  In Greaves, J. Who's who in Dickens 823.03
—Dictionaries 823.03
Dictionaries. See Dictionaries, Polyglot; Encyclopedias and dictionaries; and names of languages and subjects with the subdivision Dictionaries, e.g. English language—Dictionaries; Geology—Dictionaries
Dictionaries, Polyglot 413
Dictionary of abbreviations. Paxton, J. ed. 413
Dictionary of acronyms & abbreviations, Second. Pugh, E. 603
Dictionary of contemporary music. Vinton, J. ed. 780.3
Dictionary of fictional characters. Freeman, W. 820.3
The dictionary of foreign terms in the English language. Carroll, D. 422.03
A dictionary of geology. Challinor, J. 551.03
A dictionary of modern critical terms. Fowler, R. ed. 803
Dictionary of music, Everyman's. Blom, E. comp. 780.3
Dictionary of new English since 1963, The Barnhart 423
A dictionary of non-Christian religions. Parrinder, G. 291.03
A dictionary of politics. Laqueur, W. 909.82
Dictionary of scientific biography v9-10 920.03
Dictionary of the Christian Church, The Oxford 203
Dictionary of twentieth-century art, Phaidon 709.04
A dictionary of zoology. Leftwich, A. W. 591.03
Didion, Joan. See pages
  In Kazin, A. Bright book of life: American novelists and storytellers from Hemingway to Mailer p189-98 813.09
Diebold, John, ed. The world of the computer 001.6
Diener family. See pages
  In Thompson, T. Richie 301.43
Diet. See pages
  In The Good Housekeeping cookbook p669-90 641.5
  See also Cookery; School children—Food; Weight control
Dietetics. See Diet
Dietz, Howard. See pages
  In Green, S. The world of musical comedy p203-17 780.92
Dietz, Marjorie J. ed. 10,000 garden questions answered by 20 experts 635
A different woman. Howard, J. 301.41
Di Gaspari, Vincent M. jt. auth. See Proia, N. C. Barron's Handbook of American college financial aid 378.3
Digging up the past. Woolley, Sir L. 913
Di Giovanni, Norman Thomas, ed. Borges on writing 868
Dillard, Annie. Pilgrim at Tinker Creek 500.9
Dinosaurs. See pages
  In Life before man p62-97 560
  In Minton, S. A. Giant reptiles p3-13 598.1
Diolé, Philippe, jt. auth. See Cousteau, J. Y. Octopus and squid 594
Direct taxation. See Income tax
Directories. See classes of institutions with the subdivision Directories, e.g. Museums—Directories
A Directory of American poets 811.025
Directory of special libraries and information centers 026.025
InInIn *IIn*
Directory of the theater, The New York Times 792.01
Disaster: major American catastrophes. Hoehling, A. A. 904
Disasters 904
Discipline of children. See Children—Management
Discography. See Literature—Discography; Music—Discography
Discrimination. See Civil rights; Sex discrimination
Discrimination in education. See pages
  In DeCrow, K. Sexist justice p290-302 346.1
—Laws and regulations. See pages
  In Ross, S. C. The rights of women p116-47 346
Discrimination in employment. See pages
  In Ross, D. K. A public citizen's action manual p123-44 640.73
  In Rubin, D. The rights of teachers p122-40 344.7
—Laws and regulations. See pages
  In Ross, S. C. The rights of women p31-115, 291-341 346

Diseases. See pages
  In Marks, G. The story of medicine in America p246-61 610.9
Disney, Walt. See pages
  In Finch, C. The art of Walt Disney 791.43
Disney (Walt) Productions. See pages
  In Finch, C. The art of Walt Disney 791.43
Disraeli, Mary Anne. See Beaconsfield, Mary Anne (Evans) Disraeli, Viscountess
Distinguished company. Gielgud, Sir J. 920
Distribution of wealth. See Economics
District of Columbia. Richards, S.
  In Hatch, J. V. ed. Black theater, U.S.A. p432-36 812.08
Dittmer, Dorothy S. jt. ed. See Altman, P. L. ed. Biology data book 574.02
Dividends. See Stocks
Divination 133.3
Divine comedy. Dodson, O.
  In Hatch, J. V. ed. Black theater, U.S.A. p320-49 812.08
Diving
  See also Skin diving
—Submarine. See Skin diving
Divorce 301.42
  See also Marriage
—Laws and regulations 346.1; also pages
  In The Family legal advisor p37-80 340
  In Ross, S. C. The rights of women p208-37 346
Divorce laws. See Divorce—Laws and regulations
Dixie National Baton Twirling Institute. See pages
  In Wolfe T. ed. The new journalism p161-71 810.8
Dixon, Peter L. jt. auth. See Fleishman, N. Vasectomy, sex and parenthood 613.9
Do-it-yourself housebuilding step-by-step. Neal, C. D. 690
Dockstader, Frederick J. Indian art of the Americas 709.7
Dr Doolittle (Motion picture) See pages
  In Wolfe, T. ed. The new journalism p281-91 810.8
A documentary history of the Negro people in the United States. Aptheker, H. ed. 301.45
Documents. See Government publications
Dodgson, Charles Lutwidge. See pages
  In Auden, W. H. Forewords and afterwards p283-93 809
Dodson, Owen. Divine comedy
  In Hatch, J. V. ed. Black theater, U.S.A. p320-49 812.08
Dogs 599
The dogs bark. Capote, T. 818
The dolphin. Lowell, R. 811
Domestic animals. See names of animals, e.g. Cats; Horses; Pets
Domestic appliances. See Household equipment and supplies
Domestic arts. See Home economics
Domestic relations
  See also Divorce; Parent and child
—Laws and regulations 346.1
Domestic service. See Household employees
Donations. See Gifts
Don't you want to be free. Hughes, L.
  In Hatch, J. V. ed. Black theater, U.S.A. p262-77 812.08
Dorothy and Lillian Gish. Gish, L. 92
Dos Passos, John. See pages
  In Cowley, M. A second flowering p74-89 810.9
D'Ossoli, Sarah Margaret (Fuller) See Ossoli, Sarah Margaret (Fuller) marchesa d'
Doster, William C. ed. See Barron's How to prepare for the College Level Examination Program CLEP 378.1
Dostoevskiĭ, Fedor Mikhaĭlovich. See pages
  In Hesse, H. My belief p70-92 834
  For material by this author see Dostoevsky, Fyodor
Dostoevsky, Fyodor. Crime and punishment; criticism
  In Jackson, R. L. ed. Twentieth century interpretations of Crime and punishment 891.7
Double-speak in America. Pei, M. 422
Douglas, Stephen Arnold 92
Douglas, William O. Go East, young man: the early years 92
Douglass, Frederick. See pages
  In Rodgers, J. A. Great men of color v2 p322-49 920
Dracula. Florescu, R. 92
Dracula. Prince of Wallachia. See Vlad the Impaler, Dracula, Prince of Wallachia, 1431-1476
Drama. See pages
  In The Best plays of 1973-1974 808.82
—Collections 808.82
—History and criticism—Bibliography 016.8092
—Indexes 808.82

Drapery. See pages
 In Better Homes and Gardens Sewing for your home p28-59 646.2
Dreams. See pages
 In Hall, C. S. A primer of Jungian psychology p11-23 150.19
Dreiser, Theodore. See pages
 In Mencken, H. L. The young Mencken p552-61 818
Dress. See Clothing and dress
Dreyer, Carl Theodor. See pages
 In Solomon, S. J. ed. The classic cinema p109-27 791.43
The drinking gourd. Hansberry, L.
 In Hatch, J. V. ed. Black theater, U.S.A. p713-36 812.08
Drinks. See Beverages
Drucker, Peter F. Management: tasks, responsibilities, practices 658
Drug abuse. See pages
 In Paz, O. Alternating current p78-104 864
 In Red Cross. United States. American National Red Cross. Advanced first aid and emergency care p118-33 614.8
 In Spock, B. Raising children in a difficult time p177-91 649
 See also Drugs and youth
Drug addiction. See Drug abuse
Drugs
—Abuse. See Drug abuse
—Misuse. See Drug abuse
Drugs and youth. See pages
 In Thompson, T. Richie 301.43
The dry August. Sebree, C.
 In Hatch, J. V. ed. Black theater, U.S.A. p658-70 812.08
Dry goods. See Textile industry and fabrics
Dual personality. See Personality disorders
Dublin
—Description. See pages
 In Kane, R. S. Grand tour A to Z: the capitals of Europe p157-76 914
Dubois, Eugène. See pages
 In The First men p32-49 573
Du Bois, W. E. B. The education of Black people 373
Duckles, Vincent. comp. Music reference and research materials 016.78
Dugan, James. See National Geographic Society. World beneath the sea 551.4
Dumas, Alexandre, 1762-1806. See pages
 In Rogers, J. A. Great men of color v2 p99-108 920
Dumas, Alexandre, 1802-1870. See pages
 In Rogers, J. A. Great men of color v2 p109-22 920
Dummy. Tidyman, E. 345.7
Dunbar, Paul Laurence. See pages
 In Wagner, J. Black poets of the United States p73-125 811.09
Dunbar-Nelson, Alice. Mine eyes have seen
 In Hatch, J. V. ed. Black theater, U.S.A. p173-77 812.08
Duncan, Ronald. The gift
 In Richards, S. ed. Best short plays of the world theatre, 1968-1973 p138-51 808.82
Dunn, William J. Enjoy Europe by car 914
Dunninger, Joseph. See pages
 In Christopher, M. The illustrated history of magic p388-400 793.8
Durrell, Gerald. A bevy of beasts 591.5
Durrell, Lawrence. Vega, and other poems 821
Dutch literature
—History and criticism. See pages
 In Seymour-Smith, M. Funk & Wagnalls Guide to modern world literature p363-77 809
Duyn, Mona van. See Van Duyn, Mona
Dwellings. See Houses
Dyck, J. W. Boris Pasternak 891.7
Dyes and dyeing. See pages
 In Meilach, D. Z. Contemporary batik and tie-dye 746.4
Dylan, Bob 780.92
Dyslexia 618.9
Dyson, Anne Jane, jt. comp. See Palmer, H. H. comp. European drama criticism. Supplement I-II 016.8092
Dywasuk, Colette Taube. See Raymond, K. Adoption and after 362.7

ESP. See Extrasensory perception
Early man in America. Scientific American 970.1
Earth. See pages
 In Alter, D. Pictorial astronomy p25-55 523
East and West. See pages
 In Patai, R. The Arab mind p268-306 301.29
East India Company. See pages
 In The Horizon History of the British Empire p44-55, 68-73 942
Echnaton. See Amenhetep IV, King of Egypt

Eclipses, Lunar. See pages
 In Alter, D. Pictorial astronomy p81-90 523
Eclipses, Solar. See pages
 In Alter, D. Pictorial astronomy p81-90 523
Ecology. See Desert ecology
Economic assistance. See Underdeveloped areas
Economic conditions. See pages
 In Myrdal, G. Against the stream p182-96 330
 See also names of countries, cities, etc. with subdivision Economic conditions, e.g. United States—Economic conditions
Economic development. See Economic conditions
Economic policy. See Social policy
Economics 330; also pages
 In Pound, E. Selected prose, 1909-1965 p204-355 814
—Bibliography. See pages
 In White, C. M. Sources of information in the social sciences p181-242 016.3
Economics and the public purpose. Galbraith, J. K. 338.973
Edey, Maitland, A. The missing link 573.2
Edible plants. See Plants, Edible
Edinburgh
—Description. See pages
 In Kane, R. S. Grand tour A to Z: the capitals of Europe p177-93 914
Edmonds, Randolph. Bad man
 In Hatch, J. V. ed. Black theater, U.S.A. p241-51 812.08
Educability and group differences. Jensen, A. R. 370.15
Education
 See also Illiteracy; Library education; Private schools; also names of classes of people and social and ethnic groups with the subdivision Education, e.g. Negroes—Education
—Bibliography. See pages
 In White, C. M. Sources of information in the social sciences p425-91 016.3
—Character. See Character education
—Compulsory—Laws and regulations. See pages
 In Sloan, I. J. Youth and the law p5-14 340
—Discrimination in. See Discrimination in education
—Elementary. See pages
 In Toffler, A. ed. Learning for tomorrow p181-96 370.19
 See also Montessori method of education; Nursery schools
—Encyclopedias 370.3
—Ethical. See Character education
—Experimental methods 372.1
—Higher 378; also pages
 In Moynihan, D. P. Coping p285-313 309.173
 In Toffler, A. ed. Learning for tomorrow p272-311 370.19
—Medical. See Medicine—Study and teaching
—Philosophy. See pages
 In Dewey, J. The philosophy of John Dewey v2 p421-523 191
 In Read, H. Education through art 707
—Preschool. See Nursery schools
—Primary. See Education, Elementary
—Secondary. See pages
 In Joint Commission on Mental Health of Children. Mental health: from infancy through adolescence p264-89 155.4
—Secondary—Curricula. See pages
 In Toffler, A. ed. Learning for tomorrow p197-216 370.19
—United States. See pages
 In Diebold, J. ed. The world of the computer p203-25 001.6
 In Moynihan, D. P. Coping p167-84, 285-313, 370-94 309.173
 In Pearson, J. W. The 8-day week p68-82 331.2
 In Toffler, A. ed. Learning for tomorrow 370.19
—United States—History. See pages
 In Nye, R. B. Society and culture in America, 1830-1860 p359-99 917.3
 In Perrett, G. Days of sadness, years of triumph p104-18, 368-78 973.917
—Vocational. See Vocational education
Education and state. See pages
 In Moynihan, D. P. Coping p285-313, 370-94 309.173
Education for librarianship. See Library education
The education of Black people. Du Bois, W. E. B. 373
The education of Henry Adams. Adams, H. 92
Education of women
—Laws and regulations. See pages
 In Ross, S. C. The rights of women p116-47 346
Education through art. Read, H. 707
Educational measurements. See Educational tests and measurements

Educational psychology 370.15; also pages
  In Joint Commission on Mental Health of Children. Mental health: from infancy through adolescence p128-58, 371-431 155.4
  See also Child study
Educational sociology. See pages
  In Joint Commission on Mental Health of Children. Mental health: from infancy through adolescence p398-402 155.4
Educational tests and measurements. See pages
  In Barron's How to prepare for the College Level Examination Program CLEP 378.1
Edward IV, King of England 92
Edward, H. F. W. Job hunters
  In Hatch, J. V. ed. Black theater, U.S.A. p255-61 812.08
Edwards, Margaret A. The fair garden and the swarm of beasts 027.62
Eerdmans' Handbook to the Bible 220
Effective library exhibits. Coplan, K. 021.7
Efficiency, Household. See Home economics
Egg decorating, plain & fancy. Newsome, A. J. 745.59
Egg decoration 745.59
Egypt
—Antiquities 913.32; also pages
  In Hawkins, G. S. Beyond Stonehenge p193-218 913
—History. See pages
  In The Horizon History of the British Empire p232-47 942
—Politics and government. See pages
  In Lacouture, J. Nasser 92
Eichelberger, Clayton L. comp. A guide to critical reviews of United States fiction, 1870-1910. v2 016.813
The 8-day week. Pearson, J. W. 331.2
Eighteenth century 901.93
Eiseley, Loren. The unexpected universe; criticism
  In Auden, W. H. Forewords and afterwords p464-73 809
Eisenhower, John S. D. Strictly personal 92
Eisenhower family. See pages
  In West, J. B. Upstairs at the White House p129-90 92
Eisenstein, Sergei Mikhailovich. See pages
  In Solomon, S. J. ed. The classic cinema p65-88 791.43
Elbert, George A. The indoor light gardening book 635.9
Electioneering. See Politics, Practical
Elections
  See also Presidents—United States—Election
—United States. See pages
  In Atkins, C. G. Getting elected 329
Electric appliances. See Household appliances, Electric
Electronic apparatus and appliances. See Computers
Electric engineering. See pages
  In Graf, R. F. How it works, illustrated: everyday devices and mechanisms 621
Electronic brains. See Computers
Electronic calculating machines. See Computers
Electronic computers. See Computers
Electronic data processing 001.6
—Dictionaries 001.6
—Library science. See pages
  In Katz, W. A. Introduction to reference work v2 p217-37 025.5
Electronics. See Cybernetics
Elementary education. See Education, Elementary
Elements, Chemical. See Chemical elements
Eliot, Thomas Stearns 92
Elizabeth, Empress of Russia. See pages
  In Coughlan, R. Elizabeth and Catherine; empresses of all the Russias 92
Elizabeth and Catherine; empresses of all the Russias. Coughlan, R. 92
Ellington, Duke. See Ellington, Edward Kennedy
Ellington, Edward Kennedy. Music is my mistress 780.92
Elliott, Lawrence. I will be called John: a biography of Pope John XXIII 92
Ellison, Ralph. Invisible man; criticism
  In Hersey, J. ed. Ralph Ellison 813.09
Ellison, Ralph (as subject) See pages
  In Hersey, J. ed. Ralph Ellison 813.09
  In Kazin, A. Bright book of life: American novelists and storytellers from Hemingway to Mailer p243-55 813.09
Elonka, Stephen Michael. Standard refrigeration and air conditioning questions and answers 621.5
Embroidery 746.4
Embroidery book, Erica Wilson's. Wilson, E. 746.4
Emergencies. See First aid

Emlyn. See Owen, A Male of the species: Emlyn
Emotions. See pages
  In Skinner, B. F. About behaviorism p148-66 150.19
Empiricism. See pages
  In Dewey, J. The philosophy of John Dewey v 1 p160-207, 240-354, v2 p494-598 191
Employment discrimination. See Discrimination in employment
Employment of women. See Woman—Employment
Enamel paints. See Varnish and varnishing
Encyclopaedia Britannica 031
Encyclopedia of American art. The Britannica 709.73
Encyclopedia of banking and finance. Glenn G. Munn's. Munn, G. G. 332.03
The Encyclopedia of education 370.3
Encyclopedia of games, Scarne's. Scarne, J. 795
Encyclopedia of golf. Evans, W. comp. 796.352
Encyclopedia of golf. Golf Magazine's 796.352
Encyclopedia of the American Revolution. Boatner, M. M. 973.303
The encyclopedia of the horse. Hope, C. E. G. ed. 636.103
Encyclopedia of 20th century men's fashions. Esquire's Schoeffler, O. E. 391
Encyclopedia of world biography. The McGraw-Hill 920.03
Encyclopedias and dictionaries 031
  See also names of languages and subjects with the subdivision Dictionaries for works with definitions of words, e.g. English language—Dictionaries; Geology—Dictionaries; and subjects with the subdivision Encyclopedias for facts presented in condensed form, e.g. Sports—Encyclopedias
—Bibliography. See pages
  In Katz, W. A. Introduction to reference work v 1 p89-148, 249-86 025.5
The end of philosophy. Heidegger, M. 110
Endangered species. See Rare animals
Endowments. See Charities
Energy. See Force and energy
Energy crisis in America 333.8
Engineering
  See also Electric engineering
—History. See pages
  In The Horizon History of the British Empire p359-73 942
Engines. See Automobiles—Engines; Marine engines
The English. Priestley, J. B. 914.2
English composition. See English language—English composition
English drama
—Bibliography. See pages
  In Nicoll, A. English drama, 1900-1930 822.09
—History and criticism 822.09
English drama, 1900-1930. Nicoll, A. 822.09
English language 420
—Americanisms. See Americanisms
—Business English. See pages
  In Whalen, D. H. The secretary's handbook 651.02
—Composition and exercises 808
—Dialects. See pages
  In Laird, C. You and your language p120-35 420
  See also Americanisms
—Dictionaries 423; also pages
  In Moss, N. What's the difference? 427
—Etymology 422; also pages
  In Laird, C. You and your language p70-80 420
—Foreign words and phrases—Dictionaries 422.03
—Phrases and terms. See English language—Terms and phrases
—Slang. See pages
  In Laird, C. You and your language p109-19 420
—Terms and phrases 427; also pages
  In Pei, M. Double-speak in America 422
  See also English language—Dictionaries
English literature
—Anecdotes, facetiae, satire, etc. 817
—Bibliography 016.82
—Collections 820.8
—Dictionaries 820.3
—History and criticism. See pages
  In Seymour-Smith, M. Funk & Wagnalls Guide to modern world literature p191-223 809
English poetry 821
—Collections 821.08
—Indexes 821.08
Engravings by Hogarth. Hogarth, W. 769
Enjoy Europe by car. Duhn, W. J. 914
Ennis, Bruce. The rights of mental patients 346

AUTHOR, TITLE, SUBJECT, AND ANALYTICAL INDEX
1974 SUPPLEMENT

Enoch Pratt Free Library, Baltimore. See Coplan, K. Effective library exhibits 021.7
Entertainers. See Actors and actresses
Entertaining. See pages
  In The Good Housekeeping cookbook p735-54 641.5
  In Habeeb, V. T. The Ladies' Home Journal Art of homemaking p371-88 640
Entomology. See Insects
Environment and state. See Environmental policy
Environmental policy. See pages
  In Myrdal, G. Against the stream p197-233 330
  See also Conservation of natural resources
Environmental pollution. See Pollution
Epidemics. See names of contagious diseases, e.g. Smallpox
Episode in the life of an author. Anouilh, J.
  In Richards, S. ed. Best short plays of the world theatre, 1968-1973 p113-25 808.82
Epistemology. See Knowledge, Theory of
Equality. See pages
  In Padover, S. K. ed. Sources of democracy p55-78 321.8
Equestrian. See Horsemanship
Erdkinder. Montessori, M.
  In Montessori, M. From childhood to adolescence 371.3
Erikson, Erik H. Young man Luther; criticism
  In Auden, W. H. Forewords and afterwords p79-87 809
Ernst, Carl H. Turtles of the United States 598.1
Erosion. See pages
  In Leonard, J. N. Atlantic beaches p30-41 500.9
Eruptions. See Geysers; Volcanoes
Ervin, Samuel James 92
The escape. Brown, W. W.
  In Hatch, J. V. ed. Black theater, U.S.A. p34-58 812.08
Escape from childhood. Holt, J. 301.43
Eshleman, Ruthie. ed. See The American Heart Association cookbook 641.5
Eskimo poetry. See pages
  In Rukeyser, M. Breaking open p87-102 811
Eskimos. See pages
  In Alaska p174-205 917.98
  In Severin, T. The Horizon Book of vanishing primitive man p197-23 301.2
Espionage, American. See pages
  In Marchetti, V. The CIA and the cult of intelligence p183-240 353.007
Esquimaux. See Eskimos
Esquire's Encyclopedia of 20th century men's fashions. Schoeffler, O. E. 391
Essences and essential oils. See Perfumes
Estate tax. See Inheritance and transfer tax
Esthetics. See pages
  In Dewey, J. The philosophy of John Dewey v 1 p300-25, v2 p525-73 191
Esty, John C. Choosing a private school 371
The eternal bliss machine. Seligson, M. 392
Ethical education. See Character education
Ethics
  See also Cruelty; Sin
—Sexual. See Sexual ethics
—Social. See Social ethics
Ethnology
  See also Man, Primitive; Race; Society, Primitive; also names of races, tribes, and peoples, e.g. Negroes; and names of countries with the subdivision Social life and customs, e.g. United States—Social life and customs
—Japan. See Ainu
—Melanasia. See Melanesians
Etymology. See English language—Etymology
Eurail. See Baxter, R. Baxter's Eurailpass travel guide 914
Eurailpass travel guide, Baxter's. Baxter, R. 914
Europe
—Description and travel 914
—Hotels, motels, etc. See Hotels, motels, etc.—Europe
—Politics. See pages
  In Kissinger, H. A. American foreign policy p163-77, 269-82 327.73
Europe on a budget, Fodor's 914
European drama criticism. Supplement I-II. Palmer, H. H. comp. 016.8092
European music. See Music, European
Euthanasia 174
Evans, Charles M. The terrarium book 635.9
Evans, David Allan. ed. New voices in American poetry 811.08
Evans, Travers Moncure. The meat book 641.3
Evans, Webster, comp. Encyclopedia of golf 796.352

Everglades. See pages
  In Carr, A. The Everglades 500.9
Everyman. Everyman
  In The Oxford Anthology of English literature v 1 p388-411 820.8
Everyman's Dictionary of abbreviations. See Paxton, J. ed. Dictionary of abbreviations 413
Everyman's Dictionary of music. Blom, E. comp. 780.3
Everything a woman needs to know to get paid what she's worth. Bird, C. 331.4
Evil spirits. See Demonology
Evolution 573.2; also pages
  In Dewey, J. The philosophy of John Dewey v 1 p31-41 191
  In Life before man 560
  In Severin, T. The Horizon Book of vanishing primitive man p11-28 301.2
  See also Man—Origin and antiquity; Social change
Ewards, I. E. S. The treasures of Tutankhamun 913.32
Ewen, David. Orchestral music 785
Examinations. See Colleges and universities—Entrance requirements
Excavations (Archaeology) 913
Exceptional children. See pages
  In Stewart, M. A. Raising a hyperactive child 618.9
  In Wender, P. H. The hyperactive child 618.9
Executive order 9066: the internment of 110,000 Japanese Americans. Conrat, M. 973.7
Executive power
—United States 353.03; also pages
  In Wolff, R. P. ed. 1984 revisited p75-88 973
Executive privilege. Berger, R. 353.03
Experience. See Empiricism
Experimental methods in education. See Education—Experimental methods
Extinct animals. See Rare animals
Extrasensory perception. See pages
  In Tompkins, P. The secret life of plants p3-45 581
Extremism (Political science) See Right and left (Political science)
Eye. See pages
  In Cousteau, J. Window in the sea p110-27 574.92

Fabre, Michel. The unfinished quest of Richard Wright 92
Fabrics. See Textile industry and fabrics
Facts about the Presidents. Kane, J. N. 920
Facts of life for children. See Child Study Association of America. What to tell your child about sex 612.6
Fair employment practice. See Discrimination in employment
The fair garden and the swarm of beasts. Edwards, M. A. 027.62
Fairy tales. See pages
  In Auden, W. H. Forewords and afterwords p198-208 809
Faith. See pages
  In Hesse, H. My belief p189-201 834
The fall of America. Ginsberg, A. 811
Falling stars. See Meteors
Family. See pages
  In Joint Commission on Mental Health of Children. Mental health: from infancy through adolescence p54-63 155.4
  See also Divorce; Family life education; Parent and child
The Family Handyman Home improvement book 643
The Family legal advisor 340
Family life education. See pages
  In Landis, J. T. Building a successful marriage 301.42
  In United States. Department of Agriculture. Handbook for the home p 1-90 640
  See also Sex instruction
Family planning. See Birth control
Fantastic fiction
—History and criticism. See pages
  In Bretnor, R. ed. Science fiction, today and tomorrow p217-33 809.3
The fantasticks. Jones, T.
  In Jones, T. The fantasticks [and] Celebration p 1-95 812
The fantasticks [and] Celebration. Jones, T. 812
Farb, Peter. Word play 401
Farm buildings 728
Farm life
—United States. See pages
  In National Geographic Society. Life in rural America 917.3

Farm management. See pages
  In Logsdon, G. Homesteading 630.2
Farms. See Farm management
The fashion dictionary. Picken, M. B. 391.03
Fatigue
—Mental. See Boredom
Faulkner, William 92; also pages
  In Cowley, M. A second flowering p130-55 810.9
  In Kazin, A. Bright book of life: American novelists and storytellers from Hemingway to Mailer p21-37 813.09
Faust, Joan Lee. The New York Times Book of house plants 635.9
—ed. The New York Times Garden book 635
Favorite songs of the nineties. Fremont, R. A. ed. 784
The fearful void. Moorhouse, G. 916.6
Federal aid to libraries. See pages
  In The Metropolitan library p73-88 027.4
Feeling. See Perception
Feelings. See Emotions
Feininger, Andreas. Darkroom techniques 770
—Principles of composition in photography 770.1
Fellini, Federico. See pages
  In Solomon, S. J. ed. The classic cinema p317-38 791.43
Fellini Satyricon (Motion picture) See pages
  In Solomon, S. J. ed. The classic cinema p317-38 791.43
The feminine mystique. Friedan, B. 301.41
Feminine psychology. See Women—Psychology
Feminism. See Woman—Social conditions
The feminist papers: from Adams to de Beauvoir. Rossi, A. S. ed. 301.41
Fennimore, Keith J. Booth Tarkington 813.09
Ferdinand, Val. Blk love song #1
  In Hatch, J. V. ed. Black theater, U.S.A. p864-74 812.08
Ferlinghetti, Lawrence. Open eye, open heart 811
Fest, Joachim C. Hitler 92
Fiction
  See also American fiction; Fantastic fiction
—American. See American fiction
—Technique 808.3; also pages
  In Bretnor, R. ed. Science fiction, today and tomorrow p295-306 809.3
  In Meredith, S. Writing to sell 808
Fictional characters, Dictionary of. Freeman, W. 820.3
Fiedler, Leslie Aaron. See pages
  In Malin, I. ed. Contemporary American-Jewish literature p134-45 810.9
Field hospitals. See Medicine, Military
Fielding's Guide to traveling with children in Europe. Hadley, L. 914
Fields, W. C. W. C. Fields by himself 92
The fifth year of the Nixon watch. Osborne, J. 973.924
50 modern American & British poets, 1920-1970. Untermeyer, L. ed. 821.08
The filmgoer's companion. Halliwell, L. 791.4303
Finance
  See also Inflation (Finance)
—Encyclopedias 332.03
—Personal. See pages
  In Landis, J. T. Building a successful marriage p322-45 301.42
  See also Insurance; Investments
Finch, Christopher. The art of Walt Disney 791.43
Findhorn Foundation. See pages
  In Tompkins, P. The secret life of plants p361-71 581
Fine arts. See The arts
Finishes and finishing. See Lacquer and lacquering; Varnish and varnishing; Wood finishing
Fire. See pages
  In Asimov, I. Today and tomorrow and . . . p85-96 508
Fire Island, N.Y. See pages
  In Leonard, J. N. Atlantic beaches p58-67 500.9
The fire we can light. Marty, M. E. 277.3
Firearms
—Encyclopedias 683
—Laws and regulations 363.3
Firearms encyclopedia. Nonte, G. C. 683
Firearms industry and trade. See pages
  In Sherrill, R. The Saturday night special 363.3
First aid 614.8; also pages
  In Bridge, A. America's backpacking book p279-95 796.5
The first five years. Pomeranz, V. E. 649
The First men 573
First special report to the U.S. Congress on alcohol & health. See United States. Department of Health, Education and Welfare. Alcohol and health 613.8

Fischer, Robert
  In Horowitz, A. The world chess championship p219-84 794.1
  In Roberts, R. Fischer/Spassky: The New York Times Report on the chess match of the century 794.1
Fischer/Spassky: The New York Times Report on the chess match of the century. Roberts, R. 794.1
Fischler, Stan, jt. auth. See Beddoes, R. Hockey 796.9
Fish. See Fishes
Fishes 597; also pages
  In Villiard, P. Raising small animals for fun and profit p82-94 636.08
  See also Fishing
—United States. See pages
  In Clement, R. C. Hammond Nature atlas of America p194-219 500.9
Fishing 799.1
  See also Flies, Artificial
Fishing-flies. See Flies, Artificial
Fisk University. See pages
  In Du Bois, W. E. B. The education of Black people p41-60 378
Fitzgerald, Ella. See pages
  In Pleasants, H. The great American popular singers p168-80 780.92
Fitzgerald, Francis Scott Key. See pages
  In Cowley, M. A second flowering p19-47 810.9
Fix-it home repairs handbook, Mechanix Illustrated 643
Flayderman, Norman. Collecting tomorrow's antiques today 745.1
Fleishman, Norman. Vasectomy, sex and parenthood 613.9
Flesch, Rudolf. The art of readable writing 808
Fletcher, Colin. The new complete walker 796.5
Flies
—Artificial 799.1
The flight of the natives. Richardson, W.
  In Hatch, J. V. ed. Black theater, U.S.A. p382-89 812.08
Flight to the moon. See Space flight to the moon
Floors. See pages
  In Habeeb, V. T. The Ladies' Home Journal Art of homemaking p167-78 640
Flora. See Plants
Florescu, Radu. Dracula 92
Florida
—Natural history. See Natural history—Florida
Flower gardening. See House plants; Plants, Ornamental
The flowering of American folk art, 1776-1876. Lipman, J. 745
Flowers, Wild. See Wild flowers
Fly Blackbird. Jackson, C. B.
  In Hatch, J. V. ed. Black theater, U.S.A. p671-94 812.08
Fly-casting 799.1
Flying saucers 001.9
Fodor, Eugene, ed. See Fodor's Europe on a budget 914
Fodor's Europe on a budget 914
Folk and traditional music of the western continents. Nettl, B. 781.7
Folk art
  See also Art, Primitive
—American 745
Folk music. See Folk songs
Folk songs
—American. See Folk songs—United States
—History and criticism 781.7
—United States. See pages
  In Coffin, T. P. ed. Folklore from the working folk of America p50-111 398
Folklore
—United States 398
Folklore from the working folk of America. Coffin, T. P. ed. 398
Fontana, Vincent J. Somewhere a child is crying 362.7
Food 641.3; also pages
  In Kinkade, K. A Walden Two experiment p82-91 335
  See also Meat
—Canned. See Canning and preserving
—Frozen. See pages
  In The Good Housekeeping cookbook p703-18 641.5
—Preservation. See pages
  In The Good Housekeeping cookbook p691-726 641.5
  In Habeeb, V. T. The Ladies' Home Journal Art of homemaking p357-70 640
Food for school children. See School children —Food
Food plants. See Plants, Edible
Food preservation. See Food—Preservation

AUTHOR, TITLE, SUBJECT, AND ANALYTICAL INDEX
1974 SUPPLEMENT

Food supply. See Food—Preservation
Football. See pages
  In Wolfe, T. ed. The new journalism p240-58 810.8
For Lizzie and Harriet. Lowell, R. 811
For unborn children. Livingston, M. S.
  In Hatch, J. V. ed. Black theater, U.S.A. p184-87 812.08
Forbis, William H. See The Cowboys 978
Force and energy. See pages
  In Asimov, I. Today and tomorrow and . . . p129-40 508
Ford, Gerald R. President U.S. 92
Ford, Stephen. The acquisition of library materials 025.2
Foreign language phrases. See English language—Foreign words and phrases
Foreign policy. See names of countries with the subdivision Foreign relations, e.g. United States—Foreign relations
Foreign relations. See International relations; also names of countries with the subdivision Foreign relations, e.g. United States—Foreign relations
Forem, Jack. Transcendental meditation 181
Forensic medicine. See Medical jurisprudence
Forest reserves. See Wilderness areas
Forests and forestry. See pages
  In Knauth, P. The north woods 500.9
  See also Trees
Forewords and afterwords. Auden, W. H. 809
Fossils 560; also pages
  In Edey, M. A. The missing link p32-53 573.2
Foster home care. See Adoption
Four-day work week. See Hours of labor
The fourth year of the Nixon watch. Osborne, J. 973.924
Fowler, Roger, ed. A dictionary of modern critical terms 803
Fox, Michael W. Understanding your cat 636.8
Fraenkel, Heinrich, jt. auth. See Manvell, R. Hess: a biography 92
Fraenkel, Osmond K. The rights we have 344
France. See pages
  In National Geographic Society. The Alps p60-87 914.94
Franchise. See Suffrage
Frankenstein, Mary Shelley's. Small, C. 823.09
Franklin, Aretha. See pages
  In Pleasants, H. The great American popular singers p321-32 780.92
Franklin, John Hope. From slavery to freedom 301.45
Fraser, Antonia. Cromwell, the Lord Protector 92
Free press. See Freedom of the press
Free speech. See pages
  In Padover, S. K. ed. Sources of democracy p107-40 321.8
  In Rubin, D. The rights of teachers p48-68 344.7
  See also Libel and slander
Free thought. See Religious liberty
Free will and determinism. See pages
  In Carpenter, F. The Skinner primer: behind freedom and dignity 150.19
Freedom. See Liberty
Freedom of choice. See Free will and determinism
Freedom of conscience. See Religious liberty
Freedom of information 323.44
  See also Freedom of the press
Freedom of religion. See Religious liberty
Freedom of speech. See Free speech
Freedom of teaching. See Academic freedom
Freedom of the press. See pages
  In Padover, S. K. ed. Sources of democracy p107-40 321.8
Freedom of worship. See Religious liberty
Freeman, Larry. See Burton, J. The blue book of Broadway musicals 782.8
Freeman, William. Dictionary of fictional characters 820.3
Freezers. See Refrigeration and refrigerating machinery
Freezing. See Refrigeration and refrigerating machinery
Freidel, Frank. Franklin D. Roosevelt 92
—ed. Harvard Guide to American history 973
—Our country's Presidents 920
Fremont, Robert A. ed. Favorite songs of the nineties 784
French literature
—History and criticism. See pages
  In Seymour-Smith, M. Funk & Wagnalls Guide to modern world literature p399-419, 426-518 809
French poetry 841
Freud, Sigmund. See pages
  In Fromm, E. The anatomy of human destructiveness p439-78 152.4

Fried, Henry B. The watch repairer's manual 681
Friedan, Betty. The feminine mystique 301.41
Friedman, Bruce Jay. See pages
  In Schulz, M. F. Black humor fiction of the sixties p105-19 813.09
Friedman, Myra. Buried alive: the biography of Janis Joplin 92
Friml, Rudolf. See pages
  In Green, S. The world of musical comedy p37-47 780.92
From childhood to adolescence. Montessori, M. 371.3
From slavery to freedom. Franklin, J. H. 301.45
Fromm, Erich. The anatomy of human destructiveness 152.4
Frontier and pioneer life
  See also Cowboys
—The West. See pages
  In The Soldiers 970.5
Frost, Robert. Robert Frost on writing 811.09
Frost, Robert (as subject) 92; also pages
  In Barry, E. Robert Frost 811.09
Frozen food. See Food, Frozen; Ice cream, ices, etc.
Fruit
  See also Fruit culture
—Canning. See Canning and preserving
Fruit culture. See pages
  In Crockett, J. U. Vegetables and fruits 635
Fuller, Margaret. See Ossoli, Sarah Margaret (Fuller) marchesa d'
Fuller, R. Buckminster. Buckminster Fuller to children of earth 818
—Utopia or oblivion: the prospects for humanity 901.94
The function of the university. Montessori, M.
  In Montessori, M. From childhood to adolescence 371.3
Fund raising 361.7
Funk & Wagnalls Guide to modern world literature. Seymour-Smith, M. 809
Fur trade. See pages
  In The Great Northwest p143-51 917.95
Furniture
—Repairing 684.1

G.I.'s. See Soldiers—United States
Gable, Clark 92
Gable and Lombard. Harris, W. G. 92
Gaines-Shelton, Ruth. The church fight
  In Hatch, J. V. ed. Black theater, U.S.A. p188-91 812.08
Galaxies. See pages
  In Alter, D. Pictorial astronomy p159-253 523
  In Asimov, I. Asimov on astronomy p176-91, 205-31 523
Galbraith, John Kenneth. A China passage 915.1
—Economics and the public purpose 338.973
Gale, William, jt. auth. See Schoeffler, O. E. Esquire's Encyclopedia of 20th century men's fashions 391
Galilei, Galileo. See pages
  In Du Bois, W. E. B. The education of Black people p17-30 378
Gallico, Paul. Honorable cat 636.8
Gambling 795
Game protection. See Birds—Protection
Games 795; also pages
  In Coffin, T. P. ed. Folklore from the working folk of America p296-327 398
  See also Backgammon; Cards
Gandhi, Mohandas Karamchand. See pages
  In Myrdal, G. Against the stream p234-44 330
Garage sale. How to hold a. Ullman, J. M. 658.8
Garage sale, Kesey's. Kesey, K. 818
Garcia, F. L. See Munn, G. G. Glenn G. Munn's Encyclopedia of banking and finance 332.03
Garden book, The New York Times. Faust, J. L. ed. 635
Gardening 635
  See also Fruit culture; Greenhouses; Vegetable gardening
—Lighting 635.9
Gardens, Miniature 635.9
Gargal, Berry, jt. ed. See Katz, B. ed. Magazines for libraries: supplement 016.05
Garland, Judy. See pages
  In Pleasants, H. The great American popular singers p279-90 780.92
Garvey, Marcus. See pages
  In Rogers, J. A. Great men of color v2 p415-31 920
Gas and oil engines
  See also Automobiles—Engines
—Repairing 621.43
Gaspari, Vincent M. di. See Di Gaspari, Vincent M.

Gates, Jean Key. Guide to the use of books and libraries 028.7
Gather together in my name. Angelou, M. 92
Gathorne-Hardy, Jonathan. The unnatural history of the nanny 914.2
Gay, John. The beggar's opera
  In The Oxford Anthology of English literature v 1 p1963-2010 820.8
Gay liberation. *See* Homosexuality
Gelb, Arthur. O'Neill 92
Gelb, Barbara, jt. auth. *See* Gelb, A. O'Neill 92
Gemini project. *See* pages
  In Aldrin, E. E. Return to earth p155-87 92
Generation. *See* Reproduction
Genné, William H. jt. auth. *See* Brill, M. L. Write your own wedding 265
Geographical atlases. *See* Atlases
Geographical distribution of animals and plants. *See* Desert animals; Marine animals
Geography
  See also Atlases
  —Biblical. *See* Bible—Geography
  —Bibliography. *See* pages
  In White, C. M. Sources of information in the social sciences p139-80 016.3
  —Periodicals—Indexes 910.1
Giant reptiles. Minton, S. A. 598.1
The geography of the Bible. Baly, D. 220.9
Geology
  See also Geysers
  —Dictionaries 551.03
  —Stratigraphic. *See* Fossils
George IV, King of Great Britain 92
George IV: Prince of Wales, 1762-1811. Hibbert, C. 92
George M. Cohan: the man who owned Broadway. McCabe, J. 92
Géricault, Théodore. *See* pages
  In Clark, K. The romantic rebellion p177-97 759.05
Gerlach, Rex. Creative fly tying and fly fishing 799.1
German essays 834
German literature
  —History and criticism. *See* pages
  In Seymour-Smith, M. Funk & Wagnalls Guide to modern world literature p535-79 809
Germany
  —History—1866-1918—Pictorial works 943.08
  —History—1918-1933—Pictorial works. *See* pages
  In Lorant, S. Sieg Heil! 943.08
  —History—1933-1945—Pictorial works. *See* pages
  In Lorant, S. Sieg Heil! 943.08
  —Politics and government—1933-1945. *See* pages
  In Boldt, G. Hitler: the last ten days 940.54
  In Fest, J. C. Hitler 92
Germs. *See* Microorganisms
Gerontology. *See* Aged; Old age
Gershwin, George 780.92; also pages
  In Green, S. The world of musical comedy p109-27 780.92
Gershwin, Ira. *See* pages
  In Jablonski, E. The Gershwin years 780.92
The Gershwin years. Jablonski, E. 780.92
Gesell, Arnold. Infant and child in the culture of today 155.4
Getting elected. Atkins, C. G. 329
Gibbon, Edward 92
Gibbons, Euell. Stalking the faraway places 581.6
Gibson, Donald B. ed. Modern Black poets 811.09
Gibson, Litzka R. jt. auth. *See* Gibson, W. B. The complete illustrated book of divination and prophecy 133.3
Gibson, Walter B. The complete illustrated book of divination and prophecy 133.3
  —Hoyle's Modern encyclopedia of card games 795.4
Gielgud, Sir John. Distinguished company 920
The gift. Duncan, R.
  In Richards, S. ed. Best short plays of the world theatre, 1968-1973 p138-51 808.82
Gifts. *See* pages
  In Myers, N. Gifts from the kitchen 641.5
  —Laws and regulations. *See* pages
  In The Family legal advisor p203-14 340
Gifts from the kitchen. Myers, N. 641.5
Gillispie, Charles Coulston, ed. *See* Dictionary of scientific biography v9-10 920.03
Gilman, Charlotte (Perkins) Stetson. *See* pages
  In Rossi, A. S. ed. The feminist papers: from Adams to de Beauvoir p566-72 301.41
Gilroy, Frank D. Present tense
  In The Best short plays, 1974 p193-213 808.82
Ginder, Geri, jt. auth. *See* Blevin, M. The low blood sugar cookbook 641.5
Ginsberg, Allen. The fall of America 811
Ginsbury, Norman. The safety match
  In Richards, S. ed. Best short plays of the world theatre, 1968-1973 p241-53 808.82

Giovanni, Nikki. My house 811
—jt. auth. *See* Baldwin, J. A dialogue 301.45
Giovanni, Norman Thomas di. *See* Di Giovanni, Norman Thomas
Girls. *See* Youth
Gish, Dorothy. *See* pages
  In Gish, L. Dorothy and Lillian Gish 92
Gish, Lillian. Dorothy and Lillian Gish 92
Gitler, Ira, jt. auth. *See* Beddoes, R. Hockey 796.9
Give! Katz, H. 361.7
Glacier National Park. *See* pages
  In Walker, B. S. The Great Divide p158-79 500.9
Gladness. *See* Happiness
Glands, Ductless. *See* Hormones
Glass gardens. *See* Terrariums
Glazes 738.1
Gleeson, James C. tr. *See* Ave Ogden! Nash in Latin. Nash, O. 811
Glenn, Harold T. jt. auth. *See* Coles, C. W. Glenn's Complete bicycle manual: selection, maintenance, repair 629.28
Glenn Miller and his orchestra. Simon, G. T. 780.92
Glenn's Complete bicycle manual: selection, maintenance, repair. Coles, C. W. 629.28
Glossaries. *See* names of languages with the subdivision Dictionaries, e.g. English language
  —Dictionaries
Gnomes & occasions. Nemerov, H. 811
Gettysburg, Battle of, 1863 973.7
Gettysburg: the final fury. Catton, B. 973.7
Geysers. *See* pages
  In Walker, B. S. The Great Divide p148-57 500.9
Giant pandas. *See* Pandas
Go East, young man: the early years. Douglas, W. O. 92
Godwin, Mary (Wollstonecraft) *See* pages
  In Rossi, A. S. ed. The feminist papers: from Adams to de Beauvoir p25-40 301.41
Goethe, Johann Wolfgang von. Italian journey, 1786-1788: criticism
  In Auden, W. H. Forewords and afterwords p131-43 809
Goethe, Johann Wolfgang von (as subject) *See* pages
  In Tompkins, P. The secret life of plants p109-19 581
Gogol', Nikolai Vasil'evich. *See* pages
  In Lindstrom, T. S. Nikolay Gogol 891.7
Goin' a Buffalo. Bullins, E.
  In Hatch, J. V. ed. Black theater, U.S.A. p826-53 812.08
Going like sixty. Armour, R. 817
The gold of the gods. Däniken, E. von 001.9
Gold mines and mining. *See* Prospecting
The gold rush (Motion picture) *See* pages
  In Solomon, S. J. ed. The classic cinema p89-107 791.43
Goldbeck, David, jt. auth. *See* Goldbeck, N. The supermarket handbook 641.3
Goldbeck, Nikki. The supermarket handbook 641.3
Golden, Harry. Travels through Jewish America 301.45
Goldhurst, Richard. *See* Golden, H. Travels through Jewish America 301.45
Goidin, Horace. *See* pages
  In Christopher, M. The illustrated history of magic p293-318 793.8
Goldman, Peter. The death and life of Malcolm X 92
Golf 796.352
  —Encyclopedias 796.352
Golf Magazine's Encyclopedia of golf 796.352
Golf my way. Nicklaus, J. 796.352
The good fight. Chisholm, S. 329
The Good Housekeeping Book of cake decorating. *See* Good Housekeeping Complete book of cake decorating 641.8
Good Housekeeping Complete book of cake decorating 641.8
The Good Housekeeping cookbook 641.5
Good morning. Van Doren, M. 811
Goodell, Donald. The American bottle collector's price guide to historical flasks, pontils, bitters, mineral waters, inks & sodas 748
Goodman, Paul. Collected poems 811
Goodrum, Charles A. The Library of Congress 027.5
Goren, Chas. H. Goren's Modern backgammon complete 795
Goudge, Elizabeth. The joy of the snow 92
Gourlay, Logan, ed. Olivier 92
Gourmont, Rémy de. *See* pages
  In Pound, E. Selected prose, 1909-1965 p413-23 814
Governesses. *See* Household employees
Government. *See* Political science
Government, Resistance to. *See* Revolutions
Government and the press. *See* pages
  In Moynihan, D. P. Coping p314-33 309.173
  In White, T. H. The making of the President, 1972 p245-68 329

AUTHOR, TITLE, SUBJECT, AND ANALYTICAL INDEX
1974 SUPPLEMENT

Government publications
  See also United States—Government publications
—Bibliography. See pages
  In Katz, W. A. Introduction to reference work v 1 p317-42 025.5
Government reference books. Subject guide to. Wynkoop, S. comp. 015.73
Goya y Lucientes, Francisco Jose de. See pages
  In Clark, K. The romantic rebellion p69-95 759.05
Graf, Rudolf F. How it works, illustrated: everyday devices and mechanisms 621
Graham, Martha. The notebooks of Martha Graham 92
Grand tour A to Z: the capitals of Europe. Kane, R. S. 914
Grant, Ulysses Simpson, President U.S. See pages
  In Havighurst, W. The heartland: Ohio, Indiana, Illinois p219-32 977
Graphology 137
Graven images. Miller, M.
  In Hatch, J. V. ed. Black theater, U.S.A. p353-59 812.08
Graves, Robert. Poems, 1970-1972 821
Gray, Albert W. See The Family legal advisor 340
Gray, Michael. Song & dance man 780.92
Gray, Ronald. Franz Kafka 833.09
The great American popular singers. Pleasants, H. 780.92
Great Britain
—Biography. See pages
  In Priestley, J. B. The English 914.2
—Colonies—History. See pages
  In The Horizon History of the British Empire 942
—Commerce—History. See pages
  In The Horizon History of the British Empire p35-55, 64-87 942
—Description and travel 914.2
—History 942
—History—Wars of the Roses, 1455-1485. See pages
  In Clive, M. This sun of York; a biography of Edward IV 92
—History—Stuarts, 1603-1714—Sources. See pages
  In Pepys, S. The diary of Samuel Pepys v8 92
—History—Civil War and Commonwealth, 1642-1660. See pages
  In Fraser, A. Cromwell, the Lord Protector 92
—History, Military. See pages
  In Longford, E. Wellington 92
—National characteristics. See National characteristics, British
—Politics and government—19th century. See pages
  In Longford, E. Wellington 92
—Social conditions. See pages
  In Commager, H. S. ed. Britain through American eyes 914.2
—Social life and customs 914.2; also pages
  In Pepys, S. The diary of Samuel Pepys v8 92
The Great Divide. Walker, B. S. 500.9
Great historic places 917.3
The Great Northwest 917.95
Great songs of Broadway. The New York Times 782.8
Great Tom; notes towards the definition of T. S. Eliot. Matthews, T. S. 92
The great whales. McNulty, F. 599
Greaves, John. Who's who in Dickens 823.03
Greek literature
—History and criticism. See pages
  In Auden, W. H. Forewords and afterwords p3-32 809
—Modern—History and criticism. See pages
  In Seymour-Smith, M. Funk & Wagnalls Guide to modern world literature p681-91 809
Green, Stanley. The world of musical comedy 780.92
Green River. See pages
  In Walker, B. S. The Great Divide p60-71 500.9
The green stick. Muggeridge, M.
  In Muggeridge, M. Chronicles of wasted time v 1 92
Greenberg, David. See pages
  In Whittemore, L. H. The super cops 363.2
Greene, David, jt. auth. See Evans, T. M. The meat book 641.3
Greene, Graham. The portable Graham Greene 828
Greene, Lawrence G. See Bander, E. J. Change of name and law of names 346
Greenhouse gardening. Northen, H. T. 635.9
Greenhouses 635.9
Grene, Marjorie. Sartre 194

Griffin, Al. How to start and operate a day care home 362.7
—Motorcycles 629.22
Griffith, David Wark. See pages
  In Solomon, S. J. ed. The classic cinema p11-37 791.43
Grimké, Angelina Emily. See pages
  In Rossi, A. S. ed. The feminist papers: from Adams to de Beauvoir p282-96 301.41
Grimke, Angelina Weld. Rachel
  In Hatch, J. V. ed. Black theater, U.S.A. p137-72 812.08
Grimké, Sarah Moore. See pages
  In Rossi, A. S. ed. The feminist papers: from Adams to de Beauvoir p282-96 301.41
Grollman, Sigmund. The human body 612
Grosswirth, Marvin, jt. auth. See Rosenfeld, L. J. The truth about vasectomy 613.9
Groucho, Harpo, Chico and sometimes Zeppo. Adamson, J. 791.43
Group differences. Educability and. Jensen, A. R. 370.15
Grzimek, Bernhard. ed. Animal life encyclopedia 591.03
Guernsey, Otis L. ed. See The Best plays of 1973-1974 808.82
Guests. See Entertaining
Guide to American history. Harvard. Freidel, F. ed. 973
A guide to Anthony Trollope. Hardwick, M. 823.09
Guide to continental motoring. AA. Automobile Association 914
A guide to critical reviews of United States fiction, 1870-1910. v2. Eichelberger, C. L. comp. 016.813
A guide to Jane Austen. Hardwick, M. 823.09
Guide to modern world literature. Funk & Wagnalls. Seymour-Smith, M. 809
A guide to natural cosmetics. Krochmal, C. 668
Guide to reference books for school media centers. Wynar, C. L. 016
A guide to sources of consumer information. Thomas, S. M. 640.73
Guide to the use of books and libraries. Gates, J. K. 028.7
Guide to traveling with children in Europe. Fielding's. Hadley, L. 914
Guinness Sports record book 796.03
The Gulag archipelago, 1918-1956. Solzhenitsyn, A. I. 365
Guns. See Firearms

Habeeb, Virginia T. The Ladies' Home Journal Art of homemaking 640
Habits of animals. See Animals—Habits and behavior
Hackett, Earle. Blood 612
Hadley, Leila. Fielding's Guide to traveling with children in Europe 914
Haftmann, Werner. Marc Chagall 759.7
Haggin, B. H. The new listener's companion and record guide 780.1
The Hague
—Description. See pages
  In Kane, R. S. Grand tour A to Z: the capitals of Europe p22-51 914
Haile Selassie I, Emperor of Ethiopia. See pages
  In Rogers, J. A. Great men of color v 1 p419-31 920
Haiti
—Description and travel. See pages
  In Capote, T. The dogs bark p58-69 818
Half the world. Toynbee, A. ed. 915.1
Hall, Calvin S. A primer of Jungian psychology 150.19
Hallett, Robin. Africa since 1875 960
Halliwell, Leslie. The filmgoer's companion 791.4303
Hallucinations and illusions. See Personality disorders
Hallucinogenic drugs. See pages
  In Castaneda, C. The teachings of Don Juan 299
Halpin, Marlene, jt. auth. See Brill, M. L. Write your own wedding 265
Hamilton, Alexander, 1757-1804. See pages
  In Brodie, F. M. Thomas Jefferson, an intimate history p257-75 92
Hammarskjöld, Dag. Markings; criticism
  In Auden, W. H. Forewords and afterwords p436-49 809
Hammerstein, Oscar. 1895-1960. See pages
  In Green, S. The world of musical comedy p265-89 780.92
Hammond Nature atlas of America. Clement, R.C. 500.9
Handbook for prospectors. Pearl, R. M. 622
Handbook for prospectors and operators of small mines. See Pearl, R. M. Handbook for prospectors 622
Handbook for the home. United States. Department of Agriculture 640

Handbook of American college financial aid. Barron's. Proia, N. C. 378.3
Handbook of magic. The Stein and Day. Kaye, M. 793.8
Handbook to the Bible. Eerdmans' 220
Handbooks, manuals, etc. See subjects with the subdivision Handbooks, manuals, etc. e.g. Libraries—Handbooks, manuals, etc.
Handel, Beatrice. See The National directory for the performing arts and civic centers [1974] 790.2
Handicraft. See names of crafts, e.g. Egg decoration
Handlin, Oscar. See Freidel, F. ed. Harvard Guide to American history 973
Handwriting. See Graphology
Handy, William J. ed. Twentieth century criticism: the major statements 801
Handy key to your "National Geographics." National Geographic Magazine 051
Hannibal. See pages
In Rogers, J. A. Great men of color v 1 p98-109 920
Hansberry, Lorraine. The drinking gourd
In Hatch, J. V. ed. Black theater. U.S.A. p713-36 812.08
Hantz, Robert. See pages
In Whittemore, L. H. The super cops 363.2
Happiness 131; also pages
In Hesse, H. My belief p259-68 834
Hardwick, Michael, comp. The Charles Dickens encyclopedia 823.09
—A guide to Anthony Trollope 823.09
—A guide to Jane Austen 823.09
Hardwick, Mollie. Mrs Dizzy; the life of Mary Anne Disraeli, Viscountess Beaconsfield 92
—jt. comp. See Hardwick, M. comp. The Charles Dickens encyclopedia 823.09
Hardy, John Edward. Katherine Anne Porter 813.09
Hardy, Jonathan Gathorne-. See Gathorne-Hardy, Jonathan
Harnick, Sheldon. See pages
In Green, S. The world of musical comedy p359-69 780.92
Harris, Fred R. The new populism 330.973
Harris, Warren G. Gable and Lombard 92
Harrison, Hubert H. See pages
In Rogers, J. A. Great men of color v2 p432-42 920
Hart, Lorenz Milton. See pages
In Green, S. The world of musical comedy p141-63 780.92
Hartford, Huntington. You are what you write 137
The Harvard Concordance to Shakespeare. Spevack, M. 822.3
Harvard Guide to American history. Freidel, F. ed. 973
Harwood, Richard. Lyndon [biography of Lyndon Baines Johnson] 92
Hasidism. See pages
In Manheim, W. Martin Buber p65-91 181
Hatch, Alden. The Lodges of Massachusetts 920
Hatch, James V. ed. Black theater. U.S.A. 812.08
Hatteras, Cape. See pages
In Leonard, J. N. Atlantic beaches p135-46 500.9
Havighurst, Walter. The heartland: Ohio, Indiana, Illinois 977
Havlice, Patricia Pate. Index to artistic biography 709.2
Hawaii
—Natural history. See Natural history—Hawaii
Hawaii. Wallace, R. 500.9
Hawke, David Freeman. Paine 92
Hawkins, Gerald S. Beyond Stonehenge 913
Hayden, Robert Earl. See pages
In Gibson, D. B. ed. Modern Black poets p96-111 811.09
Haydn, Franz Joseph. See pages
In Ewen, D. Orchestral music p22-33 785
In Jacobs, A. A short history of Western music p174-84 780.9
Haydn, Joseph. See Haydn, Franz Joseph
Hayes, Bob. The Black American travel guide 917.3
Hayman, Ronald. Edward Albee 812.09
Haymarket Square Market Riot, 1886. See Chicago—Haymarket Square Riot, 1886
Healing, Mental. See Mental healing
Health care. See Medical care
Hearn, Michael Patrick. See Baum, L. F. The annotated Wizard of Oz 813.09
Heart
—Diseases 616.1
A heartbeat away. Cohen, R. M. 351.9
The heartland: Ohio, Indiana, Illinois. Havighurst, W. 977
Heathenism. See Paganism
Heidegger, Martin. The end of philosophy 110
Heirs. See Inheritance and succession
Helfer, Ray E. ed. The battered child 362.7
Heller, Joseph. Catch-22 812

Hellman, Lillian. Pentimento 92
Hell's Angels. See pages
In Wolfe, T. ed. The new journalism p340-55 810.8
Helm, Alice K. ed. See The Family legal advisor 340
Helms, Randel. Tolkien's world 828
Helsinki
—Description. See pages
In Kane, R. S. Grand tour A to Z: the capitals of Europe p194-212 914
Hemingway, Ernest. See pages
In Cowley, M. A second flowering p48-73, 216-32 810.9
In Kazin, A. Bright book of life: American novelists and storytellers from Hemingway to Mailer p 1-20 813.09
Henderson, G. N. ed. The international encyclopedia of cats 636.803
Henry James's major novels: essays in criticism. Powers, L. H. ed. 813.09
Herbert, Anthony B. Soldier 959.704
Herbert, Victor. See pages
In Green, S. The world of musical comedy p9-23 780.92
Herbert III. Shine, T.
In Hatch, J. V. ed. Black theater, U.S.A. p854-63 812.08
Herbs. See pages
In Crockett, J. U. Vegetables and fruits 635
Herdeck, Donald E. African authors 920.03
Heredity. See Blood groups
Heroines. See Women in literature and art
Herriot, James. All creatures great and small 92
—All things bright and beautiful 92
Herrmann family. See pages
In Christopher, M. The illustrated history of magic p181-97 793.8
Hersey, John, ed. Ralph Ellison 813.09
Hertzberg, Robert. The home owner handbook of electrical repairs 643
Hess, Rudolf 92
Hesse, Hermann. My belief 834
Hettinger, Karl. See pages
In Wambaugh, J. The onion field 364.1
Heureaux, Ulises. See pages
In Rogers, J. A. Great men of color v2 p279-90 920
Heye Foundation. See New York. Museum of the American Indian, Heye Foundation
Hibbert, Christopher. George IV: Prince of Wales, 1762-1811 92
—Versailles 914.4
Hide and seek. West, J. 92
High school education. See Education, Secondary
High schools. See Education, Secondary
Higham, Charles. The art of the American film, 1900-1971 791.43
—Cecil B. DeMille 92
Higher education. See Education, Higher
Hiking 796.5
See also Backpacking
Hill, Abram. Walk hard
In Hatch, J. V. ed. Black theater, U.S.A. p437-71 812.08
Hillbilly women. Kahn, K. 309.175
Himmler, Heinrich. See pages
In Fromm, E. The anatomy of human destructiveness p299-324 152.4
Hinduism. See pages
In Noss, J. B. Man's religions p84-105, 184-225 291
In Paz, O. Alternating current p122-31 864
Hispanic-American literature. See Latin American literature
Histology. See Anatomy
Historic houses, etc. See United States—Historic houses, etc.
Historical fiction
—Bibliography 016.8
Historical fiction guide. See McGarry, D. D. World historical fiction 016.8
Historiography. See pages
In Nye, R. B. Society and culture in America, 1830-1860 p101-14 917.3
History
—Ancient 930
—Bibliography. See pages
In White, C. M. Sources of information in the social sciences p83-137 016.3
—Criticism. See Historiography
—Historiography. See Historiography
—Modern. See Civilization, Modern
—Modern—20th century—Dictionaries 909.82
History. Lowell, R. 811
A history of England. Smith, G. 942
History of England. New illus. ed. Trevelyan, G. M. 942
A history of the ancient world. Starr, C. G. 930

AUTHOR, TITLE, SUBJECT, AND ANALYTICAL INDEX
1974 SUPPLEMENT

History of the British Empire, The Horizon 942
A history of the devil. Woods, W. 133.4
A history of the Swedish people. Moberg, V. 948.5
The history of world cinema. Robinson, D. 791.43
Hitchcock, Alfred Joseph. See pages
   In Higham, C. The art of the American film, 1900-1971 p227-38 791.43
   In Solomon, S. J. ed. The classic cinema p247-71 791.43
Hitchcock, H. Wiley. Music in the United States: a historical introduction 780.973
Hitler, Adolf 92; also pages
   In Boldt, G. Hitler: the last ten days 940.54
   In Fromm, E. The anatomy of human destructiveness p369-433 152.4
Hock, Barry. See Atkins, C. G. Getting elected 329
Hockey 796.9
Hoehling, A. A. Disaster: major American catastrophes 904
Hofman, Gert. On vacation
   In The Best short plays, 1974 p161-92 808.82
Hofstadter, Richard. The American political tradition, and the men who made it 973
Hogarth, William. Engravings by Hogarth 769
Holbrook, Stewart Hall. The Columbia 979.7
Holden, Donald. Art career guide 702.3
Holiday, Billie. See pages
   In Pleasants, H. The great American popular singers p157-67 780.92
Holland, Norman. The last victim
   In The Best short plays, 1974 p283-309 808.82
Hollander, John, ed. The literature of Renaissance England
   In The Oxford Anthology of English literature v 1 p503-1546 820.8
Hollander, Zander, ed. The modern encyclopedia of basketball 796 32
The Hollywood musical. Taylor, J. R. 791.43
Holt, John. Escape from childhood 301.43
The holy ghostly. Shepard, S.
   In Richards, S. ed. Best short plays of the world theatre, 1968-1973 p277-88 808.82
Holzman, Red. Holzman's Basketball: winning strategy and tactics. 796 32
Home. See Home economics
Home decoration. See Interior decoration
Home economics 640
   See also Consumer education; Cookery; Food; Household employees; Sewing
Home improvements book, The Family Handyman 643
Home repairing. See Houses—Repairing
Home to the wilderness. Carrighar, S. 92
The home owner handbook of electrical repairs. Hertzberg, R. 643
Homemaking, The Ladies' Home Journal of. Habeeb, V. T. 640
Homer. The Iliad 883
Homesteading. Logsdon, G. 630.2
Homosexuality. See pages
   In Pomeroy, W. B. Your child and sex p95-111 612.6
Honorable cat. Gallico, P. 636.8
Hoor, Elvie Ten. See Ten Hoor, Elvie
Hope, C. E. G. ed. The encyclopedia of the horse 636.103
Hope abandoned. Mandelstam, N. 92
The Horizon Book of vanishing primitive man. Severin, T. 301.2
The Horizon Concise history of Japan. Busch, N. F. 952
The Horizon History of the British Empire 942
Hormones. See pages
   In Asimov, I. The tragedy of the moon p145-55 508
Horovitz, Israel. Line
   In Richards, S. ed. Best short plays of the world theatre, 1968-1973 p81-100 808.82
Horowitz, Al. See Horowitz, I. A.
Horowitz, I. A. Learn chess quickly 794.1
—The world chess championship 794.1
Horse. See Horses
Horse racing. See pages
   In Scarne, J. Scarne's New Complete guide to gambling p32-108 795
Horsemanship
—Encyclopedias. See pages
   In Hope, C. E. G. ed. The encyclopedia of the horse 636.103
Horses
—Encyclopedias 636.103
—History 636.109
Horticulture. See Gardening
Hospitality. See Entertaining
Hospitals
—United States. See pages
   In Marks, G. The story of medicine in America p55-70 610.9
The hostile sun. Oates, J. C. 821.09
Hot springs. See Geysers

Hotels, motels, etc.
—Europe. See pages
   In Automobile Association. AA Guide to continental motoring 914
Hothouses. See Greenhouses
Houdin, Robert. See Robert-Houdin, Jean Eugène
Houdini, Harry. See pages
   In Christopher, M. The illustrated history of magic p339-67 793.8
Hour of gold, hour of lead. Lindbergh, A. M. 92
Hours of labor 331.2
House cleaning. See pages
   In Habeeb, V. T. The Ladies' Home Journal Art of homemaking p61-208 640
House decoration. See Interior decoration
House furnishing. See Interior decoration
House plants 635.9
House repairing. See Houses—Repairing
Housebuilding step-by-step, Do-it-yourself. Neal, C. D. 690
Household appliances. See Household equipment and supplies
Household appliances, Electric 643
—Repairing 643
Household employees. See pages
   In Gathorne-Hardy, J. The unnatural history of the nanny 914.2
   In Habeeb, V. T. The Ladies' Home Journal Art of homemaking p490-500 640
Household equipment and supplies. See pages
   In Graf, R. F. How it works, illustrated everyday devices and mechanisms 621
   In Habeeb, V. T. The Ladies' Home Journal Art of homemaking p72-90, 340-51 640
   In United States. Department of Agriculture. Handbook for the home p265-332 640
   See also Household appliances, Electric
Household management. See Home economics
Housekeeping. See Home economics
Housemaids. See Household employees
Houses 728.6; also pages
   In United States. Department of Agriculture. Handbook for the home p91-264 640
   See also Building
—Repairing 643
How it works, illustrated: everyday devices and mechanisms. Graf, R. F. 621
How to be your own best friend. Newman, M. 158
How to build and buy cabinets for the modern kitchen. Stevenson, R. P. 684.1
How to build cabinets for the modern kitchen. See Stevenson, R. P. How to build and buy cabinets for the modern kitchen 684.1
How to buy major appliances. Klamkin, C. 643
How to change your name, and the law of names. See Bander, E. J. Change of name and law of names 346
How to get to Europe and have a wonderful time. Rand, A. 914
How to get your car repaired without getting gypped. Carlson, M. B. 629.28
How to hold a garage sale. Ullman, J. M. 650.8
How to make money in Wall Street. Rukeyser, L. 332.6
How to prepare for the College Level Examination Program CLEP, Barron's 378.1
How to run a small business 658
How to start and operate a day care home. Griffin, A. 362.7
How to survive your husband's heart attack. Stichman, J. 616.1
Howard, Jane. A different woman 301.41
Hoyle, Edmond. See Gibson, W. B. Hoyle's Modern encyclopedia of card games 795.4
Hoyle's Modern encyclopedia of card games. Gibson, W. B. 795.4
The Hudson. Carmer, C. 974.7
Hudson River
   In Carmer, C. The Hudson 974.7
Hudson Valley
—History. See pages
   In Carmer, C. The Hudson 974.7
Hudson's Bay Company. See pages
   In The Great Northwest p143-51 917.95
Hughes, Emmet John. The living Presidency 353.03
Hughes, Langston. Don't you want to be free
   In Hatch, J. V. ed. Black theater, U.S.A. p262-77 812.08
—Little Ham
   In Hatch, J. V. ed. Black theater, U.S.A. p775-81 812.08
—A pictorial history of Blackamericans 301.45
Hughes, Langston (as subject) See pages
   In Gibson, D. B. ed. Modern Black poets p43-68 811.09
   In Wagner, J. Black poets of the United States p385-474 811.09
Human body. See Physiology
The human body. Grollman, S. 612
Human ecology. See Environmental policy; Population

Human rights. See Civil rights
Humanism
—20th century. See pages
 In Toffler, A. ed. Learning for tomorrow p132-43 370.19
Humanities. See pages
 In Toffler, A. ed. Learning for tomorrow p144-56 370.19
Humanities and science. See Science and the humanities
Humanities index 050
Hungarian literature
—History and criticism. See pages
 In Seymour-Smith, M. Funk & Wagnalls Guide to modern world literature p693-710 809
Hunting. See pages
 In Edey, M. A. The missing link p106-21 573.2
 In The First men p66-86 573
Husband-coached childbirth. Bradley, R. A. 618.2
Huxley, Julian. Memories II 92
Hyena dog. See Lycoon pictus
The hyperactive child. Wender, P. H. 618.9
Hyperactive child, Raising a. Stewart, M. A. 618.9
Hypoglycemia. See Cookery for hypoglycemics

I lost everything in the post-natal depression. Bombeck, E. 817
I never danced at the White House. Buchwald, A. 817
I will be called John; a biography of Pope John XXIII. Elliott, L. 92
Ibrahim al-Mahdi. See pages
 In Rogers, J. A. Great men of color v 1 p148-62 920
Ice cream, ices, etc. See pages
 In The Good Housekeeping cookbook p571-82 641.5
Ices. See Ice cream, ices, etc.
Icings, Cake. See Cake decorating
Idealism. See pages
 In Dewey, J. The philosophy of John Dewey v 1 p193-207 191
The idle head. Richardson, W.
 In Hatch, J. V. ed. Black theater, U.S.A. p233-40 812.08
Ikhnaton. See Amenhetep IV, King of Egypt
Ilg, Frances L. jt. auth. See Gesell, A. Infant and child in the culture of today 155.4
The Iliad. Homer 883
Illegitimacy. See pages
 In Wilkerson, A. E. ed. The rights of children p72-85, 138-49 346
Illinois
—History. See pages
 In Havighurst, W. The heartland: Ohio, Indiana, Illinois 977
Illiteracy. See pages
 In Montessori, M. Childhood education p103-37 371.3
An illustrated dictionary of jewellery. Mason, A. 739.2703
Illustrated history of England. See Trevelyan, G. M. History of England. New illus. ed. 942
The illustrated history of magic. Christopher, M. 793.8
The illustrated Walden. Thoreau, H. D. 818
Illustrated world atlas. Rand McNally 912
Imagination. See Creation (Literary, artistic, etc.)
Immigration and emigration
 See also Citizenship; also names of countries with the subdivision Immigration and emigration. e.g. United States—Immigration and emigration
Impeachment. See Recall
The impeachment and trial of Andrew Johnson. Benedict, M. L. 973.8
Impeachment: the constitutional problems. Berger, R. 351.9
The imperial Presidency. Schlesinger, A. M. 353.03
Implements, utensils, etc. See Household equipment and supplies
The importance of being Earnest. Wilde, O.
 In The Oxford Anthology of English literature v2 p1129-76 820.8
In cold blood (Motion picture) See pages
 In Capote, T. The dogs bark p393-404 818
In one era and out the other. Levenson, S. 817
In search of ancient gods. Däniken E. von 001.9
In search of Roosevelt. Tugwell, R. G. 92
In splendid error. Branch, W.
 In Hatch, J. V. ed. Black theater, U.S.A. p587-614 812.08
Inboard/outdrives. See Chilton's Repair and tune-up guide: inboard/outdrives 623.82
Incas. See pages
 In Hawkins, G. S. Beyond Stonehenge p155-172 913

Income tax 336.2
Index to artistic biography. Havlice, P. P. 709.2
Index to Black history & studies—multimedia
 In National Information Center for Educational Media. [NICEM Indexes to nonbook media] 016.3713
Index to ecology—multimedia
 In National Information Center for Educational Media. [NICEM Indexes to nonbook media] 016.3713
Index to educational overhead transparencies
 In National Information Center for Educational Media. [NICEM Indexes to nonbook media] 016.3713
Index to educational slidesets
 In National Information Center for Educational Media. [NICEM Indexes to nonbook media] 016.3713
Index to educational video tapes
 In National Information Center for Educational Media. [NICEM Indexes to nonbook media] 016.3713
Index to 8mm motion cartridges
 In National Information Center for Educational Media. [NICEM Indexes to nonbook media] 016.3713
Index to health and safety education—multimedia
 In National Information Center for Educational Media. [NICEM Indexes to nonbook media] 016.3713
Index to producers and distributors
 In National Information Center for Educational Media. [NICEM Indexes to nonbook media] 016.3713
Index to psychology—multimedia
 In National Information Center for Educational Media. [NICEM Indexes to nonbook media] 016.3713
Index to 16mm educational films
 In National Information Center for Educational Media. [NICEM Indexes to nonbook media] 016.3713
Index to the spoken arts on discs, tapes, and cassettes. Chicorel 808.8
Index to 35mm filmstrips
 In National Information Center for educational Media. [NICEM Indexes to nonbook media] 016.3713
Index to vocational and technical education—multimedia
 In National Information Center for educational Media. [NICEM Indexes to nonbook media] 016.3713
Indexes
 See also subjects with the subdivision Indexes. e.g. Artists—Indexes
—Bibliography. See pages
 In Katz, W. A. Introduction to reference work v 1 p61-86 025.5
India
—Economic conditions. See pages
 In Myrdal, G. Against the stream p234-65 330
—History. See pages
 In The Horizon History of the British Empire p64-77, 280-94 942
—Religion. See pages
 In Noss, J. B. Man's religions p84-235 291
Indian art of the Americas. Dockstader, F. J. 709.7
Indiana
—History. See pages
 In Havighurst, W. The heartland: Ohio, Indiana, Illinois 977
Indians
—Art 709.7
—Origin 970.1
The Indians 970.4
Indians of Central America
—Panama. See pages
 In Severin, T. The Horizon Book of vanishing primitive man p105-27 301.2
Indians of Mexico. See Aztecs
Indians of North America. See pages
 In Nye, R. B. Society and culture in America, 1830-1860 p208-17 917.3
—Art. See pages
 In Tanner, C. L. Southwest Indian painting 759.13
—Government relations 970.5; also pages
 In The Great Northwest p185-95 917.95
 In The Indians p150-69 970.4
—History 970.1; also pages
 In Chidsey, D. B. The Loyalists p114-27 973.3
—Legal status, law, etc. See Indians of North America—Government relations
—Pictorial works 970.1
—Religion and mythology. See pages
 In The Indians p118-49 970.4
—Wars 970.5; also pages
 In The Indians p170-233 970.4
—The West 970.4; also pages
 In The Great Northwest p107-21 917.95

AUTHOR, TITLE, SUBJECT, AND ANALYTICAL INDEX
1974 SUPPLEMENT

Indians of South America
  See also Incas
  —Brazil. See pages
    In Severin, T. The Horizon Book of vanishing primitive man p319-45 **301.2**
Individualism. See pages
  In Dewey, J. The philosophy of John Dewey v2 p608-20 **191**
Individuality. See pages
  In Dewey, J. The philosophy of John Dewey v2 p598-608 **191**
The indoor light gardening book. Elbert, G. A. **635.9**
Industrial management
  In Diebold, J. ed. The world of the computer p100-19 **001.6**
  See also Buying
  —Bibliography. See pages
    In White, C. M. Sources of information in the social sciences p181-242 **016.3**
Industries. See names of countries, cities, etc. with the subdivision Industries, e.g. United States—Industries
Industry and state
  —United States **338.973**
Inequality. See Equality
Infant and child in the culture of today. Gesell, A. **155.4**
Infants **155.4**
  —Care and hygiene **649**
  —Diseases **618.2**
The infernal grove. Muggeridge, M.
  In Muggeridge, M. Chronicles of wasted time v2 **92**
Inflation (Finance) See pages
  In Myrdal, G. Against the stream p17-32 **330**
Information, Freedom of. See Freedom of information
Information sciences
  —Dictionaries. See pages
    In Pugh, E. Second dictionary of acronyms & abbreviations **603**
Information storage and retrieval systems. See Electronic data processing; Libraries—Automation
Inge, William. Margaret's bed
  In Richards, S. ed. Best short plays of the world theatre, 1968-1973 p254-63 **808.82**
Ingres, Jean Auguste Dominique. See pages
  In Clark, K. The romantic rebellion p97-145 **759.05**
Ingrisch, Lotte. Vanilla crescents
  In The Best short plays, 1974 p215-30 **808.82**
Inhelder, Bärbel, jt. auth. See Piaget, J. Memory and intelligence **153.1**
Inheritance and succession. See pages
  In DeCrow, K. Sexist justice p140-55 **346.1**
  See also Inheritance and transfer tax; Wills
Inheritance and transfer tax. See pages
  In Stern, P. M. The rape of the taxpayer p320-41 **336.2**
Injuries. See First aid
Insane
  —Hospitals. See Mentally ill—Institutional care
Insane asylums. See Mentally ill—Institutional care
Insects. See pages
  In Clement, R. C. Hammond Nature atlas of America p220-45 **500.9**
  In Villiard, P. Raising small animals for fun and profit p44-80 **636.08**
Instinct. See pages
  In Fromm, E. The anatomy of human destructiveness p442-78 **152.4**
Institutional care. See classes of people with the subdivision Institutional care, e.g. Aged—Institutional care; Mentally ill—Institutional care
Instruction. See Teaching
Instrumental music. See Bands (Music); Orchestral music
Insurance. See pages
  In How to run a small business p125-36 **658**
  —Automobile. See pages
    In Moynihan, D. P. Coping p103-15 **309.173**
  —Laws and regulations. See pages
    In The Family legal advisor p363-92 **340**
  —Life. See pages
    In Landis, J. T. Building a successful marriage p346-67 **301.42**
  —Old age. See Old age pensions
  —Social. See Old age pensions
Intellect. See pages
  In Jensen, A. R. Educability and group differences **370.15**
  See also Reason
Intellectual freedom **323.44**
  See also Free speech
Intellectual freedom manual. American Library Association. Office for Intellectual Freedom **323.44**

Intellectual life. See names of countries, cities, etc. with the subdivision Intellectual life, e.g. United States—Intellectual life
Intelligence. See Intellect
Intelligence, Artificial. See Artificial intelligence
Intercommunication systems. See pages
  in Asimov, I. Today and tomorrow and ... p263-73 **508**
Interior decoration. See pages
  In Better Homes and Gardens Sewing for your home **646.2**
  In Habeeb, V. T. The Ladies' Home Journal Art of homemaking p22-60 **640**
Internal combustion engines. See Gas and oil engines
Internal revenue. See Income tax
The International. See pages
  In Marx, K. On the First International **335.4**
The international book of trees. Johnson, H. **582**
International Celebrity Register. See Celebrity register **920.03**
International cooperation. See International organization
The international encyclopedia of cats. Henderson, G. N. ed. **636.803**
International law. See International relations
International organization. See pages
  In Reischauer, E. O. Toward the 21st century: education for a changing world p92-105 **327**
International relations **327**; also pages
  In Myrdal, G. Against the stream p167-81 **330**
International Working Men's Association. See The International
Interplanetary communication. See Interstellar communication
Interpreting and translating. See Translating and interpreting
Interstellar communication. See pages
  In Tompkins, P. The secret life of plants p46-62 **581**
Intolerance (Motion picture) See pages
  In Solomon, S. J. ed. The classic cinema p11-37 **791.43**
Introduction to Aristotle. Aristotle **888**
Introduction to canoeing. Angier, B. **797.1**
Introduction to reference work. Katz, W. A. **025.5**
Investments **332.6**
Ionesco, Eugène. See pages
  In Lewis, A. Ionesco **842.09**
Ireland
  —History. See pages
    In The Horizon History of the British Empire p400-11 **942**
Irish in the United States **301.45**
Ironing. See Laundry
Islam. See pages
  In Noss, J. B. Man's religions p507-57 **291**
Islamic arts. See The arts, Islamic
Israel
  —Politics and government. See pages
    In Teveth, S. Moshe Dayan: the soldier, the man, the legend **92**
Israel-Arab border conflict. See Jewish-Arab relations
Istanbul
  —Description. See pages
    In Kane, R. S. Grand tour A to Z: the capitals of Europe p213-36 **914**
It all started with freshman English. Armour, R. **817**
Italian literature
  —History and criticism. See pages
    In Seymour-Smith, M. Funk & Wagnalls Guide to modern world literature p715-61 **809**
Italy. See pages
  In National Geographic Society. The Alps p120-51 **914.94**
  In Hitchcock, W. W. Music in the United States: a historical introduction p149-72 **780.973**

Jablonski, Edward. The Gershwin years **780.92**
Jackson, Arthur, jt. auth. See Taylor, J. R. The Hollywood musical **791.43**
Jackson, C. Bernard. Fly Blackbird
  In Hatch, J. V. ed. Black theater, U.S.A. p671-94 **812.08**
Jackson, G. N. jt ed. See Hope, C. E. G. ed. The encyclopedia of the horse **636.103**
Jackson, Mahalia. See pages
  In Pleasants, H. The great American popular singers p198-212 **780.92**
Jackson, Robert Louis, ed. Twentieth century interpretations of Crime and punishment **891.7**
Jacobite Rebellion, 1745-1746. See pages
  In Daiches, D. The last Stuart; the life and times of Bonnie Prince Charlie **92**

Jacobs, Arthur. A short history of Western music 780.9
Jacobus, John. See Matisse, H. Henri Matisse 759.4
Jainism. See pages
 In Noss, J. B. Man's religions p106-17 291
James II, King of Great Britain. See pages
 In Daiches, D. The last Stuart; the life and times of Bonnie Prince Charlie p10-24 92
James, Prince of Wales, the old Pretender. See pages
 In Daiches, D. The last Stuart; the life and times of Bonnie Prince Charlie p53-71 92
James, Henry. See pages
 In Powers, L. H. ed. Henry James's major novels: essays in criticism 813.09
James, William. See pages
 In Dewey, J. The philosophy of John Dewey v 1 p44-53 191
Jansen, Harry Alvin. See Dante
Japan
—Civilization. See pages
 In Toynbee, A. ed. Half the world 915.1
—History 952
—Religion. See pages
 In Noss, J B. Man's religions p308-32 291
Japan: the story of a nation. Reischauer, E. O. 952
Japanese in the United States. See pages
 In Perrett, G. Days of sadness, years of triumph p216-25 973.917
—Pictorial works. See pages
 In Conrat, M. Executive order 9066: the internment of 110,000 Japanase Americans 940.54
Japanese literature
—History and criticism. See pages
 In Seymour-Smith, M. Funk & Wagnalls Guide to modern world literature p763-810 809
Jazz music 781.5; also pages
 In Roach, H. Black American music: past and present p62-94 781.7
Jeal, Tim. Livingstone 92
Jefferson, Thomas, President U.S. 92
Jefferson and his time v5. Malone, D. 92
Jefferson the President, second term, 1805-1809. Malone, D.
 In Malone, D. Jefferson and his time v5 92
Jensen, Arthur R. Educability and group differences 370.15
Jerry Ford, up close. Vestal, B. 92
Jesus Christ 232
Jesus the Jew. Vermes, G. 232
Jewelry
—Encyclopedias 739.2703
Jewish-Arab relations. See pages
 In The Middle East 327.73
 In Patai, R. The Arab mind p258-67 301.29
Jewish literature
—History and criticism. See pages
 In Malin, I. ed. Contemporary American Jewish literature 810.9
Jews. See pages
 In Montagu, A. Man's most dangerous myth p353-77 572
—Literature. See Jewish literature
Jews in literature and art. See pages
 In Malin, I. ed. Contemporary American-Jewish literature p39-77 810.9
Jews in the United States 301.45
Jim Crow, The strange career of. Woodward, C. V. 301.45
Job discrimination. See Discrimination in employment
Job hunters. Edward, H. F. V.
 In Hatch, J. V. ed. Black theater, U.S.A. p255-61 812.08
Job resumés. See Applications for positions
Job security. Charles, M.
 In Hatch, J. V. ed. Black theater, U.S.A. p765-71 812.08
Johannsen, Robert W. Stephen A. Douglas 92
John XXIII, Pope 92
Johnson, Andrew, President U.S. See pages
 In Benedict, M. L. The impeachment and trial of Andrew Johnson 973.8
Johnson, Donald Bruce, comp. National party platforms, 1840-1972 329
Johnson, E. W. jt. ed. See Wolfe, T. ed. The new journalism 810.8
Johnson, Georgia Douglas. A Sunday morning in the South
 In Hatch, J. V. ed. Black theater, U.S.A. p211-17 812.08
Johnson, Hamish. jt. auth. See Quennell, P. Who's who in Shakespeare 822.3
Johnson, Haynes, jt. auth. See Harwood, R. Lyndon [biography of Lyndon Baines Johnson] 92
Johnson, Hugh. The international book of trees 582
Johnson, Jack. See pages
 In Rogers, J. A. Great men of color v2 p474-89 920

Johnson, James Weldon 92; also pages
 In Wagner, J. Black poets of the United States p351-84 811.09
Johnson, John Arthur. See Johnson, Jack
Johnson, Lyndon Baines, President U.S. 92
Johnson, Samuel, 1709-1784 92
Johnson, Walter, ed. See Stevenson, A. E. The papers of Adlai E. Stevenson v3-4 92
Johnson, William Weber. Baja California 500.9
Johnson family. See pages
 In West, J. B. Upstairs at the White House p283-352 92
Joint Commission on Mental Health of Children. Mental health: from infancy through adolescence 155.4
Jolson, Al. See pages
 In Pleasants, H. The great American popular singers p49-62 780.92
Jones, David Pryce- See Pryce-Jones, David
Jones, Howard Mumford. Revolution & romanticism 901.92
Jones, LeRoi, See pages
 In Gibson, D. B. ed. Modern Black poets p112-34 811.09
For other works by this author see Baraka, Imamu Amiri
Jones, Tom. Celebration
 In Jones, T. The fantasticks [and] Celebration p97-218 812
—The fantasticks
 In Jones, T. The fantasticks [and] Celebration p 1-95 812
—The fantasticks [and] Celebration 812
Joplin, Janis 92
Joplin, Scott. See pages
 In Schafer, W. J. The art of ragtime p205-25 781.5
Josephy, Alvin M. See La Farge, O. A. pictorial history of the American Indian 970.1
Journal. Yeats, W. B.
 In Yeats, W. B. Memoirs: Autobiography—first draft [and] Journal p137-278 92
Journal of a solitude. Sarton, M. 92
Journalism. See pages
 In Wolfe, T. ed. The new journalism 810.8
See also Freedom of the press; Government and the press
Journalistic photography. See Photography, Journalistic
Joy and sorrow. See Happiness
The joy of the snow. Goudge, E. 92
Juan, Don, 1891- See pages
 In Castaneda, C. The teachings of Don Juan 299
Judaism. See pages
 In Noss, J. B. Man's religions p355-416 291
Jung, Carl Gustav. See pages
 In Hall, C. S. A primer of Jungian psychology. 150.19
Jungian psychology, A primer of. Hall, C. S. 150.19
Just a country lawyer: a biography of Senator Sam Ervin. Clancy, P. R. 92
Juvenile courts. See pages
 In Wilkerson, A. E. ed. The rights of children p285-302 346

Kabaphēs, Kōnstantinos Petrou. See pages
 In Auden, W. H. Forewords and afterwords p333-44 809
Kael, Pauline. Deeper into movies 791.43
—Raising Kane; criticism
 In Sarris, A. The primal screen p111-36 791.43
Kafa Mountains. See pages
 In Abbey E. Cactus country p112-25 500.9
Kafka, Franz. See pages
 In Gray, R. Franz Kafka 833.09
Kahn, E. J. The American people 301.32
Kahn, Kathy. Hillbilly women 309.175
Kane, Joseph Nathan. Facts about the Presidents 920
Kane, Robert S. Africa A to Z 916
—Grand tour A to Z: the capitals of Europe 914
—London A to Z 914.21
—Paris A to Z 914.4
Kant, Immanuel. See pages
 In Dewey, J. The philosophy of John Dewey v 1 p13-24 191
Kaplan, Justin. Lincoln Steffens 92
Karnak, Egypt. Temple of Ammon. See pages
 In Hawkins, G. S. Beyond Stonehenge p193-218 913
Katz, Bill, ed. Magazines for libraries; supplement 016.05
Katz, Harvey. Give! 361.7
Katz, William A. Introduction to reference work 025.5
Kaye, Marvin. The Stein and Day Handbook of magic 973.8

AUTHOR, TITLE, SUBJECT, AND ANALYTICAL INDEX
1974 SUPPLEMENT

Kazin, Alfred. Bright book of life: American novelists and storytellers from Hemingway to Mailer 813.09
Kellar, Harry. See pages
  In Christopher, M. The illustrated history of magic p198-221 **793.8**
Keller, Heinrich. See Kellar, Harry
Kempe, C. Henry, jt. ed. See Helfer, R. E. ed. The battered child **362.7**
Kennedy, Adrienne. The Lennon play: In his own write
  In Richards, S. ed. Best short plays of the world theatre, 1968-1973 p289-303 **808.82**
—The owl answers
  In Hatch, J. V. ed. Black theater, U.S.A. p756-64 **812.08**
Kennedy, Joseph Patrick **92**
Kennedy, Rose Fitzgerald. Times to remember **92**
Kennedy family **92**; also pages
  In West, J. B. Upstairs at the White House p191-282 **92**
Kenner, Hugh. A reader's guide to Samuel Beckett **828**
Kent State. See Ohio. State University. Kent
Kentucky Derby **798**; also pages
  In Wolfe, T. ed. The new journalism p172-87 **810.8**
The Kentucky Derby, the first 100 years. Chew, P. **798**
Kermode, Frank, ed. Modern British literature
  In The Oxford Anthology of English literature v2 p1511-2187 **820.8**
—ed. See The Oxford Anthology of English literature **820.8**
Kern, Jerome. See pages
  In Green, S. The world of musical comedy p63-83 **780.92**
Kesey, Ken. Kesey's Garage sale **818**
Kesey, Ken (as subject) See pages
  In Wolfe, T. ed. The new journalism p204-18 **810.8**
Ketchum, Richard M. Will Rogers, his life and times **92**
Khe Sanh, Siege of, 1968. See pages
  In Wolfe, T. ed. The new journalism p85-115 **810.8**
Khrushchev, Nikita Sergeevich. Khrushchev remembers: the last testament **947.085**
Khrushchev remembers: the last testament. Krushchev, N. S. **947.085**
Kierkegaard, Soren Aabye. See pages
  In Auden, W. H. Forewords and afterwords p168-97 **809**
Kim, Il Sung. See pages
  In Salisbury, H. E. To Peking—and beyond p206-21 **915.1**
Kind and usual punishment. Mitford, J. **365**
Kindergarten. See Child study; Montessori method of education
Kindness to animals. See Animals—Treatment
King, B. B. See King, Riley B.
King, Billie Jean. Billie Jean **92**
King, Riley B. See pages
  In Pleasants, H. The great American popular singers p306-20 **780.92**
Kinkade, Kathleen. A Walden Two experiment **335**
Kinnamon, Keneth, ed. James Baldwin **818**
Kinsman, Clare D. ed. See Contemporary authors v9-12 **920.03**
Kirk, Ruth. Desert: the American Southwest **574.5**
Kissinger, Henry A. American foreign policy **327.73**
Kitchen utensils. See Household equipment and supplies
Kitchens. See pages
  In Habeeb, V. T. The Ladies' Home Journal Art of homemaking p292-310 **640**
  In Stevenson, R. P. How to build and buy cabinets for the modern kitchen **684.1**
Klamkin, Charles. How to buy major appliances **643**
Klein, Carole. The single parent experience **301.42**
Klibanoff, Elton, jt. auth. See Klibanoff, S. Let's talk about adoption **362.7**
Klibanoff, Susan. Let's talk about adoption **362.7**
Kline, Morris. Why Johnny can't add: the failure of the new math **372.7**
Klinkowitz, Jerome, ed. The Vonnegut statement **813.09**
Knauth, Percy. The north woods **500.9**
Knots and splices **623.88**
Knowing your trees. Collingwood, G. H. **582**
Knowledge, Theory of. See pages
  In Dewey, J. The philosophy of John Dewey v 1 p175-93, 207-39, v2 p355-71 **191**
  In Skinner, B. F. About behaviorism p137-47 **150.19**

Kobal, John. See Blum, D. A new pictorial history of the talkies **791.43**
Koontz, Dean R. Writing popular fiction **808.3**
Korea (Democratic People's Republic) See pages
  In Salisbury, H. E. To Peking—and beyond p189-221 **915.1**
Korean War, 1950-1953. See pages
  In Miller, M. Plain speaking; an oral biography of Harry S. Truman p265-85 **92**
  In Schlesinger, A. M. The imperial Presidency p127-76 **353.03**
Koskoff, David E. Joseph P. Kennedy: a life and times **92**
Kotz, Mary Lynn. See West, J. B. Upstairs at the White House **92**
Kramer, Hilton. The age of avant-garde **709**
Krantzler, Mel. Creative divorce **301.42**
Kreli, Dorothy, ed. See Alaska **917.98**
Krents, Harold. To race the wind. Large print book **92**
Krochmal, Connie. A guide to natural cosmetics **668**
Kruzas, Anthony T. ed. See Directory of special libraries and information centers **026.025**
Kübler-Ross, Elisabeth. Questions and answers on death and dying **128**
Kubrick, Stanley. A clockwork orange **791.43**
Kutz, Myer. Rockefeller power **361.7**

Labor
—Hours of. See Hours of labor
—Migratory. See Migrant labor
Labor and laboring classes
  See also Hours of labor; also names of classes of laborers, e.g. Miners; and names of countries, cities, etc. with the subdivisions Economic conditions and Social conditions, e.g. United States—Economic conditions; United States—Social conditions
—Insurance. See Old age pensions
—United States. See pages
  In Terkel, S. Working **331.2**
Labor saving devices, Household. See Household equipment and supplies
Labor supply. See Woman—Employment
Labor unions. See pages
  In Commager, H. S. ed. Britain through American eyes p441-50 **914.2**
Labor unions. See also names of individual unions, e.g. Brotherhood of Sleeping Car Porters
Lacey, Robert. Sir Walter Ralegh **92**
Lacouture, Jean. Nasser **92**
The Ladies' Home Journal Art of homemaking. Habeeb, V. T. **640**
The ladies should be in bed. Zindel, P.
  In The Best short plays, 1974 p135-60 **808.82**
La Farge, Oliver. A pictorial history of the American Indian **970.1**
Lagerwall, Edna, jt. auth. See Flayderman, N. Collecting tomorrow's antiques today **745.1**
Laird, Charlton. You and your language **420**
La Mare, Walter John de. See De La Mare, Walter John
Lamartine, Alphonse Marie Louis de. See pages
  In Lombard, C. M. Lamartine **841.09**
Land. See Real estate
Landis, Judson T. Building a successful marriage **301.42**
Landis, Mary G. jt. auth. See Landis, J. T. Building a successful marriage **301.42**
Landscape gardening. See Trees
Lang, Fritz. See pages
  In Solomon, S. J. ed. The classic cinema p129-48 **791.43**
Language and languages. See pages
  In The First men p96-110 **573**
  See also Translating and interpreting; also names of languages, e.g. English language
—Psychology **401**
Language arts. See Communication
The language of fabric. See Picken, M. B. The fashion dictionary **391.03**
Lapps. See pages
  In Severin, T. The Horizon Book of vanishing primitive man p283-308 **301.2**
Lacquer and lacquering. See pages
  In Brumbaugh, J. E. Wood furniture, finishing, refinishing, repairing p241-53 **684.1**
Laqueur, Walter. A dictionary of politics **909.82**

Large print books
- Armour, R. Going like sixty 317
- Curtin, S. R. Nobody ever died of old age 301.43
- Herriot, J. All creatures great and small 92
- Krents, H. To race the wind 92
- Lindbergh, A. M. Bring me a unicorn 92
- Lindbergh, A. M. Hour of gold, hour of lead 92
- Lindbergh, A. M. Locked rooms and open doors 92
- Marshall, P. Mr Jones, meet the master 252
- Montgomery, R. Born to heal 615
- Taber, G. Country chronicle 630-1
- Windeler, R. Sweetheart; the story of Mary Pickford 92

Large type books. See Large print books
Larkin, Philip, ed. See The Oxford Book of twentieth-century English verse 821.08
Larry Parks' day in court. Bentley, E.
In Richards, S. ed. Best short plays of the world theatre, 1968-1973 p224-40 808.82
La Salle, Robert Cavelier, sieur de. See pages
In Havighurst, W. The heartland: Ohio, Indiana, Illinois p15-26 977
Lasker, Emanuel. See pages
In Horowitz, A. The world chess championship p48-70 794.1
Lasser, J. K. See How to run a small business 658
Lasser, (J.K.) Institute, New York. See How to run a small business 658
A last encore. Coward, N. P. 92
Last rights. Mannes, M. 174
The last Stuart; the life and times of Bonnie Prince Charlie. Daiches, D. 92
The last victim. Holland, N.
In The Best short plays, 1974 p283-309 808.82
Last Whole earth catalog, The Updated 333.4
Latin America. See pages
In Kutz, M. Rockefeller power p220-31 361.7
Latin American literature
—History and criticism. See pages
In Seymour-Smith, M. Funk & Wagnalls Guide to modern world literature p823-39 809
Laufe, Abe. Broadway's greatest musicals 782.8
Launching the New Deal. Freidel, F.
In Freidel, F. Franklin D. Roosevelt v4 92
Laundry. See pages
In Habeeb, V. T. The Ladies' Home Journal Art of homemaking p209-91 640
Law, Sylvia. The rights of the poor 344.3
Law
—Criminal. See Criminal law
—Great Britain. See pages
In Commager, H. S. ed. Britain through American eyes p202-13 914.2
—United States 340; 344; also pages
In Ross, S. C. The rights of women p275-90 346
Lawick, Hugo van. Solo: the story of an African wild dog 599
Lawrence, David Herbert. See pages
In Oates, J. C. The hostile sun 821.09
Lawrence, L George. See pages
In Tompkins, P. The secret life of plants p46-62 581
Laws. See subjects with the subdivision Laws and regulations, e.g. Divorce—Laws and regulations
The layman's dictionary of computer terminology. Sondak, N. 001.6
Learn chess quickly. Horowitz, I. A. 794.1
Learning for tomorrow. Toffler, A. ed. 370.19
Lease and rental services
—Laws and regulations
In The Family legal advisor p349-62 340
Lease services. See Lease and rental services
Lee, Peggy
In Pleasants, H. The great American popular singers p343-57 780.92
Lee, Robert Edward
In Catton, B. Gettysburg: the final fury p72-107 973.7
Left (Political science) See Right and left (Political science)
Leftwich, A. W. A dictionary of zoology 591.03
Legacies. See Inheritance and succession; Wills
The legacy, the testament, and other poems of François Villon. Villon, F. 841
Legislation
See also Divorce—Laws and regulations
—Periodicals
In The CQ Guide to current American government 350
Legislative bodies. See United States. Congress
Legitimacy (Law) See Illegitimacy
Leisure
In National Geographic Society. Life in rural America p124-51 917.3
In Pearson, J. W. The 8-day week 331.2

Lending. See Loans
Lenin, Vladimir Il'ich 92
Lennon, John. In his own write; dramatization. See Kennedy, A. The Lennon play: In his own write
—A Spaniard in the works; dramatization. See Kennedy, A. The Lennon play: In his own style
The Lennon play: In his own write. Kennedy, A.
In Richards, S. ed. Best short plays of the world theatre, 1968-1973 p289-303 808.82
Leonard, Jonathan Norton. Atlantic beaches 500.9
Leptis Magna, Tripoli
—Antiquities
In Menen, A. Cities in the sand p67-116 913.37
Lerner, Alan Jay
In Green, S. The world of musical comedy p297-309 780.92
Le Roy, Servais
In Christopher, M. The illustrated history of magic p293-318 793.8
Lessing, Doris
In Schlueter, P. The novels of Doris Lessing 823.09
Let's murder Vivaldi. Mercer, D.
In The Best short plays, 1974 p93-133 808.82
Let's talk about adoption. Klibanoff, S. 362.7
Letter to the Soviet leaders. Solzhenitsyn, A. I. 947.085
Leukemia
—Personal narratives 616.1
Leuzinger, Elsy. The art of Black Africa 709.66
Levenson, Sam. In one era and out the other 817
Levertov, Denise. The poet in the world 818
Levine, Alan. The rights of students 344.7
Levy, Eugene. James Weldon Johnson, Black leader, Black voice 92
Levy, Harold B. Square pegs, round holes 371.9
Lewin, Lewis, jt. auth. See Holzman, R. Holzman's Basketball: winning strategy and tactics 796.32
Lewine, Richard. Songs of the American theater 784.01
Lewis, Allan. Ionesco 842.09
Lewis, Sinclair. See pages
In Lundquist, J. Sinclair Lewis 813.09
Libel and slander. See pages
In The Family legal advisor p229-44 340
Liberalism. See pages
In Dewey, J. The philosophy of John Dewey v2 p643-65 191
In Moynihan, D. P. Coping p185-94 309.173
Liberty. See pages
In Dewey, J. The philosophy of John Dewey v2 p665-79 191
In Padover, S. K. ed. Sources of democracy p41-53 321.8
See also Civil rights; Intellectual freedom
Liberty of speech. See Free speech
Liberty of the press. See Freedom of the press
Librarians
—Education. See Library education
Libraries
See also Public libraries; and names of individual libraries, e.g. United States. Library of Congress
—Automation. See pages
In Diebold, J. ed. The world of the computer p298-312 001.6
In The Metropolitan library p248-60 027.4
—Censorship. See pages
In American Library Association. Office for Intellectual Freedom. Intellectual freedom manual 323.44
—Communication systems. See pages
In The Metropolitan library p261-88 027.4
—Federal aid. See Federal aid to libraries
—Finance. See Library finance
—Handbooks, manuals, etc. See pages
In Gates, J. K. Guide to the use of books and libraries 028.7
—Public. See Public libraries
—Public relations. See Public relations—Libraries
—Reference service 025.5
—Special 026
—Special—Directories 026.025
—Young adults' 027.62
Libraries and community. See Public relations—Libraries
Libraries and readers. See Library service
Libraries and state. See Federal aid to libraries
Library acquisitions. See Acquisitions (Libraries)
Library catalogs
—Bibliography. See pages
In Katz, W. A. Introduction to reference work v 1 p39-59 025.5

AUTHOR, TITLE, SUBJECT, AND ANALYTICAL INDEX
1974 SUPPLEMENT

Library communication system. See Libraries
—Communication systems
Library education. See pages
  In The Metropolitan library p233-47 027.4
Library finance. See pages
  In The Metropolitan library p155-70 027.4
The Library of Congress. Goodrum, C. A. 027.5
Library service. See pages
  In The Metropolitan library p187-209 027.4
  See also Libraries—Reference service
Librettists. See pages
  In Green, S. The world of musical comedy 780.92
Liechtenstein. See pages
  In National Geographic Society. The Alps p88-99 914.94
Life (Periodical) See The Best of Life 051
Life (Biology) See Reproduction
The life and death of Adolf Hitler. Payne, R. 92
Life before man 560
The life, history, and magic of the horse. Braider, D. 636.109
Life in rural America. National Geographic Society 917.3
Life insurance. See Insurance, Life
Life on other planets. See Interstellar communication
Light. See pages
  In Asimov, I. The tragedy of the moon p65-75 508
Lin, Yutang. Lin Yutang's Chinese-English dictionary of modern usage 495.1
Lincoln, Abraham, President U.S. See pages
  In Havighurst, W. The heartland: Ohio, Indiana, Illinois p199-216 977
  In Nevins, A. Ordeal of the Union; selected chapter p152-87, 282-92 973.7
Lincoln, C. Eric, jt. auth. See Hughes, L. A pictorial history of Blackamericans 301.45
Lincoln, Mary (Todd) 92
Lindbergh, Anne Morrow. Bring me a unicorn 92
—Hour of gold, hour of lead 92
—Locked rooms and open doors 92
Lindstrom, Thais S. Nikolay Gogol 891.7
Line. Horovitz, I.
  In Richards, S. ed. Best short plays of the world theatre, 1968-1973 p81-100 808.82
Ling-Ling and Hsing-Hsing. Collins, L. R. 599
Linguistics. See Language and languages
Lions. See pages
  In Schaller, G. B. Serengeti: a kingdom of predators p60-109 599
Lipman, Jean. The flowering of American folk art, 1776-1876 745
Lisbon
—Description. See pages
  In Kane, R. S. Grand tour A to Z: the capitals of Europe p237-50 914
The listener's musical companion. See Haggin, B. H. The new listener's companion and record guide 780.1
Literacy. See Illiteracy
The literature of Renaissance England. Hollander, J. ed.
  In The Oxford Anthology of English literature v 1 p503-1546 820.8
Literary history of the United States 810.9
Literary prizes. See pages
  In Bonin, J. F. Prize-winning American drama 812.07
Literature
  See also Women in literature and art
—Comparative—History and criticism 809
—Dictionaries 803
—Discography. See pages
  In Chicorel Index to the spoken arts on discs, tapes, and cassettes 808.8
—History and criticism 809; also pages
  In Handy, W. J. ed. Twentieth century criticism: the major statements 801
Little, Malcolm. See Malcolm X
Little Big Horn, Battle of the, 1876. See pages
  In The Indians p210-33 970.4
  In The Soldiers p199-231 970.5
Little Ham. Hughes, L.
  In Hatch, J. V. ed. Black theater, U.S.A. p775-811 812.08
A little night music. Wheeler, H. 812
The lives of a cell. Thomas, L. 574.01
Living Black American authors. Shockley, A. A. 920.03
The living Presidency. Hughes, E. J. 353.03
Livingston, Myrtle Smith. For unborn children
  In Hatch, J. V. ed. Black theater, U.S.A. p184-87 812.08
Livingstone, David 92
Loans
—Laws and regulations. See pages
  In The Family legal advisor p313-24 340

Local color. Capote, T.
  In Capote, T. The dogs bark p21-104 818
Locked rooms and open doors. Lindbergh, A. M. 92
Lodge family. See pages
  In Hatch, A. The Lodges of Massachusetts 920
The Lodges of Massachusetts. Hatch, A. 920
Loewe, Frederick. See pages
  In Green, S. The world of musical comedy p297-309 780.92
Logan, Joshua Lockwood. See pages
  In Wolfe, T. ed. The new journalism p65-79 810.8
Logic. See Reason
Logsdon, Gene. Homesteading 630.2
Lombard, Carole. See pages
  In Harris, W. G. Gable and Lombard 92
Lombard, Charles, M. Lamartine 841.09
London
—Description 914.21; also pages
  In Commager, H. S. ed. Britain through American eyes p648-57 914.2
  In Kane, R. S. Grand tour A to Z: the capitals of Europe p251-95 914
London A to Z. Kane, R. S. 914.21
Long Island. See pages
  In Leonard, J. N. Atlantic beaches p169-79 500.9
Longford, Elizabeth. Pillar of state
  In Longford, E. Wellington v2 92
—Wellington 92
—The years of the sword
  In Longford, E. Wellington v 1 92
Look down that winding river. Burman, B. L. 917.7
Lorant, Stefan. Sieg Heil! 943.08
Lorayne, Harry. The memory book 153.1
Lorenz, Konrad Zacharias. See pages
  In Fromm, E. The anatomy of human destructiveness p19-32 152.4
Lou Gehrig did not die of cancer. Miller, J.
  In Richards, S. ed. Best short plays of the world theatre, 1968-1973 p101-12 808.82
L'Ouverture, Toussaint. See Toussaint Louverture, Pierre Dominique
The low blood sugar cookbook. Blevin, M. 641.5
The low blood sugar cookbook. Davis, F. 641.5
Lowell, Robert. The dolphin 811
—For Lizzie and Harriet 811
—History 811
Lowell, Robert (as subject) See pages
  In Perloff, M. G. The poetic art of Robert Lowell 811.09
Lowry, Malcolm. See pages
  In Costa, R. H. Malcolm Lowry 813.09
The Loyalists. Chidsey, D. B. 973.3
Loyalists, American. See American Loyalists
Lucas, Jerry, jt. auth. See Lorayne, H. The memory book 153.1
Lunar expeditions. See Space flight to the moon
Lunar exploration. See Moon—Exploration
Lunatic asylums. See Mentally ill—Institutional care
Lundquist, James. Sinclair Lewis 813.09
Lusitania (Steamship) See pages
  In Simpson, C. The Lusitania 940.4
Luxembourg
—Description. See pages
  In Kane, R. S. Grand tour A to Z: the capitals of Europe p296-308 914
Lycoon pictus. See pages
  In Schaller, G. B. Serengeti: a kingdom of predators p26-41 599
The lyrics of Noël Coward. Coward, N. 821

M (Motion picture) See pages
  In Solomon, S. J. ed. The classic cinema p129-48 791.43
Maas, Peter. Serpico 92
McArthur, Douglas. See pages
  In Miller, M. Plain speaking; an oral biography of Harry S. Truman p287-316 92
Macaulay, Thomas Babington Macauley, 1st Baron 92
Maculay: the shaping of the historian. Clive, J. 92
McCabe, John. George M. Cohan: the man who owned Broadway 92
MacCracken, Mary. A circle of children 371.9
McDermott, John J. ed. See Dewey, J. The philosophy of John Dewey 191
McGarry, Daniel D. World historical fiction guide 016.8
McGovern, George. An American journey 329
The McGraw-Hill Encyclopedia of world biography 920.03
McKay, Claude. The passion of Claude McKay 818

PUBLIC LIBRARY CATALOG
1974 SUPPLEMENT

McKay, Claude (as subject) See pages
  In Wagner, J. Black poets of the United States p197-257   **811.09**
MacKenzie, Norman. H. G. Wells   **92**
McKeon, Richard, ed. See Aristotle. Introduction to Aristotle   **888**
McKeown, Donal B. Your pet's health from A to Z   **636.08**
McNally, Raymond T. jt. auth. See Florescu, R. Dracula   **92**
MacNeil. See Owen, A. Male of the species: MacNeil
MacNeish, Richard S. comp. See Scientific American. Early man in America   **970.1**
McNulty, Faith. The great whales   **599**
Macramé   **746.4**
The macramé book. Bress, H.   **746.4**
McWhirter, Norris, comp. See Guinness Sports record book   **796.03**
Madrid
—Description. See pages
  In Kane, R. S. Grand tour A to Z: the capitals of Europe p309-31   **914**
Magazines. See Periodicals
Magazines for libraries; supplement. Katz, B. ed.   **016.05**
Magic   **793.8**
—History   **793.8**
Magicians. See pages
  In Christopher, M. The illustrated history of magic   **793.8**
The Magnificent Rockies   **917.8**
Magrill, Rose Mary, jt. auth. See Carter, M. D. Building library collections   **025.2**
Magruder, Jeb Stuart. An American life   **92**
Mahatma Gandhi. See Gandhi, Mohandas Karamchand
Mahdi. See pages
  In Rogers, J. A. Great men of color v 1 p295-309   **920**
Mail-order business
—Catalogs. See pages
  In The Updated Last Whole earth catalog   **338.4**
Mailer, Norman. Marilyn: a biography [of Marilyn Monroe]   **92**
Mailer, Norman (as subject) See pages
  In Kazin, A. Bright book of life: American novelists and storytellers from Hemingway to Mailer p69-77, 149-57   **813.09**
  In Malin, I. ed. Contemporary American-Jewish literature p81-98   **810.9**
Make-up (Cosmetics) See Cosmetics
Making movies: from script to screen. Bobker, L. R.   **778.5**
The making of the President, 1972. White, T. H.   **329**
Making your own cheese and yogurt. Alth, M.   **637**
Malamud, Bernard. See pages
  In Malin, I. ed. Contemporary American-Jewish literature p175-212   **810.9**
Malcolm X   **92**
—Drama. See pages
  In Baldwin, J. One day, when I was lost   **812**
Male of the species: Emlyn. Owen, A.
  In Richards, S. ed. Best short plays of the world theatre, 1968-1973 p186-99   **808.82**
Male of the species: Emlyn. Owen, A.
  In Richards, S. ed. Best short plays of the world theatre, 1968-1973 p194-201   **808.82**
Male of the species: MacNeil. Owen, A.
  In Richards, S. ed. Best short plays of the world theatre, 1968-1973 p179-86   **808.82**
Malin, Irving, ed. Contemporary American-Jewish literature   **810.9**
Malkoff, Karl. Crowell's Handbook of contemporary American poetry   **811.09**
Malone, Dumas. Jefferson and his time v5   **92**
—Jefferson the President, second term, 1805-1809
  In Malone, D. Jefferson and his time v5   **92**
Mammals. See pages
  In Clement, R. C. Hammond Nature atlas of America p112-39   **500.9**
  In Vanishing species p24-141   **591**
  In Villiard, P. Raising small animals for fun and profit p96-128   **636.08**
See also Whales
Man. See pages
  In Bronowski, J. The ascent of man   **501**
—Antiquity. See Man—Origin and antiquity
—Origin and antiquity   **573.2**; also pages
  In The First men   **573**
—Prehistoric   **573**; also pages
  In Däniken, E. von. In search of ancient gods   **001.9**
  In Severin, T. The Horizon Book of vanishing primitive man p11-28   **301.2**
See also Man—Origin and antiquity; Neanderthal race
—Prehistoric—Pictorial works. See pages
  In Edey, M. A. The missing link p21-31   **573.2**

—Primitive. See pages
  In Fromm, E. The Anatomy of human destructiveness p129-51   **152.4**
The man who owned Broadway. See McCabe, J. George M. Cohen: the man who owned Broadway   **92**
Management   **658**
See also Industrial management
—Automation. See pages
  In Diebold, J. ed. The world of the computer p128-57   **001.6**
—Dictionaries. See pages
  In Pugh, E. Second dictionary of acronyms & abbreviations   **603**
Management of children. See Children—Management
Management: tasks, responsibilities, practices. Drucker, P. F.   **658**
Managing your coronary. Brams, W. A.   **616.1**
Mandel'shtam, Osip Emil'evich. See pages
  In Mandelstam, N. Hope abandoned   **92**
For material by this author see Mandelstam, Osip Emilevich
Mandelstam, Nadezhda. Hope abandoned   **92**
Mandelstam, Osip Emilevich. Complete poetry of Osip Emilevich Mandelstam   **891.7**
For material about this author See Mandel'shtam, Osip Emil'evich
Mäng-tsze. See Mencius
Manheim, Werner. Martin Buber   **181**
Mankiewicz, Frank. Perfectly clear   **973.924**
Mankiewicz, Herman Jacob. See pages
  In Sarris, A. The primal screen p112-36   **791.43**
Manned undersea research stations. See pages
  In Cousteau, J. Window in the sea p31-45   **574.92**
Manners and customs. See names of countries, cities, etc. with subdivision Social life and customs, e.g. U.S.—Social life and customs
Mannes, Marya. Last rights   **174**
Man's most dangerous myth. Montagu, A.   **572**
Man's religions. Noss, J. B.   **291**
Mansell, Darrel. The novels of Jane Austen   **823.09**
Manslaughter. See Murder
Manufactures
—Catalogs   **338.4**
Manvell, Roger. Hess: a biography   **92**
Mao, Tse-tung. See pages
  In Salisbury, H. E. To Peking—and beyond p143-53   **915.1**
Maps
See also Atlases; Automobiles—Road guides; also subjects with the subdivision Maps, e.g. World War, 1939-1945—Maps
Maps. See pages
  In Bridge, R. America's backpacking book p224-33   **796.5**
—Road. See Automobiles—Road guides
Marchetti, Victor. The CIA and the cult of intelligence   **353.007**
Marcus, Frank. Blank pages
  In The Best short plays, 1974 p231-45   **808.82**
Margaret's bed. Inge, W.
  In Richards, S. ed. Best short plays of the world theatre, 1968-1973 p254-63   **808.82**
Marguerite. Salacrou, A.
  In Richards, S. ed. Best short plays of the world theatre, 1968-1973 p202-12   **808.82**
Marihuana. See pages
  In Spock, B. Raising children in a difficult time p177-91   **649**
Marine animals   **591.92**; also pages
  In Cousteau, J. Window in the sea   **574.92**
See also Fishes
Marine biology   **574.92**
See also Marine animals
Marine engines
—Repairing   **623.82**
Marine resources. See pages
  In National Geographic Society. World beneath the sea p165-78   **551.4**
Marine zoology. See Marine animals
Marinis, Louise, jt. auth. See Bobker, L. R. Making movies: from script to screen   **778.5**
Markmann, Charles Lam. The Buckleys   **920**
Marks, Geoffrey. The story of medicine in America   **610.9**
Marks, John D. jt. auth. See Marchetti, V. The CIA and the cult of intelligence   **353.007**
Marriage   **301.42**; also pages
  In Levine,, A. The rights of students p111-20   **344.7**
See also Divorce
—Annulment. See Divorce
—Laws and regulations. See pages
  In The Family legal advisor p15-36   **340**
Marriage customs and rites   **392**; also pages
  In Brill, M. L. Write your own wedding   **265**
  In Mencken, H. L. The young Mencken p453-63   **818**

AUTHOR, TITLE, SUBJECT, AND ANALYTICAL INDEX
1974 SUPPLEMENT

Marshall, George Catlett. See pages
  In Miller, M. Plain speaking; an oral biography of Harry S. Truman p338-43 **92**
Marshall, Peter. Mr Jones, meet the Master. Large print book **252**
Marshall Plan. See Reconstruction (1939-1951)
Marshes. See pages
  In Leonard, J. N. Atlantic beaches p116-33 **500.9**
  In Russell, F. The Okefenokee Swamp **500.9**
  See also Alakai Swamp
Martin, John Bartlow, jt. auth. See Minow, N. N. Presidential television **329**
Martineau, Harriet. See pages
  In Rossi, A. S. ed. The feminist papers: from Adams to de Beauvoir p118-24 **301.41**
Marty, Martin E. The fire we can light **277.3**
Marx, Karl. On the First International **335.4**
Marx Brothers. See pages
  In Adamson, J. Groucho, Harpo, Chico and sometimes Zeppo **791.43**
Marxism. See Communism
Mary Shelley's Frankenstein. Small, C. **823.09**
Maskelyne, John Nevil. See pages
  In Christopher, M. The illustrated history of magic p155-80 **793.8**
Mason, Anita. An illustrated dictionary of jewellery **739.2703**
Mass media
—Laws and regulations. See pages
  In Ross, S. C. The rights of women p148-63 **346**
Masterpieces of music and their composers, 101. Bookspan, M. **780.1**
Mathematics. See pages
  In Adler, I. Thinking machines **519.4**
—Study and teaching **372.7**; also pages
  In Silberman, C. E. ed. The open classroom reader p630-97 **372.1**
Mather, Cotton. See pages
  In Marks, G. The story of medicine in America p40-54 **610.9**
Matheus, John. 'Cruiter
  In Hatch, J. V. ed. Black theater, U.S.A p225-32 **812.08**
Matisse, Henri. Henri Matisse **759.4**
Matrimony. See Marriage
Matthews, Douglas, jt. auth. See Barone, M. The almanac of American politics **328.73**
Matthews, T. S. Great Tom; notes towards the definition of T. S. Eliot **92**
Matthews, Thomas Stanley. See Matthews, T. S.
Maupassant, Guy de. See pages
  In Wallace, A. H. Guy de Maupassant **843.09**
May, Rollo. Paulus [biography of Paul Tillich] **92**
Mayhew, Henry. London labour and The London poor; criticism
  In Auden, W. H. Forewords and afterwords p233-43 **809**
Mazda automobile. See pages
  In Dark, H. E. The Wankel rotary engine p93-103, 108-25 **629.2**
Meal planning. See Menus
Meals for school children. See School children
—Food
Meat **641.3**
The meat book. Evans, T. M. **641.3**
Mechanical brains. See Computers; Cybernetics
Mechanical movements. See pages
  In Graf, R. F. How it works, illustrated: everyday devices and mechanisms **621**
Mechanics. See Mechanical movements
Mechanix Illustrated Fix-it home repairs handbook **643**
Medical care. See pages
  In Ross, D. K. A public citizen's action manual p69-122 **640.73**
—Laws and regulations. See pages
  In Law, S. The rights of the poor p80-110 **344.3**
The medical detectives. Cooper, P. **614**
Medical education. See Medicine—Study and teaching
Medical hygiene. See Medicine, Military
Medical jurisprudence **614**
Medical research. See Medicine—Research
Medical schools. See Medicine—Study and teaching
Medical service. See Medical care
Medical technology. See pages
  In Diebold, J. ed. The world of the computer p246-73 **001.6**
Medical transplantation. See Transplantation of organs, tissues, etc.
Medici, Alessandro de'. See pages
  In Rogers, J. A. Great men of color v2 p24-33 **920**
Medicine. See pages
  In Cooper, P. The medical detectives **614**
  See also Medical technology; Physiology
—History **610.9**; also pages
  In Nye, R. B. Society and culture in America, 1830-1860 p338-56 **917.3**

—Military. See pages
  In Marks, G. The story of medicine in America p114-38 **610.9**
—Research. See pages
  In Marks, G. The story of medicine in America p273-83 **610.9**
  In Mitford, J. Kind and usual punishment p138-68 **365**
—Study and teaching. See pages
  In Marks, G. The story of medicine in America p73-113, 194-209 **610.9**
Medieval English literature. Trapp, J. B. ed.
  In The Oxford Anthology of English literature v 1 p3-500 **820.8**
Meditation, Transcendental. Forem, J. **181**
Meditations. See pages
  In Merton, T. The Asian journal of Thomas Merton **248**
Meier, August. CORE **322.4**
Meilach, Dona Z. Collage and assemblage **751.4**
—Contemporary batik and tie-dye **746.4**
Melanesians. See pages
  In Severin, T. The Horizon Book of vanishing primitive man p257-81 **301.2**
Mellow, James R. Charmed circle: Gertrude Stein & company **92**
Meltzer, Milton, jt. auth. See Hughes, L. A pictorial history of blackamericans **301.45**
Memoirs: Autobiography—first draft [and] Journal. Yeats, W. B. **92**
Memories II. Huxley, J. **92**
Memory **153.1**
Memory and intelligence. Piaget, J. **153.1**
The memory book. Lorayne, H. **153.1**
Men, beasts, and gods. Carson, G. **636.08**
Mencius. See pages
  In Pound, E. Selected prose, 1909-1965 p81-97 **814**
Mencken, H. L. The young Mencken **818**
For material about this author See Mencken, Henry Louis
Mencken, Henry Louis. See pages
  In Mencken, H. L. The young Mencken p xv-xxxii **818**
Mendelson, Mary Adelaide. Tender loving greed **362.6**
Menelik II, Negus of Abyssinia. See pages
  In Rogers, J. A. Great men of color v 1 p370-80 **920**
Menen, Aubrey. Cities in the sand **913.37**
Meng-tse. See Mencius
Menninger, Karl. Whatever became of sin? **233**
Men's clothing **391**
Mental depression. See Depression, Mental
Mental healing **615**
Mental health. See pages
  In Joint Commission on Mental Health of Children. Mental health: from infancy through adolescence **155.4**
Mental health: from infancy through adolescence. Joint Commission on Mental Health of Children **155.4**
Mental hospitals. See Mentally ill—Institutional care
Mental illness
—Laws and regulations **346**; also pages
  In The Family legal advisor p215-27 **340**
Mental institutions. See Mentally ill—Institutional care
Mental patients, The rights of. Ennis, B. **346**
Mental suggestions. See Mental healing
Mentally handicapped children
—Education **371.9**
Mentally ill
—Institutional care **362.2**
Menus. See pages
  In The Good Housekeeping cookbook p727-34 **641.5**
Mercer, David. Let's murder Vivaldi
  In The Best short plays, 1974 p93-133 **808.82**
Merciful disguises. Van Duyn, M. **811**
Mercy killing. See Euthanasia
Meredith, Scott. Writing to sell **808**
Merman, Ethel. See pages
  In Pleasants, H. The great American popular singers p333-42 **780.92**
Merton, Thomas. The Asian journal of Thomas Merton **248**
Metaphysics **110**
Meteorites. See pages
  In Alter, D. Pictorial astronomy p149-57 **523**
Meteors. See pages
  In Asimov, I. Asimov on astronomy p14-28 **523**
Methodist Church. See United Methodist Church. Board of Church and Society
Metropolitan areas. See pages
  In Pearson, J. W. The 8-day week p 1-10 **331.2**
  In The Metropolitan library **027.4**
The Metropolitan library **027.4**

PUBLIC LIBRARY CATALOG
1974 SUPPLEMENT

Mexico. See pages
  In Clark, S. All the best in [series] . . . 910.2

Microbes. See Microorganisms
Microbiology. See Microorganisms
Microorganisms. See pages
  In Asimov, I. The tragedy of the moon p107-41 **508**
  In Villiard, P. Raising small animals for fun and profit p21-41 **636.08**
Microscopic organisms. See Microorganisms
The Middle East **327.73**
Migrant labor. See pages
  In Law, S. The rights of the poor p155-76 **344.3**
Migratory workers. See Migrant labor
Military life. See United States. Army—Military life
Military medicine. See Medicine, Military
Mill, John Stuart. See pages
  In Rossi, A. S. ed. The feminist papers: from Adams to de Beauvoir p183-96 **301.41**
Miller, Glenn **780.92**
Miller, Jason. Lou Gehrig did not die of cancer
  In Richards S. ed. Best short plays of the world theatre, 1968-1973 p101-12 **808.82**
Miller, May. Graven images
  In Hatch, J. V. ed. Black theater. U.S.A. p353-59 **812.08**
Miller, Merle. Plain speaking; an oral biography of Harry S. Truman **92**
Millet, Jean François. See pages
  In Clark, K. The romantic rebellion p285-307 **759.05**
Milton, John. Samson Agonistes
  In The Oxford Anthology of English literature v 1 p1367-1412 **820.8**
Milton, John (as subject) See pages
  In Handy, W. J. ed. Twentieth century criticism: the major statements p328-38 **801**
Mind and body. See pages
  In Trilling, L. Mind in the modern world **901.94**
Mind in the modern world. Trilling, L. **901.94**
Mine eyes have seen. Dunbar-Nelson, A.
  In Hatch, J. V. ed. Black theater, U.S.A. p173-77 **812.08**
Mineralogy **549**; also pages
  In Clement, R. C. Hammond Nature atlas of America p20-39 **500.9**
Minerals. See Mineralogy
Miners. See pages
  In Kahn, K. Hillbilly women **309.175**
Mines and mineral resources. See Prospecting
Miniature gardens. See Gardens, Miniature
Minich, Quaid Walton, jt. auth. See Elonka, S. M. Standard refrigeration and air conditioning questions and answers **621.5**
Minnesota
—Natural history. See Natural history—Minnesota
Minorities. See names of races or peoples living within a country, state, or city dominated by another nationality, e.g. Irish in the United States; and names of countries with the subdivision Race relations, e.g. United States—Race relations
Minow, Newton N. Presidential television **329**
Minton, Madge Rutherford, jt. auth. See Minton, S. A. Giant reptiles **598.1**
Minton, Sherman A. Giant reptiles **598.1**
Misdemeanors (Law) See Criminal law
The missing link. Edey, M. A. **573.2**
Mississippi River **917.7**
Mississippi Valley
—History. See pages
  In Billington, R. A. Westward expansion **973**
Mr Jones, meet the Master. Large print book. Marshall, P. **252**
Mrs Dizzy; the life of Mary Anne Disraeli, Viscountess Beaconsfield. Hardwick, M. **92**
Mitchell, Lee M. jt. auth. See Minow, N. N. Presidential television **329**
Mitchell, Loften. Star of the morning
  In Hatch, J. V. ed. Black theater. U.S.A. p618-52 **812.08**
Mitford, Jessica. Kind and usual punishment **365**
Mnemonics. See Memory
Moberg, Vilhelm. A history of the Swedish people **948.5**
Mobile homes. See Travel trailers and campers
Moctezuma I. See Montezuma I, Emperor of Mexico
Moctezuma II. See Montezuma II, Emperor of Mexico
The modern age, 1890-1960. Cooper, M. ed.
  In The New Oxford History of music v10 **780.9**
Modern architecture. See Architecture, Modern
—20th century
Modern architecture. Scully, V. **724.9**
Modern art. See Art, Modern
Modern backgammon complete. Goren's. Goren, C. H. **795**

Modern Black poets. Gibson, D. B. ed. **811.09**
Modern British literature. Kermode, F. ed.
  In The Oxford Anthology of English literature v2 p1511-2187 **820.8**
Modern civilization. See Civilization, Modern
Modern civilization. Brinton, C. **901.9**
Modern dance. See Dancing
The modern encyclopedia of basketball. Hollander, Z. ed. **796.32**
Modern encyclopedia of card games. Hoyle's. Gibson, W. B. Hoyle's Modern encyclopedia of card games **795.4**
Mohammedans. See Muslims
Mojo. Childress, A.
  In Richards, S. ed. Best short plays of the world theatre, 1968-1973 p126-37 **808.82**
Molz, Kathleen, ed. See The Metropolitan library **027.4**
Monaco
—Description. See pages
  In Kane, R. S. Grand tour A to Z: the capitals of Europe p332-43 **914**
Money raising. See Fund raising
Monroe, Marilyn **92**
Montagu, Ashley. Man's most dangerous myth **572**
—The natural superiority of women **301.41**
Montauk Point. See pages
  In Leonard, J. N. Atlantic beaches p169-79 **500.9**
Montessori, Maria. Childhood education **371.3**
—Erdkinder
  In Montessori, M. From childhood to adolescence **371.3**
—From childhood to adolescence **371.3**
—The function of the university
  In Montessori, M. From childhood to adolescence **371.3**
Montessori method of education **371.3**
Montezuma I, Emperor of Mexico. See pages
  In Davies, N. The Aztecs p96-110 **970.3**
Montezuma II, Emperor of Mexico. See pages
  In Davies, N. The Aztecs p207-32 **970.3**
Montgomery, Edward. Useful knots for everyone **623.88**
Montgomery, Ruth. Born to heal **615**
Moon. See pages
  In Alter, D. Pictorial astronomy p57-78 **523**
  In Asimov, I. Asimov on astronomy p89-100 **523**
  In Asimov, I. The tragedy of the moon p3-26 **508**
  See also Tides
—Exploration. See pages
  In Asimov, I. Today and tomorrow and . . . p165-88 **508**
—Voyages to. See Space flight to the moon
Moore, Patrick. Color star atlas **523.8**
—The concise Atlas of the universe **523**
Moore, Sonia. The Stanislavski system **792**
Moorhouse, Geoffrey. The fearful void **916.6**
Moral conditions. See names of countries, cities, etc. with the subdivision Moral conditions, e.g. United States—Moral conditions
Moral education. See Character education
Morgan, John Hunt. See pages
  In Havighurst, W. The heartland: Ohio, Indiana, Illinois p233-43 **977**
Morphology. See Anatomy
Morris, Adalaide Kirby. Wallace Stevens: imagination and faith **811.09**
Morrison, Kathleen. Robert Frost **92**
Morro Castle (Steamship) See pages
  In Burton, H. The Morro Castle **910.4**
Mortimer, John. Bermondsey
  In Richards, S. ed. Best short plays of the world theatre, 1968-1973 p213-23 **808.82**
Moshe Dayan: the soldier, the man, the legend. Teveth, S. **92**
Moslems. See Muslims
Moss, Norman. What's the difference? **427**
Motion, The art of. Cousteau, J. **591.92**
Motion pictures. See Moving pictures
Motor boats. See Motorboats
Motor cycles. See Motorcycles
Motorboats **623.82**
Motorcycle troubleshooting guide, Chilton's **629.28**
Motorcycles **629.22**
—Repairing **629.28**
Mountain climbing. See Mountaineering
Mountain people, American. National Geographic Society **917.3**
Mountaineering. See pages
  In Abbey, E. Cactus country p92-105 **500.9**
Mountains. See pages
  In National Geographic Society. American mountain people **917.3**
  See also Mountaineering; Volcanoes; and names of mountains, e.g. Kafa Mountains
Movement of animals. See Animal locomotion
Movies. See Moving pictures
Moving picture cartoons **791.43**
Moving picture photography **778.5**

AUTHOR, TITLE, SUBJECT, AND ANALYTICAL INDEX
1974 SUPPLEMENT

Moving pictures 791.43; also pages
 In Bretnor, R. ed. Science fiction, today and tomorrow p46-64 809.3
 In Higham, C. Cecil B. DeMille 92
 In Wilson, G. B. Three hundred years of American drama and theatre p346-69 792.09
—Biography. See pages
 In Taylor, J. R. The Hollywood musical 791.43
—Encyclopedias 791.4303
—History 791.43
Mowat, Farley. A whale for the killing 599
—Wake of the great sealers 639
Moynihan, Daniel P. Coping 309.173
Mozart, Johann Chrysostom Wolfgang Amadeus. See pages
 In Ewen, D. Orchestral music p37-57 785
 In Jacobs, A. A short history of Western music p184-96 780.9
Mozart, Wolfgang Amadeus. See Mozart, Johann Chrysostom Wolfgang Amadeus
Muggeridge, Malcolm. Chronicles of wasted time 92
—The green stick
 In Muggeridge, M. Chronicles of wasted time v 1 92
—The infernal grove
 In Muggeridge, M. Chronicles of wasted time v2 92
Muhammedans. See Muslims
Multiple consciousness. See Personality disorders
Munich
—Description. See pages
 In Mencken, H. L. The young Mencken p251-66 818
Munn, Glenn G. Glenn G. Munn's Encyclopedia of banking and finance 332.03
Murder 364.1; also pages
 In Wolfe, T. ed. The new journalism p116-26 810.8
Murphy, Paul L. ed. See Political parties in American history 329
The muses are heard. Capote, T.
 In Capote, T. The dogs bark p161-307 818
Museum media 016
Museum of the American Indian, Heye Foundation. See New York. Museum of the American Indian, Heye Foundation
Museums
—Directories 069.025
Museums of the world 069.025
Music
 See also Jazz music; Orchestral music
—American. See pages
 In Ewen, D. Orchestral music p257-73 785
—American—Directories 780.973
—American—Handbooks, manuals, etc. 780.973
—American—History and criticism 780.973; also pages
 In Nye, R. B. Society and culture in America, 1830-1860 p126-36 917.3
—Analysis, appreciation 780.1
—Appreciation. See Music—Analysis, appreciation
—Bibliography 016.78
—British. See pages
 In Ewen, D. Orchestral music p244-53 785
—Discography. See pages
 In Bookspan, M. 101 masterpieces of music and their composers 780.1
 In Haggin, B. H. The new listener's companion and record guide 780.1
—Encyclopedias 780.3
—English. See Music, British
—European—History and criticism 780.9
—History and criticism. See pages
 In Bookspan, M. 101 masterpieces of music and their composers 780.1
—Negro. See Negro music
—Popular (Songs, etc.) 784; also pages
 In Coward, N. P. A last encore 92
 In Gray, M. Song and dance man 780.92
 In Pleasants, H. **The great American popular singers** 780.92
—Popular (Songs, etc.)—History and criticism. See pages
 In Burton, J. The blue book of Broadway musicals 782.8
—Popular (Songs, etc.)—Indexes 784.01
—Primitive—History and criticism 781.7
—Russian. See pages
 In Ewen, D. Orchestral music p124-54, 230-43 785
Music appreciation. See Music—Analysis, appreciation
Music in the United States: a historical introduction. Hitchcock, H. W. 780.973
Music is my mistress. Ellington, E. K. 780.92
Music reference and research materials. Duckles, V. comp. 016.78
Musical appreciation. See Music—Analysis, appreciation
Musical comedies. See Musical revues, comedies, etc.

Musical criticism. See Music—History and criticism
Musical revues, comedies, etc. 782.8; also pages
 In Green, S. The world of musical comedy 780.92
 In Lewine, R. Songs of the American theater 784.01
—History. See pages
 In Taylor, J. R. The Hollywood musical 791.43
Musicians. See pages
 In Chicorel Bibliography to books on music and musicians 016.78
 In Vinton, J. ed. Dictionary of contemporary music 780.3
 See also Composers; Singers
—American. See pages
 In Ellington, E. K. Music is my mistress 780.92
—American—Dictionaries 780.92
—Negro. See Negro musicians
Muslim arts. See The arts, Islamic
Muslims. See pages
 In Patai, R. The Arab mind p143-55 301.29
Mussolini, Benito 92
Mussolini, Rachele. Mussolini: an intimate biography 92
Mussulmans. See Muslims
Mutation (Biology) See Evolution
My belief. Hesse, H. 834
My house. Giovanni, N. 811
My young years. Rubinstein, A. 780.92
Myers, Norma. Gifts from the kitchen 641.5
Myrdal, Gunnar. Against the stream 330
Mysticism. See pages
 In Auden, W. H. Forewords and afterwords p49-78 809

NICEM. See National Information Center for Educational Media
[NICEM Indexes to nonbook media] National Information Center for Educational Media 016.3713
Nabokov, Vladimir. See pages
 In Kazin, A. Bright book of life: American novelists and storytellers from Hemingway to Mailer p295-318 813.09
Nader, Ralph. You and your pension 331.2
Najita, Tetsuo. Japan 952
Names
—Personal—United States—Laws and regulations. See pages
 In Bander, E. J. Change of name and law of names 346
 In DeCrow, K. Sexist justice p250-60 346.1
 In Ross, S. C. The rights of women p239-55, 348-56 346
Nanny, The unnatural history of the. Gathorne-Hardy, J. 914.2
Napier, John. Bigfoot 001.9
Narcotics and youth. See Drugs and youth
Nash, Ogden. Ave Ogden! Nash in Latin 811
Nasser, Gamal Abdel, President United Arab Republic 92
National characteristics
—American. See pages
 In Mencken, H. L. The young Mencken p283-98, 350-65 818
—British 914.2
—English. See National characteristics, British
The National directory for the performing arts and civic centers [1974] 790.2
National Geographic Magazine. Handy key to your "National Geographics" 910.1
National Geographic Society. The Alps 914.94
—American mountain people 917.3
—Life in rural America 917.3
—Wilderness U.S.A. 500.9
—World beneath the sea 551.4
—See Allen, T. B. Vanishing wildlife of North America 591.9
—See Friedel, F. Our country's Presidents 920
National Information Center for Educational Media. [NICEM Indexes to non book media] 016.3713
National parks and reserves
—United States. See pages
 In Great historic places 917.3
 In Natural wonders of America 917.3
National party platform, 1840-1972. Johnson, D. B. comp. 329
National planning. See Social policy
National Rifle Association of America. See pages
 In Sherrill, R. The Saturday night special 363.3
Nationalism. See pages
 In Stampp, K. M. ed. The causes of the Civil War p46-62 973.7

Native son. Wright, R.
  In Hatch, J. V. ed. Black theater, U.S.A. p393-431 **812.08**
Natkiel, Richard. See Young, P. ed. Atlas of the Second World War **940.54**
Natural childbirth. See Childbirth
Natural disasters. See Disasters
Natural history
—Alaska **500.9**
—Atlantic States **500.9**
—Baja California **500.9**
—Canada **500.9**
—Florida **500.9**
—Georgia **500.9**
—Hawaii **500.9**
—Minnesota **500.9**
—North America **500.9**; also pages
  In Gibbons, E. Stalking the faraway places **581.6**
—Rocky Mountains **500.9**
—Sonoran Desert **500.9**
—Southwest, New. See pages
  In Kirk, R. Desert: the American Southwest **574.5**
—United States **500.9**
—Virginia **500.9**
Natural law. See Civil rights
Natural man. Browne, T.
  In Hatch, J. V. ed. Black theater, U.S.A. p360-81 **812.08**
Natural monuments
—United States. See pages
  In Natural wonders of America **917.3**
Natural resources
  See also Conservation of natural resources
—United States **333.8**
Natural selection. See Evolution
The natural superiority of women. Montagu, A. **301.41**
Natural wonders of America **917.3**
Naturalization. See Citizenship
Nature **500.9**
Nature atlas of America, Hammond, Clement, R. C. **500.9**
Nature conservation. See Wildlife—Conservation
Nature study. See pages
  In Bridge, R. America's backpacking book p371-80 **796.5**
Neal, Charles D. Do-it-yourself housebuilding step-by-step **690**
Neale, Robert E. The art of dying **128**
Neanderthal race **573**
The Neanderthals. Constable, G. **573**
Near East
—Foreign relations—United States. See pages
  In The Middle East **327.73**
Nebulae
—Extragalactic. See Galaxies
Necrophilia. See pages
  In Fromm, E. The anatomy of human destructiveness p325-68 **152.4**
Needlework. See Embroidery; Quilting; Sewing
Negro authors
—Bio-bibliography **920.03**
Negro drama
—Collections **812.08**
Negro music. See pages
  In Schafer, W. J. The art of ragtime **731.5**
—History and criticism **781.7**
Negro musicians. See pages
  In Roach, H. Black American music: past and present **781.7**
Negro poetry
—Collections **811.08**
—History and criticism **811.09**
Negro race. See Negroes
Negro soldiers. See pages
  In Franklin, J. H. From slavery to freedom p89-96, 333-48 **301.45**
  In Hughes, L. A pictorial history of Blackamericans p172-81 **301.45**
Negro suffrage. See Negroes—Suffrage
Negroes. See pages
  In Montagu, A. Man's most dangerous myth p311-39 **572**
  In Myrdal, G. Against the stream p293-307 **330**
  In Nevins, A. Ordeal of the Union; selected chapters p373-409 **973.7**
  In Nye, R. B. Society and culture in America, 1830-1860 p218-35 **917.3**
  See also Slavery in the United States; United States—Race relations
—Biography **920**
—Civil rights. See pages
  In Anderson, J. A. Philip Randolph: a biographical portrait **92**
  In Aptheker, H. ed. A documentary history of the Negro people in the United States **301.45**
  In Hughes, L. A pictorial history of Blackamericans p302-25 **301.45**
  In Meier, A. CORE **322.4**
  In Padover, S. K. ed. Sources of democracy p79-101 **321.8**
—Drama. See pages
  In Walker, J. A. The River Niger **812**
—Education. See pages
  In Du Bois, W. E. B. The education of Black people **378**
  In Hughes, L. A pictorial history of Blackamericans p342-51 **301.45**
  In Moynihan, D. P. Coping p167-84 **309.173**
—History **301.45**; also pages
  In Perrett, G. Days of sadness, years of triumph p143-54, 310-24 **973.917**
—History—Sources **301.45**
—Political activity. See pages
  In Chisholm, S. The good fight **329**
  In Hughes, L. A pictorial history of Blackamericans p200-11 **301.45**
—Psychology. See pages
  In Baldwin, J. A dialogue **301.45**
  In Toffler, A. ed. Learning for tomorrow p56-71 **370.19**
—Segregation **301.45**
—Social conditions. See pages
  In Moynihan, D. P. Coping p344-69 **309.173**
—Southern States. See pages
  In Wolfe, T. ed. The new journalism p356-76 **810.8**
—Suffrage. See pages
  In Padover, S. K. ed. Sources of democracy p238-48 **321.8**
Negroes as soldiers. See Negro soldiers
Negroes in literature and art. See pages
  In Wagner, J. Black poets of the United States p48-72 **811.09**
Neighborhood. See Community life
Nelson, Alice Dunbar- See Dunbar-Nelson, Alice
Nemerov, Howard. Gnomes & occasions **811**
Neo-Greek literature. See Greek literature, Modern
Neolithic period. See Stone age
Neruda, Pablo. New poems (1968-1970) **861**
Nervous system. See Neurophysiology
Nettl, Bruno. Folk and traditional music of the western continents **781.7**
Neurophysiology. See pages
  In Fromm, E. The anatomy of human destructiveness p89-101 **152.4**
Nevin, David. See The Soldiers **970.5**
Nevins, Allan. Ordeal of the Union; selected chapters **973.7**
The New Cambridge Bibliography of English literature, v 1 600-1660 **016.82**
The new complete book of bicycling. Sloane, E. A. **796.6**
New Complete guide to gambling, Scarne's. Scarne, J. **795**
The new complete walker. Fletcher, C. **796.5**
The New Encyclopaedia Britannica. The Encyclopaedia Britannica **031**
The new journalism. Wolfe, T. ed. **810.8**
The new listener's companion and record guide. Haggin, B. H. **780.1**
The New Oxford History of music v7, v10 **780.9**
A new pictorial history of the talkies. Blum, D. **791.43**
New poems (1968-1970) Neruda, P. **861**
The new populism. Harris, F. R. **330.973**
The new science of skin and scuba diving. Council for National Cooperation in Aquatics **797.2**
New serial titles **016.05**
New voices in American poetry. Evans, D. A. ed. **811.08**
New words. See Words, New
New York. Museum of the American Indian, Heye Foundation. See Dockstader, F. J. Indian art of the Americas **709.7**
New York. Rockefeller Center. See pages
  In Kutz, M. Rockefeller power p46-69 **361.7**
New York. State Prison, Attica
—Riots. See pages
  In Kutz, M. Rockefeller power p232-48 **361.7**
New York (City)
—Police **363.2**; also pages
  In Maas, P. Serpico **92**
New York (State)
—Politics and government. See pages
  In Moynihan, D. P. Coping p53-68 **309.173**
—Social life and customs. See pages
  In Carmer, C. The Hudson **974.7**
New York Times
—Indexes. See pages
  In The New York Times Directory of the theater **792.01**
The New York Times Book of house plants. Faust, J. L. **635.9**

AUTHOR, TITLE, SUBJECT, AND ANALYTICAL INDEX
1974 SUPPLEMENT

The New York Times Directory of the theater 792.01
The New York Times Garden book. Faust, J. L. ed. 635
The New York Times Great songs of Broadway 782.8
The New York Times Guide to student adventures and studies abroad, 1974. Rowland, H. S. 914
The New York Times Report on the chess match of the century. See Roberts, R. Fischer/Spassky: The New York Times Report on the chess match of the century 794.1
Newman, Mildred. How to be your own best friend 158
News broadcasts. See Television broadcasting
Newsome, Arden J. Egg decorating, plain & fancy 745.59
Newsweek. See Hibbert, C. Versailles 914.4
Newton, Huey P. Revolutionary suicide 92
Nicklaus, Jack. Golf my way 796.352
Nicoll, Allardyce. English drama, 1900-1930 822.09
Nicolson, Sir Harold George. See pages
  In Nicolson, N. Portrait of a marriage 92
Nicolson, Nigel. Portrait of a marriage [biography of Victoria Mary Sackville-West] 92
Nicomachean ethics. Aristotle
  In Aristotle. Introduction to Aristotle p337-581 888
Nidetch, Jean. Weight Watchers Program cookbook 641.5
Nietzsche, Friedrich Wilhelm. See pages
  In Mencken H. L. The young Mencken p425-41 818
  In Paz, O. Alternating current p112-22 864
Nigeria
—History—Civil War, 1967-1970. See pages
  In Vonnegut, K. Wampeters, foma & granfalloons (opinions) p139-58 818
Nin, Anaïs. The diary of Anaïs Nin, 1947-1955 92
1984 revisited. Wolff, R. P. ed. 973
Nixon, Richard Milhous, President U.S. See pages
  In Mankiewicz, F. Perfectly clear 973.924
  In Ooborne, J. The fourth year of the Nixon watch 973.924
  In Osborne, J. The fifth year of the Nixon watch 973.924
  In The Presidential transcripts 351.9
  In Wolfe, T. ed. The new journalism p228-39 810.8
Nixon family. See pages
  In West, J. B. Upstairs at the White House p353-68 92
No-fault divorce. Wheeler, M. 346.1
Nobody ever died of old age. Curtin, S. R. 301.43
Noël [biography of Noël Coward]. Castle, C. 92
Nonbook materials. See Audio-visual materials
Nonprint materials. See Audio-visual materials
Nonte, George C. Firearms encyclopedia 633
Nordby, Vernon J. jt. auth. See Hall, C. S. A primer of Jungian psychology 150.19
Norse literature. See Scandinavian literature
North America
—Natural history. See Natural history—North America
North American Indians. See Indians of North America
The north woods. Knauth, P. 500.9
Northen, Henry T. Greenhouse gardening 635.9
Northen, Rebecca T. jt. auth. See Northen, H. T. Greenhouse gardening 635.9
Northwest, Pacific 917.95
—History. See pages
  In Holbrook, S. H. The Columbia 979.7
Noss, John B. Man's religions 291
Nostradamus. The prophecies of Nostradamus 133.3
Notable names in American history 920.03
The notebooks of Martha Graham. Graham, M. 92
Notredame, Michel de. See Nostradamus
The novels of Doris Lessing. Schlueter, P. 823.09
The novels of Jane Austen. Mansell, D. 823.09
Nurseries
—Day. See Day nurseries
Nursery schools. See pages
  In Diebold, J. ed. The world of the computer p225-39 001.6
  See also Day nurseries
Nursing homes. See Aged—Institutional care
Nutrition. See Diet; Food
Nye, Russel Blaine. Society and culture in America, 1830-1860 917.3

Oasis in space. Cousteau, J. Y. 574.92
Oates, Joyce Carol. Angel fire 811
—The hostile sun 821.09
Obscene literature. See Pornography
Obstetrics. See Childbirth
Ocean
  See also Seashore
—Economic aspects. See Marine resources
Ocean life. See Marine biology
Oceanography
  See also Marine biology
—Research 551.4
  See also Manned undersea research stations
O'Connor, Edwin. See pages
  In Rank, H. Edwin O'Connor 813.09
O'Connor, Flannery. See pages
  In Stephens, M. The question of Flannery O'Connor 813.09
  In Walters, D. Flannery O'Connor 813.09
O'Connor, Richard. See Burke, John
Octopus 594
Octopus and squid. Cousteau, J. Y. 594
Odes, Pinard's. Pindar 884
Offenses against the person. See Rape
Office for Intellectual Freedom. See American Library Association. Office for Intellectual Freedom
Office management
—Handbooks, manuals, etc. 651.02
Official baseball register 796.357
Official publications. See Government publications; United States—Government publications
O'Hara, Frank. The selected poems of Frank O'Hara 811
Ohio. State University, Kent. See pages
  In Davies, P. The truth about Kent State 378.1
Ohio
—History. See pages
  In Havighurst, W. The heartland: Ohio, Indiana, Illinois 977
Okefenokee Swamp. See pages
  In Russell, F. The Okefenokee Swamp 500.9
Old age 301.43
  See also Old age pensions
—Anecdotes, facetiae, satire, etc. See pages
  In Armour, R. Going like sixty 817
Old age homes. See Aged—Dwellings
Old age pensions 331.2
Olds, Sally Wendkos, jt. auth. See Stewart, M. A. Raising a hyperactive child 618.9
Olivier, Sir Laurence Kerr 92
On happiness. Teilhard de Chardin, P. 131
On the First International. Marx, K. 335.4
On the soul. Aristotle
  In Aristotle. Introduction to Aristotle p152-245 888
On vacation. Hofmann, G.
  In The Best short plays, 1974 p161-92 808.82
One-act plays 808.82
One day, when I was lost. Baldwin, J. 812
100 best songs of the 20's and 30's 784
101 masterpieces of music and their composers. Bookspan, M. 780.1
O'Neill, Eugene Gladstone 92; also pages
  In Wilson, G. B. Three hundred years of American drama and theatre p423-39 792.09
O'Neill, George, jt. auth. See O'Neill, N. Shifting gears 158
O'Neill, Nena. Shifting gears 158
The onion field. Wambaugh, J. 364.1
Ontology. See pages
  In Heidegger, M. The end of philosophy 110
The open classroom reader. Silberman, C. E. ed. 372.1
Open eye, open heart. Ferlinghetti, L. 811
Opera. See pages
  In Jacobs, A. A short history of Western music p232-54 780.9
Operetta. See Musical revues, comedies, etc.
Opie, Iona, ed. See The Oxford Book of children's verse 821.08
Opinion, Public. See Public opinion
Orage, Alfred Richard. See pages
  In Pound, E. Selected prose, 1909-1965 p437-51 814
Orange soufflé. Bellow, S.
  In Richards, S. ed. Best short plays of the world theatre, 1968-1973 p168-73 808.82
Oratory. See Public speaking
Orchestra. See pages
  In Ewen, D. Orchestral music 785
  See also Bands (Music)
Orchestral music
—History and criticism 785
The ordeal. Freidel, F.
  In Freidel, F. Franklin D. Roosevelt v2 92
Ordeal of the Union; selected chapters. Nevins, A. 973.7

Organ transplantation. See Transplantation of organs, tissues, etc.
Organic farming. See Organiculture
Organic gardening. See Organiculture
Organiculture. See pages
  In Tompkins, P. The secret life of plants p217-73 **581**
Organization
—International. See International organization
Oriental philosophy. See Philosophy, Oriental
Origin of man. See Man—Origin and antiquity
Origin of species. See Evolution
Ornamental plants. See Plants, Ornamental
Ornithology. See Birds
Orwell, George. The collected essays, journalism and letters of George Orwell; criticism
  In Sarris, A. The primal screen p287-301 **791.43**
Osborne, John, 1907- The fourth year of the Nixon watch **973.924**
—The fifth year of the Nixon watch **973.924**
Oslo
—Description. See pages
  In Kane, R. S. Grand tour A to Z: the capitals of Europe p344-63 **914**
The Osprey Guide to Anthony Trollope. See Hardwick, M. A guide to Anthony Trollope **823.09**
Ossoli, Sarah Margaret (Fuller) marchesa d'.
  See pages
  In Rossi, A. S. ed. The feminist papers: from Adams to de Beauvoir p144-58 **301.41**
Our country's Presidents. Freidel, F. **920**
Outboard motorboats. See Motorboats
Outboard motors, 30 horsepower & over. See Chilton's Repair and tune-up guide: outboard motors 30 horsepower & over **623.82**
Outdoor cookery **641.5**
Outdoor life. See Camping; Hiking; Mountaineering; Wilderness survival
Outdoor recreation. See Camping
Outer space
—Communication. See Interstellar communication
Ovington, Ray. Basic fly fishing & fly tying **799.1**
Owen, Alun. Male of the species: Corny
  In Richards, S. ed. Best short plays of the world theatre, 1968-1973 p186-99 **808.82**
—Male of the species: Emlyn
  In Richards, S. ed. Best short plays of the world theatre, 1968-1973 p194-201 **808.82**
—Male of the species: MacNeil
  In Richards, S. ed. Best short plays of the world theatre, 1968-1973 p179-86 **808.82**
Owen, Jean. See Newman, M. How to be your own best friend **158**
The owl answers. Kennedy, A.
  In Hatch, J. V. ed. Black theater, U.S.A. p756-64 **812.08**
The owl killer. Dean, P. H.
  In The Best short plays, 1974 p61-92 **808.82**
Ownership. See Property
The Oxford Anthology of English literature **820.8**
The Oxford Book of children's verse **821.08**
The Oxford Book of twentieth-century English verse **821.08**
The Oxford Companion to Canadian history and literature, Supplement to. [Story, N.] **810.3**
The Oxford Dictionary of the Christian Church **203**
Ozark Mountains
—Social life and customs. See pages
  In National Geographic Society. American mountain people p100-29 **917.3**

Pacific area
—History. See pages
  In The Horizon History of the British Empire p96-109 **942**
Pacific Northwest. See Northwest, Pacific
Pack transportation. See Backpacking
Padover, Saul K. ed. Sources of democracy **321.8**
Paganism. See pages
  In Woods, W. A history of the devil **133.4**
Page, James K. jt. auth. See Collins, L. R. Ling-Ling and Hsing-Hsing **599**
Paine, Thomas **92**
Painting
—American **759.13**
—American—History. See pages
  In Nye, R. B. Society and culture in America, 1830-1860 p173-88 **917.3**
—Modern—19th century **759.05**
Paleontology. See Fossils
Palmer, Helen H. comp. European drama criticism. Supplement I-II **016.8092**
Palmyra, Syria
—Antiquities. See pages
  In Menen, A. Cities in the sand p202-32 **913.37**

Pandas **599**
The papers of Adlai E. Stevenson v3-4. Stevenson, A. E. **92**
Paquet, Basil T. jt. ed. See Rottman, L. ed. Winning hearts & minds **811.08**
Paradise Key, Fla. See pages
  In Carr, A. The Everglades p120-31 **500.9**
Parent and child **301.42**; also pages
  In Griffin, A. How to start and operate a day care home p157-67 **362.7**
  In Holt, J. Escape from childhood **301.43**
  In Joint Commission on Mental Health of Children. Mental health: from infancy through adolescence p33-53 **155.4**
  In Spock, B. Raising children in a difficult time **649**
  See also Conflict of generations; Cruelty to children; Illegitimacy
Paris
—Description **914.4**; also pages
  In Kane, R. S. Grand tour A to Z: the capitals of Europe p364-407 **914**
Paris A to Z. Kane, R. S. **914.4**
Parkinson, R. N. Edward Gibbon **92**
Parole. See pages
  In Mitford, J. Kind and usual punishment p216-27 **365**
Parrinder, Geoffrey. A dictionary of non-Christian religions **291.03**
Parties, Political. See Political parties
The passion of Claude McKay. McKay, C. **818**
The passion of Joan of Arc (Motion picture) See pages
  In Solomon, S. J. ed. The classic cinema p109-27 **791.43**
Passos, John dos. See Dos Passos, John
Pasternak, Boris Leonidovich. See pages
  In Dyck, J. W. Boris Pasternak **891.7**
Patai, Raphael. The Arab mind **301.29**
Patchwork quilts, American. Bacon, L. I. **746.4**
Patria mia. Pound, E.
  In Pound, E. Selected prose, 1909-1965 p99-141 **814**
Patton, George Smith **92**
The Patton papers, 1940-1945. Blumenson, M. ed. **92**
Paul, Jean. See Richter, Johann Paul Friedrich
Paulus [biography of Paul Tillich]. May, R. **92**
Pavlakis, Christopher. The American music handbook **780.973**
Pawley, Thomas. The tumult and the shouting
  In Hatch, J. V. ed. Black theater, U.S.A. p475-513 **812.08**
Paxton, John, ed. Dictionary of abbreviations **413**
Payne, Robert. The life and death of Adolf Hitler **92**
Payroll taxes. See Income tax; Old age pensions
Paz, Octavio. Alternating current **864**
—Children of the mire **809.1**
Peabody, James Bishop, ed. See Adams, J. John Adams **92**
Pearl, Richard M. Handbook for prospectors **622**
Pearson, Drew. Diaries, 1949-1959 **92**
Pearson, John Ward. The 8-day week **331.2**
Pedagogy. See Teaching
Pediatrics. See Children—Care and hygiene
Pei, Mario. Double-speak in America **422**
Penal codes. See Criminal law
Penal law. See Criminal law
Penology. See Punishment
Pentimento. Hellman, L. **92**
Pensions. See Old age pensions
People's Republic of China, 1949- See China (People's Republic of China, 1949-)
Pepys, Samuel. The diary of Samuel Pepys v8: 1667 **92**
Perception. See pages
  In Skinner, B. F. About behaviorism p72-87 **150.19**
Perfectly clear. Mankiewicz, F. **973.924**
Performing arts
—Bibliography **016.7902**
—Directories **790.2**
Perfumes. See pages
  In Krochmal, C. A guide to natural cosmetics p67-90 **668**
Periodicals. See pages
  In Broadus, R. N. Selecting materials for libraries p101-09 **025.2**
  See also Science fiction—Periodicals
—Bibliography **016.05**
—Indexes **050**; also pages
  In Eichelberger, C. L. comp. A guide to critical reviews of United States fiction, 1870-1910 v2 **016.813**
Perloff, Marjorie G. The poetic art of Robert Lowell **811.09**
Perrett, Geoffrey. Days of sadness, years of triumph **973.917**

AUTHOR, TITLE, SUBJECT, AND ANALYTICAL INDEX
1974 SUPPLEMENT

Personal finance. See Finance, Personal
Personal liberty. See Liberty
Personality. See pages
  In Hall, C. S. A primer of Jungian psychology p31-56, 81-95 **150.19**
Personality disorders **616.8**
The personality of Shakespeare. Wagenknecht, E. **822.3**
Peru
—Antiquities. See pages
  In Hawkins, G. S. Beyond Stonehenge p90-172 **913**
Pesticides and wildlife. See pages
  In Allen, T. B. Vanishing wildlife of North America p103-20 **591.9**
Peter I, the Great, Emperor of Russia. See pages
  In Coughlan, R. Elizabeth and Catherine; empresses of all the Russias p23-51 **92**
Peter III, Emperor of Russia. See pages
  In Coughlan, R. Elizabeth and Catherine; empresses of all the Russias p69-94, 175-88 **92**
Peterson, Louis. Take a giant step
  In Hatch, J. V. ed. Black theater, U.S.A. p547-84 **812.08**
Petroleum industry and trade **338.2**; also pages
  In The Middle East **327.73**
Petrology. See Rocks
Petrosian, Tigran. See Petrosyan, Tigran Vartanovich
Petrosyan, Tigran Vartanovich. See pages
  In Horowitz, A. The world chess championship p177-218 **794.1**
Pets **636.08**
  See also Cats
—Diseases and pests **636.08**
Pezzulo, Ted. The wooing of Lady Sunday
  In The Best short plays, 1974 p311-46 **808.82**
Phaidon Dictionary of twentieth-century art **709.04**
Philanthropy. See Charities; Gifts
Phillips, John G. jt. auth. See Alter, D. Pictorial astronomy **523**
Philosophy **191**
  See also Metaphysics
—American. See pages
  In Nye, R. B. Society and culture in America, 1830-1860 p321-33 **917.3**
—Oriental. See pages
  In Hesse, H. My belief p377-93 **834**
The philosophy of John Dewey. Dewey, J. **191**
The photographs of Margaret Bourke-White. Bourke-White, M. **779**
Photography **770; 770.1**; also pages
  In The Best of Life **051**
  See also Moving picture photography
—Artistic. See pages
  In Bourke-White, M. The photographs of Margaret Bourke-White **779**
—Journalistic. See pages
  In Bourke-White, M. The photographs of Margaret Bourke-White **779**
—Moving pictures. See Moving picture photography
—Submarine. See pages
  In Cousteau, J. Window in the sea p46-65, 96-107 **574.92**
  In National Geographic Society. World beneath the sea p93-111 **551.4**
Physics. See pages
  In Asimov, I. Today and tomorrow and . . p97-106, 117-27 **508**
Physiology **612**
  See also Blood; Neurophysiology
Piaget, Jean. Memory and intelligence **153.1**
Piaget, Jean (as subject) See pages
  In Silberman, C. E. The open classroom reader p182-208 **372.1**
Picken, Mary Brooks. The fashion dictionary **391.03**
Pickford, Mary **92**
Pickup campers. See Travel trailers and campers
Pictorial astronomy. Alter, D. **523**
A pictorial history of Blackamericans. Hughes, L. **301.45**
A pictorial history of sea monsters and other dangerous marine life. Sweeney, J. B. **597**
A pictorial history of the American Indian. La Farge, O. **970.1**
A pictorial history of the Negro in America. See Hughes, L. A pictorial history of Blackamericans **301.45**
Pictorial history of the talkies, A new. Blum, D. **791.43**
Picture guide to beginner's chess. See Horowitz, I. A. **794.1**
Pictures
—Indexes **910.1**

Piekalkiewicz, Janusz. Secret agents, spies, and saboteurs **940.54**
Piercy, Esther J. Commonsense cataloging **025.3**
Pigmies. See Pygmies
Pilgrim at Tinker Creek. Dillard, A. **500.9**
Pillar of state. Longford, E.
  In Longford, E. Wellington v2 **92**
Pindar. Pindar's odes **884**
Pinetti, Giovanni Giuseppe. See pages
  In Christopher, M. The illustrated history of magic p82-96 **793.8**
Piranesi, Giovanni Battista. See pages
  In Clark, K. The romantic rebellion p45-59 **759.05**
Plain speaking; an oral biography of Harry S. Truman. Miller, M. **92**
Planets. See pages
  In Alter, D. Pictorial astronomy p91-135 **523**
  In Asimov, I. Asimov on astronomy p29-88, 115-26 **523**
Planned parenthood. See Birth control
Planning, National. See Social policy
Plant propagation. See pages
  In Northen, H. T. Greenhouse gardening p80-90 **635.9**
Planting. See Gardening
Plants **581**; also pages
  In Evans, C. M. The terrarium book **635.9**
  See also Gardening; House plants
—Edible **581.6**
—Ornamental **635.9**
—Propagation. See Plant propagation
—Useful. See Plants, Edible
Plath, Sylvia. See pages
  In Aird, E. M. Sylvia Plath **811.09**
Play. See pages
  In Griffin, A. How to start and operate a day care home p101-17 **362.7**
Playing cards. See Cards
Plays. See Drama—Collections
Plays in periodicals, Chicorel Theater index to **808.82**
The plays of Samuel Beckett. Webb, E. **842.09**
Plaza suite: Visitor from Forest Hills. See Simon, N. Visitor from Forest Hills
Pleasants, Henry. The great American popular singers **780.92**
Pleasure. See Happiness
Pliner, Roberta Lee. See Evans, C. M. The terrarium book **635.9**
Plutarch. See pages
  In Russell, D. A. Plutarch **888**
Poe, Edgar Allan. See pages
  In Auden, W. H. Forewords and afterwords p209-20 **809**
Poems, 1970-1972. Graves, R. **821**
The poet in the world. Levertov, D. **818**
The poetic art of Robert Lowell. Perloff, M. G. **811.09**
Poetics. Aristotle
  In Aristotle. Introduction to Aristotle p668-713 **888**
Poetry **809.1**
  See also American poetry; Negro poetry; and general subjects with the subdivision Poetry, e.g. Cats—Poetry
—Collections. See English poetry—Collections
—History and criticism. See pages
  In Hesse, H. My belief p163-76 **834**
  In Pound, E. Selected prose, 1909-1965 p357-400 **814**
The poetry of Black America. Adoff, A. ed. **811.08**
Poets
—American. See pages
  In Havighurst, W. The heartland: Ohio, Indiana, Illinois p307-24 **977**
—American—Directories **811.025**
Police
  See also Detectives; also names of cities with the subdivision Police, e.g. New York (City)—Police
—United States. See pages
  In Sherrill, R. The Saturday night special p247-68 **363.3**
Polish literature
—History and criticism. See pages
  In Seymour-Smith, M. Funk & Wagnalls Guide to modern world literature p899-914 **809**
Political corruption. See Corruption (in politics)
Political economy. See Economics
Political ethics. See Corruption (in politics)
Poilitcal parties **329**; also pages
  In Wolff, R. P. ed. 1984 revisited p113-38 **973**
Political parties in American history **329**
Political prisoners. See pages
  In Solzhenitsyn, A. I. The Gulag archipelago, 1918-1956 **365**

PUBLIC LIBRARY CATALOG
1974 SUPPLEMENT

Political science. See pages
  In Padover, S. K. ed. Sources of democracy 321.8
  See also Political parties
—Bibliography. See pages
  In White, C. M. Sources of information in the social sciences p493-563 016.3
—Encyclopedias 320.03
Politics
  See also names of countries, states, cities with the subdivision Politics and government, e.g. United States—Politics and government
Politics, Practical 329
  See also Television in politics
Pollution. See pages
  In Energy crisis in America p63-76 333.8
Polyglot dictionaries. See Dictionaries, Polyglot
Polynesians. See pages
  In Severin, T. The Horizon Book of vanishing primitive man p129-54 301.2
Pomeranz, Virginia E. The first five years 649
Pomeroy, Wardell B. Your child and sex 612.6
Poor relief. See Public welfare
Pope, Alexander. See pages
  In Auden, W. H. Forewords and afterwords p109-24 809
Popular government. See Democracy
Popular music. See Music, Popular (Songs, etc.)
Popular Science. See Graf, R. F. How it works, illustrated: everyday devices and mechanisms 621
Population. See pages
  In Asimov, I. Today and tomorrow and . . . p239-51 503
  See also names of countries, cities, etc. with the subdivision Population, e.g. United States—Population
Pornography. See pages
  In Pomeroy, W. B. Your child and sex p63-80 612.6
The portable Graham Greene. Greene, G. 828
Porter, Cole. See pages
  In Green, S. The world of musical comedy p181-201 780.92
Porter, Katherine Anne. See pages
  In Hardy, J. E. Katherine Anne Porter 813.09
  In Kazin, A. Bright book of life: American novelists and storytellers from Hemingway to Mailer p163-73 813.09
Porter, Kirk H. jt. comp. See Johnson, D. B. comp. National party platforms, 1840-1972 329
Porterfield, Christopher, jt. auth. See Cavett, D. Cavett 92
Portola Institute. See The Updated Last Whole earth catalog 338.4
Portrait of a marriage [biography of Victoria Mary Sackville-West]. Nicolson, N. 92
Portuguese literature
—History and criticism. See pages
  In Seymour-Smith, M. Funk & Wagnalls Guide to modern world literature p915-25 809
Posterior analytics. Aristotle
  In Aristotle. Introduction to Aristotle p8-111 888
Postscript with a Chinese accent. Sulzberger, C. L. 92
Potemkin, Grigoriĭ Aleksandrovich, knîaz'. See pages
  In Coughlan, R. Elizabeth and Catherine; empresses of all the Russias p273-98 92
Potemkin (Motion picture) See pages
  In Solomon, S. J. ed. The classic cinema p65-88 791.43
Pottery 738.1
Pound, Ezra. Patria mia
  In Pound, E. Selected prose, 1909-1965 p99-141 814
—Selected prose, 1909-1965 814
Powell, Gregory Ulas. See pages
  In Wambaugh, J. The onion field 364.1
Power boats. See Motorboats
Power politics. See Balance of power
Power resources. See pages
  In Energy crisis in America 333.8
Power supply. See Power resources
Powers, Lyall H. ed. Henry James's major novels: essays in criticism 813.09
Practical politics. See Politics, Practical
Pragmatism. See pages
  In Dewey, J. The philosophy of John Dewey v 1 p41-58, 207-22 191
Prayers. See pages
  In Marshall, P. Mr Jones, meet the Master. Large print book 252
Prayers in the public schools. See Religion in the public schools
Pregnancy. See pages
  In Levine, A. The rights of students p111-20 344.7
  See also Childbirth

Prehistoric man. See Man, Prehistoric
Prehistory. See Archeology
Prempeh I, King of Ashanti tribe. See pages
  In Rogers, J. A. Great men of color v 1 p394-404 920
Preschool education. See Nursery schools
Present tense. Gilroy, F. D.
  In The Best short plays, 1974 p193-213 808.82
Presents. See Gifts
Preservation of food. See Food—Preservation
Preservation of natural resources. See Conservation of natural resources
Preservation of natural scenery. See Wilderness areas
Preservation of organs, tissues, etc. See Transplantation of organs, tissues, etc.
Preservation of wildlife. See Wildlife—Conservation
Presidential television. Minow, N. N. 329
The Presidential transcripts 351.9
Presidents
—United States. See pages
  In Freidel, F. Our country's Presidents 920
  In Kane, J. N. Facts about the Presidents 920
  In Minow N. N. Presidential television 329
—United States—Election 329; also pages
  In Wolfe, T. ed. The new journalism p228-39 810.8
—United States—Family. See pages
  In West, J. B. Upstairs at the White House 92
—United States—History 353.03
—United States—Power. See Executive power
—United States
The President's wife: Mary Todd Lincoln. Ross, I. 92
Presley, Elvis. See pages
  In Pleasants, H. The great American popular singers p262-78 780.92
Press and government. See Government and the press
Press censorship. See Freedom of the press
Prevention of cruelty to animals. See Animals—Treatment
Price, Martin, ed. The Restoration and the eighteenth century
  In The Oxford Anthology of English literature v 1 p1549-2312 820.8
Prideaux, James. An American sunset
  In The Best short plays, 1974 p 1-22 808.82
Priestley, J. B. The English 914.2
The primal screen. Sarris, A. 791.43
Primary education. See Education, Elementary
Primates. See pages
  In Edey, M. A. The missing link p54-66 573.2
—Habits and behavior. See pages
  In Edey, M. A. The missing link p78-127 573.2
A primer of Jungian psychology. Hall, C. S. 150.19
Primitive art. See Art, Primitive
Primitive Christianity. See Church history—Primitive and early church
Primitive man. See Man, Primitive
Primitive society. See Society, Primitive
Principles of composition in photography. Feininger, A. 770.1
Prison poems. Berrigan, D. 811
The prisoner of Second Avenue. Simon, N. 812
Prisoners, Political. See Political prisoners
Prisons
  See also Political prisoners
—United States 365
—United States—Laws and regulations. See pages
  In Rudovsky, D. The rights of prisoners 345
Pritchett, V. S. Balzac 92
Private schools 371
Prize-winning American drama. Bonin, J. F. 812.07
Probations. See Parole
Problem children
—Education 371.9
Processing (Libraries) See Acquisitions (Libraries); Cataloging
Prochnow, Herbert V. comp. The speaker's and toastmaster's handbook 808.5
Production. See Economics
Professions. See Architecture as a profession
Program cookbook, Weight Watchers. Nidetch, J. 641.5
Proia, Nicholas C. Barron's Handbook of American college financial aid 378.3
Project Apollo. See Apollo project
Project Gemini. See Gemini project
Propagation of plants. See Plant propagation
Property. See pages
  In The Family legal adviser p271-312 340
—Real. See Real estate
Prophecies 133.3
  See also Divination

The prophecies of Nostradamus. Nostradamus 133.3
Prospecting 622
Protection of animals. See Animals—Treatment
Protection of birds. See Birds—Protection
Protection of natural scenery. See Wilderness areas
Protection of wildlife. See Wildlife—Conservation
Protestantism. See pages
  In Marty, M. E. The fire we can light 277.3
Proust, Marcel 92
—Contemporary France. See pages
  In Sansom, W. Proust and his world 92
Proust and his world. Sansom, W. 92
Pryce-Jones, David, ed. Evelyn Waugh and his world 92
Psychiatric hospitals. See Mentally ill—Institutional care
Psychoanalysis 150.19
Psychology
  See also Behaviorism (Psychology); Educational psychology; Memory; Psychoanalysis
—Applied 158
—Bibliography. See pages
  In White, C. M. Sources of information in the social sciences p375-424 016.3
—Child. See Child study
—Educational. See Educational psychology
—Methodology. See pages
  In Dewey, J. The philosophy of John Dewey v 1 p98-175 191
—Practical. See Psychology, Applied
—Social. See Social psychology
Psychotherapy. See pages
  In Joint Commission on Mental Health of Children. Mental health: from infancy through adolescence p106-22 155.4
Public assistance. See Public welfare
Public charities. See Public welfare
A public citizen's action manual. Ross, D. K. 640.73
Public documents. See Government publications
Public health. See Medical care
Public libraries 027.4
Public opinion. See pages
  In Boorstin, D. J. Democracy and its discontents p12-21 917.3
Public relations
—Libraries 021.7
Public schools and religion. See Religion in the public schools
Public speaking. See pages
  In Nye, R. B. Society and culture in America, 1830-1860 p136-46 917.3
—Handbooks, manuals, etc. See pages
  In Prochnow, H. V. comp. The speaker's and toastmaster's handbook 808.85
Public welfare. See pages
  In Moynihan, D. P. Coping p134-66 309.173
—Laws and regulations 344.3
Publishers and publishing. See pages
  In Bretnor, R. ed. Science fiction, today and tomorrow p17-44 809.3
  In Broadus, R. N. Selecting materials for libraries p33-47 025.2
  See also Book industries and trade
Publishing. See Publishers and publishing
Pugh, Eric. Second dictionary of acronyms & abbreviations 603
Punishment. See pages
  In Mitford, J. Kind and usual punishment p79-94 365
  See also Criminal law
Purchasing. See Buying
Purchasing handbook. Aljian, G. W. ed. 658.7
The purple flower. Bonner, M.
  In Hatch, J. V. ed. Black theater, U.S.A. p201-07 812.08
Purtell, Thelma C. See Clarke, Louis
Pushkin, Aleksandr Sergeevich. See pages
  In Rogers, J. A. Great men of color v2 p79-88 920
Putnam, Herbert. See pages
  In Goodrum, C. A. The Library of Congress p36-47 027.5
Pygmies. See pages
  In Severin, T. The Horizon Book of vanishing primitive man p69-92 301.2

Quennell, Peter. Samuel Johnson: his friends and enemies 92
—Who's who in Shakespeare 822.3
The question of Flannery O'Connor. Stephens, M. 813.09
Questions and answers on death and dying. Kübler-Ross, E. 128

Quilting. See pages
  In Better Homes and Gardens Sewing for your home p102-21 646.2
Quilts. See Coverlets
Quinn, Kenneth. Catullus 874.09

Rh. Zimmerman, D. R. 618.2
Rh factor. See Blood groups
Race 572
Race problems. See pages
  In Montagu, A. Man's most dangerous myth 572
  See also names of countries, cities, etc. with the subdivision Race relations, e.g. United States—Race relations
Rachel. Grimke, A. W.
  In Hatch, J. V. ed. Black theater, U.S.A. p137-72 812.08
Racing. See Horse racing
Radicals and radicalism. See Revolutions; Right and left (Political science)
Ragtime, The art of. Schafer, W. J. 781.5
The Railroaders 385.09
Railroads
—History 385.09; also pages
  In Havighurst, W. The heartland: Ohio, Indiana, Illinois p183-98 977
Railways. See Railroads
Railroads
—Europe. See pages
  In Baxter, R. Baxter's Eurailpass travel guide 914
Raising a hyperactive child. Stewart, M. A. 618.9
Raising children in a difficult time. Spock, B. 649
Raising small animals for fun and profit. Villiard, P. 636.08
Raleigh, Sir Walter 92
Ranch life. See pages
  In National Geographic Society. Life in rural America p88-107 917.3
Rand, Abby. How to get to Europe and have a wonderful time 914
The Rand McNally Concise atlas of the universe. See [Moore, P.] The concise Atlas of the universe 523
Rand McNally Illustrated world atlas 912
Rand McNally Road atlas of Europe 914
Randolph, Asa Philip 92
Randolph family. See pages
  In Daniels, J. The Randolphs of Virginia 920
The Randolph's of Virginia. Daniels, J. 920
Rank, Hugh. Edwin O'Connor 813.09
Rape. See pages
  In Ross, S. C. The rights of women p179-89 346
The rape of the taxpayer. Stern, P. M. 336.2
Rare animals 591; also pages
  In Allen, T. B. Vanishing wildlife of North America 591.9
Rationalism. See Reason
Ratner, Marc L. William Styron 813.09
Ravens. See pages
  In Capote, T. The dogs bark p117-30 818
Raymond, Louise. Adoption and after 362.7
Read, Herbert. Education through art 707
Read, Piers Paul. Alive 918
A reader's guide to Robert Browning. Crowell, N. B. 821.09
A reader's guide to Samuel Beckett. Kenner, H. 828
Reading. See pages
  In Diebold, J. ed. The world of the computer p225-39 001.6
  In Levy, H. B. Square pegs, round holes p55-74 371.9
  In Silberman, C. E. ed. The open classroom reader p535-629 372.1
  See also Books and reading
—Study and teaching. See Reading
Reading interest. See Books and reading
Real estate
—Laws and regulations. See pages
  In The Family legal advisor p245-69 340
Real lace: America's Irish rich. Birmingham, S. 301.45
The real Mussolini. See Mussolini, R. Mussolini: an intimate biography 92
Real property. See Real estate
Realism in literature. See Romanticism
Realty. See Real estate
Reason. See pages
  In Hesse, H. My belief p189-201 834
  In Skinner, B. F. About behaviorism p119-36 150.19
Recall 351.9; also pages
  In Benedict, M. L. The impeachment and trial of Andrew Johnson p26-60 973.8
Recipes. See Cookery
Reconstruction. See pages
  In Franklin, J. H. From slavery to freedom p236-67 301.45

Reconstruction (1939-1951) See pages
  In Miller, M. Plain speaking; an oral biography of Harry S. Truman p233-49 92
Recreation. See pages
  In Asimov, I. Today and tomorrow and . . . p199-209 508
  In Kinkade, K. A Walden Two experiment p246-56 335
  See also Play
Recreational vehicles. See Travel trailers and campers
Red China. See China (People's Republic of China, 1949-)
Red Cross. United States. American National Red Cross. Advanced first aid and emergency care 614.8
—Standard first aid and personal safety 614.8
The red desert (Motion picture) See pages
  In Solomon, S. J. ed. The classic cinema p273-94 791.43
Reducing (Body weight control) See Weight control
Reference books 028.7
—Bibliography 016; also pages
  In Carter, M. D. Building library collections p217-94 025.2
  In Katz, W. A. Introduction to reference work 025.5
  In Wynkoop, S. comp. Subject guide to government reference books 015.73
Reform, Social. See Social problems
Refrigeration and refrigerating machinery 621.5; also pages
  In Habeeb, V. T. The Ladies' Home Journal Art of homemaking p317-32 640
Regionalism. See Nationalism
Reischauer, Edwin O. Japan: the story of a nation 952
—Toward the 21st century: education for a changing world 327
Relief, Public. See Public welfare
Religion. See pages
  In Dewey, J. The philosophy of John Dewey v2 p696-712 191
  In Pound, E. Selected prose, 1909-1965 p45-71 814
  See also Faith; Mysticism; also names of countries, states, etc. with the subdivision Religion, e.g. United States—Religion
—Primitive. See pages
  In Noss, J. B Man's religions p3-32 291
Religion and art. See Art and religion
Religion in the public schools
  In Padover, S. K. ed. Sources of democracy p168-99 321.8
Religions 291
—Encyclopedias 291.03
Religious belief. See Faith
Religious freedom. See Religious liberty
Religious liberty. See pages
  In Padover, S. K. ed. Sources of democracy p141-99 321.8
Renoir, Jean. See pages
  In Solomon, S. J. ed. The classic cinema p149-70 791.43
Rental services. See Lease and rental services
Repair and maintenance guide: truck campers, Chilton's 629.28
Repair and tune-up guide: inboard/outdrives, Chilton's 623.82
Repair and tune-up guide: outboard motors 30 horsepower & over, Chilton's 623.82
Repairing. See Building—Repair and reconstruction; also names of appropriate subjects with the subdivision Repairing, e.g. Household appliances, Electric—Repairing
Representative government and representation. See Democracy
Representatives
—United States. See United States. Congress. House
Reproduction. See pages
  In Cousteau, J. The act of life 591.92
  In Landis, J. T. Building a successful marriage p392-423 301.42
Reptiles 598.1; also pages
  In Clement, R. C. Hammond Nature atlas of America p176-93 500.9
  In Vanishing species p154-87 591
  See also Turtles
—Fossil. See Dinosaurs
—Habits and behavior. See pages
  In Russell, F. The Okefenokee Swamp p58-67 500.9
Rescue work. See First aid
Research. See subjects with subdivision Research, e.g. Medicine—Research
Resources, Marine. See Marine resources
The Restoration and the eighteenth century. Price, M. ed.
  In The Oxford Anthology of English literature v 1 p1549-2312 820.8

Resumés (Employment) See Applications for positions
Retirement income. See Old age pensions
Return to earth. Aldrin, E. E. 92
Reviews. See Book reviews
Revolution
—American. See United States—History—Revolution
Revolution & romanticism. Jones, H. M. 92
Revolutionary suicide. Newton, H. P. 92
Revolutions. See pages
  In Jones, H. M. Revolution & romanticism 901.93
  In Paz, O. Alternating current p139-50 864
  See also United States—History—Revolution
Reykjavik
—Description. See pages
  In Kane, R. S. Grand tour A to Z: the capitals of Europe p408-18 914
Rhetoric 808
Rhodes, Daniel. Clay and glazes for the potter 738.1
Richards, Stanley, ed. See The Best short plays, 1974 808.82
—ed. Best short plays of the world theatre, 1968-1973 808.82
—District of Columbia
  In Hatch, J. V. ed. Black theater, U.S.A. p432-36 812.08
Richardson, Willis. The flight of the natives
  In Hatch, J. V. ed. Black theater, U.S.A. p382-89 812.08
—The idle head
  In Hatch, J. V. ed. Black theater, U.S.A. p233-40 812.08
Richie. Thompson, T. 301.43
Richter, Johann Paul Friedrich. See pages
  In Hesse, H. My belief p113-22 834
Riddles. See pages
  In Coffin, T. P. ed. Folklore from the working folk of America p144-73 398
Riding. See Horsemanship
Right and left (Political science) See pages
  In Sale, K. SDS 322.4
  In Wolff, R. P. ed. 1984 revisited 973
  See also Liberalism
The right of access to information from the Government. Thurman, S. D. 323.44
Rights, Civil. See Civil rights
The rights of children. Wilkerson, A. E. ed 346
The rights of mental patients. Ennis, B. 346
The rights of prisoners. Rudovsky, D. 345
The rights of students. Levine, A. 344.7
The rights of suspects. Rosengart, O. 345
The rights of teachers. Rubin, D. 344.7
The rights of the poor. Law, S. 344.3
Rights of women. See Woman—Civil rights
The rights of women. Ross, S. C. 346
The rights we have. Fraenkel, O. K. 344
Riley, Carolyn, ed. See Contemporary literary criticism 809
Rimbaud, Arthur. See Rimbaud, Jean Nicolas Arthur
Rimbaud, Jean Nicolas Arthur. See pages
  In Perloff, M. G. The poetic art of Robert Lowell p55-79 811.09
The rise and fall of the British nanny. See Gathorne-Hardy, J. The unnatural history of the nanny 914.2
Rites and ceremonies. See Marriage customs and rites
The River Niger. Walker, J. A. 812
The Riverside Shakespeare. Shakespeare, W. 822.3
Roach, Hildred. Black American music: past and present 781.7
Road atlas of Europe, Rand McNally 914
Road maps. See Automobiles—Road guides
Roads
—Maps. See Automobiles—Road guides
Robert-Houdin, Jean Eugène. See pages
  In Christopher, M. The illustrated history of magic p131-54 793.8
Robert Frost on writing. Frost, R. 811.09
Roberts, Richard. Fischer/Spassky: The New York Times Report on the chess match of the century 794.1
Robertson, Howard S. See Chanson de Roland. The song of Roland 841
Robinson, David. The history of world cinema 791.43
Rock climbing. See Mountaineering
Rockefeller Center. See New York. Rockefeller Center
Rockefeller family. See pages
  In Kutz, M. Rockefeller power 361.7
Rockefeller power. Kutz, M. 361.7
Rocks. See pages
  In Clement, R. C. Hammond Nature atlas of America p20-39 500.9
—Collectors and collecting. See pages
  In Desautels, P. E. Rocks & minerals 549

AUTHOR, TITLE, SUBJECT, AND ANALYTICAL INDEX
1974 SUPPLEMENT

Rocks & minerals. Desautels, P. E. 549
Rockwell, F. F. ed. See Dietz, M. J. 10,000 garden questions answered by 20 experts 635
Rocky Mountains 917.8
—Natural history. See Natural history—Rocky Mountains
—Social life and customs. See pages
In National Geographic Society. American mountain people p130-63 917.3
Rodgers, Jimmie. See pages
In Pleasants, H. The great American popular singers p11-25. 780.92
Rodgers, Richard. See pages
In Green, S. The world of musical comedy p141-63, 265-87 780.92
Rodin, Auguste. See pages
In Clark, K. The romantic rebellion p331-57 759.05
Rogers, J. A. World's great men of color 920
Rogers, Will 92
Romaic literature. See Greek literature, Modern
Romantic poetry and prose. Bloom, H. ed.
In The Oxford Anthology of English literature v2 p3-786 820.8
The romantic rebellion. Clark, K. 759.05
Romanticism. See pages
In Ewen, D. Orchestral music p70-123 785
In Jones, H. M. Revolution & romanticism 901.93
Romberg, Sigmund. See pages
In Green, S. The world of musical comedy p49-61 780.92
Rome, Harold Jacob. See pages
In Green, S. The world of musical comedy p241-49 780.92
Rome
—Civilization 913.37
—Description. See pages
In Kane, R. S. Grand tour A to Z: the capitals of Europe p419-49 914
—History—Empire, 30 B.C.-476 A.D. See pages
In Menen, A. Cities in the sand 913.37
Roncalli, Angelo Giuseppe, Cardinal. See John XXIII, Pope
Roosevelt, Eleanor (Roosevelt) See pages
In Roosevelt, E. An untold story [biography of Franklin Delano Roosevelt] 92
Roosevelt, Elliott. An untold story [biography of Franklin Delano Roosevelt] 92
Roosevelt, Franklin Delano, President U.S. 92; also pages
In Tugwell, R. G. In search of Roosevelt 973.917
Roosevelt family. See pages
In West, J. B. Upstairs at the White House p13-49 92
Rope. See Knots and splices
Rosenfeld, Louis J. The truth about vasectomy 613.9
Rosengart, Oliver. The rights of suspects 345
Ross, Donald K. A public citizen's action manual 640.73
Ross, Elisabeth Kübler- See Kübler-Ross, Elisabeth
Ross, Ishbel. The President's wife: Mary Todd Lincoln 92
Ross, Susan C. The rights of women 346
Rossi, Alice S. ed. The feminist papers: from Adams to de Beauvoir 301.41
Roth, Philip. Goodbye, Columbus; criticism
In Malin, I. ed. Contemporary American-Jewish literature p13-29 810.9
Rothschild family 920
The Rothschilds. Cowles, V. 920
Rottmann, Larry, ed. Winning hearts & minds 811.08
Rowland, Beatrice L. jt. auth. See Rowland, H. S. The New York Times Guide to student adventures and studies abroad, 1974 914
Rowland, Howard S. The New York Times Guide to student adventures and studies abroad, 1974 914
Rowse, A. L. Shakespeare the man 822.3
Rubin, David. The rights of teachers 344.7
Rubinstein, Arthur. My young years 780.92
Rudovsky, David. The rights of prisoners 345
Rudwick, Elliott, jt. auth. See Meier, A. CORE 322.4
Ruins. See Cities and towns, Ruined, extinct, etc.
Rukeyser, Louis. How to make money in Wall Street 332.6
Rukeyser, Muriel. Breaking open 811
Rules of the game (Motion picture) See pages
In Solomon, S. J. ed. The classic cinema p149-70 791.43
Rumford, Sir Benjamin Thompson, Count. See pages
In Chidsey D. B. The Loyalists p71-80 973.3
Rural life. See Country life; Farm life
Russell, D. A. Plutarch 888
Russell, Franklin. The Okefenokee Swamp 500.9

Russia
—Communism. See Communism—Russia
—Foreign relations. See pages
In Solzhenitsyn, A. I. Letter to the Soviet leaders 947.085
—Foreign relations—United States. See pages
In Osborne, J. The fourth year of the Nixon watch p74-105 973.924
—History. See pages
In Coughlan, R. Elizabeth and Catherine; empresses of all the Russias 92
In Warth, R. D. Lenin 92
—History—1925-1953. See pages
In Ulam, A. B. Stalin 92
—Intellectual life. See pages
In Mandelstam, N. Hope abandoned 92
—Politics and government 947.085
—Politics and government—1917- See pages
In Mandelstam, N. Hope abandoned 92
In Solzhenitsyn, A. I. The Gulag archipelago, 1918-1956 365
—Politics and government—1953- 947.085
Russian communism. See Communism—Russia
Russian literature 891.7
—History and criticism. See pages
In Seymour-Smith, M. Funk & Wagnalls Guide to modern world literature p935-83 809
Russian music. See Music, Russian

SALT. See Strategic Arms Limitation Talks
SDS. Sale, K. 322.4
SEC. See United States. Securities and Exchange Commission
Sackville-West, Hon. Victoria Mary 92
Sadism. See pages
In Fromm, E. The anatomy of human destructiveness p280-324 152.4
The safety match. Ginsbury, N.
In Richards, S. ed. Best short plays of the world theatre, 1968-1973 p241-53 808.82
Sagan, Carl, ed. See UFO's—a scientific debate 001.9
Sahara
—Description and travel 916.6
Saint Joan. Shaw, G. B.
In The Oxford Anthology of English literature v2 p1542-1612 820.8
Salacrou, Armand. Marguerite
In Richards, S. ed. Best short plays of the world theatre, 1968-1973 p202-12 808.82
Sale, Kirkpatrick. SDS 322.4
Salisbury, Charlotte Y. China diary 915.1
Salisbury, Harrison E. To Peking—and beyond 915.1
Salzman, Eric. Twentieth-century music: an introduction 780.9
Samson Agonistes. Milton, J.
In The Oxford Anthology of English literature v 1 p1367-1412 820.8
San Bernardino, Calif.
—Description. See Pages
In Wolfe, T. ed. The new journalism p304-19 810.8
San Blas Indians. See Cuna Indians
Sand, George X. The complete beginner's guide to fishing 799.1
Sanders, Marion K. Dorothy Thompson: a legend in her time 92
San Juan Mountains. See pages
In Walker, B. S. The Great Divide p72-95 500.9
Sanner, Marian, ed. See Piercy, E. J. Commonsense cataloging 025.3
Sansom, William. Proust and his world 92
Sarris, Andrew. The primal screen 791.43
Sarton, May. Collected poems (1930-1973) 811
—Journal of a solitude 92
Sarton, May (as subject) See pages
In Sibley, A. May Sarton 811.09
Sartre, Jean Paul 194; also pages
In Paz, O. Alternating current p164-78 864
Sasquatch 001.9
The Saturday night special. Sherrill, R. 363.3
Sauvin, Paul. See pages
In Tompkins, P. The secret life of plants p33-45 581
Scandinavian literature
—History and criticism. See pages
In Seymour-Smith, M. Funk & Wagnalls Guide to modern world literature p985-1031 809
Scarne, John. Scarne on cards 795.4
—Scarne's Encyclopedia of games 795
—Scarne's New Complete guide to gambling 795
Schafer, William J. The art of ragtime 781.5
Schaller, George B. Serengeti: a kingdom of predators 599
Scharff, Robert. Complete book of wood finishing 684
—See Golf Magazine's Encyclopedia of golf 796.352
Scherman, David E. ed. See The Best of Life 051

Schisgal, Murray. The Chinese
 In Richards, S. ed. Best short plays of the world theatre, 1968-1973 p152-67 808.82
Schlesinger, Arthur M. The imperial Presidency 353.03
Schlueter, Paul. The novels of Doris Lessing 823.09
Schmidt, Harvey. See Jones, T. The fantasticks [and] Celebration 812
Schoeffler, O. E. Esquire's Encyclopedia of 20th century men's fashions 391
Schoenberg, Jane, jt. auth. See Stichman, J. How to survive your husband's heart attack 616.1
Scholarships, fellowships, etc. 378.3
School children
—Food. See pages
 In Griffin, A. How to start and operate a day care home p119-33 362.7
School libraries. See pages
 In Wynar, C. L. Guide to reference books for school media centers 016
School lunches. See School children—Food
Schools. See Private schools
Schreiber, Flora Rheta. Sybil 616.8
Schulz, Max F. Black humor fiction of the sixties 813.09
Schwartz, Arthur. See pages
 In Green, S. The world of musical comedy p203-17 780.92
Science 508; also pages
 In Diebold, J. ed. The world of the computer p286-98 001.6
—History. See pages
 In Bronowski, J. The ascent of man 501
—Philosophy 501
—Social aspects. See Science and civilization
—Study and teaching. See pages
 In Silberman, C. E. ed. The open classroom reader p698-748 372.1
—United States—History. See pages
 In Nye, R. B. Society and culture in America, 1830-1860 p236-58 917.3
Science and civilization. See pages
 In Dewey, J. The philosophy of John Dewey v2 p388-97 191
Science and the humanities. See pages
 In Barzun, J. The use and abuse of art p97-122 701
Science fiction
—History and criticism 709.3; also pages
 In Asimov, I. Today and tomorrow and . . p275-315 508
—Periodicals. See pages
 In Bretnor, R. ed. Science fiction, today and tomorrow p17-44 809.3
—Study and teaching. See pages
 In Bretnor, R. ed. Science fiction, today and tomorrow p309-28 809.3
 In Toffler, A. ed. Learning for tomorrow p234-56 370.19
Science fiction, today and tomorrow. Bretnor, R. ed. 809.3
Scientific American. Early man in America 970.1
Scientists
—Dictionaries. See pages
 In Dictionary of scientific biography v9-10 920.03
—Directories 920.025
—Education. See pages
 In Toffler, A. ed. Learning for tomorrow p157-72 370.19
Scobey, Joan, jt. auth. See Myers, N. Gifts from the kitchen 641.5
Scotland
—History—Jacobite Rebellion, 1745-1746. See Jacobite Rebellion, 1745-1746
Scuba diving. See Skin diving
Scully, Vincent. Modern architecture 724.9
Sculpture
—American—History. See pages
 In Nye, R. B. Society and culture in America, 1830-1860 p164-73 917.3
Sea animals. See Marine animals
Sea labortories. See Manned undersea research stations
Sea monsters. See pages
 In Sweeney, J. B. A pictorial history of sea monsters and their dangerous marine life 597
Sea-shore. See Seashore
Seacole, Mary. See pages
 In Rogers, J. A. Great men of color v2 p262-71 920
Sealing 639
Sears, Stephen W. ed. See The Horizon History of the British Empire 942
Seashore. See pages
 In Leonard, J. N. Atlantic beaches p31-41, 91-97, 104-15, 169-79 500.9
Seasons. Borland, H. 500.9

Sebree, Charles. The dry August
 In Hatch, J. V. ed. Black theater, U.S.A. p658-70 812.08
Secession. See United States—History—Civil War—Causes
Second dictionary of acronyms & abbreviations. Pugh, E. 603
A second flowering. Cowley, M. 810.9
Secondary education. See Education, Secondary
Secret agents, spies, and saboteurs. Piekalkiewicz, J. 940.54
The secret life of plants. Tompkins, P. 581
Secret service. See World War, 1939-1945—Secret service
Secretaries. See pages
 In Whalen, D. H. The secretary's handbook 651.02
The secretary's handbook. Whalen, D. H. 651.02
Securities. See Stocks
Securities and Exchange Commission (United States) See United States. Securities and Exchange Commission
Security, Social. See Old age pensions
Seeds. See pages
 In Northen, H. T. Greenhouse gardening p63-79 635.9
Segregation. See Negroes—Segregation
Séjour, Victor. The brown overcoat
 In Hatch, J. V. ed. Black theater, U.S.A. p25-33 812.08
Selbit, P. T. See pages
 In Christopher, M. The illustrated history of magic p259-73 793.8
Selected and new poems. Berrigan, D. 811
Selected prose, 1909-1965. Pound, E. 814
Selecting materials for libraries. Broadus, R. N. 025.2
Self. See pages
 In Skinner, B. F. About behaviorism p167-88 150.19
Self-government. See Democracy
Seligson, Marcia. The eternal bliss machine 392
Semantics. See Words, New
Separation (Law) See Divorce
Serengeti: a kingdom of predators. Schaller, G. B. 599
Serengeti National Park. See pages
 In Schaller, G. B. Serengeti: a kingdom of predators 599
Serial titles newly received. See New serial titles 016.05
Serials. See Periodicals
Sermons 252
Serpico, Frank 92
Servants. See Household employees
The seventh seal (Motion picture) See pages
 In Solomon, S. J. ed. The classic cinema p223-45 791.43
Severin, Timothy. The Horizon Book of vanishing primitive man 301.2
Severus, Lucius Septimus, Emperor of Rome. See pages
 In Menen, A. Cities in the sand p134-49 913.37
Sewing 646.2
 See also Embroidery
Sewing for your home, Better Homes and Gardens 646.2
Sex. See pages
 In Landis, J. T. Building a successful marriage p270-90 301.42
 In Patai, R. The Arab mind p118-42 301.29
 See also Reproduction; Sadism
Sex discrimination. See pages
 In DeCrow, K. Sexist justice 346.1
 See also Woman—Civil rights
Sex education. See Sex instruction
Sex instruction 612.6; also pages
 In Spock, B. Raising children in a difficult time p149-64 649
Sexist justice. DeCrow, K. 346.1
Sexton, Anne. The death notebooks 811
Sexual education. See Sex instruction
Sexual ethics. See pages
 In Landis, J. T. Building a successful marriage p141-59 301.42
Sexual hygiene. See Birth control; Sexual instruction
Seymour-Smith, Martin. Funk & Wagnalls Guide to modern world literature 809
Shafer, Ronald G. See Carlson, M. B. How to get your car repaired without getting gypped 629.28
Shaka. See Chaka, Zulu chief

AUTHOR, TITLE, SUBJECT, AND ANALYTICAL INDEX
1974 SUPPLEMENT

Shakespeare, William. King Lear; criticism
  In Handy, W. J. ed. Twentieth century criticism: the major statements p95-110 801
—Macbeth; criticism
  In Handy, W. J. ed. Twentieth century criticism: the major statements p184-97, 387-402 801
—The Riverside Shakespeare 822.3
—Sonnets; criticism
  In Auden, W. H. Forewords and afterwords p88-108 809
Shakespeare, William (as subject)
—Biography 822.3
—Characters 822.3
—Concordances 822.3
—Criticism, interpretation, etc. 822.3
—Dictionaries 822.3
—Tragedies. See pages
  In Handy, W. J. ed. Twentieth century criticism: the major statements p290-302 801
Shakespeare the man. Rowse, A. L. 822.3
Shapiro, Karl Jay. Poems of a Jew; criticism
  In Malin, I. ed. Contemporary American-Jewish literature p213-28 810.9
Shaw, George Bernard. Saint Joan
  In The Oxford Anthology of English literature v2 p1542-1612 820.8
Shaw, George Bernard (as subject) See pages
  In Mencken, H. L. The young Mencken p63-77 818
Sheaffer, Louis. O'Neill 92
Shelley, Mary Wollstonecraft (Godwin) Frankenstein: criticism
  In Small, C. Mary Shelley's Frankenstein 823.09
Shelley, Mary Wollstonecraft (Godwin) (as subject) See pages
  In Walling, W. A. Mary Shelley 823.09
Shelley, Percy Bysbe. See pages
  In Small, C. Mary Shelley's Frankenstein 823.09
Shelton, Ruth Gaines- See Gaines-Shelton, Ruth
Shepard, Sam. The holy ghostly
  In Richards, S. ed. Best short plays of the world theatre, 1968-1973 p277-88 808.82
Sherrill, Robert. The Saturday night special 363.3
Shesgreen, Sean, ed. See Hogarth, W. Engravings by Hogarth 769
Shifting gears. O'Neill, N. 158
Shine, Ted. Herbert III
  In Hatch, J. V. ed. Black theater, U.S.A. p854-63 812.08
Shinto. See pages
  In Noss, J. B. Man's religions p308-32 291
Shockley, Ann Allen. Living Black American authors 920.03
Shoes and shoe industry. See pages
  In Bridge, R. America's backpacking book p132-46 796.5
Shooting. See Firearms
Shooting stars. See Meteors
Shoppers' guides. See Consumer education
Shopping. See Consumer education
A short history of Western music. Jacobs, A. 780.9
Sibley, Agnes. May Sarton 811.09
Sieg Heil! Lorant, S. 943.08
Siegel, Loren, jt. auth. See Ennis, B. The rights of mental patients 346
Signs and symbols. See pages
  In De Sola, R. Abbreviations dictionary 421.03
Sikhs. See pages
  In Noss, J. B. Man's religions p226-35 291
Silberman, Charles E. ed. The open classroom reader 372.1
Simon, Alfred, jt. auth. See Lewine, R. Songs of the American theater 784.01
Simon, George T. Glenn Miller and his orchestra 780.92
Simon, Neil. The prisoner of Second Avenue 812
—The sunshine boys 812
—Visitor from Forest Hills
  In Richards, S. ed. Best short plays of the world theatre, 1968-1973 p22-33 808.82
Simpson, Charlie. See pages
  In Wolfe, T. ed. The new journalism p127-60 810.8
Simpson, Colin. The Lusitania 940.4
Sin 233
Sinatra, Frank. See pages
  In Pleasants, H. The great American popular singers p181-97 780.92
Singer, Isaac Bashevis. See pages
  In Malin, I. ed. Contemporary American-Jewish literature p248-69 810.9
Singers 780.92
The single parent experience. Klein, C. 301.42
Sippl, Charles J. Computer dictionary and handbook 001.6
Sippl, Charles P. jt. auth. See Sippl, C. J. Computer dictionary and handbook 001.6
Sir Gawain and the Grene Knight
  In The Oxford Anthology of English literature v 1 p284-348 820.8
Sir Walter Ralegh. Lacey, R. 92
Sitting. Tobias, J.
  In The Best short plays, 1974 p247-82 808.82
Sixteenth-century verse, The Anchor Anthology of. Sylvester, R. S. ed. 821.08
Skin diving 797.2; also pages
  In National Geographic Society. World beneath the sea p71-90 551.4
Skinner, B. F. About behaviorism 150.19
  For material about this author See Skinner, Burrhus Frederic
Skinner, Burrhus Frederic. See pages
  In Carpenter, F. The Skinner primer: behind freedom and dignity 150.19
The Skinner primer: behind freedom and dignity. Carpenter, F. 150.19
Slander (Law) See Libel and slander
The slave. Baraka, I. A.
  In Hatch, J. V. ed. Black theater, U.S.A. p812-25 812.08
Slave trade. See pages
  In Franklin, J. H. From slavery to freedom p30-45 301.45
Slavery in Latin America. See pages
  In Franklin, J. H. From slavery to freedom p68-84 301.45
Slavery in the United States. See pages
  In Franklin, J. H. From slavery to freedom 301.45
  In Hughes, L. A pictorial history of Blackamericans 301.45
  In Nevins, A. Ordeal of the Union; selected chapters p15-64 973.7
  In Stampp, K. M. ed. The causes of the Civil War p101-39 973.7
  See also Abolitionists
Sloan, Irving J. Youth and the law 340
Sloane, Eugene A. The new complete book of bicycling 796.6
Slovenia. See pages
  In National Geographic Society. The Alps p152-71 914.94
Small, Christopher. Mary Shelley's Frankenstein 823.09
Small animals for fun and profit, Raising. Villiard, P. 636.08
Small arms. See Firearms
Small business 658
Small engines. See Chilton's Repair and tune-up guide: small engines 621.43
Smallpox. See pages
  In Marks, G. The story of medicine in America p213-33 610.9
Smith, Bert Kruger. Aging in America 301.43
Smith, Bessie. See pages
  In Pleasants, H. The great American popular singers p63-79 780.92
Smith, Cam, comp. See Fuller, R. B. Buckminster Fuller to children of earth 818
Smith, Goldwin. A history of England 942
Smith, Jimmy Lee. See pages
  In Wambaugh, J. The onion field 364.1
Smith, Martin Seymour- See Seymour-Smith, Martin
Smith, Sydney. See pages
  In Auden, W. H. Forewords and afterwords p152-67 809
Snorkeling. See Skin diving
Social change. See pages
  In Bretnor, R. ed. Science fiction, today and tomorrow p116-32 809.3
  In Dewey, J. The philosophy of John Dewey v2 p643-65 191
Social conditions. See names of countries, cities, etc. with the subdivision Social conditions, e.g. United States—Social conditions
Social equality. See Equality
Social evolution. See Social change
Social ethics. See pages
  In Dewey, J. The philosophy of John Dewey v2 p712-23 191
Social policy. See pages
  In Myrdal, G. Against the stream p33-51 330
  See also names of countries, cities, etc. with the subdivision Social policy, e.g. United States—Social policy
Social problems. See pages
  In Nye, R. B. Society and culture in America, 1830-1860 p32-70 917.3
  See also Divorce; Old age pensions; Woman—Employment; Woman—Social conditions
Social problems in education. See Educational sociology
Social psychology. See pages
  In Toffler, A. ed. Learning for tomorrow p3-32 370.19
  See also Violence
Social reform. See Social problems

Social sciences. See pages
   In Moynihan, D. P. Coping p259-71 309.173
   In Myrdal, G. Against the stream 330
   In Toffler, A. ed. Learning for tomorrow p75-131 370.19
—Bibliography 016.3
—Methodology. See pages
   In Dewey, J. The philosophy of John Dewey v2 p397-420 191
—Periodicals—Indexes 300.5
Social sciences & humanities index. See Humanities index 050
—See Social sciences index 300.5
Social sciences index 300.5
Social security. See Old age pensions
Social studies. See Social sciences
Social welfare. See Public welfare; Social problems
Socialism
   See also Communism
—Scotland. See pages
   In Commager, H. S. ed. Britain through American eyes p702-11 914.2
Society, Primitive 301.2
   See also Art, Primitive
Society and art. See Art and society
Society and culture in America, 1830-1860. Nye, R. B. 917.3
Sociology
   See also Educational sociology; Race problems; Social change
—Bibliography. See pages
   In White, C. M. Sources of information in the social sciences p243-306 016.3
—Educational. See Educational sociology
—Urban 301.34
Soil fertility. See Soils
Soils. See pages
   In Northen, H. T. Greenhouse gardening p50-62 635.9
Sola, Ralph de. See De Sola, Ralph
Solar system. See pages
   In Asimov, I. Asimov on astronomy p101-14 523
   See also Moon
Soldier. Herbert, A. B. 959.704
Soldiers
   See also United States. Army—Military life
—United States. See pages
   In Wolfe, T. ed. The new journalism p292-303 810.8
   See also Negro soldiers
The Soldiers 970.5
Solo: the story of an African wild dog. Lawick, H. van 599
Solomon, Stanley J. ed. The classic cinema 791.43
Solzhenitsyn, Aleksandr I. Candle in the wind 891.7
—The Gulag archipelago, 1918-1956 365
—Letter to the Soviet leaders 947.085
Somer, John, jt. ed. See Klinkowitz, J. ed. The Vonnegut statement 813.09
Somewhere a child is crying. Fontana, V. J. 362.7
Sondak, Eileen. jt. auth. See Sondak, N. The layman's dictionary of computer terminology 001.6
Sondak, Norman. The layman's dictionary of computer terminology 001.6
Sondheim, Stephen. See Wheeler, H. A little night music 812
Song & dance man. Gray, M. 780.92
A song at twilight. Coward, N.
   In Richards, S. ed. Best short plays of the world theatre, 1968-1973 p51-80 808.82
The song of Roland. Chanson de Roland 841
Songs. See pages
   In The New York Times Great songs of Broadway 782.8
   See also Music, Popular (Songs, etc.)
—American. See pages
   In Lewine, R. Songs of the American theater 784.01
   See also Folk songs—United States
—Popular. See Music, Popular (Songs, etc.)
Songs of the American theater. Lewine, R. 784.01
Sonoran Desert
—Natural history. See Natural history—Sonoran Desert
Sophocles. Antigone 882
Sources of democracy. Padover, S. K. ed. 321.8
Sources of information in the social sciences. White, C. M. 016.3
South African literature
—History and criticism. See pages
   In Seymour-Smith, M. Funk & Wagnalls Guide to modern world literature p1033-44 809

South American literature. See Latin American literature
South Pass, Wyo. See pages
   In Walker, B. S. The Great Divide p102-19 500.9
Southern States
—Economic conditions. See pages
   In Stampp, K. M. ed. The causes of the Civil War p63-78 973.7
Southwest, New
—Natural history. See Natural history—Southwest, New
Southwest Indian painting. Tanner, C. L. 759.13
Space communication. See Interstellar communication
Space flight to the moon. See pages
   In Collins, M. Carrying the fire 629.45
   See also Apollo project; Moon—Exploration
Space sciences. See pages
   In Alter, D. Pictorial astronomy p255-69 523
Spanish-American literature. See Latin American literature
Spanish essays 864
Spanish literature
   See also Latin American literature
—History and criticism. See pages
   In Seymour-Smith, M. Funk & Wagnalls Guide to modern world literature p1045-96 809
Spanish poetry 861
Spasskiĭ, Boris Vasil'evich. See pages
   In Horowitz, A. The world chess championship p219-84 794.1
   In Roberts, R. Fischer/Spassky: The New York Times Report on the chess match of the century 794.1
Spassky, Boris. See Spasskiĭ, Boris Vasil'evich
Speak to me, dance with me. De Mille, A. 92
The speaker's and toastmaster's handbook. Prochnow, H. V. comp. 808.5
Special libraries. See Libraries, Special
Speculation 332.6
Speech, Liberty of. See Free speech
Speeches, addresses, etc. 808.85
Spence, Eulalie. Undertow
   In Hatch, J. V. ed. Black theatre, U.S.A. p192-200 812.08
Spencer, Janet, ed. See The National directory for the performing arts and civic centers [1974] 790.2
Spevack, Marvin. The Harvard Concordance to Shakespeare 822.3
Spies. See pages
   In Piekalkiewicz, J. Secret agents, spies, and saboteurs 940.54
Spiller, Robert E. ed. See Literary history of the United States 810.9
Spirits. See Demonology
Spiritual life 248
   See also Faith
Spock, Benjamin. Raising children in a difficult time 649
Spofford, Ainsworth Rand. See pages
   In Goodrum, C. A. The Library of Congress p19-28 027.5
Sports. See pages
   In Cosell, H. Cosell 92
—Encyclopedias 796.03
Sports record book. Guinness 796.03
Square pegs, round holes. Levy, H. B. 371.9
Squids 594
Stabilization in industry. See Economic conditions
Stalin, Iosif 92
Stalking the faraway places. Gibbons, E. 581.6
Stampp, Kenneth M. ed. The causes of the Civil War 973.7
Standard first aid and personal safety. Red Cross. United States. American National Red Cross 614.8
Standard refrigeration and air conditioning questions and answers. Elonka, S. M. 621.5
The Stanislavski method. See Moore, S. The Stanislavski system 792
The Stanislavski system. Moore, S. 792
Stanislavskiĭ, Konstantin Sergeevich. See pages
   In Moore, S. The Stanislavski system 792
Stanton, Elizabeth (Cady) See pages
   In Rossi, A. S. ed. The feminist papers: from Adams to de Beauvoir p378-96 301.41
Star of the morning. Mitchell, L.
   In Hatch, J. V. ed. Black theater, U.S.A. p618-52 812.08
Starr, Chester G. A history of the ancient world 930
Stars. See pages
   In Alter, D. Pictorial astronomy p159-253 523
   In Asimov, I. Asimov on astronomy p153-64, 192-204 523
   See also Meteors
—Atlases 523.8

AUTHOR, TITLE, SUBJECT, AND ANALYTICAL INDEX
1974 SUPPLEMENT

The state. See Political science
State and education. See Education and state
State and environment. See Environmental policy
State governments. See pages
  In Diebold, J. ed. The world of the computer p158-71 001.6
State planning. See Social policy
State rights. See pages
  In Stampp, K. M. ed. The causes of the Civil War p42-62 973.7
States' rights. See State rights
Statistics
—Bibliography 016.31
Statistics sources 016.31
Stay of execution. Alsop, S. 616.1
Staying on alone. Toklas, A. B. 92
Steffens, Joseph Lincoln. See Steffens, Lincoln
Stein, Gertrude 92; also pages
  In Toklas, A. B. Staying on alone 92
The Stein and Day Handbook of magic. Kaye, M. 793.8
Steinitz, Wilhelm. See pages
  In Horowitz, A. The world chess championship p17-47 794.1
Steinitz, William. See Steinitz, Wilhelm
Stember, Sol. The bicentennial guide to the American Revolution 973.3
Stephens, Martha. The question of Flannery O'Connor 813.09
Stephenson, Ralph. The animated film 791.43
Sterilization (Birth control) 613.9
Stern, Philip M. The rape of the taxpayer 336.2
Stevens, Wallace. See pages
  In Morris, A. K. Wallace Stevens: imagination and faith 811.09
Stevenson, Adlai Ewing, 1900-1965. The papers of Adlai E. Stevenson v3-4 92
Stevenson, Robert P. How to build and buy cabinets for the modern kitchen 684.1
Stewart, Lawrence D. jt. auth. See Jablonski, E. The Gershwin years 780.92
Stewart, Mark A. Raising a hyperactive child 618.9
Stichman, JoAnn. How to survive your husband's heart attack 616.1
Stock exchange. See Stocks
Stockholm
—Description. See pages
  In Kane, R. S. Grand tour A to Z: the capitals of Europe p450-69 914
Stocks 332.6
Stone age. See pages
  In Fromm, E. The anatomy of human destructiveness p151-61 152.4
  See also Man, Prehistoric
Stonehenge. See pages
  In Hawkins, G. S. Beyond Stonehenge p 1-89 913
Storks. See pages
  In Carr, A. The Everglades p62-69 500.9
[Story, Norah]. Supplement to the Oxford Companion to Canadian history and literature 810.3
The story of medicine in America. Marks, G. 610.9
The strange career of Jim Crow. Woodward, C. V. 301.45
Strategic Arms Limitation Talks. See pages
  In Kissinger, H. A. American foreign policy p137-61 327.73
Strauss family. See pages
  In Wechsberg, J. The waltz emperors 780.92
Street traffic. See Traffic regulations
Streisand, Barbra. See pages
  In Pleasants, H. The great American popular singers p358-64 780.92
Strictly personal. Eisenhower, J. S. D. 92
Strimple, Earl O. jt. auth. See McKeown, D. B. Your pet's health from A to Z 636.08
Student adventures and studies abroad, 1974, The New York Times Guide to. Rowland, H. S. 914
Student aid. See Scholarships, fellowships, etc.
Student loan funds 378.3
Students
—Civil rights 344.7
Students for a Democratic Society 322.4
Studies abroad, 1974, The New York Times Guide to student adventures and. Rowland, H. S. 914
Styne, Jule. See pages
  In Green, S. The world of musical comedy p311-27 780.92
Styron, William. See pages
  In Ratner, M. L. William Styron 813.09
Subconsciousness. See Personality disorders; Psychoanalysis
Subject collections. Ash, L. comp. 026
Subject guide to government reference books. Wynkoop, S. comp. 015.73
Submarine photography. See Photography, Submarine
Submarine research stations, Manned. See Manned undersea research stations

Suburban areas. See Metropolitan areas
Sudan
—History. See pages
  In The Horizon History of the British Empire p232-47 942
Suffrage. See pages
  In Padover, S. K. ed. Sources of democracy p201-48 321.8
Suicide. See pages
  In Mannes, M. Last rights 174
Suite in three keys: A song at twilight. See Coward, N. A song at twilight
Sullivan, May Miller. See Miller, May
Sulzberger, C. L. An age of mediocrity 92
—Postscript with a Chinese accent 92
Summer homes. See Houses
Sun. See pages
  In Alter, D. Pictorial astronomy p 1-23 523
A Sunday morning in the South. Johnson, G. D.
  In Hatch, J. V. ed. Black theater, U.S.A. p211-17 812.08
Sunken treasure. See Buried treasure
Sunset. See Alaska 917.98
The sunshine boys. Simon, N. 812
The super cops. Whittemore, L. H. 363.2
The supermarket handbook. Goldbeck, N. 641.3
Superstition. See pages
  In Coffin, T. P. ed. Folklore from the working folk of America p177-257 398
Supplement to the Oxford Companion to Canadian history and literature. [Story, N.] 810.3
Survival (after airplane accidents, shipwrecks, etc.) See pages
  In Read, P. P. Alive 918
Swamps. See Marshes
Swanson, Roy Arthur. tr. See Pindar. Pindar's odes 884
Sweden
—History 948.5
Sweeney, James B. A pictorial history of sea monsters and other dangerous marine life 597
Sweetheart; the story of Mary Pickford. Windeler, R. 92
Switzerland
—Description and travel. See pages
  In Hesse, H. My belief p230-40 834
Sybil. Schreiber, F. R. 616.8
Sylvester, Richard S. ed. The Anchor Anthology of sixteenth-century verse 821.08
Szasz, Thomas S. ed. The age of madness 362.2

Taber, Gladys. Country chronicle 630.1
Table decoration. See Table setting and decoration
Table setting and decoration. See pages
  In Better Homes and Gardens Sewing for your home p154-63 646.2
Take a giant step. Peterson, L.
  In Hatch, J. V. ed. Black theater, U.S.A. p547-84 812.08
Tal', Mikhail Nekhem'evich. See Tals, Mihails
Talbott, Strobe. ed. See Khrushchev, N. S. Khrushchev remembers: the last testament 947.085
Tals, Mihails. See pages
  In Horowitz, A. The world chess championship p177-218 794.1
Tan, Leong T. Acupuncture therapy 615
Tan, Margaret Y. C. jt. auth. See Tan, Leong T. Acupuncture therapy 615
Tangier
—Description. See pages
  In Capote, T. The dogs bark p87-97 818
Tanner, Beatrice Stella. See Campbell, Mrs Patrick
Tanner, Clara Lee. Southwest Indian painting 759.13
Taoism. See pages
  In Noss, J. B. Man's religions p240-69 291
Taormina
—Description. See pages
  In Capote, T. The dogs bark p105-16 818
Tarkington, Booth. See pages
  In Fennimore, K. J. Booth Tarkington 813.09
Tasady people. See pages
  In The First men p137-47 573
Taxation
  See also Income tax
—United States. See pages
  In How to run a small business p68-79 658
  In Ross, D. K. A public citizen's action manual p146-68 640.73
Taxation of income. See Income tax
Taxation of legacies. See Inheritance and transfer tax
Taxes. See Taxation
Taylor, John Russell. The Hollywood musical 791.43
Taylor, Zack. jt. auth. See Angier, B. Introduction to canoeing 797.1

Teachers
　　See also Teaching
—Civil rights 344.7
—Political activity. See pages
　　In Rubin, D. The rights of teachers p68-81 344.7
Teaching. See pages
　　In Levy, H. B. Square pegs, round holes p159-75 371.9
　　In Read, H. Education through art p285-95 707
　　See also Montessori method of education
—Experimental methods. See Education—Experimental methods
—Freedom of. See Academic freedom
The teachings of Don Juan. Castaneda, C. 299
Technical assistance. See Underdeveloped areas
Techniques of novel writing. Burack. A. S. 808.3
Technology
—Dictionaries 603
—History. See pages
　　In Nye, R. B. Society and culture in America, 1830-1860 p258-82 917.3
Technology and civilization. See pages
　　In Boorstin, D. J. Democracy and its discontents p102-24 917.3
　　In Diebold, J. ed. The world of the computer 001.6
　　In Moynihan, D. P. Coping p210-32, 395-404 309.173
Teen age. See Adolescence; Youth
Teilhard de Chardin, Pierre. On happiness 131
Telecommunication. See Libraries—Communication systems
Telescope. See pages
　　In Alter, D. Pictorial astronomy p290-97 523
Television broadcasting. See pages
　　In Cavett, D. Cavett 92
　　In Cosell, H. Cosell 92
　　See also Television in politics
Television in politics 329
Temple of Ammon. See Karnak, Egypt. Temple of Ammon
Ten Hoor, Elvie, jt. auth. See Meilach, D. Z. Collage and assemblage 751.4
10,000 garden questions answered by 20 experts. Dietz, M. J. ed. 635
Tender loving greed. Mendelson, M. A. 362.6
Tennis
—Biography. See pages
　　In King, B. J. Billie Jean 92
Tennyson, Alfred Tennyson, 1st Baron. See pages
　　In Auden, W. H. Forewords and afterwords p221-32 809
Tents. See pages
　　In Bridge, R. America's backpacking book p173-87 796.5
Terkel, Studs. Working 331.2
The terrarium book. Evans, C. M. 635.9
Terrariums 635.9
Terrariums & miniature gardens 635.9
Terry family. See pages
　　In Gielgud, Sir J. Distinguished company p17-41 920
Tests. See Educational tests and measurements
Teveth, Shabtai. Moshe Dayan: the soldier, the man, the legend 92
Textile industry and fabrics
—Dictionaries 391.03
Tezozomoc, Fernando Alvaro. See Alvaro Tezozomoc, Fernando
Theater
　　See also Actors and actresses; Moving pictures
—Bibliography. See pages
　　In Palmer, H. H. comp. European drama criticism. Supplement I-II 016.8092
—Great Britain—History. See pages
　　In Nicoll, A. English drama, 1900-1930 822.09
—Indexes 792.01
—New York (City)—History 792.09
—New York (City)—Reviews. See pages
　　In The New York Times Directory of the theater 792.01
—United States—History 792.09; also pages
　　In Nye, R. B. Society and culture in America, 1830-1860 p146-57 917.3
—Yearbooks. See pages
　　In The Best plays of 1973-1974 808.82
Theater index to plays in periodicals. Chicorel 808.82
Theology
　　See also Spiritual life
—Doctrinal. See Meditations
—Encyclopedias. See pages
　　In The Oxford Dictionary of the Christian Church 203
Therapeutics, Suggestive. See Mental healing
They that sit in darkness. Burrill, M.
　　In Hatch, J. V. ed. Black theater, U.S.A. p178-83 812.08

Thinking. See Thought and thinking
Thinking machines. Adler, I. 519.4
Third world. See Underdeveloped areas
Thirteen: the flight that failed. Cooper, S. F. 629.45
This sun of York; a biography of Edward IV. Clive, M. 92
Thomas, Lewis. The lives of a cell 574.01
Thomas, Sarah M. A guide to sources of consumer information 640.73
Thomas Jefferson, an intimate history. Brodie, F. M. 92
Thompson, Sir Benjamin. See Rumford, Sir Benjamin Thompson, Count
Thompson, Dorothy 92
Thompson, Thomas. Richie 301.43
Thoreau, Henry David. The illustrated Walden 818
Thought and thinking. See pages
　　In Skinner, B. F. About behaviorism p102-18 150.19
　　See also Memory
Three hundred years of American drama and theatre. Wilson, G. B. 792.09
Thurman, S. David. The right of access to information from the Government 323.44
Thurston, Howard. See pages
　　In Christopher, M. The illustrated history of magic p222-40 793.8
Tibbles, Percy Thomas. See Selbit, P. T.
Tides. See pages
　　In Asimov, I. Asimov on astronomy p 1-13 523
Tidyman, Ernest. Dummy 345.7
Tillich, Paul 92
Time. See pages
　　In Asimov, I. Today and tomorrow and . . . p107-16 508
　　See also Calendars
Time-Life Books. See Abbey, E. Cactus country 500.9
—See Brown, D. Wild Alaska 500.9
—See Carr, A. The Everglades 500.9
—See Constable, G. The Neanderthals 573
—See The Cowboys 978
—See Crockett, J. U. Vegetables and fruits 635
—See Edey, M. A. The missing link 573.2
—See The First men 573
—See The Horizon History of the British Empire 942
—See The Indians 970.4
—See Johnson, W. W. Baja California 500.9
—See Knauth, P. The north woods 500.9
—See Leonard, J. N. Atlantic beaches 500.9
—See Life before man 560
—See The Railroaders 385.09
—See Russell, F. The Okefenokee Swamp 500.9
—See The Soldiers 970.5
—See Vanishing species 591
—See Walker, B. S. The Great Divide 500.9
—See Wallace, R. Hawaii 500.9
Times to remember. Kennedy, R. F. 92
Tinker vs Des Moines Independent Community School District. See pages
　　In Levine, A. The rights of students p149-60 344.7
To Peking—and beyond. Salisbury, H. E. 915.1
To race the wind. Large print book. Krents, H. 92
Tobias, John Sitting
　　In The Best short plays, 1974 p247-82 808.82
Today and tomorrow and . . . Asimov, I. 508
Toffler, Alvin, ed. Learning for tomorrow 370.19
Toilet preparations. See Cosmetics
Toklas, Alice B. Staying on alone 92
Tolkien, John Ronald Reuel. See pages
　　In Helms, R. Tolkien's world 828
Tolkien's world. Helms, R. 828
Tolson, Melvin Beaunorus. See pages
　　In Gibson, D. B. ed. Modern Black poets p84-95 811.09
Tolstoĭ, Lev Nikolaevich, Graf 92
Tolstoy, Leo. See Tolstoĭ, Lev Nikolaevich, Graf
Tompkins, Peter. The secret life of plants 581
Tools. See pages
　　In Mechanix Illustrated Fix-it home repairs handbook p23-37 643
Toomer, Jean. Balo
　　In Hatch, J. V. ed. Black theater, U.S.A. p218-24 812.08
Toomer, Jean (as subject) See pages
　　In Wagner, J. Black poets of the United States p259-81 811.09
Tories, American. See American Loyalists
Tortoises. See Turtles
Toussaint Louverture, Pierre Dominique. See pages
　　In Rogers, J. A. Great men of color v2 p227-40 920
Toward the 21st century: education for a changing world. Reischauer, E. O. 327

AUTHOR, TITLE, SUBJECT, AND ANALYTICAL INDEX
1974 SUPPLEMENT

Toye, William, ed. See [Story, N.] Supplement to the Oxford Companion to Canadian history and literature 310.3
Toynbee, Arnold, ed. Half the world 915.1
Traffic regulations. See pages
    In The Family legal adviser p393-418 340
    See also Automobiles—Laws and regulations
The tragedy of the moon. Asimov, I. 503
Trains, Railroad. See Railroads
Transcendental meditation. See pages
    In Forem, J. Transcendental meditation 181
    In Vonnegut, K. Wampeters, foma & granfalloons (opinions) p31-41 818
Transfer tax. See Inheritance and transfer tax
Translating and interpreting. See pages
    In Di Giovanni, N. T. ed. Borges on writing p103-60 868
Transplantation of organs, tissues, etc. See pages
    In Marks, G. The story of medicine in America p309-31 610.9
Trapp, J. B. ed. Medieval English literature
    In The Oxford Anthology of English literature v 1 p3-500 820.8
Trapping. See Fur trade
Travel 910.2
Travel trailers and campers
—Repairing 629.28
Travels through Jewish America. Golden, H. 301.45
Tray gardens. See Gardens, Miniature
The treasures of Tutankhamun. Edwards, I. E. S. 913.32
Trees 582; also pages
    In Gibbons, E. Stalking the faraway places p231-48 581.6
—United States. See pages
    In Clement, R. C. Hammond Nature atlas of America p40-69 500.9
Trevelyan, G. M. History of England. New illus. ed. 942
Tricks 793.8
Trilling, Lionel. Mind in the modern world 901.94
—ed. Victorian prose and poetry
    In The Oxford Anthology of English literature v2 p789-1507 820.8
Trilling, Lionel (as subject) See pages
    In Malin, I. ed. Contemporary American-Jewish literature p146-55 810.9
The triumph. Freidel, F.
    In Freidel, F. Franklin D. Roosevelt v3 92
Trojan War. See pages
    In Homer. The Illiad 883
Trollope, Anthony. See pages
    In Hardwick, M. A guide to Anthony Trollope 823.09
Truck campers. See Chilton's Repair and maintenance guide: truck campers 629.28
Truman, Harry S. 92
Truman, Margaret. Harry S. Truman 92
Truman family. See pages
    In West, J. B. Upstairs at the White House p51-127 92
The truth about Kent State. Davies, P. 378.1
The truth about vasectomy. Rosenfeld, L. J. 613.9
Tugwell, Rexford G. In search of Roosevelt 92
Tule Indians. See Cuna Indians
Tumors. See Cancer
The tumult and the shouting. Pawley, T.
    In Hatch, J. V. ed. Black theater, U.S.A. p475-513 812.08
Turner, Joseph Mallord William. See pages
    In Clark, K. The romantic rebellion p223-63 759.05
Turtles 598.1
Turtles of the United States. Ernst, C. H. 598.1
Tut-ank-Amen. See Tutenkhamûn, King of Egypt
Tutankhamen, King of Egypt. See Tutenkhamûn, King of Egypt
Tutankhaten. See Tutenkhamûn, King of Egypt
Tutenkhamûn, King of Egypt. See pages
    In Edwards, I. E. S. The treasures of Tutankhamûn 913.32
20th century bookkeeping and accounting: Advanced course. See Century 21 accounting: Advanced course 657
Twentieth century criticism: the major statements. Handy, W. J. ed. 801
Twentieth-century English verse, The Oxford Book of 821.08
Twentieth Century Fund. See Minow, N. N. Presidential television 329
Twentieth century interpretations of Crime and punishment. Jackson, R. L. ed. 891.7
Twentieth-century music: an introduction. Salzman, E. 780.9
Twin Oaks Community. See pages
    In Kinkade, K. A Walden Two experiment 335
200 years 973
Twombly, Robert C. Frank Lloyd Wright 92

UFO. See Flying saucers
UFO's—a scientific debate 001.9
U.S. News & World Report. See 200 years 973
Ujifusa, Grant, jt. auth. See Barone, M. The almanac of American politics 328.73
Ulam, Adam B. Stalin 92
Ullman, James Michael. How to hold a garage sale 658.8
Under the weather: Orange soufflé. See Below, S. Orange soufflé
Underdeveloped areas. See pages
    In Myrdal, G. Against the stream p65-132 330
Underhill, C. S. comp. See National Geographic Magazine. Handy key to your "National Geographics" 910.1
Undersea research stations, Manned. See Manned undersea research stations
Understanding. See Intellect; Knowledge, Theory of
Understanding your cat. Fox, M. W. 636.8
Undertow. Spence, E.
    In Hatch, J. V. ed. Black theater, U.S.A. p192-200 812.08
Underwater exploration 574.92; also pages
    In National Geographic Society. World beneath the sea 551.4
Underwater photography. See Photography, Submarine
Underwriting. See Insurance
Unemployed. See pages
    In Diebold, J. ed. The world of the computer p335-44 001.6
The unfinished quest of Richard Wright. Fabre, M. 92
The unheavenly city. See Banfield, E. C. The unheavenly city revisited 301.34
The unheavenly city revisited. Banfield, E. C. 301.34
Unidentified flying objects. See Flying saucers
United Methodist Church. Board of Church and Society. See Davies, P. The truth about Kent State 378.1
United States. Army
—Military life. See pages
    In The Soldiers 970.5
United States. Central Intelligence Agency 353.007
United States. Congress. See pages
    In Schlesinger, A. M. The imperial Presidency p68-99 353.03
    In Wolff, R. P. ed. 1984 revisited p88-112 973
—Directories 328.73
United States. Congress. House 328.73
United States. Congress. House. Committee on Ways and Means. See pages
    In Stern. P. M. The rape of the taxpayer p38-53. 388-97 336.2
United States. Congress. Senate. Committee on Finance. See pages
    In Stern. P. M. The rape of the taxpayer p34-59. 388-97 336.2
United States. Constitution. See pages
    In Berger, R. Impeachment: the constitutional problems 351.9
—Amendments. See pages
    In DeCrow, K. Sexist justice p25-45, 261-89 346.1
    In Ross, S. C. The rights of women p20-29 346
United States. Department of Agriculture. Handbook for the home 640
—Yearbook of agriculture 1973: Handbook for the home 640
United States. Department of Health, Education and Welfare. Alcohol and health 613.8
United States. Library of Congress. New serial titles 016.05
United States. Library of Congress (as subject) 027.5
United States. Military Academy, West Point. See pages
    In Aldrin, E. E. Return to earth p102-16 92
United States. Securities and Exchange Commission. See pages
    In Douglas, W. O. Go East, young man: the early years p257-96, 300-08 92
United States (as subject)
    See also Northwest, Pacific
—Aged. See Aged—United States
—Agriculture. See Agriculture—United States
—Architecture. See Architecture, American
—Art. See Art, American
—Artists. See Artists, American
—Bio-bibliography. See pages
    In Contemporary authors. First revision v9-12 920.03
—Biography. See pages
    In Hofstadter, R. The American political tradition and the men who made it 973
    In Notable names in American history 920.03
—Biography—Dictionaries 920.03
—Census. See pages
    In Kahn, E. J. The American people 301.32

—Cities and towns. See Cities and towns—United States
—Civilization 917.3; also pages
  In Nevins, A. Ordeal of the Union; selected chapters p65-107 973.7
  In Pound, E. Selected prose, 1909-1965 p99-166 814
—Civilization—Anecdotes, facetiae, satire, etc. 817
—Constitutional history. See pages
  In Berger, R. Executive privilege 353.03
—Constitutional law. See pages
  In Padover, S. K. ed. Sources of democracy p93-101, 127-40, 172-99 321.8
—Country life. See Country life—United States
—Description and travel 917.3; also pages
  In Stember, S. The bicentennial guide to the American Revolution 973.3
—Discovery and exploration. See The West—Discovery and exploration
—Economic conditions. See pages
  In Pound, E. Selected prose, 1909-1965 p167-85 814
—Economic conditions—20th century. See pages
  In Galbraith, J. K. Economics and the public purpose 338.973
—Economic conditions—1933-1945. See pages
  In Perrett, G. Days of sadness, years of triumph p173-85, 255-67, 299-309 973.917
—Economic conditions—1961- 330.973; also pages
  In Wolfe, T. ed. The new journalism p320-30 810.8
—Education. See Education—United States
—Elections. See Elections—United States
—Executive power. See Executive power—United States
—Farm life. See Farm life—United States
—Folk art. See Folk art, American
—Folk songs. See Folk songs—United States
—Folklore. See Folklore—United States
—Foreign policy. See United States—Foreign relations
—Foreign population. See United States—Immigration and emigration
—Foreign relations 327.73; also pages
  In Myrdal, G. Against the stream p266-92 330
  In Perrett, G. Days of sadness, years of triumph p54-66, 155-72, 186-93 973.917
  In Schlesinger, A. M. The imperial Presidency p278-330 353.03
—Foreign relations—China. See pages
  In Osborne, J. The fourth year of the Nixon watch p16-37 973.924
—Foreign relations—Near East 327.73
—Foreign relations—Russia. See pages
  In Osborne, J. The fourth year of the Nixon watch p74-105 973.924
—Galleries and museums—Bibliography. See pages
  In Museum media 016
—Galleries and museums—Directories. See pages
  In Museum media 016
—Government publications. See pages
  In Thurman, S. D. The right of access to information from the Government 323.44
—Government publications—Bibliography 015.73
—Historic houses, etc. See pages
  In Great historic places 917.3
—History 973; also pages
  In Freidel, F. Our country's Presidents 920
—History—Bibliography. See pages
  In Freidel, F. ed. Harvard Guide to American history 973
—History—Study and teaching. See pages
  In Freidel, F. ed. Harvard Guide to American history 973
—History—Revolution 973.3; also pages
  In Brodie, F. M. Thomas Jefferson, an intimate history p135-49 92
—History—Revolution—Encyclopedias 973.303
—History—1815-1861. See pages
  In Nye, R. B. Society and culture in America, 1830-1860 917.3
—History—Civil war 973.7; also pages
  In Commager, H. S. ed. Britain through American eyes p357-79 914.2
  In Franklin, J. H. From slavery to freedom p214-35 301.45
  In Hughes, L. A pictorial history of Blackamericans p156-82 301.45
  See also Slavery in the United States
—History—Civil War—Campaigns and battles. *See also* names of battles, e.g. Gettysburg, Battle of, 1863
—History—Civil War—Causes 973.7
—History—Civil War—Sources 973.7
—History—1865-1898 973.8
—History—1933-1945 973.917
—History—World War, 1939-1945. See World War, 1939-1945—United States
—History, Economic. See United States—Economic conditions
—Immigration and emigration. See pages
  In Havighurst, W. The heartland: Ohio, Indiana, Illinois p162-82 977

—Industries. See pages
  In Nevins, A. Ordeal of the Union; selected chapters p244-54 973.7
—Industry and state. See Industry and state—United States
—Intellectual life. See pages
  In Nye, R. B. Society and culture in America, 1830-1860 917.3
—Law. See Law—United States
—Literature. See American literature
—Manufactures. See United States—Industries
—Moral conditions. See pages
  In Mencken, H. L. The young Mencken p300-16, 369-85 818
—Music. See Music, American
—Musicians. See Musicians, American
—National characteristics. See National characteristics, American
—National parks and reserves. See National parks and reserves—United States
—Natural resources. See Natural resources—United States
—Painting. See Painting, American
—Philosophy. See Philosophy, American
—Poets. See Poets, American
—Police. See Police—United States
—Politics and government 973
—Politics and government—Encyclopedias. See pages
  In Blevins, L. W. The young voter's manual 320.03
—Politics and government—Periodicals. See pages
  In The CQ Guide to current American government 350
—Politics and government—Yearbooks. See pages
  In Barone, M. The almanac of American politics 328.73
—Politics and government—1815-1861. See pages
  In Johannsen, R. W. Stephen A. Douglas 92
—Politics and government—20th century. See pages
  In Clancy, P. R. Just a country lawyer; a biography of Senator Sam Ervin 92
  In Moynihan, D. P. Coping p3-52, 185-94, 248-58 309.173
  In Pearson, D. Diaries, 1949-1959 92
  In Stevenson, A. E. The papers of Adlai E. Stevenson v3-4 92
—Politics and government—1919-1933. See pages
  In Freidel, F. Franklin D. Roosevelt 92
—Politics and government—1933-1945. See pages
  In Perrett, G. Days of sadness, years of triumph p41-53, 287-94 973.917
—Politics and government—1945-1953. See pages
  In Miller, M. Plain speaking; an oral biography of Harry S. Truman 92
  In Truman, M. Harry S. Truman 92
—Politics and government—1961- 973.924; also pages
  In Chisholm, S. The good fight 329
  In Harwood, R. Lyndon [biography of Lyndon Baines Johnson] 92
  In McGovern, G. An American journey 329
  In Magruder, J. S. An American life 92
  In White, T. H. The making of the President, 1972 329
—Population 301.32
—Presidents. See Presidents—United States
—Prisons. See Prisons—United States
—Public documents. See United States—Government publications
—Race relations 301.45; also pages
  In Moynihan, D. P. Coping p195-209, 344-69 309.173
  In Nye, R. B. Society and culture in America, 1830-1860 p208-35 917.3
  In Perrett, G. Days of sadness, years of triumph p143-54, 310-24 973.917
—Religion 277.3; also pages
  In National Geographic Society. Life in rural America p152-73 917.3
  In Nye, R. B. Society and culture in America, 1830-1860 p283-320 917.3
—Science. See Science—United States
—Sculpture. See Sculpture, American
—Social conditions 309.173; also pages
  In Harris, F. R. The new populism 330.973
  In Howard, J. A different woman 301.41
  In Pearson, J. W. The 8-day week 331.2
  In Perrett, G. Days of sadness, years of triumph 973.917
  In Terkel, S. Working 331.2
  In Wolff, R. P. ed. 1984 revisited 973
—Social life and customs 917.3; also pages
  In Birmingham, S. Real lace: America's Irish rich 301.45
  In Wolf, T. ed. The new journalism p377-94 810.8
—Social policy. See pages
  In Moynihan, D. P. Coping 309.173
—Soldiers. See Soldiers—United States
—State governments. See State governments
—Taxation. See Taxation—United States
—Territorial expansion 973

AUTHOR, TITLE, SUBJECT, AND ANALYTICAL INDEX
1974 SUPPLEMENT

—Women. See Women in the United States
—World War, 1939-1945. See World War, 1939-1945—United States
The unnatural history of the nanny. Gathorne-Hardy, J. 914.2
Untemeyer, Louis, ed. 50 modern American & British poets, 1920-1970 821.08
An untold story [biography of Franklin Delano Roosevelt]. Roosevelt, E. 92
Update of nonbook media. See National Information Center for Educational Media. [NICEM Indexes to nonbook media] 016.3713
The Updated Last Whole earth catalog 338.4
Upstairs at the White House. West, J. B. 92
Urban areas. See Metropolitan areas
Urquhart, Fred, ed. See Freeman, W. Dictionary of fictional characters 820.3
The use and abuse of art. Barzun, J. 701
Useful knots for everyone. Montgomery, E. 623.88
Utensils, Kitchen. See Household equipment and supplies
Utopia or oblivion: the prospects for humanity. Fuller, R. B. 901.94
Utopias 335

Vacation houses. Cobb, B. 728.6
Van Beethoven, Ludwig. See Beethoven, Ludwig van
Van Doren, Mark. Good morning 811
Van Duyn, Mona. Merciful disguises 811
Vanilla crescents. Ingrisch, L.
  In The Best short plays, 1974 p215-30 808.82
Vanishing animals. See Rare animals
Vanishing species 591
Vanishing wildlife of North America. Allen, T. B. 591.9
Van Lawick, Hugo. See Lawick, Hugo van
Varnish and varnishing. See pages
  In Brumbaugh, J. E. Wood furniture, finishing, refinishing, repairing p229-40 684.1
Vasectomy. See Sterilization (Birth control)
Vasectomy, sex and parenthood. Fleishman, N. 613.9
Vega, and other poems. Durrell, L. 821
Vegetable gardening 635
Vegetable kingdom. See Plants
Vegetables
  See also Vegetable gardening
—Canning. See Canning and preserving
Vegetables and fruits. Crockett, J. U. 635
Veith, Ilza, jt. auth. See Tan, Leong, T. Acupuncture therapy 615
Veneers and veneering. See pages
  In Brumbaugh, J. E. Wood furniture, finishing, refinishing, repairing p94-132 684.1
Vermes, Geza. Jesus the Jew 232
Versailles. See pages
  In Hibbert, C. Versailles 914.4
Vertebrates. See Amphibians; Mammals; Reptiles
Vertigo (Motion picture) See pages
  In Solomon, S. J. ed. The classic cinema p247-71 791.43
Vestal, Bud. Jerry Ford, up close 92
Veterinary medicine. See pages
  In Herriot, J. All creatures great and small 92
  In Herriot, J. All things bright and beautiful 92
Victorian prose and poetry. Trilling, L. ed.
  In The Oxford Anthology of English literature v2 p789-1507 820.8
Vieira, Antonia. See pages
  In Rogers, J. A. Great men of color v2 p40-53 920
Vienna
—Description. See pages
  In Kane, R. S. Grand tour A to Z: the capitals of Europe p475-96 914
Vietnam. See pages
  In Salisbury, H. E. To Peking—and beyond p222-32 915.1
Vietnam War, 1961- See Vietnamese Conflict, 1961-
Vietnamese Conflict, 1961- See pages
  In Kissinger, H. A. American foreign policy p99-135 327.73
  In Osborne, J. The fourth year of the Nixon watch p6-15, 59-78 973.924
  In Schlesinger, A. M. The imperial Presidency p177-207 353.03
  In Wolfe, T. ed. The new journalism p292-303 810.8
  See also names of battles and sieges, e.g. Khe Sanh, Siege of, 1968
—Personal narratives 959.704
Villiard, Paul. Raising small animals for fun and profit 636.08
Villon, François. The legacy, the testament, and other poems of François Villon 841

Vinton, John, ed. Dictionary of contemporary music 780.3
Violence. See pages
  In Fromm, E. The anatomy of human destructiveness 152.4
Virginia
—Natural history. See Natural history—Virginia
Vision. See Eye
Visitor from Forest Hills. Simon, N.
  In Richards, S. ed. Best short plays of the world theatre, 1968-1973 p22-33 808.82
Vivariums. See Terrariums
Vlad the Impaler. Dracula, Prince of Wallachia, 1431-1476 92
Vocabulary. See Words, New
Vocational education. See pages
  In Du Bois, W. E. B. The education of Black people p61-82 378
Vogel, Marcel. See pages
  In Tompkins, P. The secret life of plants p17-32 581
Volcanoes. See pages
  In The Great Northwest p55-65 917.95
  In Wallace, R. Hawaii p34-67 509.9
Von Bernewitz, M. W. See Pearl, R. M. Handbook for prospectors 622
Von Däniken, Erich. See Däniken, Erich von
Von Goethe, Johann Wolfgang. See Goethe, Johann Wolfgang von
Vonnegut, Kurt. Between time and Timbuktu 812
—Wampeters, foma & granfalloons (opinions) 818
Vonnegut, Kurt (as subject) See pages
  In Klinkowitz, J. ed. The Vonnegut statement 813.09
  In Schultz, M. F. Black humor fiction of the sixties p43-65 813.09
The Vonnegut statement. Klinkowitz, J. ed. 813.09
Voting. See Suffrage
Voyages to the moon. See Space flight to the moon

W. C. Fields by himself. Fields, W. C. 92
Wagenknecht, Edward. The personality of Shakespeare 822.3
Wagner, Jean. Black poets of the United States 811.09
Wagner, Richard. See pages
  In Auden, W. H. Forewords and afterwords p244-55 809
The waiting room. Bowen, J.
  In Richards, S. ed. Best short plays of the world theatre, 1968-1973 p264-76 808.82
Wake of the great sealers. Mowat, F. 639
The Wakefield Second Shepherd's play
  In The Oxford Anthology of English literature v 1 p368-88 820.8
Walden. See Thoreau, H. D. The illustrated Walden 818
A Walden Two experiment. Kinkade, K. 335
Walk hard. Hill, A.
  In Hatch, J. V. ed. Black theater, U.S.A. p437-71 812.08
Walker, Bryce S. The Great Divide 500.9
Walker, Joseph A. The River Niger 812
Walking. See Hiking
Wallace, A. H. Guy de Maupassant 843.09
Wallace, Robert. Hawaii 500.9
Wallace Stevens: imagination and faith. Morris, A. K. 811.09
Wallant, Edward Lewis. See pages
  In Malin, I. ed. Contemporary American-Jewish literature p229-41 810.9
Walling, William A. Mary Shelley 823.09
Walters, Dorothy. Flannery O'Connor 813.09
The waltz emperors. Wechsberg, J. 780.92
Wambaugh, Joseph. The onion field 364.1
Wampeters, foma & granfalloons (opinions). Vonnegut, K. 818
Wankel engine. See pages
  In Dark, H. E. The Wankel rotary engine 629.2
The Wankel rotary engine. Dark, H. E. 629.2
War. See names of wars, battles, etc. e.g. United States—History—Revolution; Gettysburg, Battle of, 1863
War of the American Revolution. See United States—History—Revolution
War poetry. See pages
  In Rottmann, L. ed. Winning hearts & minds 811.08
Ward, Douglas Turner. Day of absence
  In Hatch, J. V. ed. Black theater, U.S.A. p695-710 812.08
  In Richards, S. ed. Best short plays of the world theatre, 1968-1973 p34-50 808.82
Ward, Theodore. Big white fog
  In Hatch, J. V. ed. Black theater, U.S.A. p278-319 812.08

Warga, Wayne. See Aldrin, E. E. Return to earth 92
Wars of the Roses, 1455-1485. See Great Britain—History—Wars of the Roses, 1455-1485
Warth, Robert D. Lenin 92
Washing. See Laundry
Washington, Booker Taliaferro. See pages
  In Rogers, J. A. Great men of color v2 p383-98 920
Washington, George, President U.S. See pages
  In Schlesinger, A. M. The imperial Presidency p208-77 353.03
The Washington Post. See The Presidential transcripts 351.9
The Washington Post (as subject) See pages
  In Bernstein, C. All the President's men 351.9
Wasserman, Paul, ed. See Museum media 016
—ed. See Statistics sources 016.31
The watch repairer's manual. Fried, H. B. 681
Water. See pages
  In Asimov, I. Today and tomorrow and . . . p73-83 508
  See also Geysers
Water animals. See Marine animals
Water sports. See Canoes and canoeing; Fishing
Watergate Affair, 1972- 351.9; also pages
  In Clancy, P. R. Just a country lawyer; a biography of Senator Sam Ervin p263-92 92
  In Magruder, J. S. An American life 92
  In Mankiewicz, F. Perfectly clear 973.924
  In Osborne, J. The fifth year of the Nixon watch 973.924
  In White, T. H. The making of the President, 1972 p269-98 329
—Sources 351.9
Watergate; chronology of a crisis 351.9
Waters, Ethel. See pages
  In Pleasants, H. The great American popular singers p80-96 780.92
Watson, George, ed. See The New Cambridge Bibliography of English literature, v 1 p600-1660 016.82
Waugh, Evelyn. A little learning; criticism
  In Auden, W. H. Forewords and afterwords p492-524 809
Waugh, Evelyn (as subject) 92
The way of the world. Congreve, W.
  In The Oxford Anthology of English literature v 1 p1673-1733 820.8
Webb, Eugene. The plays of Samuel Beckett 842.09
Wechsberg, Joseph. The waltz emperors 780.92
Weddings. See Marriage customs and rites
Weddington, Bernardine, jt. auth. See Thomas, S. M. A guide to sources of consumer information 640.73
Weight control. See pages
  In Nidetch, J. Weight Watchers Program cookbook 641.5
  See also Diet
Weight Watcher Program cookbook. Nidetch, J. 641.5
Weill, Kurt. See pages
  In Green, S. The world of musical comedy p251-63 780.92
Weinheimer, Gail. See Rosengart, O. The rights of suspects 345
Weintraub, Stanley. Whistler 709.2
Welcome to Andromeda. Whyte, R.
  In The Best short plays, 1974 p23-60 808.82
Weld, Angelina Emily Grimké. See Grimké, Angelina Emily
Wellesz, Egon, ed. The age of enlightenment, 1745-1790
  In The New Oxford History of music v7 780.9
Wellington, Arthur Wellesley, 1st Duke of 92
Wells, H. G. See Wells, Herbert George
Wells, Herbert George 92
Wells, Orson. Citizen Kane: criticism
  In Sarris, A. The primal screen p111-36 791.43
Wells, Orson (as subject) See pages
  In Higham, C. The art of the American film, 1900-1971 p207-26 791.43
  In Solomon, S. J. ed. The classic cinema p171-97 791.43
Wender, Paul H. The hyperactive child 618.9
West, J. B. Upstairs at the White House 92
West, Jessamyn. Hide and seek 92
The West
  See also Northwest, Pacific
—Discovery and exploration. See pages
  In The Great Northwest p133-41 917.95
—History. See pages
  In Billington, R. A. Westward expansion 973
  In The Railroaders 385.09
West Indian literature
—Bio-bibliography. See pages
  In Herdeck, D. E. African authors p497-507 920.03
West Point. See United States. Military Academy, West Point

Westbrook, Max, jt ed. See Handy, W. J. ed. Twentieth century criticism: the major statements 801
Westrup, Sir Jack. See Blom, E. comp. Everyman's Dictionary of music 780.3
Westward expansion. Billington, R. A. 973
A whale for the killing. Mowat, F. 599
Whalen, Doris H. The secretary's handbook 651.02
Whalen, George J, jt. auth. See Graf, R. F. How it works, illustrated: everyday devices and mechanisms 621
Whales 599
Whaley, Barton. Codeword BARBAROSSA 940.54
What every woman needs to know about abortion. Arnstein, H. S. 613.9
What to tell your child about sex. Child Study Association of America 612.6
What women should know about the breast cancer controversy. Crile, G. 616.9
Whatever became of sin? Menninger, K. 233
What's the difference? Moss, N. 427
Wheeler, Hugh. A little night music 812
Wheeler, Keith. See The Railroaders 385.09
Wheeler, Michael. No-fault divorce 346.1
Whipsnade Park. See Zoological Society of London. Gardens, Whipsnade Park
Whistler, James Abbott McNeill 709.2
White, Carl M. Sources of information in the social sciences 016.3
White, Margaret Bourke- See Bourke-White, Margaret
White, T. Harriman, jt. auth. See McGarry, D. D. World historical fiction guide 016.8
White, Theodore H. The making of the President, 1972 329
White's Conspectus of American biography. See Notable names in American history 920.03
Whitman, Walt. See pages
  In Gibson, D. B. ed. Modern Black poets p43-56 811.09
Whittemore, L. H. The super cops 363.2
Whole earth catalog. See The Updated Last Whole earth catalog 338.4
Who's who in Dickens. Greaves, J. 823.03
Who's who in Shakespeare. Quennell, P. 822.3
Why Johnny can't add: the failure of the new math. Kline, M. 372.7
Whyte, Ron. Welcome to Andromeda
  In The Best short plays, 1974 p23-60 808.82
Widow. Caine, L. 301.42
Widows 301.42
Wiene, Robert. See pages
  In Solomon, S. J. ed. The classic cinema p39-64 791.43
Wild Alaska. Brown, D. 500.9
Wild flowers. See pages
  In Clement, R. C. Hammond Nature atlas of America p70-111 500.9
Wild life
—Conservation. See Wildlife—Conservation
Wilde, Oscar. The importance of being Earnest
  In The Oxford Anthology of English literature v 2 p1129-76 820.8
—Letters; criticism
  In Auden, W. H. Forewords and afterwords p302-24 809
Wilder, Thornton Niven. See pages
  In Cowley, M. A second flowering p114-29 810.9
Wilderness areas. See pages
  In National Geographic Society. Wilderness U.S.A. 500.9
Wilderness cooking. Berglund, B. 641.5
Wilderness survival. See pages
  In Gibbons, E. Stalking the faraway places 581.6
Wilderness U.S.A. National Geographic Society 500.9
Wildlife
—Conservation 591.9; also pages
  In Leonard, J. N. Atlantic beaches p158-67 500.9
  See also Rare animals
Wildlife and pesticides. See Pesticides and wildlife
Wilkerson, Albert E. ed. The rights of children 346
Will. See Free will and determinism
Will Rogers, his life and times. Ketchum, R. M. 92
Williams, Bert. See pages
  In Rogers, J. A. Great men of color v2 p373-82 920
Williams, Hank. See pages
  In Pleasants, H. The great American popular singers p227-46 780.92
Williams, Tennessee. Confessional
  In Richards, S. ed. Best short plays of the world theatre, 1968-1973, p 1-21 808.82
Wills
  See also Inheritance and succession
—Laws and regulations. See pages
  In The Family legal advisor p159-92 340

AUTHOR, TITLE, SUBJECT, AND ANALYTICAL INDEX
1974 SUPPLEMENT

Wilson, Erica. Erica Wilson's Embroidery book 746.4
Wilson, Garff B. Three hundred years of American drama and theatre 792.09
Winchester, Alice, jt. auth. See Lipman, J. The flowering of American folk art, 1776-1876 745
Windeler, Robert. Sweetheart; the story of Mary Pickford 92
Window gardening. See House plants
Window in the sea. Cousteau, J. 574.92
Wine and wine making 663; also pages
  In The Good Housekeeping cookbook p613-20 641.5
Wine in the wilderness. Childress, A.
  In Hatch, J. V. ed. Black theater, U.S.A. p737-55 812.08
The wines of America. Adams, L. D. 663
Winning hearts & minds. Rottmann, L. ed. 811.08
Witcover, Jules, jt. auth. See Cohen, R. M. A heartbeat away 351.9
Wilder, Billy. See pages
  In Higham, C. The art of the American film, 1900-1971 p239-52 791.43
Witney, Dudley, jt. auth. See Arthur, E. The barn 728
Wolfe, Thomas. See pages
  In Cowley, M. A second flowering p156-90 810.9
Wolfe, Tom, ed. The new journalism 810.8
Wolff, Robert Lee, jt. auth. See Brinton, C. Modern civilization 901.9
Wolff, Robert Paul, ed. 1984 revisited 973
Wollstonecraft, Mary. See Godwin, Mary (Wollstonecraft)
Wolves. See pages
  In Allen, T. B. Vanishing wildlife of North America p80-89 591.9
Woman 301.41
  See also Women in astronautics; Women in literature and art; Women in the United States
—Civil rights 346; also pages
  In DeCrow, K. Sexist justice 346.1
  In Rossi, A. S. ed. The feminist papers: from Adams to de Beauvoir 301.41
—Employment 331.4; also pages
  In DeCrow, K. Sexist justice p64-139 346.1
—Employment—Laws and regulations. See pages
  In Ross, S. C. The rights of women p31-115, 291-341 346
—Equal rights. See Woman—Civil rights
—History and condition of women. See Woman —Social conditions
—Psychology. See pages
  In Toffler, A. ed. Learning for tomorrow p33-55 370.19
—Rights of women. See Woman—Civil rights
—Social conditions 301.41; also pages
  In Asimov, I. Today and tomorrow and . . . p217-27 508
—Suffrage. See Woman—Civil rights
Women in astronautics. See pages
  In Asimov, I. Today and tomorrow and . . . p189-98 508
Women in industry. See Woman—Employment
Women in literature and art. See pages
  In Bretnor, R. ed. Science fiction, today and tomorrow p278-92 809.3
  In Kinnamon, K. ed. James Baldwin p77-95 818
  In Malin, I. ed. Contemporary American-Jewish literature p156-74 810.9
Women in the United States 301.41; also pages
  In DeCrow, K. Sexist justice 346.1
  In Kahn, K. Hillbilly women 309.175
Women's lib. See Women's Liberation Movement
Women's Liberation Movement. See pages
  In Rossi, A. S. ed. The feminist papers: from Adams to de Beauvoir 301.41
Women's rights. See Woman—Civil rights
Wood. See pages
  In Brumbaugh, J. E. Wood furniture, finishing, refinishing, repairing p57-93 684.1
Wood finishing 684; also pages
  In Brumbaugh, J. E. Wood furniture, finishing, refinishing, repairing 684.1
Wood furniture, finishing, refinishing, repairing 684.1
Woodward, Bob, jt. auth. See Bernstein, C. All the President's men 351.9
Woodward, C. Vann. The strange career of Jim Crow 301.45
Woods, William. A history of the devil 133.4
The wooing of Lady Sunday. Pezzulo, T.
  In The Best short plays, 1974 p311-46 808.82
Woolf, Leonard. Beginning again; criticism
  In Auden, W. H. Forewords and afterwords p492-524 809
Woolley, Sir Leonard. Digging up the past 913

Wooten, James T. jt. auth. See Herbert, A. B. Soldier 959.704
Word play. Farb, P. 401
Words, New. See pages
  In Pei, M. Double-speak in America 422
—Dictionaries 423
Work 331.2
Working. Terkel, S. 331.2
Working day. See Hours of labor
Working women. See Woman—Employment
World beneath the sea. National Geographic Society 551.4
The World book encyclopedia 031
The world chess championship. Horowitz, A. 794.1
World economics. See Economic conditions
World historical fiction guide. McGarry, D. D. 016.8
The world of musical comedy. Green, S. 780.92
The world of the computer. Diebold, J. ed. 001.6
World politics
  See also International relations; also names of countries with the subdivisions Foreign relations and Politics and government, e.g. United States—Foreign relations; United States—Politics and government
—Dictionaries 909.82
World War, 1939-1945
—Campaigns and battles 940.54; also pages
  In Blumenson, M. ed. The Patton papers, 1940-1945 92
—Drama 812
—Evacuation of civilians—Pictorial works 940.54
—Germany. See pages
  In Whaley, B. Codeword BARBAROSSA 940.54
—Maps 940.54
—Personal narratives 940.54
—Reconstruction. See Reconstruction (1939-1951)
—Russia. See pages
  In Whaley, B. Codeword BARBAROSSA 940.54
—Secret service 940.54
—United States. See pages
  In Perrett, G. Days of sadness, years of triumph 973.917
  In Schlesinger, A. M. The imperial Presidency p100-26 353.03
World's great men of color. Rogers, J. A. 920
Wounded, First aid to. See First aid
Wright, Frances. See pages
  In Rossi, A. S. ed. The feminist papers: from Adams to de Beauvoir p86-99 301.41
Wright, Frank Lloyd 92
Wright, Richard. Native son
  In Hatch, J. V. ed. Black theater, U.S.A. p393-431 812.08
Wright, Richard (as subject) 92; also pages
  In Bakish, D. Richard Wright 813.08
Write your own wedding. Brill, M. L. 265
Writing popular fiction. Koontz, D. R. 808.3
Writing to sell. Meredith, S. 808
Wyeth, N. C. N. C. Wyeth: the collected paintings, illustrations, and murals 759.13
Wynar, Christine L. Guide to reference books for school media centers 016
Wynkoop, Sally, comp. Subject guide to government reference books 015.73

Xanvante Indians. See Chavante Indians

Yaqui Indians
—Religion and mythology 299
The years of the sword. Longford, E.
  In Longford, E. Wellington v 1 92
Yeats, W. B. Autobiography
  In Yeats, W. B. Memoirs: Autobiography— first draft [and] Journal p19-134 92
—Journal
  In Yeats, W. B. Memoirs: Autobiography— first draft [and] Journal p137-278 92
—Memoirs: Autobiography—first draft [and] Journal 92
Yellow fever. See pages
  In Marks, G. The story of medicine in America p234-45 610.9
Yellowstone National Park. See pages
  In Walker, B. S. The Great Divide p128-57 500.9
Yeti 001.9
Yogurt 637
You and your language. Laird, C. 420
You and your pension. Nader, R. 331.2
You are what you write. Hartford, H. 137
Youmans, Vincent. See pages
  In Green, S. The world of musical comedy p129-39 780.92

Young, Margaret Labash, ed. See Directory of special libraries and information centers 026.025
Young, Peter, ed. Atlas of the Second World War 940.54
The young Mencken. Mencken, H. L. 818
The young voter's manual. Blevins, L. W. 320.03
Your child and sex. Pomeroy, W. B. 612.6
Your pet's health from A to Z. McKeown, D. B. 636.08
Youth 301.43
   See also Adolescence
—Political activity. See pages
   In Moynihan, D. P. Coping p116-33 309.173
   In Wolff, R. P. ed. 1984 revisited p11-39 973
Youth and drugs. See Drugs and youth
Youth and the law. Sloan, I. J. 340

Zarca, Albert. See Mussolini, R. Mussolini: an intimate biography 92
Zenobia, Queen of Palmyra. See pages
   In Menen, A. Cities in the sand p240-50 913.37
Zimmerman, David R. Rh 618.2
Zinberg, Len. Walk hard—talk loud; dramatization. See Hill, A. Walk hard
Zindel, Paul. The ladies should be in bed
   In The Best short plays, 1974 p135-60 808.82
Zoological Society of London. Gardens, Whipsnade Park. See pages
   In Durrell, G. A bevy of beasts 591.5
Zoology
—Encyclopedias 591.03
Zoroastrianism. See pages
   In Noss, J. B. Man's religions p336-54 291

DIRECTORY OF PUBLISHERS AND DISTRIBUTORS

A.L.A. American Library Association, Publishing Services, 50 E Huron St, Chicago, Ill. 60611

Abelard-Schuman. See Crowell

Abrams. Harry N. Abrams, Inc, 110 E 59th St, New York, N.Y. 10022

Am. Forestry Assn. American Forestry Association, 1319 18th St, N.W, Washington, D.C. 20036

Am. Heritage. American Heritage Publishing Company, Inc, 1221 Av. of the Americas, New York, N.Y. 10020
  Also distributed by McGraw and other publishers

Am. Photographic Bk. Pub. Co. American Photographic Book Publishing Company, Inc, (AMPHOTO), East Gate & Zeckendorf Blvds, Garden City, N.Y. 11530

Am. Tech. Soc. American Technical Society, 848 E 58th St, Chicago, Ill. 60637

Am. West. American West Publishing Company, 599 College Av, Palo Alto, Calif. 94306

Anchor Bks. See Doubleday

Anchor Press. See Doubleday

Archon Bks. See Shoe String

Arco. Arco Publishing Company, Inc, 219 Park Av, S, New York, N.Y. 10003

Assn. Press. Association Press (Natl. Council of Y.M.C.A.'s) 291 Broadway, New York, N.Y. 10007

Atheneum Pubs. Atheneum Publishers, 122 E 42d St, New York, N.Y. 10017

Audel. Theodore Audel & Company, 4300 W 62d St, Indianapolis, Ind. 46208

Bankers Pub. Bankers Publishing Company, 89 Beach St, Boston, Mass. 02111

Barnes, A.S. A. S. Barnes & Company, Forsgate Dr, Cranbury, N.J. 08512

Barnes & Noble. See Harper

Barnhart. See Harper

Barrons Educ. Ser. Barron's Educational Series, Inc, 113 Crossways Park Dr, Woodbury, N.Y. 11797

Basic Bks. Basic Books, Inc, Publishers, 10 E 53d St, New York, N.Y. 10022

Beacon Press. Beacon Press, Inc, 25 Beacon St, Boston, Mass. 02108

Belknap Press. See Harvard Univ. Press

Black Orpheus Press. Black Orpheus Press, Inc, 322 New Mark Esplanade, Rockville, Md. 20850

Black Sparrow Press. Black Sparrow Press, Box 25603, Los Angeles, Calif. 90025

Bobbs. Bobbs-Merrill Company, Inc, 4300 W 62d St, Indianapolis, Ind. 46268

Bounty Bks. See Crown

Bowker. The R. R. Bowker Company, Xerox Education Group, 1180 Av. of the Americas, New York, N.Y. 10036

Braziller. George Braziller, Inc, 1 Park Av, New York, N.Y. 10016

Cambridge. Cambridge University Press, 32 E 57th St, New York, N.Y. 10022

Century House. Century House, Inc, Watkins Glen, N.Y. 14891

Charterhouse Bks. Charterhouse Books, Inc, 750 3d Av, New York, N.Y. 10017

Chicorel Lib. Pub. Corp. Chicorel Library Publishing Corporation, 275 Central Park West, New York, N.Y. 10024

Child Study Press. The Child Study Press, 50 Madison Av, New York, N.Y. 10010

Chilton Bk. Co. Chilton Book Company, Chilton Way, Radnor, Pa. 19089

Citadel Press. Citadel Press, 120 Enterprise Av, Secaucus, N.J. 07094

City Lights Bks. City Lights Books, 1562 Grant Av, San Francisco, Calif. 94133

Collier Bks. See Macmillan Pub. Co.

Collins + World Pub. Co. William Collins + World Publishing Company, Inc, 2080 W 117th St, Cleveland, Ohio 44111

Columbia Univ. Press. Columbia University Press, 562 W 113th St, New York, N.Y. 10025

Congressional Quarterly. Congressional Quarterly, Inc, 1735 K St, N.W, Washington, D.C. 20006

Cornell Univ. Press. Cornell University Press, 124 Roberts Pl, Ithaca, N.Y. 14850

Coward, McCann & Geoghegan. Coward, McCann & Geoghegan, Inc, 200 Madison Av, New York, N.Y. 10016

Crane, Russak. Crane, Russak & Company, 52 Vanderbilt Av, New York, N.Y. 10017

Crescendo Pub. Crescendo Publishing Company, 48-50 Melrose St, Boston, Mass. 02116

Crowell. Thomas Y. Crowell Company, 666 Park Av, S, New York, N.Y. 10019

Crown. Crown Publishers, Inc, 419 Park Av, S, New York, N.Y. 10016

Day. The John Day Company, 257 Park Av, S, New York, N.Y. 10010

Delacorte Press. See Dell

Dell. Dell Publishing Company, Inc, 1 Dag Hammarskjöld Plaza, 245 E 47th St, New York, N.Y. 10017

Denison. T. S. Denison & Company, Inc, 5100 W 82d St, Minneapolis, Minn. 55437

Dial Press. The Dial Press, 1 Dag Hammarskjöld Plaza, 245 E 47th St, New York, N.Y. 10017

Dodd. Dodd, Mead & Company, Inc, 79 Madison Av, New York, N.Y. 10016

Doubleday. Doubleday & Company, Inc, 245 Park Av, New York, N.Y. 10017

Dover. Dover Publications, Inc, 180 Varick St, New York, N.Y. 10014

Drake Pubs. Drake Publishers, Inc, 381 Park Av, S, New York, N.Y. 10016

Drama Bk. Specialists/Pubs. Drama Book Specialists/Publishers, 150 W 52d St, New York, N.Y. 10019

Dutton. E. P. Dutton & Company, Inc, 201 Park Av, S, New York, N.Y. 10003

DIRECTORY OF PUBLISHERS AND DISTRIBUTORS

Eerdmans. William B. Eerdmans Publishing Company, 255 Jefferson Av, S.E, Grand Rapids, Mich. 49502

Encyclopaedia Britannica, Inc, 425 N. Michigan Av, Chicago, Ill. 60611

Evans, M.&Co. M. Evans & Company, Inc, 216 E 49th St, New York, N.Y. 10017

Farrar, Straus. Farrar, Straus & Giroux, Inc, 19 Union Sq, W, New York, N.Y. 10003

Federation of American Societies for Experimental Biology. Federation of American Societies for Experimental Biology, 9650 Rockville Pike, Bethesda, Md. 20014

Field Enterprises. Field Enterprises Educational Corporation, 510 Merchandise Mart Plaza, Chicago, Ill. 60654

Fielding Publications. Fielding Publications, Inc, 105 Madison Av, New York, N.Y. 10016

Four Winds. The Four Winds Press, 50 W 44th St, New York, N.Y. 10036

Free Press. The Free Press, 866 3d Av, New York, N.Y. 10022

Freeman. W. H. Freeman & Company, Publishers, 660 Market St, San Francisco, Calif. 94104

Funk. Funk & Wagnalls Publishing Company, Inc, 666 5th Av, New York, N.Y. 10019

Gale Res. Gale Research Company, 700 Book Tower, Detroit, Mich. 48226

Gambit. Gambit, Inc, 53 Beacon St, Boston, Mass. 02108

Good Housekeeping Bks. See Hearst Bks.

Grosset. Grosset & Dunlap, Inc, 51 Madison Av, New York, N.Y. 10010

Grossman Pubs. Grossman Publishers, Inc, 625 Madison Av, New York, N.Y. 10022

Hall, G.K.&Co. G. K. Hall & Company, 70 Lincoln St, Boston, Mass. 02111

Hammond. Hammond, Inc, 515 Valley St, Maplewood, N.J. 07040

Handel & Co. Handel & Company, Inc, 2800 Routh, Suite 231, Dallas, Tex. 75201

Harcourt. Harcourt, Brace, Jovanovich, Inc, 757 3d Av, New York, N.Y. 10017

Harmony Bks. See Crown

Harper. Harper & Row, Publishers, 10 E 53d St, New York, N.Y. 10022

Harpers Mag. Press. Harper's Magazine Press, 2 Park Av, New York, N.Y. 10016

Harvard Univ. Press. Harvard University Press, 79 Garden St, Cambridge, Mass. 02138

Hawthorn Bks. Hawthorn Books, Inc, 260 Madison Av, New York, N.Y. 10016

Hearst Bks. Hearst Books, 250 W 55th St, New York, N.Y. 10019

Hearthside Press. Hearthside Press, Inc, 445 Northern Blvd, Great Neck, N.Y. 11021

Hill & Wang. Hill & Wang, 19 Union Sq, W, New York, N.Y. 10003

Holt. Holt, Rinehart & Winston, Inc, 383 Madison Av, New York, N.Y. 10017

Horizon Press. Horizon Press, 156 5th Av, New York, N.Y. 10010

Houghton. Houghton Mifflin Company, 2 Park, St, Boston, Mass. 02107

Ind. Univ. Press. Indiana University Press, 10th & Morton Sts, Bloomington, Ind. 47401

Information Resources Press. Information Resources Press, 2100 M St, N.W, Washington, D.C. 20037

Knopf. Alfred A. Knopf, Inc, 201 E 50th St, New York, N.Y. 10022

Lane Bk. Co. Lane Magazine & Book Company, Willow Rd. at Middlefield Rd, Menlo Park, Calif. 94025

Lib. of Congress. See U.S. Lib. of Congress

Libs. Unlimited. Libraries Unlimited, Inc, Box 263, Littleton, Colo. 80120

Lippincott. J. B. Lippincott Company, E Washington Sq, Philadelphia, Pa. 19105

Little. Little, Brown & Company, Inc, 34 Beacon St, Boston, Mass. 02106

Littlefield. Littlefield, Adams & Company, 81 Adams Dr, Totowa, N.J. 07512

Liveright. Liveright Publishing Corporation, 386 Park Av, New York, N.Y. 10016

Longman. Longman, Inc, 72 5th Av, New York, N.Y. 10011

La. State Univ. Press. Louisiana State University Press, University Station, Baton Rouge, La. 70803

Luce, R.B. Robert B. Luce, Inc, 2000 N St, N.W, Suite 103, Washington, D.C. 20036

MIT Press. Massachusetts Institute of Technology Press, 28 Carleton St, Cambridge, Mass. 02142

McGraw. McGraw-Hill Book Company, Inc, 1221 Av. of the Americas, New York, N.Y. 10020

McKay. David McKay Company, Inc, 750 3d Av, New York, N.Y. 10017

Macmillan (N Y) See Macmillan Pub. Co.

Macmillan Pub. Co. Macmillan Publishing Company, 866 3d Av, New York, N.Y. 10022

Meredith Corp. Meredith Corporation, 1716 Locust St, Des Moines, Iowa 50336

Mich. State Univ. Press. Michigan State University Press, 1405 S Harrison Rd, East Lansing, Mich. 48823

Morrow. William Morrow & Company, Inc, Publishers, 105 Madison Av, New York, N.Y. 10016

Mus. of the Am. Indian. Museum of the American Indian, Heye Foundation, Broadway & 155th St, New York, N.Y. 10032

DIRECTORY OF PUBLISHERS AND DISTRIBUTORS

Natl. Geographic Soc. National Geographic Society, 17th & M Sts, N.W, Washington, D.C. 20036

Natl. Information Center for Educational Media. National Information Center for Educational Media, University of Southern California, University Park, Los Angeles, Calif. 90007

Naturegraph. Naturegraph Publishers, 8339 W Dry Creek Rd, Healdsburg, Calif. 95448

New Directions. New Directions Publishing Corporation, 333 Av. of the Americas, New York, N.Y. 10014

New Viewpoints. New Viewpoints, 845 3d Av, New York, N.Y. 10022

N.Y. Graphic. New York Graphic Society, Publishers, Ltd, 140 Greenwich Av, Greenwich, Conn. 06830

Newsweek. Newsweek, Inc, 444 Madison Av, New York, N.Y. 10022

Norton. W. W. Norton & Company, Inc, Publishers, 500 5th Av, New York, N.Y. 10003

Oceana. Oceana Publications, Inc, 75 Main St, Dobbs Ferry, N.Y. 10522

Ohio Univ. Press. Ohio University Press, Administrative Annex, Athens, Ohio 45701

Overlook Press. See Viking

Oxford. Oxford University Press, Inc, 200 Madison Av, New York, N.Y. 10016

Pantheon Bks. Pantheon Books, 201 E 50th St, New York, N.Y. 10022

Parker Pub. Co. Parker Publishing Company, Englewood Cliffs, N.J. 07632

Playboy Press. Playboy Press, 919 N. Michigan Av, Chicago, Ill. 60611

Poets & Writers. Poets & Writers, Inc, 201 W 54th St, New York, N.Y. 10019

Potter, C.N. Clarkson N. Potter, Inc, Publishers, 419 Park Av, S, New York, N.Y. 10016

Praeger. Praeger Publishers, Inc, 111 4th Av, New York, N.Y. 10003

Prentice-Hall. Prentice-Hall, Inc, Route 9W, Englewood, N.J. 07632

Princeton Univ. Press. Princeton University Press, Princeton, N.J. 08540

Putnam. G. P. Putnam's Sons, 200 Madison Av, New York, N.Y. 10016

Quadrangle Bks. See Quadrangle/The N.Y. Times Bk. Co.

Quadrangle/The N.Y. Times Bk. Co. Quadrangle/The New York Times Book Company, 10 E 53d St, New York, N.Y. 10022

Rail-Europe. Rail-Europe, Box 3255, Alexandria, Va. 22302

Rand McNally. Rand McNally & Company, Box 7600, Chicago, Ill. 60680

Random House. Random House, Inc, 201 E 50th St, New York, N.Y. 10022

Regnery. Henry Regnery Company, 114 W Illinois St, Chicago, Ill. 60610

Rodale. Rodale Press, Inc, 33 E Minor St, Emmaus, Pa. 18049

Ronald. The Ronald Press Company, 79 Madison Av, New York, N.Y. 10016

Routledge. Routledge & Kegan Paul, 9 Park St, Boston, Mass. 02108

Rowman & Littlefield. Rowman & Littlefield, Publishers, 81 Adams Dr, Totowa, N.J. 07512

Rutgers Univ. Press. Rutgers University Press, 30 College Av, New Brunswick, N.J. 08901

St Martins. St Martin's Press, Inc, 175 5th Av, New York, N.Y. 10010

Sams. Howard W. Sams & Company, 4300 W 62d St, Indianapolis, Ind. 46268

Saturday Review Press. See Dutton

Scarecrow. Scarecrow Press, Inc, 52 Liberty St, Metuchen, N.J. 08840

Schocken. Schocken Books, Inc, 200 Madison Av, New York, N.Y. 10016

Scribner. Charles Scribner's Sons, 597 5th Av, New York, N.Y. 10017

Shoe String. The Shoe String Press, Inc, 995 Sherman Av, Hamden, Conn. 06514

Simon & Schuster. Simon & Schuster, Inc, Publishers, 630 5th Av, New York, N.Y. 10020

South-Western Pub. South-Western Publishing Company, 5101 Madison Rd, Cincinnati, Ohio 45227

Southern Ill. Univ. Press. Southern Illinois University Press, Box 3697, Carbondale, Ill. 62901

Sporting News. Sporting News, 2018 Washington Av, St Louis, Mo. 63166

Stackpole Bks. Stackpole Books, Cameron & Kelker Sts, Harrisburg, Pa. 17105

State Univ. of N.Y. Press. State University of New York Press, 99 Washington Av, Albany, N.Y. 12210

Stein & Day. Stein & Day Publishers, Scarborough House, Briarcliff Manor, N.Y. 10510

Sterling. Sterling Publishing Company, Inc, 419 Park Av, S, New York, N.Y. 10016

Straight Arrow Bks. Straight Arrow Books, 625 3d St, San Francisco, Calif. 94107

Sunrise Bks. See Dutton

Supt. of Docs. Superintendent of Documents, Government Printing Office, Washington, D.C. 20402

Taplinger. Taplinger Publishing Company, Inc, 200 Park Av, S, New York, N.Y. 10003

Temple Univ. Press. Temple University Press, Broad & Montgomery Sts, Philadelphia, Pa. 19122

Time-Life Bks. Time-Life Books, Time & Life Bldg, Rockefeller Center, New York, N.Y. 10020

Tuttle. Charles E. Tuttle Company, Inc, 28 E Main St, Rutland, Vt. 05701

Twayne. See Hall, G.K.&Co.

DIRECTORY OF PUBLISHERS AND DISTRIBUTORS

U.S. Lib. of Congress. United States. Library of Congress, Washington, D.C. 20540

U.S. News & World Report. U.S. News & World Report, Inc, 2300 N St, N.W, Washington, D.C. 20037

Underhill, C.S. Charles S. Underhill, Box 127, East Aurora, N.Y. 14052

Ungar. Frederick Ungar Publishing Company, Inc, 250 Park Av, S, New York, N.Y. 10003

Unicorn Press. Unicorn Press, Inc, Box 3307, Greensboro, N.C. 27402

Univ. of Ariz. Press. The University of Arizona Press, Box 3398, Tucson, Ariz. 85722

Univ. of Calif. Press. University of California Press, 2223 Fulton St, Berkeley, Calif. 94720

Univ. of Chicago Press. University of Chicago Press, 5801 Ellis Av, Chicago, Ill. 60637

Univ. of Ill. Press. University of Illinois Press, Urbana, Ill. 61801

Univ. of Mass. Press. The University of Massachusetts Press, 505 E Pleasant St, Amherst, Mass. 01002

Univ. of Mich. Press. University of Michigan Press, 615 E University Av, Ann Arbor, Mich. 48106

Univ. of Minn. Press. University of Minnesota Press, 2037 University Av, S.E, Minneapolis, Minn. 55455

Univ. of N.Mex. Press. University of New Mexico Press, Albuquerque, N.Mex. 87131

Univ. of Okla. Press. University of Oklahoma Press, 1005 Asp Av, Norman, Okla. 73069

Univ. of Pittsburgh Press. University of Pittsburgh Press, 127 N Bellefield Av, Pittsburgh, Pa. 15260

Univ. of Wash. Press. University of Washington Press, 1405 N.E. 41st St, Seattle, Wash. 98105

Univ. Press of Ky. University Press of Kentucky, Lexington, Ky. 40506

Van Nostrand-Reinhold. Van Nostrand-Reinhold Company, 450 W 33d St, New York, N.Y. 10001

Viking. The Viking Press, Inc, 625 Madison Av, New York, N.Y. 10022

Walker & Co. Walker & Company, 720 5th Av, New York, N.Y. 10019

Watson-Guptill. Watson-Guptill Publications, 1 Astor Plaza, New York, N.Y. 10036

Watts, F. Franklin Watts, Inc, 730 5th Av, New York, N.Y. 10019

Westminster Press. The Westminster Press, Witherspoon Bldg, Philadelphia, Pa. 19107

Weybright & Talley. Weybright & Talley, Inc, 750 3d Av, New York, N.Y. 10017

White. David White Company, Publishers, 60 E 55th St, New York, N.Y. 10022

Wilson, H.W. The H. W. Wilson Company, 950 University Av, Bronx, N.Y. 10452

Winchester Press. Winchester Press, 460 Park Av, New York, N.Y. 10022

Winthrop Pubs. Winthrop Publishers, Inc, 17 Dunster St, Cambridge, Mass. 02138

World Pub. See Collins + World

Writer. The Writer, Inc, 8 Arlington St, Boston, Mass. 02116

Writers Digest. Writer's Digest, 9933 Alliance Rd, Cincinnati, Ohio 45242

Z
1035
W77
Supp.
1974